THE
ONE THAT
GOT AWAY

ABOUT THE EDITORS

MARTIN H. GREENBERG, who has been called "the King of the anthologists," now has 306 books to his credit, of which 241 are anthologies. He is co-editor of *A Treasury of American Mystery Stories, Cloak & Dagger: A Treasury of 35 Great Espionage Stories, On the Diamond: A Treasury of Baseball Stories, Weird Tales: 32 Unearthed Terrors,* and many others. He is professor of regional analysis and political science at the University of Wisconsin–Green Bay, where he also teaches a course in the history of science fiction.

CHARLES G. WAUGH is a leading authority on science fiction and fantasy and has collaborated on more than 100 anthologies and single-author collections with Martin H. Greenberg and other assorted colleagues.

THE
ONE THAT
GOT AWAY

A TREASURY OF FISHING STORIES AND LORE BY
ERNEST HEMINGWAY • ZANE GREY • RODERICK L. HAIG-BROWN •
PHILIP WYLIE • NICK LYONS • AND MANY OTHERS

EDITED BY

MARTIN H. GREENBERG
AND
CHARLES G. WAUGH

BONANZA BOOKS

New York

This 1989 edition is published by Bonanza Books,
distributed by Outlet Book Company,
Inc., a Random House Company,
225 Park Avenue South, New York, New York 10003,
by arrangement with Martin H. Greenberg.

Printed and bound in the United States of America

Library of Congress Cataloging-in-Publication Data

The One that got away: a treasury of fishing stories and lore/by Ernest Hemingway
. . . [et al.] : edited by Martin H. Greenberg and Charles G. Waugh.
1. Fishing—Literary collections.   2. Fishing stories.   I. Hemingway, Ernest, 1899–
1961.   II. Greenberg, Martin Henry.   III. Waugh, Charles.
PN6071.F47054   1989
808.83'9355—dc19   88-30777
                                                                                          CIP
ISBN 0-517-67675-3

10 9 8 7 6 5 4 3

ACKNOWLEDGMENTS

Hemingway—Ernest Hemingway, "Big Two-Hearted River" (parts I & II) from *The Short Stories of Ernest Hemingway.* Copyright 1925 by Charles Scribner's Sons; copyright renewed 1953 by Ernest Hemingway. Reprinted with the permission of Charles Scribner's Sons, an imprint of Macmillan Publishing Company.

Grey—"Where Rolls the Rogue," copyright 1928 by Harper & Brothers, copyright © renewed 1956 by Lina Elise Grey; renewal assigned to Zane Grey Inc., 1956. Reprinted by permission of Zane Grey, Inc.

Pertwee—"The River God," copyright 1928 by The Curtis Publishing Company. Reprinted from *The Saturday Evening Post.* Reprinted by permission of The Curtis Publishing Company.

Haig-Brown—"The Unexpected Fish," copyright 1951 by Roderick L. Haig-Brown. Excerpted from *Fisherman's Spring* with the permission of Nick Lyons Books, New York, and Douglas & McIntyre, Vancouver.

Lyons—"Brannigan's Trout," copyright © 1978 by Nick Lyons. Originally published in *Gray's Sporting Journal.* Reprinted by permission of the author.

Blaisdell—"Of Trout and Men," copyright © 1969 by Tom Harold Blaisdell. Excerpted from *The Philosophical Fisherman* with the permission of Nick Lyons Books, New York.

Benét—"Daniel Webster and the Sea Serpent," copyright 1937 by Stephen Vincent Benét, copyright © renewed 1965 by Thomas C. Benét, Stephanie B. Mahin and Rachel Benét Lewis. Reprinted by permission of Brandt & Brandt Literary Agents, Inc.

Slocum—"Gathering of the Clan," reprinted from *Ye Gods and Little Fishes* by Eugene E. Slocum.

Blaisdell—"Where the Grass Is Really Greener," copyright © 1969 by Tom Harold Blaisdell. Excerpted from *The Philosophical Fisherman* with the permission of Nick Lyons Books, New York.

Haig-Brown—Excerpt from *A River Never Sleeps,* copyright 1946, copyright © renewed 1974 by Roderick L. Haig-Brown. Reprinted by permission of Nick Lyons Books and Harold Ober Associates Incorporated.

Caroline Gordon—"Old Red," from *The Collected Stories of Caroline Gordon.* Copyright © 1961, 1963, 1977, 1981 by Caroline Gordon. Reprinted by permission of Farrar, Straus & Giroux, Inc.

Smith—"Weather Prophet," reprinted by arrangement with James W. Smith.

Ford—"The Trout," copyright © 1961 by Jesse Hill Ford. First published in *The Atlantic*. Reprinted by permission of Harold Ober Associates Incorporated.

Waldrop—"God's Hooks!" by Howard Waldrop. Copyright © 1982 by Terry Carr. From *Universe 12*, Doubleday & Company, 1982. Reprinted by permission of the author.

Arthur Gordon—"The Sea Devil," copyright © 1983 by Arthur Gordon. Reprinted from *Through Many Windows* published by Fleming H. Revell Co., Old Tappan, NY 07675. Reprinted by permission of the author.

Wylie—"Spare the Rod," copyright 1940 by Philip Wylie. Copyright © renewed 1968. Reprinted by permission of Harold Ober Associates Incorporated.

Wylie—"Once on a Sunday," copyright 1943 by Philip Wylie. Copyright © renewed 1971. Reprinted by permission of Harold Ober Associates Incorporated.

Blaisdell—"Labrador-Ungava," copyright © 1969 by Tom Harold Blaisdell. Excerpted from *The Philosophical Fisherman* with the permission of Nick Lyons Books, New York.

Zelazny—"The Doors of His Face, the Lamps of His Mouth," copyright © 1965 by Mercury Press, Inc. From *The Magazine of Fantasy and Science Fiction*. Reprinted by permission of the author, Roger Zelazny.

CONTENTS

BIG
TWO-HEARTED
RIVER

ERNEST HEMINGWAY

PART ONE

The train went on up the track out of sight, around one of the hills of burnt timber. Nick sat down on the bundle of canvas and bedding the baggage man had pitched out of the door of the baggage car. There was no town, nothing but the rails and the burned-over country. The thirteen saloons that had lined the one street of Seney had not left a trace. The foundations of the Mansion House hotel stuck up above the ground. The stone was chipped and split by the fire. It was all that was left of the town of Seney. Even the surface had been burned off the ground.

Nick looked at the burned-over stretch of hillside, where he had expected to find the scattered houses of the town and then walked down the railroad track to the bridge over the river. The river was there. It swirled against the log spiles of the bridge. Nick looked down into the clear, brown water, colored from the pebbly bottom, and watched the trout keeping themselves steady in the current with wavering fins. As he watched them they changed their positions by quick angles, only to hold steady in the fast water again. Nick watched them a long time.

He watched them holding themselves with their noses into the current, many trout in deep, fast moving water, slightly distorted as he watched far down through the glassy convex surface of the pool, its surface pushing and swelling smooth against the resistance of the log-driven piles of the bridge. At the bottom of the pool were the big trout. Nick did not see them at first. Then he saw them at the bottom of the pool, big trout looking to hold themselves on the gravel bottom in a varying mist of gravel and sand, raised in spurts by the current.

Nick looked down into the pool from the bridge. It was a hot day. A kingfisher flew up the stream. It was a long time since Nick had looked into a stream and seen trout. They were very satisfactory. As the shadow of the kingfisher moved up the stream, a big trout shot upstream in a long angle, only his shadow marking the angle, then lost his shadow as he came through the surface of the water, caught the sun, and then, as he went back into the stream under the surface, his shadow seemed to float down the stream with the current, unresisting, to his post under the bridge where he tightened facing up into the current.

Nick's heart tightened as the trout moved. He felt all the old feeling.

He turned and looked down the stream. It stretched away, pebbly-bottomed with shallows and big boulders and a deep pool as it curved away around the foot of a bluff.

Nick walked back up the ties to where his pack lay in the cinders beside the railway track. He was happy. He adjusted the pack harness around the bundle, pulling straps tight, slung the pack on his back, got his arms through the shoulder straps and took some of the pull off his shoulders by leaning his forehead against the wide band of the tumpline. Still, it was too heavy. It was much too heavy. He had his leather rod-case in his hand and leaning forward to keep the weight of the pack high on his shoulders he walked along the road that paralleled the railway track, leaving the burned town behind in the heat, and then turned off around a hill with a high, fire-scarred hill on either side onto a road that went back into the country. He walked along the road feeling the ache from the pull of the heavy pack. The road climbed steadily. It was hard work walking up-hill. His muscles ached and the day was hot, but Nick felt happy. He felt he had left everything behind, the need for thinking, the need to write, other needs. It was all back of him.

From the time he had gotten down off the train and the baggage man had thrown his pack out of the open car door things had been different. Seney was burned, the country was burned over and changed, but it did not matter. It could not all be burned. He knew that. He hiked along the road, sweating in the sun, climbing to cross the range of hills that separated the railway from the pine plains.

The road ran on, dipping occasionally, but always climbing. Nick went on up. Finally the road after going parallel to the burnt hillside reached the top. Nick leaned back against a stump and slipped out of the pack harness. Ahead of him, as far as he could see, was the pine plain. The burned country stopped off at the left with the range of hills. On ahead islands of dark pine trees rose out of the plain. Far off to the left was the line of the river. Nick followed it with his eye and caught glints of the water in the sun.

There was nothing but the pine plain ahead of him, until the far blue hills that marked the Lake Superior height of land. He could hardly see them, faint and far away in the heat-light over the plain. If he looked too steadily they were gone. But if he only half-looked they were there, the far-off hills of the height of land.

Nick sat down against the charred stump and smoked a cigarette. His pack balanced on the top of the stump, harness holding ready, a hollow molded in it from his back. Nick sat smoking, looking out over the country. He did not need to get his map out. He knew where he was from the position of the river.

As he smoked, his legs stretched out in front of him, he noticed a grasshopper walk along the ground and up onto his woolen sock. The grasshopper was black. As he had walked along the road, climbing, he had started many grasshoppers from the dust. They were all black. They were not the big grasshoppers with yellow and black or red and black wings whirring out from their black wing sheathing as they fly up. These were just ordinary hoppers, but all a sooty black in color. Nick had wondered about them as he walked, without really thinking about them. Now, as he watched the black hopper that was nibbling at the wool of his sock with its fourway lip, he realized that they had all turned black from living in the burned-over land. He realized that the fire must have come the year before, but the grasshoppers were all black now. He wondered how long they would stay that way.

Carefully he reached his hand down and took hold of the hopper by the wings. He turned him up, all his legs walking in the air, and looked at his jointed belly. Yes, it was black too, iridescent where the back and head were dusty.

"Go on, hopper," Nick said, speaking out loud for the first time. "Fly away somewhere."

He tossed the grasshopper up into the air and watched him sail away to a charcoal stump across the road.

Nick stood up. He leaned his back against the weight of his pack where it rested upright on the stump and got his arms through the shoulder straps. He stood with the pack on his back on the brow of the hill looking out across the country, toward the distant river and then struck down the hillside away from the road. Underfoot the ground was good walking. Two hundred yards down the hillside the fire line stopped. Then it was sweet fern, growing ankle high, to walk through, and clumps of jack pines; a long undulating country with frequent rises and descents, sandy underfoot and the country alive again.

Nick kept his direction by the sun. He knew where he wanted to strike the river and he kept on through the pine plain, mounting small rises to see other rises ahead of him and sometimes from the top of a rise a great solid island of pines off to his right or his left. He broke off some sprigs of the heathery sweet fern, and put them under his pack straps. The chafing crushed it and he smelled it as he walked.

He was tired and very hot, walking across the uneven, shadeless pine plain. At any time he knew he could strike the river by turning off to his left. It could not be more than a mile away. But he kept on toward the north to hit the river as far upstream as he could go in one day's walking.

For some time as he walked Nick had been in sight of one of the big islands of pine standing out above the rolling high ground he was crossing. He dipped down and then as he came slowly up to the crest of the ridge he turned and made toward the pine trees.

There was no underbrush in the island of pine trees. The trunks of the trees went straight up or slanted toward each other. The trunks were straight and brown without branches. The branches were high above. Some interlocked to make a solid shadow on the brown forest floor. Around the grove of trees was a bare space. It was brown and soft underfoot as Nick walked on it. This was the over-lapping of the pine needle floor, extending out beyond the width of the high branches. The trees had grown tall and the branches moved high, leaving in the sun this bare space they had once covered with shadow. Sharp at the edge of this extension of the forest floor commenced the sweet fern.

Nick slipped off his pack and lay down in the shade. He lay on his back and looked up into the pine trees. His neck and back and the small of his back rested as he stretched. The earth felt good against his back. He looked up at the sky, through the branches, and then shut his eyes. He opened them and looked up again. There was a wind high up in the branches. He shut his eyes again and went to sleep.

Nick woke stiff and cramped. The sun was nearly down. His pack was heavy and the straps painful as he lifted it on. He leaned over with the pack on and picked up the leather rod-case and started out from the pine trees across the sweet fern swale, toward the river. He knew it could not be more than a mile.

He came down a hillside covered with stumps into a meadow. At the edge of the meadow flowed the river. Nick was glad to get to the river. He walked upstream through the meadow. His trousers were soaked with the dew as he walked. After the hot day, the dew had come quickly and heavily. The river made no sound. It was too fast and smooth. At the edge of the meadow, before he mounted to a piece of high ground to make camp, Nick looked down the river at the trout rising. They were rising to insects come from the swamp on the other side of the stream when the sun went down. The trout jumped out of water to take them. While Nick walked through the little stretch of meadow alongside the stream, trout had jumped high out of water. Now as he looked down the river, the insects must be settling on the surface, for the trout were feeding steadily all down the stream. As far down the long stretch as he could see, the trout were rising, making circles all down the surface of the water, as though it were starting to rain.

The ground rose, wooded and sandy, to overlook the meadow, the stretch of river and the swamp. Nick dropped his pack and rod-case and looked for a level piece of ground. He was very hungry and he wanted to make his camp before he cooked. Between two jack pines, the ground was quite level. He took the ax out of the pack and chopped out two projecting roots. That leveled a piece of ground large enough to sleep on. He smoothed out the sandy soil with his hand and pulled all the sweet fern bushes by their roots. His hands smelled good from the sweet fern. He smoothed the uprooted earth. He did not want anything making lumps under the blankets. When he had the ground smooth, he spread his three blankets. One he folded double, next to the ground. The other two he spread on top.

With the ax he slit off a bright slab of pine from one of the stumps and split it into pegs for the tent. He wanted them long and solid to hold in the ground. With the tent unpacked and spread on the ground, the pack, leaning against a jackpine, looked much smaller. Nick tied the rope that served the tent for a ridge-pole to the trunk of one of the pine trees and pulled the tent up off the ground with the other end of the rope and tied it to the other pine. The tent hung on the rope like a canvas blanket on a clothesline. Nick poked a pole he had cut up under the back peak of the canvas and then made it a tent by pegging out the sides. He pegged the sides out taut and drove the pegs deep, hitting them down into the ground with the flat of the ax until the rope loops were buried and the canvas was drum tight.

Across the open mouth of the tent Nick fixed cheesecloth to keep out mosquitoes. He crawled inside under the mosquito bar with various things from the pack to put at the head of the bed under the slant of the canvas. Inside the tent the light came through the brown canvas. It smelled pleasantly of canvas. Already there was something mysterious and homelike. Nick was happy as he crawled inside the tent. He had not been unhappy all day. This was different though. Now things were done. There had been this to do. Now it was done. It had been a hard trip. He was very tired. That was done. He had made his camp. He was settled. Nothing could touch him. It was a good place to camp. He was there, in the good place. He was in his home where he had made it. Now he was hungry.

He came out, crawling under the cheesecloth. It was quite dark outside. It was lighter in the tent.

Nick went over to the pack and found, with his fingers, a long nail in a paper sack of nails, in the bottom of the pack. He drove it into the pine tree, holding it close and hitting it gently with the flat of the ax. He hung the pack up on the nail. All his supplies were in the pack. They were off the ground and sheltered now.

Nick was hungry. He did not believe he had ever been hungrier. He opened and emptied a can of pork and beans and a can of spaghetti into the frying pan.

"I've got a right to eat this kind of stuff, if I'm willing to carry it," Nick said. His voice sounded strange in the darkening woods. He did not speak again.

He started a fire with some chunks of pine he got with the ax from a stump. Over the fire he stuck a wire grill, pushing the four legs down into the ground with his boot. Nick put the frying pan on the grill over the flames. He was hungrier. The beans and spaghetti warmed. Nick stirred them and mixed them together. They began to bubble, making little bubbles that rose with difficulty to the surface. There was a good smell. Nick got out a bottle of tomato catchup and cut four slices of bread. The little bubbles were coming faster now. Nick sat down beside the fire and lifted the frying pan off. He poured about half the contents out into the tin plate. It spread slowly on the plate. Nick knew it was too hot. He poured on some tomato catchup. He knew the beans and spaghetti were still too hot. He looked at the fire, then at the tent, he was not going to spoil it all by burning his tongue. For years he had never enjoyed fried bananas because he had never been able to wait for them to cool. His tongue was very sensitive. He was very hungry. Across the river in the swamp, in the almost dark, he saw a mist rising. He looked at the tent once more. All right. He took a full spoonful from the plate.

"Chrise," Nick said, "Geezus Chrise," he said happily.

He ate the whole plateful before he remembered the bread. Nick finished the second plateful with the bread, mopping the plate shiny. He had not eaten since a cup of coffee and a ham sandwich in the station restaurant at St. Ignace. It had been a very fine experience. He had been that hungry before, but had not been able to satisfy it. He could have made camp hours before if he had wanted to. There were plenty of good places to camp on the river. But this was good.

Nick tucked two big chips of pine under the grill. The fire flared up.

He had forgotten to get water for the coffee. Out of the pack he got a folding canvas bucket and walked down the hill, across the edge of the meadow, to the stream. The other bank was in the white mist. The grass was wet and cold as he knelt on the bank and dipped the canvas bucket into the stream. It bellied and pulled hard in the current. The water was ice cold. Nick rinsed the bucket and carried it full up to the camp. Up away from the stream it was not so cold.

Nick drove another big nail and hung up the bucket full of water. He dipped the coffee pot half full, put some more chips under the grill onto the fire and put the pot on. He could not remember which way he made coffee. He could remember an argument about it with Hopkins, but not which side he had taken. He decided to bring it to a boil. He remembered now that was Hopkins's way. He had once argued about everything with Hopkins. While he waited for the coffee to boil, he opened a small can of apricots. He liked to open cans. He emptied the can of apricots out into a tin cup. While he watched the coffee on the fire, he drank the juice syrup of the apricots, carefully at first to keep from spilling, then meditatively, sucking the apricots down. They were better than fresh apricots.

The coffee boiled as he watched. The lid came up and coffee and grounds ran down the side of the pot. Nick took it off the grill. It was a triumph for Hopkins. He put sugar in the empty apricot cup and poured some of the coffee out to cool. It was too hot to pour and he used his hat to hold the handle of the coffee pot. He would not let it steep in the pot at all. Not the first cup. It should be straight Hopkins all the way. Hop deserved that. He was a very serious coffee drinker. He was the most serious man Nick had ever known. Not heavy, serious. That was a long time ago. Hopkins spoke without moving his lips. He had played polo. He made millions of dollars in Texas. He had borrowed carfare to go to Chicago, when the wire came that his first big well had come in. He could have wired for money. That would have been too slow. They called Hop's girl the Blonde Venus. Hop did not mind because she was not his real girl. Hopkins said very confidently that none of them would make fun of his real girl. He was right. Hopkins went away when the telegram came. That was on the Black River. It took eight days for the telegram to reach him. Hopkins gave away his .22 caliber Colt automatic pistol to Nick. He gave his camera to Bill. It was to remember him always by. They were all going fishing again next summer. The Hop Head was rich. He would get a yacht and they would all cruise along the north shore of Lake Superior. He was excited but serious. They said good-bye and all felt bad. It broke up the trip. They never saw Hopkins again. That was a long time ago on the Black River.

Nick drank the coffee, the coffee according to Hopkins. The coffee was bitter. Nick laughed. It made a good ending to the story. His mind was starting to work. He knew he could choke it because he was tired enough. He spilled the coffee out of the pot and shook the grounds loose into the fire. He lit a cigarette and went inside the tent. He took off his shoes and trousers, sitting on the blankets, rolled the shoes up inside the trousers for a pillow and got in between the blankets.

Out through the front of the tent he watched the glow of the fire, when the night wind blew on it. It was a quiet night. The swamp was perfectly quiet. Nick stretched under the blanket comfortably. A mosquito hummed close to his ear. Nick sat up and lit a match. The mosquito was on the canvas, over his head. Nick moved the match quickly up to it. The mosquito made a satisfactory hiss in the flame. The match went out. Nick lay down again under the blanket. He turned on his side and shut his eyes. He was sleepy. He felt sleep coming. He curled up under the blanket and went to sleep.

PART TWO

In the morning the sun was up and the tent was starting to get hot. Nick crawled out under the mosquito netting stretched across the mouth of the tent, to look at the morning. The grass was wet on his hands as he came out. He held his trousers and his shoes in his hands. The sun was just up over the hill. There was the meadow, the river and the swamp. There were birch trees in the green of the swamp on the other side of the river.

The river was clear and smoothly fast in the early morning. Down about two hundred yards were three logs all the way across the stream. They made the water smooth and deep above them. As Nick watched, a mink crossed the river on the logs and went into the swamp. Nick was excited. He was excited by the early morning and the river. He was really too hurried to eat breakfast, but he knew he must. He built a little fire and put on the coffee pot.

While the water was heating in the pot he took an empty bottle and went down over the edge of the high ground to the meadow. The meadow was wet with dew and Nick wanted to catch grasshoppers for bait before the sun dried the grass. He found plenty of good grasshoppers. They were at the base of the grass stems. Sometimes they clung to a grass stem. They were cold and wet with the dew, and could not jump until the sun warmed them. Nick picked them up, taking only the medium-sized brown ones, and put them into the bottle. He turned over a log and just under the shelter of the edge were several hundred hoppers. It was a grasshopper lodging house. Nick put about fifty of the medium browns into the bottle. While he was picking up the hoppers the others warmed in the sun and commenced to hop away. They flew when they hopped. At first they made one flight and stayed stiff when they landed, as though they were dead.

Nick knew that by the time he was through with breakfast they would be as lively as ever. Without dew in the grass it would take him all day to catch a bottle full of good grasshoppers and he would have to crush many of them, slamming at them with his hat. He washed his hands at the stream. He was excited to be near it. Then he walked up to the tent. The hoppers were already jumping stiffly in the grass. In the bottle, warmed by the sun, they were jumping in a mass. Nick put in a pine stick as a cork. It plugged the mouth of the bottle enough, so the hoppers could not get out and left plenty of air passage.

He had rolled the log back and knew he could get grasshoppers there every morning.

Nick laid the bottle full of jumping grasshoppers against a pine trunk. Rapidly he mixed some buckwheat flour with water and stirred it smooth, one cup of flour, one cup of water. He put a handful of coffee in the pot and dipped a lump of grease out of a can and slid it sputtering across the hot skillet. On the smoking skillet he poured smoothly the buckwheat batter. It spread like lava, the grease spitting sharply. Around the edges the buckwheat cake began to firm, then brown, then crisp. The surface was bubbling slowly to porousness. Nick pushed under the browned under surface with a fresh pine chip. He shook the skillet sideways and the cake was loose on the surface. I won't try and flop it, he thought. He slid the chip of clean wood all the way under the cake, and flopped it over onto its face. It sputtered in the pan.

When it was cooked Nick regreased the skillet. He used all the batter. It made another big flapjack and one smaller one.

Nick ate a big flapjack and a smaller one, covered with apple butter. He put apple butter on the third cake, folded it over twice, wrapped it in oiled paper and put it in his shirt pocket. He put the apple butter jar back in the pack and cut bread for two sandwiches.

In the pack he found a big onion. He sliced it in two and peeled the silky outer skin. Then he cut one half into slices and made onion sandwiches. He wrapped them in oiled paper and buttoned them in the other pocket of his khaki shirt. He turned the skillet upside down on the grill, drank the coffee, sweetened and yellow brown with the condensed milk in it, and tidied up the camp. It was a good camp.

Nick took his fly rod out of the leather rod-case, jointed it, and shoved the rod-case back into the tent. He put on the reel and threaded the line through the guides. He had to hold it from hand to hand, as he threaded it, or it would slip back through its own weight. It was a heavy, double tapered fly line. Nick had paid eight dollars for it a long time ago. It was made heavy to lift back in the air and come forward flat and heavy and straight to make it possible to cast a fly which has no weight. Nick opened the aluminum leader box. The leaders were coiled between the damp flannel pads. Nick had wet the pads at the water cooler on the train up to St. Ignace. In the damp pads the gut leaders had softened and Nick unrolled one and tied it by a loop at the end of the heavy fly line. He fastened a hook on the end of the leader. It was a small hook; very thin and springy.

Nick took it from his hook book, sitting with the rod across his lap. He tested the knot and the spring of the rod by pulling the line taut. It was a good feeling. He was careful not to let the hook bite into his finger.

He started down to the stream, holding his rod, the bottle of grasshoppers hung from his neck by a thong tied in half hitches around the neck of the bottle. His landing net hung by a hook from his belt. Over his shoulder was a long flour sack tied at each corner into an ear. The cord went over his shoulder. The sack flapped against his legs.

Nick felt awkward and professionally happy with all his equipment hanging from him. The grasshopper bottle swung against his chest. In his shirt the breast pockets bulged against him with the lunch and his fly book.

He stepped into the stream. It was a shock. His trousers clung tight to his legs. His shoes felt the gravel. The water was a rising cold shock.

Rushing, the current sucked against his legs. Where he stepped in, the water was over his knees. He waded with the current. The gravel slid under his shoes. He looked down at the swirl of water below each leg and tipped up the bottle to get a grasshopper.

The first grasshopper gave a jump in the neck of the bottle and went out into the water. He was sucked under in the whirl by Nick's right leg and came to the surface a little way down stream. He floated rapidly, kicking. In a quick circle, breaking the smooth surface of the water, he disappeared. A trout had taken him.

Another hopper poked his face out of the bottle. His antennae wavered. He was getting his front legs out of the bottle to jump. Nick took him by the head and held him while he threaded the slim hook under his chin, down through his thorax and into the last segments of his abdomen. The grasshopper took hold of the hook with his front feet, spitting tobacco juice on it. Nick dropped him into the water.

Holding the rod in his right hand he let out line against the pull of the grasshopper in the current. He stripped off line from the reel with his left hand and let it run free. He could see the hopper in the little waves of the current. It went out of sight.

There was a tug on the line. Nick pulled against the taut line. It was his first strike. Holding the now living rod across the current, he brought in the line with his left hand. The rod bent in jerks, the trout pumping against the current. Nick knew it was a small one. He lifted the rod straight up in the air. It bowed with the pull.

He saw the trout in the water jerking with his head and body against the shifting tangent of the line in the stream.

Nick took the line in his left hand and pulled the trout, thumping tiredly against the current, to the surface. His back was mottled the clear, water-over-gravel color, his side flashing in the sun. The rod under his right arm, Nick stooped, dipping his right hand into the current. He held the trout, never still, with his moist right hand, while he unhooked the barb from his mouth, then dropped him back into the stream.

He hung unsteadily in the current, then settled to the bottom beside a stone. Nick reached down his hand to touch him, his arm to the elbow under water. The trout was steady in the moving stream, resting on the gravel, beside a stone. As Nick's fingers touched him, touched his smooth, cool, underwater feeling he was gone, gone in a shadow across the bottom of the stream.

He's all right, Nick thought. He was only tired.

He had wet his hand before he touched the trout, so he would not disturb the delicate mucus that covered him. If a trout was touched with a dry hand, a white fungus attacked the unprotected spot. Years before when he had fished crowded streams, with fly fishermen ahead of him and behind him, Nick had again and again come on dead trout, furry with white fungus, drifted against a rock, or floating belly up in some pool. Nick did not like to fish with other men on the river. Unless they were of your party, they spoiled it.

He wallowed down the stream, above his knees in the current, through the fifty yards of shallow water above the pile of logs that crossed the stream. He did not rebait his hook and held it in his hand as he waded. He was certain he could catch small trout in the shallows, but he did not want them. There would be no big trout in the shallows this time of day.

Now the water deepened up his thighs sharply and coldly. Ahead was the smooth dammed-back flood of water above the logs. The water was smooth and dark; on the left, the lower edge of the meadow; on the right the swamp.

Nick leaned back against the current and took a hopper from the bottle. He threaded the hopper on the hook and spat on him for good luck. Then he pulled several yards of line from the reel and tossed the hopper out ahead onto the fast, dark water. It floated down towards the logs, then the weight of the line pulled the bait under the surface. Nick held the rod in his right hand, letting the line run out through his fingers.

There was a long tug. Nick struck and the rod came alive and dangerous, bent double, the line tightening, coming out of water, tightening, all in a heavy, dangerous, steady pull. Nick felt the moment when the leader would break if the strain increased and let the line go.

The reel ratcheted into a mechanical shriek as the line went out in a rush. Too fast. Nick could not check it, the line rushing out, the reel note rising as the line ran out.

With the core of the reel showing, his heart feeling stopped with the excitement, leaning back against the current that mounted icily his thighs, Nick thumbed the reel hard with his left hand. It was awkward getting his thumb inside the fly reel frame.

As he put on pressure the line tightened into sudden hardness and beyond the logs a huge trout went high out of water. As he jumped, Nick lowered the tip of the rod. But he felt, as he dropped the tip to ease the strain, the moment when the strain was too great; the hardness too tight. Of course, the leader had broken. There was no mistaking the feeling when all spring left the line and it became dry and hard. Then it went slack.

His mouth dry, his heart down, Nick reeled in. He had never seen so big a trout. There was a heaviness, a power not to be held, and then the bulk of him, as he jumped. He looked as broad as a salmon.

Nick's hand was shaky. He reeled in slowly. The thrill had been too much. He felt, vaguely, a little sick, as though it would be better to sit down.

The leader had broken where the hook was tied to it. Nick took it in his hand. He thought of the trout somewhere on the bottom, holding himself steady over the gravel, far down below the light, under the logs, with the hook in his jaw. Nick knew the trout's teeth would cut through the snell of the hook. The hook would imbed itself in his jaw. He'd bet the trout was angry. Anything that size would be angry. That was a trout. He had been solidly hooked. Solid as a rock. He felt like a rock, too, before he started off. By God, he was a big one. By God, he was the biggest one I ever heard of.

Nick climbed out onto the meadow and stood, water running down his trousers and out of his shoes, his shoes squelchy. He went over and sat on the logs. He did not want to rush his sensations any.

He wriggled his toes in the water, in his shoes, and got out a cigarette from his breast pocket. He lit it and tossed the match into the fast water below the logs. A tiny trout rose at the match, as it swung around in the fast current. Nick laughed. He would finish the cigarette.

He sat on the logs, smoking, drying in the sun, the sun warm on his back, the river shallow ahead entering the woods, curving into the woods, shallows, light glittering, big water-smooth rocks, cedars along the bank and white birches, the logs warm in the sun, smooth to sit on, without bark, gray to the touch; slowly the feeling of disappointment left him. It went away slowly, the feeling of disappointment that came sharply after the thrill that made his shoulders ache. It was all right now. His rod lying out on the logs, Nick tied a new hook on the leader, pulling the gut tight until it grimped into itself in a hard knot.

He baited up, then picked up the rod and walked to the far end of the logs to get into the water, where it was not too deep. Under and beyond the logs was a deep pool. Nick walked around the shallow shelf near the swamp shore until he came out on the shallow bed of the stream.

On the left, where the meadow ended and the woods began, a great elm tree was uprooted. Gone over in a storm, it lay back into the woods, its roots clotted with dirt, grass growing in them, rising a solid bank beside the stream. The river cut to the edge of the uprooted tree. From where Nick stood he could see deep channels, like ruts, cut in the shallow bed of the stream by the flow of the current. Pebbly where he stood and pebbly and full of boulders beyond; where it curved near the tree roots, the bed of the stream was marly and between the ruts of deep water green weed fronds swung in the current.

Nick swung the rod back over his shoulder and forward, and the line, curving forward, laid the grasshopper down on one of the deep channels in the weeds. A trout struck and Nick hooked him.

Holding the rod far out toward the uprooted tree and sloshing backward in the current, Nick worked the trout, plunging, the rod bending alive, out of the danger of the weeds into the open river. Holding the rod, pumping alive against the current, Nick brought the trout in. He rushed, but always came, the spring of the rod yielding to the rushes, sometimes jerking under water, but always bringing him in. Nick eased downstream with the rushes. The rod above his head he led the trout over the net, then lifted.

The trout hung heavy in the net, mottled trout back and silver sides in the meshes. Nick unhooked him; heavy sides, good to hold, big undershot jaw, and slipped him, heaving and big sliding, into the long sack that hung from his shoulders in the water.

Nick spread the mouth of the sack against the current and it filled, heavy with water. He held it up, the bottom in the stream, and the water poured out through the sides. Inside at the bottom was the big trout, alive in the water.

Nick moved downstream. The sack out ahead of him sunk heavy in the water, pulling from his shoulders.

It was getting hot, the sun hot on the back of his neck.

Nick had one good trout. He did not care about getting many trout. Now the stream was shallow and wide. There were trees along both banks. The trees of the left bank made short shadows on the current in the forenoon sun. Nick knew there were trout in each shadow. In the afternoon, after the sun had crossed toward the hills, the trout would be in the cool shadows on the other side of the stream.

The very biggest ones would lie up close to the bank. You could always pick them up there on the Black. When the sun was down they all moved out into the current. Just when the sun made the water blinding in the glare before it went down, you were liable to strike a big trout anywhere in the current. It was almost impossible to fish then, the surface of the water was blinding as a mirror in the sun. Of course, you could fish upstream, but in a stream like the Black, or this, you had to wallow against the current and in a deep place, the water piled up on you. It was no fun to fish upstream with this much current.

Nick moved along through the shallow stretch watching the banks for deep holes. A beech tree grew close beside the river, so that the branches hung down into the water. The stream went back in under the leaves. There were always trout in a place like that.

Nick did not care about fishing that hole. He was sure he would get hooked in the branches.

It looked deep though. He dropped the grasshopper so the current took it under water, back in under the overhanging branch. The line pulled hard and Nick struck. The trout threshed heavily, half out of water in the leaves and branches. The line was caught. Nick pulled hard and the trout was off. He reeled in and holding the hook in his hand, walked down the stream.

Ahead, close to the left bank, was a big log. Nick saw it was hollow; pointing up river the current entered it smoothly, only a little ripple spread each side of the log. The water was deepening. The top of the hollow log was gray and dry. It was partly in the shadow.

Nick took the cork out of the grasshopper bottle and a hopper clung to it. He picked him off, hooked him and tossed him out. He held the rod far out so that the hopper on the water moved into the current flowing into the hollow log. Nick lowered the rod and the hopper floated in. There was a heavy strike. Nick swung the rod against the pull. It felt as though he were hooked into the log itself, except for the live feeling.

He tried to force the fish out into the current. It came, heavily.

The line went slack and Nick thought the trout was gone. Then he saw him, very near, in the current, shaking his head, trying to get the hook out. His mouth was clamped shut. He was fighting the hook in the clear flowing current.

Looping in the line with his left hand, Nick swung the rod to make the line taut and tried to lead the trout toward the net, but he was gone, out of sight, the line pumping. Nick fought him against the current, letting him thump in the water against the spring of the rod. He shifted the rod to his left hand, worked the trout upstream, holding his weight, fighting on the rod, and then let him down into the net. He lifted him clear of the water, a heavy half circle in the net, the net dripping, unhooked him and slid him into the sack.

He spread the mouth of the sack and looked down in at the two big trout alive in the water.

Through the deepening water, Nick waded over to the hollow log. He took the sack off, over his head, the trout flopping as it came out of water, and hung it so the trout were deep in the water. Then he pulled himself up on the log and sat, the water from his trouser and boots running down into the stream. He laid his rod down, moved along to the shady end of the log and took the sandwiches out of his pocket. He dipped the sandwiches in the cold water. The current carried away the crumbs. He ate the sandwiches and dipped his hat full of water to drink the water running out through his hat just ahead of his drinking.

It was cool in the shade, sitting on the log. He took a cigarette out and struck a match to light it. The match sunk into the gray wood, making a tiny furrow. Nick leaned over the side of the log, found a hard place and lit the match. He sat smoking and watching the river.

Ahead the river narrowed and went into a swamp. The river became smooth and deep and the swamp looked solid with cedar trees, their trunks close together, their branches solid. It would not be possible to walk through a swamp like that. The branches grew so low. You would have to keep almost level with the ground to move at all. You could not crash through the branches. That must be why the animals that lived in swamps were built the way they were, Nick thought.

He wished he had brought something to read. He felt like reading. He did not feel like going on into the swamp. He looked down the river. A big cedar slanted all the way across the stream. Beyond that the river went into the swamp.

Nick did not want to go in there now. He felt a reaction against deep wading with the water deepening up under his armpits, to hook big trout in places impossible to land them. In the swamp the banks were bare, the big cedars came together overhead, the sun did not come through, except in patches; in the fast deep water, in the half light, the fishing would be tragic. In the swamp fishing was a tragic adventure. Nick did not want it. He did not want to go down the stream any further today.

He took out his knife, opened it and stuck it in the log. Then he pulled up the sack, reached into it and brought out one of the trout. Holding him near the tail, hard to hold, alive, in his hand, he whacked him against the log. The trout quivered, rigid. Nick laid him on the log in the shade and broke the neck of the other fish the same way. He laid them side by side on the log. They were fine trout.

Nick cleaned them, slitting them from the vent to the tip of the jaw. All the insides and the gills and tongue came out in one piece. They were both males; long gray-white strips of milt, smooth and clean. All the insides clean and compact, coming out all together. Nick tossed the offal ashore for the minks to find.

He washed the trout in the stream. When he held them back up in the water they looked like live fish. Their color was not gone yet. He washed his hands and dried them on the log. Then he laid the trout on the sack spread out on the log, rolled them up in it, tied the bundle and put it in the landing net. His knife was still standing, blade stuck in the log. He cleaned it on the wood and put it in his pocket.

Nick stood up on the log, holding his rod, the landing net hanging heavy, then stepped into the water and splashed ashore. He climbed the bank and cut up into the woods, toward the high ground. He was going back to camp. He looked back. The river just showed through the trees. There were plenty of days coming when he could fish the swamp.

TROUTING
ALONG THE
CATASAUQUA

FRANK FORESTER

"And this 'clattering creek,' what sort of water is it?" asked Frank; "that I may learn at once the whole lay of the land."

"A real mountain burn."

"I'm thinking of trying it myself tomorrow," said Robins. "Mr. Langdale tells me it can only be fished with bait, and that's what I'm best at. Besides, there are bigger fish in it."

"But fewer," answered Langdale. "No, Robins, I'd advise you to stick to the 'Stony,' unless you'll try a cast of the fly with us over the pool and down the Catasauqua."

"No, no," replied St. Clair, half indignantly, "none of your flies for me, and no canoe-work. But why do you advise me against it? You said there were no trees, bait-fishing and big fish. What is there against it?"

"The toughest crag-climbing and the most difficult fishing you ever tried."

"What like fishing is it, Lancelot?" asked Frank.

"Exactly what that capital sportsman, Colquhoon of Luss, describes in his excellent book, the 'Moor and Loch,' under the title of the 'Moorburn'."

"I remember," replied Frank. "Is it as bad as that?"

"Worse; but the fish much larger. I have caught them up to two pounds."

"I should like to hear about that. Can't you read it to me?" asked the Wall-street man, eager for information.

"I've no objection," said Langdale, "if Frank has not. He has read it fifty times already."

"I'm convenient," answered Frank, laying down his knife and fork, the last duck having disappeared.

"Well, then, here goes. Now, Scipio, look alive and clear away the table; bring us our pipes and coffee; and then we'll to bed, for we must be afoot by day-break."

And with the word he rose, and, after turning over a few volumes on his crowded shelves, brought down the volume in question, with its pages underlined, and interlined, and filled with marginal notes and references. This done, he ensconced himself in the chimney corner, threw on a fresh log, and read as follows:

" 'In most of the small Highland burns, there is a succession of cataracts and pools, with a parapet of rock rising perpendicularly on each side, and often scarcely footing enough for a dog to pass. The greater proportion of picturesque-looking brethren of the angle would almost start at the idea of continuing their pastime under such disadvantages. They therefore make a circuit, and come down again upon the burn, where it is more easy to fish, and the ground less rugged. The trout in these places are thus left until many of them grow large, and each taking possession of a favorite nook, drives all the smaller fry away. The difficulty of reaching these places is, I admit, often great, the angler having sometimes to scramble up on his hands and knees, covered with wet moss or gravel, and then drag his fishing-rod after him. These lyns should always be fished up-stream, otherwise the moment you appear at the top of the waterfall or rock, the trout are very like to see you, and slink into their hiding-place. The burn, however, must always be low, as at no other time can you distinguish the snug retreat of these little tyrants, which, indeed, they often leave, during the slightest flood, in search of prey. By fishing up the stream, your head will be on a level with the different eddies and pools, as they successively present themselves, and the rest of your person out of sight. Hold the baited hook with the left hand, jerking out the rod, underhanded, with your right, so as to make the bait fall softly at the lower end of the pool. The trout always take their station either there or at the top where the water flows in, ready to pounce on worms, snails, slugs, etc., as they enter or leave the pool. Should a trout seize the bait, a little time may be given to allow it to gorge, which it will most likely do without much ceremony. If large, care must be taken to prevent it from getting to the top of the lyn, which may probably harbor another expectant. The best plan is, if possible, to persuade it to descend into the pool below. Having deposited the half-pounder in your creel, you will now crawl upon hands and knees, just so near the top of the lyn as will enable you to drop the bait immediately below the bubbling foam, nearly as favorite a station for an overgrown, monopolizing trout as the other. Except in such situations, the burn trout seldom exceeds a quarter of a pound, and may be pulled out with single gut, without much risk of breaking it. In these lyns, however, I have occasionally taken them upward of a pound, which is easily accounted for. As soon as the trout grows to a sufficient size to intimidate his pigmy neighbors, he falls back into the best pool for feeding, not occupied by a greater giant than himself, and as these lyns are almost always in precipices very difficult of access, he remains undisturbed and alone, or with a single companion, driving all others away, until he may at last attain to a pound weight.'

"Now, I fear, brother angler, that you are in some respects what the indefatigable Gael would call a 'picturesque angler'; so I advise you in good faith, stick to the 'Stony Brook'; fish it from the long fall carefully down. Scipio shall attend you with the landing-net and plenty of worms and minnows; the last, hooked through the lip and back fin, will do you yeoman service in the lower pools; and Frank and I will join you in the afternoon."

"Agreed," said Mr. Robins; "I'll take your advice, I believe; and now I guess I'll turn in. Good night."

"Time, too," said Frank, laughing. "He was beginning to get a little white about the gills. Could that be his old Otard; he did not drink so much of it."

"Lord help you, no! he'd drink a gallon of it and no hurt. No! But he will persist in smoking Cavendish tobacco and kinnikinnic, because he has seen me do it, and, I believe, imagines that it confers some special powers of trout-catching. But come, suppose we turn in, too; you'll be tired after your journey, and a good night's rest will give a steady hand and clear eye tomorrow."

"Volontiers."

So they incontinently joined the Wall-street man, who declared, half asleep, that the bed was not so very bad, after all; while Frank, once ensconced in the fragrant sheets, swore, by the great god Pan, patron of hunters, that never had bed so sweet, so soft, so warm, in every way so excellent, received the limbs of weary hunter. And so, indeed, it proved; for, until Scipio made his entree, with his announcement, "Breakfast soon be ready, Massa; sun h'em 'mose up now," no one stirred or spoke during the livelong night.

Thereon they all turned, like the Iron Duke, not over, but out. Their sporting toilets were soon made; but Frank and Lancelot, in their old shepherd's plaid jackets and trews and hob-nailed fishing shoes, could not but exchange glances and smiles at the elaborate rig of their friend, which some Broadway artist had, it was evident, elaborated from a Parisian fashion-plate, the high boots of exquisitely enamelled leather, the fine doeskin trousers, the many-pocketed, pearl-buttoned shooting jacket of fawn-colored silk plush, the batiste neckerchief and waist-coat, point device, with green and silver fishes embroidered on a blue ground, and, to complete the whole, a cavalier hat, in which, but that it lacked the king's black feather, Rupert might well have charged at Marston Moor or Naseby. He seemed, however, so happy, that it would have been as useless as ill-natured to indoctrinate him; for evidently, as an angler, the man was hopelessly incurable, though, as Frank observed, for Wall-street, he was wonderfully decent.

His weapon was a right good Conroy's general-fishing rod, but without reel, and having its line, an unusually stout silk one, with a superb salmon-gut bottom, which, in good hands, would have held a twenty-pounder, made carefully fast to the top funnel; eschewing all use of the ring and destroying all chance of the rod's regularly bending to its work. But again, to counsel would have been to offend; so our friends held their peace.

The smoked venison ham, broiled troutlings, dry toast and black tea, which furnished their morning meal, were soon finished; and forth they went into the delicious, breezy air of the quiet summer morning, not a sound disturbing the solitude, except the plash and rippling of the rapid waters, the low voices of the never-silent pine-tops, and the twittering of the swallows, as they skimmed the limpid pool.

Up the gorge of the Stony Brook, followed by Scipio, with bait of all kinds enough to have kept the kraten fat for one day at least, a large creel at his back, and gaff and landing-net in hand, away went St. Clair Robins, gay and joyous and confident; and then, but not till then quoth Forester—

"And whither we?"

"To the other side of the pool. You may see the big fish rising under the alders, there, in the shadow of the big hill, from this distance. That shadow will hang there until noon, while all this side of the basin will be in blazing sunshine. Not a fish will bite here, I warrant me, until three o'clock, while we'll fill our basket there with good ones, certain. The best fish in the pool lies under that round-headed stone, just in the tail of the strong eddy, where the 'Clattering Creek' comes in, in the broken water. I rate him a six-pounder, and have saved him for you all the spring. As soon as the sun turns westward, and the hemlocks' shadows cross the white water, you shall kill him, and then we'll away to the Wall-street man"; and therewith the larger birch canoe was manned, paddled gently over to the shady side of the pool and moored in about twenty-foot water, and then, the rods being put together, the reels secured and the lines carried duly through the rings, the following colloquy followed:

"What flies do you most affect here, Lancelot?" asked Frank.

"Any, at times, and almost all," answered Langdale. "In some weather I have killed well with middle-sized gaudy lake flies; but my favorites, on the whole, are all the red, brown, orange, and yellow hackles, and the blue and yellow duns. And yours?"

"My favorite of all is a snipe feather and mouse body; next to that the black and the furnace hackles."

"And will you use them today?"

"I will; the snipe wing for my stretcher. I mean to kill the big chap with him this evening."

"Be it so! to work."

And to work they went; but, though most glorious the sport to enjoy, or even to see performed gnostically, to read of it described, is as little interesting as to describe it is difficult. Suffice it to say, that before the sun had begun to turn westward, sixteen brace and a half were fairly brought to basket by our anglers, one a three-pound-and-a-halfer, three two-pounders, there or there about; not a fish under a pound, all smaller were thrown back unscathed, and very few so small as that, all beautifully fed fish, big-bellied, small-headed, high in color, prime in condition. At one o'clock, they paddled leisurely back to the cabin, lunched frugally on a crust of bread and a glass of sherry, and awaited the hour when the hemlock's shadow should be on the white water.

At the moment they were there; and lo! the big trout was feeding fiercely on the natural fly.

"Be ready, Frank, and when next he rises drop your fly right in the middle of his bell."

"Be easy, I mean it." His line, as he spoke, was describing an easy circle around his head; the fish rose not. The second revolution succeeded; the great trout rose, missed his object, disappeared; and, on the instant, right in the centre of the bell, ere the inmost circle had subsided, the snipe feather fell and fluttered. With an arrowy rush, the monster rose, and as his broad tail showed above the surface, the merry music of the resonant click-reel told that Frank had him. Well struck, he was better played, killed unexceptionably; in thirteen minutes he lay fluttering on the greensward, lacking four ounces of a six-pounder. The snipe feather and mouse body won the day in a canter. So off they started up the Stony Brook, to admire the feats of P. St. Clair Robins. It was not long ere they found him; he had reached the lower waters of the brook, full of beautiful scours, eddies, whirlpools and basins, and was fishing quietly down it, wading about knee deep with his bait, he was roving with a minnow, some ten yards down the stream, playing naturally enough in the clear, swirling waters. Some trees on the bank hung thickly over his head; a few yards behind him was a pretty rocky cascade, and above that an open upland glade, lighted up by a gleam of the westering sun; and, altogether, with his gay garb, he presented quite a picturesque, if not a very sportsmanly appearance.

"After all," said Frank, as unseen themselves, they stood observing him, "he does not do it so very badly as one might have expected."

But before the words had passed his lips, a good fish, at least a pounder, threw itself clear out of the water and seized his minnow. In a second, in the twinkling of an eye, by a movement never before seen or contemplated by mortal angler, he ran his right hand up to the top of the third joint of his rod, which he held perpendicularly aloft, and with his left grasped his line, mid length, and essayed to drag the trout by main force out of his element. The tackle was stout, the stream strong, the bottom slippery, the fish active, and, before any one could see how it was done, hand and foot both slipped, the line parted, the rod crashed in the middle, the fish went over the next fall with a joyous flirt of his tail, and the fisherman, hapless fisherman, measured his own length in the deepest pool of the Stony Brook.

He was soon fished out, equipped in dry rigging, comforted with a hot glass of his favorite cognac; but he would not be consoled. He was off at daylight the following morning, and, for aught that I have heard, Cotton's Cabin beheld him nevermore.

WHERE ROLLS
THE ROGUE

ZANE GREY

The happiest lot of any angler would be to live somewhere along the banks of the Rogue River, most beautiful stream of Oregon. Then, if he kept close watch on conditions, he could be ready on the spot when the run of steelhead began. This peculiar and little-studied trout travels up streams and rivers flowing into the Pacific, all the way from northern California to British Columbia. During the run, which occurs at varying seasons according to locality, the steelhead are caught in abundance, on bait, salmon eggs, spinners, and spoons. But so far as I can learn they will rise to a fly in only two rivers, the Eel and the Rogue, particularly the latter. The Rogue is probably the outlet of Crater Lake, and is the coldest, swiftest, deepest stream I ever fished.

The singular difference in steelhead of different localities is probably a matter of water. The steelhead that runs up the Klamath, which is a stream of rather warm, yellow, muggy water, is less brilliantly colored than the Rogue steelhead, and certainly not to be compared with him as a game fish. Many anglers claim that rainbow trout and steelhead trout are one and the same species. My own theory is that the rainbow is a steelhead which cannot get to the sea. He is landlocked. And a steelhead is a rainbow that lives in the salt water and runs up freshwater streams to spawn. Once the whole western part of the continent was submerged. As the land became more and more elevated through the upward thrust of the earth the salt water receded, landlocking fish in lakes and streams. The rainbow might be a species that survived.

The relation of the two fish has never been satisfactorily established.

But one thing seems assured—to fly fishermen who know the Rogue River, the steelhead is the most wonderful of all fish.

I first heard of steelhead through Mr. Lester, a salmon fisherman of long experience. He was visiting Long Key, Florida, and happened to tell me of his trip to Oregon and his adventure on the Rogue. He said he could not hold these steelhead—that when they were hooked they began to leap downstream through the rapids, and had to be followed. The big ones all got away. They smashed his tackle. Now this information from a noted salmon angler was exceedingly interesting. That happened six years ago. I made a trip to Oregon and found the Rogue beautiful beyond compare, but there seemed to be no fish in it. Two years ago R.C. and I ventured again, along about the end of June. Forked-tail trout and Chinook salmon had begun to appear, but no steelhead. They were expected any time. R.C. and I could not catch even the less desirable fish that had already come. We persevered, but all to no purpose.

The summer, 1922, recorded a different story. Upon our return from Vancouver and Washington we reached Grants Pass, Oregon, just when the run of steelhead was on. This was in September, and Lone Angler Wiborn had accompanied us. Fishermen friends we had made there assured us that we had struck it just right and were in for the sport of our lives. Fred Burnham, of California, surely one of the greatest of fly fishermen, was there, and he, in company with several of the native experts, kindly took upon themselves the burden of showing us how and where.

We had the finest of tackle, but only two fly-rods in the collection that would do for steelhead. Too light! And not one of our fly-reels would hold a third enough line. There were no reels of American manufacture that would do for this great fish. We had to have English reels that would hold a hundred yards of linen line besides the thirty or forty yards of casting line. These steelhead ran, we were told. All our flies were too small. Number fours and sixes were used, and Royal Coachman, Professor, Brown Hackle were advised as a start. I had a very old Kosmic fly-rod, nine and a half feet, eight ounces, that took the eye of these gentlemen anglers. Burnham had a hundred rods, but said he would cheerfully steal my Kosmic if I did not sleep with it. We rigged up seven-ounce Hardy rods for R.C. and Lone Angler. All this fuss and care and deliberation over a lot of fishing-tackle seems to many people an evidence of narrow, finicky minds. It is nothing of the kind. It is unalloyed joy of anticipation, and half of pleasure. If anyone should claim it a remarkably expensive procedure, I could not gainsay that.

Next morning we got up in the dark, and had breakfast at five o'clock in a little all-night restaurant, and were on the way up the river to Pierce Riffle before daylight. The morning was cool and gray. Forest fires were burning in the mountains and the fragrant odor of pine filled the air. Gradually the day broke, and when we turned off the road and ran down to the river the red of sunrise tipped the timbered peaks. A fringe of trees bordered the river and hid it from sight until we penetrated them.

The roar of swift, heavy waters greeted me before I saw the long green-and-white rapid that bore the name Pierce Riffle. Upstream the broad river glided round a wooded curve, and hurrying and constricting its current slid into a narrow channel with a mellow roar. A long flat bar of gravel led down to the water, and on the other shore the current rushed deep and strong, chafing at a rocky willow-skirted bank. The whole disturbance of water was perhaps a quarter of a mile long. Below the riffle opened out a magnificent broad stretch of river. The white water poured into it. There was a swift current, and dancing waves for a hundred yards, after which the water quieted and glided smoothly on toward the curve where the river disappeared. A faint violet light glimmered over the river. Most striking of all, however, were the significant widening circles and agitated spots of the placid surface upstream, and the hard splashes in the swift current before us, and below at the head of the big pool the sight of many fish breaking water, frequently several at once, trout of varying size, and steelhead that showed their beautiful colors, and occasionally a huge salmon. Certain it was that, what with trying to see all this and rig my tackle at the same time, I missed threading my line through at least two guides on my rod.

Lone Angler, true to his instincts, slipped off alone downstream; R.C. headed for the middle of the riffle, while Wharton led me up to the wide sweep of water where the river glided into the rapids. I had only hip boots and could not wade far out. Wharton wore waders and went in above his waist. Then he began to cast his fly, reaching fifty, sixty, and even seventy feet. Out there in the middle and beyond was where the steelhead lay. Even had I been able to wade out there I could not have cast far enough. At once I saw the very high degree of skill required. My spirits and hopes suffered a shock, and straightaway I felt discouraged. Nevertheless, for a while I divided my time between trying to cast my fly afar and watching Wharton at work. He claimed he was not a fine fly-caster, although he could reach the distance. But that morning the steelhead were not striking. After long patient efforts he tried one of the tiny brass spinners, without any better success. Eventually the sun grew hot and the fish stopped breaking and playing on the surface. R.C. and Lone Angler had found no luck. We gave up

and started back to town. Wharton advised us to try it in the afternoon, from four o'clock until dark.

The day grew very hot and oppressive. The mountains appeared
shrouded in smoke. Oregon was in the grip of a very severe hot, dry
spell of weather, and was sadly in need of rain.

By two o'clock we were on our way up the river, and this time we
strolled beyond Pierce Riffle to see an irrigation dam where, we had
heard, salmon and steelhead congregated in great numbers and were
visible. The concrete structure was indeed a fine piece of work, but we
hardly more than glanced at it.

A board walk crossed the river on top of this dam. From the road,
high up, we could see the fish leaping, and we ran over one another to
get down on that bridge. Water was streaming through cracks in the
gates. Evidently this dam had been built across a rocky formation in
the river bed. Below stood up narrow ridges of rocks, and between two
of these ran a channel of swift water, dropping every few rods over a
ledge. This channel was alive with steelhead. First we saw them leaping up the white foamy falls; then we found them in corners and eddies
of the channel, and lastly we stood right over a place where we could
see hundreds of these wonderful fish. Not more than thirty feet below
us! Shallow swift water ran over smooth rock, and swirled in a deep
eddying pool, and then rushed on to take the first fall. Here had congregated the mass of steelhead. They had gone the wrong side of the
dam to get up, for the fish ladder was at the other shore of the river.
Every moment a steelhead would dart up the swift water and leap
against the concrete wall, to fall back. The average weight of these fish
appeared to be about six to seven pounds, but we saw many of ten and
twelve pounds, and a few larger still. They were of different colors,
some dark-backed, others yellow, most of them speckled gray-green.
Whenever one turned on his side, then we caught the beautiful pink
and silver gleam.

We crossed the river to find on the other side a wide deep pool below
the apron of the dam, and up out of this led the zigzag fish ladder, an
admirable waterway of many little steps, whereby the fish could get up
over the dam. By watching sharply, we were able now and then to see
the dark flash of fish in the white water. Hovering and wavering in the
pool were large purple shadows, big salmon waiting for night to take
their turn at the fish ladder. Occasionally one of these huge salmon
would swoop up in the current, and lazily expose his back to the sun
and to our fascinated gaze. One would have weighed more than sixty
pounds. As he loomed up he gleamed purple, then darker, shading to
brown, and when he came out into the light he seemed to have a
greenish-black back covered with dots, and his tail looked a foot wide.

"Say, if we could only drop a line to him!" ejaculated R.C.

Speech was inadequate to express what I felt. Almost I regretted the law and the huge white sign which forbade fishing within four hundred feet of this dam. We idled there watching, and then we went back across the dam to where the steelhead were leaping and splashing. At last R.C. and Wiborn had to drag me away from there.

Five o'clock was it instead of four when we arrived at Pierce Riffle. Dusky and hot lay the somber smoky glare over the river. But the water would be like ice.

No fish appeared to be breaking. Possibly the steelhead had moved upstream. We were told that they arrived in schools, tarried at a riffle or rapid, and passed on during the night. But any day might bring a new and fresher school.

We were on our own hook, so to speak, this afternoon, and therefore more leisurely, more independent, and less keyed up. R.C. was at the head of the riffle in less time than it takes to tell it; Lone Angler took a long while to get into new waders; and I wasted a good deal of time over my tackle. This afternoon I wore hobnailed shoes over stockings, dispensing altogether with rubber, and I was rather loath to enter that ice-cold water. Still the day had been so hot that I should have welcomed the coldest of water. My brother started out with a spinner, and he had not made a dozen casts before he raised a fish.

We did not need his yell to gather that he had apparently hooked a moving avalanche underwater. His rod jerked down and shook like a buggy-whip swinging a heavy lead. I could not hear his reel, but I did not have to hear it to know his line was flying off. Floundering out with great strides, he began to run down the gravelly shore. Right even with us then we saw a black threshing fish split the white water and disappear. R.C.'s rod sprang up like a released sapling. Gone! He waved a sorrowful hand at us and began to reel in. R.C. waded back as far as he dared into the swift heavy current, and began again to cast, quartering across the river, so that his line bagged and drifted down the current, dragging the spinner.

Lone Angler and I waded in at the head of the great pool. Industriously I plied my fly, cast after cast, sometimes executing a good one, until in half an hour I grew tired and discouraged. Steelhead began to leap in the shadow of the willow bank just opposite me. I waded in to my hips, until I had difficulty in keeping my balance in that swift current, and I cast desperately to reach the coveted distance. But always I fell short several yards.

Presently a newcomer appeared on the scene, a little man in farmer garb, with an old straw hat and a pointed beard. He had a cane pole fully twenty feet long. At the butt he had a reel attached, and I saw the big shiny spinner dangling from his line. Some rods above us he labored out on a rocky point, and thrust the enormous pole out over the river. It seemed as though it might reach across. The spinner floated down the length of line he had out, about as long as his pole, and sank from sight. Then this native fisherman stood motionless like Ajax defying the lightning. I wondered skeptically and disdainfully what he imagined he was going to catch. Then in about two minutes he gave a jerk and his long pole bent. Something was pulling mighty hard on his line. But he made short shift of that fish, dragged it ashore and up on the bank, a steelhead of about five pounds. Again he thrust the huge telegraph pole out over the river. Fascinated, I watched him. Just as I feared, pretty soon he had another strike. I saw the pole jerk and curve. This fish was heavier and a fighter. I saw it smash the current and scoot through the water like an arrow. The native endeavoured to be as ruthless and violent as with his first fish. He tried literally to drag the steelhead out. I had hard work to control myself, to keep from yelling to him to play the fish. But he bent the huge pole double, dragged a big white tumbling fish in among the rocks in shallow water, and floundered after it. Disaster attended his awkward and uncouth attempt. The steelhead broke the line and got away. Then the old Oregonian exhibited some peevishness. He looked and acted as if a shabby trick had been played upon him. I was tickled and could almost hear him mutter: "Wal, by Jimmy! I'd 'a' hed thet one if he hedn't busted my line."

He disappeared in the willows and I went back to my own fishing. But presently I heard a sousing splash near me, and looked around to see another native standing in the water above me, holding out a cane pole fully as long as the other fellow's. What was more and worse, that pole was bent. This native had hooked a fish. Suddenly I felt the line rub along my legs. Amazed and angry, I waded back. Then I heard the well-known swish of a taut line cutting water. The man waded down and back, lifted his line over my head, and went ashore. He followed that fish along the shore, and presently pulled it out on the sand, a fine steelhead. Then he approached his former position. I saw him stick some kind of bait on his spinner. When he got to his place above me he cast this out and let it down, and held his rod stationary. I could see his line and it was not three feet from where I stood.

Now what would happen? I looked for Lone Angler and R.C. Both of them waved at me, and not at all sympathetically. In a few moments that native angler hooked another steelhead right by my feet. And he went ashore, and downstream with it, landing a seven-pounder in less than seven minutes. He came back, and soon he had another on. This was too much. It filled me with despair. I changed my fly for a spinner and began to cast that. It seemed to me that I might just as well have had an onion on for bait. Presently the native picked up another steelhead, right off my boots, and this one turned out to be a big one. It made a leap on the first run, a splendid diving leap, came out again fifty feet farther down, and churned the water white again. The fisherman was not able to get ashore quickly enough, so that he could run and follow this fish and it took out all his line and broke off.

"Thet there was a twelve-pounder," he told me as he came back. "Ketched two like him yestiddy down below. Ain't you hevin' any luck?"

I acquainted him with the direful state of my angling fortunes, whereupon he gave me a small crawfish and told me to put that on. Gratefully I did so. I fished alongside of him with great expectancy, but nothing happened to either of us. The steelhead had quit biting.

Sunset had passed, and the dusky violet and purple lights fell over mountains and river. R.C. reported a fish hooked and lost, and Lone Angler said he had not caught anything but scenery.

The next day found us faithfully on the job, but the morning yielded nothing. In the afternoon we went again to the dam to see the steelhead and salmon. Again we were delighted and dejected by sight of wonderful schools of fish. We idled there for two hours, and then we returned to Pierce Riffle.

The sun was westering low and showed a dull magenta through the pall of smoky haze. The river seemed a moving medium of rose and lilac, incredible to the eye. Hot and oppressive, the dry air was full of odorous penetrating fragrance. Not a single fisherman marred the beautiful landscape for us. The loneliness, the charm of the place, the mellow changing roar of the rapids, and the leaping of steelhead everywhere inspired us once more to hope and action.

R.C. got there first, and on his initial cast he raised something big. I saw his spoon hit the water, and then something strike it. A wide breaking swirl attested to the power of the fish. How incredibly fast he shot downstream! R.C. had no time to move out of his tracks before the fish was gone.

I was the last to get ready, and before I stepped into the water R.C. had another strike—missed—and Lone Angler had a steelhead on. It took him the whole length of the swift water, and farther still, not a leaping fish, but a good one of five pounds. This sudden windfall of luck changed the aspect of things. With thrilling zest we went at it, and I held to my desire to catch a steelhead on a fly. The difficulties I had discovered at first hand, and the fact that few steelhead, comparatively, were taken on a fly, spurred me on to an accomplishment of that worthy feat.

R.C. soon struck another snag in the shape of a salmon. One of the heavy Chinook appropriated his spoon and started away from that place. Valiantly and wondrously my brother performed and pursued, but that salmon had a jaw of iron and an unconquerable spirit. He could not be held.

"Looks as if I were going to get mine today," said R.C. to me. "Thought I could lick anything with this tackle."

He had rigged up one of my green Leonard bait-rods, nine and one half feet, ten ounces, that I had built for bonefish, with a good-sized reel full of silk line. He waded in above me, made a wonderful cast clear across the river into the shade of the willows, and a big steelhead leaped out with the spoon in his mouth. Sharp and hard R.C. came up on him, and out he sprang again, a curved quivering opal shape, flashing the ruddy diamond drops of water. I let out a whoop and R.C. yelled, "Run, you son-of-a-gun—run!"

R.C. never moved from his tracks. He held his rod well up, and apparently lightly thumbed the reel. I could hear it screech—screech —screech. Below us stretched the hundred yards of swift water, white and choppy close at hand, and gradually quieting down into the broad deep pool. That steelhead tumbled over the white waves in the most bewildering exhibition I had ever seen. He did not seem to go under at all. He danced like a will-o'-the-wisp, like a twisting light, over and over, with a speed unbelievable. He surely ran that hundred yards in less than ten seconds. He ended this run with a big high leap. Then he sounded.

R.C. came wading down to me. His face was beaming in spite of its tensity. His eyes were alight.

"Say, did you ever see the beat of that? Sure, this steelhead game has got me," he said. "Run, you Indian! That's what all this line is for."

Before the steelhead slowed down he ran off another hundred yards of line. Then R.C. waded out and went with him downstream. Lone Angler accompanied him, and then I, unable to withstand the temptation, waded out, laid down my tackle, and joined them. R.C. gave an admirable performance with that steelhead, handling him perfectly, and eventually beaching him far around the curve of the big pool. Seven and one half pounds!

We went back to the rapid, and in a very few moments R.C. had hooked another, a different kind of fighter. He did not leap and he wanted to go upstream. What with bucking that swift current and R.C.'s strain on the line he soon tired, and gradually dropped down to the still water. There he was dragged over the shoal and landed. Six and one half pounds.

My ethical ambition expired for the time being and I put on a spinner. I made, more or less, nine hundred casts without avail. Then as I was letting my line drift, looking back at Lone Angler, totally unprepared for anything, I had a most tremendous strike. Thirty yards of fly-casting line went by the board in a flash and the green linen line followed. I burned my fingers and thumbs. All the hundred yards of linen line whizzed off the reel. Then this thunderbolt of a fish slowed up. Seizing the opportunity, I nearly drowned myself wading ashore below where I should have gone. Then I ran along the river, downstream. Soon I found that my fish had snagged the line on the bottom. How sickening was that realization! I worked for a long time to save the line, and finally did so, but the steelhead was gone. Never will I forget that strike.

The run of a bonefish, after he is hooked, is certainly great, but this strike of a steelhead is all run. You have no choice but to run yourself. That day indeed was a red-letter day along the Rogue.

Next day Burnham took us up the river, five miles beyond the dam, to a place he called the Suspension Bridge. A couple of wire cables sagged across the water between high banks, and to these were attached loops of chicken-fence wire, which in turn supported some rotten loose boards. The contrivance must have been as old as the oldest Oregon pioneer; it swayed at every step, and was certainly alarming to one unused to it. Burnham had a lot of fun leading us across this bridge, and I was sure he started it swaying by his own movements.

The stretch of Rogue River here was Burnham's favorite place. No wonder! It surpassed any stretch of fishing water I ever encountered. The bank from which we had crossed was high, a rocky rugged cliff, green with moss and vines, and covered on top with heavy timber, consisting in part of giant pines. The bank we approached was high, too, but sloping, and we descended it through thickets to the shallow rocky-floored stream. A narrow riffle roared at the head of this stretch, and sent its swift current along the far shore under the cliff, and through deep channels cut in the flat of the stream bed.

R.C. and Wiborn waded out to the riffle. I saw the former hook and lose a steelhead in the white water. Then I essayed to follow Burnham. I had a task. He stood over six feet tall and wore seven-league wading-boots, and deep or shallow was all the same to him. He worked downstream.

Nevertheless, here was a place where I could wade out as far as I liked and reach all but the farthermost spots. For a hundred yards out the water ran scarcely a foot deep over level rock, and led to where the deep ruts and channels and lanes could be reached. These deeper aisles in the rocky formation of the river bed were wonderful places to fish. The water ran dark and eddying through them. The river here was very wide, bank full, so that no bars or gravel beds or ragged rocks showed from one green shore to the other. The farther down we progressed the more beautiful grew the forest-topped cliff. Meadow larks and orioles sang melodiously in the trees, accompanied by the low murmur of the swift water. White ships of clouds sailed in the blue sky, and the sunlight shone golden on the foliage.

The steelhead were not there or would not rise. Burnham said this stretch seldom failed and we should keep on. What a wonderful sight to see him cast a fly! It fascinated me. It seemed so easy. His fly gleamed like a spark of gold in the sun. It shot out and back, forward and back, and his line seemed to wave, to undulate, to sweep up in a great curve, and at last stretch out low over the water, to drop the deceiving wisp of feathers like thistledown. He always cast quartering a little across the channel so that the bag in his line would drag the fly faster than the current. He said a steelhead rose to a fly and followed it downstream, and struck it so hard that it hooked itself. Twice he raised fish, and both times he let out a lusty yell. But he missed them, to my great disappointment.

Toward the lower end of that magnificent stretch of river the water deepened somewhat and the channels appeared harder for me to reach with a fly. I could not cast over into the shady ruts under the cliff, and it was here that Burnham was raising fish. I would make half a dozen attempts, and that meant at least six sweeps of my rod for each cast, and then I would rest my tired arm and watch Burnham.

I came to a place Burnham had left for me, a joining of two dark channels above a flat rock, behind which swirled and eddied the most haunting and beautiful little pool imaginable. It was fully sixty feet away, a prodigious cast for me. But I essayed it, more in the persistence and pride of practice than in a hope of raising a fish. Straining nerve and muscle, I swept my rod forward and back, forward and back, watching my fly, letting out more line, until I reached the limit. The fly dropped perfectly. I saw it sink and float under the surface, and then as the current caught the bag of line it dragged my fly a little more swiftly. The sight pleased me.

Then out of the dark eddying depths of that pool loomed a shape, dim at first, gathering color and life, until it became the reality of a steelhead, huge and broad as he swerved half over to follow the fly, shining pink and silver through the water. My heart leaped to my throat. Just as he reached the fly I jerked—and pulled it away from him. The action was involuntary. Then one instant I thrilled and shook, and the next my heart turned to lead and I groaned at my stupidity. Many and many a time I cast again over that pool, but all to no avail.

Suddenly my attention was attracted by Burnham's yell, and then shouts of onlookers up on the cliff opposite his position. He had hooked a steelhead. I saw it leaping. He called for me to hurry down and take the rod. I yelled back no. But he insisted. By the time I covered the goodly stretch of distance between us the fish had stopped leaping. But he had out nearly all of Burnham's line. So I took his rod, much to the amusement and interest of the audience on the cliff, and I waded after that steelhead. It took me fully a quarter of an hour to get back that line, and longer to lead the steelhead ashore. My left arm felt dead. The fish was not large, but on Burnham's light rod he was indeed heavy.

After that we fished down to the end of the stretch of good water, with no success. Then we waded to the narrow shore and headed back toward the bridge.

Next day the three of us tried Pierce Riffle again, and struck another off day. The following morning we left at daylight to motor twenty-five miles down the river to meet Burnham at the end of the road.

Our drive over the rugged bluffs above the Rogue, and the accidents we had, and the times we lost the way, would make a story. All I have space for is mention of the picturesque beauty of the Rogue River below Grants Pass. The farther we went and the higher we climbed the more beautiful grew the vistas of river, seen through the iron-walled gorges, or winding white-wreathed between dark and lofty timbered mountains, or meandering through a wide fertile valley of golden cornfields and fertile orchards.

Eventually we found the end of the road and the ranch where Burnham was staying. Late that afternoon he took us to a place called Chair Riffle, where the night before he and a Mr. Carlon had taken a dozen steelhead.

Naturally we were both excited and elated. Chair Riffle owed its name to a chair-shaped stone, on which an angler could sit and fish to his heart's content. This stretch of the Rogue revealed a long wide sweep of water, running four feet deep over gravel beds, where the steelhead lay in certain currents. They loved swift water. Burnham said it was necessary to learn where they lay. This evening, however, they did not lie anywhere in that riffle. They had moved on. We were too late. But I enjoyed sitting in the stone chair, watching, and listening to the river. This was wild country. I saw cougar and bear tracks along the shore, and deer were numerous. The mountains were high, cone-shaped, heavily timbered on some slopes. From this point on through the Coast Range to the Pacific there was unsettled rugged country, full of game and fish.

Next day Burnham and Mr. Carlon extended themselves in efforts to see that I hooked a steelhead on a fly. I enjoyed these kindly sportsman-like offices, but in my secret heart I did not believe the fish god himself could connect me with a steelhead. But you never can tell!

Toward sunset we motored several miles back upstream from the ranch, to Mr. Carlon's favorite fishing water. It was at the foot of a rapid that foamed in many white channels around and between many little islands, all of which were covered by a long heavy green grass. Burnham took Lone Angler and R.C. up above this rapid, while Mr. Carlon rowed a skiff through tortuous swift channels and in all kinds of difficult places in order to get me just where he wanted me. In half a dozen spots he held the boat and instructed me to cast here and there. What swirling eddies, and holes under shelving rocks, and little deep pools overhung by willows! Always behind us on the other side of the ledges of rock was the main roaring white channel.

At last this genial and indefatigable gentleman hauled the boat up on the edge of a rocky island, right in the middle of the lower fall of the rapid. Below us a long irregular sunken ledge of rock divided the deep-heavy water from the eddies and pools on the other side.

"Never have I failed to catch a steelhead here," he said. "You must cast farther. Watch me."

Then he swept his line out over the water without letting it touch, farther and farther, with a wonderful grace and skill. It undulated as had Burnham's, only in longer higher waves, and it seemed instinct with life. Reeling in, he took a position directly behind me, and grasping my rod hand he gave my wrist quick powerful jerks, getting my line out with the sweep that had characterized his. In a few moments he had taught me the swing of it.

"Now try it," he said, finally, turning toward the channel of swift deep water. "Cast across and down. Don't drop your fly until it is as far out as you can cast. Then let it float down along that ledge."

I complied to the best of my new-found ability, succeeding fairly well in reaching the spot designated. But I did not see my fly float under the ledge. The ruddy glow of sun on the water dazzled my eyes.

"There! You raised one!" shouted Carlon.

Then my rod sprang down, straightened by a violent tug, so energetic and electrifying that I was astounded. The scream of my reel told me what had happened. I swept up the rod to feel the strong pull of a steelhead taking line. Carlon called something that I could not distinguish above the roar of the water. But I thought he said the fish was leaping. Facing directly in the sun, I was dazzled and could not see downstream. My fish took a hundred yards of line, out into that swift channel, and there he hung. As good luck would have it, R.C. and Lone Angler with Burnham came along down the rocky shore and provided me with an inspiring audience.

If moments could be wholly all-satisfying with thrills and starts, and dreads and hopes, and vague, deep, full sense of the wild beauty of environment, and the vain boyish joy in showing my comrades my luck and my skill—if any moments of life could utterly satisfy, I experienced them then. It took what seemed a very long time to tire and lead that steelhead, but at last I accomplished it. When he bored under the ledge of rock he alarmed me considerably, and evidently worried Carlon, who wanted to take me in the boat and row around the ledge. This I feared might be needful, and was about to comply when the steelhead came out where I could lead him over the ledge. For five minutes he swam in the shallows below me, showing plainly, dark-backed, rosy-sided, gradually slowing in action until he turned on his side, his broad tail curling, his fins waving. That was the moment to have released him. I had the motive, but not the unselfish appreciation of him and his beautiful Rogue—not that time. He had been too hard to catch and there across the river stood those comrades of mine. Instead I lifted him up in the sunlight for them to see.

THE FISHING HOLE

GUY DE MAUPASSANT

nflicting blows and wounds causing death. Such was the charge on which M. Léopold Renard, upholsterer, appeared before the assizes.

In court were the chief witnesses, Mme Flamèche, widow of the victim; Louis Ladureau, cabinetmaker; and Jean Durdent, plumber: while close to the accused was his wife, in black—small, ugly, like a monkey dressed up as a woman.

And here is Renard (Léopold)'s account of the drama.

"As God is my witness, this is a catastrophe where, far from being the cause, I was all along the chief victim. The facts speak for themselves, My Lord. I am a decent man, a hard-working man, upholsterer these sixteen years in the same street, known, liked, respected, well thought of by all, as you've heard the neighbors say, even the houseporter, who speaks a sane word now and then. I'm fond of work, I'm fond of thrift, I'm fond of honest folk and of harmless pleasures. That's been my undoing, worse luck. Still, as I did nothing of intent, I feel no shame.

"Well, every Sunday for five years my wife here and I have spent the day at Poissy. That takes us into the open air—to say nothing of our love of fishing. Why, we're as keen on that as on spring onions! Mélie's the one that gave me the craze, the wretch, and that she's madder on it than I am, the sinner, you can see from all this trouble having come about through her, as assuredly it did, as you'll learn.

"As for me, I'm no soft one, yet I'm easy-going, without a pennyworth of wickedness. But as for her, well, well! You'd think her quite harmless, she's so small and skinny. Let me tell you, though, she's more spiteful than a cat. I'm not denying that she has her points; indeed she has, and important ones for one like me in business. But her disposition! Just you ask the neighbors, and even the house-porter, who put in a word for me a moment ago—she can tell you things.

"Day in day out she kept harping on about my softness. 'I wouldn't put up with this. I wouldn't put up with that.' Had I listened to her, My Lord, I'd have been in three scraps a month at least."

Mme Renard cut in: "Keep on. He laughs best who laughs last."

He turned towards her, not mincing his words: "Oh well, I can say what I like about you, seeing it's not you that's on trial, you."

Then turning to the judge again, he said:

"I proceed. We always went, then, to Poissy on Saturday evenings to be able to start our fishing next morning at daybreak. That custom became a kind of second nature, as the saying goes. Three years past this summer I discovered a swim—and such a swim! Shaded, eight feet of water at the least, perhaps ten. What a spot it was with its hollows under the bank—a regular lair of fishes! Talk about an angler's heaven! This hole, My Lord, I could look on as my own, seeing I was its Christopher Columbus. Everyone in the district knew it for mine, everyone—not a soul to dispute it. 'That, oh, that's Renard's spot,' they'd say, and nobody dreamt of going there, not even M. Plumeau, who is notorious, and no offence meant in saying it, for pinching the places of others.

"Well, certain always of my place, I went back and back to it just like an owner. The moment I arrived on Saturdays I boarded *Dalila* with my wife. *Dalila*, I should explain, is a Norwegian boat I had made for me by Fournaise—light yet strong. I was saying, then, that we boarded *Dalila*, and we would set about baiting the swim. As for baiting, there's no one to touch me, and well my pals all know it. You want to hear what I bait with? Well, I can't tell you. It has nothing to do with the case, I just can't tell you. It's my secret. Hundreds have asked me for it. I've been offered drinks and dainties no end to make me part with it. But just go and see if the chub come! Oh yes, they've tried to pet my patent out through my tummy. But not another soul knows it apart from my wife, and she won't tell it any more than I shall. Isn't that so, Mélie?"

The judge interrupted: "Just get to the point as soon as you can."

Whereupon the accused went on: "I'm getting to it, I'm getting to it. Well, on Saturday, the 8th of July, we left by the 5:25 train, and, as we always did on Saturdays, went before dinner to bait the swim. The weather promised to be fine. I said to Mélie: 'Great work tomorrow, great work.' And she answered: 'Looks like it.' We never talk more than that to each other.

"Then we came back to dinner. I was feeling good, and I was dry. That's where the whole trouble began, My Lord. I said to Mélie: 'Look here, Mélie, I think it would be an idea if I had a bottle of "nightcap." ' That's a light white wine we've christened so, because, if you drink too much of it, it keeps you awake and is just the opposite of a nightcap. You get the idea?

"She replied: 'Have your way, but you'll be upset again and won't be able to get up tomorrow.' There for you was truth, wisdom, prudence, discernment—I own it. Still I couldn't resist, and back I knock the bottle. Whence the whole trouble.

"Well, I couldn't sleep. Good Lord! that grape-juice nightcap kept me awake till two in the morning. Then in a twinkling, over I go, and so soundly that I'd have been deaf to the last trump itself.

"To be brief, my wife woke me at six. Out of bed I spring. On in a jiffy with my trousers and jersey, a dash of water on my mug, and into *Dalila* we jump. Too late. When I get to the swim it is already taken. Never had that happened before, My Lord, never in three years. Why, I was being robbed before my very eyes! 'Well I'm damned, I'm damned, I'm damned,' I cried. And then my wife began to rail at me: 'That's your nightcap for you. Get out, you soaker. Are you satisfied now, you stupid fool?'

"I answered nothing. Everything she said was true.

"I went ashore, however, near the spot, by way of making the best of a bad job. Perhaps the fellow wouldn't catch anything after all, and would clear out.

"He was a little skinny chap, in white drill and with a large straw hat. His wife was with him, a fat woman, who was sitting behind, sewing.

"When she saw us taking up our position near the spot, what do you think she muttered?

" 'Is this, then, the only place on the river?'

"And my wife, fuming, replied:

" 'People of ordinary decency usually make a point of finding out local ways. It keeps them off others' preserves.'

"As I didn't want a row, I said to her:

" 'Hold your tongue, Mélie. Don't answer back, don't answer back. We'll see about this all right.'

"Well, we had tied up *Dalila* under the willows and had got out and were fishing side by side, Mélie and I, right beside the other two.

"Here, My Lord, I must go into detail.

"We hadn't been there five minutes, when down went my neighbor's line twice, thrice, and lo and behold, he hauled out a chub, big as my thigh, a bit less perhaps, but not much! My heart gave a jump, my brow broke into a sweat, and Mélie cried: 'Hi, you toper, did you see that?'

"Just then, M. Bru, the grocer of Poissy, a dab with the gudgeon, passed by in his boat and shouted:

" 'So somebody's taken your place, M. Renard?' 'Yes, M. Bru,' I replied, 'there are some toughs in this world who don't know how to behave.'

"The little fellow in drill at my side pretended not to hear. His fat lump of a wife likewise, the cow."

The judge interrupted a second time: "Careful of your language. You insult the widow, Mme Flamèche, here."

Renard made excuse: "Pardon me, pardon me, my feelings ran away with me."

"Well, a quarter of an hour had hardly gone, when what should the little devil in drill do but yank out another fish, a chub, and then another on top of it, and still another five minutes later.

"I tell you I was on the verge of tears, and I could sense Mme Renard bursting with rage. She kept on rating me without pausing for breath: 'You miserable fool, don't you see you're being robbed of your fish? Don't you see it? You'll catch nothing, you, nothing, nothing, not even a frog. Don't my hands itch merely to think of it?'

"All I said, and to myself, was: 'Just wait till noon. He'll go to lunch then, this poaching fellow, and you'll get back your place.' You see, My Lord, we lunch every Sunday on the spot. We bring food with us in *Dalila*.

"Bah! Twelve struck. The wretch had a chicken wrapped up in a newspaper, and, would you believe it, while he ate he actually caught another chub!

"Mélie and I had a crumb, hardly anything. As things were, we didn't feel like it.

"Then to aid digestion I took up my newspaper. Every Sunday I read *Gil Blas* like that in the shade by the waterside. Sunday is Columbine's day, Columbine, you know, who writes articles in *Gil Blas*. I've a way of infuriating Mme Renard by pretending to know this Columbine. It's all a yarn. I don't know her at all, have never even seen her. Still she writes well, hits out and to the point, for a woman. She suits me down to the ground. After all, there're not so many of her kind.

"Well, then, I began ragging my wife, but at once she got angry, furiously angry, and then angrier still. So I said no more.

"Just at this moment our two witnesses here, M. Ladureau and M. Durdent, appeared on the other bank. We know each other by sight.

"The little fellow had begun fishing again and to such tune that I shook from sheer vexation. Then his wife said: 'This is a thundering good spot, we'll keep on coming here, Désiré.'

"A cold shiver ran down my spine, and Mme Renard kept on saying: 'Call yourself a man, call yourself a man! You chicken heart!'

" 'Look here,' I said quickly, 'I'd rather clear out. I shall only do something I'll regret.'

"She hissed as if she'd scald me: 'Call yourself a man! Now you're running away, giving up your place! Run away then, you Bazaine!'

"That went home. Still I did not wince.

"Then what does the other fellow do but drag out a bream! Never had I seen such a thumper before. Never.

"And now my wife began to talk out loud—pretending to be merely thinking. You see what a she-devil she is. 'This is what one might call stolen fish,' she said, 'seeing it was we who baited the swim. They ought at least to pay us for the bait.'

"Whereupon the little drill-clad bloke's fat wife chipped in: 'Is it us you're getting at madam?'

" 'I'm getting at fish thieves, those who profit by what's been spent by others.'

" 'Are you calling us fish thieves then?'

"Then they began explaining—then slanging. Good Lord! they knew the words all right—real stingers. They bawled so, that our two witnesses, who were on the other bank, called out by way of a joke: 'Hi, you, over there, less row, you'll spoil your husbands' sport!'

"The fact is that the little fellow in drill and myself remained stock still. We stuck where we were, our noses glued to the water, as if we'd never heard.

"But Lord help me, we heard all right!

" 'You're nothing but a liar.'—'And you a strumpet.'—'And you a trollop.'—'And you a trull.' And so on and so on. A sailor couldn't have beat them.

"Suddenly I heard a noise behind me and turned round. There was the other woman, the great fat thing, belaboring my wife with her parasol. Whack! whack! Mélie took a couple. But now she was fairly roused, and when Mélie's roused she lams about, I tell you. She seized the fat dame by the hair and then smack! smack! smack! the blows fell like a shower of ripe plums.

"I'd have left them to it—the women to themselves, the men to themselves. Why mix the thing? But up like a devil comes the little drill-suit chap making to spring at my wife. 'No, no, hardly that, my hearty,' says I, and I received the old cock-sparrow flush on the end of my fist. Biff! biff! One on the nose, the other in the guts. Up go his arms, up go his legs, and he falls on his back clean in the river, right in the middle of the swim.

"Most certainly I would have fished him out, My Lord, if I'd had the time just then. But now, to crown all, the fat woman gained the upper hand and was making mincemeat of Mélie. I know well I shouldn't have rescued her while the other was drinking his fill. Still I didn't think he would be drowned. I said to myself: 'Ugh! that'll cool him down.'

"I ran, then, to separate the women. I was pommelled, scratched, bitten. Good Lord, what vixen!

"The long and the short of it was that it took me a good five minutes, nearer ten, perhaps, to part this pair of clingers.

"I turned round. There was nothing to be seen. The water was as smooth as a lake. And the fellows on the other bank kept shouting: 'Fish him out, fish him out.'

"That was all very well, but I can't swim, much less dive, believe me.

"At last, after more than a quarter of an hour it would be, the lockkeeper came along and two men with boat-hooks. They found him at the bottom of the pool, under eight feet of water, as I have said, but there he was, the little fellow in his drill suit.

"These are the facts as I swear to them. On my word of honor I am innocent."

The witnesses having testified in the same sense, the accused was acquitted.

THE RIVER GOD

ROLAND PERTWEE

When I was a little boy I had a friend who was a colonel. He was not the kind of colonel you meet nowadays, who manages a motor showroom in the West End of London and wears crocodile shoes and a small mustache and who calls you "old man" and slaps your back, independent of the fact that you may have been no more than a private in the war. My colonel was of the older order that takes a third of a century and a lot of Indian sun and Madras curry in the making. A veteran of the Mutiny he was, and wore side whiskers to prove it. Once he came upon a number of Sepoys conspiring mischief in a byre with a barrel of gunpowder. So he put the butt of his cheroot into the barrel and presently they all went to hell. That was the kind of man he was in the way of business.

In the way of pleasure he was very different. In the way of pleasure he wore an old Norfolk coat that smelt of heather and brine, and which had no elbows to speak of. And he wore a Sherlock Holmesy kind of cap with a swarm of salmon flies upon it, that to my boyish fancy was more splendid than a crown. I cannot remember his legs, because they were nearly always under water, hidden in great canvas waders. But once he sent me a photograph of himself riding on a tricycle, so I expect he had some knickerbockers, too, which would have been that tight kind, with box cloth under the knees. Boys don't take much stock of clothes. His head occupied my imagination. A big, brave, white-haired head with cherry-red rugose cheeks and honest, laughing, puckered eyes, with gunpowder marks in their corners.

People at the little Welsh fishing inn where we met said he was a
bore; but I knew him to be a god and shall prove it.

I was ten years old and his best friend.

He was seventy something and my hero.

Properly I should not have mentioned my hero so soon in this nar-
rative. He belongs to a later epoch, but sometimes it is forgivable to
start with a boast, and now that I have committed myself I lack the
courage to call upon my colonel to fall back two paces to the rear,
quick march, and wait until he is wanted.

The real beginning takes place, as I remember, somewhere in
Hampshire on the Grayshott Road, among sandy banks, sentinel firs
and plum-colored wastes of heather. Summer-holiday time it was, and
I was among folks whose names have since vanished like lizards under
the stones of forgetfulness. Perhaps it was a picnic walk; perhaps I
carried a basket and was told not to swing it for fear of bursting its
cargo of ginger beer. In those days ginger beer had big bulgy corks
held down with a string. In a hot sun or under stress of too much
agitation the string would break and the corks fly. Then there would
be a merry foaming fountain and someone would get reproached.

One of our company had a fishing rod. He was a young man who,
one day, was to be an uncle of mine. But that didn't concern me. What
concerned me was the fishing rod and presently—perhaps because he
felt he must keep in with the family—he let me carry it. To the fisherman born there is nothing so provoking of curiosity as a fishing rod in
a case.

Surreptitiously I opened the flap, which contained a small grass
spear in a wee pocket, and, pulling down the case a little, I admired
the beauties of the cork butt, with its gun-metal ferrule and reel rings
and the exquisite frail slenderness of the two top joints.

"It's got two top joints—two!" I exclaimed ecstatically.

"Of course," said he. "All good trout rods have two."

I marveled in silence at what seemed to me then a combination of
extravagance and excellent precaution.

There must have been something inherently understanding and noble about that young man who would one day be my uncle, for, taking
me by the arm, he sat me down on a tuft of heather and took the
pieces of rod from the case and fitted them together. The rest of the
company moved on and left me in Paradise.

It is thirty-five years ago since that moment and not one detail of it
is forgotten. There sounds in my ears today as clearly as then, the
faint, clear pop made by the little cork stoppers with their boxwood
tops as they were withdrawn. I remember how, before fitting the pieces
together, he rubbed the ferrules against the side of his nose to prevent

them sticking. I remember looking up the length of it through a tunnel of sneck rings to the eyelet at the end. Not until he had fixed a reel and passed a line through the rings did he put the lovely thing into my hand. So light it was, so firm, so persuasive; such a thing alive—a scepter. I could do no more than say "Oo!" and again, "Oo!"

"A thrill, ain't it?" said he.

I had no need to answer that. In my new-found rapture was only one sorrow—the knowledge that such happiness would not endure and that, all too soon, a blank and rodless future awaited me.

"They must be awfully—awfully 'spensive," I said.

"Couple of guineas," he replied offhandedly.

A couple of guineas! And we were poor folk and the future was more rodless than ever.

"Then I shall save and save and save," I said.

And my imagination started to add up twopence a week into guineas. Two hundred and forty pennies to the pound, multiplied by two—four hundred and eighty—and then another twenty-four pennies—five hundred and four. Why, it would take a lifetime, and no sweets, no elastic for catapults, no penny novelty boxes or air-gun bullets or ices or anything. Tragedy must have been writ large upon my face, for he said suddenly, "When's your birthday?"

I was almost ashamed to tell him how soon it was. Perhaps he, too, was a little taken aback by its proximity, for that future uncle of mine was not so rich as uncles should be.

"We must see about it."

"But it wouldn't—it couldn't be one like that," I said.

I must have touched his pride, for he answered loftily, "Certainly it will."

In the fortnight that followed I walked on air and told everybody I had as good as got a couple-of-guineas rod.

No one can deceive a child, save the child himself, and when my birthday came and with it a long brown paper parcel, I knew, even before I had removed the wrappers, that this two-guinea rod was not worth the money. There was a brown linen case, it is true, but it was not a case with a neat compartment for each joint, nor was there a spear in the flap. There was only one top instead of two, and there were no popping little stoppers to protect the ferrules from dust and injury. The lower joint boasted no elegant cork hand piece, but was a tapered affair coarsely made and rudely varnished. When I fitted the pieces together, what I balanced in my hand was tough and stodgy, rather than limber. The reel, which had come in a different parcel, was of wood. It had neither check nor brake, the line overran and backwound itself with distressing frequency.

I had not read and reread Gamages' price list without knowing something of rods, and I did not need to look long at this rod before realizing that it was no match to the one I had handled on the Grayshott Road.

I believe at first a great sadness possessed me, but very presently imagination came to the rescue. For I told myself that I had only to think that this was the rod of all other rods that I desired most and it would be so. And it was so.

Furthermore, I told myself that, in this great wide ignorant world, but few people existed with such expert knowledge of rods as I possessed. That I had but to say, "Here is the final word in good rods," and they would accept it as such.

Very confidently I tried the experiment on my mother, with inevitable success. From the depths of her affection and her ignorance on all such matters, she produced:

"It's a magnificent rod."

I went my way, knowing full well that she knew not what she said, but that she was kind.

With rather less confidence I approached my father, saying, "Look, father! It cost two guineas. It's absolutely the best sort you can get."

And he, after waggling it a few moments in silence, quoted cryptically:

"There is nothing either good or bad but thinking makes it so."

Young as I was, I had some curiosity about words, and on any other occasion I would have called on him to explain. But this I did not do, but left hurriedly, for fear that he should explain.

In the two years that followed I fished every day in the slip of a back garden of our tiny London house. And, having regard to the fact that this rod was never fashioned to throw a fly, I acquired a pretty knack in the fullness of time and performed some glib casting at the nasturtiums and marigolds that flourished by the back wall.

My parents' fortunes must have been in the ascendant, I suppose, for I call to mind an unforgettable breakfast when my mother told me that father had decided we should spend our summer holiday at a Welsh hotel on the river Lledr. The place was called Pont-y-pant, and she showed me a picture of the hotel with a great knock-me-down river creaming past the front of it.

Although in my dreams I had heard fast water often enough, I had never seen it, and the knowledge that in a month's time I should wake with the music of a cataract in my ears was almost more than patience could endure.

In that exquisite, intolerable period of suspense I suffered as only childish longing and enthusiasm can suffer. Even the hank of gut that

I bought and bent into innumerable casts failed to alleviate that suffering. I would walk for miles for a moment's delight captured in gluing my nose to the windows of tackleists' shops in the West End. I learned from my grandmother—a wise and calm old lady—how to make nets and, having mastered the art, I made myself a landing net. This I set up on a frame fashioned from a penny schoolmaster's cane bound to an old walking stick. It would be pleasant to record that this was a good and serviceable net, but it was not. It flopped over in a very distressing fashion when called upon to lift the lightest weight. I had to confess to myself that I had more enthusiasm than skill in the manufacture of such articles.

At school there was a boy who had a fishing creel, which he swapped with me for a Swedish knife, a copy of *Rogues of the Fiery Cross,* and an Easter egg which I had kept on account of its rare beauty. He had forced a hard bargain and was sure he had the best of it, but I knew otherwise.

At last the great day dawned, and after infinite travel by train we reached our destination as the glow of sunset was graying into dark. The river was in spate, and as we crossed a tall stone bridge on our way to the hotel I heard it below me, barking and grumbling among great rocks. I was pretty far gone in tiredness, for I remember little else that night but a rod rack in the hall—a dozen rods of different sorts and sizes, with gaudy salmon flies, some nets, a gaff and an oak coffer upon which lay a freshly caught salmon on a blue ashet. Then supper by candlelight, bed, a glitter of stars through the open window, and the ceaseless drumming of water.

By six o'clock next morning I was on the river bank, fitting my rod together and watching in awe the great brown ribbon of water go fleetly by.

Among my most treasured possessions were half a dozen flies, and two of these I attached to the cast with exquisite care. While so engaged, a shadow fell on the grass beside me and, looking up, I beheld a lank, shabby individual with a walrus mustache and an unhealthy face who, the night before, had helped with our luggage at the station.

"Water's too heavy for flies," said he, with an uptilting inflection. "This evening, yes; now, no—none whateffer. Better try with a worrum in the burrun."

He pointed at a busy little brook which tumbled down the steep hillside and joined the main stream at the garden end.

"C-couldn't I fish with a fly in the—the burrun?" I asked, for although I wanted to catch a fish very badly, for honor's sake I would fain take it on a fly.

"Indeed, no," he replied, slanting the tone of his voice skyward. "You cootn't. Neffer. And that isn't a fly rod whateffer."

"It is," I replied hotly. "Yes, it is."

But he only shook his head and repeated, "No," and took the rod from my hand and illustrated its awkwardness and handed it back with a wretched laugh.

If he had pitched me into the river I should have been happier.

"It is a fly rod and it cost two guineas," I said, and my lower lip trembled.

"Neffer," he repeated. "Five shillings would be too much."

Even a small boy is entitled to some dignity.

Picking up my basket, I turned without another word and made for the hotel. Perhaps my eyes were blinded with tears, for I was about to plunge into the dark hall when a great, rough, kindly voice arrested me with:

"Easy does it."

At the thick end of an immense salmon rod there strode out into the sunlight the noblest figure I had ever seen.

There is no real need to describe my colonel again—I have done so already—but the temptation is too great. Standing in the doorway, the sixteen-foot rod in hand, the deer-stalker hat, besprent with flies, crowning his shaggy head, the waders, like seven-league boots, braced up to his armpits, the creel across his shoulder, a gaff across his back, he looked what he was—a god. His eyes met mine with that kind of smile one good man keeps for another.

"An early start," he said. "Any luck, old fellar?"

I told him I hadn't started—not yet.

"Wise chap," said he. "Water's a bit heavy for trouting. It'll soon run down, though. Let's vet those flies of yours."

He took my rod and whipped it expertly.

"A nice piece—new, eh?"

"N-not quite," I stammered; "but I haven't used it yet, sir, in water."

That god read men's minds.

"I know—garden practice; capital; nothing like it."

Releasing my cast, he frowned critically over the flies—a Blue Dun and a March Brown.

"Think so?" he queried. "You don't think it's a shade late in the season for these fancies?" I said I thought perhaps it was. "Yes, I think you're right," said he. "I believe in this big water you'd do better with a livelier pattern. Teal and Red, Cock-y-bundy, Greenwell's Glory."

I said nothing, but nodded gravely at these brave names.

Once more he read my thoughts and saw through the wicker sides of my creel a great emptiness.

"I expect you've fished most in southern rivers. These Welsh trout have a fancy for a spot of color."

He rummaged in the pocket of his Norfolk jacket and produced a round tin which once had held saddle soap.

"Collar on to that," said he; "there's a proper pickle of flies and casts in that tin that, as a keen fisherman, you won't mind sorting out. Still, they may come in useful."

"But, I say, you don't mean—" I began.

"Yes, go in; stick to it. All fishermen are members of the same club and I'm giving the trout a rest for a bit." His eyes ranged the hills and trees opposite. "I must be getting on with it before the sun's too high."

Waving his free hand, he strode away and presently was lost to view at a bend in the road.

I think my mother was a little piqued by my abstraction during breakfast. My eyes never, for an instant, deserted the round tin box which lay open beside my plate. Within it were a paradise and a hundred miracles all tangled together in the pleasantest disorder. My mother said something about a lovely walk over the hills, but I had other plans, which included a very glorious hour which should be spent untangling and wrapping up in neat squares of paper my new treasures.

"I suppose he knows best what he wants to do," she said.

So it came about that I was left alone and betook myself to a sheltered spot behind a rock where all the delicious disorder was remedied and I could take stock of what was mine.

I am sure there were at least six casts all set up with flies, and ever so many loose flies and one great stout, tapered cast, with a salmon fly upon it, that was so rich in splendor that I doubted if my benefactor could really have known that it was there.

I felt almost guilty at owning so much, and not until I had done full justice to everything did I fasten a new cast to my line and go a-fishing.

There is a lot said and written about beginners' luck, but none of it came my way. Indeed, I spent most of the morning extricating my line from the most fearsome tangles. I had no skill in throwing a cast with two droppers upon it and I found it was an art not to be learned in a minute. Then, from overeagerness, I was too snappy with my back cast, whereby, before many minutes had gone, I heard that warning crack behind me that betokens the loss of a tail fly. I must have spent half an hour searching the meadow for that lost fly and finding it not. Which is not strange, for I wonder has any fisherman ever found that lost fly. The reeds, the buttercups, and the little people with many legs who run in the wet grass conspire together to keep the secret of its hiding place. I gave up at last, and with a feeling of shame that was only proper, I invested a new fly on the point of my cast and set to work again, but more warily.

In that hard racing water a good strain was put upon my rod, and before the morning was out it was creaking at the joints in a way that kept my heart continually in my mouth. It is the duty of a rod to work with a single smooth action and by no means to divide its performance into three sections of activity. It is a hard task for any angler to persuade his line austerely if his rod behaves thus.

When, at last, my father strolled up the river bank, walking, to his shame, much nearer the water than a good fisherman should, my nerves were jumpy from apprehension.

"Come along. Food's ready. Done any good?" said he.

Again it was to his discredit that he put food before sport, but I told him I had had a wonderful morning, and he was glad.

"What do you want to do this afternoon, old man?" he asked.

"Fish," I said.

"But you can't always fish," he said.

I told him I could, and I was right and have proved it for thirty years and more.

"Well, well," he said, "please yourself, but isn't it dull not catching anything?"

And I said, as I've said a thousand times since, "As if it could be."

So that afternoon I went downstream instead of up, and found myself in difficult country where the river boiled between the narrows of two hills. Stunted oaks overhung the water and great boulders opposed its flow. Presently I came to a sort of natural flight of steps—a pool and a cascade three times repeated—and there, watching the maniac fury of the waters in awe and wonderment, I saw the most stirring sight in my young life. I saw a silver salmon leap superbly from the caldron below into the pool above. And I saw another and another salmon do likewise. And I wonder the eyes of me did not fall out of my head.

I cannot say how long I stayed watching that gallant pageant of leaping fish—in ecstasy there is no measurement of time—but at last it came upon me that all the salmon in the sea were careering past me and that if I were to realize my soul's desire I must hasten to the pool below before the last of them had gone by.

It was a mad adventure, for until I had discovered that stout cast, with the gaudy fly attached in the tin box, I had given no thought to such noble quarry. My recent possessions had put ideas into my head above my station and beyond my powers. Failure, however, means little to the young and, walking fast, yet gingerly, for fear of breaking my rod top against a tree, I followed the path downstream until I came to a great basin of water into which, through a narrow throat, the river thundered like a storm.

At the head of the pool was a plate of rock scored by the nails of fishermen's boots, and here I sat me down to wait while the salmon cast, removed from its wrapper, was allowed to soak and soften in a puddle left by the rain.

And while I waited a salmon rolled not ten yards from where I sat. Head and tail, up and down he went, a great monster of a fish, sporting and deriding me.

With that performance so near at hand, I have often wondered how I was able to control my fingers well enough to tie a figure-eight knot between the line and the cast. But I did, and I'm proud to be able to record it. Your true-born angler does not go blindly to work until he has first satisfied his conscience. There is a pride, in knots, of which the laity knows nothing, and if, through neglect to tie them rightly, failure and loss should result, pride may not be restored nor conscience salved by the plea of eagerness. With my trembling fingers I bent the knot and, with a pummeling heart, launched the line into the broken water at the throat of the pool.

At first the mere tug of the water against that large fly was so thrilling to me that it was hard to believe that I had not hooked a whale. The trembling line swung round in a wide arc into a calm eddy below where I stood. Before casting afresh I shot a glance over my shoulder to assure myself there was no limb of a tree behind me to foul the fly. And this was a gallant cast, true and straight, with a couple of yards more length than its predecessor, and a wider radius. Instinctively I knew, as if the surface had been marked with an X where the salmon had risen, that my fly must pass right over the spot. As it swung by, my nerves were strained like piano wires. I think I knew something tremendous, impossible, terrifying, was going to happen. The sense, the certitude was so strong in me that I half opened my mouth to shout a warning to the monster, not to.

I must have felt very, very young in that moment. I, who that same day had been talked to as a man by a man among men. The years were stripped from me and I was what I was—ten years old and appalled. And then, with the suddenness of a rocket, it happened. The water was cut into a swath. I remember a silver loop bearing downward—a bright, shining, vanishing thing like the bobbin of my mother's sewing machine—and a tug. I shall never forget the viciousness of that tug. I had my fingers tight upon the line, so I got the full force of it. To counteract a tendency to go headfirst into the spinning water below, I threw myself backward and sat down on the hard rock with a jar that shut my teeth on my tongue—like the jaws of a trap.

Luckily I had let the rod go out straight with the line, else it must have snapped in the first frenzy of the downstream rush. Little ass that I was, I tried to check the speeding line with my forefinger, with the result that it cut and burnt me to the bone. There wasn't above twenty yards of line in the reel, and the wretched contrivance was trying to be rid of the line even faster than the fish was wrenching it out. Heaven knows why it didn't snarl, for great loops and whorls were whirling, like Catherine wheels, under my wrist. An instant's glance revealed the terrifying fact that there was not more than half a dozen yards left on the reel and the fish showed no sign of abating his rush. With the realization of impending and inevitable catastrophe upon me, I launched a yell for help, which, rising above the roar of the waters, went echoing down the gorge.

And then, to add to my terrors, the salmon leaped—a winging leap like a silver arch appearing and instantly disappearing upon the broken surface. So mighty, so all-powerful he seemed in that sublime moment that I lost all sense of reason and raised the rod, with a sudden jerk, above my head.

I have often wondered, had the rod actually been the two-guinea rod my imagination claimed for it, whether it could have withstood the strain thus violently and unreasonably imposed upon it. The wretched thing that I held so grimly never even put up a fight. It snapped at the ferrule of the lower joint and plunged like a toboggan down the slanting line, to vanish into the black depths of the water.

My horror at this calamity was so profound that I was lost even to the consciousness that the last of my line had run out. A couple of vicious tugs advised me of this awful truth. Then, snap! The line parted at the reel, flickered out through the rings and was gone. I was left with nothing but the butt of a broken rod in my hand and an agony of mind that even now I cannot recall without emotion.

I am not ashamed to confess that I cried. I lay down on the rock, with my cheek in the puddle where I had soaked the cast, and plenished it with my tears. For what had the future left for me but a cut and burning finger, a badly bumped behind, the single joint of a broken rod and no faith in uncles? How long I lay there weeping I do not know. Ages, perhaps, or minutes, or seconds.

I was roused by a rough hand on my shoulder and a kindly voice demanding, "Hurt yourself, Ike Walton?"

Blinking away my tears, I pointed at my broken rod with a bleeding forefinger.

"Come! This is bad luck," said my colonel, his face grave as a stone. "How did it happen?"

"I c-caught a s-salmon."

"You what?" said he.

"I d-did," I said.

He looked at me long and earnestly; then, taking my injured hand, he looked at that and nodded.

"The poor groundlings who can find no better use for a river than something to put a bridge over think all fishermen are liars," said he. "But we know better, eh? By the bumps and breaks and cuts I'd say you made a plucky fight against heavy odds. Let's hear all about it."

So, with his arm round my shoulders and his great shaggy head near to mine, I told him all about it.

At the end he gave me a mighty and comforting squeeze, and he said, "The loss of one's first big fish is the heaviest loss I know. One feels, whatever happens, one'll never—" He stopped and pointed dramatically. "There it goes—see! Down there at the tail of the pool!"

In the broken water where the pool emptied itself into the shallows beyond, I saw the top joints of my rod dancing on the surface.

"Come on!" he shouted, and gripping my hand, jerked me to my feet. "Scatter your legs! There's just a chance!"

Dragging me after him, we raced along by the river path to the end of the pool, where, on a narrow promontory of grass, his enormous salmon rod was lying.

"Now," he said, picking it up and making the line whistle to and fro in the air with sublime authority, "keep your eyes skinned on those shallows for another glimpse of it."

A second later I was shouting, "There! There!"

He must have seen the rod point at the same moment, for his line flowed out and the big fly hit the water with a plop not a couple of feet from the spot.

He let it ride on the current, playing it with a sensitive touch like the brushwork of an artist.

"Half a jiffy!" he exclaimed at last. "Wait! Yes, I think so. Cut down to that rock and see if I haven't fished up the line."

I needed no second invitation, and presently was yelling, "Yes—yes, you have!"

"Stretch yourself out then and collar hold of it."

With the most exquisite care he navigated the line to where I lay stretched upon the rock. Then:

"Right you are! Good lad! I'm coming down."

Considering his age, he leaped the rocks like a chamois.

"Now," he said, and took the wet line delicately between his forefinger and thumb. One end trailed limply downstream, but the other end seemed anchored in the big pool where I had had my unequal and disastrous contest.

Looking into his face, I saw a sudden light of excitement dancing in his eyes.

"Odd," he muttered, "but not impossible."

"What isn't?" I asked breathlessly.

"Well, it looks to me as if the joints of that rod of yours have gone downstream."

Gingerly he pulled up the line, and presently an end with a broken knot appeared.

"The reel knot, eh?" I nodded gloomily. "Then we lose the rod," said he. That wasn't very heartening news. "On the other hand, it's just possible the fish is still on—sulking."

"Oo!" I exclaimed.

"Now, steady does it," he warned, "and give me my rod."

Taking a pair of clippers from his pocket, he cut his own line just above the cast.

"Can you tie a knot?" he asked.

"Yes," I nodded.

"Come on, then; bend your line onto mine. Quick as lightning."

Under his critical eye, I joined the two lines with a blood knot. "I guessed you were a fisherman," he said, nodded approvingly and clipped off the ends. "And now to know the best or the worst."

I shall never forget the music of that check reel or the suspense with which I watched as, with the butt of the rod bearing against the hollow of his thigh, he steadily wound up the wet slack line. Every instant I expected it to come drifting downstream, but it didn't. Presently it rose in a tight slant from the pool above.

"Snagged, I'm afraid," he said, and worked the rod with an easy straining motion to and fro. "Yes, I'm afraid—no, by Lord Bobs, he's on!"

I think it was only right and proper that I should have launched a yell of triumph as, with the spoken word, the point at which the line cut the water shifted magically from the left side of the pool to the right.

"And a fish too," said he.

In the fifteen minutes that followed, I must have experienced every known form of terror and delight.

"Youngster," said he, "you should be doing this, by rights, but I'm afraid the rod's a bit above your weight."

"Oh, go on and catch him," I pleaded.

"And so I will," he promised; "unship the gaff, young un, and stand by to use it, and if you break the cast we'll never speak to each other again, and that's a bet."

But I didn't break the cast. The noble, courageous, indomitable example of my river god had lent me skill and precision beyond my years. When at long last a weary, beaten, silver monster rolled within reach of my arm into a shallow eddy, the steel gaff shot out fair and true, and sank home.

And then I was lying on the grass, with my arms round a salmon that weighed twenty-two pounds on the scale and contained every sort of happiness known to a boy.

And best of all, my river god shook hands with me and called me "partner."

That evening the salmon was placed upon the blue ashet in the hall, bearing a little card with its weight and my name upon it.

And I am afraid I sat on a chair facing it, for ever so long, so that I could hear what the other anglers had to say as they passed by. I was sitting there when my colonel put his head out of his private sitting room and beckoned me to come in.

"A true fisherman lives in the future, not the past, old man," said he; "though, for this once, it 'ud be a shame to reproach you."

I suppose I colored guiltily—at any rate, I hope so.

"We got the fish," said he, "but we lost the rod, and a future without a rod doesn't bear thinking of. Now"—and he pointed at a long wooden box on the floor, that overflowed with rods of different sorts and sizes—"rummage among those. Take your time and see if you can find anything to suit you."

"But do you mean—can I—"

"We're partners, aren't we? And p'r'aps as such you'd rather we went through our stock together."

"Oo, sir," I said.

"Here, quit that," he ordered gruffly. "By Lord Bobs, if a show like this afternoon's don't deserve a medal, what does? Now, here's a handy piece by Hardy—a light and useful tool—or if you fancy green-heart in preference to split bamboo—"

I have the rod to this day, and I count it among my dearest treasures. And to this day I have a flick of the wrist that was his legacy. I have, too, some small skill in dressing flies, the elements of which were learned in his company by candlelight after the day's work was over. And I have countless memories of that month-long, month-short friendship—the closest and most perfect friendship, perhaps, of all my life.

He came to the station and saw me off. How I vividly remember his shaggy head at the window, with the whiskered cheeks and the gunpowder marks at the corners of his eyes! I didn't cry, although I wanted to awfully. We were partners and shook hands. I never saw him again, although on my birthdays I would have colored cards from him, with Irish, Scotch, Norwegian postmarks. Very brief they were: "Water very low." "Took a good fish last Thursday." "Been prawning, but don't like it."

Sometimes at Christmas I had gifts—a reel, a tapered line, a fly book. But I never saw him again.

Came at last no more cards or gifts, but in the *Fishing Gazette,* of which I was a religious reader, was an obituary telling how one of the last of the Mutiny veterans had joined the great majority. It seems he had been fishing half an hour before he died. He had taken his rod down and passed out. They had buried him at Totnes, overlooking the River Dart.

So he was no more—my river god—and what was left of him they had put into a box and buried it in the earth.

But that isn't true; nor is it true that I never saw him again. For I seldom go a-fishing but that I meet him on the river banks.

The banks of a river are frequented by a strange company and are full of mysterious and murmurous sounds—the cluck and laughter of water, the piping of birds, the hum of insects, and the whispering of wind in the willows. What should prevent a man in such a place having a word and speech with another who is not there? So much of fishing lies in imagination, and mine needs little stretching to give my river god a living form.

"With this ripple," says he, "you should do well."

"And what's it to be," say I—"Blue Upright, Red Spinner? What's your fancy, sir?"

Spirits never grow old. He has begun to take an interest in dry-fly methods—that river god of mine, with his seven-league boots, his shaggy head, and the gaff across his back.

THE
UNEXPECTED
FISH

RODERICK L. HAIG-BROWN

nevitably there is great satisfaction in catching the exact fish one is
fishing for; a big fish of his kind, yet not extravagantly big, rising or
lying precisely where he should be, coming to the fly confidently and
smoothly, fighting with anticipated vigor, sliding at last to net or gaff
or beach in the calculated place. This is the reward of experience and
performance, good to watch and good to achieve. Presumably it is the
principal objective of going fishing. Yet the fish one remembers are not
these noble creatures of orthodoxy and perfection but the unexpected
fish, the almost impossible fish, that catch one with tackle and body off
balance, and force improvisation and shocked, stumbling, cross-legged
incompetence.

It is impossible to create such fish deliberately, by going out with
inadequate tackle for instance, because their essence is to be unexpected. The closest one can come to it is to go out and fish calmly and
conscientiously for fifteen- or sixteen-inch trout in a stream that also
has a run of big steelhead or Atlantic salmon; but even this fails after
two or three times, because experience steps in and makes the unexpected more than half-expected. One cannot do it with steelhead kelts
in a spring trout stream, with a giant halibut or ling cod when looking
for salmon or with an oversize Dolly Varden in a lake of small trout,
because these are all pretty much undesirables and it is essential that
the unexpected fish be very much desired. There is no harm in hoping,
in an offhand way, for an unexpected fish, but any too precise opti-
mism will destroy him in advance by making him expected.

One unexpected fish that leaves me a little cold is the great, unyielding brute who takes a wet fly on 2 or 3X gut when it is at fullest stretch downstream, just as one starts to recover line; about all he adds up to is a solid pull, a lost fly and a moment of annoyance; one hasn't even time to blame oneself for heavy-handedness. His broad-backed brother, who shoulders suddenly out of a fast little run where a two-pounder should have been lying and seems to break 4X gut against the friction of the line on the water, is almost as bad. There is a limited hope that either fish may come again, but usually one can only mark the place and season for future caution. To resolve upon perpetual caution, a constant delicate anticipation of the unexpected, is to inter-fere too much with the easy pleasure of fishing though the shades of the mentors of one's youth will try to argue that this should be the lesson learned.

The first August steelhead I ever caught in the Campbell was the ideal of the unexpected fish. I was working a No. 6 Silver Brown with a 2X leader on a long slow swing across the tail of the Canyon Pool, expecting nothing more than a three- or four-pound cutthroat, secured in the expectation by the experience of six or eight seasons. The big fish took midway on the swing right at the surface, with a slash that sent a spout of water several inches into the air above the smooth pool. I let the drag of the line strike him and he ran upstream from the pull, keeping well to the middle, away from all trouble, wearing down his first surge of strength and giving me time to realize what it was all about. He could have broken me at any time during the first ten min-utes and would have been well within his rights in doing so. After that he was under the control of the rod, though still dangerously heavy and strong. If he had flipped over and broken the gut as I beached him I should probably not have blamed myself much. He did not, and he weighed sixteen pounds.

I caught three or four more August and September steelheads of ten or twelve pounds in seasons after that before I realized that the river had a small late run of big summer fish. They are no longer altogether unexpected, but the run is too sparse for one to go out and deliberately fish for them. It is a time to look for two- or three-pound trout, with appropriate tackle, so the big fish retain many of the exciting qualities of the unexpected.

A fish need not be extremely large to qualify in the unexpected class. I shall remember a brown trout of my boyhood, not over a pound in weight, which escaped into a weed bed and broke me. He stayed where he was, head burrowed into the weeds and only an inch or two of his back showing intermittently as the long green strands moved in the current over it. I waded cautiously toward him from downstream, the net ready in my hand, though I hadn't any very clear idea of what I intended to do; I had tried and failed before to net trout out of weed beds. When I was still six or eight feet below him he came suddenly to life, darted out of the weed bed and a little way upstream. For a moment he rested there uncertainly, then turned and came downstream for his holt like a bullet. I thrust the net toward the line of his flight in a forlorn reflex action and felt a surge of astonished triumph as he thudded into it. He was my fish all right, with my little ginger quill trailing broken 4X gut from his mouth.

Last winter was cold, so cold that I shouldn't write of it in a book of springtime fishing. Towards the end of January I finished a book and felt I had to go fishing, though the weather was around zero and there was four feet of snow on the ground. Ann told me to be sure and get a fish because it was a long while since we had had one. I knew I shouldn't be fishing long in any sort of comfort, so I waded in a few yards above a good lie and began to work my fly out over it as quickly as possible. A fine fish took the fly almost at once, well out in the fast water, and ran strongly seventy or eighty yards downstream. There was ice in the rings of the rod already and when the wet backing began to come in I saw that it was coated with ice, so I began to worry a little and handle the fish carefully. The splice between backing and fly line jammed in the ice of the top ring, but I broke it through and felt a fine sense of relief when it came on to the reel. He took it out again twice and caused me plenty of other trouble and anxiety, but I had him at last within reach of the gaff and fairly quiet. I was standing among large boulders, in two or three feet of moderate current, but I knew I had to gaff him there because I dared not take him nearer the ice at the edge of the river.

I was standing awkwardly and the fish was lying awkwardly, head a little down and still upright. I judged him about fifteen pounds and thought several things one has no business to think when about to gaff a fish. I thought: that hook's got a light hold. If I try to shift him he'll run again and he might shake the hook or even get into the ice along the shore. I want him very much, because it's going to be tough fishing from here on, with ice just about solid in the rings and on the line, and forming faster than you can break it loose. With him on the bank it won't matter much—at least I can relax and enjoy myself. . . . So I reached the gaff backhandedly over him and made the stroke. It was a bad one, too far forward and not solid, but it pierced the gill cover and I lifted the fish, swung him across and started towards the bank, holding him out of the water on the gaff. As I made the first step, the point of the gaff broke off and the fish fell back into the water. I saw the gut was wrapped around the broken hook of the gaff.

For one quick moment as I tried to free the gut, the fish was quiet.

Then he gulped water and expelled a cloud of blood from his gills, turned and ran. I made one last move to free the gut, then it broke and he was gone.

In spite of my successive stupidities, I managed to feel quite sorry for myself, and at the same time disgusted. I knew from that cloud of blood I had killed the fish—fish don't have much blood to lose. So he was wasted. And the chance of another with the freezing line that would no longer shoot a yard was pretty small.

Out of my shame, in an unpromising attempt to reduce it a little, I developed the idea that I might find the fish if he died quickly. The river was quite low and for a hundred yards or more below me the current set slightly towards the bank, running at an uneven three to five feet among big boulders. I started fishing again, but watched the water below me.

After about five minutes of fishing I saw a faint white reflection in the water a few feet below where my fly was working. I lost it, then saw it again. It was far too easy to account for—the white rock, I told myself, in the lower lie. But I kept watching, and after a while it showed again, thirty or forty feet farther downstream. I admitted it was too far out to do me any good, but fished on a little faster and still kept watching. It disappeared, showed again, disappeared again. I was casting in a sort of a way, but paying no attention to the fly and hurrying over the big round boulders in a way that threatened to put me off my feet at any moment. Then the flash showed again, still farther down but close to water that might not be over my waders. I knew it was my fish now, because I had seen the twisting shape of his body as he came up through the water, and I knew it was my last hope, because the current set out again just below where he was. I reeled up and hurried.

When I got to where he should have been there was no sign of him. I didn't want to be too hopeful, because the whole affair seemed moderately unlikely, but at the same time I was quite determined to stay with the fish as long as there was any hope at all.

He showed suddenly, starting from the bottom belly up in a twisting effort that carried him almost to the surface, a few feet out from me and a few feet below. Then he sank slowly back and disappeared. I waded out and down, on tiptoe in the current, with an occasional flick of ice water slopping over the waders against my chest. I peered down into the water and saw the fish, right side up, curved against the upstream side of a rock, held against it by the current. Then I remembered the point of the gaff was broken off. I thought of lowering my fly down on the tip of my rod, decided against it and pushed the broken gaff towards him. It meant putting my arm in up to the shoulder but I reached him, got the remains of the hook well under him, and heaved. It didn't go home, but he came up on it almost to the surface, then slipped off. I raked the broken gaff along the length of him, hoping it might catch in the gills. It did. I lifted his head clear of the water, set my fingers in his gills and waded ashore. He weighed fourteen pounds, which is not large for a winter fish, and any triumph I could claim was born of clumsiness and poor judgement. But he rates high among my unexpected fish.

If doing the wrong thing can make an unexpected fish, it is far more certain that an unexpected fish can make one do the wrong thing. Not so long ago I was standing under April sunshine in a shallow, sandy slough at the head of a big lake. There were trout in the slough, handsome green-backed cutthroats up to two pounds or so, but they weren't moving much at that time of day. So I was wading cautiously along, hoping to see one against the pale sand. I was watching the edges of the slough mostly, expecting the fish to be close under the matted tangle of swamp brush that hung down into the water, so I did not see the big fish until he was almost opposite me.

He was swimming majestically, calmly, very slowly, right up the center of the slough. He was broad and deep and long, and I will say he weighed seven pounds, though I am quite sure he weighed over ten pounds. I have never knowingly put a fly over a cutthroat even nearly so big.

He passed me without a tremor of his fins to suggest he had seen me and I remained for a long moment in frozen hesitation. I thought of only two things: that I was going to put a fly over him and that I mustn't move to do so until he was far enough away. I did not manage to remember that I was fishing a No. 14 variant on 4X gut in my search for two-pounders, nor that the big fish was now trapped between me and the head of the slough, so that I could easily take time to change my rigging on the certainty I would find him again. I simply waited until his lazy swimming had carried him ten or twelve yards beyond me, then began to put out line in cautious but rapid false casts.

He was about sixty feet away when I gave it to him. I had the sense to set the fly to one side and a little ahead of him and the luck to make a shepherd's crook that kept the gut farther from him than the fly. As a cast, it was a pretty smooth operation all through—at one moment the flat, calm surface of the slough was empty, in the next my fly was there without a ripple to show how it had arrived. The big trout saw it and turned instantly towards it, probably wondering how the nymph had passed up through the water without being seen. There was no change of pace, only of direction. Very slowly he came, nudged the fly with his nose, took it down. I tightened on him and thought I was quite a fisherman.

Right in the second the little fly hit him, the fish knew he had no business in the slough and I began to suspect I had no business being hooked up to him. He was past me, trailing slack line, before I could turn around, and the line was tight again and the reel running before I could begin stumbling after him. Just for a moment he kept to the open slough and I kidded myself I still had a chance. Then the drag of the reel worried him and he cut over among the drowned tips of the swamp brush. The reel ran out a few more yards and stopped. I saw the flash of a broad, bright side in the brush, a splash and that was the end of it. I felt very lonely.

If they ever come to writing life insurance under water, the unexpected fish will be a pretty good risk. But I'd rather lose one honest example of the type than land a hundred orthodox creatures. It's nice to be reminded that one cannot put a line in the water without tempting the unknown.

BRANNIGAN'S
TROUT

NICK LYONS

After the crackup, he was hospitalized for six months. Twice the doctors warned Jane that they might lose him. Then, when they saved him, they warned that there was probably brain damage. When he was released, in November, they told him he'd be paralyzed on his right side for life. Four doctors confirmed the verdict.

There was nothing for it.

Perhaps there was a slight chance, but not likely, that regular exercise, steady exercise over a period of several years, might restore some small portion of his mobility. Not much. Possibly none. Frankly, Brannigan was not inclined to try. Why go through all the effort? So he sat silent and sullen in the wheelchair that grey afternoon and allowed the men in white to push him to the car, lift and place him into the front seat, collapse the chair and put it in the back, then tell Jane how he was to get in and out, how she was to rig the contraption and place it for him. Like a baby.

He said not a word on the long trip through the sere, dead countryside. Jane told him about the boys, and which friends had called; Mike Novak might come over that evening. He didn't even nod. His great black-haired head thrown back and tilted to one side, he watched with dead eyes the fleeting fields of withered cornstalks, leafless trees, dark scudding clouds. There was nothing for it. He was forty-six and it was over. He couldn't sell books or anything else anymore; he didn't know whether he could drink beer with his friends, chop wood, tend his garden, drive, smoke, sing, read, write; and certainly the fishing season was over for him. Permanently.

The crash in all its stark detail, the fluky chance of it, kept flashing through his brain: Johnny Wohl driving, across the seat from him, saying, seconds before, "Well, Billy, we made a day of it, didn't we? I never saw the river so alive." And Mike in the back, laughing wildly and about to say something about having caught three Hendricksons. Then the rasp of brakes, the black car coming just that moment smoothly out of the side road, the jolt of fear, his hands flying up, his back thrusting backward against the seat, then hurtling forward—and darkness, and stabbing, raw pain in his shoulders, his head. Then nothing. Johnny Wohl and the two teenagers in the black car had been killed instantly. Mike came out of it with his right pinky broken. Well, good for him. Good for old Mike.

As for himself, it would have been better to have had it over then, right then when it happened. Quick. No more pain to die than to live, then. He need merely not have come out of the coma. After that first, searing pain, poof. For good. And they all said he'd only lived because he wanted to live. So he lived—like a half-squashed worm.

He saw suddenly in his mind the 20-gauge shotgun in the cabinet in his den. Would Jane have removed it? This was no time to ask. That night, when the boys were doing their homework, he'd wheel in by himself and just take a look-see. He'd take it out, break it open . . . take a look-see.

At dinner, Jane talked constantly—about the Murphys' new Brittany spaniel; the good batch of slab wood Frank had hauled from the lumber yard, piece by piece, and cut himself; the threat of an early snow. Brannigan looked up now and then from his plate, spread his lips slightly in the best he could do for a smile, and nodded. He said nothing. He was still not sure what the cracked, alien sound of his voice—what remained of speech—would be to these people, whether he could put together all the words needed for one whole sentence. Whenever he raised his head and looked toward one of his sons, Frank to his right, fifteen, Junior on his left, a year older and dark-haired too, rebellious, they were looking at their own plates. They knew everything. When he looked back at his own plate and prepared his next strategy to get a piece of meat to his mouth, he thought he saw, peripherally, their heads raise slightly and turn toward him. He didn't think he could bear it. Not that. He'd come through Normandy without a scratch; he'd never been seriously ill in his life.

Working diligently with the fork in his left hand, like they'd taught him in the hospital, he speared a piece of the steak Jane had cut for him, shifted the fork carefully in his hand, and brought it to his mouth. He chewed the meat slowly for a few moments, then lowered the fork to get another. But the prongs pressed against the gristle, slipped, and flicked the chunk of meat onto the floor. Brannigan looked after it, heard Jane say, "I'll pick it up later, dear," then slammed the fork down on his plate. Frank and Junior raised their hunched shoulders and looked up sharply. Jane took a deep breath.

"Nuff," muttered Brannigan. "Nuff." He pushed the wheelchair away, turning it, and, his hand on the wheel-rail, glided into the living room and toward his den—hearing Frank say something low that ended with "like that," and Junior's heavier voice, and then Jane telling them in a normal voice to finish quickly and go upstairs: they'd talk of it later.

He negotiated the living room and came to the door of his den. His room. The door was closed but he came against it sideways, took his left hand from the wheel-rail and reached out for the knob. As he did so, the chair slipped back a few inches and he was only able to touch a bit of the knob. He gritted his teeth, pounded his left hand down on the armrest, wheeled himself close again, and tried another time. Again the chair slipped back a bit and he couldn't, hard as he strained, even touch the knob. *Damned. Damned.* He sat in the chair, breathing heavily for a few moments, then tried again, got it, flung the door open, gave the wheel-rail a sharp thrust forward, and was in his room. *His* room.

God, how many good hours he'd spent there. The soft old armchair. His own mount of the four-pound brook trout he'd caught in Canada that summer with Mike and Johnny. The humidor with those long black dago-ropes he loved so much. Fireplace. Little fly-tying table— just like he'd left it. Silver rod cases in the cabinet he'd built himself. The old black-bear rug he'd bought, over Jane's hilarious objections. *His room.*

It was a room to which he slunk after a knockdown argument with Jane, a lousy road trip; he went there to plan his selling strategies, realign the world, read quietly in the evening or tie flies. He'd had most of his serious talks with his boys in this room; and he'd laughed and drunk beer and told stories half the night with Johnny and Mike here. Useless now. There was not one thing in the room, as he looked around, that he wanted.

The shotgun.

His eyes shifted sharply to the oak cabinet with the V-back that fitted into the corner so snugly. It was there. He went to his fly-tying table, opened the middle drawer, and felt with his hand among the capes and bobbins until his fingers found and closed tightly around the long brass key. Then, holding the key in the palm of his left hand, he used his fingers to push the chair over to the cabinet.

He had only that one gun, a beautiful 20-gauge with polished walnut stock, grey shoulder cushion, twin slate-grey barrels. He liked the feel of it in his hands, the power with which it jerked back when he shot. He'd gotten his first grouse with it last winter. Sam, Johnny's Brittany, had frozen on a point, Johnny had called for the flush, and the grouse, a single, had exploded with a whirr from the underbrush. "Yours!" shouted Mike, and he'd swung, led, and watched the bird pause, sputter, and fall. He remembered the deep satisfaction he'd felt from that connection, that force which shot out from him and dropped that bird.

The shotgun.

Another moment and he'd have it in his hands, feel its sleek powerful lines, its smooth stock. The gun held power, energy, force; merely to have it in your hands was to feel some electrical current, some charge of strength shot into your veins, your body. "Look-see," he said, flinching at the cracked, strange sound of his voice, inserting the key into the lock and turning, then opening the cabinet door slowly.

It was not there. The cabinet was empty.

His eyes blazed and he slammed the door shut. It was not there. She had taken it. Grasping the wheel-rail he thrust downward and began to roll across the carpet toward the closed door to the living room. She had taken it. "Gun," he said, his voice a rasping growl. "Gun. Gun." Then, opening the door, he let his head fall, and he muttered, "Did she . . . really . . . think . . ."

"So the point is that *I* asked Jane for your goddam shotgun because mine is at the gunsmith and I ain't got one to use next week," Mike said ten minutes later when they were alone in the den. "She didn't want to let me have it. Nope. 'Mike,' she says, 'Billy loves that rifle.' That's what she called it, a rifle, 'and I don't think I can let you have it.' "

Brannigan frowned. He looked intently at the bronze, hearty face of his friend, that bullish chest above toothpick legs, the straight black, always greasy and carefully combed hair, the mechanic's hands, stained black.

"I says: 'Look, Janie, he may not be out until after Christmas and I know he'd want me to put a few notches on it for him. One thing about Billy, he don't like a good rod or shotgun lying around. Offends his Scotch-Irish blood.' "

"Lie."

"I was going to take it out to the range, test it on some clays, but if you'd like it back, got some special use for it, I'll . . ." He broke off, lowered his voice, and said: "It's been rough, ain't it, kiddo?"

"Ruh-uf."

"Yeah," said Mike, turning his back and walking across the room to look at the big, bright male brook trout on the wall. "Remember when you got that one, Billy?" he said without turning around. "You'd cast that big funny fly from New Zealand, the Red Setter, looked like a whore's hairdo, into the swirls below the falls. I was behind you. I'd gotten one about three pounds that morning and you was burning mad. Didn't even speak to me at lunch. Well, maybe I was being a bit rotten about it." He came and sat down in the soft old armchair. "I must've turned and the next thing I know your rod's bent like a crescent moon and you're yelling like a banshee. Johnny thinks you've fallen in or got bit by a snake, so he comes running up, and by this time there's the goddamnedest smug look on your face! You've got the fish well hooked, you've seen him roll, and you know the size of him—and you know you got the greatest audience any mug ever had."

He watched Brannigan's eyes. They changed as he told the story.

"You're using this ten-pound-test leader and can't possibly lose that fish unless it gets into the rapids, and you're acting just as cockeyed cool as a cock of the roost. Johnny and me, we may be a little green around the gills but we're sitting polite as you please, murmuring a few friendly words of praise now and then—like, 'Did *that* lemon have to get it?'—and you keep playing him gently, making maybe a bit too much of a show of fear when it heads downstream. Cool. Very cool, Billy. And when Johnny wants to net him for you, with the big net, what do you do? Wave him away, and fuss with that minnow net you carry."

The faintest trace of a smile began to struggle around the corners of Brannigan's twisted mouth and eyes.

"So this absolute monster of a brookie, the biggest trout any of us has ever seen, is beat, and over on its side, and you're swiping at it with your net—probably trying to get it to rush off so's the show can go on—and first you get the tail in, right?"

Brannigan nodded.

"Then when it flops out, you try to bend it in, from the middle, but the monster won't be bent, so you go for the head, which barely fits into that guppy net, and then you've got it head first to about the gills and sort of clamp your hand down on the rest and come yelping out of the water, the line and rod and net and you all tangled together, and you fall on it. God, that fish was gorgeous—and there he is. That the way it happened, Billy? Something like that?"

Brannigan raised his left hand in a little shrug. "Ha-pinned . . . like . . . that."

"So the point is, you got one. You got one bigger than any of us ever got, even Johnny, God rest his soul, and now you figure, 'The big bird's crapped on me. I've caught my last big fish and shot my last grouse.' That it?"

"Tha-z-it."

"Johnny doesn't make it and you ain't satisfied to be here. Instead of being pleased I come tonight, passing up some very possible quail, you're going to stew in your own bile, right?"

"Rrr-ight."

"There's no one in particular to hate for it, so you figure you'll spread the hate around, to Jane and the boys, and especially yourself, and maybe you'll get lucky and not be around too much longer to be a burden to anyone. Well, I see your point, Brannigan. Lot of logic to it. They say maybe there's a chance in a couple hundred thousand that you get anything back on that right side, so you say, 'Bad odds.' " He walked to the fly-tying table, picked up one of the capes, a pale ginger, and bent back the hackle of one feather. "A good one, Billy. First-rate dry-fly neck. Good small size, too." Then he went to the humidor and drew out one of the twisted black cigars. "You don't mind?" Brannigan, watching him closely, did not change his expression. Mike put the cigar in the center of his mouth, struck a match, and got the tip of the cigar glowing like a little coal. "Good cigar, Billy." He puckered his lips, held the cigar in three fingers, and took a long puff.

Brannigan kept watching him. He had not moved his chair from the moment Mike had come in. *Quail. Big trout. A grouse or two. Lives for that. Two wives, maybe have ten more. Funny guy. The way he holds that cigar—like he owned the world, all of it. Shotgun. Ask.*

"So the point is, it would break my sweet heart if you wasn't around, kiddo. Know what I mean? You know what I did when they told me you was"—he put out his hand, palm down, and rocked it slightly—"maybe not going to make it? I prayed. Me. Prayed. I said, 'Oh, God, let old Billy come through with *anything,* any goddamit thing at all, so long as he's here and I can brag to him now and then about what quail I'm snatching—anything, God, just so long as he's here where I can see his ugly black-haired head now and then' "—he puffed hard at the cigar—"when the quail ain't flying and the trout is down. It's rough, right?"

Ask about shotgun.

"Suddenly the rules is all changed."

The gun.

"So the point is," he said, puffing hard, exhaling three times in rapid succession—"Hell, I don't know what the point is, Billy, but it will be awfully lonely next May when the Hendricksons start popping not to . . . Here, catch this"—and he tossed a softball, underhand, directly at Brannigan's chest. The left hand went up and forced the ball against the right shoulder. The right shoulder, limp and loose, twitched ever so slightly toward the ball. Brannigan held the ball for a moment, then took it in his left hand and tossed it back. Then he felt his right shoulder and slowly dug his fingers into the muscle. "Not . . . much-left."

"You'll cast lefty," said Mike. "Once knew an old poacher name of Sven who had to learn because there was bad brush on the right side. Dry-fly purist of a poacher." And the story went on for twenty minutes, and included a patrol dog named Wolf, five pound rainbows, two delicious young women, the true origin of "Sven's left curve drop cast," which only lefties could use, and then, just before the point of it all, Mike simply said, "It's eleven. The quail will have flown. I'll bring the 20-gauge tomorrow, eh?"

Brannigan smiled, a slow, deep smile that spread into his cheeks and eyes, and stayed, even when the twitch started. He nudged his right hand out with his left, so Mike could take and hold it, and Mike took it and held it in both of his own, rubbing the lifeless thing vigorously, then turning quickly for the door. Before he got there, Brannigan said: "The gun . . . yours."

The limbs remember, he thought, working the rake lightly across the soil he'd just fitted with seed, *and so does the earth. It remembers what it must do to these seeds, and the seeds, someplace deep within them, knew what they must do.*

Back and forth he moved the rake, holding it firmly in his left hand, using his nearly useless right to steady it. The May sun was warm but not bright, and kneaded his broad naked shoulders. He could walk without the cane now—somewhat. With that bizarre arc. His hair had gone snow white, which he liked, but otherwise, if he didn't move and didn't talk, he looked nearly the same.

Everyone else had planted a week or two ago but he'd worked more slowly, as he had to—long patient hours, setting his fertilizer, running the hand plow steadily across the small garden he'd staked out last spring, seeding the soil. This would be a good year. He could feel it. He'd learned how to coax green from the brown soil, how important it was, always, to be patient—to lay the proper foundation, however long that took, before you could expect anything to grow. Tomatoes, cucumbers, carrots, radishes, onions—he'd had these last year; now he added kale, zucchini, tarragon, other herbs. Each day now he would work on his garden for several hours, bending down to it, plucking, feeling, watering, watching. It all mattered. Even the watching. Every day. He'd increased the size of his garden by a third this year. It would require more work but he could do it. He still forgot many things—

names, events, people he had known; but he forgot nothing connected to his garden. It would be a good garden this year, as fruitful as anyone's garden. Maybe better.

Got it all in now, he thought, leaning against the rake, *and Mike will be here soon to take us a-fishing.* It would be good to be in the car, on a trip, listening to Mike's excited patter; it would be good to try the river again. Mike had said the Hendricksons had started.

Three years. Days, weeks, months had ticked by, minute by minute, and imperceptibly the changes had come. The insurance had kept them from bankruptcy, Jane had begun to work for a real-estate agent in town—and had blossomed with it. Junior was earning his way in college, his own man, and Frank was a senior in high school and working part-time at Mike's garage. They didn't need what he'd once earned; he knew that what they needed most he could give them only after he had given it to himself.

He had done the exercises the men in white advised, with barbells and bicycle—over and over and again; he hated to do them and stopped when it came time to work in his garden. Several times last spring Mike had taken him to the West Branch, which they'd often fished together, before he got wrecked. At first he merely found a rock, sat down, and watched. But he had not been able to resist the tug, deep inside him, to be on the stream, part of it, fishing. Wasn't that *really* why he'd done all those endless, tedious exercises, up and down, back and forth, hour after hour, all those months?

It had been impossible at first, after nearly two years. He had slipped twice on the rocks before he even reached the river. Even with the cane his right leg would not hold on broken terrain. Then he slipped again when he took his first tentative step into the water, careening badly, catching himself on his left arm. "No help, no help," he'd said when Mike stepped toward him. Then he'd been unable to strip line and cast left-handed, and finally, after several mad minutes he had given it up and fallen again on his way out, slamming his chin into a rock, cutting it sharply. No. It was not possible. He could not do it.

But it was a warm May morning and Mike would be there soon and it would be better this year. He'd earned it. Perhaps he'd even take his first trout since the crash.

Mike came promptly at twelve, and in a few minutes they were in the car racing toward the West Branch. "Magnificent day, Billy," Mike said, pushing the pedal harder. "The Hendricksons will be on in all their glory. They'll be popping out and the birds will be working, and we're going to get us a few. The cornfield run. I can feel a certain fat old brownie just waiting for you there today."

Mike parked along a small dirt turnoff and they got out and began
to rig their rods, put on their waders. Mike was suited up and ready
before Brannigan had worked one leg into his hip boots. "Go on,
Mike. I'll be there . . . when I'm there."

"So you're tired of my company. Fine. I'm going upstream, you
take the middle of the run, where the current slows. Take your time:
we're a half hour early. Lousy luck, kiddo."

Brannigan watched him stride off, his bull back bouncing even in
waders. Then he finished raising his boots, strapped them to his belt,
and got out his vest. He could use his right hand as a support now, to
hold one section of the rod firmly enough for his left to insert the other
section; he managed it, with guides aligned, on only the second try.
Then he strung the line slowly through the guides until the end of the
fly line and all of the leader were outside the tip top. It was well he had
practiced all winter.

He got out a Hendrickson he'd tied before the crash, kept in moth-
balls, and held it as firmly as he could with his right fingers. Then he
tried to insert the point of the leader. It would not go. He kept shoving
it off to the side, or shaking the fly. Finally he dropped the fly in the
grass and had to bend down, slowly, to look for it. When he found it,
he stayed on the ground in the shadow of the car and held the fly up to
the sky so that the light-blue would show through the hole and he
could better fit in the leader. The operation took him five minutes.

As he began to walk along the edge of the cornfield toward the river,
his right leg came up in a large, jerky arc, and then down again, one
step after the other. Slowly. There was no rush. There was plenty of
time. Mike had coaxed him out several more times last summer and
fall, and each time he fell but there was some slight improvement. Not
much. Not enough for him to know he could do it, like he could
garden, not enough to get a line out far enough to tempt a trout—but
some. You had to connive. You had to be cunning and crafty, and to
forget how it once was. You had to remember always that it would not
all come back, not ever. You had to work within the fixed knowledge
that you could continue to improve, always, and that this counted, but
that even at your very best, some day, you would be, by the world's
standards, a lemon.

Perhaps he'd get one today. His first. It would be wonderful if he
could get into a really large trout, perhaps seventeen or eighteen
inches. You didn't have to make many casts, just the right one at the
right time. He'd practiced on the lawn and he knew he now could get
enough distance to reach the lip of the current in the cornfield pool.
He'd once fished it many times. There was room for a decent backcast,
and the shallow bar on his side of the run was hard earth and rubble,

with only a few rocks that might trip him up. Mike had made a good choice; he'd be fishing upstream, in the fast water where the Hendricksons hatched, but there'd be plenty of fish falling back into the pool to pick up the duns as they floated down, especially once the hatch really got going.

One step at a time—the right leg out first, and down, out and down. No hurry. You couldn't rush a walk anymore than you could a garden. You couldn't rush anything. Anyway, you saw more when you walked this slow—those crows pecking at corn seeds, that huge growth of skunk cabbage, lush and green and purple, the fuzzy green on the boughs of the willows. A gorgeous day, only slightly overcast now, perfect for Hendricksons.

As he neared the row of trees that bordered the river, he could see Mike upstream, wading deep; his rod was held high and had a sharp arc. *Good old Mike. Got one already.* Up and out, then down. Then again. And again. He worked his way through the alders to the edge of the river. The water was perfect—dark and alive, flecked with bubbles and eddies where the current widened and slowed. Like he'd dreamed it all winter. Yes, that was a fish. And another. He looked to the sky and saw four or five tan flies flutter and angle off into the trees. *Yes. Yes.*

He took a tentative step into the water and felt a touch of fear as he left the firmness of the earth. No matter. It would pass. All the old feeling was there; he could still feel, deep within him, something in him reaching out to the life of the river—its quick faceted run above, the long flat pool below; its translucent dark green and gliding shadows. Flowing, always moving. Changing. The same and not the same. He picked out a dun and watched it bound, like a tiny tan sailboat, over the tail of the riffle, then swirl and float into slower water where it vanished in a sudden pinching of the surface.

Yes, they were moving today. He could see six, seven fish in fixed feeding positions, rising steadily. There was plenty of time. *Don't rush. Do it very, very slowly.* They'd be going good for another hour; he wanted to pick out one good fish, near enough for him to reach with his short cast. Only one good fish. He didn't want a creelful. Only one.

Upstream, Mike was into another trout, and a few minutes later, while Brannigan still eased slowly, steadily into deeper water, inch by inch, Mike had another. *We've caught one of those magical days,* he thought. *Another foot or so . . .* At last, deep as he dared go, he stood on firm hard rubble in water up to his thighs. He stripped line deliberately by raising and lowering his right hand; then, holding the loose line as best he could, he made an extremely short cast. *Good. Much better this year.* Then he stood, rod poised, watching the spreading circles of feeding fish. There were two twelve-inchers in the middle current lane, feeding freely, and two small fish back ten feet; he couldn't reach any of those anymore, though they'd once have been easy enough casts. He could never have fished to that rise in the far eddy, though: the currents were too tricky, the cast too long. Too bad. That was a large fish.

Then he saw the steady sipping rise directly upstream from him, not thirty feet away. Sometimes the largest fish rose like that, but so did fingerlings. It was time to try. He could reach that fish.

His first cast was too short and too hard. His next was off to the right and too hard. The next two were not bad but the fish both times rose to a natural a second before his fly floated past. On his next cast, the trout rose freely, took, and, gripping line and handle with his left hand, as he'd practiced, he struck and had the fish on. A good one. A bright, large leaper that came out, shaking its spots at him and falling back, and then streaking up into the current, across to the far bank, boring deep, and then leaping again.

"Mike!" He usually didn't talk while he fished but he wanted his friend to see this. He hadn't shouted very loud and above him, Mike, busy with still another fish, did not hear. Again the fish came out. "A beauty," he said, audibly. "A fine brown." Again the fish raced across the current, stripping line from the reel, arching the rod sharply. *Got to get it. Can't lose this one.*

In ten minutes he could tell the trout was tiring. But it was still on the opposite side of the current. As he began to retrieve the line slowly, the fish came into the current and allowed itself to be carried downstream. Then, suddenly, it bolted directly toward him and the line went slack. "No, no," he said, struggling but unable to strip back line quickly enough.

When he regained control, the fish was gone. He drew the line back slowly until he could see the bedraggled fly. The fish had merely pulled out on the slack line—because of his goddam right arm. His right arm —which might as well not be there.

He was sitting in the car, all his equipment packed away, when Mike came back. Mike had caught seven fish, all of size but none as large as the one Brannigan had lost, and said it was the best day he could remember, except of course the day he'd gotten the three-pound brookie in Canada and Brannigan that lucky male. Brannigan offered a weak smile but said nothing, and Mike looked at him and then said nothing as he took off his vest and waders.

In the car, heading home, he turned to Brannigan and asked quietly, "How'd you do, Billy? Take any?"

"I lost one . . . Mike. Pretty good fish. Then I decided I'd better quit because at least I hadn't fallen in. Like every other time. So I headed . . . out. Slowly. Praising myself all the time . . . that at least I hadn't taken . . . a bath this time."

"You took some bad ones last year, Billy."

"I'd lost a good one, a really good fish, and that didn't make . . . me feel too cheery . . . Yet I'd hooked it and played it a long time . . . which I . . . never did before, not since I got wrecked, and I figured . . . if I could get out without a spill, I'd . . . still be ahead."

"Was it a really good fish, Billy?"

"Big. Very big brown."

"Sixteen inches?"

"More."

"That's a big fish."

"So I was one step or two from the bank, smiling and praising myself . . . that I . . . hadn't fallen, when . . . I went into a pothole."

"Hell!"

"So I went down and over, ass . . . over teakettle. Almost drowned."

"Billy!"

"Almost. My head went under . . . and I was on my right side and couldn't . . . get leverage, and sort of forced my head out, and went under again, and gagged. Knew I was going to die. I felt the rasp of brakes . . . in my brain. I suddenly . . . did not want to die. The water was shallow . . . but it was deep enough. Deep enough, Mike. I did not want to die," he said quietly. "So finally I managed to twist over onto my left side. Broke my rod. Slammed my bone badly. Barely . . . got out of it."

Mike looked over at his friend who had lost his fish, nearly ended it all. He had not one word to cheer him with. Brannigan was sitting in the same seat he'd been in when the accident smashed him, and there was a curious grin on his face. "Maybe we . . . really shouldn't go anymore, Billy," Mike said soberly. "Know what I mean?" He had hoped desperately that Brannigan would get one good trout, that this day might be a new beginning. He had for three years said everything he knew to say. He had no words left.

Faintly, as a slight pressure first and then a firm grip, Mike felt his friend's left hand on his shoulder. "No," he heard Brannigan say. And when he turned: "We're going . . . to keep going . . . back."

CROCKER'S HOLE

R. D. BLACKMORE

PART ONE

The Culm, which rises in Somersetshire, and hastening into a fairer land (as the border waters wisely do) falls into the Exe near Kilerton, formerly was a lovely trout stream, such as perverts the Devonshire angler from due respect toward Father Thames and the other canals round London. In the Devonshire valleys it is sweet to see how soon a spring becomes a rill, and a rill runs on into a rivulet and a rivulet swells into a brook; and before one has time to say, "What are you at?"—before the first tree it ever spoke to is a dummy, or the first hill it ever ran down has turned blue, here we have all the airs and graces, demands and assertions of a full-grown river.

But what is the test of a river? Who shall say? "The power to drown a man," replies the river darkly. But rudeness is not argument. Rather shall we say that the power to work a good undershot wheel, without being dammed up all night in a pond, and leaving a tidy back stream to spare at the bottom of the orchard, is a fair certificate of riverhood. If so, many Devonshire streams attain that rank within five miles of their spring; aye, and rapidly add to it. At every turn they gather aid, from ash-clad dingle and aldered meadow, mossy rock and ferny wall, hedge-trough-roofed with bramble netting, where the baby water lurks, and lanes that coming down to ford bring suicidal tribute. Arrogant, all-engrossing river, now it has claimed a great valley of its own; and whatever falls within the hill scoop sooner or later belongs to itself. Even the crystal "shutt" that crosses the farmyard by the woodrick, and glides down an aqueduct of last year's bark for Mary to fill the kettle from; and even the tricklets that have no organs for telling

or knowing their business, but only get into unwary oozings in and
among the water grass, and there make moss and forget themselves
among it—one and all, they come to the same thing at last, and that is
the river.

The Culm used to be a good river at Culmstock, tormented already
by a factory, but not strangled as yet by a railroad. How it is now the
present writer does not know, and is afraid to ask, having heard of a
vile "Culm Valley Line." But Culmstock bridge was a very pretty
place to stand and contemplate the ways of trout; which is easier work
than to catch them. When I was just big enough to peep above the rim,
or to lie upon it with one leg inside for fear of tumbling over, what a
mighty river it used to seem, for it takes a treat there and spreads
itself. Above the bridge the factory stream falls in again, having done
its business, and washing its hands in the innocent half that has
strayed down the meadows. Then under the arches they both rejoice
and come to a slide of about two feet, and make a short, wide pool
below, and indulge themselves in perhaps two islands, through which
a little river always magnifies itself and maintains a mysterious middle.
But after that, all of it used to come together, and make off in one
body for the meadows, intent upon nurturing trout with rapid stickles,
and buttercuppy corners where fat flies may tumble in. And here you
may find in the very first meadow, or at any rate you might have
found, forty years ago, the celebrated "Crocker's Hole."

The story of Crocker is unknown to me, and interesting as it doubtless was, I do not deal with him, but with his Hole. Tradition said that
he was a baker's boy who, during his basket rounds, fell in love with a
maiden who received the cottage loaf, or perhaps good "Households,"
for her master's use. No doubt she was charming, as a girl should be,
but whether she encouraged the youthful baker and then betrayed him
with false role, or whether she "consisted" throughout—as our cousins across the water express it—is known to their *manes* only. Enough
that she would not have the floury lad; and that he, after giving in his
books and money, sought an untimely grave among the trout. And
this was the first pool below the bread walk deep enough to drown a
five-foot baker boy. Sad it was; but such things must be, and bread
must still be delivered daily.

A truce to such reflections—as our foremost writers always say,
when they do not see how to go on with them—but it is a serious thing
to know what Crocker's Hole was like; because at a time when (if he
had only persevered, and married the maid, and succeeded to the
oven, and reared a large family of short-weight bakers) he might have
been leaning on his crutch beside the pool, and teaching his grandson
to swim by precept (that beautiful proxy for practice)—at such a time,

I say, there lived a remarkable fine trout in that hole. Anglers are notoriously truthful, especially as to what they catch, or even more frequently have not caught. Though I may have written fiction, among many other sins—as a nice old lady told me once—now I have to deal with facts; and foul scorn would I count it ever to make believe that I caught that fish. My length at that time was not more than the butt of a four-jointed rod, and all I could catch was a minnow with a pin, which our cook Lydia would not cook, but used to say, "Oh, what a shame, Master Richard! They would have been trout in the summer, please God! if you would only a' let 'em grow on." She is living now and will bear me out in this.

But upon every great occasion there arises a great man; or to put it more accurately, in the present instance, a mighty and distinguished boy. My father, being the parson of the parish, and getting, need it be said, small pay, took sundry pupils, very pleasant fellows, about to adorn the universities. Among them was the original "Bude Light," as he was satirically called at Cambridge, for he came from Bude, and there was no light in him. Among them also was John Pike, a born Zebedee if ever there was one.

John Pike was a thickset younker, with a large and bushy head, keen blue eyes that could see through water, and the proper slouch of shoulder into which great anglers ripen; but greater still are born with it; and of these was Master John. It mattered little what the weather was, and scarcely more as to the time of year, John Pike must have his fishing every day, and on Sundays he read about it, and made flies. All the rest of the time he was thinking about it.

My father was coaching him in the fourth book of *The Aeneid* and all those wonderful speeches of Dido, where passion disdains construction; but the only line Pike cared for was of horsehair. "I fear, Mr. Pike, that you are not giving me your entire attention," my father used to say in his mild dry way; and once when Pike was more than usually abroad, his tutor begged to share his meditations. "Well, sir," said Pike, who was very truthful, "I can see a green drake by the strawberry tree, the first of the season, and your derivation of 'barbarous' put me in mind of my barberry dye." In those days it was a very nice point to get the right tint for the mallard's feather.

No sooner was lesson done than Pike, whose rod was ready upon the lawn, dashed away always for the river, rushing headlong down the hill, and away to the left through a private yard, where "No Thoroughfare" was put up and a big dog stationed to enforce it. But Cerberus himself could not have stopped John Pike; his conscience backed him up in trespass the most sinful when his heart was inditing of a trout upon the rise.

All this, however, is preliminary, as the boy said when he put his father's coat upon his grandfather's tenterhooks, with felonious intent upon his grandmother's apples; the main point to be understood is this, that nothing—neither brazen tower, hundred-eyed Argus, nor Cretan Minotaur—could stop John Pike from getting at a good stickle. But, even as the world knows nothing of its greatest men, its greatest men know nothing of the world beneath their very nose, till fortune sneezes dexter. For two years John Pike must have been whipping the water as hard as Xerxes, without having ever once dreamed of the glorious trout that lived in Crocker's Hole. But why, when he ought to have been at least on bowing terms with every fish as long as his middle finger, why had he failed to know this champion? The answer is simple—because of his short cuts. Flying as he did like an arrow from a bow, Pike used to hit his beloved river at an elbow, some furlong below Crocker's Hole, where a sweet little stickle sailed away downstream, whereas for the length of a meadow upward the water lay smooth, clear, and shallow; therefore the youth, with so little time to spare, rushed into the downward joy.

And here it may be noted that the leading maxim of the present period, that man can discharge his duty only by going counter to the stream, was scarcely mooted in those days. My grandfather (who was a wonderful man, if he was accustomed to fill a cart in two days of fly fishing on the Barle) regularly fished downstream; and what more than a cartload need anyone put into his basket?

And surely it is more genial and pleasant to behold our friend the river growing and thriving as we go on, strengthening its voice and enlarging its bosom, and sparkling through each successive meadow with richer plenitude of silver, than to trace it against its own grain and good will toward weakness, and littleness, and immature conceptions.

However, you will say that if John Pike had fished upstream, he would have found this trout much sooner. And that is true; but still, as it was, the trout had more time to grow into such a prize. And the way in which John found him out was this. For some days he had been tormented with a very painful tooth, which even poisoned all the joys of fishing. Therefore he resolved to have it out and sturdily entered the shop of John Sweetland, the village blacksmith, and there paid his sixpence. Sweetland extracted the teeth of the village, whenever they required it, in the simplest and most effectual way. A piece of fine wire was fastened round the tooth, and the other end round the anvil's nose, then the sturdy blacksmith shut the lower half of his shop door, which was about breast-high, with the patient outside and the anvil within; a strong push of the foot upset the anvil, and the tooth flew out like a well-thrown fly.

When John Pike had suffered this very bravely, "Ah, Master Pike," said the blacksmith, with a grin, "I reckon you won't pull out thic there big vish"—the smithy commanded a view of the river—"clever as you be, quite so peart as thiccy."

"What big fish?" asked the boy, with deepest interest, though his mouth was bleeding fearfully.

"Why, that girt mortial of a vish as hath his hover in Crocker's Hole. Zum on 'em saith as a' must be a zammon."

Off went Pike with his handkerchief to his mouth, and after him ran Alec Bolt, one of his fellow pupils, who had come to the shop to enjoy the extraction.

"Oh, my!" was all that Pike could utter, when by craftily posting himself he had obtained a good view of this grand fish.

"I'll lay you a crown you don't catch him!" cried Bolt, an impatient youth, who scorned angling.

"How long will you give me?" asked the wary Pike, who never made rash wagers.

"Oh! till the holidays if you like; or, if that won't do, till Michaelmas."

Now the midsummer holidays were six weeks off—boys used not to talk of "vacations" then, still less of "recesses."

"I think I'll bet you," said Pike, in his slow way, bending forward carefully, with his keen eyes on this monster; "but it would not be fair to take till Michaelmas. I'll bet you a crown that I catch him before the holidays—at least, unless some other fellow does."

PART TWO

The day of that most momentous interview must have been the 14th day of May. Of the year I will not be so sure; for children take more note of days than of years, for which the latter have their full revenge thereafter. It must have been the 14th, because the morrow was our holiday, given upon the 15th of May, in honor of a birthday.

Now, John Pike was beyond his years wary as well as enterprising, calm as well as ardent, quite as rich in patience as in promptitude and vigor. But Alec Bolt was a headlong youth, volatile, hot, and hasty, fit only to fish the Maelstrom, or a torrent of new lava. And the moment he had laid that wager he expected his crown piece; though time, as the lawyers phrase it, was "expressly of the essence of the contract." And now he demanded that Pike should spend the holiday in trying to catch that trout.

"I shall not go near him," that lad replied, "until I have got a new collar." No piece of personal adornment was it, without which he would not act, but rather that which now is called the fly cast, or the gut cast, or the trace, or what it may be. "And another thing," continued Pike; "the bet is off if you go near him, either now or at any other time, without asking my leave first, and then only going as I tell you."

"What do I want with the great slimy beggar?" the arrogant Bolt made answer. "A good rat is worth fifty of him. No fear of my going near him, Pike. You shan't get out of it that way."

Pike showed his remarkable qualities that day, by fishing exactly as he would have fished without having heard of the great Crockerite. He was up and away upon the millstream before breakfast; and the forenoon he devoted to his favorite course—first down the Craddock stream, a very pretty confluent of the Culm, and from its junction, down the pleasant hams, where the river winds toward Uffculme. It was my privilege to accompany this hero, as his humble Sancho; while Bolt and the faster race went up the river ratting. We were back in time to have Pike's trout (which ranged between two ounces and one half pound) fried for the early dinner; and here it may be lawful to remark that the trout of the Culm are of the very purest excellence, by reason of the flinty bottom, at any rate in these the upper regions. For the valley is the western outlet of the Black Down range, with the Beacon hill upon the north, and Hackpen long ridge to the south; and beyond that again the Whetstone hill, upon whose western end wark portholes scarped with white grit mark the pits. But flint is the staple of the broad Culm Valley, under good, well-pastured loam; and here are chalcedonies and agate stones.

At dinner everybody had a brace of trout—large for the larger folk, little for the little ones, with coughing and some patting on the back for bones. What of equal purport could the fierce rat hunter show? Pike explained many points in the history of each fish, seeming to know them none the worse, and love them all the better, for being fried. We banqueted, neither a whit did soul get stinted of banquet impartial. Then the wielder of the magic rod very modestly sought leave of absence at the teatime.

"Fishing again, Mr. Pike, I suppose," my father answered pleasantly; "I used to be fond of it at your age; but never so entirely wrapped up in it as you are."

"No, sir; I am not going fishing again. I want to walk to Wellington, to get some things at Cherry's."

"Books, Mr. Pike? Ah! I am very glad of that. But I fear it can only be fly books."

"I want a little Horace for eighteenpence—the Cambridge one just published, to carry in my pocket—and a new hank of gut."

"Which of the two is more important? Put that into Latin, and answer it."

"*Utrum pluris facio? Flaccum flocci. Viscera magni.*" With this vast effort Pike turned as red as any trout spot.

"After that who could refuse you?" said my father. "You always tell the truth, my boy, in Latin or in English."

Although it was a long walk, some fourteen miles to Wellington and back, I got permission to go with Pike; and as we crossed the bridge and saw the tree that overhung Crocker's Hole, I begged him to show me that mighty fish.

"Not a bit of it," he replied. "It would bring the blackguards. If the blackguards once find him out, it is all over with him."

"The blackguards are all in factory now, and I am sure they cannot see us from the windows. They won't be out till five o'clock."

With the true liberality of young England, which abides even now as large and glorious as ever, we always called the free and enlightened operatives of the period by the courteous name above set down, and it must be acknowledged that some of them deserved it, although perhaps they poached with less of science than their sons. But the cowardly murder of fish by liming the water was already prevalent.

Yielding to my request and perhaps his own desire—manfully kept in check that morning—Pike very carefully approached that pool, commanding me to sit down while he reconnoitered from the meadow upon the right bank of the stream. And the place which had so sadly quenched the fire of the poor baker's love filled my childish heart with dread and deep wonder at the cruelty of women. But as for John Pike, all he thought of was the fish and the best way to get at him.

Very likely that hole is "holed out" now, as the Yankees well express it, or at any rate changed out of knowledge. Even in my time a very heavy flood entirely altered its character; but to the eager eye of Pike it seemed pretty much as follows, and possibly it may have come to such a form again:

The river, after passing through a hurdle fence at the head of the meadow, takes a little turn or two of bright and shallow indifference, then gathers itself into a good strong slide, as if going down a slope instead of steps. The right bank is high and beetles over with yellow loam and grassy fringe; but the other side is of flinty shingle, low and bare and washed by floods. At the end of this rapid, the stream turns sharply under an ancient alder tree into a large, deep, calm repose, cool, unruffled, and sheltered from the sun by branch and leaf—and that is the hole of poor Crocker.

At the head of the pool (where the hasty current rushes in so eagerly, with noisy excitement and much ado) the quieter waters from below, having rested and enlarged themselves, come lapping up round either curve, with some recollection of their past career, the hoary experience of foam. And sidling toward the new arrival of the impulsive column, where they meet it, things go on which no man can describe without his mouth being full of water. A V is formed, a fancy letter V, beyond any designer's tracery, and even beyond his imagination, a perpetually fluctuating limpid wedge, perpetually creneled and rippled into by little ups and downs that try to make an impress but can only glide away upon either side or sink in dimples under it. And here a gray bough of the ancient alder stretches across, like a thirsty giant's arm, and makes it a very ticklish place to throw a fly. Yet this was the very spot our John Pike must put his fly into, or lose his crown.

Because the great tenant of Crocker's Hole, who allowed no other fish to wag a fin there, and from strict monopoly had grown so fat, kept his victualing yard—if so low an expression can be used concerning him—without above a square yard of this spot. He had a sweet hover, both for rest and recreation, under the bank, in a placid antre, where the water made no noise, but tickled his belly in digestive ease. The loftier the character is of any being, the slower and more dignified his movements are. No true psychologist could have believed—as Sweetland the blacksmith did, and Mr. Pook the tinman—that this trout could ever be the embodiment of Crocker. For this was the last trout in the universal world to drown himself for love; if truly any trout has done so.

"You may come now, and try to look along my back," John Pike, with a reverential whisper, said to me. "Now, don't be in a hurry, young stupid; kneel down. He is not to be disturbed at his dinner, mind. You keep behind me, and look along my back; I never clapped eyes on such a whopper."

I had to kneel down in a tender reminiscence of pastureland and gaze carefully; and not having eyes like those of our Zebedee (who offered his spine for a camera, as he crawled on all fours in front of me), it took me a long time to descry an object most distinct to all who have that special gift of piercing with their eyes the water. See what is said upon this subject in that delicious book, *The Gamekeeper at Home.*

"You are no better than a muff," said Pike, and it was not in my power to deny it.

"If the sun would only leave off," I said. But the sun, who was having a very pleasant play with the sparkle of the water and the twinkle of the leaves, had no inclination to leave off yet, but kept the rippling crystal in a dance of flashing facets, and the quivering verdure in a steady flush of gold.

But suddenly a May fly, a luscious gray drake, richer and more delicate than canvasback or woodcock, with a dart and a leap and a merry zigzag, began to enjoy a little game above the stream. Rising and falling like a gnat, thrilling her gauzy wings, and arching her elegant pellucid frame, every now and then she almost dipped her three long tapering whisks into the dimples of the water.

"He sees her! He'll have her as sure as a gun!" cried Pike, with a gulp, as if he himself were "rising." "Now can you see him, stupid?"

"Crikey, crokums!" I exclaimed, with classic elegance; "I have seen that long thing for five minutes; but I took it for a tree."

"You little"—animal quite early in the alphabet—"now don't you stir a peg, or I'll dig my elbow into you."

The great trout was stationary almost as a stone, in the middle of the V above described. He was gently fanning with his large clear fins, but holding his own against the current mainly by the wagging of his broad-fluked tail. As soon as my slow eyes had once defined him, he grew upon them mightily, molding himself in the matrix of the water, as a thing put into jelly does. And I doubt whether even John Pike saw him more accurately than I did. His size was such, or seemed to be such, that I fear to say a word about it; not because language does not contain the word, but from dread of exaggeration. But his shape and color may be reasonably told without wounding the feeling of an age whose incredulity springs from self-knowledge.

His head was truly small, his shoulders vast; the spring of his back was like a rainbow when the sun is southing; the generous sweep of his deep elastic belly, nobly pulped out with rich nurture, showed what the power of his brain must be, and seemed to undulate, time for time, with the vibrant vigilance of his large wise eyes. His latter end was consistent also. An elegant taper run of counter, coming almost to a cylinder, as a mackerel does, boldly developed with a hugeous spread to a glorious amplitude of swallowtail. His color was all that can well be desired, but ill described by any poor word palette. Enough that he seemed to tone away from olive and umber, with carmine stars, to glowing gold and soft pure silver, mantled with a subtle flush of rose and fawn and opal.

Swoop came a swallow, as we gazed, and was gone with a flick, having missed the May fly. But the wind of his passage, or the skir of wing, struck the merry dancer down, so that he fluttered for one instant on the wave, and that instant was enough. Swift as the swallow, and more true of aim, the great trout made one dart, and a sound, deeper than a tinkle, but as silvery as a bell, rang the poor ephemerid's knell. The rapid water scarcely showed a break; but a bubble sailed down the pool, and the dark hollow echoed with the music of a rise.

"He knows how to take a fly," said Pike; "he has had too many to be tricked with mine. Have him I must; but how ever shall I do it?"

All the way to Wellington he uttered not a word, but shambled along with a mind full of care. When I ventured to look up now and then, to surmise what was going on beneath his hat, deeply set eyes and a wrinkled forehead, relieved at long intervals by a solid shake, proved that there are meditations deeper than those of philosopher or statesman.

PART THREE

Surely no trout could have been misled by the artificial May fly of that time, unless he were either a very young fish, quite new to entomology, or else one afflicted with a combination of myopy and bulimy. Even now there is room for plenty of improvement in our counterfeit presentment; but in those days the body was made with yellow mohair, ribbed with red silk and gold twist, and as thick as a fertile bumblebee. John Pike perceived that to offer such a thing to Crocker's trout would probably consign him—even if his great stamina should overget the horror—to an uneatable death, through just and natural indignation. On the other hand, while the May fly lasted, a trout so cultured, so highly refined, so full of light and sweetness, would never demean himself to low bait, or any coarse son of a maggot.

Meanwhile Alec Bolt allowed poor Pike no peaceful thought, no calm absorption of high mind into the world of flies, no placid period of cobbler's wax, floss silk, turned hackles, and dubbing. For in making of flies John Pike had his special moments of inspiration, times of clearer insight into the everlasting verities, times of brighter conception and more subtle execution, tails of more elastic grace and heads of a neater and nattier expression. As a poet labors at one immortal line, compressing worlds of wisdom into the music of ten syllables, so toiled the patient Pike about the fabric of a fly comprising all the excellence that ever sprang from maggot. Yet Bolt rejoiced to jerk his elbow at the moment of sublimest art. And a swarm of flies was blighted thus.

Peaceful, therefore, and long-suffering, and full of resignation as he was, John Pike came slowly to the sad perception that arts avail not without arms. The elbow, so often jerked, at last took a voluntary jerk from the shoulder, and Alex Bolt lay prostrate, with his right eye full of cobbler's wax. This put a desirable check upon his energies for a week or more, and by that time Pike had flown his fly.

When the honeymoon of spring and summer (which they are now too fashionable to celebrate in this country), the heyday of the whole year marked by the budding of the wild rose, the start of the wheat ear from its sheath, the feathering of the lesser plantain, and flowering of the meadowsweet, and, foremost for the angler's joy, the caracole of May flies—when these things are to be seen and felt (which has not happened at all this year), then rivers should be mild and bright, skies blue and white with fleecy cloud, the west wind blowing softly, and the trout in charming appetite.

On such a day came Pike to the bank of Culm, with a loudly beating heart. A fly there is, not ignominious, or of cowdab origin, neither gross and heavy-bodied, from cradlehood of slimy stones, nor yet of menacing aspect and suggesting deeds of poison, but elegant, bland, and of sunny nature, and obviously good to eat. Him or her—why quest we which?—the shepherd of the dale, contemptuous of gender, except in his own species, has called, and as long as they two coexist will call, the Yellow Sally. A fly that does not waste the day in giddy dances and the fervid waltz, but undergoes family incidents with decorum and discretion. He or she, as the case may be—for the natural history of the riverbank is a book to come hereafter, and of fifty men who make flies not one knows the name of the fly he is making—in the early morning of June, or else in the second quarter of the afternoon, this Yellow Sally fares abroad, with a nice well-ordered flutter.

Despairing of the May fly, as it still may be despaired of, Pike came down to the river with his masterpiece of portraiture. The artificial Yellow Sally is generally always—as they say in Cheshire—a mile or more too yellow. On the other hand, the Yellow Dun conveys no idea of any Sally. But Pike had made a very decent Sally, not perfect (for he was young as well as wise), but far above any counterfeit to be had in fishing-tackle shops. How he made it, he told nobody. But if he lives

now, as I hope he does, any of my readers may ask him through the
G. P. O. and hope to get an answer.

It fluttered beautifully on the breeze, and in such living form that a
brother or sister Sally came up to see it, and went away sadder and
wiser. Then Pike said: "Get away, you young wretch," to your humble
servant who tells this tale; yet, being better than his words, allowed
that pious follower to lie down upon his digestive organs and with
deep attention watch. There must have been great things to see, but to
see them so was difficult. And if I huddle up what happened, excitement also shares the blame.

Pike had fashioned well the time and manner of this overture. He
knew that the giant Crockerite was satiate now with May flies, or
began to find their flavor failing, as happens to us with asparagus,
marrow-fat peas, or strawberries, when we have had a month of them.
And he thought that the first Yellow Sally of the season, inferior
though it were, might have the special charm of novelty. With the skill
of a Zulu, he stole up through the branches over the lower pool till he
came to a spot where a yard-wide opening gave just space for spring of
rod. Then he saw his desirable friend at dinner, wagging his tail, as a
hungry gentleman dining with the Lord Mayor agitates his coat. With
one dexterous whirl, untaught by any of the many books upon the
subject, John Pike laid his Yellow Sally (for he cast with one fly only)
as lightly as gossamer upon the rapid, about a yard in front of the big
trout's head. A moment's pause, and then too quick for words was the
thing that happened.

A heavy plunge was followed by a fearful rush. Forgetful of the
current the river was ridged, as if with a plow driven under it; the
strong line, though given out as fast as might be, twanged like a harp
string as it cut the wave, and then Pike stood up, like a ship dismasted,
with the butt of his rod snapped below the ferrule. He had one of those
foolish things, just invented, a hollow butt of hickory; and the finial
ring of his spare top looked out, to ask what had happened to the rest
of it. "Bad luck!" cried the fisherman; "but never mind, I shall have
him next time, to a certainty."

When this great issue came to be considered, the cause of it was
sadly obvious. The fish, being hooked, had made off with the rush of a
shark for the bottom of the pool. A thicket of saplings below the alder
tree had stopped the judicious hooker from all possibility of following;
and when he strove to turn him by elastic pliance, his rod broke at the
breach of pliability. "I have learned a sad lesson," said John Pike,
looking sadly.

How many fellows would have given up this matter, and glorified
themselves for having hooked so grand a fish, while explaining that

they must have caught him, if they could have done it! But Pike only told me not to say a word about it, and began to make ready for another tug of war. He made himself a splice rod, short and handy, of well-seasoned ash, with a stout top of bamboo, tapered so discreetly, and so balanced in its spring, that verily it formed an arc, with any pressure on it, as perfect as a leafy poplar in a stormy summer. "Now break it if you can," he said, "by any amount of rushes; I'll hook you by your jacket collar; you cut away now, and I'll land you."

This was highly skillful, and he did it many times; and whenever I was landed well, I got a lollipop, so that I was careful not to break his tackle. Moreover he made him a landing net, with a kidney-bean stick, a ring of wire, and his own best nightcap of strong cotton net. Then he got the farmer's leave, and lopped obnoxious bushes; and now the chiefest question was: What bait, and when to offer it? In spite of his sad rebuff, the spirit of John Pike had been equable. The genuine angling mind is steadfast, large, and self-supported, and to the vapid, ignominious chaff, tossed by swine upon the idle wind, it pays as much heed as a big trout does to a dance of midges. People put their fingers to their noses and said: "Master Pike, have you caught him yet?" and Pike only answered: "Wait a bit." If ever this fortitude and persever-ance is to be recovered as the English Brand (the one thing that has made us what we are, and may yet redeem us from niddering shame), a degenerate age should encourage the habit of fishing and never de-spairing. And the brightest sign yet for our future is the increasing demand for hooks and gut.

Pike fished in a manlier age, when nobody would dream of cowering from a savage because he was clever at skulking; and when, if a big fish broke the rod, a stronger rod was made for him, according to the usage of Great Britain. And though the young angler had been de-feated, he did not sit down and have a good cry over it.

About the second week in June, when the May fly had danced its day and died—for the season was an early one—and Crocker's trout had recovered from the wound to his feelings and philanthropy, there came a night of gentle rain, of pleasant tinkling upon window ledges, and a soothing patter among young leaves, and the Culm was yellow in the morning. "I mean to do it this afternoon," Pike whispered to me, as he came back panting. "When the water clears there will be a splendid time."

The lover of the rose knows well a gay voluptuous beetle, whose pleasure is to lie embedded in a fount of beauty. Deep among the incurving petals of the blushing fragrance, he loses himself in his joys sometimes, till a breezy waft reveals him. And when the sunlight breaks upon his luscious dissipation, few would have the heart to oust him, such a gem from such a setting. All his back is emerald sparkles, all his front red Indian gold, and here and there he grows white spots to save the eye from aching. Pike put his finger in and fetched him out, and offered him a little change of joys, by putting a Limerick hook through his thorax, and bringing it out between his elytra. *Cetonia aurata* liked it not, but pawed the air very naturally, and fluttered with his wings attractively.

"I meant to have tried with a fern web," said the angler; "until I saw one of these beggars this morning. If he works like that upon the water, he will do. It was hopeless to try artificials again. What a lovely color the water is! Only three days now to the holidays. I have run it very close. You be ready, younker."

With these words he stepped upon a branch of the alder, for the tone of the waters allowed approach, being soft and sublustrous, without any mud. Also Master Pike's own tone was such as becomes the fisherman, calm, deliberate, free from nerve, but full of eye and muscle. He stepped upon the alder bough to get as near as might be to the fish, for he could not cast this beetle like a fly; it must be dropped gently and allowed to play. "You may come and look," he said to me; "when the water is so, they have no eyes in their tails."

The rose beetle trod upon the water prettily, under a lively vibration, and he looked quite as happy, and considerably more active, than when he had been cradled in the anthers of the rose. To the eye of a fish he was a strong individual, fighting courageously with the current, but sure to be beaten through lack of fins; and mercy suggested, as well as appetite, that the proper solution was to gulp him.

"Hooked him in the gullet. He can't get off!" cried John Pike, laboring to keep his nerves under. "Every inch of tackle is as strong as a bell pull. Now, if I don't land him, I will never fish again!"

Providence, which had constructed Pike, foremost of all things, for lofty angling—disdainful of worm and even minnow—Providence, I say, at this adjuration, pronounced that Pike must catch that trout. Not many anglers are heaven-born; and for one to drop off the hook halfway through his teens would be infinitely worse than to slay the champion trout. Pike felt the force of this, and rushing through the rushes, shouted: "I am sure to have him, Dick! Be ready with my nightcap."

Rod in a bow, like a springle riser; line on the hum, like the string of Paganini; winch on the gallop, like a harpoon wheel, Pike, the headcenter of everything, dashing through thick and thin, and once taken overhead—for he jumped into the hole, when he must have lost him else, but the fish too impetuously towed him out, and made off in passion for another pool, when, if he had only retired to his hover, the angler might have shared the baker's fate—all these things (I tell you, for they all come up again, as if the day were yesterday) so scared me of my never very steadfast wits, that I could only holloa! But one thing I did, I kept the nightcap ready.

OF TROUT
AND MEN

HAROLD F. BLAISDELL

Some men complain that their wives don't understand them, but my wife understands me all too well. She has me so well doped out that she usually knows what I'm going to do before I know it myself. To her, I'm not merely an open book; I'm an open *primer.*

The only thing about me she can't figure out is my love of fishing, and particularly my passion for trout fishing. She accepts my affinity for trout and wishes me well in my fishing. But she does so in much the same spirit as that in which one indulges a child's whim.

She is not alone in her inability to account for the strange fascination some men find in trout. In spite of all that is proclaimed for bass, pike, walleyes and other game fish, trout are accorded a romantic distinction which, to fishermen, sets them apart from all other species of freshwater fish. Whether trout actually merit this distinction is a question of little real significance. Worthy or not, the trout is the sentimental favorite, its position so firmly established that it is quite beyond serious challenge.

To try to explain my own sentimental leaning toward trout, I can offer nothing more substantial than that they seem to me to be the "wildest" of all the fish in our lakes and streams. They are the quickest to sense danger and take flight. No other freshwater fish can match them in flashing speed and fluid grace. They are the least tolerant of the effects of civilization. Finally, they are of a distinctive appearance which suggests their quality of wildness.

This is not as much suggested by coloration or body shape as by the distinctive appearance of the head. The distinction is not lost on artists who paint pictures of fish, for their paintings of trout and salmon invariably capture that fierce and haughty mien that is seen in the heads of the hawk and the eagle. Paintings and drawings of other fish lack this quality. The vacancy of expression in the smallmouth bass, for instance, is in sharp contrast to the aristocratic hauteur which is implicit in the appearance of trout and salmon.

Trout are different from other game fish when classified more objectively. On the evolutionary scale they rate as "primitive" fish, while such species as perch and bass are regarded as "advanced" forms of fish life. This superiority is accorded because of anatomical specializations not manifest in trout: sharp spines in the fins, a more protective scale covering and a more efficient fin arrangement.

These differences constitute biological advantages, and it is clearly evident that fish in possession of these specializations are able to survive where trout perish. But to the fisherman these evolutionary advances have an aspect of coarseness which he instinctively deplores. He finds it hard to recognize exotic qualities in fish for which the problem of survival has been so successfully resolved. He is drawn to trout, again instinctively, by the very deficiencies which make their continued existence uncertain.

At any rate, men fish for trout for reasons which can only be defined in terms of romanticism. This being the case, it is not surprising that the methods of trout fishing incorporate both practical measures and those designed to be ritually symbolic of the proper degree of devoutness. This often tends to dismay the beginner, for as intended, it conveys the impression that trout fishing is extremely complex and difficult. Since the beginner cannot distinguish between necessity and affectation, he may be overwhelmed by their sum total.

Trout are quite unaware of their exalted status. All the romance of trout fishing exists in the mind of the angler and is in no way shared by the fish. It is not a game in which the opponents agree upon certain rules and then engage in a contest in which such rules are binding. Nevertheless, the trout fisherman likes to think that such a circumstance exists. It pleases him to believe that trout are aware of his efforts to outsmart them and are equally determined to outsmart him. As in checkers, where a piece must be jumped when proffered, he comes to feel that trout are under much the same sort of obligation to rise to his fly whenever he presents it properly. This is at least true in my case, for I indulge in just this sort of whimsy when I fish for trout.

One evening recently I worked my way upstream on nearby Furnace Brook (a stream about which I shall have more to say later) to a run that to me had become an enigma. A leaning tree afforded abundant shade at the head of the run, and a deeply undercut bank along one side virtually assured the presence of trout. Yet during one evening after another, I had failed to raise a trout in this extremely likely stretch.

I was absolutely certain that there were trout there, and the conviction that they were deliberately and consciously resisting my best efforts deepened with each unsuccessful attempt to take them.

A thick screen of long grass drooped from the undercut bank and trailed in the water. I drifted my fly within inches of this canopy as usual, and as usual it was ignored. Finally, I overshot my cast a bit, and the fly disappeared behind the curtain of trailing grass. I was on the verge of yanking the fly back before the leader snagged on the grass, when I noticed that the pliant tips allowed the leader to pass beneath them. I let the hidden fly continue on its way, and suddenly heard a resounding *blurp* from behind the grassy screen. I set the hook, and a dandy brown trout came rocketing out of his hiding place and jumped all over the run as certain rare browns have a habit of doing.

My elation at taking that particular fish was quite beyond rational justification. I experienced an illusion of triumph which contained not only the impression that I had finally succeeded in outfoxing a shrewd and calculating adversary, but that the trout had been made to know the humiliation of defeat.

This shows how silly it's possible to become. Trout do not play games; they have no concept of conquest or defeat, and unlike fishermen, they have no sense of pride to be guarded against puncture. Trout simply exist, possessed of sufficient natural shyness and prudence to avoid both obvious and subtle dangers, but vulnerable enough to fall for ruses which camouflage the danger signals. No trout has brains enough to realize that he is being "fished for," but the trout fisherman enhances his sport by picturing them as fully aware of this circumstance.

By way of example, consider the thoughts which usually accompany the choice of a fly. Let's say that no insects are hatching, no fish showing and the angler is forced to make an arbitrary choice. After considerable deliberation, usually pointless, he settles on a No. 14 Quill Gordon as his selection.

What is he thinking? That perhaps the trout in the stream have made a conscious resolution somewhat as follows: "Today we will scorn all patterns of artificial flies with the exception of the Quill Gordon. We will make things even tougher by ruling out everything but No. 14 Quill Gordons. Fishermen who fail to guess our preference will be out of luck. But if a fellow *does* tie on a No. 14 Quill Gordon we will all rise to it, for we are jolly good sports and always play by the rules."

For obvious reasons, fishermen do not admit, even to themselves, that they entertain any such naive and childish notions. But if they refuse to dignify these notions by admission, they subconsciously nurture nebulous and unexpressed versions of these and other absurdities. For while the trout fisherman's efforts are ostensibly aimed at taking trout, his preoccupation is concerned with preserving the illusion that his elaborate methodology is at all times justified. He satisfies himself on this score by refusing to see trout for what they actually are, but as creatures endowed with imaginary characteristics which serve to create the desired image.

I have mentioned the nearby Chittenden Reservoir, and that on rare occasion it yields a huge trout. Since this does happen—although the chances against it are probably more than a thousand to one—those who fish the lake invariably have the possibility in mind and hair-raising tales of lunkers hooked and lost are extremely common. When you have heard one such yarn you have heard them all, for the teller invariably asserts in essence: "He was so big I just couldn't do a thing with him!"

This declaration is made in all seriousness, despite the fact that the fisherman had more than a hundred yards of stout spinning line on his reel and an open lake in which to play the fish. By declaring that he "couldn't do a thing with him," he means he couldn't do what he idiotically elected to try: to horse the big fish ashore by brute strength, moments after it was hooked.

But the tendency toward romanticism is so strong among fishermen that these tales are accepted at face value. The obvious truth—that the fisherman had only himself to blame—is rejected in order to preserve the titillating legend that the Chittenden Reservoir is the home of awesome monsters possessed of inexorable brute strength.

A fisherman leaves a stream with an empty creel and declares to one and all that he "tried everything he had but couldn't find the fly they wanted." This clearly implies the notion that trout always "want" a fly of a particular pattern and substantiates my observation that trout fishermen tend to regard trout fishing as a game in which the trout consciously participate.

The defeated fisherman never lacks a sympathetic audience, for listeners share his quaint belief that all that stood between him and success was the trouts' jealously guarded secret. They have often found themselves in the same boat and are fully aware of the limits to which trout will go in order to fool fishermen. Here again, the possibility of failure because of commonplace reasons is instinctively dismissed. The unique ardor of the trout fisherman is best complimented by blaming failure, not on his own ineptness, but on the devastating cunning of his wily antagonist.

Such flights of fancy are not to be denounced, for it is by their indulgence that trout fishing becomes most keenly enjoyable. If we delude ourselves, as indeed we must, our harmless pretense serves a worthy cause. But although we may gain greater pleasure, this does not gainsay the fact that we have taken liberties with reality in order to do so.

Large brown trout are usually very hard fish to catch, and this has won them a reputation for intelligence and cunning which I strongly suspect is undeserved. Once a brown reaches trophy size he becomes more and more a night feeder and is hard to take during hours of daylight largely because he spends much of the day in a state of suspended animation, almost completely indifferent to food carried by the current and thus indifferent to any imitations offered by fishermen. Fishermen like to believe that big browns survive because they are wise enough to resist temptation, but I am inclined to believe that their survival is accomplished largely by settling into a daily stupor which places them beyond the reach of temptation.

The true test of a brown's sagacity comes when he is on the feed at night, or when he has been roused from his daytime lethargy by some unusual circumstance such as a hatch of exceptionally large flies or a sudden rise of water. Then, when he is on the alert and actively seeking food, he is likely to demonstrate no greater wisdom than do trout of other species.

Years ago I was worm fishing a stream on a hot day and had almost nothing to show for it. The water was low and clear, and although I drifted my bait into shaded pockets and under windfalls, I had caught only a pair of very small trout.

Finally I came to a favorite pool and worked it carefully and thoroughly. Time and again I guided my bait through the deepest part, but no trout grabbed it.

In the meantime, a heavy thunderstorm was in progress upstream from where I was fishing. Lightning zigzagged against a backdrop of purple clouds, the heavens rumbled ominously and I was prepared to make a run for my car at any moment. But it proved to be one of those storms which are violent but soon over. Before it could reach me the thunder died down and the dark clouds dispersed. I counted myself lucky to escape a soaking and then forgot about it.

A short time later, while I was still stubbornly fishing the same pool, I became conscious of a swelling sound in the upstream direction. I looked up and saw a minor flood of brown water rushing toward me.

Bare rocks disappeared beneath the roily water, and soon the heavy flow swept into the pool.

I clamped on a heavier sinker, and put my biggest night crawler on the hook. Then I flipped the bait into the now brawling current at the head of the pool. The crawler was grabbed almost instantly, and I set the hook in a three-pound brown trout.

This fish had undoubtedly seen my bait each time it drifted through the pool, but the theory that he refused it because he was too smart can hardly be defended in the face of what happened eventually. Until the flood came along, the brown was in a characteristic daytime trance which gave me nothing to work on. Once his interest in food was awakened by the sudden rise in water, he became a pushover for a tumbling night crawler.

With prolonged experience, most trout fishermen reach the point where the taking of trout on bait becomes relatively unattractive. This dim view of bait fishing supposedly arises because of the conviction that it is unsportsmanlike, but I doubt very much that this is the true reason. It is suspect if for no other reason than it implies a nobility and gentility to which few trout fishermen, I least of all, can lay honest claim.

In my own case, I think the reason I am reluctant to use bait on trout is that it simplifies the process. When I take a trout on a worm I am keenly aware of the prosaic nature of the operation and no longer able to see trout in the romantic perspective essential to maximum enjoyment. Fly fishing permits and encourages this sentimental distortion of view, for its complexities are sufficient to disguise a certain amount of romantic liberty. A trout is a trout, whether taken on a worm or on a tiny dry fly, yet my concept of a trout while I am bait fishing is considerably less glamorous than the concept I have of the same fish while I am fly fishing. I am sure that my preference for fly fishing is due, in part, to this purely selfish consideration, and not at all in deference to the dictates of "sportsmanship."

No two people have the same sense of values, and I'm sure there are many fishermen who enjoy taking trout on bait fully as much as I enjoy taking them on flies. The same holds true for spinning enthusiasts, and for those whose persuasions lie at various points along this scale of preference.

Remember the old calendar pictures in which a lavishly equipped fly fisherman was caught in the act of furtively slipping a kid a five-spot for a lunker trout the kid had caught on his alder pole? These pictures have disappeared from the scene, and in all probability their ponderous humor was an exaggeration. Yet they contained the seeds of certain truths which are worthy of study.

Along the banks of trout streams will be forked sticks at the edges of deep pools, left by bait fishermen who propped their rods in the forks. Like the kid in the calendar picture, they lob out heavily weighted baits and then do nothing but sit and wait. This technique is looked down on by more sophisticated trout fishermen, but during the course of a season these bank fishermen usually haul more big trout from a given stream than do all the other fishermen combined.

In the first place, they use tempting bait—usually one or more night crawlers. In the second place, they unconsciously conceal the unnatural influence of the line on the bait, the biggest bugaboo in hook and line fishing.

They heave out their baits with complete disregard for the splash made by the heavy sinker and the fact that it probably alarms every trout in the pool. They do not expect early returns, however; they look on that single cast as a long-term investment. Once it is made, they intend only to sit tight.

The night crawler plunges to the bottom and lies there. The pool is deep and slow moving, so this is exactly what trout expect any night crawler to do. If the slow current acts on the line to any extent, its slight influence is absorbed by the heavy sinker. The drag factor is thus completely eliminated.

Absolute quiet prevails. Trout that may have been alarmed by the disturbance of that one cast gradually relax and once more go about their business. And the normal business of large trout, whenever they are interested in food, includes making periodic inspections of their domain, which consists of a slow and deliberate tour of their respective pools, with the intent of discovering something substantial in the form of food.

I have sat and watched enough quiet pools to learn that this is standard behavior among large trout, although it is a characteristic which escapes general attention. I suspect that while smaller trout can depend on stream currents to bring sufficient food past a single location, large trout find the same amount of food inadequate. To satisfy their greater needs they are forced to seek out food over a wide area.

These cruising fish usually show little interest in the surface, focusing their attention almost exclusively on the bottom. They dip down to make close inspection of any item which attracts their interest and gobble it if it proves edible.

The bank fisherman, in all likelihood, is quite unaware of this habit. He sips through one can of beer and goes to work on a second. He is pleasantly relaxed and places his trust entirely in what he imagines to be luck. To recast, move to another spot or otherwise attempt to engineer his own success is contrary to his philosophy. Success, as far as he's concerned, rests in the hands of fate, and he is content to let it lie there.

No conscious technique could be more deadly, for a lunker trout has set out to make the rounds of the pool. He probes here and there, a circumstance of which the fisherman remains blissfully unaware. Eventually the big trout comes over the night crawler, turns quickly and scoops it up without the least hesitation. And why not? There is absolutely nothing in the night crawler's presence or appearance to arouse suspicion.

The fisherman comes awake in a hurry when his rod takes on a slow bend as the trout, the night crawler already swallowed, resumes his cruise. The fisherman gives a mighty heave, and for the next few moments all is commotion. Finally, more thanks to stout tackle than angling finesse, the trout is hauled ashore. The elated fisherman admires his prize and cheerfully attributes his success to a remarkable stroke of luck.

It is ironic that the trout fishing method held in the lowest esteem embodies all that is required to take trout, even the largest: inducement that is innocent of visible (to the trout) cause for suspicion and caution. It is equally ironic that the majority of those who employ it are ignorant of the reason for its deadly potential and fish with the impression that they are merely taking potluck.

Although bottom fishing will account for large trout that are not easily fooled by other methods, few fishermen care to fish that passively and patiently. As soon as they fish more aggressively, natural presentation must be achieved by manipulation. Otherwise, drag will have the same adverse effect that it has in dry fly fishing.

Unsuccessful bait fishermen are usually those who fail to appreciate the significance of drag, while those who consistently make good catches do everything possible to eliminate it. They use light leaders (in the interest of flexibility), as little sinker weight as possible (none at all whenever conditions permit) and fish with hooks of the smallest practical size. And in most cases these drag-conscious fishermen prefer to fish upstream for the same reason that dry fly fishermen do so: to allow the bait to drift with the current with the least possible restraint.

Another thing which distinguishes the accomplished bait fisherman is his realization that worms are not the most fetching bait he can use on trout. More trout are caught on worms than on all other natural baits combined, but only because worms are the bait most commonly used.

Actually, trout have little opportunity to feed on earthworms, other than on those that are draped on hooks. Under normal conditions, streams contain virtually no earthworms, and in spite of popular belief, I doubt that any substantial number is washed into streams by even the heaviest rains. Proof of scarcity becomes evident with the examination of stomach contents. Worms are found in few trout gullets, including those of trout caught in high, roily water. That trout look on worms as highly desirable food is beyond question, but the fact remains that earthworms are not common to their experience, and this element of strangeness can reasonably be assumed to constitute a negative factor.

On the other hand, every stream supports many forms of life which trout regard as equally delectable, if not even more desirable. And it stands to reason that an advantage is gained by using bait that is fully as attractive as a worm and, at the same time, reassuringly familiar.

It is for this reason that some of the most successful fishermen I have known spend considerable time along streams with a dip net, turning over rocks in the riffles and scooping up a variety of organisms which they use on trout with deadly effect. It is because of the attraction that these forms of life hold for trout, and other fish, that they are forced to hide under rocks in order to survive. Consequently, any that can be hung on a hook usually make superlative trout bait.

Among such baits are hellgrammites, small crayfish, salamanders, sculpins and any nymphs or larvae large enough to thread on a tiny hook. Most common of all are the stick caddis larvae which cling to the upper sides of rocks at the bottom of the stream. That they can survive in plain view is proof that trout do not relish them to any extent when protected by their tough covering, but when this is removed, and the larva lightly impaled on a No. 12 hook, they will take trout where the juiciest worm may go begging.

In addition to these items, others will turn up which may defy classification but which may produce spectacular results when used as bait.

One fisherman told me of finding gelatinous masses (possibly salamander eggs) on the undersides of rocks at the mouth of a tiny feeder stream. Out of curiosity he tried hanging small gobs on his hook, and discovered that they were tough enough to stay put if handled gently. He also discovered that the trout couldn't seem to leave this unconventional bait alone. Unfortunately, he declared sadly, his supply was soon exhausted and no amount of searching could produce more.

The same fisherman also showed me a sample of some large larvae he had discovered in another small stream. They were dark, fat and rubberlike in appearance. They were outside my experience, and the best I could do was hazard a guess that they were larvae of the crane fly. I suspect, however, that this was incorrect.

Whatever they were, according to my fisherman friend, trout went for them as eagerly as they had gone for the egg masses. Again, his supply was small and irreplaceable—but he murdered the trout while it lasted.

There was a time when I found fascination in just such experimental bait fishing, but it has lost most of its appeal because of a personal eccentricity which I have already mentioned. But I learned much about trout during this period, as will others who explore the same possibilities.

When spinning first became popular in this country, immediately after the end of World War II, I turned to it with enthusiasm. But this enthusiasm has also waned. Nowadays I resort to bait fishing and spinning for trout only when conditions make these moves imperative. Only within the contexts of fly fishing can I picture trout as I wish to perceive them. I am not ashamed to indulge my whims in the interest of pleasure, but I feel better about it for doing so knowingly.

Most bewildering of all to the beginner, perhaps, is the matter of fly patterns. What he reads and hears creates the impression that the secret of success is in selecting precisely the proper fly at any given time. He infers that trout of the moment will rise to one particular pattern, and that one only. Therefore, by some mysterious means, he must select that single pattern from among a staggering number of possibilities. He also comes to believe that if by some miracle he hits on the right choice, the battle is virtually won.

The probable truth is that he would do just as well to make a blind choice. Many fishermen have written at great length about such things as matching the hatch, favorite patterns, imitative equivalents and much, much more. Put all of these observations together, and there emerges a hodgepodge of confusing nonsense.

In *The Fisherman's Handbook of Trout Flies,* written by Donald Du Bois, there is a listing that contains no less than 5939 different trout fly patterns. The text is fascinating, and I enjoyed it thoroughly. Most intriguing are the author's calculations by which he identifies the astronomical number of patterns that is theoretically possible. Since each fly is supposedly tied to meet a particular need, this presupposes a day, an hour or a minute, during which each of the 5939 will be preferred by the trout over the remaining 5938. Experience will prove that trout can be discriminating and selective to an exasperating degree. But as common sense would lead one to suspect, their selectivity is not such that 5939 alternatives are required to assure its satisfaction.

While selectivity is supposedly a critical factor in all fly fishing, I am inclined to believe that it is of relatively minor importance in most phases and of major significance only in dry fly fishing. Even in this area, trout do not regularly exhibit the narrowly defined preferences with which they are generally credited. Periods of maximum selectivity are relatively rare, and at the other extreme are interludes when they will rise to almost anything. In between lies a middle ground, marked by a willingness to respond to well-presented flies which vary considerably in pattern and size. Happily, this circumstance prevails much of the time.

When my son Mike was very young, he pestered me to take him fly fishing. There is a deep hole in Furnace Brook which local youngsters use as a swimming hole, but it is heavily populated with trout which seem undisturbed by the swimming, and which rise all over the pool most evenings after the last swimmer has left. They would give Mike something to cast to, I knew, so we approached the pool one evening at dusk.

I had rigged Mike's line with the stub of a tapered leader, discounting that he would hook a trout in any event, but figuring that he would snag plenty of brush in his flailing. And in the same vein, I took along a box of bedraggled dry flies which I had discarded as having no value, save for the hooks.

Small trout were in evidence everywhere, and Mike had at them excitedly. Just as I expected, I was busy freeing his fly from the brush behind him much of the time, but between hang-ups he was happily doing what he imagined to be dry fly fishing for rising trout.

I was sharing his enjoyment when a lunker of a brown trout suddenly rose majestically in the center of the pool. His rise was that slow head-and-tail roll which large trout make, so deliberate that I could make out the big red spots against the rich golden color of his exposed side. He moved upstream a bit and came up again, cruised toward the side of the pool and showed himself once more.

I grabbed the rod away from Mike and made a frantic search of my sorry collection of flies for something that might bring him up when tied to the stubby leader. The best bet seemed a heavily palmered No. 8, a big powderpuff of a fly that I had tied for some long-forgotten reason. I put it on as quickly as possible, and then waited. When the big brown came up again, I dropped the bushy fly a bit upstream from him and quickly handed the rod to Mike.

The gob of hackle drifted over the fish, and he rolled up and took it without the slightest show of either haste or hesitation. Mike, who had never hooked a fish on a dry fly in his life, simply stood transfixed. I let out a yell that may have been heard all over town, and Mike heaved on the rod. But it was too late; the brown had already found feathers not to his liking and had spat them out.

The irony of the situation was almost too painful to bear, and I shall not dwell on it. Suffice it to say that the brown's willingness to rise to that particular fly illustrates the fact that the fisherman usually enjoys much more latitude in the matter of pattern selection than is generally acknowledged.

For here was a huge brown trout, supposedly the most selective of all trout, rising to mayflies. This was clearly apparent, for a brisk hatch of mayflies was in progress and they were all of one type and size. By all the sacred rules of fly fishing, the only way to have taken that trout on a dry fly was to select a pattern and size which matched the appearance of the living insects. Yet this "necessity" was rudely refuted by what transpired. Instead of "matching the hatch," a ritual supposedly of sacramental importance, I tied on a fly that bore not the slightest resemblance to the hatching insects. And in spite of this act of heresy, the trout promptly rose and took it.

There is a catechism of trout fishing which is rich in contrived complexities, and which the inexperienced tend to accept without question and hold in reverence. Actually, fly fishing for trout is considerably less complicated than the romantic notions which it tends to inspire. It has its profundities, but these are encountered in a context that is relatively simple. True, trout are so difficult to fool that far more resist the fisherman's best efforts than are taken in by them. Yet the fisherman has usually done his best, and can do no more, when he has observed principles that are relatively few in number and fundamental in nature.

Most important by far, in my opinion, is the matter of presentation. Unfortunately, this often receives too little attention because of the prior belief that the "right" fly is the panacea, and that a "wrong" choice of pattern dooms one to failure. As for me I have long since resigned myself to fishing the wrong fly, for the simple reason that I doubt very much that there is ever a right fly. Even if there were, I'd much rather fish the wrong fly right than to fish the right fly wrong. I have strong faith in *any* dry fly that is fished without drag, and very little faith in any pattern that is allowed to drag.

In dry fly fishing, the prevention of drag is the big problem—and there is no stock solution. It is not nearly as much a matter of leader length, tippet diameter or even casting skill, as that of correctly appraising the water in advance and deducing the probable effect of its various currents on line and leader. This is a knack that comes only with experience, but once it is acquired the fisherman sizes up each new situation in this light as a matter of course.

He will strive for perfect presentation, but this is usually an impossibility. The course over which a dry fly drifts is almost always marked by various means of judging the degree to which the fly responds to the influence of the current: bubbles, flecks of foam and the flow of the water itself. Close observation will invariably disclose a discrepancy between the pace of the fly and that of the water. A fleck of foam, for instance, will either pass the drifting fly, or the fly will pull ahead of the foam. Almost never do the two maintain the constant positional relationship that would be proof of a drag-free float.

Even if perfection is beyond attainment, success can be won by a sufficiently close approach to perfection. The secret of closing this gap so that it falls within the limits of trout tolerance is largely a matter of realizing what must be done. In other words, the fisherman who recognizes the imperative nature of this requirement will shift his position or modify his cast to avoid the drag. And he will fool trout by virtue of this single circumstance.

Of less importance than presentation, but considerably more important than the choice of pattern, is the matter of size. During much of the time that trout are feeding at the surface they will rise to a No. 12 or No. 14 dry fly which gives them no cause for alarm. There are other times, however, when they will only rise to flies that are much smaller. This tendency increases as the fishing season advances, probably because the mayflies which hatch late in the season are usually much smaller than those of May and June.

Trout must be hard put to derive sustenance from these tiny insects, and it seems logical to assume that they would welcome the appearance of more substantial items. The mysteries of trout fishing often defy logic, however, as they do in this case. For trout feeding on midges will usually ignore a No. 12 or a No. 14 dry fly, and although the reason may lie beyond human understanding, it is a fact which the fisherman must honor if he is to take the trout in question. Instinctively he welcomes the need to use tiny flies, as they provide him with romantic pride in any subsequent success. As a result, he tends to exaggerate the frequency with which the need for tiny flies arises, and he also tends to exaggerate the success he achieves by their employment.

Nonfishing friends sometimes drop in when I'm tying flies, and I bask in the amazement they express when I show them the smallest flies I have in stock.

"Yes, indeed," I say grandly when they ask me if it is really possible to catch trout on such tiny hooks. Then I exploit their gullibility by a dissertation which implies that while ordinary fishermen could scarcely hope to, I, by virtue of great skill, land many whoppers without difficulty.

It is now late August. Streams have held at good levels, thanks to a wet summer, and the hatches of larger flies have continued longer than usual. It has been only in the past couple of weeks that I have had to use really small flies, and I estimate the result of my "great skill" about as follows:

Of the trout I have raised to midges I have hooked less than half. Of the half that I have raised, I have popped the leader against one out of every five, and nearly half of those safely hooked have come off before I could land them. As for the "whoppers," the biggest of those taken has been all of thirteen inches long.

Those whose knowledge of dry fly fishing consists largely of what they read, often entertain the belief that the demand of late-season, low-water fishing can be met at no cost to production. The fisherman simply ties tippets of 6X or 7X to his leader, bends on a No. 20 fly and goes on taking as many trout as before. In actual practice, it doesn't work out that way.

Late summer action usually begins at dusk, a time when it is almost impossible to see a No. 18, or smaller, dry fly on the water. The fisherman is seldom certain of his fly's location, so the rise of a taking fish usually comes at an unanticipated spot. This causes a split second of delay in setting the hook, for which the angler attempts to compensate with a harder than usual yank. Providing the fish is hooked at all, this is often more than his wispy tippet can take.

In any event, the hooks are so tiny they fail to grab a good share of the time. When they do, their bite is so superficial that they often pull out or work free in spite of every effort to be gentle. Fishing with extremely small dry flies is a fascinating facet of trout fishing, but its reputation of efficiency is due largely to the fisherman's tendency to forget the many fish that are missed, broken off and otherwise lost, and to remember only those (relatively few) that he manages to land. The fishermen who can reconcile themselves to this high incidence of loss are few in number. Thus, while many acclaim this phase of fly fishing in the abstract, those who actually practice it are but a small fraction of those who sing its praises.

In spite of all testimony to the contrary, the least important consideration in fly fishing is the choice of pattern. In this respect, the term "pattern" should not be construed to include sharp departures from conventional design, for unique differences do sometimes result in deadly effectiveness. The term "pattern" is used here to designate variations of color, materials, and the like among standard fly forms: streamers, bucktails, dry flies and wet flies.

To suggest that pattern is of relatively small importance is to flout one of trout fishing's oldest and most sacred beliefs. It has long been accepted as gospel, for instance, that brook trout, particularly wilderness brookies, are especially fond of gaudy wet flies such as the Parmachene Belle, Silver Doctor, Montreal, Royal Coachman and the like. The Gray Ghost streamer supposedly casts a spell over land-locked salmon, and the Quill Gordon is often described as the "most killing" of all dry fly patterns. Yet I suspect that there is little in fact to substantiate such notions, and that if the truth were known it would indicate that the choice of pattern matters far less than fishermen are pleased to believe.

Visiting fishermen sometimes ask me what patterns I recommend for particular Vermont streams, and they are visibly shocked when I tell them that I don't think it makes much difference what patterns they use. Of course, mine is just one opinion against many, and quite possibly wrong. But I have sufficient faith in my skepticism to test it from time to time. Results to date have tended to solidify my convic-tion that the belief that for each day, or hour, there is a single pattern of ultimate appeal is nothing more than a myth.

Because of this conviction I have always intended to tie a supply of scarlet dry flies, or purple or orange; wings, hackles, tails and bodies all the same outrageous color, and fish with nothing else for a spell. I've never got around to it, but only because I'm too lazy. I may be wrong, but I have a strong suspicion that these flies would account for fully as many trout as would the most painstaking selection from among standard patterns.

What I *have* done many times is to switch from a pattern that is producing to one that is markedly different. If the trout are coming well to an Adams, for instance, and I break it off in a fish or in the brush, I replace it with a fanwing Royal Coachman to see what will happen. And what invariably happens is that I take trout as readily on the fanwing as I had been doing on the completely different Adams.

Few fishermen get to see this side of the picture, for fishing time for most is too precious to waste on experimentation. When they run into a streak of luck they wouldn't change to another pattern for love or money, for they are hooked on the conviction that the pattern they are using is responsible for their success. They come away with a good catch, and the ingrained belief that with no other pattern could they have done as well.

The next time out they tie on the same pattern, and perhaps fail to raise a fish. They try others with the same result. Do they sensibly conclude that the fish simply aren't feeding? Very seldom. Instead, they entertain the belief that the trout have transferred their prefer-ence to some other pattern which would work wonders if only they, the fishermen, could come up with it.

In much the same vein, I have often ignored the advice of guides and tied on a streamer pattern other than the one landlocked salmon allegedly were "taking." As nearly as I can judge, this deliberate contrariness has paid off about as well as has compliance with popular preference. If a guide tells me that salmon are hitting a Goldenhead, I am happy to believe him. For then I feel pretty sure that they will also hit just about any streamer I choose to tie on.

Here again, the supposedly supereffectiveness of a particular pattern is seldom put to the test. Few fishermen are brash enough to tie on anything but the local favorite at what they imagine to be the unnecessary risk of failure. Thus, while a particular streamer pattern may account for virtually all the salmon taken on a lake during a spell of hot fishing, this circumstance is robbed of significance by the failure to give other patterns a try. Unless I miss my guess, dozen of others would have produced as well.

Trout fishing has little justification other than the enjoyment one derives from it, and it is probably true that many trout fishermen gain maximum enjoyment by entertaining beliefs that are little other than romantic. It is not my intention to belittle the traditional fallacies which add to the fascination of trout fishing. I lean on them heavily myself, and my pleasure is intensified by the realization that I am playing make-believe for the sheer fun of it.

What this amounts to is that in the actual business of taking trout I am guided by the relatively few basic principles upon which I believe success depends. These principles do, indeed, make exacting demands upon the fisherman, but they are nothing more than common sense concessions to the powers of discrimination which trout possess and manifest. At the same time, I *picture* trout as much shrewder, far more wary and ever so much more capricious than they really are. Although I take trout by ordinary means, I delude myself by pretending to believe that there is an element of magic in my methods, and by regarding trout as fish which can be fooled only by occult maneuvers.

THE ANGLER

WASHINGTON IRVING

It is said that many an unlucky urchin is induced to run away from his family, and betake himself to a seafaring life, from reading the history of Robinson Crusoe; and I suspect that, in like manner, many of those worthy gentlemen who are given to haunt the sides of pastoral streams with angle rods in hand, may trace the origin of their passion to the seductive pages of honest Izaak Walton. I recollect studying his *Compleat Angler* several years since, in company with a knot of friends in America, and moreover that we were all completely bitten with the angling mania. It was early in the year; but as soon as the weather was auspicious, and that the spring began to melt into the verge of summer, we took rod in hand and sallied into the country, as stark mad as was ever Don Quixote from reading books of chivalry.

One of our party had equalled the Don in the fullness of his equipments; being attired *cap-à-pie* for the enterprise. He wore a broad-skirted fustian coat, perplexed with half a hundred pockets; a pair of stout shoes and leathern gaiters; a basket slung on one side for fish; a patent rod, a landing-net, and a score of other inconveniences, only to be found in the true angler's armory. Thus harnessed for the field, he was as great a matter of stare and wonderment among the country folk, who had never seen a regular angler, as was the steel-clad hero of La Mancha among the goatherds of the Sierra Morena.

Our first essay was along a mountain brook, among the highlands of the Hudson; a most unfortunate place for the execution of those piscatory tactics which had been invented along the velvet margins of quiet English rivulets. It was one of those wild streams that lavish, among our romantic solitudes, unheeded beauties, enough to fill the sketch book of a hunter of the picturesque. Sometimes it would leap down rocky shelves, making small cascades, over which the trees threw their broad balancing sprays, and long nameless weeds hung in fringes from the impending banks, dripping with diamond drops. Sometimes it would brawl and fret along a ravine in the matted shade of a forest, filling it with murmurs; and, after this termagant career, would steal forth into open day with the most placid demure face imaginable; as I have seen some pestilent shrew of a housewife, after filling her home with uproar and ill-humor, come dimpling out of doors, swimming and courtseying, and smiling upon all the world.

How smoothly would this vagrant brook glide, at such times, through some bosom of green meadow-land among the mountains; where the quiet was only interrupted by the occasional tinkling of a bell from the lazy cattle among the clover, or the sound of a woodcutter's axe from the neighboring forest.

For my part, I was always a bungler at all kinds of sport that required either patience or adroitness, and had not angled above half an hour before I had completely "satisfied the sentiment," and convinced myself of the truth of Izaak Walton's opinion, that angling is something like poetry—a man must be born to it. I hooked myself instead of the fish; tangled my line in every tree; lost my bait; broke my rod; until I gave up the attempt in despair, and passed the day under the trees, reading old Izaak; satisfied that it was his fascinating vein of honest simplicity and rural feeling that had bewitched me, and not the passion for angling. My companions, however, were more persevering in their delusion. I have them at this moment before my eyes, stealing along the border of the brook, where it lay open to the day, or was merely fringed by shrubs and bushes. I see the bittern rising with hollow scream as they break in upon his rarely invaded haunt; the kingfisher watching them suspiciously from his dry tree that overhangs the deep black millpond, in the gorge of the hills; the tortoise letting himself slip sideways from off the stone or log on which he is sunning himself; and the panic-struck frog plumping in headlong as they approach, and spreading an alarm throughout the watery world around.

I recollect also, that, after toiling and watching and creeping about for the greater part of a day, with scarcely any success, in spite of all our admirable apparatus, a lubberly country urchin came down from the hills with a rod made from a branch of a tree, a few yards of twine, and, as Heaven shall help me! I believe a crooked pin for a hook, baited with a vile earthworm—and in half an hour caught more fish than we had nibbles throughout the day!

But, above all, I recollect the "good, honest, wholesome, hungry" repast, which we made under a beech-tree, just by a spring of pure sweet water that stole out of the side of a hill; and how, when it was over, one of the party read old Izaak Walton's scene with the milk-maid, while I lay on the grass and built castles in a bright pile of clouds, until I fell asleep. All this may appear like mere egotism; yet I cannot refrain from uttering these recollections, which are passing like a strain of music over my mind, and have been called up by an agreeable scene which I witnessed not long since.

In a morning stroll along the banks of Alun, a beautiful little stream which flows down from the Welsh hills, and throws itself into the Dee, my attention was attracted to a group seated on the margin. On approaching, I found it to consist of a veteran angler and two rustic disciples. The former was an old fellow with a wooden leg, with clothes very much but very carefully patched, betokening poverty, honestly come by, and decently maintained. His face bore the marks of former storms, but present fair weather; its furrows had been worn into an habitual smile; his iron-gray locks hung about his ears, and he had altogether the good-humored air of a constitutional philosopher who was disposed to take the world as it went. One of his companions was a ragged wight, with the skulking look of an arrant poacher, and I'll warrant could find his way to any gentleman's fish-pond in the neighborhood in the darkest night. The other was a tall, awkward, country lad, with a lounging gait, and apparently somewhat of a rustic beau. The old man was busy in examining the maw of a trout which he had just killed, to discover by its contents what insects were seasonable for bait; and was lecturing on the subject to his companions, who appeared to listen with infinite deference. I have a kind feeling towards all "brothers of the angle," ever since I read Izaak Walton. They are men, he affirms, of a "mild, sweet, and peaceable spirit"; and my esteem for them has been increased since I met with an old *Tretyse of fishing with the Angle,* in which are set forth many of the maxims of their inoffensive fraternity. "Take good hede," sayeth this honest little tretyse, "that in going about your disportes ye open no man's gates, but that ye shet them again. Also ye shall not use this forsayd crafti disport for no covetousness to the encreasing and sparing of your money only, but principally for your solace, and to cause the helth of your body and specyally of your soule."

I thought that I could perceive in the veteran angler before me an exemplification of what I had read; and there was a cheerful contentedness in his looks that quite drew me towards him. I could not but remark the gallant manner in which he stumped from one part of the brook to another; waving his rod in the air, to keep the line from dragging on the ground, or catching among the bushes; and the adroit-ness with which he would throw his fly to any particular place; some-times skimming it lightly along a little rapid; sometimes casting it into one of those dark holes made by a twisted root or overhanging bank, in which the large trout are apt to lurk. In the meanwhile he was giving instructions to his two disciples; showing them the manner in which they should handle their rods, fix their flies, and play them along the surface of the stream. The scene brought to my mind the instructions of the sage Piscator to his scholar. The country around was of that pastoral kind which Walton is fond of describing. It was a part of the great plain of Cheshire, close by the beautiful vale of Gess-ford, and just where the inferior Welsh hills begin to swell up from among fresh-smelling meadows. The day, too, like that recorded in his work, was mild and sunshiny, with now and then a soft-dropping shower, that sowed the whole earth with diamonds.

I soon fell into conversation with the old angler, and was so much entertained, that, under pretext of receiving instructions in his art, I kept company with him almost the whole day; wandering along the banks of the stream, and listening to his talk. He was very communica-tive, having all the easy garrulity of cheerful old age; and I fancy was a little flattered by having an opportunity of displaying his piscatory lore; for who does not like now and then to play the sage?

He had been much of a rambler in his day, and had passed some years of his youth in America, particularly in Savannah, where he had entered into trade and had been ruined by the indiscretion of a part-ner. He had afterwards experienced many ups and downs in life, until he got into the navy, where his leg was carried away by a cannon-ball, at the battle of Camperdown. This was the only stroke of real good fortune he had ever experienced, for it got him a pension, which, together with some small paternal property brought him in a revenue of nearly forty pounds. On this he retired to his native village where he lived quietly and independently; and devoted the remainder of his life to the "noble art of angling."

I found that he had read Izaak Walton attentively, and he seemed to have imbibed all his simple frankness and prevalent good humor. Though he had been sorely buffeted about the world, he was satisfied that the world, in itself, was good and beautiful. Though he had been as roughly used in different countries as a poor sheep that is fleeced by every hedge and thicket, yet he spoke of every nation with candor and kindness, appearing to look only on the good side of things; and, above all, he was almost the only man I had ever met with who had been an unfortunate adventurer in America and had honesty and magnanimity enough to take the fault to his own door, and not to curse the country.

The lad that was receiving his instructions, I learnt, was the son and heir apparent of a fat old widow who kept the village inn, and of course a youth of some expectation, and much courted by the idle gentleman-like personages of the place. In taking him under his care, therefore, the old man had probably an eye to a privileged corner in the taproom, and an occasional cup of cheerful ale free of expense.

There is certainly something in angling, if we could forget, which anglers are apt to do, the cruelties and tortures inflicted on worms and insects, that tends to produce a gentleness of spirit, and a pure serenity of mind. As the English are methodical, even in their recreations, and are the most scientific of sportsmen, it has been reduced among them to perfect rule and system. Indeed, it is an amusement peculiarly adapted to the mild and highly cultivated scenery of England, where every roughness has been softened away from the landscape. It is delightful to saunter along those limpid streams which wander, like veins of silver, through the bosom of this beautiful country; leading one through a diversity of small home scenery; sometimes winding through ornamented grounds; sometimes brimming along through rich pasturage, where the fresh green is mingled with sweet-smelling flowers; sometimes venturing in sight of villages and hamlets, and then running capriciously away into shady retirements. The sweetness and serenity of nature, and the quiet watchfulness of the sport, gradually bring on pleasant fits of musing, which are now and then agreeably interrupted by the song of a bird, the distant whistle of the peasant, or perhaps the vagary of some fish, leaping out of the still water, and skimming transiently about its glassy surface. "When I would beget content," says Izaak Walton, "and increase confidence in the power and wisdom and providence of Almighty God, I will walk the meadows by some gliding stream, and there contemplate the lilies that take no care, and those very many other little living creatures that are not only created, but feed (man knows not how) by the goodness of the God of nature, and therefore trust in him."

I cannot forbear to give another quotation from one of those ancient champions of angling, which breathes the same innocent and happy spirit:

> Let me live harmlessly, and near the brink
> Of Trent or Avon have a dwelling-place,
> Where I may see my quill, or cork, down sink,
> With eager bite of pike, or bleak, or dace;
> And on the world and my Creator think:
> Whilst some men strive ill-gotten goods t' embrace;
> And others spend their time in base excess

Of wine, or worse, in war, or wantonness.
Let them that will, these pastimes still pursue,
And on such pleasing fancies feed their fill;
So I the fields and meadows green may view,
And daily by fresh rivers walk at will,
Among the daisies and the violets blue,
Red hyacinth and yellow daffodil.

On parting with the old angler, I inquired after his place of abode, and happening to be in the neighborhood of the village a few evenings afterwards, I had the curiosity to seek him out. I found him living in a small cottage, containing only one room, but a perfect curiosity in its method and arrangement. It was on the skirts of the village, on a green bank, a little back from the road, with a small garden in front, stocked with kitchen herbs, and adorned with a few flowers. The whole front of the cottage was overrun with a honeysuckle. On the top was a ship for a weathercock. The interior was fitted up in a truly nautical style, his ideas of comfort and convenience having been acquired on the berth-deck of a man-of-war. A hammock was slung from the ceiling, which, in the daytime, was lashed up so as to take but little room. From the center of the chamber hung a model of a ship, of his own workmanship. Two or three chairs, a table, and a large seachest, formed the principal moveables. About the wall were stuck up naval ballads, such as "Admiral Hosier's Ghost," "All in the Downs," and "Tom Bowling," intermingled with pictures of sea-fights, among which the battle of Camperdown held a distinguished place. The mantlepiece was decorated with sea-shells, over which hung a quadrant, flanked by two wood-cuts of most bitter-looking naval commanders. His implements for angling were carefully disposed on nails and hooks about the room. On a shelf was arranged his library, containing a work on angling, much worn, a Bible covered with canvas, an odd volume or two of voyages, a nautical almanack, and a book of songs.

His family consisted of a large black cat with one eye, and a parrot which he had caught and tamed, and educated himself, in the course of one of his voyages; and which uttered a variety of sea phrases with the hoarse brattling tone of a veteran boatswain. The establishment reminded me of that of the renowned Robinson Crusoe; it was kept in neat order, everything being "stowed away" with the regularity of a ship of war; and he informed me that he "scoured the deck every morning, and swept it between meals."

I found him seated on a bench before the door, smoking his pipe in the soft evening sunshine. His cat was purring soberly on the threshold, and his parrot describing some strange evolutions in an iron ring that swung in the center of his cage. He had been angling all day, and gave me a history of his sport with as much minuteness as a general would talk over a campaign; being particularly animated in relating the manner in which he had taken a large trout, which had completely tasked all his skill and wariness, and which he had sent as a trophy to mine hostess of the inn.

How comforting it is to see a cheerful and contented old age; and to behold a poor fellow, like this, after being tempest-tost through life, safely moored in a snug and quiet harbor in the evening of his days! His happiness, however, sprung from within himself, and was independent of external circumstances; for he had that inexhaustible good nature, which is the most precious gift of Heaven; spreading itself like oil over the troubled sea of thought, and keeping the mind smooth and equable in the roughest weather.

On inquiring further about him, I learnt that he was a universal favorite in the village, and the oracle of the tap-room; where he delighted the rustics with his songs, and, like Sinbad, astonished them with his stories of strange lands, and shipwrecks, and sea-fights. He was much noticed, too, by gentlemen sportsmen of the neighborhood; had taught several of them the art of angling; and was a privileged visitor to their kitchens. The whole tenor of his life was quiet and inoffensive, being principally passed about the neighboring streams, when the weather and season were favorable; and at other times he employed himself at home, preparing his fishing tackle for the next campaign, or manufacturing rods, nets, and flies, for his patrons and pupils among the gentry.

He was a regular attendant at church on Sundays, though he generally fell asleep during the sermon. He had made it his particular request that when he died he should be buried in a green spot, which he could see from his seat in church, and which he had marked out ever since he was a boy, and had thought of when far from home on the raging sea, in danger of being food for the fishes—it was the spot where his father and mother had been buried.

I have done, for I fear that my reader is growing weary; but I could not refrain from drawing the picture of this worthy "brother of the angle"; who has made me more than ever in love with the theory, though I fear I shall never be adroit in the practice, of his art; and I will conclude this rambling sketch in the words of honest Izaak Walton, by craving the blessing of St. Peter's master upon my reader, "and upon all that are true lovers of virtue; and dare trust in his providence: and be quiet; and go a angling."

DANIEL WEBSTER AND THE SEA SERPENT

STEPHEN VINCENT BENÉT

It happened, one summer's day, that Dan'l Webster and some of his friends were out fishing. That was in the high days of his power and his fame, when the question wasn't if he was going to be President but when he was going to be President, and everybody at Kingston depot stood up when Dan'l Webster arrived to take the cars. But in spite of being Secretary of State and the biggest man in New England, he was just the same Dan'l Webster. He bought his Jamaica personal and in the jug at Colonel Sever's store in Kingston, right under a sign saying ENGLISH AND WEST INDIA GOODS, and he never was too busy to do a hand's turn for a friend. And, as for his big farm at Marshfield, that was just the apple of his eye. He buried his favorite horses with their shoes on, standing up, in a private graveyard, and wrote Latin epitaphs for them, and he often was heard to say that his big Hungarian bull, Saint Stephen, had more sense in his rear off hoof than most politicians. But, if there was one thing he loved better than Marshfield itself, it was the sea and the waters around it, for he was a fisherman born.

This time, he was salt-water fishing in the Comet, well out of sight of land. It was a good day for fishing, not too hazy, but not too clear, and Dan'l Webster enjoyed it, as he enjoyed everything in life, except maybe listening to the speeches of Henry Clay. He'd stolen a half-dozen days to come up to Marshfield, and well he needed the rest, for we'd nearly gone to war with England the year before, and now he was trying to fix up a real copper-riveted treaty that would iron out all the old differences that still kept the two countries unfriendly. And that was a job, even for Dan'l Webster. But as soon as he stepped aboard the Comet, he was carefree and heartwhole. He had his real friends around him and he wouldn't allow a word of politics talked on the boat—though that rule got broken this time, and for a good reason, as you'll see. And when he struck his first cod, and felt the fish take the hook, a kind of big slow smile went over his features, and he said, "Gentlemen, this is solid comfort." That was the kind of man he was.

I don't know how many there were of them aboard—half a dozen or so—just enough for good company. We'll say there were George Blake and Rufus Choate and young Peter Harvey and a boy named Jim Billings. And, of course, there was Seth Peterson, Dan'l's boat captain, in his red flannel shirt, New England as cod and beach plums, and Dan'l Webster's fast friend. Dan'l happened to be Secretary of State, and Seth Peterson happened to be a boat captain, but that didn't make any difference between them. And, once the Comet left dock, Seth Peterson ran the show, as it's right that a captain should.

Well, they'd fished all morning and knocked off for a bite of lunch, and some had had segars and snoozes afterward, and some hadn't, but in any case, it was around midafternoon, and everybody was kind of comfortable and contented. They still fished, and they fished well, but they knew in an hour or so they'd be heading back for home with a fine catch on board. So maybe there was more conversation than Seth Peterson would have approved of earlier, and maybe some jokes were passed and some stories told. I don't know, but you know how it is when men get together at the end of a good day. All the same, they were still paying attention to their business—and I guess it was George Blake that noticed it first.

"Dan'l," he said, breathing hard, "I've got something on my line that pulls like a Morgan horse."

"Well, yank him in!" sang out Dan'l, and then his face changed as his own line began to stiffen and twang. "George," he said, "I beat you! I got something on my line that pulls like a pair of steers!"

"Give 'em more line, Mr. Webster!" yells Seth Peterson, and Dan'l did. But at that, the line ran out so fast it smoked when it hit the water, and any hands but Dan'l Webster's would have been cut to the bone. Nor you couldn't see where it went to, except Something deep in the waters must be pulling it out as a cat pulls yarn from a ball. The veins in Dan'l Webster's arm stood out like cords. He played the fish and played the fish; he fought it with every trick he knew. And still the little waves danced and the other men gaped at the fight—and still he couldn't bring the Something to time.

"By the big elm at Marshfield!" he said at last, with his dark face glowing and a fisherman's pride in his eyes. "Have I hooked on to a frigate with all sails set? I've payed out a mile of my own particular line, and she still pulls like ten wild horses. Gentlemen, what's this?"

And even as he said it, the tough line broke in two with a crack like a musket-shot, and out of the deep of ocean, a mile away, the creature rose, majestic. Neighbors, that was a sight! Shaking the hook from its jaw, it rose, the sea serpent of the Scriptures, exact and to specifications as laid down in the Good Book, with its hairy face and its furlong on furlong of body, wallowing and thrashing in the troubled sea. As it rose, it gave a long low melancholy hoot, like a kind of forsaken steamboat; and when it gave out that hoot, young Jim Billings, the boy, fainted dead away on the deck. But nobody even noticed him—they were all staring at the sea serpent with bulging eyes.

Even Dan'l Webster was shaken. He passed his hand for a moment across his brow and gave a sort of inquiring look at the jug of Jamaica by the hatch.

"Gentlemen," he said in a low voice, "the evidence—the ocular evidence would seem to be conclusive. And yet, speaking as a lawyer—"

"Thar she blows! I never thought to see her again!" yells Seth Peterson, half driven out of his mind by the sight, as the sea serpent roiled the waters. "Thar she blows, by the Book of Genesis! Oh, why ain't I got a harpoon?"

"Quiet, Seth," said Dan'l Webster. "Let us rather give thanks for being permitted to witness this glorious and unbelievable sight." And then you could see the real majesty of the man, for no sooner were the words out of his mouth than the sea serpent started swimming straight toward the Comet. She came like a railway train and her wake boiled out behind her for an acre. And yet, there was something kind of skittish about her, too—you might say that she came kind of shaking her skirts and bridling. I don't know what there was about her that made you sure she was a female, but they were all sure.

She came, direct as a bullet, till you could count the white teeth shining in her jaws. I don't know what the rest of them did—though doubtless some prayers were put up in a hasty way—but Dan'l Webster stood there and faced her, with his brow dark and his eyes like a sleepy lion's, giving her glance for glance. Yes, there was a minute, there, when she lifted her head high out of water and they looked at each other eye to eye. They say hers were reddish but handsome. And then, just as it seemed she'd crash plump through the Comet, she made a wide wheel and turned. Three times she circled the boat, hooting lonesomely, while the Comet danced up and down like a cork on the waves. But Dan'l Webster kept his footing, one hand gripping the mast, and whenever he got a chance, he fixed her with his eye. Till finally, on the third circuit, she gave one last long hoot—like twenty foghorns at once, it was, and nearly deafened them all—and plunged back whence she'd come, to the bottomless depths of the sea.

But even after the waters were calm again, they didn't say anything for quite a while. Till, finally, Seth Peterson spoke.

"Well, Mr. Webster," he said, "that one got away"—and he grinned a dry grin.

"Leviathan of the Scriptures! Give me paper and pen," said Dan'l Webster. "We must write this down and attest it." And then they all began to talk.

Well, he wrote an account of just what they'd seen, very plain and honest. And everybody there signed his name to it. Then he read it over to them again aloud. And then there was another silence, while they looked at one another.

Finally, Seth Peterson shook his head, slow and thoughtful.

"It won't do, Dan'l," he said, in a deep voice.

"Won't do?" said Dan'l Webster, with his eyes blazing. "What do you mean, Seth?"

"I mean it just won't do, Dan'l," said Seth Peterson, perfectly respectful, but perfectly firm. "I put it up to you, gentlemen," he said, turning to the others. "I can go home and say I've seen the sea serpent. And everybody'll say, 'Oh, that's just that old liar, Seth Peterson.' But if it's Dan'l Webster says so—can't you see the difference?"

He paused for a minute, but nobody said a word.

"Well, I can," he said. He drawled out the words very slow. "Dan'l Webster—Secretary of State—sees and talks to a sea serpent—off Plymouth Bay. Why, it would plumb ruin him! And I don't mind being ruint, but it's different with Dan'l Webster. Would you vote for a man for President who claimed he'd saw the sea serpent? Well, would you? Would anybody?"

There was another little silence, and then George Blake spoke.

"He's right, Dan'l," he said, while the others nodded. "Give me that paper." He took it from Dan'l Webster's hand and threw it in the sea.

"And now," he said in a firm voice, "I saw cod. Nothing but cod. Except maybe a couple of halibut. Did any gentleman here see anything else?"

Well, at that, it turned out, of course, that nobody aboard had seen anything but cod all day. And with that, they put back for shore. All the same, they all looked over their shoulders a good deal till they got back to harbor.

And yet Dan'l Webster wasn't too contented that evening, in spite of his fine catch. For, after all, he had seen the sea serpent, and not only seen her but played her on the line for twenty-seven minutes by his gold repeater, and, being a fisherman, he'd like to have said so. And yet, if he did—Seth was right—folks would think him crazy or worse. It took his mind off Lord Ashburton and the treaty with England— till, finally, he pushed aside the papers on his desk.

"Oh, a plague on the beast!" he said, kind of crossly. "I'll leave it alone and hope it leaves me alone." So he took his candle and went up to bed. But just as he was dropping off to sleep, he thought he heard a long low hoot from the mouth of Green Harbor River, two miles away.

The next night the hooting continued, and the third day there was a piece in the Kingston paper about the new Government foghorn at Rocky Ledge. Well, the thing began to get on Dan'l Webster's nerves, and when his temper was roused he wasn't a patient man. Moreover, the noises seemed to disturb the stock—at least his overseer said so— and the third night his favorite gray kicked half the door out of her stall. "That sea serpent's getting to be an infernal nuisance," thought Dan'l Webster. "I've got to protect my property." So, the fourth night he put on his old duck-shooting clothes and took his favorite shotgun, Learned Selden, and went down to a blind at the mouth of Green Harbor River, to see what he could see. He didn't tell anybody else about his intentions, because he still felt kind of sensitive about the whole affair.

Well, there was a fine moon that night, and sure enough, about eleven o'clock, the sea serpent showed up, steaming in from ocean, all one continuous wave length, like a giant garden hose. She was quite a handsome sight, all speckled with the moonlight, but Dan'l Webster couldn't rightly appreciate it. And just as she came to the blind, she lifted her head and looked sorrowfully in the direction of Marshfield and let out a long low soulful hoot like a homesick train.

Dan'l Webster hated to do it. But he couldn't have a sea serpent living in Green Harbor River and scaring the stock—not to speak of the universal consternation and panic there'd be in the countryside when such a thing was known. So he lifted Learned Selden and gave her both barrels for a starter, just a trifle over her head. And as soon as the gun exploded, the sea serpent let out a screech you could hear a mile and headed back for open sea. If she'd traveled fast before, she traveled like lightning now, and it wasn't any time before she was just a black streak on the waters.

Dan'l Webster stepped out of the blind and wiped his brow. He felt sorry, but he felt relieved. He didn't think she'd be back, after that sort of scare, and he wanted to leave everything shipshape before he went down to Washington, next morning. But next day, when he told Seth Peterson what he'd done, he didn't feel so chipper. For, "You shouldn't have done that, Mr. Webster," said Seth Peterson, shaking his head, and that was all he would say except a kind of mutter that sounded like "Samanthy was always particular set in her likes." But Dan'l didn't pay any attention to that, though he remembered it later, and he was quite short with Seth for the first time in their long relationship. So Seth shut up like a quahog, and Dan'l took the cars for Washington.

When he got there he was busy enough, for the British treaty was on the boil, and within twenty-four hours he'd forgot all about the sea serpent. Or thought he had. But three days later, as he was walking home to his house on Lafayette Square, with a senator friend of his, in the cool of the evening, they heard a curious noise. It seemed to come from the direction of the Potomac River.

"Must have got a new whistle for the Baltimore night boat," said the senator. "Noisy too."

"Oh, that's just the bullfrogs on the banks," said Dan'l Webster steadily. But he knew what it was, just the same, and his heart sank within him. But nobody ever called Dan'l Webster a coward. So, as soon as he'd got rid of the senator, he went down to the banks of the Potomac. Well, it was the sea serpent, all right.

She looked a little tired, as well she might, having swum from Plymouth Bay. But as soon as she saw Dan'l Webster, she stretched out her neck and gave a long low loving hoot. Then Dan'l knew what the trouble was and, for once in his life, he didn't know what to do. But he'd brought along a couple of roe herring, in a paper, just in case; so he fed them to her and she hooted, affectionate and grateful. Then he walked back to his house with his head bowed. And that very night he sent a special express letter to Seth Peterson at Marshfield, for, it seemed to him, Seth must know more about the business than he let on.

Well, Seth got to Washington as fast as the cars would bring him, and the very evening he arrived Dan'l sent him over to interview the serpent. But when Seth came back, Dan'l could see by his face that he hadn't made much progress.

"Could you talk to her, Seth?" he said, and his voice was eager. "Can she understand United States?"

"Oh, she can understand it all right," said Seth. "She's even picking up a few words. They was always a smart family, those Rock Ledge serpents, and she's the old maid of the lot, and the best educated. The only trouble with 'em is, they're so terrible sot in their ways."

"You might have warned me, Seth," said Dan'l Webster, kind of reproachful, and Seth looked uncomfortable.

"Well, to tell you the truth," he said, "I thought all of 'em was dead.

Nor I never thought she'd act up like this—her father was as respectable a serpent as you'd see in a long summer's day. Her father—"

"Bother her father!" said Dan'l Webster and set his jaw. "Tell me what she says."

"Well, Mr. Webster," said Seth, and stared at his boots, "she says you're quite a handsome man. She says she never did see anybody quite like you," he went on. "I hate to tell you this, Mr. Webster, and I feel kind of responsible, but I think you ought to know. And I told you that you oughtn't to have shot at her—she's pretty proud of that. She says she knows just how you meant it. Well, I'm no great hand at being embarrassed, Mr. Webster, but, I tell you, she embarrassed me. You see, she's been an old maid for about a hundred and fifty years, I guess, and that's the worst of it. And being the last of her folks in those particular waters, there's just no way to restrain her—her father and mother was as sensible, hard-working serpents as ever gave a feller a tow through a fog, but you know how it is with those old families. Well, she says wherever you go, she'll follow you, and she claims she wants to hear you speak before the Supreme Court—"

"Did you tell her I'm a married man?" said Dan'l. "Did you tell her that?"

"Yes, I told her," said Seth, and you could see the perspiration on his forehead. "But she says that doesn't signify—her being a serpent and different—and she's fixing to move right in. She says Washington's got a lovely climate and she's heard all about the balls and the diplomatic receptions. I don't know how she's heard about them, but she has." He swallowed. "I got her to promise she'd kind of lie low for two weeks and not come up the Potomac by daylight—she was fixing to do that because she wants to meet the President. Well, I got her to promise that much. But she says, even so, if you don't come to see her once an evening, she'll hoot till you do, and she told me to tell you that you haven't heard hooting yet. And as soon as the fish market's open, I better run down and buy a barrel of flaked cod, Mr. Webster—she's partial to flaked cod and she usually takes it in the barrel. Well, I don't want to worry you, Mr. Webster, but I'm afraid that we're in a fix."

"A fix!" said Dan'l Webster. "It's the biggest fix I ever was in in my life!"

"Well, it's kind of complimentary, in a way, I guess," said Seth Peterson, "but—"

"Does she say anything else?" said Dan'l Webster, drawing a long breath.

"Yes, Mr. Webster," said Seth Peterson, his eyes on his boots. "She says you're a little shy. But she says she likes that in a man."

Dan'l Webster went to bed that night, but he didn't sleep. He worked and worked those great brains of his till he nearly wore out the wheels, but he still couldn't think of a way to get rid of the sea serpent. And just about the time dawn broke, he heard one long low hoot, faithful and reminiscent, from the direction of the Potomac.

Well, the next two weeks were certainly bad ones for him. For, as the days wore on, the sea serpent got more and more restive. She wanted him to call her Samanthy, which he wouldn't, and she kept asking him when he was going to introduce her into society, till he had to feed her Italian sardines in olive oil to keep her quiet. And that ran up a bill at the fish market that he hated to think of—besides, her continually threatening to come up the Potomac by day. Moreover, and to put the cap on things, the great Webster-Ashburton treaty that was to make his name as Secretary of State had struck a snag and England didn't seem at all partial to admitting the American claims. Oh, it was a weary fortnight and a troublesome one!

The last afternoon of the fortnight, he sat in his office and he didn't know where to turn. For Lord Ashburton was coming to see him for a secret conference that night at nine, and he had to see the sea serpent at ten, and how to satisfy either of them he didn't know. His eyes stared wearily at the papers on his desk. He rang the bell for his secretary.

"The corvette Benjamin Franklin reports—" he said. "This should have gone to the Navy Department, Mr. Jones." Then he glanced at the naval report again and his eyes began to glow like furnaces. "By the bones of Leviathan! I've got it!" he said, with a shout. "Where's my hat, Mr. Jones. I must see the President at once!"

There was a different feeling about the house on Lafayette Square that evening, for Dan'l Webster was himself again. He cracked a joke with Seth Peterson and took a glass of Madeira and turned it to the light. And when Lord Ashburton was announced—a nice, white-haired old gentleman, though a little stiff in his joints—he received him with all the courtesy of a king.

"I am glad to see you so much restored, Mr. Webster," said Lord Ashburton, when the greetings had been exchanged. "And yet I fear I bring you bad news. Concerning clauses six and seven of the proposed treaty between Her Majesty's Government and the United States of America, it is my duty to state—"

"My lord, let us drop the clauses for a moment and take the wider view," said Dan'l Webster, smiling. "This is a matter concerning the future welfare and peace of two great nations. Your government claims the right to search our ships; that right we deny. And our attitude seems to you preposterous. Is that not so?"

"I would hesitate to use the word 'preposterous,' " said Lord Ashburton cautiously. "Yet—"

"And yet," said Dan'l Webster, leaning forward, "there are things which may seem preposterous, and yet are not. Let me put a case. Let us say that Great Britain has the strongest navy afloat."

"Britannia rules the waves," said Lord Ashburton, with a noble smile.

"There were a couple she didn't rule in 1812," said Dan'l Webster, "but let that pass. Let me ask you, Lord Ashburton, and let me ask you solemnly, what could even the power and might of Britain's navy avail against Leviathan?"

"Leviathan?" said Lord Ashburton, rather coldly. "Naturally, I understand the Biblical allusion. Yet—"

"The sea serpent," said Dan'l Webster, kind of impatient. "What could all Britain's navy do against the sea serpent out of the Scriptures?"

Lord Ashburton stared at him as if he had gone mad. "God bless my soul, Mr. Secretary!" he said. "But I fail to see the point of your question. The sea serpent doesn't exist!"

"Doesn't he—I mean she?" said Dan'l Webster, calmly. "And suppose I should prove to you that it does exist?"

"Well, 'pon my word! God bless my soul!" said Lord Ashburton, kind of taken aback. "Naturally—in that case—however—but even so—"

Dan'l Webster touched a bell on his desk. "Lord Ashburton," he said, kind of solemn, "I am putting my life, and what is dearer to me, my honor and reputation, in your hands. Nevertheless, I feel it necessary, for a better understanding between our two countries."

Seth Peterson came into the room and Dan'l nodded at him.

"Seth," he said, "Lord Ashburton is coming with us to see Samanthy."

"It's all right if you say so, Mr. Webster," said Seth Peterson, "but he'll have to help carry the sardines."

"Well, 'pon my word! Bless my soul! A very strange proceeding!" said Lord Ashburton, but he followed along.

Well, they got to the banks of the Potomac, the three of them, and when they were there, Seth whistled. Samanthy was lying mostly under water, behind a little brushy island, but when she heard the whistle, she began to heave up and uncoil, all shining in the moonlight. It was what you might call a kind of impressive sight. Dan'l Webster looked at Lord Ashburton, but Lord Ashburton's words seemed sort of stuck in his throat.

Finally he got them out. "Bless my soul!" he said. "You Americans are very extraordinary! Is it alive?"

But then all he could do was goggle, for Samanthy had lifted her head, and giving a low friendly hoot, she commenced to swim around the island.

"Now, is that a sea serpent or isn't it?" said Dan'l Webster, with a kind of quiet pride.

"Indubitably," said Lord Ashburton, staring through his eyeglass. "Indubitably," and he kind of cleared his throat. "It is, indeed and in fact, a serpent of the sea. And I am asleep and in bed, in my room at the British Embassy." He pinched himself. "Ouch!" he said. "No, I am not."

"Would you call it sizable, for a sea serpent?" persisted Dan'l Webster.

Lord Ashburton stared again through his eyeglass. "Quite," he said. "Oh, yes, quite, quite!"

"And powerful?" asked Dan'l.

"I should judge so," said Lord Ashburton, faintly, as the sea serpent swam around and around the island and the waves of its wake broke crashing on the bank. "Yes, indeed, a very powerful engine of destruction. May I ask what it feeds upon?"

"Italian sardines, for preference," said Dan'l. "But that's beside the point." He drew a long breath. "Well, my lord," he said, "we're intending to commission that sea serpent as a regular and acknowledged war vessel in the United States Navy. And then, where's your wooden walls?"

Lord Ashburton, he was a diplomat, and his face didn't change expression as he stared first at the sea serpent and then at the face of Dan'l Webster. But after a while, he nodded. "You need not labor the point, Mr. Secretary," he said. "My government, I am sure, will be glad to reconsider its position on the last two clauses and on the right of search."

"Then I'm sure we can reach an agreement," said Dan'l Webster, and wiped the sweat from his brow. "And now, let's feed Samanthy."

He whistled to her himself, a long musical whistle, and she came bounding and looping in toward shore. It took all three of them to heave her the barrel of sardines, and she swallowed it down in one gulp. After that, she gave a hoot of thanks and gratitude, and Lord Ashburton sat down on the bank for a minute and took snuff. He said that he needed something to clear his mind.

"Naturally," he said, after a while, "Her Majesty's Government must have adequate assurances as to the good conduct of this—this lady." He'd meant to say "creature" at first, but Samanthy rolled her eye at him just then, and he changed the word.

"You shall have them," said Dan'l Webster, and whistled Samanthy even closer. She came in kind of skittish, flirting her coils, and Lord Ashburton closed his eyes for a minute. But when Dan'l Webster spoke, it was in the voice that hushed the Senate whenever he rose.

"Samanthy," he said, "I speak to you now as Secretary of State of the United States of America." It was the great voice that had rung in the Supreme Court and replied to Hayne, and even a sea serpent had to listen respectful. For the voice was mellow and deep, and he pictured Samanthy's early years as a carefree young serpent, playing with her fellows, and then her hard life of toil and struggle when she was left lone and lorn, till even Seth Peterson and Lord Ashburton realized the sorrow and tragedy of her lonely lot. And then, in the gentlest and kindest way you could ask, he showed her where her duty lay.

"For, if you keep on hooting in the Potomac, Samanthy," he said, "you'll become a public menace to navigation and get sat upon by the Senate Committee for Rivers and Harbors. They'll drag you up on land, Samanthy, and put you in the Smithsonian Institution; they'll stick you in a stagnant little pool and children will come to throw you peanuts on Sundays, and their nurses will poke you with umbrellas if you don't act lively enough. The U.S. Navy will shoot at you for target practice, Samanthy, and the scientists will examine you, and the ladies of the Pure Conduct League will knit you a bathing suit, and you'll be bothered every minute by congressmen and professors and visitors and foreign celebrities till you won't be able to call your scales your own. Oh, yes, it'll be fame, Samanthy, but it won't be good enough. Believe me, I know something about fame and it's begging letters from strangers and calls from people you don't know and don't want to know, and the burden and wear and tear of being a public character till it's enough to break your heart. It isn't good enough, Samanthy; it won't give you back your free waters and your sporting in the deep. Yes, Samanthy, it'd be a remarkable thing to have you here in Washington, but it isn't the life you were meant for and I can't take advantage of your trust. And now," he said to Seth Peterson, "just what does she say?"

Seth Peterson listened, attentive, to the hootings.

"She says the Washington climate isn't what she thought it was," he said. "And the Potomac River's too warm; it's bad for her sciatica. And she's plumb tired of sardines."

"Does she say anything about me?" asked Dan'l Webster, anxiously.

"Well," said Seth Peterson, listening, "she says—if you'll excuse me, Mr. Webster—that you may be a great man, but you wouldn't make much of a sea serpent. She says you haven't got enough coils. She says —well, she says no hard feelings, but she guesses it was a mistake on both sides."

He listened again. "But she says one thing," he said. "She says she's got to have recognition and a husband, if she has to take this Lord Ashburton. She says he doesn't look like much, but he might get her introduced at Court."

A great light broke over Dan'l's face and his voice rang out like thunder. "She shall have them both," he said. "Come here, Samanthy. By virtue of the authority vested in me as Secretary of State, and by special order of the President of the United States and the Secretary of the Navy, as witness the attached commission in blank which I now fill in with your name, I hereby attach you to the United States Navy, to rank as a forty-four-gun frigate on special duty, rating a rear admiral's flag and a salute of the appropriate number of guns, wherever encountered in American waters. And, by virtue of the following special order, I hereby order you to the South Seas, there to cruise until further orders for the purpose of seeking a suitable and proper husband, with all the rights, privileges, duties and appurtenances pertaining to said search and said American citizenship, as aforesaid and Hail Columbia. Signed John Tyler, President. With which is subjoined a passport signed by Daniel Webster, Secretary of State, bidding all foreign nations let pass without hindrance the American citizen, Samanthy Doe, on her lawful journeys and errands." He dropped his voice for a moment and added reflectively, "The American corvette, Benjamin Franklin, reports sighting a handsome young male sea serpent on February third of the present year, just off the coast of the Sandwich Islands. Said serpent had forty-two coils by actual count, and when last sighted was swimming SSW at full speed."

But hardly had he spoken when Samanthy, for the last time, lifted her head and gave out a last long hoot. She looked upon Dan'l Webster as she did so, and there was regret in her eye. But the regret was tinctured with eagerness and hope.

Then she beat the water to a froth, and, before they really saw her go, she was gone, leaving only her wake on the moonlit Potomac.

"Well," said Dan'l Webster, yawning a little, "there we are. And now, Lord Ashburton, if you'll come home with me, we can draw up that treaty."

"Gladly," said Lord Ashburton, brushing his coat with his handkerchief. "Is it really gone? 'Pon my soul! You know, for a moment, I imagined that I actually saw a sea serpent. You have a very vivid way of putting things, Mr. Webster. But I think I understand the American attitude now, from the—er—analogy you were pleased to draw between such a—er—fabulous animal and the young strength of your growing country."

"I was confident that you would appreciate it, once it was brought to your attention," said Dan'l Webster. But he winked one eye at Seth Peterson, and Seth Peterson winked back.

And I'll say this for Dan'l Webster, too—he kept his promises. All through the time he was Secretary of State, he saw to it that the forty-four-gun frigate, Samanthy Doe, was carried on a special account on the books of the Navy. In fact, there's some people say that she's still so carried, and that it was her give Ericsson the idea for building the Monitor in the Civil War—if she wasn't the Monitor herself. And when the White Fleet went around the world in Teddy Roosevelt's time—well, there was a lookout in the crow's-nest of the flagship, one still calm night, as they passed by the palmy isles of the South Seas. And all of a sudden, the water boiled, tremendous and phosphorescent, and there was a pair of sea serpents and seven young ones, circling, calm and majestic, three times around the fleet. He rubbed his eyes and he stared, but there they were. Well, he was the only one that saw it, and they put him in the brig for it next morning. But he swore, till the day he died, they were flying the Stars and Stripes.

GATHERING OF
THE CLAN

EUGENE E. SLOCUM

Our lives are altogether too short; that's certain. As soon as we get fairly started here, away we have to go somewhere else. Worse still, our very limited existence is mostly splotched with worries and responsibilities. The dull drab of business environment is accepted by custom as being its necessary hue. Murders, thuggery, scandals, embezzlements, political chicanery and all other evils of mankind are spread bountifully before us by the daily press like an endless exhibit in a chamber of horrors. Reeking with such atmosphere, it is no wonder that imagination is becoming atrophied. Our milieu carries us farther and farther away from the blithesome realm of fancy. Never more may we hope to have our own "Arabian Nights."

And yet, let one of our present day anthropomorphists cast off his formal mantle and go a-fishing in the wilderness if you would behold him transformed completely into a real man; a happy child of nature. In the twinkling of an eye the millionaire is mentally estranged from all his wealth and its worries; he is elevated to the peerage of sportsmanship on an equal footing with the chastened spirits of the pedantic schoolmaster, the unassuming accountant, the overtired doctor, the underpaid preacher, the grandiloquent lawyer and all the rest who make up the congenial brotherhood of the mountain stream. Once freed from their irksome shackles, these untrammeled grown-ups are in really, truly fairyland.

Behold them now! They are loafing at ease on the spacious porch at general headquarters after a perfect day with the trout, followed by a satisfying dinner. The shades of evening have been drawn very slowly;

153

twinkling stars without number are beginning to cast their glittering
sparks through pure air that has never been breathed before. It is
inhaled with the fragrant tobacco of many pipes and given back fervently like burnt offerings to a deity. The time for story telling is at
hand. There is the guttural sound of a throat being cleared for action.
At once all desultory conversation ceases. The slumbering moon,
aroused by the resonance which stirs the rarefied air, peeps inquiringly
over the distant rim of the world and stays to listen.

It is the clergyman whom the spirit naturally moves first; his duty,
he feels, is to lead his flock.

"My friends," he begins, then pauses impressively. "My friends," he
repeats, "I have today passed through an experience so strange and
still so convincing that we may look for it to revolutionize our methods of trout fishing." Again he pauses, fearful of the effect upon his
spotless reputation if, perchance, any one present should doubt the
truth of what he wishes to reveal. Were he speaking from his pulpit,
then all must go well. His fishing coat is orthodox enough but his faith
in its power to supply the proper background for his almost unbelievable story is not reassuring. If he could now only feel the satisfying
discomfort of his clerical collar! He holds the warm bowl of his smoking pipe close in his left hand and with his right he grasps an object
lying across his knees, unseen by the rest in the gathering darkness.
These employments give him courage and he resumes:

"I was working up through the Hopkins pasture where I found the
cattle taking their midday drink and cool-off in the brook. All of them
moved deliberately away as I came along except one Jersey heifer. She
stood belly deep in the pool just below the leaning beech and seemed
perfectly content to stay there. In fact, when she turned her head
toward me there was in her great, round, fawnlike eyes a pleading look
which induced me to sit on the bank and rest until she might leave of
her own accord. While admiring her sleek side and flank my attention
was carried to her bag by a series of odd movements there. At first I
thought they were nervous twitchings or perhaps were aimed volun-
tarily at dislodging some pestering fly."

"I can feel that my credulity is about to get stretched," softly
breathes the ruddy faced advertising agent, as he settles back to more
fully enjoy the process.

Without appearing to hear the interruption, the narrator continues:

"My friends, as we approach the climax you are to understand that
I disclaim the privilege of the antinomian. I firmly believe that an
untruth might send me to perdition. Now then: riveting my gaze intently upon the udder, I saw that it was being pressed up and pulled
down with the same movement as though made by a sucking calf. The

cause I could not discern, for the lower portion of the bag was submerged. It must be the work of some water animal, a mink or muskrat, I thought. Yet I dared not approach closer for fear of scaring it off before solving the mystery. I knew that my voice would not carry into the water, so I shouted at the heifer and she took a few steps forward. As she moved into shallower water the surging ceased and with her next step I beheld hanging to one of her teats like grim death a brown trout all of two feet long!"

The men are now leaning forward openmouthed listening with straining ears to this most unusual recital. The advertising agent is pressing something to his lips.

"By rapid observation," continues he of the cloth, "I took in at a glance the intentness of the fish and even hoped that I might capture it. Acting at once upon this impulse, I stole forward cautiously, crouching like an Indian. To my intense gratification I saw that the fish's eyes were closed tightly in complete absorption like a hungry babe at its mother's breast. A stride and I was within reach! A deft sweep of the net and the monster was mine! I firmly gripped both sides of the landing net, suspending its great weight, and turned sharply toward shore. I then had only one idea in mind. While I well knew that none of you would doubt for a moment what had been revealed to me, I should feel much better to open the trout in your presence and permit you to see the milk gush from its distended paunch. Alas, friends, such was not to be. A strong rap of its tail tore the net from rim to bottom and through it the trout went. As it dropped on its belly against the surface of the stream a perfect geyser of milk spurted from its mouth. Some of it spattered my waders. You are at liberty, my friends, to examine them, as well as the ruined net which I have brought to you as further evidence."

It is apparent that every one believes the minister's story, for no one accepts his invitation. The advertising agent passes something to the doctor, who tilts back his head, which, with an arm, is silhouetted against the everlasting firmament.

"You stated in the beginning that your experience might revolutionize trout fishing," remarks the schoolmaster eagerly. "Do you mean that in future we shall need equip ourselves with long-handled gaffs?"

"No; with heifers," answers the minister.

The ambient air becomes laden with an odor of artificial purity as a tall, thin man rises from his seat. He has evidently used carbolic soap through force of habit while washing his hands after manipulating the unsterilized knives, forks and spoons at the dinner table. The more emphatic pungency of iodoform is not required to firmly establish the nature of his profession in the minds of those present. Furthermore, the impress of suffering humanity is plainly seen by the light of the moon to have been stamped indelibly upon his sympathetic face. As he takes a commanding position against one of the porch pillars in the direct line of the waiting ellipsoid, his companions know instinctively that he is a shining light either of medicine or of surgery. . . .

In a voice that is modulated to the proprieties of the sick-room, he now starts the development of his apocalypse.

"It is not my intention to insert a spirit of gloom into this delightful gathering, but in order to prepare your minds for a full comprehension of the phenomenal scientific discovery which I plan to lay before the next International Medical Congress I must remind you that some day we all must die."

"Atta boy," chirps up the life insurance solicitor, shamelessly.

"Is this to be a fish story or sob stuff?" The question is peevishly shot from the far end of the porch against a muffled drum, for the ear that is turned in the insurgent direction ceased to function long ago.

"It seems most appropriate for me to bring this world-important matter first to the knowledge of this imposing group of men, especially as it has to do with both trout and turtles, though its deep significance relates to the *bono beefum*."

Sweeping the nonplussed audience with a look of superior intelligence, the pedantic schoolmaster explains, "Meaning the human body."

"Precisely," adds the doctor courteously. "Five years ago I became run down from overwork and went up into the White Mountains to rest and recuperate next to the very heart of nature. It rained every day I was there but this did not deprive me of my daily walk, on one of which tramps I ran across a perfectly beautiful little foamy brook. Strangely enough for that wild country, I found no trout in it, but, nevertheless, I fell in love with its active water. After inducing the owner of the farm through which it ran to sell me the fishing rights for twenty-five years, which I then thought would fully cover the unused span of my life, I got him to accept my check covering the entire period, fearing that he or his heirs might otherwise back out because of what I planned to do. With his receipt stowed safely in my wallet, I sent at once to a private hatchery for a dozen cans of trout fry and when they arrived I dumped them in. There must have been millions of them. I then had no idea of the disastrous result of overcrowding a stream with fish.

"Like waiting patiently for your block of mining stock to make you rich," he continues with a wan smile, "I stayed away from them religiously until last summer, estimating that those four-year-old trout would then average nearly a foot and a half long. What I beheld when I anxiously reached the place where I had given the little fish their freedom went straight to the pit of my stomach like the shock of a crushed finger. I found, to my dismay, that my beautiful brook was as dry as a bone and grass was growing where it had flowed! When the honest farmer explained to me my egregious blunder I had my own stupidity alone to blame. My plans had gone so far askew that the kindly soul had not had the heart to write me about their failure. It seems that I had planted many times more fish than the stream could care for. During the first year, the farmer said, they had plenty of water to play about in after drinking all they wanted. During the second summer their thirsts kept exact pace with the supply. The following year they naturally demanded more drink than ever because of their increased size. This kept narrowing the stream in its bed until there was only room enough for them to shoulder against each other in close formation. The backs of those at the ends of the ranks were out of the water and these fish suffered cruelly from sunburn during July and August; then the skin peeled off, causing them to die right in their tracks like heroic soldiers. Only the center files were left for the fourth year. While you might think these remaining fish were the fortunate ones, their torture was the worst of all. They fought for drink like thirst-crazed men at a scant waterhole in a desert, standing on their heads to reach the precious and constantly diminishing trickle between the stones in the bottom of what was surely becoming an arroyo. Finally, the last one of them perished. As the sympathetic farmer told me this sad tale he was often compelled to cover his face with his handkerchief."

Tears are one of the evidences of a tender heart. The last remark of the doctor seems to have furnished an excuse for the use of many handkerchiefs, though the sobs are strangely hysterical, coming, as they do, from full grown men.

"Why didn't the water reach its former level again after there were no fish to drink it?" asks the student.

"That appeared odd to me, too, until the farmer explained it. During their final fight for life some of the fish, unfortunately, discovered all of the various spring sources and they sucked at these water veins so hard that in every case a vacuum was formed, stopping the flow permanently."

The uncanny laugh of a roystering loon on a nearby pond is startlingly inopportune, but the doctor resumes without apparent concern.

"And now I come to the turtle part of my story—the part that has to do with the *bono beefum*. There are already too many painless ways for ending life, but science has thus far been able only to scratch the surface of life extension. Biology proved long ago that characteristics of one organism may be transmitted to another of a different kind, but when it came to inserting the element of old age into mankind there was nothing from which to extract it. This problem of all the past ages, my friends, I have solved! Today, in the light of my discovery, there is no reason why, if we overcome the attacks of disease, we may not live so long as to look back at Methuselah as one who died in childhood."

The noise of shifting chairs is punctuated by exclamations that continue for some minutes.

"It is a fact of common knowledge that turtles attain to perhaps the greatest age of any living creature, and yet the oldest recorded age of any of these chelonia is about one hundred and sixty years. Therefore, as was proven in the case of Thomas Parr, who died in England at one hundred and fifty-two years, mankind enjoys so closely the honors of age with the lowly turtle that science has recognized no material gain in transferring to the human body the living cells of turtle protoplasm for this purpose, though I believe that a turtle serum is injected into fishermen who frequent the Adirondacks and Canada in June to make them more adept at snapping the black flies that hover about their faces.

"When I found my stream dried up I decided to spend a few days loafing, making my home with the farmer. One morning he led me into his woods for a stroll. There was one tree, a silver beech, into the trunk of which he had affectionately carved his initials when a boy. A pretty sentiment, I thought. Presently he pointed out to me a turtle, which of course reminded me at once of the transfusion theory with which I had already made him familiar. The farmer remarked that it looked like a pretty old one and I was about to pass on when it hissed at me like an angry gander. Surprised at this crotchety exhibition of temper, I then noticed that it was, indeed, a very aged specimen, for its head was warty and misshapen, and a film covered its dull eyes. Looking still closer, I became interested in a design on its back; so, giving it a tap with my stick, which tap was quickly followed by the withdrawal of its head into its shell, I picked it up and, to my uncontrollable joy, I was able to decipher, notwithstanding the erosion of thirty-eight hundred centuries, the unquestionable date of its birth in the handiwork of its Maker. As plainly as I now see you all before me, there is to be seen emblazoned upon the topmost shield of this real, living organism, which is now being fed on mushrooms in my laboratory at home, the momentous inscription, '1880 B.C.'"

The Supreme Court judge is whispering to the prosecuting attorney sitting next to him. The latter rises suddenly and, pointing an accusing finger at the guileless doctor, asks in the manner of one of authority:

"Doctor, will you now state to the jury—I say," lowering his threatening hand, "will you please tell us the name of this farmer?"

"Certainly. I can never forget it because of his striking resemblance to his name. He has a very ruddy complexion and one of his legs is bent. His name is Brandywine Cruikshank."

"Thank you. That's all. Next!"

The portly toy importer becomes popular at once by saying, "I know very little about trout fishing." Some of his hearers get up from their seats and look through the twilight to see who has had the frankness to make such an extraordinary admission.

"I have heard a friend of mine tell for years what a wonderful sport it is and so I decided to try it. I always thought there was nothing to it. Now I know it.

"But when it comes to salt-water fishing, ask me. I'll bet my car against one of the gadgets you call flies that I can get more pounds of fish in a morning down in Peconic Bay when the weaks or blues or porgies are running than this whole crowd can catch of trout in an entire season. And I haven't got to tramp all over hellangone to do it either. All I have to do is to sit pretty in a wicker chair on the poop of my yacht. My hook is baited for me and thrown overboard. I don't even have to bother with a pole. I just pull 'em up hand over hand and sit back resting while they are taken off. That's what I call sport. And you've got something to show for your time besides a few little runts such as I use for bait."

"Does salt water fishing afford one the same opportunity for study and experiment as the dainty brook trout?" asks the student.

"Sure. Why, I've just bought a farm in the mountains and have it already stocked with codfish."

"A farm stocked with codfish!" several exclaim in a single voice.

"Sure. I've got a brook a mile long. At my upper line I've had a wooden trough built and sunk across the stream. Lots of holes are bored through both sides and it is kept full of rock salt. The brook has got to flow through the salt and of course the water becomes briny. I had my man keep boring holes through the trough while I tasted the water that passed through until it got just as salty as the ocean. Then it was ready. Talk about study and experiment! It takes some taster to do this right; not too little and not too much. Yesterday just before I started to motor up here, the fish came that I bought from the Government. There were 10,000 fingerling codfish. At that age they call 'em codlets. They were dumped into the creek and are now having the time of their young lives."

"Who told you that this method of propagating the cod can be done successfully?" inquires the brain specialist.

"Why, the real estate agent who sold me the place."

"Speaking of real estate agents," pipes up the financial editor of *The Universe,* "reminds me of how one of them helped me beat a competitor to a sale when I was a young man on the road for a wholesale drug house. Another drummer happened to get off the same train with me in a village down in Arkansas, named Wideners. It was so small and snuggled so close to the St. Francis River that you might have shoved it off the bank without creating any noise or making the water any muddier. After we had made our call upon the only druggist in town and had done no business except buy a couple of good five-cent cigars from him, we went to the hotel to wait for the stage.

"We listened to all our genial host had to tell us about the natural gas boom in that region and of the wonderful bass fishing they had in the river until the coming of the last freshet which tore out the bridge that crossed to Madison on the other side and carried all boats away down into the Mississippi. He had started to give us the exact measurements of some of these monster fish when the telephone bell interrupted. I recall that I felt relief at my escape from being made an accessory to what I perceived was his contemplated crime of exaggeration. Shortly I heard our boniface say, 'Yes, Kunnel Phinizy; two of 'em heah right now.'

"You know how a thing of no real importance will impress itself upon your mind when you've got nothing else to think about. It's like all hands aboard ship getting excited about a little bird that's lost at sea. Then I heard him say, 'Ah suttonly will,' and hang up the receiver.

"He came back to the bar and looked us both over thoughtfully. I perceived that he was trying to make up his mind about something that concerned us. If there was to be any favoritism I was willing to pay for it. So I invited the boss and my competitor as well to have a drink, and at that moment a real estate agent breezed into the party and was made welcome. I liked the fellow from the start. He seemed to believe in himself, and his business card added confirmation. It read, 'I'm Mosby of Memphis'—no initials, no local address. His main business was selling farms, but the first step was the sale of gas machines to the farm owners. With each machine he gave without extra charge a sheet of printed directions telling how to set it up underground and how to pipe from it to distant points close to the surface the alluring odor of natural gas for the frenzied speculators to smell.

"The proprietor squared his obligation by placing another round before us in order that he might feel free to play fair. Then he said, 'Mah friends, thah's a big awdah waitin' for you-all at Phinizy's drug-sto' 'cross the rivah, an' he's jess bin a-tellin' me the fust one that gits thah gits it.'

"Here was indeed a problem. With all the boats by now out in the Gulf and the bridge gone, the quickest way across the St. Francis was by stage south fifteen miles to Park Place, then west by train ten miles to Marianna, then by another train north fifteen miles to Forrest City, and finally east to Madison. I suggested to my rival that only one of us make the trip and that we split the commission.

"While he hesitated Mosby dropped me a wink and I followed him outside. 'Brother,' he said, 'I reckon I can get you across in a jiffy. You don't need to split no commission with nobody. You can pay me $25 if you use my idea and not a guldurned cent if you don't.'

"Of course, $25 would be only a flea bite out of my commission on the big order that was clamoring to be filled; so I promptly agreed. Then I announced to my contender that I would not bother going all that distance to get an order which I might lose, and that if he got it he was welcome.

"As soon as he had hopped onto the stage, Mosby notified me that all was ready. He escorted me to the river bank where he had installed the mortar that the village used every Fourth to let the world know it was on the map. He had fed its capacious maw with a pound of gunpowder. Next he had coiled into it a stout fishline with a stub of old lead pipe attached to one end; the other end was tied to the axle. At every two feet along the line there was a baited tarpon hook. The gun was pointed high toward the opposite bank.

"All this I noted with curiosity; it meant nothing at all to me except that this man was wasting my valuable time. I was anxious to get to Madison but refrained from betraying my annoyance. Without bother-ing to explain, Mosby lit the fuse. 'Boom!' went the squat thunderer and away went the pipe stub to the Madison side of the river. Trailing behind, followed the baited line through the air in a parabolic curve as graceful as a swan's neck."

The narrator pauses, then digresses with a tone of apology and mental penance. He thumbs the coins in his vest pocket as though they were a rosary.

"No matter what the hotel man may have intended to tell us about the size of bass in the St. Francis River, he could not possibly have exaggerated. That day I learned my lesson to never again doubt a fish story, and I never have since questioned one for a moment. That was thirty years ago."

Picking up the thread of his yarn, he says:

"The line had no sooner stretched itself on the water than it became transformed into a huge, twisting, writhing, tumultuous cable of gigantic bass, strung from shore to shore! They raged at their captivity like ferocious lions, tugging this way and that, spending their enormous energy futilely like people in a panic. Mosby knew; he had this all figured out ahead. If instead, they had all of them rushed up or all rushed down the river in a body they would certainly have carried the mortar along with them like a pebble. The surface of the water below was covered with foam; it must have been froth from their mouths, they were that frenzied. After a while they began to calm down. One by one each of the fish keeled over on its broad side and then came my realization that what I beheld was something more than a mere spectacle arranged for my entertainment.

"Mosby keenly observed that his idea had at last penetrated my dull brain.

"With a graceful sweep of both arms and a low bow with hat in hand, he said, 'Welcome, sir, to Madison.' Instead of paying him in bills I counted out twenty-five silver dollars to lighten my weight. Taking up my sample-case, I walked confidently across this pontoon bridge of bass without even wetting my shoes!"

"Wonderful! Marvelous! Stupendous!" shout the delighted grownup children.

"By the way," inquires the student, "what held the lead pipe end of the line while you were crossing?"

"It caught in the crotch of a tree."

"Did you ever learn the fate of the other salesman?" asks the minister.

"No; not ultimately. God alone knows that. He grew suspicious because I did not leave town with him and came back to investigate. While looking about for me he heard the explosion and hurried to the river in time to see me step safely onto the other shore.

"Idiot that he was, he started after me on a run. He ought to have known that the rhythmic impact would set the bridge vibrating and cause its utter destruction. Well, when the line broke he managed to get clear of the pontoons all right and I thought he was going to come through. I climbed up the bank where I could watch him better. He weighed about two hundred pounds and, swimming toward me in his linens, looked for all the world like a big yellow-back frog with all four legs going in a most irresistible manner.

"Just as I was on the point of turning around to beat him to the drugstore I was horrified beyond my power to move or cry out! I give you my word, gentlemen, one of those St. Francis River bass came up and scooped him right off the surface as neatly as you might skim a money-bubble from a cup of tea!"

"How much profit did you make from your sale to the druggist over the $25 you paid Mosby," casually asked the certified public accountant from force of habit.

"I sold Col. Phinizy 1/12 doz. bottles of ague bitters for $1.13 less 50, 50 and 10. He also took a shine to a sample bottle of nerve tonic, so I gave it to him with my compliments."

During the foregoing recital one of the party who was forced to take an overflow perch on the edge of the veranda with his legs dangling off, has begun pacing back and forth noiselessly on the grass. This is the very man who is saving millions of smokers from nicotine poisoning. Modestly avoiding notoriety and honors, his whole life is secretly devoted to making synthetic tobacco from alfalfa and tonka-beans. He now comes to a stop and, under the benign influence of the radiant heavens, proves himself an unselfish benefactor to the guild of bass fishermen.

"You all know," he declares, "that lakes which are near enough to reach for weekends during the summer have little to offer nowadays except boating and bathing. The fish have become too darned wise. If ever one is caught by chance it is because it has lost an eye and can't see the boat. So many of them were yanked out and then put back years ago through the demands of the law that the present generation has learned by instinct that a boat means a man and a man means danger. Even the shadow of a boat will scare them away as far as they can get.

"I have a camp on just such a bass lake in the Adirondacks. Up to last year I used to fish as everybody else did and still does. Filled with hope in spite of absolute failure the day before, I would each morning scan both sky and water critically and, for no good reason at all other than a hunch, point the bow of my boat toward some far-distant place.

"My equipment included every kind of bait I could think of, most of which had been secured at great pains from a couple of hundred miles away. Being a veteran, I knew what a capricious fish the bass is. On the welcome arrival of my bait I carefully salvaged each precious morsel that had not passed away in transit.

"You men who fish for bass know just what it means to row from place to place only to find that the fish have gone elsewhere. On a seat which grows harder by the minute you simmer in the broiling sun by the hour and by the end of the day your back seems bent for life. In the silent company of what remains of your hellgramites, crickets, frogs, worms, bass-bugs, minnows, grasshoppers, stoner bullheads and crawfish you return to camp tired and disappointed, swearing that you are through forever. But after dinner and a rest it suddenly occurs to you that you forgot to take along lamper-eels! How odd you never thought of lamper-eels! With the keyed-up tension of a setter on a point, you are sure this is the one bait the bass are waiting for. An order by wire brings a fine supply in three days. Off you start again with the same old hope, ending with the same old result.

"Year after year my summers have been made up of these bitter experiences. Finally I concluded to try out my theory that the fish were there to be caught if not scared to death by a boat. The decision solved the whole problem, for the rest was easy. Ever since, I have been supplying fish to all my friends who have cottages around the lake. I am now known up there as the greatest bass fisherman on earth."

"Do you intend letting us into the secret?" cautiously asks the student.

"Of course," assures the speaker. "My place includes two points of land jutting into the lake, and an intervening cove. These two points are half a mile apart. Lined up between them is a long, rocky reef about six feet beneath the surface, an ideal feeding place for bass. I have a water-spaniel that has an appetite which would be worth a million dollars if it were mine immanently instead of by proxy. He is always ready to eat. My first step was to train him to expect food whenever a white flag was waved. The flag was a sheet tied to a long, bamboo pole. I provided two of these. Next I rigged up a pair of traces to snap onto his collar and to these traces I attached a six-foot spreader, or you might call it a whiffletree, with three strong lines three feet apart. These lines were one hundred feet long and to each of them were suspended and weighted with small sinkers ten imitation minnows on swiveled lines, each two feet in length. These were applied to only the last fifty feet of the main lines, which left them five feet apart.

"Talk about a mine-sweeper! It proved to be a Golconda finder! My wife became so excited about it that she took entire charge of the camp terminal, while I went around by trail to the other point, taking with me a furled flag, a bag and a meaty bone. As soon as she saw me on the distant shore she snapped the traces into rings at either side of Nero's collar, straightened out the lines, and pointed me and my waving flag out to him.

"Into the water he leaped. He was a strong swimmer and was only mildly impeded by the constant shocks as the fish grabbed unengaged minnows. After all berths had been taken he pulled the load more steadily and brought it in without sweating a hair. I quickly unsnapped his collar, drew the thirty bass to the shore, bagged them and laid down in the shade while Nero finished his bone and dreamed of more food. When the faithful dog had rested sufficiently I snapped the sweeper to his collar, shouted to my expectant wife, who waved the flag and off he paddled for camp. I reached there with my load in time to take thirty more bass from the hooks."

"A rare piece of headwork," comments the attorney, "but it is my impression that the law does not permit two persons to take sixty bass in a day."

"True, but it says nothing about how many a dog may catch."

Evidently the gray-haired stockbroker has something on his mind. He shifts uneasily in his seat and then gets up. He can think more readily on his feet. In that position he has no feeling of being under compression.

"I spent my entire boyhood," he begins, "on my father's farm in Connecticut. The growing season is pretty short up there in the Litchfield Hills and dad had a hard time to keep his little family in food and clothes. I went barefoot every summer to save shoe leather. As I became old enough to go to school I also got big enough to help with chores. Still, we could not get ahead. I remember that mother was almost worried to death. Nothing had been paid against the mortgage and she realized that the dream of her life, sending me to college, must be abandoned. When the time came I went to high school but had to walk five miles twice a day to do it.

"The winters there come early and stay late. One day while on my way to school through unbroken roads piled high with snow, goaded by our poverty to try to find a way out of it all, I formulated a plan which first paid off our mortgage and later put me through college."

There come expressions of sincere interest from some of the listeners. The moon, now fully risen, seems to lend a sympathetic ear to this recital of deprivation and hardship, finally to be overcome by what is now to be divulged.

"We had a fine brook on the farm and there were lots of trout in it in those days. By the end of the following summer I started my scheme working. First I put a barrel into our cellar safe from frost when winter came, and filled it with peat moss and sand. Then I dug thousands of angleworms and dumped them into the barrel. They worked down through the moss and sand which I sprinkled with a quart of milk every day or so. This was food for the worms. Then I waited more anxiously than ever before for the first cold spell. Meanwhile I had been in correspondence with the swellest hotels in many different cities and found there would be no doubt about marketing my product.

"When the first tightening weather came in November I found, as I had expected, that the worms had grown strong and tough from the milk ration and moss scouring. With a big wad of them nestled against my leg in a pocket of my pants to keep them warm, I went down to the stream."

"Pants?" interrupts the pedant.

"Yes; we did not wear trousers in those days. One of the lusty worms I dropped onto the thin, transparent ice which was forming rapidly and, sure enough, a big trout immediately glued his nose so rigidly against the ice in the expectation that the worm would drop into his mouth that he soon became frozen in beyond his gills and could not have gotten loose if he had tried. Then I quickly disposed more worms every six inches over an area two feet wide by four feet long. I observed with great satisfaction that beneath each of the thirty-two worms a good sized trout was gradually being preserved in all its natural beauty and for as long a time as the ice might be made to last."

"You did not have to inject ether through holes in the ice into their mouths to keep them still while they were being frozen?" the dentist inquires, adding mechanically, "Did it hurt?"

The speaker does not consider the questions relevant and therefore declines to answer. "By next morning the ice was eighteen inches thick. I then sawed out the block."

"Some weather!" comments the potato baron from Houlton, Maine.

"Yes, indeed. I never saw such a beautiful sight as that block of crystal ice with its precious cargo of speckled trout all headed the same way. They looked just as natural as life. Even the expression of eager interest was frozen on their faces.

"I had the cake already sold for a dollar a pound. It was to be used as a restaurant window display. Of course, I wanted to surprise mother and dad with my good fortune, so I had no help to lift it onto the bobsled and deliver it at the station for shipment. Within a few days I was overjoyed to receive my first check. It was for exactly one hundred dollars and came from the Waldorf-Astoria. As soon as I got my plant well under way the money kept piling in on me from hotels and fancy restaurants all over the country. Just as fast as the trout-filled cakes were cut out others were formed in their places. Before spring arrived I had sold a hundred cakes at a dollar per pound, just ten thousand dollars altogether. This paid off the mortgage, bought mother an organ on which she learned to play 'Home, Sweet Home' first of all, and there was plenty left to put me through college.

"It is perfectly wonderful what golden opportunities lie right at our feet if we only have the sense to pick them up."

"Very true," agrees the construction engineer, "but few of us are strong enough to lift a cake of ice two by four by one and one-half feet, which weighs six hundred and ninety pounds."

"Of course, you found out later that you got shortchanged by five hundred and ninety dollars on each cake," observes the nimble-minded accountant.

"I believe you are right, now I come to think of it," concurs the unruffled broker.

"Let's see; when was the Waldorf-Astoria built?" innocently muses the architect.

"Did I say the Waldorf-Astoria? Perhaps it was the old Astor House," suggests the storyteller helpfully. "Yes, of course it was. Isn't it getting a little cool out here? What do you say, boys? Shall we call it a day?"

WHERE THE GRASS IS REALLY GREENER

HAROLD F. BLAISDELL

Rotary clubs are habitually hard up for speakers, at least this seems to be the case in my neck of the woods. I'm basing this opinion on the fact that they sometimes ask me to give a talk on fishing.

My shortcomings as a public speaker are sufficient to make me apprehensive about such assignments, but my queasiness is compounded by the knowledge that not all Rotarians are fishermen. In my audience are bound to be those who look on fishing as a foolish enterprise, and an acute awareness of them dampens any small enthusiasm I might otherwise have for the job. Even when speaking to groups made up entirely of fishermen, I never feel confident of hitting on any common denominator of interest. To the many people who fish, fishing is a great many different things, and what one fisherman sees as its greatest charms may be in sharp contrast to the views of other anglers of equal enthusiasm.

One beautiful June day, several years ago, Pete Terwilliger and I were fishing Attean Rips, a stretch of rapids on the Moose River near Jackman, Maine. Fishing at the head of the rips, or the "top of the pitch" as it is called in Maine, we took brook trout up to a two-pound top, plus several land-locked salmon which weighed between two and three pounds. All had risen to dry flies, so it was fishing that left little to be desired.

Our guide was a hardened veteran of the Maine woods named Walter Wilson. Walter had guided me on several previous trips, and I had come to value and appreciate his expert services.

But Walter wasn't one you'd pick as your guide on the strength of appearances. He was well past seventy, and his lined and angular face seemed to bespeak a deep-seated cynicism toward everything and everybody, giving the impression that he was patiently waiting for the world to get the comeuppance he believed it richly deserved.

Just to watch him paddle a canoe was enough to bring on strong feelings of depression. He hunched himself over his paddle in a manner which seemed to reflect the accumulated weariness of more than a half century of paddling, while his face took on the dour expression of a man who has just discovered a leak in his waders. To anyone the least bit sensitive to human suffering, the idea of pursuing pleasure in the presence of such abject misery seemed almost indecent.

I hadn't fished long from Walter's canoe, however, before discovering that I was always exactly where I wanted to be: in comfortable casting range of the most likely places. In the meantime, although in the manner of one discharging an odious duty, Walter drew on decades of experience to point out the precise spots where I should drop my fly. By the end of the first day I knew that he had done his darndest to put me on fish. When I got to know him better, I came to realize that he actually got a big kick out of doing so.

That morning, however, Pete and I needed no help from Walter. We fished in waders, the fish were on the move and all we had to do was to lay about us with high-riding dry flies. Walter watched us a spell, then ambled downstream to the big pool at the base of the rips where we had beached the canoe. He'd holler when lunch was ready, he told us.

There was a rustic table and shelter overlooking the pool, and I can think of no pleasanter setting for a noon cookout. This, plus the exuberance brought about by the splendid fishing, impelled Pete and me to praise Walter's culinary efforts to the skies. The broiled chops were delicious beyond all previous experience, the pan-fried potatoes and onions superb and the heady flavor of the boiled coffee—which only Maine guides seem able to achieve—was out of this world.

If Walter reacted to our praise, it was without visible sign. He stared out over the broad pool in silence, and then, if such were possible, his face took on a more pained expression than usual.

"There was a feller I used to guide years ago," he said, plunking down each word as though glad to be rid of it. "He wanted to catch a trout of five pounds or more. Had his heart set on having one that big mounted, but wouldn't settle for anything smaller. He caught quite a few trout that weighed over four pounds, but darned if I could ever get him one that weighed five.

"One spring he showed up with his uncle, an old feller who had never caught a trout in his life. We came up here to the rips, and the young feller told me to look out for the old man while he fished the top of the pitch.

"I put the uncle in the canoe and paddled up to the head of this pool in front of us. Tied on a streamer for him, stripped out some line and then handed him the rod and told him to keep twitching it.

"Pretty soon a fish hit that streamer a helluva belt, and I finally managed to net it. It was a trout that weighed five pounds and two ounces. I worked out line again and gave the old man the rod. Another helluva wallop, and *another* trout of over five pounds!

"You should have seen the young feller's face when he saw that pair of fish. But before he could say anything, the uncle wanted to know where I planned to have him fish after lunch.

" 'You and I are going right back where we were this morning,' I told him.

" 'What for?' he wanted to know. 'We fished there all morning and only caught two.' "

Walter continued to stare out over the pool, tortured by the resurrection of irony too painful for a man to bear. Finally, still lost in glum reflection, he silently went about gathering up dishes and the few leftovers from our lunch.

If nothing else, this yarn illustrates the degree to which the charm of fishing lies in the eye of the beholder. Although some see it clearly, others see it not at all, raising for philosophical debate the question of whether it is real or imaginary.

Even among those who dearly love to fish, a divergence of viewpoint has developed in recent years, threatening to alter the traditional concept of the sport. This new concept has evolved, I suspect, as a result of the quickening tempo of life with which we seem obliged to keep pace.

What I have chosen to call the traditional point of view or concept is that which concerns itself largely with nearby waters and the problems involved in taking fish that have been well educated by persistent attempts on their lives. Within this framework the gross thrill of taking large numbers of big fish is not a paramount goal. Instead, the principal objective is to achieve modest success under circumstances sufficiently demanding to make this a reliable and gratifying reflection of angling skill.

The modern concept has little patience with this quiet challenge. The foremost goal, to its swelling ranks of adherents, has become that of reaching remote waters which have seen little or no fishing, and where even the tyro can expect to catch more fish than he can carry.

It is both natural and practical for editors and writers to capitalize on the glamour of far-off places, and much that is published about fishing nowadays has to do with the spectacular fishing which can be found only in the most remote regions. Such material has its effect on the reader. Local attractions have less appeal as he reads of virgin fishing and big fish, and his angling ambitions come to include little else than the desire to fish the romantic waters he reads about.

How well does this modern concept serve the fisherman's need? If he was bitten by the same fishing bug that long ago bit me, it tends to tantalize far more than to satisfy.

When I was a kid, a small group of men in my hometown made annual trips to a wilderness pond in northern Vermont, which involved a drive of less than a hundred miles, plus a hike through the woods of a dozen more. For these modest efforts they were rewarded with virginal fishing. They never failed to return with big catches of trout that ran up to three and four pounds in weight, to say nothing of yarns calculated to make a youngster squirm with envy. Needless to say, a good road now leads straight to the pond, and the fishing has been a put and take proposition for many years.

Years later I enjoyed somewhat the same kind of fishing in Maine. The demands had become greater, however: a drive of nearly four hundred miles, then plane flights to wilderness ponds and lakes. A few years later, Pete and I drove over a good road to a pond I had previously visited by plane. Where my friends and I had caught a trout on about every fourth cast, Pete and I worked an entire afternoon to catch a dozen.

Three years ago, Pete and I drove four hundred miles to Bangor, Maine. From there we flew nearly a thousand miles to a camp in western Labrador. From the base camp, we hopped another two hundred and fifty miles northeast to a river on the Labrador coast. With that distance behind us, we finally stood where few men have fished. In a huge pool which teemed with big arctic char, fresh from the sea, we finally found fishing which matched our wildest dreams.

But that was three long years ago. We haven't returned to that wild and wonderful river, and the chances are good that we never will. The memories of that trip still make my scalp prickle, but they are no answer to my basic fishing need which, above all else, is to fish as frequently as the mood strikes. This is likely to be on any balmy evening, and by the time I have eaten dinner and assembled my fishing gear there is scarcely time to reach the northern coast of Labrador.

For this reason alone, the theory that the answer to a fisherman's needs can be found in the blessings of modern transportation is largely an illusion. Anybody who hopes to find virgin fishing that can be easily reached, even by plane, is entertaining a pipe dream. Any easily approached fishing is soon reduced to mediocrity, and only those places which can be reached with difficulty remain truly beyond the frontier.

This does not detract from the thrills to be found beyond these frontiers, but it does compress them into the infrequency with which the necessary trips can be made—if they can be made at all. And what fisherman can be at peace with the world if he must confine his fishing to an occasional trip, or even worse, to dreams of making such a trip?

There is a bit more to it than that. Once the fisherman reaches waters that are everything he has dreamed of, he finds that the game suddenly changes. Big fish that are easily caught tend to lose significance, just as gold would lose its glamour if gold nuggets were as common as pebbles.

Two years ago Pete and I fished the George River in northern Quebec. We were after Atlantic salmon, and we were lucky enough to arrive when the run of these dynamic fish was on. But along with the salmon, brook trout of several pounds rose to our flies, as did lake trout that weighed up to ten pounds. The composite result was fishing that was as close to the ultimate as any fisherman could hope for.

But Pete and I came to look on strikes from big brookies and lake trout almost as intrusions, even though we do most of our fishing where a foot-long brook trout is a rare prize, and the fisherman who takes a ten-pound laker gets his picture in the papers. With eyes only for salmon, fish that normally would set our hearts to pounding became victims of a sliding scale of values.

This feeling suggests that the thrills of fishing are not tied in directly with the size and number of fish, caught, but are determined by the relativity fish have to the context in which they are encountered. In other words, spectacular success in an atmosphere of extravagance is not necessarily more satisfying than substantially lesser achievements made under more modest circumstances.

There is a stream only a few miles from my home in which there is a long stretch of quiet water which is perfect for dry fly fishing. It teems with wild brookies, and the only disparaging thing to be said about it is that the trout run to small size. I have caught as many as forty in a single evening, not one of which was more than nine inches long.

One evening last summer I reached the upstream limit of this stretch before darkness had closed in and decided to fish downstream toward my car. I tied on a fairly large Cooper Bug, and as I sloshed my way back I skittered this fly across some of the better holes.

Small trout made abortive passes at the thing, but none had the courage to grab it. Suddenly, in a particularly deep hole, a fish broke behind it with a tremendous swirl. I could feel my hackles rise, for I knew by the size of the swirl that the trout was *fully a foot long!*

Adding to my excitement was the feeling that the "lunker" would take on the next cast.

Sure enough, he attacked the bug almost the instant it hit the water a second time, and I'm completely honest in saying that my heart hammered for fear that he would come off before I could get him in the net. Although he proved to be a wee bit short of the estimated twelve inches, he was one of the "biggest" brook trout I have ever taken.

Was I kidding myself? Does fishing admit a line of demarcation between those thrills which are somehow absolute and those which are merely affectations? I doubt that any such line can be drawn that will stand the test of objectivity.

In support of this contention I'll pass along a yarn told to me by Bev Weatherby of Grand Lake Stream, Maine. Bev and his wife Alice own and operate a popular fishing camp on Grand Lake, and for a string of years I have enjoyed wonderful fishing for both smallmouth bass and landlocked salmon with their camp as my headquarters. In addition, I've been privileged to listen to Bev tell stories, and thanks to his rare talent for yarning, this has been no small consideration.

According to Bev, there was this fisherman of advanced age who, for years, had tried in vain to hang an Atlantic salmon in the Maine rivers which still have limited salmon runs. At long last the miracle came to pass; a big salmon rose to his fly and was securely hooked.

The water was low and the shoreline a jumble of large boulders. And since the salmon made many long runs, the old fellow was forced to chase upstream and down to avoid the calamity of a cleaned reel.

This went on for some time, during which the angler showed increasing signs of wear and tear. He had fallen several times, shedding patches of skin and some blood as the result of rough contact with raw granite. Eventually he seemed on the verge of collapse, from exertion and from his high state of excitement.

At this point a native, who had watched the proceedings with interest and amusement, felt obliged to intercede. He arose, drew up alongside the battered and wildly excited fisherman and pointed toward the salmon with the stem of his pipe.

"It ain't really none of my business," he said, "but before you kill yourself I want to remind you that the thing out there on the end of your line ain't nothing but a fish."

It can be argued that the man with the pipe missed the point, that, to a fisherman, an Atlantic salmon is not "just a fish" but a thing of enormous worth. While this may be true, the salmon's magnificence is a reality only in the sense that it is an emotional conviction which fishermen happen to share.

Many years ago I helped land a bluefin tuna which weighed nearly seven hundred pounds. The power and speed of this huge fish were incredible to behold, and perhaps they should have made me contemptuous of the relatively puny fighting qualities of freshwater fish. Actually, the epic battle with the huge fish had no such effect. Although I still remember how the tuna all but yanked three of us over the stern —this was in the days when tuna fishing off the coast of Maine was in its experimental stages—I can refer to the "terrific" battle put up by a trout or salmon without feeling the slightest bit ridiculous.

This story brings into focus what I believe to be the fisherman's salvation: his ability to adjust to the situation at hand, and to realize through relativity the satisfactions which otherwise lie beyond his reach. Fishing is such that the ultimate becomes a mirage for those who seek it deliberately and exists as an attainable reality only for those who do not consciously engage in its pursuit. The man who fishes with only modest expectations experiences the ultimate whenever these are exceeded. This tends to happen quite frequently, for it takes no more than a fifteen-inch trout or a three-pound bass to turn the trick. The fisherman who sets loftier goals not only renounces his principal source of triumph, but dooms himself to almost constant disappointment.

There is a limit, of course, to the kind of fishing that will furnish the satisfaction the fisherman craves. I like to fish for bluegills, crappies, perch and bullheads, but I would be the last to suggest that panfish are a satisfactory substitute for game fish. Fortunately, few fishermen are so compromised that they have only panfish to turn to. All of us have a much greater area within easy reach than is generally realized, and this area almost always holds unappreciated potential.

In this day and age a distance of fifty miles has become trivial—a mere hour's drive. The Battenkill is that distance from my home, and I don't hesitate to drive to it for the evening fishing—whenever I get the vain and foolish notion that my skill is a match for its sophisticated trout.

Actually, most fishermen, myself included, think nothing of driving much farther to fish, but to be on the conservative side, let's assume that all waters within fifty miles constitute a fisherman's home base. This base establishes an imaginary circle of rather surprising area. Applying the formula $A = \pi r^2$, the area of a circle of fifty-mile radius comes out to be 7857 plus square miles!

There is no denying the inroads made upon fishing by pollution, construction, urbanization and other forces, but an area of nearly 8000 square miles is a mighty large chunk of territory. In spite of the many negative factors, I believe it would be next to impossible to find an area of this size which didn't contain at least some worthwhile fishing.

But proximity, like familiarity, breeds both contempt and indifference, and the more one associates glamour with remoteness, the more he is inclined to dismiss the potential of that to which he has easy access. As a result, local opportunities often go begging simply because of the widespread assumption that they cannot, and therefore do not, exist.

Several years ago a colony of beavers set up housekeeping on a tiny stream only five miles from my home, almost within sight of heavily traveled U.S. Route 7. Long before their appearance, I had checked out the stream, hardly more than a trickle, and came away convinced that it held no fish of any description, let alone trout. So, although aware of the beaver flowage, I wrote it off as unworthy of investigation. Others who knew about it apparently did the same, for it existed for several years, without attracting the attention of a single fisherman.

In the meantime, brook trout somehow became established in the pond, prospering and fattening without interference from the fishermen who sped along the nearby highway. I'm sure that among these were many who, like myself, have kicked themselves since for not taking the trouble to investigate.

Finally, on last opening day, one angler who refused to take things for granted gave the flowage an off-chance try. He was richly rewarded for this slight effort with brookies which were as deep bellied as bass and which had reached lengths as great as eighteen inches.

Inconceivable as it seems, this lucky fisherman blabbed of his discovery, and hordes of eager citizens converged on the flowage. It took only a week to rid it of its trout, but they totaled several hundred, almost none of which was under a foot long.

Where did those trout come from? The question is rendered pointless by virtue of the fact that they were there awaiting discovery. The fellow who found them made out gloriously while the rest of us were either headed for or dreaming of more distant places.

Although I goofed this chance, I have made comparable finds. About ten years ago beavers dammed another nearby stream. The resulting flowage covered many acres and was so large that it could be explored by canoe. The stream had always catered to a population of brook trout, and this led Pete and me to believe that a concentration of brookies existed somewhere in the expanse, brookies that would be growing steadily bigger and fatter. But although we acted on our hunch and probed all sections of the flooded area on successive years, we never found our dreamed-of bonanza. Two or three small trout per trip were the best we could do.

Eventually the flowage threatened to flood the nearby highway, and apprehensive town fathers dynamited the dam repeatedly until the beavers finally gave up and moved. This action left our unsolved mystery dangling, and whenever I had nothing better to do, and often when I had, I'd fret about the trout we'd never been able to track down but in whose existence I had never lost faith.

Then one spring evening, I took my setter out for some exercise and decided to see if the woodcock had returned to some of our favorite covers. The route home took me along the border of what had been the beaver flowage, but what was now a stark expanse of dead trees which rose above a tangle of weeds and vines. With the remote hope of finding signs of reconstruction, I pulled off the road and forced my way through the tangle to the remains of the dam.

There was no evidence of rebuilding, but the dynamiting had not destroyed the dam so completely but that a pool of some size and depth remained. As I morosely surveyed the wreckage of the dam, a trout rolled up to suck in a mayfly only a few yards up the pool. This rise was followed by another, and the pool soon boiled with rises as a hatch developed. These were the deliberate, bulging rises of bulky fish —trout that had grown sleek and fat somewhere in the flowage, exactly as Pete and I had suspected. Now, they had been forced to take up residence in the only remaining pool large enough to accommodate them.

Needless to say, I was back there the following evening with the appropriate tools. Although cars buzzed steadily past, no more than a couple of hundred yards away, not a boot print marred the border of the trout-jammed pool. As for the trout, they were as gullible and unsophisticated as those of unfished wilderness waters. So what followed was almost too easy; my dry fly hardly had time to settle on the water before one of those fat squaretails had it.

As a consequence, I actually got a bigger kick from finding those trout than I did from catching them. The rare chance to take trout after trout without changing position was a pleasant experience, but sole possession of the knowledge of their whereabouts was a source of even greater pleasure.

Strange as it may seem, and I presume in much the same way that a miser is ever reluctant to dip into his hoard, I found myself reluctant to press the advantage of my discovery. I never did return to that trout-filled pool throughout the remainder of the season, and from this asceticism I derived unaccountable pleasure and satisfaction.

My mood had become more realistic by the beginning of the next fishing season. Unfortunately, however, I returned to find the pool filled with silt and the trout long gone. In accord with the old saying, I had my cake for quite a spell, but without getting to eat much of it.

To continue with the same metaphor, the rare finds such as I have mentioned are but frosting on a cake which is usually thoroughly palatable by itself. In other words, one need not discover secret pockets of fish to enjoy good fishing in local waters. The extent to which fishermen neglect nearby fishing opportunities is often nothing short of amazing.

Until recent years, certain stretches of fast water in Vermont's Otter Creek furnished some of the finest trout fishing in New England. These stretches, in the vicinity of Middlebury, are only twenty-five miles from Pittsford, so for many years Pete and I were able to pay them the attention they deserved. Along these stretches we enjoyed some of the most glorious dry fly fishing we have ever had anywhere.

The fish were predominantly rainbows, intermixed with a scattering of browns. Their forage was so rich that scale samplings revealed that they grew to lengths as great as eighteen inches over a period which included only three winters. They were crammed to the gills with energy, as is the case with rainbows that have grown rapidly in big water, and we took as many as two hundred of these gorgeous fish per season—practically all of which we released.

Yet in spite of such fishing it was not uncommon to fish an entire afternoon and evening and never see another fisherman. Most of those we did encounter were out-of-state anglers who drove hundreds of miles to fish waters neglected by local fishermen. We got to know several who regularly made long trips to fish there, and they never failed to marvel at the lack of competition. Most of them erroneously accounted for it by picturing Vermont fishermen as a quaint subspecies which angling evolution had passed by. They attributed their absence to a lack of interest in fly fishing and visualized them as worm dunkers who stuck to pasture brooks.

Nothing could have been further from the truth. Skillful and dedicated fly fishermen are not lacking among Vermont anglers, all of whom would have found the fishing every bit as rewarding as we did. The only reason they stayed away was that they simply didn't know that that particular fishing existed. Otter Creek is the longest stream contained wholly within Vermont, and over most of its length it is sluggish and virtually devoid of trout. Consequently, most fishermen wrote it off without investigation. Very, very few knew that it contained stretches of fast water which teemed with wild trout. As binding proof of the extent of this oversight, these stretches, which furnished some of the finest trout fishing in the east, were classed as open (nontrout) water by the Vermont Fish and Game Service. They are still classed as such, and to the best of my knowledge no effort has been made to restore the once heavy populations of trout.

Although the number of trout has dwindled, the same stretches afford another possibility that is virtually ignored. They always held large numbers of smallmouth bass, even when the trout were abundant, and the bass are still there. One afternoon last summer Mike and I caught over fifty smallmouths on fly rod poppers in only a short stretch of river. We never saw another fisherman.

Although I mourn the trout's passing too much to take comfort in the undiminished bass population, I'm sure that less prejudiced fishermen would be happy with a spot that yielded fifty bass in a single afternoon. Yet such spots go largely unattended, on the theory that there is little of value to be found in that which is readily accessible.

For a substantial number of years I have done a fair amount of fishing in Maine. Typically enough, most of my efforts have been aimed at reaching waters as remote as possible. Trips have involved plane flights, wilderness canoe trips and long hikes to get "back in" to where fishing pressure is minimal. The result has been many memorable experiences, and sometimes, but by no means always, fishing which has lived up to expectations.

As far as expectancy is concerned, probably nothing builds it up as does a flight over miles of seemingly impenetrable wilderness before dropping down to a forest-rimmed lake that shows no sign of habitation. The romantic promise of wild, virgin fishing is implicit in such a circumstance. Pete and I have experienced it many times—enough to know that it can be very misleading and disappointing. We have racked up big scores in such places, but we have also had our high hopes shattered.

Any fishing enterprise which involves a reasonable hope of getting "beyond the beyond" induces an excitement which justifies the attempt, even when results are abortive. In line with the intent of this chapter, however, it is significant to point out that some of the best fishing Pete and I have had in Maine has been along the outskirts, and in the very center, of the village of Bingham.

This village is situated on the banks of the Kennebec River, a few miles below the Wyman Dam. I don't know the population, but it is a community with a business section which boasts several restaurants, a concentration of stores, garages, filling stations, motels and the like. It is not an outpost which marks a jumping-off place for wilderness fishing.

On our return trips from Jackman—which is precisely such an outpost—Pete and I often dined in a modern restaurant and then had wonderful fishing by driving no more than a few hundred yards to the river.

The rainbow is something of a rarity in Maine, but this section of the Kennebec holds an established and self-sustaining population of these fish. Like all big water rainbows, they are fairly bursting with strength and energy. The river also holds enough landlocked salmon to make a strike from one of these wild leapers an interesting possibility. Neither Pete nor I have ever taken a brown trout there, but huge browns are snagged by lucky fishermen on rare occasion, and there is a scattering of brook trout to complete the picture.

Pete and I have discovered several good spots along the river, and as I have indicated, one is smack in the center of town. There, in the community's backyard, Pete and I have stood among rising fish, busted our leaders on whoppers and enjoyed wild and woolly fishing without seeing another fisherman.

Is this because State of Mainers are not interested in trout fishing? Hardly! Unless I miss my guess, while Pete and I fished in the center of town, any number of resident fishermen were battling black flies on wilderness ponds and bogs that could be reached only by punishing a jeep to the limit and then walking miles beyond the jeeping-off place.

This contention was borne out by gabbing with local fishermen. Few shared our enthusiasm for the nearby river, but most were ready with suggestions concerning spots that could be reached only with difficulty. We were even gullible enough to act on one particularly strong recommendation and spent an entire morning getting ourselves and our canoe to a bog where we were assured our sweating and straining would be rewarded by a hefty catch of squaretails. Instead, while we could have been fighting reel-running fish almost in sight of our car, we caught two trout that were all of eight inches long.

Indifference to that which lies handy seems to be typical of fishermen. As a result, many of those who bemoan the lack of good fishing do so without good reason and actually are victims of this strange form of blindness.

Otter Creek passes through the town of Pittsford, and within less than a mile of my home. Here it is slow-moving, snag-infested and overhung by the soft maples and willows which line its high, steep banks. Among the snags, and in the shaded pockets, northern pike lie in wait for fish, frogs and other forms of life to come within easy reach of their long snouts. The setup is ideal for float fishing and, over the years, Mike, Pete and I have taken hundreds of these pike by casting to them from a canoe.

Although northerns do not enjoy a favorable reputation in all quarters, I have yet to see a fisherman react with anything but excitement when a big pike savagely assaults his lure. This is particularly true if the lure is an oversize popping bug. We have bugged and landed pike of over ten pounds in weight and have lost larger ones. Most important of all, pike fishing tends to be at its best during the low water periods when trout fishing is poorest. We have come to hold pike in high esteem, if for no other reason than that they keep us in business when trout fishing falls off.

But in spite of this opportunity, I know of only one or two other local fishermen who fish Otter Creek seriously for pike. I have written articles about it which have appeared in national magazines, and these have inspired a substantial number of fishermen to drive long distances to fish Otter Creek for pike—usually with good results. Nevertheless, the creek doesn't exist as far as most local fishermen are concerned. Naturally, I am not unhappy with this state of affairs. Yet I cannot help but feel sorry for those who don't know what they're missing.

If all this seems to identify me as a wise and crafty character who profits because of a human failing to which he is immune, let me hasten to admit that I can be, and often am, as blind and blockheaded as the next fellow. If I have learned to take fuller advantage of nearby opportunities, it is only because I have lived long enough for the obvious to finally penetrate my thick skull, at least to a degree.

For the past twenty years I have lived almost within sight and sound of that remarkable little trout stream, Furnace Brook. It rises high in the mountains and is fed by bountiful springs which keep its water cool and maintain a trout-sustaining level of flow during even the hottest and driest months of the year. A couple of miles before joining Otter Creek it tumbles down a gorge carved from solid rock, furnishing a waterpower potential which attracted Pittsford's first settlers.

Only the barest traces of ancient dams and mills remain, and the Furnace has long since ceased to be of industrial significance. But because of its past attractions in this respect, a very happy and fortunate state of affairs exists for those who now live in the community: a magnificent little trout stream flowing through the center of town, providing a recreational facility which no expenditure of effort and money could duplicate.

I moved to Pittsford at the end of World War II and like many other recently discharged G.I.'s at the time found that cars were completely unavailable. I was without private means of transportation throughout an entire spring and summer, and for that reason my trout fishing was confined almost completely to Furnace Brook. As a result, I probably caught more trout than I have caught in any season since.

Most were rainbows, all wild fish that ran from eight-inchers to a top limit of around sixteen inches; twelve-inch fish were common. Fish of that size are not exactly lunkers, but I submit that happiness is to be found wherever foot-long rainbows come regularly to a dry fly. The stream also held a lesser number of brown trout, and some of these grew to considerably larger size. During that summer I took a few browns that measured more than twenty inches.

I owned a car by the following spring, but one might conclude that I saw little need to burn gasoline in search of trout fishing. Yet this was not the case. To all intents and purposes I ignored Furnace Brook and drove far afield with the instinctive conviction that I could better my lot simply by putting distance behind me.

This ridiculous notion persisted for years. On many occasions I returned from all-day jaunts with little to show for my efforts, when, as my wife always took it upon herself to point out, I could have filled my limit on the Furnace in a fraction of the time and with far less effort.

Actually, this was precisely why I *didn't* fish Furnace Brook, but I could never explain this to my wife's satisfaction. Now, when I perhaps have a bit more common sense than I did then, I can appreciate her inability to understand.

I have also learned to appreciate Furnace Brook. This has been due in part to the fact that while trout fishing has declined in general, the Furnace has remained almost as productive as ever. Also, I have revised my formerly held opinion that the only way to fish for trout was to set out at daylight, or before, and fish until dark.

I suppose that this turnabout is an involuntary concession to the aging process. At any rate, my goal now is to enjoy the best hours without wearing myself out long before they arrive.

The best hours of trout fishing, at least in my opinion, are those between sundown and darkness. This is the best part of the trout fishing day, but it is impossible to enjoy it to the fullest if one is already weary from hours of wading and casting. But it can be a truly wonderful period to the fellow who is just starting out.

This is particularly true when an evening's fishing comes at the close of a trying day. One thing after another may have gone wrong until life seems nothing more than a hopeless assault of insurmountable obstacles. But if one can step into a stream that evening, just as the trout are beginning to rise, the next few hours will make life seem worth living after all.

This feeling of rejuvenation seldom can be gained on opening day, or even for several weeks thereafter. Magazine articles appear each spring which purport to reveal the secrets of taking trout during April and early May, and I have written several such pieces myself. But the truth is that early spring trout fishing is usually a slow, cold business, distinguished largely by excesses of enthusiasm and apathy manifested respectively by fishermen and trout.

For me, the real opening day arrives when streams finally come to life, an event that is not tied in with any date set by law. This day of transformation cannot be circled on the calendar, but its arrival can be felt instantly in the bones.

There is that period following the formal opening of trout fishing when harsh traces of winter linger in the air. Streams are open and fishable, and angling enthusiasm is at fever pitch. But the water has a hard and brittle look to it, and an experienced hand can tell by its appearance that his prospects are slim.

Finally, there comes a day that is as soft as a down pillow, and this is the day that trout fishing turns a corner. Water temperatures rise, trout metabolism shoots upward, mayflies begin to hatch and pools that seemed to hold nothing but ice water are suddenly dotted with the rings of rising fish.

This phenomenon is worthy of special mention, for it illustrates the mistake one makes by judging streams against early season results. April skunkings are often blamed on a lack of trout, but a stream that appears to be fishless in April can break out in a rash of fish a few weeks later when the water has warmed and insects have begun to hatch.

Last spring, the soft day I had been waiting for fell in the middle of the week. Warm air had begun drifting in from the south the previous afternoon, and the temperature had risen steadily during the night. By morning it was easy to tell that the looked-for time had come; trout would be gorging on mayflies that evening as surely as the sun would set.

After supper I drove to a favorite stretch of Furnace Brook, a drive which took all of five minutes. From where I entered the stream I could see a church spire bathed by the last rays of the setting sun, a golden beacon above surrounding homes already overtaken by the soft neutrality of dusk. I could see cars passing along the street on which I live and hear the cheers of a crowd watching a ball game at the school's ball field. As I tied on a fly, I heard Nimrod, my big Bluetick coonhound, bawl his approval as Mike brought him his supper. I was that close to home.

I make a point of stressing the proximity, for it was this very factor which had once made me contemptuous of the Furnace; that and confidence that I could take trout without any great difficulty. To show the extent to which this prejudice robbed me of good fishing, I'll recount the highlights of the evening.

Even as I looped on a leader, a nine-footer tapered to 4X, and tied on a No. 12 Nearenuf, I could see a good fish rising. He had taken cover under an apron of debris that had lodged against a fallen tree and was busily gulping flies along the edge of this cover. This is a situation that is both easy and difficult. On the easy side, the trout is effortlessly approached and is very likely to gather in any dry fly which bumps along the edge of the debris. What makes it hard is that the fly *must* trickle along this edge, and in so doing it runs a fifty-fifty chance of snagging.

My fly was fresh out of the box and high riding, so it nudged along the border of the debris without hanging. The trout was lying with his nose only inches from the barrier and scarcely had to move to suck in my fly. But while the rise was a very quiet affair, that which immediately followed was quite the opposite. I jabbed the barb home, and an estimated fourteen inches of rainbow trout promptly went berserk. He made one wild leap after another, and by the time I brought him to the net he was utterly exhausted.

I removed the fly and held the helpless fish upright until he regained sufficient strength to take off. I looked on it as a particularly grand beginning, for I have a special love and respect for the rainbow. It is sometimes argued that the rainbow is not particularly distinguished as a scrapper, that the smallmouth actually packs more punch, and so on. I have always suspected that those who hold this view have never caught rainbows under ideal conditions, or perhaps have never caught wild rainbows at all. It has been my experience that naturally propagated rainbow trout, taken while at their physical peak—just as water temperatures are becoming optimum, will dish out more thrills per inch of fish than any brown, brookie or smallmouth that ever swam. In fact, I rate them ahead of the landlocked salmon, although the landlocked is admittedly the more spectacular leaper.

Feeling real good, I worked on upstream. Trout showed in almost every pool and run, and I took several nice browns—eleven- and twelve-inch fish—in pleasantly swift succession. Then, in a long, flat pool which usually gave me trouble, I came up against a better fish that wasn't so easily fooled.

He was rising steadily in the glassy flat near the tail of the pool, and although my fly seemed to drift over him faultlessly, he would have none of it. In the meantime, he continued to feed on the abundant naturals with tantalizing regularity.

I was reluctant to spend time on an obstinate fish when there were plenty of more willing takers, so I marked the trout down for future reference and continued upstream. I ran my total up to ten fish, and with my yen for quantity somewhat satisfied my thoughts returned to the difficult trout I had given up on. Nagged by challenge, I reeled up and returned to the long, flat pool.

The trout was rising steadily in the very same location, and now I had the patience to tie on a 6X tippet and a No. 16 fly. These refinements had no immediate effect; the fish went on ignoring my fly as before.

Yet this time I fished with considerable confidence. Doing so was more than a hunch, for it was conditioned by much past experience in similar situations. I wouldn't have been at all confident earlier in the day, but time was working in my favor. Light was dwindling rapidly, and the time would soon come when the finicky trout would no longer be able to distinguish the small flaws of presentation which, to this point, had accounted for his steady refusal. If I just kept putting the fly over him . . .

I could no longer see my fly when the trout finally took it, as indeed he did, but I could see the boil of the rise. I set the hook gently, a discretion which I do not always observe, and the reel buzzed as the trout ran the length of the pool. Then things settled down to a dogged, rod-thumping struggle which seemed to leave no doubt that the fish was a brown. When I finally had him in the net I was surprised to find that he was a beautiful, heavy-bodied squaretail. I laid him on the grass, still in the net, and held the tape of my De-Liar above him before releasing him. I needed the help of my flashlight to see that he was fully fifteen inches long.

A squaretail is a rarity in Furnace Brook, and particularly a fifteen-incher. I had additional reasons to prize this particular fish, however, for the previous year I had caught and released a half-dozen brookies in the same spot. Investigation disclosed that cold spring water seeped and trickled into the pool along one bank, and this undoubtedly accounted for the presence of brook trout. At any rate, it pleased me to think that the fifteen-inch fish was one of those I had put back the year before. (I caught three more during the season, and all were larger than the six I had released a year earlier.)

It was almost completely dark by that time, and perhaps I should have deemed the brookie the fitting close of a perfect evening. But I wasn't quite ready to call it quits. Instead, I replaced my tapered leader with a six-foot strand of eight-pound test monofilament and tied on a big rubber-hackled fly about which I shall have more to say in a later chapter.

The rubber monstrosity would have scared the wits out of any sensible trout in daylight, but trout, particularly browns, become bold under cover of darkness to a degree that many fishermen fail to appreciate. I spatted the big fly down on the calm surface of the pool and retrieved it with erratic jerks. Nothing happened during the first half-dozen retrieves, but I gradually lengthened line and when it finally landed near the tail of the pool I felt the electrifying yank of a savage strike. The big hook took its bite, and all was commotion for a spell thereafter. After a dingdong battle—always an exciting and uncertain bit of business in pitch darkness—I brought the trout into the beam of my light and netted him. He was a beautiful brown of well over two pounds in weight.

Had I chosen to stick at it, perhaps I could have donged up more, and possibly bigger, browns with my after-dark prescription, but suddenly I felt the urge to call a halt and bask in the culmination of perfection. The delights of the past few hours simmered within me as I made my way back to my car, giving rise to a feeling of well-being and contentment that nothing but a perfect evening of fishing could have aroused.

In only a short time I had caught what must have been nearly ten pounds of wild trout. They were all back in the stream, little the worse for wear, with plenty of others to keep them company. Most of them would be there when I next decided to fish, and best of all, only five minutes away from my front door. How could I have once been so stupid that I was blind to such a blessing!

Before counting me as specially lucky—few fishermen have a stream like Furnace Brook almost in sight of their homes—remember that all who live within twenty-five miles of the same stream are equally fortunate. All could be on the Furnace in a half-hour or less. The city of Rutland is a mere ten miles from Pittsford, and its population of over 25,000—a metropolis by Vermont standards—includes many fishermen. Yet all the time I was busy taking trout I *never met another fisherman!*

This is a circumstance which I in no way deplore. In fact, if I thought what I wrote here would bring fishermen flocking to Furnace Brook, I wouldn't set down a word. I'm sure it will have no such effect. But to be on the safe side, I hasten to add that the Furnace doesn't give up its trout as easily as reported except when conditions are unusually favorable. Like all other streams it usually makes a fisherman work for his trout, and once the peak of the season is past it yields fish grudgingly only to those who know their business.

Actually, what I have written about Furnace Brook hasn't been about the Furnace at all. Instead, it has been about the many "Furnace Brooks" that are largely neglected by the fishermen who live closest to them. They need not be trout streams. They can be bass ponds, pickerel bogs, pike waters, catfish holes, panfish hotspots and opportunity in other guises.

In my own case, although I greatly prefer trout fishing, I depend on the totality of local opportunity to satisfy my inborn hankering to fish. Each year, between ice-out and freeze-up, I figure to get in my licks at trout, landlocked salmon, smallmouths, largemouths, walleyes, northern pike, bullheads, catfish, yellow perch, calicoes and any other species I can track down in nearby waters.

As a result, I have come to know a good many "Furnace Brooks." I value all of them highly, for while I often relive the more spectacular fishing I've had elsewhere, it is upon these close-to-home spots that I depend for sustenance. I find it far more satisfying to fish frequently for whatever lies within easy reach than to reconstruct glorious experiences of the past, or try to live on the uncertain hope that they can be repeated.

A RIVER
NEVER SLEEPS:
JANUARY—JUNE

RODERICK L. HAIG-BROWN

JANUARY

It is easy to forget about the river in winter, particularly if you are a trout fisherman and live in town. Even when you live in the country, close beside it, a river seems to hold you off a little in winter, closing itself into the murky opacity of freshet or slipping past ice-fringed banks in shrunken, silent flow. The weather and the season have their effect on the observer too, closing him into himself, allowing him to glance only quickly with a careless, almost hostile, eye at the runs and pools that give summer delight. And probably his eyes are on the sky for flight of ducks or geese or turned landward on the work of his dogs. Unless he is a winter fisherman, he is not likely to feel the intimate, probing, summer concern with what is happening below the surface.

In the south of England our school holidays might have been planned to emphasize this break in interests. The Easter and summer holidays were times when the duns and sedges hatched and trout rose in every favorite holt of the quiet chalk streams. The Christmas holidays left us free for a full two thirds of each January, but trout rods were stored away and we hoped that tact and good behavior might win us permission to go out with shotguns. Fortunately—it seems now—the center of things, the pheasant-stocked coverts on the downs, the windy stubbles and root fields where partridges were wild and wise as geese, was kept for our elders and betters; the easiest-won permission was for a day in the water meadows after snipe and ducks, with the exciting chance of an old cock pheasant in any one of a dozen cropped and tended willow beds. They were good for many things, those winter days in the frost-browned water meadows. Plentiful game never yet made a good hunter, and we walked all day to spend a dozen shells. We learned where to look for snipe, how to walk them, and how to drive them. We learned where the ducks fed and when, how to test the wind and stalk them cautiously, how to hide ourselves along a line of flight at dusk or dawn. And we learned in sharp surprise that the duns hatched and the trout rose even in midwinter, even in the January frosts that brought the snipe south to us.

Perhaps the knowledge was profitless to us—certainly we could not turn back to the trout rods then, for trout were always left free to attend to their own affairs between October and April in those good waters. But the upright float of pale-winged flies on the winter-dark water and the heavy suck of a rising trout spreading on an overfast run were somehow even more thrilling and enticing to the mind than they were in summer. In the happy misery of cold and wet—for we were often cold and nearly always wet—under the gray skies and leafless trees of soaking or frost-brown meadows, one felt an affinity with the rising fish, a bond of hardihood that permitted one a share in this secret off-season life of his. In spring or summer he rose expectedly, and other fishermen watching there might see him and know his ways; probably they would be able to see, not merely the circle of his rise but his long, thick body also, poised close to the surface and waiting the float of the duns. In this winter water he was unseen, of a size only to be judged from the manner of his rise to an unknown hatch; but you judged him big, bigger perhaps than any fish you had ever seen in the river, a winter wanderer from the dark depths of some deep weir hole half a mile farther down. And you wondered about him: Did the roiled water seem good to him? Had he spawned and was he now growing back to condition for April? Did he feel the rain and the heavy sky as you did? Would he wander farther or find a summer holt near where you had seen his rise?

On those snipe-shooting days I marked down many good trout that I found later on fishing days, and it was borne in upon me that the life of the river is only slightly less full through the winter months. Inevitably this suggested winter fishing. But our Dorset river, unlike most south of England chalk streams, had no pike or grayling in it where we fished—a virtue that I regretted at the enthusiastic age of twelve or thirteen, though it probably made for better trout fishing. Pike, certainly, are a menace to a trout stream, and they seldom grow large enough in such water to make really interesting fishing; but grayling are another matter altogether. True, they compete with trout for the available food and so presumably reduce the river's yield of trout and the average size, but they are noble fish themselves and really test a fly-fisherman. Further, their competition is limited by somewhat different feeding habits, so it is likely that the total yield of the stream is increased, even though its yield of trout may be reduced. If you admire and respect grayling and if you want late fly-fishing when the trout have turned to spawning, you are better off with them in the stream; if you want only trout, presumably you are worse off, except that all the finest south-country trout streams have them. Anyhow, I was sorry that we had no grayling, and I still am because I am quite sure I should have learned a lot by fishing for them.

Apart from trout, the best fish we had in our river were the dace. Dace are little fish, seldom as large as a pound, never larger than a pound and a half, but they are bright, cheerful, quick little fish—the name is from the Old English dare or dart—and they spawn in April, so they were in prime condition during the Christmas holidays. And to make matters better still, we acquired merit by catching them because grandfather reckoned them as evil as other trout-stream owners reckon the grayling.

Most of our dace spent their days feeding over a long reach of shallow water between a big pool we called the Hatch Hole and a lesser pool known as the Trough Bridge for a wooden trough that crossed it to carry water to the meadows. They did not school as closely as I believe dace do in the Thames and other rivers but scattered out over the gravel and worked a slow way upstream, not independently, but in spaced formations of seldom more than five or six individuals. Each formation had its favorite beat of ten or fifteen yards and would work slowly up it, feeding steadily, then swim back down and start again.

Dace like worms and grubs and bottom feed of all kinds, and probably I should have done well with them had I been expert with such baits. But they also rose to surface flies, not steadily and regularly as trout do, but often enough, so I stayed with what I knew, and there were several winter days when I caught six or eight of them on a small dry fly. They are pretty fish with their big tight scales, bright silver on belly and lower sides, faintly olive or lemon gold on their backs, and they fought well when they were hooked. Fishing for them I learned many things. They would take a dragged fly that would have scared the wits out of a sensible trout, yet they were fussy risers, often coming up in important, satisfying dimples that left the fly to float away untouched. A strike to such a rise did not send them scurrying away in instant flight; the effect was far more irritating and educational. The little group that a moment before had seemed so friendly, accommodating and unsuspicious suddenly became aloof and contemptuous; it fed on in its own way, perhaps rising to surface flies less often, certainly disregarding anything I could offer.

Under the Trough Bridge one winter day I caught a dace that weighed fifteen ounces. That was the largest, though I suspect there may have been larger ones there. Sometimes as I fished for them in January, a good trout rose within reach and the temptation was too great; occasionally I made an honest mistake and covered a trout where I thought there was only a dace. Faithfully and always I turned such fish back, but they taught me that some of the trout whose rises we saw on snipe shooting days were clean and bright and hard in winter as they ever were in summer.

The dace introduced me to winter fishing and confirmed me as a winter fisherman. From them I learned that fishing is pleasant and the river worth knowing even when water from the line forms ice in the rings of the rod; and the lesson made me look for other winter fishing. In *The Fishing Gazette* I read often of the great Scottish salmon rivers where twenty- and thirty-pounders run in January and strong men go out in breast waders to catch them on huge flies thrown by sixteen- or eighteen-foot rods. I dreamed of those fish and that fishing and should still like my chance at it one day. It is difficult to imagine a stronger fishing experience than that of handling a big rod against the drive of wind and snow and hooking a thirty-pounder on the fly amid the fierce tumble of a great January river. But Scotland was far away, and I knew of no one who would ask me to fish such a river, so I thought again of pike and grayling.

To hear the owners of trout and salmon rivers talk of pike and grayling, you might well suppose that they would turn out the butler and a couple of footmen and welcome with open arms anyone who expressed a desire to catch either of those fish in their waters. This isn't exactly what happens, but one can usually get permission in the end through an introduction or a distant connection or something of that sort. Sometimes the permission is given very graciously, sometimes suspiciously; usually in my case it was given suspiciously, because a teen-age boy is not unreasonably expected to be about as dangerous as a good-sized pike on a closely preserved trout water. I think that for this reason I never had a really good winter grayling day—I was always limited to some minor stretch of water or to times that did not give me a real chance. The pike fishing was better, and I have had January days in private lakes and in the slow, heavy water of salmon rivers that I should hesitate to trade for anything short of a really fine chance of salmon.

It was January when I came with a rod to my first river in North America—the Pilchuck near Snohomish in Washington. My good friend Ed Dunn took me there, and we caught nothing, at least partly because neither of us knew very much about the fish we were after; but I cannot forget the day, because it was the first day and it started me thinking of steelhead—a habit I haven't grown out of yet. Two or three days later we went to the Stillaguamish, and I remember that day too, though the river was roaring down in tawny flood and I suppose we hadn't a chance of a fish even if we had known all there was to know. But there were dead salmon along the banks, and I saw and loved a fine Pacific coast river, so that day also is remembered.

And now, if all goes well and the Campbell, on whose bank I live, does not rise in full freshet, I know January for the best of all winter steelhead months. The fish have come in in good numbers by that time, but they are still fresh and silver and clean. There may be snow on the ground, two feet of it or more; and if so, the river will be flowing darkly and slowly, the running water below freezing but not ice, just flowing more slowly, as though it meant to thicken into ice—which it never does. Steelhead fishing can be good then, and there is a strange satisfaction in the life of the river flowing through the quiet, dead world. On the bank the maples and alders are stark and bare, drawn into themselves against the cold. The swamp robin moves among them, tame and almost bold for once, and perhaps an arctic owl hunts through them in heavy flight whose softness presses the air until the ear almost feels it. On the open water of the river are mergansers and mallards, bluebills, butterballs, perhaps even geese and teal. Under it and under the gravel, the eggs of the salmon are eyed now; the earliest of the cutthroat trout are beginning their spawning, and the lives of a thousand other creatures—May flies, stone flies, deer flies, dragonflies, sedges, gnats, water snails and all the myriad forms of plankton—are slowly stirring and growing and multiplying. But the steelhead, with the brightness of the sea still on him, is livest of all the river's life. When you have made your cast for him, you are no longer a careless observer. As you mend the cast and work your fly well down to him through the cold water, your whole mind is with it, picturing its drift, guiding its swing, holding it where you know he will be. And when the shock of his take jars through to your forearms and you lift the rod to its bend, you know that in a moment the strength of his leaping body will shatter the water to brilliance, however dark the day.

About Steelhead

I cannot remember now what I expected of steelhead before I ever saw one. The name almost certainly gave me a mental picture of a fish whose back was a polished blue-gray like steel and whose strength was all that steel implies. One could do a lot worse than that. Cobb says the name probably comes from the hardness of the steelhead's skull, which forces the net fishermen to use several blows of a club to kill him when they bring him into the boat; and a steelhead fresh from the sea has a blued-steel back whose color is deepened by a brightness of silver below the lateral line. Matching his skull, all the bones of a steelhead are thicker and harder and stronger than the bones of Pacific salmon, and perhaps his strength is greater for that.

I do remember very well that I had preconceived ideas about fishing for steelhead. All I had heard of them suggested that their habits and life history were almost exactly those of Atlantic salmon—yet, I was told, only salmon eggs would catch them. I didn't know how to use salmon eggs and had the strongest of prejudices against using them, so I easily persuaded myself that ordinary methods of fishing for Atlantic salmon should be successful for steelhead. Perhaps not the fly, I told myself; that would be expecting too much, but certainly minnow or prawn or spoon.

Those two first days on the Pilchuck and the Stillaguamish did nothing to prove my theory, but they did nothing to disprove it either, because I didn't see the salmon eggs catching anything and I had fished out plenty of blank days for Atlantic salmon with minnow or prawn. Soon after that I went up to work at a logging camp near Mount Vernon in Washington, first as a scaler and then as a member of the survey crew. There was plenty of good fishing near camp—for cutthroat trout and largemouthed bass in Lake Cavanaugh—and plenty of steelhead talk. But the steelhead talk was distant; the fish ran in June and July, which were six months away, to Deer Creek, a good many miles away through the woods. The steelhead talk was mixed in with hunting talk of bears and cougars, much of it designed to impress rather than to enlighten. I led with a chin that asked incessant questions about fishing and hunting and got less than I deserved. I am still amazed at the kindness of those men to an immigrant greenhorn—Red

Wayne, the scaler who broke me in, Ed Phipps, the timekeeper, Jim Curtis, the bull bucker, Jack Murray, the bridge foreman, Frank Breslich and Johnny O'Leary of the survey crew and a dozen others. Americans generally seem much kinder and more friendly toward an immigrant than my Canadian brothers and sisters, and I think it must be because they are more sure of themselves in their country and yet at the same time more conscious of being themselves immigrants or of immigrant stock. When I had been in camp only a week or two, a little old Irishman whom we called Frank Skagway showed me the strength and passion with which America grips her immigrants. In the bunkhouse one evening a few of us were talking of Europe and America and the differences in the life of the two continents. Probably I said my say for Old England—I don't remember now—but being only two or three months away from her, I must have. Frank had been listening without offering a word, but suddenly he looked over at me, his lined and long-jawed Irish face serious as I had never seen it.

"Lad," he asked, "do you know what country this is?"

"No," I said doubtfully.

"It's the land of the free and the home of the brave."

Frank's voice was steady and calm and sure and kind. He wasn't boasting, he wasn't correcting me; he was simply stating a solemn, unshakable fact. Nobody laughed, even though there was white moonshine in the bunkhouse.

The cougar and bear and steelhead stories were kind and gentle as Frank's fine statement of his belief. You can string a greenhorn along and make him pretty miserable if you want—it's an easy sport and not without its attractions I suppose—but no one ever tried to do that to me. The evening after I came down from Camp 10 to Camp 7 to start work with the survey crew, Jack Murray told me, "You'd better watch how you go out to that new bridge tomorrow."

"Why's that?" I asked him.

"They brought in a windfall bucker from up there tonight. Badly scratched up he was—by a cougar. If his partner hadn't been there with an ax, he'd 'a' been killed, likely."

I believed him and wanted to see the windfall bucker, which made Jack happy. I could have gone on believing such stories for weeks and making everyone very happy if Jack hadn't suggested snipe hunting a few nights later.

"Ever been snipe hunting?" he asked.

"Sure, lots of times."

That wasn't the expected answer, and one of the boys had to help Jack out a little.

"He means with a gun," he explained. "Not the way we do it here, Jack."

I had to admit that was true, and Jack gave the rest of the explanation.

"Snipe won't fly at night," he said. "So all we do is get one guy to stand at the lower end of a gully with an open gunny sack and have the rest of the bunch walk down toward him. We'll let you take the sack, seeing its your first time, but you'll have to stand awful still and quiet."

I had seen snipe fly at night many times in the Dorset water meadows; but even so, this was a new country and probably a different kind of snipe, and for a moment I wasn't sure. Then I was sure, quite sure, and I thought, "If I'm at the foot of the gully, they'll have to go up at least a little way, and I can be back in camp ahead of them and say I took the snipe to the cookhouse." So I said sure I'd go. But no one could find a sack and the show was off. Jack told me afterward that they had realized I knew the score.

That made me suspicious of the hunting stories, but the steelhead stories all seemed to have the silk thread of the genuine article and many of them were firsthand. Ed Phipps told me he had gone into Deer Creek the previous July, hooked a steelhead and lost rod, reel and line before he had time to think of moving. It was easy to believe that when he showed me the counterpart of the lost outfit—a hollow steel telescope rod, a tiny multiplying reel and less than fifty yards of heavy cutty-hunk. Someone else, crossing a Deer Creek log jam, had seen a group of yard-long gray shapes lying under it. Someone else again knew of a party of sportsmen who had gone in to the creek and come out with a fabulous catch of big fish. Most of the stories had the same moral—they'll take you for everything you've got; you just can't hold them. I felt I could hold them but wondered if I could hook them and if I'd get the chance to try.

The chance came at last in June. The survey crew—Johnny and Ray and Frank and myself—had gone out to camp about four miles from Deer Creek. Johnny and Frank were both quite newly married and liked to get back to Camp 7, the main camp, over each weekend; Ray generally went with them. That left me free to get away for Deer Creek sometime on Saturday afternoon and stay there until almost dark on Sunday night.

The first of those weekends was in many ways the best of them all, partly because the whole experience was new to me and partly because of the bears. Our camp, like Deer Creek itself, was some twelve or thirteen hundred feet above sea level, but the country immediately around it was a big flat which the bears seemed to like. We saw signs of them all the time along the preliminary line on which we were work-ing. On the way out to the creek that Saturday afternoon I met a female bear and a cub along the trail about a mile from camp. I stopped, looking for a second cub, and she seemed to watch me with solemn unfrightened eyes for a long time. Then the cub moved as if to pass her and come on toward me. The old bear swept one forepaw sideways and knocked the cub rolling into the salal brush. He picked himself up with a frightened, half-angry squeal and ran. She followed him. I ran ahead in the hope of seeing them again; then I began to think once more of the second cub. I don't know what persuaded me that there was a second cub, but I was persuaded and Jack Murray's stories began to do their work. I decided I was probably somewhere between the female and this theoretical second cub, and for the next mile or so along the trail I was constantly turning back to make sure that she wasn't after me.

I came to Deer Creek at a fine pool above a log jam. Upstream the river swung over to the foot of a round timber-covered hill about two thousand feet high; downstream, below the jam, it twisted its way between heavy green timber on the left and a slope of alders on the right. The river was a lot bigger than the word "creek" had led me to expect, and it was beautiful, clear and bright and fast, tumbled on rocks and gravel bars. I was standing on a wide gravel bar which gave me every chance to cast and fish as I wished, and my heart beat hard and my fingers trembled as I dumped my pack and began to put my rod up—they do that even today when I come to the bank of a river I have not fished before and find the reality of it better than anything I had dared hope.

I had brought in with me a nine-foot casting rod, a silex reel and a boxful of the spoons and devon minnows and phantoms we had used for salmon on the Dorsetshire Frome. As soon as the rod was up and the line was threaded, I went up to the head of the pool and began to fish. I made cast after cast across the swift water, working down a step or two at each cast, swinging the minnow across as slow and deep as I could. The pool became slower and deeper, and I really began to expect a fish. The minnow touched bottom several times among the big round rocks, and I knew I was deep enough. I made a cast whose swing carried the minnow almost under the log jam and felt a sharp, heavy strike. This was it, I told myself, a steelhead at last. The fish ran almost instantly from the strike, and I held hard to turn him from the log jam. It was a strong run, clear across the river; then he came back a little, and I began to think of the stories. In spite of anything I could do, he would run again under the log jam and break me there. He ought to jump soon; all the stories said they jumped like mad things. I began to walk him upstream, away from the jam, and at first he came quietly enough. Then he seemed to decide that he wanted to go that way anyhow, and he ran steadily and smoothly right up to the head of the pool. Still there was no jumping and no sign of the fierce strength of a good fish that raps the handle of the reel against your knuckles and makes you think you really have lost control this time.

I put pressure on him, and he came into the shallow water at the foot of the gravel bar steadily and quietly. I walked close and lifted him to the surface; he struggled and bored away once, came back and was finished, quiet on his side on top of the water. I ran him up on the beach without difficulty and stooped down to look him over. He was a fish of about four pounds, silver gray all over, very little darker on the back than on the belly; he was thick and fat, and along his sides there were pale lemon-colored spots.

I didn't think he was a steelhead. I almost hoped he wasn't, because he was so far from what I had looked forward to, in strength, size, fighting quality, beauty, everything. Yet no one had warned me to expect any other fish but steelhead in Deer Creek, and it was hard to believe that such a good-sized, handsome fish as this certainly was could be overlooked. Doubtfully I went back to my fishing.

I caught three more fish that evening, all almost exactly like the first one. Not one of them had jumped; but all had fought well enough for their size, and at least they made something to take back to camp. I went up from the creek a little before dark and made camp beside a small stream that ran down to it. About fifty feet below my camp the stream ran shallow under a big log, and I threw the fish down there, thinking it was cool and shaded and they would keep well through the heat of the next day. Then I made supper and rolled happily into my single blanket, tired, thoroughly contented, in love with Deer Creek and fully determined that it should show me a steelhead the next day.

I woke in the quiet dim light before sunrise. For once I didn't want to go on sleeping. There was a whole day of Deer Creek ahead, and I sat straight up in my blanket. Below me, near the log where my fish were, I saw a movement. It was a bear, a fine, handsome black bear who hadn't the slightest idea I was within a hundred miles of him. For a moment I was more pleased than scared; then I realized he was eating my good fish. I yelled in fury. He looked up at me, and I thought he looked calm and contented, as he very well may have. I reached for my boots and yelled again, and he turned round then, lifting his forepaws from the ground in that lovely liquid movement bears have. I drew back a boot to throw at him—a logger's calked boot at fifty feet is something of a weapon—but he didn't wait for that. I pulled on my boots and went down to look at the wreck of my fish. His meal had not really been disturbed; my first yell had come merely as a grace at the end of it.

I was a little worried when I got down to the creek after breakfast. The bear story was a honey, but I should never dare to tell it unless I had fish to take back with me, or the boys would write it up as the record fisherman's alibi of all time. The first cast reassured me; another lemon-spotted three- or four-pounder took hold and came in to the beach.

During the morning I worked a long way up the river and caught three more Dolly Vardens, for that was what, months later, I found they were. Then I rested for a long while on a gravel bar in the warm sun and wondered what to do next. The river seemed to have an endless succession of pools, nearly every one of them good for at least a strike. I decided at last to fish down over the same water, because the steelhead could be there as well as anywhere else and possibly I had fished through most of it too fast. Several more Dollies took hold as I worked down, but I gave them slack line; or if that wasn't enough to free them, I turned them loose when they were played out. I came to a pool near the foot of the round mountain just as the sun was going down. It was a good pool, with the deep water on my side and a long sloping beach of pale gravel on the far bank. I had worked about halfway down it when a fish took, out in midstream, right on the swing of the minnow. There was no question of striking; he was away before I had the rod point up, taking line with a speed that made the ratchet of the reel echo back from the timber. Then he jumped three times, going away, and the sunset was gold on his side each time. He turned after the third jump and started back across the pool, and suddenly I knew I was reeling in a slack line with only a devon at the end of it.

I caught my first steelhead in Deer Creek two or three weeks later— a fish of seven pounds. A summer fish, of course, caught in June, not in January. Probably I shouldn't have written of this Deer Creek fishing at all under a January heading, but it has always seemed to me that I started fishing for that June steelhead back in January on the Pilchuck and the Stillaguamish.

All this was in 1927. In 1928 I caught a real January steelhead in the Kla-anch River on Vancouver Island. The Kla-anch, which is sometimes called the Upper Nimpkish, is the largest stream flowing into Nimpkish Lake and is a hard river to know for several reasons. It is a very long river, with scattered pools that are not often easy to approach; it comes into heavy freshet rather quickly and easily, and it is an isolated river in a totally unsettled area, so that few people have fished it and anyone who goes there to fish must gather his own local knowledge as he goes along. But I think it is almost certainly a very fine winter steelhead river, and I know that very large fish run to it. One day the road will reach in there, and then fishermen will learn the river and name the pools.

By January, 1929, I had found my way to the real Nimpkish, a seven-mile stretch of big river that runs from Nimpkish Lake to the sea. Like the Kla-anch, the Nimpkish is little known to steelhead fishermen, and I had to build my own local knowledge there. I had learned my way about the river in two summers of trout and salmon fishing, but I do not, even to this day, know its steelhead lies properly; I am not even sure to what extent steelhead do lie there in preference to running straight on through to the lake. The Nimpkish is a fairly difficult river to travel and, except at low water, a very difficult one to wade. It is further complicated by two long, slow, deep pools, either one of which can only be searched thoroughly by the better part of a day's fishing; and if you fish them through and find them blank, you still have learned little, because you can always tell yourself that the water was perhaps too high or too low for the fish to be holding in them, or that the fish were not taking that day, or that you may have missed the best lie in the place or failed to bring your bait properly across it. That's the way steelhead fishing is; a great number of variable factors enter into it, and sure knowledge comes only from the hooking and killing of a fish and decently close observation of the place and conditions of the catch.

But one pool of the Nimpkish, at least partly because it was more accessible to me than most of the others, gave me results in January, 1929, that let me feel I had grown into something of a veteran winter steelhead fisher. This was the Canyon Pool, the first pool above tidewater, a long, straight, very deep reach between high, steep banks. The river enters it from a sharp rapid through a narrow throat choked by a great pinnacle of rock that thrusts up from the bottom. The heavy water, surging against this solid obstruction, breaks into a complication of currents and eddies and whirls that I never could fish properly, and I am still not sure whether steelhead lie in that upper part of the pool. A hundred feet or so below the rock, the pool widens, and on fairly low river the currents sort themselves out into some sort of order. Steelhead kelts lie there on the edge of the eddy, but so far as I know fresh fish do not. All the fresh fish I caught were lying near the tail of the pool, where the river divides to pass round a large island.

January, 1929, was a cold month on Vancouver Island, and my partners and I were busy with a series of trap lines. Since there was the perfectly legitimate argument that we needed fresh fish for trap bait, I took a day out every once in a while to work the river. One cold, windy Sunday I took the skiff and poled up into the Canyon Pool. We knew steelhead were running to the river because we had found them trapped by the falling tide in the pool behind the Indian Island, but I was not feeling optimistic. Snow began drifting in coldly from the north, and the line kept freezing in the rings of the rod. After half an hour of it my fingers were so cold and stiff that I could hardly turn the reel to bring the bait in. I thought of going home but made another cast instead and hunched down into my mackinaw to watch the swing of the ice-hung line as the rod top followed the bait around. The fish took with a jolt that snapped the ice fragments yards away. He ran straight upstream, deep down, jumped as he was opposite me and fell back on his tail. My stiff fingers fumbled wildly to recover line and failed miserably—only the drag of the current on the belly of the line kept a strain on him. A moment later I was trying as frantically to find the drum of the reel and check his heavy run to the tail of the pool. I had the feeling that a big fish in his first runs should give one—a feeling of temporary helplessness, of being a little late for every move he makes, dependent on a break of luck to reduce his strength until it is evenly matched to the strength of the tackle. This fish seemed determined to run right on out of the pool and down the rapid, and my only hope was to follow him in the skiff. I began to run and stumble toward it over the difficult, icy footing. Then he jumped again, just above the rapid. Without help from me he turned and held almost still in five or six feet of heavy water. I tightened on him gently and began to walk slowly backward to where I had hooked him. He came, slowly and quietly, and from then on I had a measure of control.

He kept me busy for ten or fifteen minutes after that. I filled my boots with ice water, stumbled after him, checked his rushes, watched his jumps and at last brought him close enough to set the gaff. He was clean and beautiful, so strongly marked with deep-water colors that he might have been caught in salt water. And he weighed twenty-two pounds, the only steelhead of over twenty pounds that I have yet caught.

One thing that had given me some hope when I first came to the pool that day was the sight of two seals up near the big rock. For some reason the seals run right through Nimpkish River to the lake and spend a great deal of their time in fresh water when fish are running; it is the only river I know where they do that. In January only steelhead could be running. I saw the seals again after I had killed the big fish and partly for that reason went on fishing. For a long while nothing moved to my minnow, and I almost decided to go home and get out of the misery of my wet boots. But I had a brand-new artificial prawn and I wanted to try it. I did and hooked a fish almost at once, the only one I have ever hooked on an artificial prawn. It wasn't a big fish and seemed to be coming nicely under control; then something jolted it into the wildest, fastest run of its life. It crossed the pool without a check in spite of the strongest pressure my cold fingers could put on the reel. Close under the far bank the run ended in a tremendous flurry of silver, of round, gleaming bronze and black and of broken water. Then my line was cutting the water behind something heavy and strong that fled with a rhythm of movement subtly different from anything I had felt before. I looked down at the reel and saw the gleam of its metal drum under the few remaining thin turns of line. I pressed my fingers tight on it and for a moment thought that the run would turn. Then everything broke at once—the rod at the first ferrule and the top joint, the line somewhere out in the water. I stood in frozen, horrified amazement and watched what I had seen before only in the broken water of a rapid, never against the still surface of a pool—a seal jumping, head, flippers, body and tail free from the water, several clear feet above the surface of it. I could see his thick body suspended there in the falling snow long after it had slipped back into the water again; but I did not see—perhaps at that distance I could not have seen—the scarlet artificial prawn that must have hooked itself somewhere into his tough hide.

A Fish for Firmin

Firmin wrote that he would like to come up and try for steelhead around February seventh. Firmin has to come some three hundred miles by car and boat and he is a busy man. He is also a very good and keen fisherman, and I was in his debt by reason of a fine day on the Green River down in Washington the previous summer. So I wanted to be able to write back: "Come along. The river is in good shape and there are lots of fish. We'll look for you about dinner time on the sixth."

But when his letter came, there had been no fish at all and the river was high. I watched as it fell through a few fine days, and on January twenty-seventh it seemed just low enough to get out to the Island Pools. January twenty-eighth was perfect, warm, brightly sunny and with a light breeze from the west, such a winter's fishing day as seldom comes when the water is right. I packed up and started out.

The Island Pools are fishermen's water in a way that the rest of the river is not. The Canyon Pool and the Sandy Pool are all right; they are big, deep, heavy-water pools that hold steelhead well. But much of the Sandy Pool fishes best from a boat; and unless you can cross to the far side you must fish the Canyon Pool from one single point of rock, by shorter and longer casts at varying angles. The Island Pools are swift water, sparkling and broken, seldom deep, and you can wade down them and fish the day through without more than covering them properly.

I always like to start out for the Island Pools. They seem remote from everywhere, and few people go up to them, but forty minutes of good walking from my house takes me there, and I know that I shall see nothing all day long except bright water and heavy green timber, eagles, mergansers, mallards, perhaps water ousels and almost certainly fish. In the winter, particularly, it is good, and on this day, because it was the first time of the season and because the sun was on the alder trunks and on the wet dead leaves under them, it had the quality of rich and full experience.

I passed the Sandy Pool with scarcely a glance at the water. It had been fished heavily for several days, ever since the water came to fair fishing height, and had not given a fish. No part of the river had yet given a fish, nor even a good solid strike from a fish, though it was six or eight weeks past the time when the first of the run should have come in. That it had not come I was pretty sure; I had tried hard for a fish early in January, in the only other short period when the water was low enough. And the General had written a few days before to say that the rivers down on his part of the Island had missed their usual January run. No theory seemed to account for it, but they had to come sooner or later. The return of salmon and steelhead is inevitable as the spring of grass or the fall of leaves; it may be delayed a little, reduced from year to year, affected in many ways, but it cannot suddenly and mysteriously fail altogether.

So I came past the Sandy Pool and past the stretch of rapid above it to the mouth of the Quinsam, that swift, considerable tributary of the Campbell, oversensitive to rain in the hills and always an uncertain quantity when you start for the Island Pools in winter. If you are lucky, you can wade it just above the mouth; if you are unlucky, you will have to plow half a mile upstream through the brush to the crossing log, then half a mile back again to the main river.

This was one of the doubtful days. It looked just possible, but an error in judgment means a day of wet feet, and I hesitated. I thought of the trip up to the log, then of the Island Pools and how much I wanted to be up there and fishing them. I found a heavy stick for a wading staff and started into the water; it surged about two inches from my boot tops on the upstream side, where the current piled against them. It would be all right if the high water hadn't washed the center channel deeper and if I could keep my footing. I worked across, well up on the toes of my felt-soled sandals, weight on the staff as much as possible. It went well—no more than a quart of water in the left boot as I edged over the deepest place. I let the current take my staff and made the last few easy steps to the far bank.

A little water in one boot, even at the start of a winter's day, doesn't mean much if you have a pair of dry socks in your bag. But don't put them on at once. I took off the wet boot and emptied it, then wrung out the wet socks, shook them and put them on again; then the boot. While I walked up to my pools, the damp wool socks would keep me warm enough and would soak up the last of the water in the boot—you can never drain it all. Then there would be dry socks to go into a dry boot before I started fishing.

Coming up to the Islands on a fine day is beautiful. As you come opposite the downstream end of the Lower Island your troubles with brush and hard going are over. You can wade across to the island quite easily and walk up the center of it, on freshet-swept gravel and grass among tall spruces and distorted crab-apple trees. At the head of the island you come suddenly round a great log jam and upon the pools.

The upstream end of the Lower Island tapers away in round rocks and willow clumps to the water's edge and slants on under the water in a shallow bar three or four hundred yards to the downstream end of the Upper Island. This bar, with its broken water, big rocks and hard, fast runs, is at once the head and one slanting side of the Upper Pool. The pool itself is a broad stretch of water that nurses the leaping waves of the rock-broken current to a smoothness of strong deep flow, then collects the full force of the river and hurls it over a narrow tumble of rocks into the Lower Pool. The current runs strongly through the Lower Pool, against a cut bank on the far side, but spreading and slowing behind the protecting shoulder of the island. And there, not far from the head of the pool and only a little toward the island from the edge of the current, is where the fish lie.

I had a big fly rod with me and a short bait-casting rod as well. This was a day in search of fish, not merely fishing, and unless I could find fish, I should have to write Firmin not to come. I felt in my bones that he had picked a good time, that the river would be fishable then and would have fish in it. But if today was blank, what could I say? Not a fish caught this year; come on up; I'm sure it will be good? You couldn't say that to a man who had to pick his fishing holidays carefully. I wanted fish.

So I changed to the dry socks and almost regretfully put up the casting rod. It was a beautiful day for the fly, warm air, clear water and a fair, full flow to work it over the best lying places. But the devon minnow was the right thing to start with; one knows that it gets well down to them, gives them a real chance to take hold.

I treat the Lower Island Pool with respect and fish it carefully, every inch of water right down from the head. The record rod-caught steelhead for the whole of British Columbia came from there a few years ago—a fish of twenty-four pounds, dressed weight—and there always seems to be the outside chance that it may happen again. My minnow curved out in the sun, halfway out over the heavy water and a little upstream of straight across. It swung round, came deep into the easy water behind the shoulder of the island, and I brought it slowly back to me. Two steps; another cast. Half a dozen more, moving down, and I was coming into the best of the water. It isn't much, that best part of the pool; three casts cover it fully, though one always tries more than that. I made the first cast and brought the minnow back, slow and deep. Then the second, and as it swung smoothly across the easy water, something struck at it. It was a gentle touch, almost certainly a small trout I told myself. But it had come in the best spot in the whole pool, the surest steelhead lie in the river. I sent the minnow over once again, then fished on down the pool to give him a rest.

When the pool was fished out, I came back and ate my lunch near the head of it. So far there was nothing to put in a letter, and I wondered what to do. A smaller minnow perhaps and a lighter lead to let it fish slower? But if that, why not the fly? I put up the big thirteen-foot rod and threaded the heavy fly line through the rings. Three yards of good gut, well soaked, and what fly? It stared up at me from the first box I opened, Preston Jennings's Lord Iris, on a long, slim hook, silver bodied and very handsome with the orange hackle and the built wing of blue, green, yellow, red, the furnace hackle laid along and jungle-cock cheeks. I knew how it would look in the water, slender and full of life, with the orange showing up well and the dark streak of the furnace hackle along the side. The minnow had had its chance. There could be no magic in it that the Iris had not also.

I started down the pool happily, rolling the fly out into the tumbled water, mending the line upstream to give it a chance to sink well down. A little more line and a little more, until I was covering the water at the angle I wanted to. The fly came over the loaded place, and I held it there in the quiet water at full stretch of the line with the long rod pointing straight downstream. I recovered line slowly, two yards, four yards, moved my two steps down, cast again. Again it swung into the quiet water, and I held it there, knowing how it hung, how it looked, how the water plucked at it and gave it life. I moved my left hand up to recover line, and the pull came, heavy and solid, then slack in the same moment. A great swirl boiled up to the surface below the fly. I brought the line in slowly and moved back from the water. The fly was all right. He was just a lucky fish, not even a short riser, but lucky to take the fly so that it came freely away from him.

The only thing was to rest him and leave the last few yards of the pool until later. I knew now that he was a really good fish and I knew also that the fly was all right, so I left the casting rod behind and went on to the Upper Pool.

The river was too high, and it was a fight to get up against the current along the bar. The big run in the middle of the bar was too deep and too heavy to cross, so the best part of the pool was unfishable. I cast a long line across the run, well upstream, and fished with the rod held high. In this way the fly covered some of the good water before the heavy flow caught the line and dragged it out, but nothing moved to it. I worked on down, slowly and carefully, and once again there was a good pull, strong and straight below me. The reel ran and the fish came out twice, bright and clean in the sunshine; five pounds, perhaps a little more, perhaps less—less, I thought as I saw him, more I was sure when I felt him taking the line out and across. The pressure turned him, and he came back up the pool, swimming slowly against the current. Still fifteen yards below me, he turned and ran again, but the big rod stopped that quickly and humored him up again. Not five pounds, I knew now. Over that weight they don't humor so easily. I held hard, lifting his head and drawing him up on his side along the surface. He came within reach, and I got a good hold of the shank of the fly; a steelhead, all right, probably just under four pounds. I twisted the fly out, and he turned and swam off with the current; the game laws protect fish under five pounds until after March 1.

Fishing on down the pool I hooked and freed four others of about the same size. Each time the heavy pull, the strong run, then the revealing leap, and I knew there was little chance of a sizable fish in that part of the water. The small ones were early, but that is where they always lie when they are in. The big fish prefer the deeper water beyond the main run in the center of the bar.

I came out of the water and went down to the Lower Pool again. It had been satisfying to fish the big pool through like that, with a long line out and the quick, heavy rises straight below. It would be something to tell Firmin. But what of the big fish, the real January run? Perhaps the fish of the heavy pull and the big boiling rise in the Lower Pool was just another five-pounder. The time was short now, and the chances of the day were almost gone. I started in only a little above where he had come to me and fished each cast slowly and carefully, with only a step between them. The fourth cast came round into the easy water, and I left the fly there, straight downstream, with no movement from rod or line. The fish came suddenly, and the big rod was suddenly bent in its long curve against the sunny sky, the reel ratcheting out, the heavy line taut and flinging fine spray from it. He ran out for the heavy water and jumped far clear, flung over by the drag of the line. A thick, deep fish; the sun made a rainbow along his side, but only the palest of rainbows, so that one knew he was fresh and would be beautiful out of the water. The first run was very strong, and I slipped my fingers round onto the drum of the reel to increase the pressure. I felt the backing come up, and he was still in the strongest water, traveling, really traveling, down the pool. Briefly there was the feeling of helplessness and frailty that a really big, strong fish can give one. I thought of the gut, heavy, but three seasons old, and of the light iron and small barb of the fly hook. Then he jumped twice again, but not with the strength of that first jump. He turned, and I began to work him up the pool.

He came well up, and there was fly line back on the reel before he turned and ran again. I checked the second run short and felt I had him. He came up very easily but still in the strong water, tiring himself that way, but in good shape to turn and run again as far as the first time. He did run again, but this time came over into the easy water at the end of it. He was still strong, and I brought him up gently. He swam past me, fifteen feet away and near the surface so that I saw him clearly and knew that he was real fish, long as well as deep and thick, fifteen pounds anyway. Now that he was upstream of me and tired, I had only to pull him over, off balance, and lead him back past me to the gaff. A fish for Firmin, I said, the first of the season and a good one. I looked down to free the gaff and get it into my hand. Then the rod sprang straight and the fly was trailing its orange across the surface of the water. The fish turned very slowly out into the fast water.

I sat down on a rock and swore, picked up the fly, saw that barb and point were perfect and swore again. "Dear Firmin, I lost a good fish yesterday. Saw him clearly, a really good one, so I know the winter run is in the river all right." Well, it might do, but it wasn't right. I cut off the fly and knotted it to the gut again. That hold had had all the strain it should be asked to take.

The rest of the pool was worth a dozen more casts and a prayer. It wasn't so very late, but by the time I got down to the pool above the Quinsam or the Sandy Pool it would be, and neither pool really offered a better chance than those twelve more casts in the Lower Island Pool. I waded in, worked a short line over where the fifteen-pounder had taken, lengthened it and was into a fish. A crazy fish this time. He ran straight upstream in the heaviest part of the run and made three jumps, one below me, one dead opposite, one above me almost in the white water just below the Upper Pool. There was no strain on him except the drag of the drowned line, and I recovered as fast as I could, hand-lining through the rings of the rod. The line came tight between fish and rod, and a foot of gut showed with the fast water cutting against it. I moved out a little, took the loose line onto the reel, then lifted on the rod and tumbled him back down. He let me pull him into the quiet water behind the shoulder of the island, and I kept him there, drew him past me, set the gaff and carried him ashore. Not more than two or three days from the sea, a little fish—perhaps eight pounds— but perfect of his sort, with the sharp-cut line of three years' deepwater life along his side between the polished steel of back and brilliant silver of belly.

I loosed the gut from the line and coiled it away, then took down the rods and started for home. "Dear Firmin," I wrote in my mind, "had a really good day yesterday. Only hooked two big fish and only killed one of them, but both were on the fly. The weather is fine and the river is going down nicely. By the time you get here, it should be about perfect."

FEBRUARY

February, like January, is a fine steelhead month, in some ways the better month of the two. January can be cold and dry, but it can also be a very wet month, a month of heavy rain or quick thaw and freshet-guarded rivers. February is more dependable, at least on the Campbell. And February is likely to have splendid days of bright sun after frost, with the first faint feeling of spring in them, for the sap is rising in the maples again and the willow shoots are scarlet with it and the alders and fruit trees budded with it. By the middle of February some of the December and January fish may have lost the perfection of their ocean loveliness, but it is not likely that you will catch a really ugly fish, and fresh fish are still running steadily. This is February's great advantage over March, for in March—certainly after the fifteenth—you stand a very good chance of hooking fish that have actually started to spawn, and these fish have no beauty of shape or color left in them. Even when you return them safely and see them swim away almost strongly, you feel that you have done an unnecessary thing, an evil thing—which you probably have. I like almost everything about fishing, but I hate to catch an ugly fish, particularly a trout or a salmon that has lost even the ferocious beauty of spawning time and become a miserable thing with health and color and nearly all of life itself gone out of him.

February is a good month too because Washington was born on the twenty-second, and that means that my brother-in-law Buck Elmore will probably be able to take time out and come up to try for a fish. Buckie is not a polished fisherman—he won't mind my saying that because he hasn't been long at the business and he doesn't get much time for it—but he is as enthusiastic and determined as any fisherman I have ever known and likes to look at new water just as well as he likes to catch fish. In the war year of 1942, Washington's Birthday got Buckie two free days from an otherwise unbroken succession of seventy-hour weeks, and he used them to come up to us. On the first day we caught a fish or two in the Islands Pools, and I mentioned a theory that an exceptionally long period of high water had drawn the fish up the Quinsam, a large tributary of the Campbell, more quickly than usual. You can fish the Quinsam, but it is a little river with the pools far apart and small when you get to them; the banks are thick with alder and crab apple and salmonberry and logging debris along all the miles of it that I had worked. I told Buckie this and that I thought the fish might have traveled on through the lower pools to the falls.

"Where're the falls?" Buckie asked.

I didn't know exactly. I had never been in there, and no one I knew seemed able to tell me much about them. They weren't big falls and fish did get over them. I knew that because I had seen steelhead farther up the stream.

"There's a new forestry road that goes somewhere around where they're supposed to be," I said. "I've been meaning to try it out for nearly a year now."

"May as well do that," Buckie said.

We did, and we had one of the best days we've ever had. It blew from the north and tried to snow. We climbed a hill and tried to judge where the falls would be, picked out the rocky forestry road from among half a dozen abandoned logging roads and found that it took us to within a hundred yards of the falls. From the falls we fished down a reach of broken water without a touch, then a swift pool under a high cut bank which also held nothing, then a long, quiet, deep reach that seemed a certain place for fish but turned out to be as empty as the rest of the river. We were both happy enough, but I began to think we should have turned up from the falls instead of down. They were very little falls, certainly no obstacle to fish except in the lowest of low water, and there had been nothing of that sort for months.

Below the quiet stretch there was a huge log jam, a mountainous pile of charred and battered tree trunks that had been building itself for two or three hundred years, if the bleached and rock-hard bones of dead trees at the lower end were evidence. Below the log jam the river split to pass over an alder flat where the beaver were working. And below the flat, where the streams joined again, was a pool that made the day one of useful as well as pleasant discovery. It was a long pool, eighty or a hundred yards of even flow and even depth to a right-angle bend against a rock face and from there thirty or forty yards of deep, slow flow to the draw of the little rapid at the tail.

We began to fish it with enthusiasm, but we had to admit that we wished we were fishing a summer evening instead of a February afternoon, working up with the dry fly instead of down with minnow and wet fly. That first eighty yards was almost like a stretch of fine chalk stream, with rushes on the far side and the smooth surface creased here and there by the thrust of boulders from the bottom. Even in February one could imagine a score of big trout scattered through it, rising steadily to a good hatch of flies. But it held no steelhead, and perhaps it is a little shallow for them. We fished the deep water at the bend more carefully, and once a fish of some kind took the minnow firmly but did not hold on to it.

It was getting late, but the next pool down looked good (as the next pool always does), so we had to try it. As we walked across the shallow breakoff from the big pool, a steelhead tried to swim up between us, turned in a surge of water and went back down the rapid. We tried for him, and while we were doing so, another steelhead jumped in the big pool near where the fish had touched the minnow. It was almost dark then, and we had to cross two miles of logging slash to get back to the car.

"One thing," Buckie said, "we'll know where to start in next time."

"I'm coming back before next steelhead season," I told him. "I want to see a good trout rising along by the rushes and put a brown sedge over him."

That is a promise I still have to keep, now in this coming summer of 1946. The war years lasted a long time and the Quinsam and all its pools have been far out of reach for me ever since that day.

The times with Buckie are always a little bit different from other fishing times. Two or three years ago he came, not on Washington's Birthday, but on March first. I had been up the river a few days earlier and found few steelhead but plenty of cutthroats, so I told him we'd make a day of starting the trout season and not bother much about steelhead. We came to the Lower Island Pool, and I said, "Start in there, Buckie. You might pick up a couple, and then we'll go on to the Upper Pool and really make a killing."

Buckie started in with a trout fly and a 2X leader, and when I looked up again he was fast in a ten-pound steelhead, which broke him in short order.

The next season it was Washington's Birthday and the steelhead were in. We came to the Lower Island Pool again, and I put up the minnow rod.

"Take a few practice swings, Buck," I said, "up here at the head of the pool. There's never a fish here; they always lie half a dozen casts farther down."

The practice swings didn't work out quite right, so I took the rod to see if I could adjust the reel a little for him. I made one cast, right into the broken, shallow water, and a bright steelhead came from nowhere and took the minnow almost as it fell. Buckie fished the rest of the pool and I fished it, and there wasn't another fish anywhere.

But that day ended well. We crossed the river at the Upper Pool—a nice achievement at the best of times and a matter for wholehearted applause if your boots have plain rubber soles as Buckie's had—and went on from there to the Canyon Pool. On fairly low river the Canyon Pool can be a winter fisherman's hell. With the water at a good height the fish lie well up in the pool, and you can reach them from the rock ledges. But on low water they lie at the tail, and you can only reach the tail properly from a bar about fifteen yards out. To get to the bar, you have to wade over the tops of thigh boots, and even when you get there, the least wavelet slops in—though that doesn't really matter much perhaps. Buckie went out there while I built a fire to dry him off. In half a dozen casts he hooked a twelve-pounder that took his line round a rock and traveled on down the rapid. We took the gaff to him instead of bringing him to the gaff, so that was all right. But Buckie said, "That's not going to happen again."

I started back toward the fire, and Buckie hooked another fish, a five- or six-pounder this time. It happened to be one of those fish that swim right up to you before making up their minds where they really want to go. Those might have been pretty fair tactics if Buckie had been in another mood. Unluckily for the five-pounder, Buck was remembering what he had said as the first fish was gaffed. He reached down quickly, grabbed the leader short and hung on to his fish.

"Get his gills, Buckie," I shouted, "or he'll break the hooks out."

Buckie made a grim, solid effort, got his fingers in the fish's gills and sat down in three feet of water. Twice more on the way in toward the bank the slippery boots let him down, but when he came ashore the fish was still with him. We got part-way dry in front of the fire and laughed till we were warm clear through. That's why I like fishing with Buckie. I hope he'll be here again when Washington's Birthday comes round.

About Pike

To create a legend, time is needed. There must be time for stories to grow and men's minds to work upon them and build them larger yet, time for eyes and minds made receptive by tales already told to collect and magnify new fragments of evidence, time for partisans of the growing myth to raise about its essential points a hedge of protecting dogma. So a fish, to make a good subject for a legend, must belong to one of those species that stay put—migratory fish, such as salmon, haunting a single locality at most for the brief span of a season, have little chance to become legendary.

Brown trout are excellent subjects of minor legend. Almost any village public house in the British Isles has its monstrous, hog-backed hero who is seen from time to time through the dark depths of a great pool or under the dim center arch of the nearest road bridge. Carp, because they are long-lived and cautious fish, are favorites of some storytellers. But no fish has inspired such legends as the pike. He has every necessary quality—size, strength, ferocity, a cruel cold eye, a wicked head and a love of dark, still waters.

Because, as I have said, it takes time to cultivate good stories, it is natural that the oldest ones should be the best. In 1497 the famous Mannheim pike was caught, a neat little fish nineteen feet long and 267 years old. The age was readily ascertained from a brass ring in its gills, which was inscribed as follows: "I am the first fish that was placed in this pond by the hand of Frederick II, Governor of the World, on the 5th October, 1230." The skeleton of the fish and the ring were preserved in Mannheim Cathedral for many years in clearest proof of the tale. True, some busybody checked the skeleton and found that it had been lengthened by the addition of a number of vertebrae, but the Mannheim pike has found its way into more printed records than most fish, and the debunker's name is quite lost.

Sir John Hawkins slipped a fine pike story into several of his editions of *The Compleat Angler.* This fish, which weighed 170 pounds, was taken from a pool near Newport that had been drained, and a contemporary newspaper report has the following note:

> Some time ago the clerk of the parish was trolling in the above pool, when his bait was seized by this furious creature, which by a sudden jerk pulled him in, and doubtless would have devoured him also, had he not by wonderful agility and dexterous swimming escaped the dreadful jaws of this voracious animal.

The fishing writers tell that one without a single debunking note, but it is a long drop down to the next monster—the Kenmure pike, of seventy-two or sixty-one pounds, depending on who is telling the tale. From examination of the measurements of the skull, Tate Regan believes the fish really may have weighed that much.

Irish pike stories are innumerable and for a long while they were regarded with the greatest suspicion by all the authorities. Then the late R. B. Marston, editor of *The Fishing Gazette,* offered a prize of ten pounds for any properly authenticated Irish pike of fifty pounds or over. This was probably the best-spent ten pounds on record and the kindest service ever done for pike fishers throughout the British Isles, because in 1923 John Garvin caught a pike of fifty-two pounds in Lough Conn and received the reward. This gives substance to all the records and reports of Irish thirty- and forty-pounders and makes the ninety-six-pound fish from Killaloe and the sixty-pounder from the Ballina Lakes well worth thinking about.

Nearly all these big fish have fine tales built around them; but the fish are unnecessarily big, for a twenty-pounder, under the right circumstances, can do just as well. There is so much about a pike for the imagination to work on—the lean swift body, the love of dark, deep places, the flat head and long jaws filled with sharp teeth, the cold, upward-staring eyes, even the mottled green and olive brown of his sides and back which allow him to melt into invisibility against an underwater background of reeds and rushes. A pike lurks—that is the perfect word—in wait for his prey. When it moves close enough to him, he springs forward or upward upon it. He seizes it crosswise in his huge jaws and sometimes shakes it. When he is ready to do so, he turns it and swallows it. He has a boldness in pursuit that leads him to reach for ducks and grebes on the surface of the water, for a swimming rat and perhaps for other and larger creatures that come within reach. In Svend Fleuron's book about a great pike, his heroine (Grim is her name) graduates into legend through a splendid series of crimes. One unfortunate angler falls from his boat in the excitement of reaching to gaff her and is drowned as she tangles the line about his legs. Another, who unwisely chooses to go swimming when sport is slow, almost loses a leg to the slash of her great teeth. Later she drags down a roe deer fawn that has come to drink at the edge of the lake and after that a swimming dog. She learns to lie in wait at the drinking holes of the cattle and to seize and tear the noses of steers and horses. As her fame spreads through the villages, she becomes a serpent, a dragon, a crocodile. A milkmaid saw her as she shot up out of the deep water and shook herself. The jingling of the scales in her mane was clearly to be heard. Ole, the wheelwright, saw her too. "Such a head! As big as a calf's! And the skin round the corners of its mouth all in great thick folds!"

This is the very stuff of good pike legend: crocodile, serpent, dragon; lurking, lying in wait, dangerous, mysterious; of the swampy marges and the blackest depths; seen only in breathtaking, terrorizing glimpses. There must, I think, be American and Canadian pike legends. I have found a trace of one in a book by William Senior, the famous "Red Spinner" of the angling periodicals: "Captain Campbell of the Lake Ontario Beaver Line informs me that he once brought over in a whiskey cask the head of a muskinlonge from the St. Lawrence that was said to weigh one hundred and forty pounds." There are the bare bones of a fine story, and it would seem that there should be others to be found in lands which have not only the common pike but the pickerel and the muskellunge as well. After all, the muskie commonly attains weights that are the outside limit for ordinary pike. Or perhaps a country that breeds the gator and the catamount, to say nothing of Paul Bunyan and Mike Fink and Daniel Boone and sidehill gougers, need not concern itself with mere fish.

Though I have listened faithfully to all pike stories, I have never yet come close enough to one of these fabled monsters to go out after it myself. I have many times fished waters where every cast gave me a chance of a salmon of forty or fifty pounds, and probably I have never shown a bait to a pike much larger than twenty pounds. But pike fishing has always given me a strange excitement. It is a different excitement, musty as folklore, yet with some of the radiance of mythology, built on curiosity and a sense of vague possibilities rather than on the expectation of a great fish and an uncontrollable fight.

Once I built my own myth. It was only a little myth and all my own, but it was very satisfying and there was room for doubt in the end of it, as there should be in all good myths. It started in a south of England railroad train which stopped, unaccountably, between stations. I saw that my carriage was on a steel bridge over a slow, dark river and stood up to look out of the window. The guard came along as I did so and I asked him, "How long?"

"About ten minutes," he said.

"Can I get out? I'd like to take a look at the river."

He hesitated a moment, then said, "All right. Don't be long. Not more than five minutes."

I climbed out and went to the side of the bridge to look down. The river was big and deep as it passed under the bridge, and I realized that I should not be able to see what I had vaguely hoped to see—a big spring salmon passing upstream. Then the long curve of a backwater caught my eye, and I thought of pike. It was a perfect place, stirring in tiny whirlpools where the easy current swung round against the river's flow, its surface hidden under a raft of little dead sticks and leaves and rushes near the bank. I saw the pike as the guard called me back to the train. A long, still shape, four or five feet down in the water, wide-backed, bronze against the darkness beneath him. I turned away and ran for the train. All the way to London I thought about that pike, and perhaps, as good pike do, he began to grow. Anyhow, I mentally weighed him at twenty-five pounds as I waited for a taxi at Waterloo.

It took me over a year to get back to the backwater under the railroad bridge. The river, as I had known all along, was closely preserved salmon water. But there was a hotel in a nearby town where one could stay and get day tickets on the water to fish for pike and coarse fish of all kinds. A bad case of mumps earned me a February holiday, and I persuaded Mother to spend it with me at this hotel. In the hotel lobby a great pike looked down from a glass case. I began to ask about the fishing. Pike like that were a thing of the past, I was told; the river wasn't what it used to be. I might get something around five or six pounds, but not much more than that.

To reach the main river, we had to cross the millstream at the mill. I stopped to fish through the milltail, and the miller came out to watch me. He was a pale but cheerful man, with flour-whitened clothes and a stoop from lifting heavy sacks. He watched my fishing intently, his head a little on one side as though sizing up what I could do. I asked him about pike, and he gave depressing answers. After a little he said, "There's zalmon up t' river now." His voice was suddenly much softer than it had been.

"I haven't got a salmon ticket," I said. "Only pike."

"If so be 'ee should get one on, 'ee wouldn't think to turn un loose, would 'ee?"

I made another cast. "What else could I do?"

"There's sacks to the mill. There wouldn't be no one the poorer if 'ee was to send t' lady back after one."

I laughed then, because I didn't think I'd hook a salmon. But the miller was too friendly and his conspiracy too flattering for me to turn him down.

"I'll remember that," I said, "if I hook one."

He went back into the mill, and in a little while Mother and I started across the wet meadows toward the main river. I was not in a hurry to try for my big pike, but I began at once to look for the black steel bridge under which he had been lying. We were about half a mile above the railroad, and there were two bridges, one over the millstream, the other over the main river. I realized that I wasn't sure which was the right one. We decided to fish down the main river, then cut back along the railroad to the bridge over the millstream. I told Mother I was sure I could recognize the place as soon as I saw the water.

The big river was a disappointment. Not that it wasn't a fine river—it was, broad and strong and deep in wide, flat meadows that climbed almost sharply into low timbered hills a mile or so away on either side. But it was in flood, not in heavy flood, but full to the height of its low banks and soaking back into the meadows so that one could only approach it properly where there was a slight rise in the flat ground. I plowed in with knee boots and got wet almost at once. After making a few casts I had to circle back into the meadow to move on; then I could make a few more casts and circle another wet place. So it went, and Mother said, "Why don't you leave it and go back to the millstream? It's just right there."

I thought I knew better. The big river looked like big fish, and in spite of the high water there were beautiful places for pike to lie. I was using a big bait too, something new, the first pike plug I had ever owned. With a one-ounce lead and my silex reel I could get it well across the river and search some of the likely places, but I was not fishing as I had been taught to, moving down only a step or two between casts and working the bait so that it covered the whole river from side to side in slow, careful arcs. The wet places that forced me back from the bank prevented this and made me uneasy and uncomfortable.

When we came to the bridge, I had caught only a single pike, a little fish of about four pounds, which is the same as nothing at all if you are used to such rivers as the Frome and the Dorsetshire Stour, and this was a river at least as famous as either of them. I looked hopefully at the water just above the bridge and tried to see in it the place I had looked down on from the railroad bridge. Mother asked me, "Is this it?"

"No," I said. "I'm sure it isn't. Lord, I hope we find it."

"It must be on the millstream, then," Mother said sensibly. "And that's lucky because you'll be able to get to it without any trouble."

So we crossed to the millstream, and that was it and I could fish it. The wide eddy was under the far bank, almost as I had seen it a year before, with the same scum of little sticks and broken reeds on the surface and the same little whirls where the current turned back. I can never look at such a place in any river without thinking of pike and now I found that my fingers were shaking as I held the plug in my hands and looked carefully at the hooks.

"Do you think he's still there?" Mother said. "I do hope he is."

I nodded. "He's still there—or another one just as big. It's too good a place for them to give a little fish a chance."

I made the first cast carefully and accurately into the upstream tip of the eddy. The plug sidled down into the black water, and I could feel the gentle throb as it worked, suddenly stronger as it came out of the eddy into the current. I fished the eddy for an hour and I don't think I made a bad cast the whole time. I tried every different angle, worked different depths, brought the bait to me at different speeds. I changed the plug to a big rubber wagtail, blue and silver; from that to a brown and gold phantom; from that to a little silver reflex minnow. Nothing touched any of them and at last I had to give up. Mother takes it hard when I don't get what I want. "What a shame!" she said. "He must have moved, or else somebody has caught him."

"Nobody's caught him," I said quickly. That idea hurt. "He's still there. If he wasn't, we'd have caught a little fish like the one we've got. It's too good a place to be empty."

We went back to the mill and ate our lunch of blue vinny cheese with thick, crusty white bread, yellow butter and Dorset beer for a Dorset cheese. The miller came out to us and I offered him the little pike. He accepted it gratefully.

"And 'ee haven't zee'd no zalmon?" He shook his head and clicked his tongue. "Must be that 'ere bait's too durn big for un."

I tried to say again that we were fishing for pike, not salmon. Then he looked at my rod and saw the little silver devon on it, and his face lighted in a great smile. He winked one eye solemnly as he turned away. "Don't 'ee forget where to come fer t' zack, will 'ee?"

After lunch we went up above the mill and began fishing where the stream split to pass a reedy island. In spite of the miller's confidence in me, I changed the minnow for a wagtail, which has always been my favorite pike bait. The millstream was big, almost as big as the main river itself, but the banks were dry, and I could drop the bait comfortably across it to within six inches of the rushes of the island. To be fishing properly was satisfying in itself, and I was scarcely thinking of fish as I cast across to the mouth of the lesser stream at the lower end of the island. A good fish took the wagtail before it had traveled six feet from the bank. He ran well, and Mother asked, "Is it a salmon?"

"No," I said. "But it's a bigger pike than they said we'd get at the hotel."

"You must get him, my dear. It may be your only chance."

But I didn't feel that when he was on the bank, a fine thick fish of thirteen pounds.

"That's just a beginning for us," I said confidently. "This river grows fish big enough to make a meal of him."

Mother looked at the big, flat head and sharp, backward-pointing teeth as I cut the hooks out. She was used to Frome trout.

"I call him an ugly brute," she said. "I don't think I'd like to see one very much bigger."

For some reason, perhaps because the wagtail was battered and twisted, I changed back to the plug again. For half a dozen casts nothing moved to it; then there was a broad silver flash close behind it under the far bank. I felt nothing and did not strike, but I knew what it was and moved down half a dozen paces before I cast again. I asked Mother if she had seen anything.

"No," she said. "What was it?"

"The miller's salmon," I said. "The bait's too big for him and he only showed at it, but we'll try him again in a minute with something smaller."

"We shouldn't really," Mother said. But it was only a formal protest.

I felt salmon excitement strong in me, and it was hard to keep on and fish out the rest of the pool before going back to him; but I knew he should be rested, and it was easier to keep fishing than to stand quietly on the bank and wait out the time. Then a four-pound chub took the plug at the end of the pool and filled in more time. When he was safely on the bank, I changed to the two-inch silver reflex again, and I was as shaky as I had been when we found the eddy by the bridge. The river was famous for big pike, all right, but it was famous for even bigger salmon.

I had the place exactly marked, but I started a few casts above it and worked down. The minnow was easier and pleasanter to cast than the plug, and it began to spin the moment it hit the water, so that one could work it down deep and slow even under the far bank. The salmon took it there, deep down, with a heavy, solid pull, and started straight out on a run that made the reel talk its loudest.

"I've got him," I said triumphantly.

"Oh, no, my dear," Mother said. "What are we going to do?"

Then the fish broke water, twice and splendidly. He was big and silver and beautiful. Mother started down the river toward the mill.

"We must tell the miller," she said. "We promised him we would."

For another five minutes the fish played me, then I began to feel on top of the fight. Guiltily I looked behind me across the broad meadows. There was a man in the distance coming down toward me. I saw Mother disappear into the mill. The salmon ran again, jumped again, then let me bring him slowly back. The unknown was closer now, and I felt sure he was a keeper or a water bailiff. Mother came out of the mill, and the miller was with her. The salmon was directly below me, lying almost quietly, but not on his side. I knelt on the bank where I could see him very clearly and knew he was nearer thirty pounds than twenty. It might be a chance to tail him; by getting him out that way I should still be free to slip him back if the unknown man upstream of me was too close. I reached down, just touched him and sent him away on another fine run.

He had run against the stream and against heavy pressure and out at the end he rolled over, obviously tiring. He came slowly back, making short downward rushes whenever he felt the surface of the water too close. I looked downstream, then up, and knew that Mother would reach me with the miller and his incriminating sack at almost exactly the same time as the unknown man. The salmon was at my feet again now, really played out, and there seemed only one thing to do. I reached into a pocket for my pliers and knelt down once more. The minnow had been blown up the trace and jammed on the lead, and there was only a single small hook in the side of the salmon's jaw. I gripped it in the pliers, twisted sharply, and he was free. But he lay there quietly under the bank, just moving his great tail. Twice he opened his mouth and forced water out through his gills. Then he began to swim slowly down and away in the dark water. I looked upstream: the unknown man had turned off toward the main river. The miller came up panting, a hundred yards ahead of Mother.

"'Ee didn't lose un, did 'ee? I came as fast as I could."

"No," I said. "Turned him loose. I had to. That fellow up there," and I pointed to the unknown man out in the middle of the meadow now, "was coming straight down at me. What is he? The keeper?"

The miller snorted in disgust. "Yon's nowt but Jim Ford, going over to look at t' hatches. How big was t' zalmon?"

"Twenty-five pounds," I said. "Perhaps more."

The miller clicked his tongue. "A fi' pun note," he said. "A fi' pun note. That's what 'ee throwed away."

I pointed to the pike on the bank. "How's that one?"

"Yon's big," the miller said. "For what they do be 'ere nowadays.

But her beant like the ones they used to catch. And her beant no zalmon neither."

He went sadly back to his mill, and we fished on down. Mother said, "Perhaps it was just as well you let the salmon go. I felt all the time we shouldn't do it, but it was so exciting when he got on I just had to go."

I hooked another small pike of six or seven pounds above the mill, and Mother took the rod and killed him. Below the mill we caught another big chub, and a fair-sized pike came at the bait and missed it. So we came again to the railroad bridge. I stopped to straighten the hooks of the wagtail, and Mother went a little ahead. She said quickly, almost in a whisper, "Look! He's there now."

I looked across and the pike was there, my pike, straight and still as a thick bronze rod, not a foot under the water. He was lying at the lower end of the eddy, nose almost touching the main stream, body slanting in toward the bank. Mother came quietly and slowly back to where I was standing—she knows about fish.

"Do you think you can catch him?"

"Not from this side," I said. "I'll go up on the railway and round. You wait here and tell me what he does."

It must have taken me ten minutes to cross the bridge and get to where I wanted to fish from.

"He hasn't moved at all," Mother said.

I made the first cast right across the stream from well above the eddy, so that the wagtail would swing round to my side opposite the upstream end of the eddy and well away from the waiting pike. I meant to fish right down the length of the eddy step by step that way, so that he would see the bait first at a distance, then gradually closer and closer to him. The second cast swung round. As the line straightened, I let it hang for a minute, then began to reel quite fast. I heard Mother say, "He's gone," and there was a splash and a great swirl in the water twenty or thirty feet below me, directly behind the wagtail. He hadn't touched it, and I let the bait hang there again, then brought it slowly up to me until I was sure he was not following. I lifted it out and felt despair. All too often when a big pike misses the first time, he does not come again. Then Mother said, "He's back in his old place."

"Exactly the same?"

"Exactly the same, except perhaps a little deeper now. I can only just see him."

I supposed I ought to wait and rest him, but I couldn't do it. We had two more days to fish, but he might not be in the mood to take again. I fished on down the eddy, bringing the bait to the edge of it at each cast from clear across the stream. I thought he would come, if he were coming at all, when it swung in three or four feet above him. But he didn't; and he didn't come at the next cast or the next. Mother said, "He doesn't seem to see it even," and I was sure then that we wouldn't get him. I took two steps down and cast again. The bait swung in ten or twelve feet below the eddy, and I began to recover it in quick jerks and stops. He took when it was right opposite him, within two feet of his nose. I don't think I struck. He just ran, pulling the rod down in my hands, tearing at the reel as the salmon had. Fifty or sixty yards down, right under the bridge, he jumped, not like a pike, half out and shaking his head, but like a trout or salmon, clear out so that the drag of the line flopped him over on his side with a splash that echoed splendidly from the bridge girders. There was much more to it than that: at least three good runs, several sulky, head-shaking jumps, a long straining and reaching with the gaff from the high bank above the eddy. But I had him at last and held him up on the hook of the spring balance for Mother to see.

"He's twice as big as the other one," she said. "He must be even bigger than you thought."

But he wasn't; the needle of the spring balance wouldn't quite come down to the eighteen-pound mark. And I still don't know whether he was the same fish I had made into a twenty-five-pounder on Waterloo Station or whether someone had caught that fish and let another take his place. Probably it was the same though; spring balances are notoriously unfriendly to legends.

The day that all this happened was February 22, 1926. I was eighteen years and one day old at the time and still six or eight months away from American soil, so I probably didn't realize it was Washington's Birthday.

"Where to Fish"

The North American is probably the luckiest fisherman in the world. He can range a whole continent of lakes and streams and up and down along the shores of two oceans; he can catch salmon and trout and char, bass and pike and muskie, sailfish and tarpon and tuna, and seldom enough run up against man or sign that seeks to bar his way. As a result he flourishes in his millions, learns his craft, finds his happiness and the growth of soul that his sport yields.

In Great Britain, too, anglers flourish, not merely in thousands or tens of thousands, but again in millions. This is hard to believe. Sitting here and knowing it, I still find it hard to believe. Yet there is ample evidence. Consider only the quantity and quality of British fishing tackle that has been used for years on this continent; an export trade such as that grows only from something that a home demand has created, and maintains its standard only under the exacting criticism of a lively home use.

Great Britain is tiny and crowded, it is heavily industrialized, cross-hatched with roads and plagued with private ownership of sporting rights, all circumstances that mark the ruin of fishing for the average man in North America. They have their effect in Great Britain, but it is a double-edged effect. Good angling waters have been ruined by pollution and overfishing. Against that, the people of the country are wise and strong in their efforts toward conservation, and there is powerful legislation directed against pollution. Private ownership prevents the access of the great body of anglers to the best salmon and trout fishing. But against that, it has done much to preserve and improve the resource, and with the increase of fishing clubs of all kinds, more and more anglers have access to fishing that might no longer exist had it always been in public hands. The island is small, tiny when measured against the hugeness of the North American continent; but this means that a man can reach a lot of fishing without the expense of traveling far from home. It may be pleasant for the New Yorker to be able to regard the fine streams of Montana or Oregon as part of his birthright, but he can hardly feel that he has free access to them when he is writing the check for his traveling expenses.

Perhaps the garden quality of England is the greatest single factor in the country's yield of good fishing. Heavy rainfall and the lay of the land make for a multitude of river systems. Dense and long-established settlement has tended to conserve and increase this total acreage of water; everywhere there are man-made lakes and ponds, and almost every stream or river is controlled by weirs and hatches that hold and turn the water to irrigate fields and drive mills. Such water is stocked with fish and often cultivated as carefully as any garden, and every fish that swims is used by the angler. For the moment—but only for the moment—write off trout and salmon as preserved for the wealthy or the fortunate. There are still pike, perch, roach, dace, rudd, carp, tench, eels, grayling, chub and even the tiny six-inch gudgeon, all of which provide sport satisfying enough to draw men out from their firesides.

Perhaps the most popular fish in England, where the mass of British anglers live and do their fishing, is the roach. And most roach fishermen are craftsmen—mechanics, carpenters, plumbers, miners, blacksmiths, skilled workers of every kind who have learned their trade through slow and careful apprenticeship. Perhaps for this reason, roach fishing is an art whose mastery requires long apprenticeship and a high degree of natural skill. A real roach fisherman is an artist, and his art commands the respect and admiration of any angler—it most certainly has all of mine.

For one thing, roach fishermen use the lightest and finest of tackle. A friend of mine at Oxford, a plumber whose name was Tom, had six 2-pound roach in handsome glass cases. They were silvery fish, deep-bodied and scarlet-finned, and in the case beside each one was the hook and a length of the gut that had caught it. Tom was partial to a No. 18 hook and 6X gut, which makes the dry-fly fisherman with his No. 16 fly and 4X gut just plain crude, if not clumsy. The rod Tom used was what is called a "roach pole," fourteen feet long and weighing rather less than an ounce to the foot, but stiff and quick. At home over a pot of tea or elsewhere over a pint of ale, Tom was happy and easygoing to a fault; he loved a belly laugh and indulged himself frequently, to the disquiet of the heavy gilt watch chain that looped across his broad and upborne waistcoat. By the river he was silent, still, intent and deadly. He would set up his fishing stool by a favorite swim, usually a twenty- or thirty-foot length of easy current about six feet deep, throw in his ground bait of bread paste and bran and aniseed oil, then bait his tiny hook with an even more succulent variation of the same mixture and begin to fish. Tom used a slender quill float with enough line below it to carry his hook to within an inch or two of the bottom of the river. Three or four small split shot sank the hook and cocked the float, and the lightest of light lines ran back from the quill through the rings of the rod to the reel that he always called a winch.

Silent on his stool, he would make each cast with a slow, easy swing that dropped the paste gently at the top of the swim; as the float cocked and started its journey, his concentration became thick as gloom. The strike is the roach fisherman's art, for roach have tiny suspicious mouths and love to nibble at a bait or take it in and eject it so quickly that the movement scarcely shows in a quiver on the float. Such playful creatures were never safe with Tom. His eyes were hard on his float, and his whole body was hunched toward it, keeping the rod top as nearly as possible above it right through the length of the swim. The tiniest check meant a swift, sure strike and generally a fish securely hooked. I watched him many times before going off with my fly rod to look for chub, and occasionally I tried my hand with his tackle. Whenever I did so, I learned humility; again and again I would strike too late or too hard or fail to strike at all. And Tom would take the rod and show me. "There. You see 'ow easy it is. Just keep your

eye on the quill and 'it 'im as soon as it checks." As he spoke, he
would have struck to a check that only his spirit could have seen—his
eyes were no better than mine and I had not seen it—and be fast in a
good fish. He played them as he fished for them, with a minimum of
fuss and movement, generally on a tight line and following the runs
and struggles of the fish by keeping his rod top as nearly as possible
directly over it. With the fish on the bank, he would say, "You could
do it, easy, if you'd keep at it. It ain't nothing but practice and a little
patience. You'll come to it when you're older and not so flighty. Now
you've got to be running up and down and flicking a fly abaht all the
time or else you don't think you're doing any good." Tom would laugh
then. "Young stuff," he'd say. "That's the ticket, boy. Keep running
just so long as there's a jot or run left in you. Go on now and catch
some of them there durn old chub. They're more your mark."

Roach fishing, as Tom went about it, takes skill and patience and a
developed sixth sense; above all it takes concentration. There are thousands upon thousands of fishermen like Tom in the Midland and south
of England angling clubs, and they match their skill in championship
competitions that make the Puget Sound salmon derbies look like little
family gatherings, though the prizes are nothing more than cups and
medals. This, then, is the rock-solid base of British angling. For myself, I would choose to try for many other fish before roach—salmon,
trout, pike, grayling, perch and chub, to name only a few—but I feel
always that the roach fisherman is the highest and most orthodox
symbol of all the great body of coarse fishermen, and that these men of
the float and paternoster and ledger are more truly representative of
British angling than all the trout and salmon fishermen about whom
the books are written.

You can find coarse fishing in almost any part of England—in the
Norfolk broads and the Cumberland lakes, in the Thames and in the
fine rivers of the West Country, in the Ouse and Trent of the Midlands,
in the Tyne and the Tees of the North, in hundreds upon hundreds of
lakes and ponds all over the country. Sometimes this fishing is open to
the public without question or payment of any kind. More often it is
necessary to buy a daily or weekly or season ticket to the water, nearly
always at a nominal cost, from some local angling club. Sometimes it
is necessary to ask permission from a landowner or his agent, and the
permission is usually given for coarse fish. This means that in spite of
private ownership and dense population a keen angler, even though he
happens to be a poor man, can find a lot of fishing in England if he
knows where to look for it and whom to ask.

There is a little book in gray cardboard covers, put out by The Field
Press, which gives a tremendous amount of information of this sort.

The book is called simply *Where to Fish.* My copy is the fifty-fourth edition, dated 1923–24, and I have had a lot of fishing out of it, both riverside and fireside fishing. Someday I shall get a later edition— preferably a postwar edition, because there surely will be one—just to see how much has changed, but I shall never discard the old fifty- fourth, which was the first edition to be published after the First World War. The book starts out with a glance back to angling affairs of the previous year or so and slides quickly on to "A List of Notable Fish," about a dozen pages of them, and, what I mean, they *are* nota- ble fish: salmon from 50 pounds to 69¾, trout from 7 pounds to 39½, pike from 30 pounds to 53, and so on through the whole list; then to England and Wales, county by county and town by town; then to Scotland, Ireland, Africa, Canada, the United States; back through France, Norway, Iceland; thence to the Balkans, Australia, and even the Fiji Islands.

I like the parts about England and Scotland best because the au- thors, most of whom are local tackle dealers, really know their subject. There is page after page of "The hotel has six miles of water reserved for guests"; "Good pike and perch in Blank Lake—permission from the owner of Blank Manor"; "Good trouting; the proprietor of the King's Arms gives permission when properly applied to"; "Salmon and trout; fishing free for eight miles below the town; water above the town strictly preserved, but permission can sometimes be obtained"; "Chub, dace, pike, perch, good fishing; day tickets 1/-, season tickets 10/-, from Hon. Sec. Willow Bottom Angling Association." It is so easy to expand the pictures. You go to Willow Bottom, settle yourself in the warm and comfortable Black Swan or perhaps the Stuffed Pike, then search out the Hon. Sec. He is a large and cheerful individual, busy, but glad to take time out for a pint or several pints at the inn of your choice. Yes, the fishing is good. Be sure to give the Weir Pool a try—there's a big one there, always lies near the broken willow on the far bank; Joe Gain hooked him last month and broke in him. And the Long Wood Pool—be sure you don't miss that. . . .

Where would you fish and what would you fish for? Name it, be- cause nothing is impossible. Perhaps the Dee in Scotland for salmon? Look under Braemar: "By staying at the Fife Arms Hotel, salmon fishing can be had in over seven miles of water, or Invercauld Arms has two miles." Or perhaps the Tay—the Tay, after all, has produced its sixty-pounders, while the Dee has only fifty-pounders to boast of. See under Aberfeldy: "By staying at the Breadalbane Arms, 4½ miles of the Tay can be fished free." Come down to the south of England. Really good trout fishing? How about the Kennet, where Sir Aubone Fife caught, in 1903, on the May fly, sixteen trout weighing fifty-six

pounds? No river has such a May-fly hatch or such monster trout as
the Kennet. "Hungerford," the gray book says, "Kennet and Dunn.
The river is preserved and well stocked with trout and grayling; appli-
cation for season ticket to be made to Mr. L. H. Beard and for day
ticket to T. G. Freeman. May and June reserved for S. T. holders, fly
only; no Sunday fishing. Commoners' days [I'm not sure what this
means, but it sounds hopeful for you and me] Monday, Thursday and
Saturday." Not the Kennet, something really hard? The Test at Stockbridge, the finest stretch of dry-fly water in the world, preserved, developed and used by the ancient and fabulous Houghton Club. The
gray book admits it's not too easy: "Preserved by the Houghton Club
above and below the town." Then the ray of hope: "Below, most of the
free holders of Stockbridge have the right of fishing in the marsh on
one side of the river for half a mile; leave from one of these." So, even
this can be done.

Perhaps all this hasn't much to do with a day's fishing in February;
I don't think Tom bothers his roach much in February, and all the
season tickets in the world will not let you catch a February trout in
the Kennet or the Test. But for some reason I think I have turned to
the gray book most often in February. It was a February day in London when Gerry came up to my Redesdale Street room. He circled the
big, paper-littered table contemptuously, then pointed to half a dozen
pipes in an ash tray.

"You're ruining your health," he said. "All you do is sit in here and
swot your head off and smoke your lungs black. You look pale and
sickly. You need to get out."

"Well," I said, "when did you get the call?"

"No, I really mean it. You'll kill yourself if you go on like this.
You've got to go out somewhere—go fishing or something like that."

"Yeah?" I said. "Where for instance? Off Battersea Bridge?"

"No, really get away somewhere. Devonshire's pretty nice. You
could find fishing in Devonshire this time of year, couldn't you?"

"Probably," I said suspiciously. "Whereabouts in Devonshire?"

"Oh, anywhere. Ever hear of a place called Totnes?"

"Yes, I have. Why Totnes?"

"I just like the sound of it."

"There must be a woman there," I said, but I reached behind me for
the gray book.

"No, there's not. Not a woman. I mean, of course, there's a woman
there, lots of women, but that's not it. I just want to see you get out of
this work rut you're in before you kill yourself."

"Well, there's the Dart at Totnes. Salmon start on the fifteenth. It's kind of good sometimes. I've been there before, higher up than Totnes. But I'm not going now. I'm broke."

"Don't think about that, old man; it's my party—get your health back and all that. Besides, I want to catch a Dart salmon. Always have wanted to."

"Up till a couple of minutes ago you didn't know Totnes was on the Dart, and you didn't know there were salmon in the river."

The end of it was that I went with him, not for the sake of my health, which was perfectly good, but because the Dart was a strong temptation in February London and because Gerry obviously had some plan that needed his presence and mine at or near Totnes. We settled in at a place near Buckfastleigh, where the gray book had taken me once before. I was up early on the first morning (we had arrived at dark the night before) and tried to move Gerry to enthusiasm over the possibilities of a Dart salmon.

"Can't go with you today, old man. Got to see a man about some business. Take my rod and I'll join you this afternoon if I can."

That was final. I took his rod gladly—it was a thirteen-foot split cane and half the weight of my old greenheart—and went out by myself. It was a sunny day, too sunny, but I couldn't mind that because the whole air smelled of spring and sunshine belonged there. The river danced and sparkled and begged for a fly to play with as our deep, quiet Dorsetshire Frome never does. I went down to the first pool, a wide stretch broken by big rocks, and found salmon showing there. I covered fish after fish without a touch until at last something took near the tail of the pool; it was a twelve-pound kelt and I freed him to find the sea. All day it was the same story, fish showing everywhere, but only kelts were taking hold. The afternoon went on, and Gerry did not come down. I felt sure now that it must be a woman. Seeing him in town, walking down Sloane Street, you might have doubts about Gerry; he is likely to be wearing a bowler perched on one side of his head, a light gray overcoat of quite spectacular beauty, pale-yellow chamois gloves and an umbrella of the slender, tightly rolled kind that we used to call dieted. But he can be a really grim and determined fisherman. Bad weather means nothing to him, and dangerous wading is only a challenge; a new river should have hurried him through any business with a man in no time at all. I tried to guess my part in the affair and decided comfortably that I was just a convincing piece of camouflage. Then, at dusk, I hooked a fresh-run ten-pounder and forgot about Gerry.

That fish rounded out the day perfectly. You do not, or at least I do not, really, deep in the heart, expect great things of places found in the gray book; they may be as good as they seem or they may not; the only way to be sure is to go and fish and find out; and if you have taken a blind chance on such things as the state of the water and the weather and the arrival or nonarrival of migratory fish, you really deserve a disappointment. So I went back to the farmhouse in a pleasant glow of satisfaction and ate a lazy and contented dinner before I began to worry about Gerry again. He came in almost as I started worrying, and I could see at once that his day had not been wholly wasted. Gerry, as he quite often is, was excited.

"Hello, old man," he said. "How was the fishing? Let's have a drink on it. Great place this, isn't it?"

I hadn't had a chance to tell him about the fish or anything else, so I took it that the roses of his day were bright enough to color mine for him. I began to mix the drinks.

"How did you make out?" I asked. "Fix things up O.K.?"

"Yes. It wasn't the way I thought at all. Gosh, she's fine. I want you to meet her."

"Gerry," I said reproachfully, "you said it wasn't a woman."

"She isn't either—not the way you say that. You don't know how awful you make it sound—as if a girl has to be a mistress or something."

"I'm sorry. But you didn't tell me much about it."

"We'll tell you the whole thing tomorrow. You've simply got to meet her—she's wonderful."

"So's the fishing," I said. "You're not going to miss it all, are you? If it's cloudy tomorrow, we ought to be able to murder them."

"I'll get down there with you early tomorrow—really I will. Just as soon as I've got everything straight. Mix another drink now; I feel like celebrating a bit."

The next day was cloudy. Gerry took the car and went off about his affairs quite early, and I went to the top pool and started in. The top pool is wide and fairly fast, with a current badly broken up so that you have to do a real job of fishing to bring your fly properly through each little pocket that may hold a fish. There are high, steep banks on each side, but the right bank, from which I was fishing, is clear of trees, and for some reason I decided to fish from the top of it instead of going down to the water and using a roll cast. It is a contemptible practice and a lazy one, to stand up high like that when you don't have to, but that day it brought me a reward. I had fished through nearly three quarters of the pool, using a big Silver Wilkinson, thoroughly enjoying myself because I could watch the fly work through each cast and feel that I was really learning the pool. Over on the far side the river deepened under the roots of a big sycamore. I drew line off the reel, made a cast well short of the deep place, let it fish a little way round, then lifted and really reached out. The fly rolled over in a satisfying curve and laid itself in the water within inches of the sycamore's upstream root. I kept the rod point high to give it a chance to come slowly over the deep water. Then two things happened at once: the sun broke through the clouds, and I saw a big salmon rise slowly, slowly through the water, seeming to balance through his whole rise with head and tail absolutely level. He had judged the swim of the fly perfectly, and I saw his gills show scarlet as he opened his mouth to take it. The pull of the line struck him, and he went away upstream at once in a run that made Gerry's rod bend like a birch sapling in a gale of wind.

He was one of those bullheaded, unspectacular fish, but it wasn't altogether easy to fight him from the high bank. I could see every move of his fight, even see that he was hooked well back in the corner of the mouth as the sun caught the blue and magenta hackle of the fly. He seemed to know the rocks and worked his way sullenly from one to another, boring down under each and every one until the lift of the rod moved him on. He came in under my own bank at last and held there, still a strong fish, close under a willow stump. I worked my way cautiously down, keeping a tight line on him, worried because I had no tailer, and no gaff is allowed on the Dart in February. He moved up a little, clear of the stump; his head was hidden from me behind a clump of dead bracken, but I could see his back almost to the dorsal fin. His big tail was moving slowly and easily and his head was down against the lift of the rod; it was no time to try for him, but I managed to lie down along the bank without jerking the rod. Still keeping the strain on him I reached out my right hand, slid it into the water and got a firm grip on the wrist of his tail. He tried to go, but I have a big hand, and the tail of an Atlantic salmon has a slender wrist that a man can really hold on to. I held him and lifted, dragged him on to the bank and rolled on top of him. He was a cock fish of twenty-one pounds.

It was a good start—so good that I felt I was hardly entitled to anything more. I knew even then that the vivid sunlit picture of that big fish coming up to the fly was one that I should hold and cherish forever. I can see it clearly now, more than ten years after. And I know now what I did not know then, that I had risen and struck my first salmon by the greased-line method; for that was what it was, in spite of the big fly and my ungreased line.

The next two pools gave me only a single kelt and a half-hearted rise from another fish. Then I came to the Abbey Pool, a fine pool in a rock basin under the high wall of the Abbey. Two brown-robed monks were leaning over the wall watching the pool as I came up. I said good morning to them and began to fish. One of the monks moved away, but the other stayed to watch me. He was a big man, with a broad, heavy face on which his beard showed blackly in spite of close shaving, but his blue eyes were interested and his fine big mouth seemed made for laughing. The monks of Buckfastleigh, as all the world knows, are craftsmen—masons, carpenters and architects who have hewn and raised and placed every stone of the magnificent Abbey.

I nodded toward the pool and asked him, "Fish?"

He smiled and held up three fingers. "They're lying together. Your fly crossed a few feet above them."

I let out line and cast again. "The outside one is following," the monk said. "No, he's turned away from it."

I cast again and looked up at him, but he shook his head and smiled. I cast a slack line to let the fly work down deeper, but still it was no good. I moved position to bring it across from a different angle, tried to hang it near them, took in line and swept the fly across short of them, worked it fast and slow, smoothly and in jerks.

"They don't seem interested," the monk said. "Let out a little more line and bring it across behind their tails."

I stripped line from the reel and made the cast. The monk said, "Now!" and I missed the rest in the thrill of the savage take. That fish was both lively and spectacular. He jumped almost as he took, then began a run that took him out of the short pool in a moment. "Quickly," I heard the monk say. "Follow him." I was already following, holding hard because I didn't know what was below or how far I could follow. The strain checked the run in fifty or sixty yards and though the fish ran again several times I brought him out at last, still under the Abbey wall. I looked up to thank the monk and ask what he thought of the fish, but he was gone, and I heard a bell somewhere beyond the wall. Perhaps he was wondering, as he knelt in the choir stalls, how it had all come out.

The fish was smaller than the first one, and my battered spring balance made him just under seventeen pounds. I went back to the pool and decided to give it a rest; the sun, which had been in and out of clouds all day, seemed to be permanently out now and it was warm. I went up a little from the pool and lay where I could look across the river at a sloping bank covered by dark firs and silver-barked birches. I thought I could see faint, pale green on the birch branches, and daffodils were blooming golden here and there under the trees. Up the valley, on the line of the river, there was a distant sight of Dartmoor. Beside me, bright and clean and beautiful, lay my two fish.

Because of all this I was, perhaps, in a receptive mood when I first saw the girl. But even so, she was really beautiful. I thought of her at once as a blue-black girl; that may not have been the color of her hair, but it certainly was its quality. Her eyes were deep blue, almost violet, and showed strongly in her dark face. I think there were freckles about her nose, rather large ones and dark, but that was only an impression that I never had time to confirm for looking at the rest of her. She was wearing a blue, brushed-wool sweater, a pleated gray skirt and square-heeled shoes that she set firmly and confidently against the sloping ground.

I stood up, and she said, "You must be Gerry's friend. He'll be along in a minute—he went down at the other pool to make sure you weren't there. Oh, look what you've caught. Aren't they beautiful?" And she knelt beside the fish to look at them.

Gerry came then and brought things back to ground level by introducing us more or less formally.

"Joan and I are going to get married," he said. "Surprise you?"

"Well," I said, "you haven't given me much chance to be anything but surprised."

Joan laughed, and it was a good laugh to hear, happy, yet strong and full without a trace of giggle anywhere about it.

"Will you tell him, Gerry, or shall I? Perhaps I'd better. It's all my fault." She lay back on one elbow and crossed her ankles. "You see, Gerry asked me to marry him in London, the first night I met him. I didn't think it was very sensible to decide something like that all at once, but I didn't want to say no, so I told him a fine story about having a fierce family that wouldn't hear of suitors—you know, an angry papa and man-eating big brothers. It was fun telling him."

"Scared me to death," Gerry said. He picked up the rod and began playing with the fly. "Those are real fish. Any more where they came from?"

"It didn't scare him too much, though," Joan said. "He came down here to abduct me."

I looked at Gerry. "You were going to take a girl forcibly from the bosom of her family?" I said. "Abduct her? Ride away to the west with her, shaking off pursuit and all that sort of stuff?"

"You were going to help," Gerry said. "Lower ropes over walls, place ladders against casements, drive the panting vehicle of escape, attend to all the mundane details of making sure that the marriage was legal." He got up, dropped the fly into the water and began to pay out line.

"That's nice," I said. "That would have been good for my failing health." I looked at Joan. "Yes," I said, "I think it might have. How was it all this action didn't take place?"

Joan laughed again. "I haven't got a fierce family, I'm afraid. Just a very normal and gentle white-haired father and no brothers at all."

Gerry had let out a good length of line and he rolled it over in a graceful, easy cast. A good fish took hold at once. Joan scrambled to her feet and went over to him.

"Oh, Gerry," I heard her say. "You're wonderful. You do things so easily."

MARCH

Whatever else may be happening in Pacific coast streams, their task of raising and fostering the salmon runs goes on; it is their huge main theme, fading into the background at times, while other movements become more obvious, but always dominant and controlling. March is the alevin month, as January is the hatching month. You may never see them, but they are there, the millions of tiny salmon, each with the supporting yolk sac pendent on its belly, no longer egg but still not quite fish. At least fifty days must pass between the time they first break from the egg and the time they become free-swimming fry, the last of the yolk sac having been taken into them as food—fifty days at an average water temperature of fifty degrees Fahrenheit. For each degree of temperature below fifty, five days longer. The Campbell is a cold river in the winter months, often a shade below freezing, seldom above forty degrees Fahrenheit; so the whole period from the burying of the eggs in the gravel to the emergence of the alevins is a long one. But the clusters of fry in every eddy of the river in April tell the story of March, and occasionally there is the direct evidence of alevins in the stomachs of steelheads or cutthroats. If you have the heart for it, you may also dig in the gravel and find them. I have not—their troubles are enough without my curiosity.

It is interesting to wonder how generally March could be considered the alevin month in the Northern Hemisphere. There is so much variation on the Pacific coast alone. Salmon run to most of the streams, from the Yukon in Alaska to the Sacramento in California, but spawning times vary and times of hatching and full development must vary with the tremendous variation of winter temperature. And what of Japan and Siberia where Pacific salmon also run? The brown trout and Atlantic salmon of England and Scotland are late-fall spawners, so alevins should be working up through the gravel there, too, sometime in March. Generalizations about fish are shoddy and dangerous, doubly dangerous for one so little given to mathematical calculation and solid search of reference books as I am. But I like this picture of myriad tiny atoms, in rivers all around the world, struggling through silt and gravel to start their growth to trout or salmon at about the same time.

March, certainly for most Northern Hemisphere fishermen, is the start of the trout season. Sometimes I think it should not be. Trout are hungry in March; there has been little for them in streams and lakes through the cold months, and now there is enough moving surfaceward to stir them into activity. In England, where the brown trout spawn in October and November, March fish are seldom in good condition, and many streams are closed until April first. On the Pacific coast, the noblest cutthroats spawn in January and February, and they are thin, sad, ravenous creatures in March. Even in May they are not fully recovered, and anyone who really loves beautiful fish slips them back to search the estuaries for sandhoppers and the aquatic cousins of the wood louse. And the nonmigratory rainbows have May for a spawning month, so that you must always catch some of them red and full of spawn in March or April.

Perhaps a too close consideration of spawning times is not sound. I have seen rainbow trout spawning magnificently in July, and in August every year I work my hardest to catch the big cutthroats that ascend the Campbell to hold in the Canyon Pool until they come to ripeness in January or February. The winter steelhead are full of spawn in the months they run to the river, and even the summer fish are developing fast toward the business of October or November. Catch a yearling trout of any species tomorrow, and you have made sure that he will not come to his mating in two or three years' time. I think a closed season should be measured rather in terms of the rest it gives to a fishery, so many months in which trout may not be and are not caught, so that the angler's total catch over a full year may be less; this for the sake of the fish. And for the sake of the angler it is best to pick a closed time when the trout are in poor condition and least inclined to respond to attractive angling methods. This means the winter months and leaves spring and summer and early fall as the trout fisher's season; but not too early in the spring nor too late in the fall, or the rest cannot be long enough for the fish. I have never felt that the Pacific coast cutthroats are given a fair chance. Their British Columbia open season runs from March first to November fifteenth in nontidal waters and all the year round in tidal waters. March fifteenth to October fifteenth in all waters should be enough, and more than enough, time for the anglers to do their work.

Yet I have fished for trout in March and greatly loved the fishing. There is a breathless expectancy about the start of a new season. Fishing the big steelhead flies through the pools in January and February, one may feel and see fine trout again and again. Sometimes a run of small steelhead is in, fish just under the five-pound mark, which makes them safe for the time being. I have seen the Main Island Pool so full of these in February that one dared not let the fly rest near the head or in the lesser runs at all, but had to fish only the flattening of the heavy water toward the tail—I went out eagerly on March first that year.

March is a good month for fishing beaver ponds. The water is high then for trout to climb into them from the lakes, and the shallow reservoirs, almost motionless, warm more quickly to release creatures still held by winter cold in other waters. If you are a fisherman at all or a woodsman at all, you have to like beaver ponds. Their variety of size and shape is almost infinite: they may be as large as full-sized lakes or nothing more than mudholes in tiny creeks; they may be sloughs cutting back from the head of a big lake; they may be whole segments of a lake or wandering backwaters from a river or a series of fine, flowing pools. Always there are deciduous trees around them, alder and willow, perhaps crab apple and barberry. Always the water seems rich, with deep pockets of mystery and a promise of big fish. Because the water looks fit for them, I often think of huge bass and pike laying in wait under the lily pads or among the waterlogged sticks on the bottom. In western waters they aren't there—only trout. But several times I have worked a good fly over a likely place and seen a fish surge at it with all the wicked swiftness of pike or bass. Once it was a cutthroat trout, monstrous-headed, black-backed, cruel-jawed, his body nowhere wider than between his gill covers, nowhere deeper than the depth of his head; he weighed three pounds for his hungry twenty-eight-inch length. Once it was another type of cutthroat, green-backed, white-bellied, strong and altogether perfect; his hog-backed eighteen inches weighed three pounds, and five others exactly like him came in the next dozen casts.

But at the start of the season I always remember a beaver pond that cut back from the Anutz River, above Nimpkish Lake. With Tommy Dickinson I started several seasons there, creeping on cold gray days into a slimy, fire-blackened dugout whose sole virtue was that it floated with the seats above water—that was a real virtue, because it was no craft to stand up in. The trout seemed to be schooled at that time. They were not big fish, and we caught nothing that would quite draw down to the two-pound mark; but they were clean and bright and sufficiently uncertain to be interesting. Sometimes the ponds were covered with a hatch of small blue May flies, and the schools cruised swiftly among them and responded eagerly to a small dry fly. At other times the ponds were still and seemed empty of fish; yet one could find them with a slow, deep wet fly or, strangely, with the same small dry fly. I remember two dry-fly patterns that I used there, a blue quill variant and that old chalk-stream stand-by, Tup's indispensable; it seemed strange to be setting that one out from a crazy dugout among the beaver houses under the white spires of drowned cedar trees.

There can be sunny days in March, mild and full of spring, but I do not think of such days when I think of March trout fishing. Instead, I remember a day of cold, heavy rain driven by an equinoctial gale that lifted spray from the crests of the current waves. I was standing thigh deep in the Sandy Pool, a few steps above the mouth of the little creek that comes in on the south side. Suddenly there were May flies on the water, out-of-place creatures on the black surface, torn at by the wind, seeming to cling with their feet to keep from being blown away upstream. A big trout rose untidily, then another smaller one, then another. I changed quickly from my wet fly and began to cover the rises. The wind picked my fly away from where I had tried to drop it above the big fish, hurled it upstream and in toward the bank, picked it up again and dropped it almost in the rings of a rising fish. I caught that fish and tried a hundred casts to cover the big fish; when I did cover him, he wouldn't come up to it. I tried again, and again he let it go by, rising contemptuously to a natural fly. I raised the rod top, and the wind caught the line and flicked the fly over above him again. This time he took, and I felt the small hook solidly into him. As he came to the net, the rain turned to sleet, and a great Douglas fir crashed down on the far bank of the river. But I fished on until dusk, when the hatch failed, and caught fish steadily. Then I came up out of the water and turned my face into the wind for home and a March fireside.

There is never the hardness and bitter cold of winter fishing in March, but the month has a wild competitive savagery of strength suddenly aroused from sleep. Under it, somewhere, the alevins shelter and grow.

House Hunting

When Ann and I first decided to get married, we did not worry greatly about where we should live or how. In Canada, we knew, and not in a city. The rest would take care of itself; after all, the first place need not be the last, and people always had found places to live. Since our freedom of choice was practically unlimited by any other factor, it seemed sensible enough to look for a place in good hunting and fishing country. Years of living with prospectors and trappers and stump ranchers had even persuaded me there was good economic reason for doing so, and I had known more than one household where regular visits to the butcher shop were considered outright self-indulgence, bordering on immorality when there was meat to be found in the woods and streams. I am not quite sure now whether I had actually adopted this belief myself or whether it was convenient to have an economic justification for hunting and fishing; but I know that for a long while I reckoned an empty larder the signal to go and look out a rod or a rifle.

We were not worrying, as I say. We were mainly concerned about getting married and we were more than satisfied that we could solve any and every problem that came up after that. But as time went on, I began to worry a little, all by myself. Ann was living and working in Seattle and would be until we were married; I was going my way about Vancouver Island, and Vancouver Island was where we would live, certainly at first. So the business of finding a house was rather squarely up to me. The prospect was a little frightening. I had never owned a house other than a cabin or rented a house or paid much attention to houses. I doubted whether I knew what to look for, and it seemed as though a house should be chosen to suit the fancies and foibles of a wife rather than those of a husband.

This problem was fairly well forward in my mind toward the end of March, 1933. I had spent the winter hunting cougars, trying to polish my knowledge of them to the point that would let me write a book, and now the snow was gone and the best of the hunting was over. Reg Pidcock came along then and reminded me of my promise to go up and fish for steelhead with him in the Campbell.

"Heck," I said, "I've got to start in and write a book."

"You've got all summer for that," he said. "Besides, I want to see if you can catch steelhead. It takes a good fisherman to catch steelhead."

"I'll catch 'em, if they're there." The implied doubt of my competence was more than enough excuse to delay the painful start of a new book. "When do we start?"

"Right now," Reg said. And we got in the car and went.

Reg is a bachelor of sixty or so, a retired logger and a native son of Vancouver Island. He loves hunting and fishing with a deep and quiet intensity grown out of a lifetime of taking both sports for granted. He lived then and lives now on the bank of the Campbell River, five or ten minutes' walk below the Sandy Pool. The Sandy Pool, naturally enough, was the first place he took me to on the morning after we arrived, and he left me there to see what I could do while he went to arrange about getting a boat for later fishing.

I could see at once that it was a truly great pool, one of the rare ones that deserve something more than a merely local name. In a sense it is two pools. The river comes roaring out of the rapid at the head in a strong race under the far bank, leaving a wide eddy that drops sand to a sloping beach. The race spreads gradually through a hundred yards or more until it covers the full width of the river bed just above the big rocks. Twenty or thirty yards below the rocks is the tail of this first pool, a wide place, shallow enough for big sunken boulders to mark the surface. Almost at once the shallow drops away into ten or twelve feet of strong water, and this is really the lower part of the pool, more properly called Pidcock's Pool. It is deep through fifty or sixty yards, then widens into a broad fine sweep of current, almost even from bank to bank and a wonderful lying place for fish.

I had been able to see all this as I walked up the length of the pool under the tall bare alders on the south bank of the river. The far bank was beautiful; great dark Douglas firs growing away from the water through a steep slope, dead maple leaves showing brown under their banked green. A single tree, one of the largest, had recently fallen into the river and was held there, almost squarely across the current, by the grip of its big flat roots in the gravel; thirty or forty feet of the top had broken away and gone on down the river, but there were still green branches on the upper side. I was in a hurry to start fishing; but I didn't know the pool, and Reg had been discouraging about its possibilities unless one had a boat. "You can fish from the sandy beach at the top, but the best fishing is at the lower end and it's much too deep to wade there."

I started just below the rapids and began to fish carefully down, casting well across and spinning a devon minnow, moving down two or three steps between each cast. Rather quickly I caught a dark and ugly fish which I turned loose. That was a disappointment because I had suspected all along that it might be rather late in the season, though Reg was confident we should find bright fish. It began to rain as I got down to the big rocks, an unkind rain, cold and with snow in it, and I could see the stirrings of a southeaster in the tops of the tall trees across the river. I came to the lower part of the pool and was already wet and cold. Wading in thigh boots was impossible. Alders and small brush grew right out to the edge of the water and the bottom was steeply sloping sand that crept away from underfoot until water flooded over the waders and one clambered, gasping, up the slope again.

I found a fairly clear spot on the bank at last and managed a good cast well out into the deep water just below the fallen tree. I paid out a little line to let the minnow well down, felt it start nicely on its swing; then a good fish took. He jumped after a short run, and I saw that he was silver and I wanted him badly. There was much trouble he could get into; a good run downstream would have taken him among the boulders in the heavy current of the tail or perhaps beyond and into the rapid. Bringing him back would have been difficult in any case, almost impossible if he had chosen to swing over to my own bank, because a matted clump of spirea grew out into the water fifty yards below me. For some reason he chose to fight well out in midstream, almost opposite me most of the time. Once he seemed inclined to run up under the log, but I brought him back from that and in a little while I had him.

The first fish from a strange water is always a triumph. It is difficult not to be greatly hopeful of a new stream, but one learns to temper hope with skepticism and loses nothing by doing so. The thrill of expectancy is there as one starts to fish, the fine delight of picking this place or that as a good lie, of visualizing the swim of bait or fly through a swell of dark current or across the eddy behind a dimly seen rock. And then, when a fish comes up and is caught, there is a surprised sense of achievement, a feeling that something new has been found and is held proved for the future—one will never again fish through that spot without hope and confidence.

I should have gone home then, I suppose, but I didn't. I fished on and hooked another good fish and lost him as he rolled on the surface twenty or thirty feet out from the bank. Then I did go home. Reg was in the house when I got there.

"Did you get the boat?" I asked. "That pool needs it."

"Sure. We'll take it up tomorrow. How did you make out?"

"I got one."

"No," he said. "Did you?" He came out, and I showed him the fish.

"You did all right; I didn't think you'd have much chance without the boat."

"Lost another," I said. "If I hadn't been so wet, I'd have tried it a while longer."

"You'd better come in and take a hot bath. I'll have supper on by the time you're ready."

The bath was really hot, and the bathroom was steamy and warm. As I lay in the water, I realized slowly that in six years on Vancouver Island this was the first house I had been in that had proper plumbing —running hot and cold water, bathtub, wash basin, inside toilet. The rest of the house was good too. It had a full basement, a small comfortable living room with an open fireplace, a neat kitchen with the sink just off it in a convenient pantry, two downstairs bedrooms and a large attic. But I did not immediately connect all this comfort with my search for a house. I don't think I had seriously considered Campbell River as a place to live; it had seemed to me a place where tourists came to fish for tyee salmon, and tourist places too seldom have a real life of their own.

As I fished and lived with Reg during the next few days, I began to think more sensibly. There was more to Reg's place than a comfortable house; there were ten or twelve acres of pasture land and alders, a good red barn, an orchard, a small vegetable garden with an asparagus bed and the fine river flowing by. There was more to Campbell River than the tourists; there were quiet, fine people there, fishing, farming, logging, running garages and stores, some of them attending to the tourists for two or three months in the year, but all very much concerned with other things through the rest of the time. And there was more to the fishing than just the Sandy Pool. There was the Canyon and the Islands, the tidal water below the bridge and a whole world of lakes and streams above the falls in the Campbell; good hunting country, too.

There are few men like Reg, in Campbell River or anywhere. I have fished and hunted and cut wood and lived alongside him for ten years now and I have never known him as anything but generous and gentle and overfair. This very afternoon I am going up to the Sandy Pool with him. He will fish the minnow, and I shall follow him down with the fly, and probably we shall both catch steelhead, because the river is in comfortable shape. Those fishing days in 1933 were wonderful. From the boat we caught many fish in the Sandy Pool and learned, in some surprise, that they were nearly all lying just above or just below the fallen tree—rather interesting evidence of the adaptability of migratory fish, because they had seldom held in that part of the pool before, and since 1935, when the tree went out, they have gone back to their old lying places at the tail of the pool. We went up and fished the Canyon Pool, and I caught two beautiful fish there, then hooked bottom about forty yards out and broke a brand new line at the rod top.

The next day after that was the last day, and we went to the Sandy Pool again. We wanted fish to take back to Comox with us and felt sure we could get them. It didn't occur to me to worry about my line. It was brand new, twelve pounds breaking strain, and I had had a hundred and thirty yards of it on the reel, so there was plenty left. We started in just above the fallen tree and hooked the first fish almost at once. He was a good one, about fifteen pounds and bright, and he ran strongly down to get under the tree. I tried to hold him, actually did hold him and felt him coming back to me, then the line broke.

"Damn it," I said. "Held him too hard."

"No," Reg said. "Your line's too light. That's a foolish little line to use for steelhead."

"It casts well and I've held plenty of them with it the last few days. It's just that I didn't feel this one right. Too clumsy."

So I cast again and hooked another, a little fish of six pounds which I handled lightly and Reg netted for me. Two or three casts later—the whole of this affair took only a very short time—I hooked yet another, a fish of about ten pounds, and he also went down for the tree. But I held him and humored him up, and at last Reg slipped the net under him. "This one's ours anyway," he said as he lifted. He swung the long handle to bring the fish into the boat, but there was a faulty place in the net and the fish slipped through, into the water, and the line broke again.

"Told you that line was no good," Reg said.

"Don't blame my line," I said. "It's your net that's bad."

"Well, you'd better get the next one if we're going to have anything to take down with us. How many fish do you think there are in this pool anyway?"

I hooked the next one without much difficulty, steered him gently away from the log, brought him almost up to the boat, humored him through two or three short runs and decided he was about ready for the net. Then the line broke once again. This time there was nothing at all to confuse the issue; it was a bad line and I knew it was a bad line. Reg didn't say a word. I sat down in the boat and began to take the line apart, pulling gently on it between thumb and forefinger of each hand until I had broken away ten or twelve yards in small pieces. Then it became decently strong again.

"A fisherman like you ought to know better than fish with a line like that," Reg said.

"It's a new line," I told him. "Never been used till I came up here this time." But I knew that didn't let me out.

That, I suppose, was a fairly depressing afternoon of fishing; we didn't even hook another fish. But even so, it must have had something, because on the way home I asked Reg, "How's chances to rent your house this summer?"

I rented it that summer, and Ann and I lived there for three good years after, until we bought the house we now live in and moved a hundred yards farther up the river.

Picking Favorites

Two or three days ago the editor of a sporting magazine wrote and asked me to name my favorite trout flies, wet, dry and streamer, and my favorite trout water. That sounds straightforward enough; a man ought to be able to answer questions like that almost without thinking. But I found myself mulling them over and over. I'd be thinking while I milked the cow, thinking while I was up the river, thinking in the bathtub or while the children were saying their prayers, or even in court while one of the boys from our local Tortilla Flat was explaining how he came to have a couple of extra beers Saturday night and set himself up against the uniformed force of the law. At the end of something like a week of odd-moment thinking, I sent in my answers; and I found that two of the flies I had named were old favorites that I hadn't used for years. They were good flies, the Gammarus fly and the brown and white bi-visible to be exact, but I know they'll catch fish under most conditions, so I don't bother with them much.

That made me wonder again: Just what is a favorite fly, one you use or one you don't use? The answer is that it's neither, but the one you'd fall back on if you were to have no other, something like the one book you'd take along to a desert island. I found myself answering that one too, back in 1939 when I thought I'd get myself into a fighting army within a matter of days. I didn't make the army, but if I had, I should have taken with me Taine's *History of English Literature*. It's a good long book, thirteen or fourteen hundred pages, packed with quotations and references that would call back to memory a thousand other books and give a taste of something for almost any need or mood. But you can't say all that for some particular fly or even for some particular trout water. Generally I choose or make a fly because it fits an idea. And my favorite fishing water would always be the one I know best. For some reason there is more pleasure in catching a fish where you have caught one before and know one ought to be lying than in catching one, more or less blind, from an unknown water. And obviously there must be greater pleasure and merit in learning a new thing about a well-known stream than in learning half a dozen new things in one day about a strange water.

There is something foolish about trying to name favorites and ideals —the whole business has the schoolgirl's giggle strongly in it. Yet there is a lot in it that appeals to human nature. There must be, because we go on year after year naming beauty queens and most useful ballplayers and men of the year and most worthy citizens, and there's never much let-up of interest. Much of the appeal is in the scope given the imagination: think of any girl you like, any one at all; look the whole world over for your man; name any fly you like of all the thousands or millions that anglers have made from silk and wool and hairs and feathers. For once your mind can really go to town, without any petty limits at all. And sometimes the choice is easy and clear—Joe DiMaggio in baseball a couple of years ago for instance. I have a fly like that, a natural—Preston Jennings's Lord Iris for winter steelhead. It must be about three seasons now since I tied one on to a 4/5 leader and I've hardly wetted another fly for winter steelhead since then. That fly catches fish, and that's all I need to know for winter steelhead, because I think there is so much more in the way the fly is worked for them than in the pattern itself that I don't feel a need for change.

The selection-of-favorites racket can become contentious at times. King Arthur's knights put on some ferocious shows to decide just who was the ideal girl, and presumably the zoot-suited knights of today feel as strongly about favorite hepcats. The sports writers have had their prickings of conscience some years about picking Joe Gordon over Ted Williams or vice versa. I don't think I could get fighting mad over a choice of flies, but talking up one's favorite fishing water—well, that's something else again. I'm likely to get in trouble right at the start, because I automatically rule out all lakes and the salt water; only a river can give what I really want.

When it comes to choosing between rivers of different types I feel less sure. I have never yet seen a river that I could not love. Moving water, even in a pipeline or a flume, has a fascinating vitality. It has power and grace and associations. It has a thousand colors and a thousand shapes, yet it follows laws so definite that the tiniest streamlet is an exact replica of a great river. This has always been important to me. I can lie for an hour at a time and watch the flow of a little stream, dropping pieces of dry sticks into it to trace the current movements, following the midwater drift of clumps of diatoms or algae torn from the bottom, marking the way sand builds behind a pebble and the current eddies there. It is easy, in the mind, to magnify such a stream to the proportions of a full river, and it is highly profitable for an angler to do so, because the secret vagaries of current are clearly revealed here. Later, drifting a sunk fly past the edge of a big boulder, it may be valuable to remember how the current sucked in and turned back on the downstream side of the pebble in the streamlet.

Very often there is small-scale fish life in the little stream. On the Pacific coast probably there will be orange-tailed coho salmon fry, swift and active little fish that sample every passing fragment of drift. It is not so safe to magnify these into full-scale trout, for the trout's movements will be slower and more closely circumscribed; but there is much to be learned from the choice of a lie or the approach to a morsel of plankton. In a small stream's pools it is possible also to watch the free and natural movement of water insects, the crawling caddis-fly and stone-fly nymphs, the flat May-fly nymphs that cling by preference to the underside of stones, free-swimming Callibeatis, quick and fussy beetles, menacing water striders. This also is trout fisher's education and any man's entertainment.

A fold or break of current, a burst of bubbles or the ripple of a stone in a little stream, sharply and vividly matched to some known part of a big river, releases in me a flood of satisfaction that must, I think, be akin to that which a philosopher feels as his mind is opened to a profound truth. I feel larger and better and stronger for it in ways that have nothing to do with any common gain in practical knowledge. I have tried to rationalize this as growing from a sense of unity between the great and the small or perhaps merely from the godlike position that finds a full, wide river between my feet, my own body magnified as my mind has magnified the stream. Certainly there is a spell there that I break reluctantly and that hangs with me as I turn away to walk toward home across the fields or through the woods; and perhaps one day I may know truly what and why it is.

All these qualities of moving water help make up my preference for rivers over other fishing places. Next to fishing a river I think I should choose to wade the surf of a California beach and hurl a long line out into it to find what is there; but that too is moving water, and I have never tried surf fishing, so I don't really know. Of rivers I should always choose clear ones; not the glass clearness of the mountain streams nor the peat-brown clearness of Scottish burns, but something between the two, a clearness that gives the water its proper depth.

That is the clearness of the English chalk streams and also the clearness of Pacific coast rivers below the lakes, a satisfying, natural clearness, revealing and yet not staring.

Chalk-stream fishing is beautiful. The gentle, chuckling current, the long, trailing wave of dark-green weeds, the fine trees and rich meadows, all these form a lovely setting. The trout themselves are fast and strong and wise, and they rise with noble freedom to the droves of natural flies that sail the river's surface. Ancient stone bridges, weirs and hatch holes and deep-ditched carriers all make for variety in the fishing. It is difficult to name any preference ahead of chalk-stream fishing, and to do so is to deny the water that most challenges every phase of an angler's skill. And yet, I like to wade. I like to reach out across a big river; I like to use the wet fly sometimes; I like the exciting possibilities of sea-run fishing and the sharp seasonal changes that test one's most intimate knowledge of rivers open to the sea. I like winter fishing and I like, perhaps perversely, to know that I am fishing water open to all men, not preserved for a favored few. No waters that I know fill all these conditions more exactly than do the rivers of Vancouver Island.

I have said that I like to wade. You can wade the English chalk streams (many anglers do so), but it is wise to wade them as little as possible because the big brown trout are easily disturbed, and clumsy wading may put a big fish down from surface feeding for several days. Besides, there is no challenge to chalk-stream wading; the bottom is easy and the current smooth and even. The young rivers of Vancouver Island have strong, white water piling over rapids, and there is dark, gliding depth in many of their pools. Generally these rivers have floors of tumbled, round boulders, slippery and treacherous under fast water, dismaying to the overcautious, positively dangerous to the clumsy. Very often it is necessary to wade a deep run of really fast water to reach good fishing. Sometimes one has to work and shift position for an hour or more with body braced into a little dam that builds the water a foot higher on the upstream side. The sound and feel and look of all this is satisfying. It is a test of strength and confidence, and the rewards are great. The water is free and open to all, but there can still be fair and equal ways of opening a little more to yourself than to the next man.

Not that I am a really bold wader. I wear breast-high waders and use them to their limit when I need to. Occasionally I use them a little beyond the limit, and I have more than once ridden with them through a length of water that was stronger than I judged it. Down in Oregon I believe there are men who don't find mere waders enough. They wear also waterproof windbreakers, securely zipped up to the neck and drawn tight over their high waders; then, when need arises, they plant their feet firmly and actually shoulder their way neck-deep across a fast run. I haven't got a waterproof windbreaker and, though I sometimes think of getting one, I should prefer to watch the exact technique of these artists once or twice before I try it out. The possibilities are attractive—for summer fishing anyway.

Chalk-stream fishing gives some perfect moments of sport that are given by no other type of fishing. There is the difficult stalk of a big fish rising surely in an awkward place; the clear visibility of so many of the fish one covers or attempts to cover; the certainty that they are wise fish, educated to nice distinctions; above all the quiet loveliness of the meadows during the evening rise and their sweet, heavy richness in the early summer months. And a fly-fisherman must always love the brown trout for the free riser that he is.

There is evening peace, too, on the western rivers, though it is threatened sometimes by the prospect of a hard trip home. They have a richness directly and peculiarly their own—the glory of the salmon runs. Their beauty has a rugged strength and leaping vitality of youth rather than any calm serenity of mellowed age. Something of this is in western fish also. The golden cutthroat seems always such a workman-like fish. He goes after his food with a slashing ferocity, hunting it through the tide flats, mounting the rapids to meet it where white water sweeps it from the rocks above the pools. The rainbow is an individualist, a pioneer searching always wider scope; mere rivers confine him, and he goes out with the salmon into the breadth of the sea, to grow himself to the silvered nobility of the steelhead.

Both types of river test a fisherman, the one more subtly than the other. But there are other kinds of trout waters, each with its own joys and fascinations. I have narrowed my choice, inevitably, I think, to the types I know best. In my earliest fishing years I fished between the chalk hills of Dorset until any change in the river Frome or the fish that swam in it or the duns that hatched from its weed beds marked itself instantly upon my mind. In the years since then I have fished one or two Vancouver Island rivers until I know them as well as I know the Frome; I feel at home on them, and everything I see in them or about them has its meaning for me, as the life of the Frome meadows had. These waters are favorites because they are the waters I know best; the choice is an artificial one really, having little to do with the merits of the streams themselves measured against the qualities and merits of other streams. In the same way and for the same reasons my final choice is an artificial one. Because I go out to find her fresh-run steelheads on a named day in December; because I know her big cutthroats will chase the humpback fry in April and climb the river again behind the first of the adult humpbacks in August; because the little summer steelhead lie thick in the Island Pools in May; because I live beside her and can learn something new about her each time I go out, my favorite trout stream is—the Campbell.

APRIL

Whatever one may say of March, April is the true opening month of the trout season. I have caught plenty of out-of-condition trout in April, brown trout not yet built back to shape by the release of underwater life in the warmer temperatures, cutthroats hardly finished with their spawning, rainbows full ripe and ready to begin theirs. April days can be as cold and wet and miserable with wind as December days. April rivers can be swollen and thick with flood. But April is still as beautiful as its name, the true spring month that breaks our world out of winter into something nearly summer. It could not be right to keep anglers away from their rivers at such a time, and I think they seldom are kept away, unless by the ice of a high altitude or a late year.

There is a tale that the willow and the alder are two anglers who offended the powers by fishing on Sunday and were transformed, to stand beside the river evermore. It would have been in April, I think, that this happened. The alder woods are a bright, fresh mist of pale green then; the willow whips are tall and supple, with the sap swelling under green and yellow bark and red and white buds thrusting forth. April, perhaps because it is the spring month, is a month of little pictures vividly remembered. I remember the high, wild, crying wedges of geese swinging splendidly northward, sometimes with the sunlight bright on their wings; and once, at dusk, three geese circling the house and looking for a place to light. I remember the bright mating plumage of the mallards and the drake mergansers all up and down the river and once, along the road, the first goldfinch of the year all black and sunlit yellow just ahead of me. I remember the approach to the Sandy Pool—under the white-barked alders a floor of freshet-swept sand pierced by bleeding heart and a thousand trilliums and the pink Easter lilies just breaking out of bud. Once, going up to the Canyon Pool along the far bank of the river, I crossed a little swamp where skunk cabbage flowers sprang strongly from black ooze in spaced and loveliest yellow. There is pink almond blossom in April and heavy white cherry blossom against blue and white skies. There are killdeer and yellowlegs on the tide flats, meadow larks on the fence posts, red-winged blackbirds in the swamps. Not to go out and meet all this would be a denial of the year's hope.

The humpback fry are out in the Campbell in April—other fry too, for that matter—but one notices the humpbacks because of their bright silver scales quite without parr marks. It seems to me I always see them first swimming about in the current within inches of my waders, half a dozen quick little fish, heads upstream, holding maybe, but going down very shortly. Then I look harder and see others, whole schools clustered in the eddies. The big cutthroats find them out and feed greedily—it pays to drop a fly in places where no fish lies through the rest of the year. Obviously a silver-bodied fly is the thing, fished fast; but that is a shade too obvious. It will take fish, yes, and sometimes take them better than anything else. But the cutthroats are seldom as single-minded as they seem. Many times I have opened up a catch of ten or twelve fish, taken in April when the river was full of salmon fry, and found that only one or two of my fish had been really feeding on fry, and sometimes not even one or two. Of the others, several perhaps would have fry in them, but well mixed with other feed, and at least half the catch would have been concerned with anything and everything except fry—May flies, caddis grubs, beetles, caterpillars, bees, even bullheads, but not fry. I suspect that free-swimming fry are overquick and difficult to catch. Not every fish can be bothered with them when the current brings other and better things straight to the open jaws.

So I seldom fish my silver fly very fast; I let it drift weakly, crossing the current but making no headway against it, tumbling down rather and, I like to think, rolling clear over sometimes. And I do not stay always with the silver fly or even with the wet fly. The trout are feeding, on the lookout, and I have risen April fish after April fish to the dry fly in pools where every little backwater was packed with fry.

I remember April fishing days, like other April happenings, in quick sunlit flashes. I remember an English garden, built narrowly along a trout stream, a thorn hedge, a narrow border, an edge of lawn, a red-graveled path, another strip of lawn, and then the river, and on the far bank, tall and graceful willows in wild growth. The river was shallow and straight through the garden, broken into three little falls by logs staked across it. Close under the far side of the center fall, in a deeper place where the bubbles showed white in green water, I could see the long dark shape of a big trout. He was a thin fish with a great wedge-shaped head, and he showed up very clearly against the pale sand of

the river bottom. Grandfather, walking up the garden a few days earlier, had seen him and decided that he was a ne'er-do-well, a cannibal,
who must be taken out by any method; and I was ordered to attend to
the matter.

I had a medium olive quill tied on a No. 16 hook—double-o, we
called it—and 4X gut. The chance of moving the fish to that, clear up
from the bottom, didn't seem very great, but at least he deserved his
chance. I dropped down on one knee and began to let out line in false
casts. Then I saw the other fish, a pale, thick, hog-backed fish lying
two or three feet over from the dark fish, well up in the water, his nose
almost touching the little log that made the fall. As I watched, his
body tilted slightly and his nose just broke water to suck in a fly.

I thought quickly over all the implications and complications; there
were plenty of both. The pale fish was really big and really beautiful—
I wanted him badly. He was a stranger, perhaps not yet settled into a
permanent summer holt, and if I left him or disturbed him this time I
might not find him again. He was difficult; the fall of water over the
log made a close back eddy, perhaps five or six inches wide and running the full length of the little fall. He was taking flies held in this
back eddy, and to catch him, I must drop my first cast so that the fly
pitched almost exactly on his nose, with a slack line behind it to delay
the pull of the stream which would eventually whip the fly out of the
eddy in an unnatural drag that would scare the wits out of him. I
considered a longer cast above the fall that would let the fly drift down
on him, but decided against that because the fly might be drowned or,
worse still, the longer drift might use up the precious slack line and
bring the drag on the fly just as it came into his vision.

Then there was Grandfather to be considered. Grandfather wanted
his cannibal caught and would have a good deal to say about it if he
was not caught—Grandfather hadn't a very high opinion of fishing as
a sport, though he felt that one possibly had some excuse for indulging
in it if one did a good job. Catching the pale fish would almost certainly disturb the cannibal and make him impossible to move. But I
still wanted the pale fish and I promised myself that the affair of the
cannibal would work itself out somehow.

I lengthened my line and dropped the fly on the water once, well
behind both fish. The pale fish came up in one of his tiny, tidy, fastidi-
ous rises as I did so; his back looked six inches wide, which it was not
and could not have been, but the impression made me want him still
more. I let out more line, then took my long chance and aimed the fly
for the narrow eddy. It came perfectly to the water, perhaps three
inches to one side of his nose. He turned to it slowly, so slowly that I
knew from the poise and set of his body rather than from actual

movement that he was interested. The little olive danced there on the curling water in the April sunlight; I moved my rod point cautiously to delay the drag of the line until the last possible moment. Then he came, confidently and calmly, and the fly was gone. For a tiny fraction of time his back was broad again and quite still in the bright water. Then I touched the hook home. He did the right thing, by Grandfather and by me. Instead of turning across or down he went straight up, over the log like an explosion and on almost to the tail of a fine weed bed, where the rod turned him. I brought him back, and he ran again as he felt his tail come out over the log. Three times he did that; then I tumbled him down, and we fought it out in water well below the cannibal's lie. On the bank he was as perfect as I had hoped he would be, his red spots splendid against his pale coat, his body far too thick for my hand's grip.

And the black fish was still where he had been. I dried the fly and dropped it over him, but he made no move. I tried it again, half a dozen times, then a freak of the current smoothed the surface and I saw his head most clearly. Around the eye there was a circle of dead whiteness; I knew he was blind. I drowned the fly and dropped it to him again, several times. Once he moved, the slight restless movement that brown trout make when they are deciding it's about time to move out for some favorite hiding place. I crept back from the bank and made myself wait for ten or fifteen minutes, then changed the little dry fly to a much larger wet fly, for the small hook would not sink down to him. The big fly went down well, and I tried drifting it a foot or two away from him at first, hoping he would sense it and come across. I brought it closer and closer to him with each cast, and still he would not move. Then I dropped it squarely above him. It sank and slid down; it brushed his nose so that he turned away; it crept along his body, passed his tail—then he turned like a pike, his great white mouth opened and he had it. Grandfather looked over both fish as they lay in state on the hall table and was impressed.

Two other April days come sharply into my mind, and both are sunny days of fish seen clearly in bright April water. On the Nimpkish River we kept the gas boats tied to a rough landing two or three hundred yards below the house. One morning we went down to work on them, and as we worked, a good fish rose again and again with solemn, solid plops close under the bushes just above us. Buster said at last, "Go and catch him."

I started on him, using a small iron blue; and as he came to it, another fish rose twenty or thirty yards farther up. I netted the first fish, a green-backed, solid cutthroat of two and a half pounds. Little dark-blue May flies poured down the river in a narrow stream close under the bushes, and the second fish still rose. I went up to him, and as I cast for him, a third fish rose twenty yards beyond him. An hour later I came out of the water opposite the house, and I had with me ten white-bellied, green-backed cutthroats with not an inch in length nor a quarter of a pound in weight between them. I laid them out in the sunlight on the short grass of the bank. Buster was coming up to the house for lunch and saw me there. "You're a hell of a guy," he said. "I ought to have known better than let you go off the job." Then he came closer and saw the fish. "Oh, boy!" he said softly. "Oh, boy!"

Since Ann and I have filled the house with children, we go up the river together too seldom. But there was an April day a year or two ago when we arranged things and went. "We shan't find much," I said. "The fish seem to have moved up out of the Island Pools this year. I think the river's low for them. But it's a swell day and it will be fun up there."

So I went out into the main pool and hooked almost at once a thick golden cutthroat that looked to me like a four-pounder and fought me till I was trembling with the fear that I should never get him to the scales to find out. I have caught only one sea-run cutthroat of over four pounds in the Campbell, and he doesn't count because I was fishing for steelhead when he took hold. The fish came to the net at last, and I carried him proudly ashore. "He's a four-pounder," I told Ann.

She shook her head. "I don't think so. I've seen you catch them as big as that before."

The scales made him three and three-quarter pounds.

I fished lazily, bouncing a deer-hair dry fly down over the fast water of the pool, and caught other fish. We lay in the sun and ate lunch and talked. I went far out on the bar at last, because it seems wrong to go all the way up to the Islands and not try it out properly, however lazy the day. Just above the main run a great, bright steelhead took my fly. He seemed to love the fast, clear water and ran and played in it with little care for all I could do with my trout rod. Ann saw me in trouble and came out along the bar toward me. The fish came back, more or less of his own free will, and carelessly let himself into slack water behind a rock. I held hard, reached down and slipped a finger in his gills. I held him up, looking back toward Ann against the sun, then freed the hook and slipped him back. I heard Ann laugh and knew that the Island Pool was a good place to be on a spring day.

H. M. Greenhill

As I look back on them now it seems to me that my male elders in Dorset fell into two astonishingly well-defined groups. There were the Victorians, men in their seventies and eighties: Grandfather and his two brothers; Thomas Hardy; Squire Sheridan, Grandfather's neighbor; Mr. Shepherd, the village carpenter; Knight, the river keeper on the club water. These make a cross section of examples. They were small, spare, wiry men, usually with short gray beards—though Hardy and my two great-uncles had only gray mustaches—very quick and keen, both physically and mentally. Dorset is kind to old men, or was before the world wars began. Squire Sheridan was well over eighty when I last saw him, but he was standing waist deep in the river, cutting weeds with great sweeping strokes of his scythe. Grandfather had to break his ankle twice in the hills to be convinced that eighty is too old for hard shooting days. Knight was walking his twelve or fourteen miles a day through the water meadows, summer and winter, when he was well into the eighties. Hardy, though the scope of his labors bore little relation to that of these mere mortals, was in no greater haste to lay down his burden than they were; his greatness did not fail him in his lifetime and his stature grows steadily now that he is dead.

Among these men there was something of the closeness that there is among the elder citizens of an American small town. Grandfather and my great-uncles had been at Dorchester Grammar School with Hardy, and though the way of the three brothers branched widely from Hardy's way after their school days, there was much that held them together. Grandfather loved Dorset county as Hardy loved Dorset people and he respected Hardy with a sincerity that was wholly admirable in such a practical and autocratic old gentleman. I think he rarely missed a quarterly teatime visit to Max Gate, and I know that when he took me with him, we entered the house and met the great and gentle little man with a humility that seemed to reduce Grandfather to my own schoolboy age. Between Grandfather and Squire Brinsley Sheridan there was a different respect, grudging and born out of a lifetime of disagreements, but real. Mr. Shepherd and Grandfather met squarely as equals, craftsman to trader, though one was employer and the other employed, and I think the fraternity of old age was stronger between these two than between any of the others. Knight was Knight, the friend of every keen fisherman, wise in the life of his water meadows and a truer countryman than any of the others. Knight could not read or write properly, and he regretted it. Once he told me, "I ain't never learned 'ee. My zister, her can do 'un, but her beant so oold as I be. You zee, when they passed this 'ere law 'bout 'avin' to 'ave schoolin' it du zeem I were just too old for 'un." I often wondered how great was the loss through that, not Knight's loss, for he was great in his work as were the other Victorians I have listed, but the country's. Sixty years of walking the meadows is a long time, sixty years of knowing birds and beasts and fish and seeing them with sharp gray eyes that never needed spectacles is time to have yielded much knowledge. An educated Knight might have been another such as William Lunn, the inspired keeper and manager of the Houghton Club water. He might even have been a Gilbert White or a Jefferies.

The other group of my elders was Edwardian, as clearly as Grandfather's group was Victorian. They were big, heavy, broad-shouldered men, often soldiers, black-mustached and deep-voiced, lovers of all forms of sport. Nearly all of them were magnificent with the shotgun, most of them were cricketers, and some were good fishermen. I can think easily over a long list of names—Colonel Saunders, Major Radclyffe, the Hambro brothers of banking fame, my uncle Alec who died of wounds in 1919 and John Kelly, the wonderful Irish gardener who was as truly a Dorset man as William Barnes himself. Of them all, none was truer to type than Major Greenhill, and from Greenhill I learned most of those things about fishing and wing shooting that a boy generally learns from his father.

The First World War took hold of my father when I was six years old and held him until he was killed at Bapaume in March, 1918. Nearly all my Mother's eleven brothers were kept busy during the war and for some years after. As a result, I grew up beside a fine trout stream and in the midst of good shooting country with only the crudest ideas of how to go about either business. I caught a few fish by most reprehensible methods and stalked rabbits and pigeons, even partridges and mallards, with a variety of weapons at once less effective and less artistic than the shotgun. In the summer of 1922, when I was fourteen, one of my uncles—the best and keenest fisherman of them all —was at home long enough to teach me the elements of dry-fly fishing. And during the Christmas holidays of the same year Greenhill came, it seemed to me from nowhere, and took over.

At that time Greenhill was already a heroic figure to me. He had always been held up to me as one of the best wing shots in England,

and I knew he was a fine salmon fisherman. He was a huge man, an inch or two over six feet and weighing about 220 pounds, which he seemed to carry mainly on his chest and shoulders. I had seen him play a brave part on the cricket field, lifting the ball in full-shouldered drives to bounce its way among the mounds of the cemetery. Seated in glory at the edge of the ring, I had watched him referee the army boxing tournaments. And now his talented bulk rested itself deep in one of the dining-room chairs, and his strong, heavy voice told Mother that he would look after my sporting education. Someone, he said, had to make up for the war.

He taught as good teachers do, by example, by opportune and unhurried explanation, by occasional strong direction. The strongest lesson he taught, though he never named it, was complete concentration on, and devotion to, the matter in hand. I learned quickly that if there was a chance of going shooting on a certain day, I must not tie myself to anything else; that while we were out I must see everything and know everything—the identity of birds by their flight, the line that rabbits would take in bolting from a certain place, any shift of wind, the change of a field from stubble to plow, any lowering or raising of the river by a farmer's manipulation of irrigation hatches. I must never tire, because I was younger and stronger in proportion to my weight than he was—a point that it was not difficult for me to recognize. No walk must be too long, no hour of creeping in wet meadows too painful, if there was a chance of a shot at the end of it. Above all, I must be ready when game flushed; I could miss and be forgiven, provided I offered no excuse for missing. But if I failed to get my gun off at a fair chance, I must walk with it unloaded through the rest of the day. Safety was provided for by an even stiffer penalty; if I fired a dangerous shot, if I failed to break my gun before climbing a fence or crossing a hedge, I must go home at once in disgrace. But this penalty was never invoked, because I had been already well trained in safety.

Such an account of penalties and forfeits makes our shooting days sound gloomy, but they were not. I made him angry perhaps half a dozen times in all the years we fished and shot together—two or three times because I was lazy or fainthearted, two or three times because I missed, through sheer carelessness, golden chances we had worked hard for, once because I lied to him. It was a simple thing, this last, yet it taught me clearly, as nothing else has, the urgency of being honest with yourself if you want to learn. I had planned to take the ferrets and terriers out one day to kill off the rats that infested a corn rick. The day turned out badly, with a southwesterly gale and driving rain, but I wanted to go anyway and I asked Greenhill to go with me. "No use," he said. "Rats won't bolt a day like this. You'll get your ferrets all bitten up and you'll just be wasting your time." I went anyway, with a couple of friends; and my favorite ferret got badly bitten, the rats wouldn't bolt and we finished the day with six or eight dead rats instead of a hundred or more. A few days later he asked me how it had been.

"All right," I said. "We didn't do badly."

Greenhill snorted. "Bet you didn't get half a dozen rats."

"Yes, we did," I said. "More than that."

"How many? Twenty? Thirty?"

I nodded. "About that," I said, and he said nothing more until the next day. Then he said, "You lied to me about those rats, young fellow. You only got six or seven the whole day."

I tried to get out of it, but there was no way. He was really angry then and so was I, angry and afraid. But what he meant was clear enough: rats and rabbits won't bolt well to ferrets on a bad day—that is a piece of knowledge by which one must be guided again and again in planning a day. Any exception to it is important, for it may disclose some other factor that has entered into the business. A lie such as I had told is aimed at the roots of useful knowledge.

One other incident taught me early just what sort of training I was under. Greenhill had a Labrador bitch named Dinah, and Dinah was a model retriever. By some standards she was too sedate and dignified and slow, but her calm eyes and mind missed nothing. Greenhill could stand and drop a dozen birds, with Dinah moving only her head behind him to watch the flight and fall of each one. Then, when the drive was finished, he would move her out, and she would pick up every one of them on her own, without help unless there happened to be an exceptionally bad runner. She was the same in the meadows, phlegmatic about the rise of a bird, unmoved by the shot, unconcerned about the retrieve until he ordered her out. Early one January we had a quick spell of hard weather, a light fall of snow and more frosts. Working the meadows for snipe, we found a flock of mallards on the river, stalked them and killed four. Two fell in the water on the far side of the river and were caught up by low-hanging willow branches. We picked up the other two, and I waited for him to send Dinah across. He didn't. Instead he said, "All right, young fellow, get on with it."

"Get on with what?"

"Go across and pick 'em up. It's too cold for Dinah; she's getting old."

The nearest bridge was a mile upstream, and the water was high and dirty in spite of the frosts.

"You mean swim?" I asked. "It's too cold."

"If you want to come out with me you do what I say and don't argue."

"I haven't got anything to dry myself with."

"You've got a handkerchief, haven't you?"

I took my clothes off and fetched the ducks, and the handkerchief did its job well enough. That wasn't the last time I worked for Dinah.

"She works hard enough for you," Greenhill said. "You can do something for her once in a while."

Because he infinitely preferred shooting and salmon fishing and because I knew my way about the river well enough, Greenhill did not come trout fishing with me very often at first. As a matter of fact I began, in my dry-fly man's arrogance, to discount him as a trout fisherman. My uncles and my father had, so far as I knew, used nothing but the dry fly on Grandfather's lengths of the Frome and the Wrackle and on the Club water as well. The uncle who taught me to fish had taught me only dry-fly fishing, and I was, at fourteen, a hidebound purist. To make matters worse, I got pretty good at the business and kept on improving steadily, which was natural enough because I had every opportunity to know the water well and had a fanatical keenness as well as a complete disregard for weather conditions or discomfort of any kind. Such things simply didn't register.

I am not sure just when or how I discovered that Greenhill was not a very experienced dry-fly fisherman. Certainly he never told me or admitted it by remotest inference, nor did he ever attempt to suggest that the wet fly was a better method. But I knew somehow; and after the original shock of surprise, the knowledge gave me a very pleasant sense of superiority—there was at least one thing in which I could match him. Greenhill took whatever offensiveness I had to offer—I can't remember any of it exactly, but I am sure it was plenty—and began to fish with me more often. He used the dry fly for the most part, out of respect for the unwritten rule of the water, but occasionally turned to the wet fly. Very offhandedly he began to explain to me and show me some of the difficulties and complications of wet-fly fishing. We treated it as something of a joke, a method to play with occasionally, just for a change. I was glad to keep it that way because I was in no hurry to lose my sense of superiority. Wet-fly fishing was chuck-and-chance-it, a fair-enough method for the little trout of the Scottish burns or the Devonshire streams, but mild sacrilege on a chalk stream, even on a minor edition of a chalk stream such as the Frome was. But unfortunately for my sense of superiority, I liked fishing and I liked to know about fish; watching Greenhill and trying the method occasionally myself I began to see that there were satisfactions and difficulties in it as great as those of dry-fly fishing; more important, trout responded differently to a fly moved across or against the current than they did to one floating on the surface. Fishing the wet fly, one found trout in unexpected places; they came to it sometimes over the top of weed beds in great smooth arrows of disturbed water that checked sharply into a boiling rise. The sudden direct pull of a fish on the line and back into the hand was fully as exciting as the gentle dimple in which a dry fly disappeared.

The Frome fish were every bit as shy as chalk-stream fish are likely to be—any clumsy approach would put a feeding fish down for the rest of that day and perhaps for longer. Fishing a dry fly, one learned to kneel and crawl upstream, spotting rises carefully, studying the approach, working carefully into position for the cast. Upstream nymph fishing was fascinating and profitable, as I already knew, and the upstream wet fly offered most of the same advantages, except that the fish usually turned to follow it downstream before taking and so would sometimes see the rod or simply turn in disgust from the too swift swimming of the fly. But Greenhill wanted me to fish the downstream wet fly, and that was really difficult with shy fish. It meant an altogether more intense form of crawling and creeping, a closer study of lies and approaches and current, longer and in some ways more accurate casting. Greenhill was good, and I wanted to be as good myself; so I began to work at it.

As soon as I had thoroughly committed myself to learning the method, Greenhill began to rule and guide my learning as he ruled what I did when we were shooting. I started out with one bad fault, an almost unbreakable habit of recovering line in my hand, developed by years of upstream fishing. This brought the fly across too fast and too shallow, and Greenhill, after a period of patient explanation, began to take the rod away from me whenever I fell in to it. In a little while we were fishing with only one rod between us, changing over whenever one or other of us hooked a fish and whenever I made a clumsy or careless cast or fished the fly badly. I became a respectable wet-fly fisherman rather quickly, and from then on Greenhill was little concerned about whether I fished wet or dry or with the nymph.

All this, I realize now, was his way of preparing me for salmon fishing. Greenhill was not by any means a rich man; he lived frugally in the barracks at Dorchester and spent what little money he had where it would give him the most of the sports he loved. He had a pair of beautiful guns and loaded his own cartridges. His salmon rods were greenheart that he had made up himself; he made all his own traces and flights and minnows and prawn tackles, though not, I think, his flies. The one extravagance he allowed himself was the renting of a stretch of salmon water on the lower reaches of the Frome, between

Wool and Wareham. During the season he fished there almost every day, alone or with his friend Charlie Baunton, with whom he shared the water.

At that time the Frome, like several other fine salmon rivers in the south of England, was slowly and painfully recovering after bad days. Early in the nineteenth century it had been a great river with a magnificent run of fish. Uncontrolled netting and some pollution had made it almost worthless, but evidently the run of fish was not quite killed out. I don't know the exact history of its recovery, whether the riparian owners bought off some of the nets, as they did on the Wye, or whether the scarcity of salmon simply discouraged the net fisherman, but the recovery was a fine thing. In the early 1920's there was a good run of fish in the spring months, and they were really large fish—over twenty pounds as often as not and thirty-pounders were common. One April, during the Easter holidays, Greenhill suddenly told me that I was to come salmon fishing with him, not just once or twice, but every day I wanted to. This was like a sudden opening of heaven's gate. For years I had listened to my uncle's talk of salmon fishing and read books about salmon fishing and dreamed dreams of it. Now I was to start fishing with the almost certain chance of really big fish, and I knew I should be learning the business properly.

The Frome is a slow, deep river in its lower reaches, and the meadows through which it runs are wilder and rougher than those farther up. Strong weeds and sedges grow up in the pasture land, and the irrigation ditches are deep and wide; the river was not tidal where we fished it, but as I remember it now the country had some measure of the bigness and wildness of the tide flats at the mouths of British Columbia rivers that I have known since. There were ravens there and big hawks and ducks and wading birds of many kinds. Small birds were there also, sedge warblers and reed buntings and black-headed buntings, pippits and pert wagtails; they sang and mated and nested in the reeds and the rough grass, the wagtails fussing and fluttering and strutting at the edge of the river. And always things were happening in the wide meadows and the willow beds: a nesting plover would be chasing a raven, or two ravens chasing a hawk; a polecat would be glimpsed hunting a hedge; or a sudden rush of wings would reveal a sparrow hawk's stoop at a bunting.

But the river itself was the greatest fascination. Its slow current hid things that I could only vaguely imagine: the lies of great pike and salmon, deep silent places from which they might fiercely turn at any moment to seize the fly or minnow or prawn that I dared to hang there. I was almost genuinely afraid at times, afraid of dragging the fly away from some crashing rise or of jamming the reel as a great fish jumped or of doing any of the hundred other things I could do to throw away a golden chance that might better have been in Greenhill's capable hands.

Wisely, Greenhill started me with the fly. The Frome is not a really good river for the fly; for the most part it is too slow and too deep for attractive fishing, though many fine fish have come to the torrish or Jock Scott or green highlander. But I was given the fly rod because it was easy—minnow and prawn were for those experienced and fortunate individuals who knew the bottom of the river as well as its surface and could handle them properly.

We started fishing at an off time. Fish were being caught in the pool below Bindon Mill. We heard about them and even saw them caught as we passed the mill each day. But in the rest of the river there was little moving; in a full week's fishing I had moved two fish to the fly, and Greenhill had felt perhaps five or six touch his prawn, only one of them hard enough to take out line. We had not even killed a good-sized pike, something I had hoped for, though Greenhill had warned me carefully that we were not fishing for pike and should not catch them unless we fished too fast for salmon. Before the end of the week I had tried prawn and minnow several times, gladly and hopefully, but they had done little more for me than the fly—one good hard pull to the minnow in the Railway Pool.

On the morning of the ninth day we got to the river late and found that Charlie Baunton had killed two beautiful fish on the fly before we got there. We caught nothing. On the tenth day we took out only the spinning rod and fished alternately. The Railway Pool was blank and so was the next pool below it. That brought us to the Ivy Pool, a deep pool where the fish sometimes lie well in under the bank in a sort of cave that the river has cut away. Greenhill worked his prawn into this place and hooked a fish. For once all went well, and I gaffed it for him ten minutes later—a fourteen-pounder.

I worked down the rest of the pool, fishing my most careful best, dropping the prawn within six inches of the other bank, swinging it across deep and slow, holding it as long as I could wherever the fish should be lying. Greenhill watched closely and once or twice nodded his head in approval. I wanted that because I knew that a bad cast plopping down in midstream or a few turns of the reel too fast in bringing the prawn through a good lie would be his signal to take the rod away for half an hour. But fish how I would, the rest of the pool was blank.

The next pool was the Hut Pool, a pool on a curve and shallow at the head, so shallow that I could see the prawn as I brought the first cast around. I moved two steps and cast again. Again I saw the prawn coming up to me under my own bank; then there was a fish behind it, a silver-gray fish, big and beautiful. He came in a wave and turned in a boil, and then Greenhill was shouting anxious directions to me.

He was only a ten-pounder, and Greenhill lifted him on the gaff five or six minutes after I had hooked him. He half-apologized, half-scolded me, "I wanted you to get the first one, young fellow. Next time you can play him out and bring him to the gaff properly."

I don't think I cared whether I fished at all in the rest of that day. My salmon was on the bank, clean silver and beautiful, with the violet sheen of the sea faint on his scales. Greenhill fished on, and we came to the long pool called the Salmon Water. He was fishing as only he could, swinging the prawn out easily, letting it almost brush the reeds of the far bank in its fall, working it deep down to the floor of the river before he began the slow recovery. His big shoulders hunched over the rod, his hands on rod and reel were ready and sensitive, his whole being seemed projected out into the swim of his prawn, concentrated on what it was doing down there on the bottom of the river. Beside him Dinah sat in trembling concentration as tense as his own. Suddenly, almost in the exact moment that he began the recovery of a cast, he lifted the rod in a heavy strike. Dinah stood up, ears pricked forward. Right under the far bank a big fish crashed to the surface in a heavy, shattering jump. The fish ran as the others had not, deep down and strongly, taking out a lot of line. For fully twenty minutes he bored and struggled and twisted, while we followed him as closely as we could along the bank. Then Greenhill brought him to the gaff, and I saw he was big, so big I didn't want the gaffing of him for fear I would muff it. I reached over, slowly and carefully, then struck and felt the gaff slide solidly home; I lifted and the fish was on the bank.

"Well done," Greenhill said.

"Gosh," I said. "What does he weigh? Forty pounds?"

Greenhill shook his head and smiled. "Not quite thirty. We'll see when we get back to the mill." He began to mount a new prawn. "You get on and fish before it's too late. You won't get many days like this one."

So I fished out the rest of the Salmon Water, and near the tail of it an eighteen-pounder took me, and I killed him, properly and alone as a salmon fisherman should, even gaffing him myself. As we walked back up toward the mill along the railroad, I felt my face hot and my knees weak from sheer joy; the thirty-pound weight of salmon slung clumsily on my back was something I remembered only because it was salmon—salmon Greenhill and I had caught.

I fished many more days with Greenhill. Once I gaffed a forty-pounder for him, and within an hour of that he gaffed a twenty-eight-pounder for me. But right up until the last day I fished with him, I fished on probation. Sometimes, despairing of salmon, I would fish the minnow a little faster in the hope of attracting a big pike. "When you come out with me for salmon, don't waste time fishing for pike," he would say. "Give me that rod." Or, when I made a clumsy cast, "What are you trying to do? Knock their brains out? They don't want it on top of their heads." I think I learned the lessons. I know I still think of him almost every time I fish a pool and try to cover it as carefully and cunningly as he would have.

The very last day I fished with him we fished for pike in the river Stour near Wimborne. We often went out in high hopes of big pike during the winter months, and I was not surprised when he suggested the Stour because I knew a forty-pounder had been killed there years earlier. We crossed the river on a bridge some way above where we were to fish and saw it was high but in good shape. "You ought to get a twenty-pounder today, young fellow," he said. At the farm where we left the car, they told us the river might be flooded over its banks in places, but it should be fishable. This was accurate enough, and I killed a ten-pounder in the first few minutes by wading over the tops of my boots. I offered Greenhill the rod, but he shook his head. "I want to see you catch fish today," he said.

I caught them. An eight-pounder, a fourteen-pounder, two or three small ones, then a sixteen-pounder. Each time I offered him the rod, and each time he refused it. He stood behind me all the time, leaning on the long handle of his gaff, watching closely and yet not whole-heartedly interested in the fate of every cast as he usually was. It was still early in the day when the sixteen-pounder was on the bank. Greenhill said, "You know, I was born a few miles from here."

I was surprised; I hadn't known that. I think I realized then how little I did know about him. He said, "You've got all the fish you want. I'd like to drive round and look at two or three places."

So we took the rod down and went back to the car. He directed as I drove along narrow lanes until we came to the gates of a big stone house in a fine park. I stopped the car, and he looked at it for a long time. I knew it was the house where he was born and I asked, "Who lives there now?" But he didn't answer. Later we drove on farther, to a cemetery, and he showed me the graves where his mother and father were buried. After that we drove home. I felt I had been taken close to him, but I couldn't understand why and I held back into myself a little, afraid. After a while, he said, "Sorry I took you away from your fishing, young fellow. But it's not like salmon fishing; it was only pike." I hadn't minded about the fishing, but I knew it was strange that he had wanted to leave it and strange that he hadn't taken the rod all day. At seventeen I was perfectly willing to call a thing strange without wondering much just why it was strange.

Three weeks later Greenhill went up to shoot pigeons in a wood on a windy hill. He died there, and Dinah howled beside him through the night and part of the next morning.

Little Lakes

The little lakes of Vancouver Island and the British Columbia coast are uncountable. If they were to be counted, someone would have to lay down a law that distinguished between a lake and a pothole and a pond and a swamp. Then all the ground would have to be resurveyed and all the maps drawn again to make quite sure that no little lake, anywhere, was left out. And that would be an awful job because they nestle in a thousand unexpected places—on the breasts of mountains, in wide river flats, up draws and gullies, on forgotten plateaus and on the round tops of big hills.

To be little, I think a lake should be not more than a mile or two long. To be a lake at all, it should have a respectable flow of water into it and out of it; some lakes, I know, are fed by springs and drained by underground streams; but a little lake that has nothing more than an overflow channel leading from it is in grave danger of being reckoned a pond. Swamps, very often, are lakes filled in by the slow deposit of each year's algal bloom and weed growth until reeds and hardhack can spread their roots out into it and still keep their heads above water. It is not always too easy to decide when a lake has ceased to be a lake and become a swamp. Potholes, for my purpose, are flood pools in the swamps and wide places in the creeks where there is just room for a few ducks to light and feed. Beaver ponds usually are something all their own, good places to fish, but still more nearly potholes than lakes.

Most of the little lakes on the British Columbia coast have trout in them, and the time to go to them first is in April. May can be a good month too, but in July and August, even in June, the water is likely to be too warm for good fish or good fishing. In late September and early October, when cool nights have lowered the water temperature, they are good again. Generally the trout in the lakes are cutthroats, generally they will come well enough to the fly and generally there will be plenty of them; but that's about all the generalizing it is safe to do because little lakes can vary in fascinating ways, even when they are on the same watershed.

I like them best when they are back in the standing timber. They are secret and silent then, closed in, and few people go to them. It is a great moment when you come down through the woods to such a lake. You stand there and look at it, judging its shore line, measuring its islands, noticing a deep bay here, a sloping beach there, a rock bluff across on the other side; it is untried water then and it looks full of promise. Every windfall, thrusting out into the water, may be the haunt of a big fish; the shallow water behind the island, where the lily pads show, will surely be a good place for the fly; the mouth of the stream at the head will be worth trying; the deep, still water may hide anything, even a short, thick ten-pounder, perhaps a whole round dozen of them. True, that miracle never happens, but a man would be a queer sort of fisherman if he did not let his mind play with the idea of it at every first sight of new water.

There is a whole chain of little lakes above the fourteen-mile length of Nimpkish Lake—Anutz, Hustan, Atluck, Wolf, Crescent, Loon, to name only the larger ones. Each lake, and its fishing, is sharply different from the others, and each has its surprises. I fished Anutz for a whole year before I caught anything much bigger than a pound. Then one day I ran a canoe clear to the head and pulled it up on a gravel bar where the stream came in. I had meant to take the trail and go on through to Hustan Lake, but as I watched there was a quiet little rise at the edge of the fast run of water that poured into the lake. I got ready lazily to fish over it, but because the day was bright I put up a 4X leader and a No. 17 greenwell nymph. The fish rose again while I was tying on the fly, but I still didn't suppose he was particularly big. I cast upstream of the rise, saw a faint movement underwater and struck into something solid. The fish rolled out as he felt the hook, then turned and ran down into the lake until he had half the backing off the reel. He weighed over four pounds when I netted him, and I caught two others of about the same size without moving from the gravel bar. The next week I caught three more in the same place and with the same fly, one of them only a few ounces under five pounds. I can't recall that I saw any others or lost any, and each rise meant a fish fairly and solidly hooked. The little greenwell does its work well.

Hustan lies farther in toward the high mountains and is more beautiful than Anutz. It is almost two lakes, divided by a thirty-foot neck of moderate current. The best fishing is in this neck, good, free-rising little cutthroats running from three quarters of a pound up to a pound and a quarter at most. The lower half of the lake is a great jam of floating logs and smaller drift, sucked in against an underground outlet. There are two layers of splendidly arched limestone caves, the upper layer bone dry and with funnels that lead down to the river on the lower level. There were fish here in the semidarkness, little, thin half-pounders that took the fly greedily and fought gamely for their size. They were not blind, even far down the caves where only a shadow of light penetrated, and it was strange to hook them and play them and net them entirely by feel.

Little lakes have a way of hiding themselves in the woods, and it is easy to pass within a few hundred feet of one and not see it, particularly if it has an underground outlet, as is very often the case in limestone country. Unknown Lake is within a hundred yards of the main trail to Buttle Lake, or what was the main trail until logging destroyed it a year or two ago. Even though a stranger passing may see light on the water through the trees, he will not suspect there is a lake there because he has just passed a great wide backwater of the Buttle River and it is easy to imagine that the trail has curved to pass the head of this. I heard reports of Unknown Lake long before I found it, and wonderful reports they were too: the trout took with fierce carelessness; they were hog fat from feeding on nothing but leeches; they averaged three pounds or more in weight. The truth, when I found it, differed somewhat from the reports, but was almost as spectacular. The truth was not revealed the first time I found the lake—only suggested. It was a hot day in July, and Edward and I ran down from the trail on our way out from Buttle Lake. The lake lay in the sun without a ripple, and all over its surface there played great mottled-wing dragonflies, mating and hunting and feeding. They swooped and dove and pounced and hovered, and the warm, still air seemed to nestle under their wings and click with their sharp maneuvering. There were other, smaller dragonflies among them and gray and blue damsel flies also, but not a trout moved anywhere that we could see. We found an old dugout at the lower end of the lake; but it was leaky and waterlogged, and we had only an hour or so to fish, so we worked along the shore, wading in where the bottom was right. We caught and killed three fish that weighed about a pound each and returned two others that were smaller. All of them came up from deep water, in fine slashing rises, but after that fought poorly. Fortunately I had a thermometer with me, and when I read the water temperature at sixty-eight degrees Fahrenheit, I knew we had not given the lake a fair chance. When I examined the stomachs of the fish we had caught and found them packed with beetles and caddis larvae and chironomid nymphs, in hundreds, and fresh-water clams and dragonfly larvae, I knew the lake had possibilities.

So we tried it again the next year, in April, before the water had time to get warm. One or two fish showed far out, near the islands, while we were putting our rods up. I tied on a fly and flipped it out along the log I was standing on. It was taken fiercely and at once by a fish about fifteen inches long. All around the lake it was the same: the second a fly touched the water, a fish had it. They came to wet fly or dry, to fly worked or simply sinking down through the water, to fly cast well out or flicked in close to shore. Often three or four fish came at once, and the disappointed waited their chance until the barbless and pointless hook—for we cut away barbs and points almost at once—dropped away from the first fish. We caught no three-pounders—a pound and a half was the largest; but we caught no really small fish, nothing much smaller than ten inches long. Later I went into the lake again and built a raft so that we could fish the deep water in the center and the shoals near the islands. We tried in May and in September, but still we could find no three-pounders even though we tried a little halfhearted trolling for them.

Burnt Lake is another lake with no outlet and only a small stream running into it in times of heavy rain. It is a tiny lake, not more than twenty acres, and I first heard of it from hunters ten or twelve years ago. A wonderful place for big bucks, they said, if you can find it. It's somewhere in the flat above the Quinsam, not more than a mile or so from the road and nearer the bluffs than the river, probably draining into Coal Creek.

Then the timber was cut away, and the hunters seemed even more vague than they had been about it. So I took time out one day when I was hunting willow grouse and found it myself. It wasn't really so very hard to find, because there were a few tall, slim trees standing around it amidst all the devastation of high-lead logging; and when one marked their line from Coal Creek, it was fairly obvious that the lake was near them. It was a calm day, and the surface of the lake was not stirred by the least ripple. I watched it for nearly an hour and saw no sign of fish.

A week or two later I took the rubber boat in there and learned a little more about it. I fished with everything—flies and spinners and even worms—and could not move a fish of any kind. I took soundings and found over seventy feet of water in the center, with depths sloping almost evenly down to that from every side. The lake was quite cool enough for fish—fifty-two degrees Fahrenheit at six feet, forty-two degrees Fahrenheit at twenty-four feet—and I found many kinds of good trout feed in it. It seemed a perfect chance for an experiment in stocking. I made a few calculations and decided that an annual planting of about 500 fry should keep the lake producing a steady harvest of two- and three-pound fish. Kamloops trout would be the best prospect, because they will seldom spawn without running water, and I felt confident that the intermittent flow of the creek at the head would not be sufficient encouragement for them. So long as there was no natural spawning to confuse things, it should not be difficult to keep the lake exactly controlled.

I reckoned without the freehandedness of the powers that be. I wrote and asked them for the first stocking, 500 fry. When the cans came up, they had in them a thousand little fish instead of five hundred, three-inch fingerlings instead of one-inch fry, and all were solemnly dumped into poor little Burnt Lake. This meant a survival far in excess of anything I had counted on, and I saw that my hope of two- and three-pounders was gone. The next year, which was 1928, the powers sent along 500 more fingerlings in the spring, and then, during the summer, a great forest fire swept down Vancouver Island. For two or three days Burnt Lake was in the hottest heart of the fire. The last few standing trees burned away, the salal brush burned and the hardhack around the edges of the lake, and the soil burned away from the gravel of the ridges. Even great Douglas fir stumps were burned to nothing, leaving three or four deep holes in the ground where their largest roots had gone down.

I saw Burnt Lake soon after the fire passed through. Its whole surface was covered with a gray scum of ashes, and I tried to imagine it as it had been in the fire, with the red glare all around it and reflected from it and smoldering pieces of bark and debris, wind-borne, falling into it and hissing their heat away into the water. I wondered if any fish still lived. Such a little lake in the midst of such a huge fire seemed no more than a kettle on a hot stove, but I remembered that heat goes up, not down, even in water, and that the lake was seventy feet deep. There would have been plenty of cool water down there. Then I wondered about the ash, whether it would choke the oxygen out of the water or perhaps sink down and clog the gills of the fish. I felt less certain about this; it might not kill them all but surely would affect a fair number, and that would be no bad thing for my hope of three-pounders.

I fished the lake the following April. It was full of fish, lively little nine- and ten-inch Kamloops that came hungrily to any fly. I waited a year and tried again; there were eleven- and twelve-inch fish now, rather thin and dark, but red-fleshed, pretty and lively. Many of them were fully ripened to spawn and some of the females had begun to reabsorb their eggs, I thought.

I still go occasionally to Burnt Lake. It isn't so pretty since the fire, but there is something attractive about its small, almost perfect round-

ness and the way the ridges circle it close and hide it. The salal and
Oregon grape are starting to grow again, with yellow violets among
them; willows are creeping down again from the swamp that feeds the
creek; and not all the hardhack along the edge of the lake was killed.
The fish are still there, and I keep very quiet about them and the lake.
I don't think anyone has remembered to stock it since the war started,
and in time the surplus stock of fish should die out. Then, if there has
been even a little successful natural spawning, there may be a chance
of two- and three-pounders. I like to think of that and I like to think,
too, that the ridges all around the lake will be green again with salal,
perhaps even with the start of fir and hemlock and cedar. Some day,
hunters may talk again of the little lake lost in the woods on the wide
flat above the Quinsam. "A fine place for a big buck," they'll say.
"And there's big fish in the lake too; you can see 'em jump sometimes,
if you watch."

Ax and fire and logging machinery come to nearly all the little lakes
of Vancouver Island sooner or later. Some are still lost in the deep
woods, a few are protected in parks, rugged mountain country guards
others; but the near ones, those one lives with, are passing through the
change or must pass through it soon. And the change is not all loss. I
wonder often about logged-off land, whether or not love of it is an
acquired taste. The first days and months of the change are shocking
—scarred earth, splintered stumps, dead, brown treetops, broken saplings, everything torn and shattered and flattened into a chaos of
waste. The summer sun bleaches the raw red scars, dries the glistening
sap where the bark is torn away, shrivels the needles from the broken
tops; in the fall there is fire, and the waste becomes black logs and
stumps against red gravel. Sooner or later after that the healing starts.
Little shoots of salal and Oregon grape show the earliest green, and
then the brambles and bracken and fireweed make light ground cover
out of the exhausted soil; after these, willows and poplars in the creek
bottoms and along the lines of swamps, spreading out even to dry
ground where the country is fairly flat. Dogwoods spring from old
stumps on the slopes, and in a few favored places the broad-leaved
maples seed thickly and grow to tree height in a few short years.
Wherever there are seed trees left alive after the burning, Douglas fir
and hemlock and cedar show again; often the white pine comes, far
more thickly than before the logging. But no fire kills blister rust. Its
spores settle from the high air, and one by one the little pine trees
wither and bleed and die. Slowly the old botanical wars fight themselves out again, and the forest builds back to itself through a changing
loveliness surely as satisfying as the heavy magnificence of virgin timber.

The first little lake I ever saw on Vancouver Island was Theimar Lake, and my first duty was to stake out the line of the logging railroad that harvested its timber. Our line ran eight hundred or a thousand feet from the lake, but I went down there the first day. Mac, a little Irishman who was working on the same crew, came down with me, and I asked him about the fish. "Lots of them," he said. "The boys go out from camp every Sunday. We can come back and try it after supper if you like."

We did that, and the fishing was pretty good. It was an exciting lake too, deep and fairly wide at the upper end, suddenly narrow where an island came up out of the deep water and little more than river width from there down through a mile or more of swamp. I wanted to explore, and Mac was willing enough, so we poled the clumsy old raft all over it until the sun was down and the moon was up. Then we hit back for camp, and the moon went in and we lost ourselves somehow between the lake and our survey line. We walked around a little until I fell over a twenty-foot bluff and told Mac I meant to stay put until there was some light. Soon after that the moon came out again, and we found the line and saw lanterns along it—our boss had come out with the skidder rigger to look for us. Mac didn't like being kidded and he was pretty gloomy on the way home. "We'll never hear the last of this," he said. "The only way is to pull right out of camp tomorrow." But we survived it somehow and both of us were still working on the same crew a full year later.

I fished Theimar Lake a good many times during the next several years and learned the full length of the little stream that runs from it down to the salt water. There were beaver dams in the stream where big sea-run cutthroats sometimes lay, and in October a fine run of coho salmon came through to the lake to spawn. In the winter months I shot ducks and geese in the marshy lower end of the lake, and once, at dusk, half a dozen swans circled the island where I was hidden. I remember the work of the graders and steel gangs as they put in the railroad along the line we had laid out; I remember the fallers coming behind them and how I worked myself to load the logs on the cars as the yarding donkey brought them up to the track from the edge of the lake. I felt then that the lake was almost dead and finished. There was scrub timber still around the heronry and the swampy lower end of the lake, scrub timber around the swamps at the head; but the main part of the lake was stripped bare, and dead tops lay dismally out in the water in all the little bays we had fished. I fished it no more, though I passed it often on the way to other fishing places, and in fall and winter I hunted in it and near it for ducks and geese and grouse and deer.

Then I was away from that country for two or three years. The April after I got back I thought of lake fishing. Theimar Lake was only four or five miles away across the logging slash, so I took blankets and a light pack and went there. On the way to the lake I passed through two heavy hailstorms, cold lashing storms from black clouds, but the clouds blew over and the sun came out again in a blue and white sky. I began to notice how the logging slash had healed: alders were thick along the grades, willows and young conifers grew in the old settings, the raw red earth of the skid roads was weathered and overgrown by brambles, and salal brush was thick and glossy green among the burned stumps.

Even so, I did not expect that the lake would please me; the trees had been cut away from it, and the slope of Mount Holdsworth was bare for two thousand feet above it. I could see how the benches and gullies had logged out to the railroads we had laid along them and across them. I came upon the lake almost suddenly. It was blue and white, broken by the wind, very clean and clear in the sunlight. On the islands and at the far end the scrub timber was still standing; the swamp grass was thick, still brown from winter frosts, and Hudson's Bay tea grew in the drier places. At the head was the long, level swamp, and at the upper end of that stood the tall white pines that had not been reached by the high-lead machine. The lake seemed as fine as it had ever seemed, and now it was lonely and lost in the logging slash as little lakes are lonely and lost in the Scottish moors. The loggers who had taken the timber had moved far away; the steel and the ties were stripped from the railroads, and there was no threat of ax or donkey whistle or saw. No one wanted the country or the lake or anything in it, so it was mine as it never had been before. I was suddenly conscious of the other little lakes that lay near by, Soo Lake and Roselle Lake, and of the length of Theimar Creek toward the salt water and the sweep of land over toward the mountains along Nimpkish Lake. It was a big empty country, left to its own devices, to its own fascinating growth back into something that some day men would want again.

It was late afternoon when I came to the lake, and I had decided to build a raft because I knew the old ones would be waterlogged and falling apart. I made camp quickly near the larger of the two creeks that came in at the head of the lake, then walked two or three hundred yards up to the old logging trestle. The lean-to shelter where Sam Ford's bridge crew had cooked their lunches was still there, and I found a handful of spikes, as I was pretty sure I would. Then I picked out two of the sawed bridge ties left on the deck and dragged them down to the lake. There was enough shiplap lumber lying around the trestle to floor my raft, so I packed that down too. Then I put up my rod and caught two or three fish for supper.

The wind died down at dusk and a full moon was in the sky almost at once; it was a still night, crystal bright in the stars and the moon and the water. All day long the big blue grouse had been hooting in the logging slash and the ruffed grouse drumming in the swamps; now the hooters were silent, but the ruffed grouse drummed and courted all around me in the moonlight. I lay and listened to them and thought of Sam's good bridge crew—Roy Davis, Curly Brown, George Boxall, Ozzie, the engineer, Sam himself. I knew where some of them were and could guess at what they were doing. I wondered if they ever thought of this one of the many, many logging trestles they had built together, this one near the head of little, lost Theimar Lake.

I made my raft the next morning, dapping the bridge ties across three slender, sharply pointed cedar poles, nailing the shiplap deck to the ties. By the time I had finished the wind was strong again, blowing up from the foot of the lake. I poled my raft up to the island, drifted back and caught a few fish, poled up again, drifted once more and caught a few more fish. But it was hard work and uncomfortable, so I decided to wait for the calm of the next morning and spent the rest of that afternoon in walking to Soo Lake and Roselle Lake to see how they looked with the timber away from them.

In the calm of the next morning the fish were really feeding, coming freely to the surface in deep water all down the center of the lake. I used a small, dry iron blue on 3X gut and kept everything larger than fourteen inches. It was fine fishing, exactly what I had come for, and by the time the first ripple of wind came up the lake I had twelve or fourteen good, clean fish on the raft. None of them was larger than a pound and a half, but I was not looking for large fish because I had learned long before that Theimar Lake's big ones were dark and thin in April. I was near the island, almost a mile from my camp, when the wind began to freshen. I hooked another fish, and by the time he was in the net there were whitecaps all over the lake. I thought I saw a quiet rise on the slope of one and cast to it. A fish took the little fly at once and ran with a solid determination that told me he was big. Had he broken me or shaken loose in that first run, I should hardly have cared, because I was certain I knew his type—twenty-four inches long, a bare two pounds in weight, dark, with a big head and red on his gill covers. But he came back from the run and ran again, near the surface this time, so that I saw his broad, clean side under the crest of a whitecap. Then everything was difficult. The fish went down, and the raft wanted to drift over the line. I paddled awkwardly with one hand, holding the rod in the other. The waves swept over the shiplap floor of my raft, and the raft itself creaked and groaned. I couldn't raise the fish in the water; then I could raise him and he came back to me, but I couldn't net him. And the raft drifted over him again and I straightened that out, but he ran again, strongly, upwind, and I dared not hold him on the light rod and the light gut. Then the raft jarred suddenly, hard on the shore at the head of the lake. I jumped out into the shallow water and knew that the fish was tiring. Two or three minutes later he was on his side, with the swells lifting him as I slipped the net under. I looked at him a long time when I had him, because he was the only really fine fish I ever caught in Theimar Lake—nearly four pounds and fat as a fish from the Test in June. I forced the hook from his jaw and loosed the gut from my line. It was no time to make another cast.

MAY

In May the Kamloops trout spawn. Most of the spawners are four-year-old fish, and they migrate from their lakes into the feeder streams exactly as their steelhead cousins on the coast move from salt water into the rivers. The Kamloops trout has made a great name for himself as a game fish, and he deserves it: I know of no other freshwater fish that runs more strongly than he does or jumps with a finer freedom and recklessness. A two- or three-pounder hooked on a fly cast over the shoals of some interior lake is the spectacular model of all that a fighting fish should be. And three-pound Kamloops are common enough in the interior of British Columbia, ten- and twelve-pounders are not absolutely rare and forty-pounders have been caught, though not, so far as I know, on the fly.

Yet the Kamloops is a simple product of environment. He differs from the steelhead and the Pacific coast rainbow (which differ from each other not at all) only in that he has rather smaller scales, 145 or so along the lateral line instead of about 135. Even this superficial difference can be wiped out in a single generation by hatching the eggs of Kamloops trout at slightly higher temperatures than those normally prevailing in interior streams.

The Kamloops at his best should be compared to the early summer-run steelhead, which is the coast rainbow at his best, a fish built to full strength and vigor by two or three years of sea feeding and not yet slowed by the drain and weight of developed ovaries or milt sacs. One catches the summer steelhead in rivers, usually in fine, sparkling, swift rivers whose current and obstacles give him great advantage. The Kamloops at his best is usually a lake fish; but there is no other lake fish like him, and if the tackle is anywhere weak or the hand on the rod too clumsy, he will find it out.

Though the Kamloops spawns in May, running then, gravid and red, to the streams, May is also one of the best months in which to catch him. One is not concerned with the spawning four-year-olds— they are in the streams, out of the way. The three-year-olds, still a year away from spawning, are coming into their noble prime. Dark-gray backed and silver-bellied from a full winter of deepwater feeding, they come to the surface as the ice breaks up and by May, unless the lake is a very high and cold one, they are feeding well on the shoals and over the chara-weed beds. There is plenty for them in the lime-rich water that few other fresh-water fish can hope to find: Gammarus, the fresh-water shrimp, Daphnia, the water flea, many sedges, dragonfly nymphs and damsel-fly nymphs, craneflies and midges, stone flies and snails and leeches, all in the abundance that grows Kamloops trout to three, six, twelve, even eighteen pounds in three or four years.

Many of the wonderful interior lakes were troutless only a few years ago, their masses of feed multiplying in chara-weed beds, feeding upon one another in a never-ending cycle of productivity too small for human interest. A few trout from a lake with a natural stock, painfully transplanted by some local enthusiast, often built a cycle of fish upon the teeming cycles of insect life, and anglers from all over the world began to find that the Kamloops trout lakes held great things for them. Knouff Lake and Paul Lake came into their famous days; and by that time things were on a more organized basis, and the government took a hand, with hatcheries and large-scale plantings. More and more lakes came into production, and fishermen learned to watch and wait for them. "Peter Hope ought to be pretty hot next year," they'd say. "They've made some big plantings there." Or, "Tawheel's going to be open this season. Boy! I'm sure going to try that one out."

It isn't all just perfect, by any means. Nearly always the plantings of fish are made "blind," that is, without proper survey of the lakes to be stocked and without consideration for the type of fishing most needed. Once stocked, a lake is usually left to control itself. Further plantings of fish will probably be made, but there will be no effort to limit natural spawning. As a result, many of the lakes quickly spoil themselves. For a few years they give great fishing; then natural spawning produces an overstock, and the average size drops far down, or the lake becomes unbalanced, with an overstock of fish one year and a small stock the next. This uses up lakes pretty fast, and one soon hears that "X lake isn't what it was," or, "You can't get big fish in B lake any more." But there are plenty of lakes in British Columbia, and more and more of them become accessible all the time, so that the feast of plenty goes through its extravagant courses and only a few of us worry. There's good fishing, the Lord knows; there's always good fishing.

That is why I always feel happy at Paul Lake. Paul Lake is one lake that is controlled, because there is a hatchery at Paul Creek where all the spawners are caught up. Their eggs are hatched artificially, and the fry are shipped out to other less fortunate lakes. Only a set and limited number is turned back into Paul Lake, and that number is just enough to yield plenty of fish between one and three pounds. Paul is a beautiful lake, set narrowly in the mountains, with fine shallows where the trout come splendidly to the fly and deep beds of chara where feed of all kinds multiplies. Two men are closely identified with it for me, and they always will be. One was a great fisherman—Bill Nation. The other is a great fishman—Charlie Mottley.

Charlie is a biologist with soaring vision; he has all a biologist's patience for detail, for controlled experiment, exact proof. But his mind does not stop there; it leaps ahead to put to use what has been learned. Working at Paul Lake, Charlie learned a lot, and from what he learned he developed the stocking formula that keeps the lake producing some ten thousand fish a year with a total weight of about five tons. The formula is simple enough and would apply to all the artificially stocked lakes of the interior. But Charlie, like many another good man, has left British Columbia for the United States, and no one bothers to apply his formula elsewhere than at Paul Lake.

Bill Nation was a wise, gentle, wholehearted angler. He was Paul Lake's best guide and the best guide to a hundred other interior lakes. Bill was no scientist, though he sometimes liked to set himself up as one. But he knew how to fish for Kamloops trout; he knew where to look for them, knew what they would be feeding on, knew how to give them a close enough imitation of whatever that feed might be. Bill's mind, like Charlie's, loved to take long flights ahead of sure knowledge, using a base of knowledge for imaginative and often very effective experiment. Bill's vivid theories lacked the close, hard logic that Charlie's ideas always had. Bill loved a poetic flight for its own sake— a wet fly, for instance, tied to represent mating damsel flies and fished several inches under water, on the supposition that the fish, by some process of their own, would reverse the relationship of the fly's position to the surface of the water and consider that it was flying some inches out in the free air, yet strike at the submerged improbability. Of course, the fly caught fish and caught them well, so Bill's idea must have had something.

Charlie learned a great deal from Bill, poetic flights and all, and Bill learned a great deal from Charlie; I was lucky enough to come between and learn from both of them. But I don't remember them for their work or their theories, but for their companionship and for what they gave to the lake. A day at Paul might start with a big batch of trout to be checked over, a sample of the previous day's catch. We would be curious about what their feed had been, and for an hour or more we would open stomachs, identify and count insects. Always there were surprises in this—perhaps a selective feeder with a stomach full of nothing but copepods or Daphnia; what had persuaded him to take bright fly on a No. 6 hook? Or a fish of more catholic tastes, crammed to the gullet and beyond with every variety of feed the lake offered; how had he supposed he could take and hold one more thing? Perhaps one or two of the fish would be spawners of the previous year, carrying Charlie's numbered tags in their tails. Bright fish, but thin and not brave when you hooked them as the maiden fish were. The spring balance told the tale of these, for almost without exception they weighed less than they had when running to spawn the previous year. And their scales under the microscope repeated the story—a ragged edge eating back into four good years of growth, with nothing at all formed beyond it. "They're nothing but a drain on the lake," Charlie would say. "A spawner recovering won't put back two ounces while a maiden fish is putting on five. Kill them, cut their swim bladders, turn them back for the sedge larvae to feed on."

Later in the morning we might go up to the traps in the creek to weigh and mark fish, and all the time we'd talk of fish, not only of Kamloops trout, but of brown trout and cutthroats, of Pacific salmon, of herrings or grayling or kokanees or anything else that balances itself on fins.

On the way back down the lake from the creek we would almost certainly fish, but lazily, because the afternoon would be hot and the lake calm and we would be thinking of cool beer back at the camp and some intricate argument we wanted to settle with reference book or microscope.

Toward evening we would go on down the lake to the lodge for a quiet drink with Bill and some of the guests and hear talk of the day's fishing. Bill would develop some new theory of imitating dragonflies, a new tying of an old fly perhaps, or simply a new and more realistic method of working the fly through the water. About then someone would start kidding, and Bill would answer in his soft voice and stories would begin to grow tall. And then it would be time to go down to dinner.

After dinner we would go to the boats, a little excited by the thought of the best fishing hour of the day ahead of us, the time when two- and three-pounders, perhaps bigger fish, came boldly onto the shallows near the outlet. "There's no hurry," Bill would say gently. "No hurry. They won't start to move much for half an hour yet."

But we would climb into the boats and start off anyway, cruising gently over the still water. In our boat Bill himself would have a rod, trailing one of his big dragon-nymph imitations on a long line while Charlie stood in the stern and I used some fly of which Bill did not approve from the bow. Sunset took the color from the water, leaving it gray and black, rippled by the movement of oars and boats but otherwise still: some fish rising, but nothing really big within reach; a good rise well down toward the outlet, just in the gentle draw of the current. Bill swung the boat to it, and we covered it, Charlie and I. Then Bill's rod jumped—the big dragon nymph, fishing deep, had moved him. By the time he was netted, it was real dusk. Bill picked up the oars again and moved the boat gently and silently back to its hunting. I covered a good rise and hooked a fish of nearly two pounds. Charlie dropped a fly beside my hooked fish and struck at once to a solid pull. By the time both fish were in the boat, we were across the outlet, within casting distance of the far shore. It was harder to see now and difficult to judge distance.

I covered the little dimple of a rise under a bush that leaned out from the shore, but the fish would not take. I brought the fly in. "Going to put on a dry sedge," I said.

Bill shook his head. "No. Waste time. Too late to change. Keep fishing."

But I changed anyway and was lucky enough to get it done quickly in the dim light. The rise had come again near the bushes, twice, but Charlie's wet fly had not moved him. I shot the sedge into the rings of a third dimple, saw it disappear and tightened. A silver Kamloops caught the last light as he walked the water in five great jumps. "You were right," Bill said. "I was wrong." The reel talked as it had not through all that day, and the fish twisted his body against the pull of the line, deep down now. Suddenly he was at the surface again, jumping and jumping back toward the boat. I hand-lined fast and came up with him—lucky. A little while longer and he was on his side and Bill slipped the net under.

"Might be three pounds. We'll have to weigh him."

Charlie laughed. "When you check a batch for me, you say you can guess the weight close enough."

"Little fish," Bill said. "All about the same. Weigh two or three and you've weighed them all. Go on fishing. There's time to catch another on the way back to the float."

So the boat stole on, and we cast to the rises we could reach until Charlie hooked the last good fish of the evening, and we netted it with the lights shining brightly out from the lodge.

Bill has had the chance now that he sometimes used to talk about— a chance to size up the fish and fishing qualities of the Styx. Charlie's excursion into mythology has taken him only as far as Ithaca, where he watches Cayuga's waters and plans for the Finger Lakes, but even that is overfar for the good of the Kamloops lakes. Paul Lake is a monument to both men—to Charlie's fish sense and Bill's fishing sense, but whatever the fish may do, should they become twice as numerous and grow twice as large, a day there can never be quite so full and good again.

Sea-Run Cutthroats

May is a great and generous month for the trout fisherman. In the English chalk streams the fish are coming to their best and the hatching May flies drift in squadrons and flotillas and armadas, their proudly upright wings a mark that stirs both fish and fisherman. In the Adirondacks and the Catskills trout fishermen are out with the Hendrickson. Here in British Columbia the interior lakes are warm enough, but not too warm, for good fly-fishing, and the great native-stock Kamloops trout come up out of Shuswap Lake to their fierce feeding on sockeye and spring salmon yearlings at Little River and off the mouth of Adams. On the coast the summer steelhead are running. In May each year I used to return to General Money his big thirteen-foot salmon rod; through the winter months it was mine because, the General said, he was too old to give it proper work to do, but by mid-May he would be thinking of early summer fish in the Stamp and would take the big rod over there to fish its easy, graceful way down the Junction Pool or the General's Pool. In May I turn to a smaller rod and go to the Island Pools to find our own run of summer fish, little fish seldom over five pounds, seldom under two, but sea-run steelhead just the same and brave fish that hit the fly hard and jump freely in the broken water. The twenty-fourth of May, a good Canadian holiday, is a day I have often celebrated with the little steelheads of the Island Pools.

The Pacific coast is great trout country. If we consider the chars as separate from trout—and I am quite certain that we should—there are in the world only three species of trout, the brown, the rainbow and the cutthroat. Of these, two are native to the Pacific coast and the slope of water west of the Rocky Mountains. This, by itself, seems to argue that the Pacific watershed has in full measure whatever it is that trout need and like; all the testing and sorting processes of evolution have left it with two trouts and given only one to all the rest of the world. The variations of environment in the watershed have developed at least two subspecies of each of these native species: the rainbow or steelhead of the coast proper becomes the Kamloops trout at medium elevations and the mountain Kamloops at high elevations; the Yellowstone cutthroat and the mountain cutthroat, as their names suggest, bear similar relationship to the coast cutthroat, the type of the species.

I suppose it is most improper to talk of degrees of nativeness. A fish or a bird or a mammal is native to a country or not native, and that is all there is to it. But for many reasons, most of them emotional and quite illogical, I feel that the cutthroat is the most native of Pacific coast game fish, just as I feel that the ruffed grouse is the most native of the continent's game birds and the cougar and the raccoon are the most native of the mammals. The cutthroat, the coast cutthroat of tidal waters particularly, is such a down-to-earth, workaday, unspectacular fish; he fits his environment so perfectly and makes such good, full use of it, following the tides and the salmon runs and the insect hatches to the limit of their yield; and he has not been, as the rainbow has, more or less successfully transplanted to all parts of the world. He lives in his own place in his own way and has his own special virtues. He is a little like the burned stumps and slash and new growth of the old logging works in that one must know and deeply love the country to appreciate him properly.

In writing of the "Game Fish of British Columbia," Professor J. R. Dymond gives an opinion of cutthroat trout that is undoubtedly shared by many anglers:

> Were it not that it (the cutthroat) occurs in the same area as two of the hardest fighting game fish known, its qualities would be more highly regarded. At times it does leap from the water when hooked, and often puts up quite a prolonged struggle before being landed. It generally rises quite readily to the fly, although as a rule it takes the fly sunk and drawn as a minnow, more readily than the dry fly.

The implication of this is that the cutthroat is not to be compared with either the Kamloops or the steelhead as a game fish. My own opinion is that, at his best, he is in every way comparable; and under some circumstances a discerning angler may even find him superior.

The qualifying phrase "at his best" is important, because the cutthroat is too often caught when he is not at his best. When the humpback fry are running in March and April, anglers catch two- and three-pound cutthroats that are thin and feeble after spawning. Many cutthroats are caught in low-producing lakes where the average fish are too small to give a good account of themselves and the larger fish are always in poor condition; and many are caught, quite unnecessarily, with spinner and worm or other such clumsy gear and have no chance to show what they can do. The cutthroat is at his best in a river that is open to the sea; he should then be a short, thick fish of two pounds or more, not too long in fresh water, with a clean white belly and a heavily spotted, green- or olive-brown back. Such a fish will come nobly to wet fly or dry—better to the dry fly than will Kamloops trout and far better, certainly, than steelhead—and when you set the hook he will run as boldly as any fish of his size, and probably he will jump too. Beyond this he has a way of his own that is fully as dangerous to tackle as the more spectacular antics of the Kamloops, a way of boring down and out into the heaviest stream against the lift of a fly rod and sometimes twisting his body and shaking his head in solid, sulky strength. I have had more moments of straining anxiety with big cutthroat trout half played out than I have with any fish, except, perhaps, big brown trout among the weed beds and other obstructions of the chalk streams.

The cutthroat's habit of going to sea is what makes him a really fine game fish. There are good cutthroats and good cutthroat fishing in the cold mountain streams that drain into the big lakes and even in ordinary landlocked rivers that owe nothing to lake or stream; but the true sea-run cutthroat is a very special fish and makes very special fishing. He is not truly migratory, like the steelhead and the salmon: that is, he does not run out to sea from his river in early youth and range freely through deep water until grown to full maturity. He is at once less businesslike about his migration and more practical. Somewhere toward the end of his first or second year he finds that the food available to him in fresh water is not enough, and he simply moves downstream to find more. In tidal water or in the sea just beyond the mouth of his river he finds what he is seeking, so he stays there awhile and feeds; sometimes he moves on out as far as five or ten miles from the mouth of his river, feeding as he goes; he may even (though I am not sure of this) school with other cutthroats to feed for a while off the mouth of some stream quite distant from his own—certainly schools of big cut-throats lie at certain times off the mouths of little creeks that seem far too small to support them even as a spawning run.

But in spite of all this wandering there seems to be no sharp break between the salt-water and fresh-water life of the migratory cutthroat. He may return to the fresh-water pools of his river at any time: in spring when the salmon fry hatch, in fall when the ripe salmon run, in summer when the sedge nymphs crawl thickly over the round rocks of the stream bed. And he is seldom beyond reach of the fly-fisherman's search; by studying the tides and his movement in them you may catch him at his feeding in the estuary; by knowing a favorite bay or sandbar and his chosen time there you may even find him right out in salt water. In Puget Sound keen cutthroat fishermen search water as far as six or seven miles from any stream, trolling a small spinner until they hook the first fish, then changing over to the fly.

My own first meeting with sea-run cutthroats was in the Nimpkish River. I was working in a logging camp seven or eight miles away and started out for the river immediately after work on my second Saturday in camp. I took a blanket and enough food for a meal or two and promised myself a well-spent Sunday. On Saturday evening I fished one pool in the short hour or so before dark and caught three fish of about a pound. The Sunday was a bright, warm day and I started early. The Nimpkish is a broad, fine river, fast and fierce in most places, but with a few long, slow pools. On the first of these pools I wasted far too much time, but there was a strong deep run below it that spread into something less than a pool, no more, really, than a slackening in the rapid. Right in the deepest and fastest water a fine fish took, and I landed a three-pound cutthroat. At the head of the next pool was another deep, broken run, and there the second fish, a little larger than the first, came boldly to my fly. From then on I fished the fast, heavy water whenever I could find it, and by the end of the day I had four cutthroats and two rainbows, all over three pounds and one of them over four.

Since then I have caught sea-run cutthroats in the salt water, off the mouths of tiny creeks, over the tide flats of big rivers, in fresh-water pools and in the brackish water of shrunken river channels on the ebb tide. About ten years ago I used to fish the mouth of the Campbell regularly with Cliff Whitaker, who was my next-door neighbor at that time. Cliff had learned to fish and hunt in Alaska and was a good man at both sports, aggressive and determined, a fine woodsman and a tireless walker. He also loved human competition in hunting and fish-ing, which I do not, but we found a way around that which left both of us happy and comfortable.

There are half a dozen or more good places to catch cutthroats in the tidal part of the Campbell; two of them are sloughs, which make dull fishing; three of the good places are best fished from a boat; and only one offers the real variations and complications of current that one hopes for in river fishing and can, at the same time, be fully covered by wading. On a fair run-out of tide the river breaks into a sharp rapid just below the upper slough, and this runs for two hundred yards or more—water where there is always a chance of picking up one or two fish on the wet fly. At the tail of the rapid a small creek comes in, and since the creek has a run of cohos, the cutthroats wait near its mouth when the fry are moving down. But the best of the fishing was in a fairly big pool below the rapid. The main current of the pool swung away from the bank from which we fished and left a wide eddy where feed collected; this was a good place. The run of current itself was fairly good and became very good where it spread out among the short butts of rotten piles at the tail of the pool. All this water was uncertain; on a good tide during April or May the fish were sure to come into it, but just where they would be and how they would be feeding depended on the stage of the tide, the strength of the river and the type of feed that was most available. The mood of the fish also seemed to depend on just what kind of hunting they had had during the full tide before the ebb—a fish with a really fine bellyful of sand launce or sow bugs or sand hoppers could be a very fussy feeder when he came into the pool.

Cliff and I made a habit of going down to the pool whenever there was a good tide, and it wasn't long before we were getting very fine results on the last two hours of the ebb. We caught most of our fish on flies of the streamer type, tied, not in the American way on a long single hook, but on two or three small hooks in tandem, what the English and Scottish sea-trout fishers call "demons" or "terrors." Several Hardy patterns were very deadly: one with long dark badger hackles laid back to back, two tinsel-covered hooks and a red tag on the second hook; another with long blue hackles, strips of light mallard and three hooks each tinsel-covered and with a red tag; a third, called the "dandy" and made up of two hooks, mallard strips and a red hackle at the throat, was deadliest of all. But in the course of this fishing two things became evident: first, that streamer-type flies were altogether too effective under certain conditions, particularly when fish were taking freely on the last of the ebb; and second, that we were not catching fish at all well on the start of the flood, though big ones commonly moved up into the pool and began a lazy sort of feeding at that time.

Cliff and I discussed the deadliness of the streamers and agreed that we had better limit ourselves by giving up their use. At about the same time we discovered we could pick off some of the lazy feeders of the flood tide very nicely with a dry fly. From then on, all Cliff's competitive instinct was directed toward catching the fish by more and more delicate methods. We almost gave up fishing the ebb and always gave our main attention to the glassy slide of water near the piles at the tail of the pool; as soon as the tide began to slow the current there, we went down and waited for some sign of fish moving in.

They came early one day, and Cliff saw a quiet rise just behind the lowest pile. He dropped a brown and white bi-visible into the rings and hooked his fish almost as the fly touched the water; it was a three-pounder. His fly was hardly out free and dried off again when another fish rose within reach; Cliff covered him, played him and netted another three-pounder. Ten minutes later he dipped his net under a third of the same size. "That bi-visible's too deadly," he said. "Guess we'll have to quit using it."

And we did. The bi-visible we had been using was brown and white, tied on a size 9 or 10 hook. We turned to other flies on size 15 and 16 hooks and did less well with them, though still well enough. And we finally went one stage farther still, to upstream nymph fishing with flies as small as size 17. The nymphs were more attractive to the fish than were the small dry flies, but the fishing was actually more exciting and more difficult, because light and water conditions made it hard to tell when a fish had taken the nymph; we were usually wading deep and looking toward the sun across smooth water whose reflecting surface concealed the faint flash of a moving fish that the nymph-fisherman generally depends on.

That seems to show that you can go to almost any refinement of fly-fishing and still find sea-run cutthroats willing to meet you halfway. But in spite of the sport they give in tidal waters, I still prefer to catch them when they have left the estuaries for the fresh-water pools. Tidal waters can be very beautiful. I remember an evening below the falls of Theimar Creek, when the sunset light was blood red on the shiny wet sand of the tide flats and big cutthroats were rising in the narrow channel all down the length of a seaweed-covered log. I remember an August sunrise in the mouth of the Campbell, off the point of the Spit, when big cutthroats in perfect condition came to our flies so fast and hard that we each had a limit within an hour or two; outside the tyee fishermen were passing up and down in their white rowboats, and a little westerly wind came up to scuff the water of Discovery Passage as the full daylight made it blue; behind us the mountains of Vancouver Island were black and white with rock and snow, and across from us the Coast Range was jagged and tall and endless from farthest south to farthest north. Those were good times. But in the comings and goings of the cutthroats in fresh water there is something more than good fishing, something more than any simple beauty of surroundings. Each movement is an outward sign of a change in the year's cycle; more than a sign, it is an actual part of both change and cycle. And knowledge of the movements in any particular river is the seal of one's intimacy with the country at least as much as it is a test of one's knowledge as a fisherman.

In March and April and on into May the cutthroats are there because the salmon fry are coming up from the gravel and moving down; the fishing is often quick and fierce, with a big wet fly quickly cast to a slashing rise and worked back fast. Fish show in unexpected places, in short eddies behind rocks in the rapids, off the mouths of little creeks, and in all the expected places as well. Sometimes the May flies hatch thickly, and not a trout will stir to a wet fly, though fish after fish will come to a dry blue quill or a little iron blue. Then on some hot day in May, the big black ants put out their wings and make their brief mating flight; for a day, or perhaps two days, the river is full of drowned or drowning ants, and the fish feed on them and come to a dry fly that is not too tidily tied and not too well greased, something bedraggled and half-drowned like the ants themselves. After that there is a change, and there seem few cutthroats in the fresh-water pools of the Campbell. I used to say of June and July: it's hardly worth going up—there won't be any fish. But the days are so good and the river is so bright that one goes sometimes just for the pleasure of being out in the sun and the summer, with running water all about one and the trees green on the banks.

I have been surprised so many times now that I am careful what I say about June and July. It was a June afternoon that I went up to the head of the Sandy Pool, lay on the beach for a while in the sun and at last walked lazily down into the water to make a few casts before going home. Just as soon as my fly reached out into the fast water a trout took hold, a good trout, short and thick and over two pounds. I went on fishing and soon hooked a second fish, the most beautiful cutthroat, I think, that I have ever hooked; he was a two-pounder, like the first one, but shorter still and thicker, splendidly marked with a rich pattern of heavy spots all over the deep and shining green of his back and sides. That was all for that afternoon, but it was enough to leave the short June hour as clear and sharp in my memory as any fishing time.

Two years ago a July day looked good, and I went to the Island Pools, just to look them over. I told myself that the fish wouldn't come in for a couple of weeks yet. So I worked along the bar and floated a

Mackenzie River bucktail down the runs, dancing it back to me from wave top to wave top on the upstream wind, lowering my rod to slack the line and let the fly ride the rough water down again. It seldom finished the ride. The big cutthroats, three-pounders, some of them nearly four pounds, came at it like fiercer creatures than any fish, leapt right out of the water with it, fought me for possession of it and yielded only to utter exhaustion and the lift of the net.

So I have no wisdom that will let me write of June and July, even in my own river that I know well. And the wisdom I once had for August and September is shaken a little and likely to grow shakier yet as I grow older and learn to watch more closely. Sometimes in the second week of August the humpback salmon run into the river. With them, I used to say, come the big cutthroats that are maturing to spawn in the following February—magnificent fish that have attained their full weight and strength and a cunning or dourness that makes them hard to catch on bright August days in the Canyon Pool. I argued that they came into the river because of their maturity, following the maturity of the humpbacks rather than in any hope of feeding on salmon eggs that would not be dropped to the gravel for another two months. It was a nice theory, but in the last two or three years I've noticed the cutthroats before the humpbacks. I asked General Money about that, and he had noticed the same thing. So I no longer know why they come in then—I only know that I try to get away to the Canyon Pool as soon as I can after the first of August.

That August fishing in the Canyon Pool is the finest cutthroat fishing I have had anywhere. The fish are very big—I have killed several that weighed within an ounce of four pounds and have lost some that I know were over five pounds—and they can be superlatively difficult. They are not feeding, for only very rarely is there so much as a Mayfly nymph in a stomach; they lie in water six or eight feet deep, unrippled by the slightest stir of wind and burnished by the full glare of summer sun. When they rise, they come right up from the bottom, and every cast that covers them is a really long cast. When they feel the hook, they turn and run with a pull that makes every one seem a ten-pounder, and at the end of that first long run, well down at the tail of the pool, they jump with a coho's wildness. That part is easy. Coaxing them back up the pool again, trying to keep them from disturbing the rest of the water, meeting their plunging, boring, heavy resistance and yielding no more than must be yielded to save 2X gut is the hard part, the part that makes fingers clumsy and trembling and the heart quick in the chest when it's time to reach for the net.

After August you may perhaps find cutthroats again in October, when the cohos run up on the first heavy fall rains. They seem less important then, because their season is almost over and you're fishing a big fly and heavy gut for the cohos anyway—tackle too clumsy for a trout—so you turn them back to live and spawn. And again in steelhead time, in December and January and February, they are there, heavy with spawn now, dark, with red gill covers and golden bellies. I hold them hard and bring them in fast, then reach down for the shank of the hook and twist the barb quickly away from them so that they can go back without harm to their important affairs. But recently a few big cutthroats have been caught and killed as steelheads in the Campbell. I saw one two seasons ago that weighed six and a half pounds. This season there was one that weighed well over seven pounds. I hope that next August, or one August soon, in the Canyon Pool . . .

The Big Salmon Water

The Columbia River is not, from my point of view, an angler's river. An angler's river is one that can be covered and searched for fish from bank to bank by wading and casting. I don't mean that a single, long cast should reach clear across it, but that by fishing it from both sides and using all his skill and water wisdom, a good fisherman should have at least an outside chance of reaching every lie and holding place. When a river is much larger than that, one is fishing only a part of it, not the whole river. There must be channels and lies and bars and eddies only a little distance away of which one can know nothing; and a really big river, like a lake, has its secret depths.

But a big river has all the beauties and intricacies and delights of a smaller river, and has them on a scale so vast that the imagination is awed and staggered as it is when one turns eyes and mind from the earth on a clear night to look into the infinity of the stars. The Columbia is a big, grand river in this sense, one of the truly great rivers of the world, and the country it drains is immeasurably beautiful, vast and varied and full of the stories of men. The Columbia is also a great salmon river, the greatest of all Chinook salmon rivers, and so when I wanted to write a story of the Chinook run, it was quite obvious that I had to draw my salmon from the Columbia watershed.

When I was ready to start the book, I knew something of the Columbia; I had followed the river in several places and had seen many of its tributaries. I also knew a good deal about Columbia River Chinooks, because so much of scientific research has been directed toward the Columbia runs. But I had never seen the dams at Bonneville and Grand Coulee, I had not seen the Snake River or the Salmon, where thousands upon thousands of Chinooks turn off from the Columbia in each spawning migration, and I had never looked at any part of the watershed with this particular book in mind. I felt I could write a book without going down, but that if I did so, it would be less than the book it should be; and since the Columbia was only three or four hundred miles away, there seemed no slightest excuse for this. So I wrote two chapters and a synopsis and sent them off to New York with the hope that enough money would be advanced to make the trip. The weeks went by and I waited for news. I wrote slowly ahead as far as the end of Chapter 6, then came to a dead stop; thus far my salmon had not left the pool of her birth, but now she had to find her way down to salt water through lengths of river I had never seen. It is one thing in writing to invent when you must, to think into people's thoughts or plan their actions or describe their houses and how they live in them—there is generally enough real knowledge to limit and control the imagination; if not, then to be honest one must go out and search or else find some other way to state one's point. There was no other way to state mine, though I had hoped there might be. And in any case, the difficulties and distances of the search were not such as to justify evasion.

I left the book alone and turned to all the odds and ends of jobs that could be done around the house and the farm. One wet afternoon, because there seemed nothing else to do, I spent in cleaning and polishing Ann's kettles until they shone as the makers had never meant them to. As if that had been a virtuous deed instead of an angry expression of frustration, there was a letter from New York the next day. The money for the trip would be through in a few days.

So Ann and I went down in May, which is a fine month for the purpose, and saw the Columbia and most of its tributaries between Astoria and Grand Coulee Dam. We were in the spirit of the thing as deeply as it is possible to be; we knew the framework of the watershed, we knew the whole essential outline of the Chinook salmon's life history; we had only to fill in the gaps, and we knew where the gaps were and what we must find to fill them; we had only to travel the country, look carefully and see properly.

We started with some of the tributaries on the Washington side, then turned from these down to Astoria. Astoria was not fishing, though the spring run of Chinooks had passed through and the summer run was due to start any day. The scattered piling of the fish traps was gaunt and dreary, but beyond it the river was wide and strong with tide and spring flood—too wide to seem a river. Above Astoria, where the big islands are, we felt it a river; and above the islands it narrows again, though deep-sea ships still climb against it and the little gill-net boats are lonely and lost within sight of the highway.

We stopped in Portland because there were people to see and things to learn about the river there. Portland is a Coast League baseball town too, so we took time out for a double-header on Sunday. I'm for the Seattle Rainiers myself and feel strongly about it, but I can always see virtue in the Hollywood team, and the Portland Beavers were playing to an affectionate crowd and stealing bases in a way that the form sheet said they should not, so the game was fine. On Monday, with slight prickings of conscience, we hurried to Bonneville.

Bonneville is worth any fisherman's time and thought. It is worth any human being's time and thought, for that matter. Here, where the dam is built, the river has found its way through the Cascade Range, yet the ocean tides run up almost to the foot of the dam, so low is the pass. There is an island at the site of the dam, Bradford Island, and the power dam itself spans Bradford Slough, between the island and the Oregon bank, while the spillway dam closes off the rest of the river between the island and the Washington bank. Being river-minded rather than mechanically minded, I prefer the spillway dam to the power dam. It is a long and noble structure, with many slanting buttresses that gleam white in the sun and dark-steel sluice gates between them. The gates open from the bottom to let the surplus water away in a thunder of foam and spray and great waves that translate into visible form the mighty weight and strength of fifty or sixty solid feet of Columbia River water piled behind the dam.

This race of savage, tumbled water drew the fish when we saw it and wondered at it, for there was only a single turbine turning in the powerhouse. They worked against it, unseen, until tiring muscles turned them toward the sheltered water at either side of the dam, where they found the easier draw of current escaping from the ladders. At Bonneville there are at least three ladders and three sets of elevators, or fish locks, as well as many passes and chutes by which the young fish can find their way to the sea, but the finest of all these is the Bradford Island ladder. A full river of water flows down its curving length, breaking white on the steps, filling the rest pools between them, sending a hidden, twisting flow of current through the gaps in each step which are the main passageway of the fish. We followed the ladder up, walking slowly along it, stopping often to watch. Occasionally we saw a fish, usually a steelhead, jump clear out. Once or twice we saw the shining dark back of a big Chinook curve over, but for the most part they were passing unseen, six or seven feet below the bubbled, white-veined surface of the water.

At the counting fence they had to come up. The water was smoother and slower here, and the shapes of big fish showed clearly in it, pressing their noses against the feel of the current through the bars of the steel grating, searching along until they came to the counting gap, coming up over the white plate under the counter's box, hesitating, sometimes going back to turn and come again, sometimes going forward to pass over the plate and on into the dark water above. Fish of different kinds came through as we watched—big steelheads, suckers, lampreys and, more numerous than any, the Chinooks. The fish were nervous but not frightened. They passed steadily, almost with an air of knowing the way, and as a matter of fact they did know it, because in spite of dams and ladders it was the same old upstream way, a way that must be made against the current flow clear up from the sea to the spawning bed.

There has been great concern about Bonneville. Thousands upon thousands of words have been written—naturally enough, perhaps, since the dam is so far down the river, well below most of the best spawning areas—to show that the runs will be destroyed or will not be destroyed, that the mature fish would not go up the ladders, that the small downstream migrants could not survive the passage through the ice chutes or through the turbines, that they would fail to find the by-passes especially designed for them. It seems safe to say now that the fishways and by-passes of Bonneville have proved themselves. The fish go up and come down and return again at least as well as they ever did. And from the concept of Bonneville dam, from the first realization that the dam would be a threat to a great fishery, men began to notice properly the other evils, individually small, but collectively greater than any the dam could cause, that had been damaging the runs for years. There was pollution, the effluent of mines and mills and cities that poisoned the spawning streams. There were the hundreds, if not thousands, of petty dams which barred off the acres upon acres of good gravel beds that had built and maintained the runs, dams built without a thought of the passage of fish or with wretched, impossible ladders that filled the letter of some law of man but served the runs not at all. And there were the irrigation ditches, turning the streams out into farmers' fields and orchards and drawing the migrants down to die in mud. These conditions and excessive fishing were the drain. The threat of Bonneville drew attention to them. Now many of the useless little dams have been torn out, and over others there are proper ladders that take the spawning fish to the gravel beds again. Hundreds of irrigation ditches and power intakes have been screened so that the

migrants cannot pass down them—though many still remain un-
screened. Pollution? Perhaps that has been improved a little, though
there is still far to go. Overfishing? They take them as they can get
them, and until the fisherman can find no one but himself to blame, he
will probably go on trying to catch more fish than he safely should.

I like to think that Bonneville is not the first dam that has helped
the salmon runs of the Columbia. A little above Bonneville is a stretch
of water, still fast and strong in spite of the dam, which is called the
Cascades. The break of the Cascades is caused by a tumbled mass of
rock on the river bed—the wreckage of what was once, perhaps, a
great natural bridge across the river. F. H. Balch has written of this in
a book called *The Bridge of the Gods*. In his preface he says:

> Everywhere along the mid-Columbia the Indians tell of a great
> bridge that once spanned the river where the Cascades now are,
> but where at that time the placid current flowed under an arch of
> stone; that this bridge was *tomanowos*, built by the gods; that the
> Great Spirit shook the earth and the bridge crashed down into the
> river, forming the present obstruction of the Cascades. . . .
>
> "Ancutta (long time back)," say the Tumwater Indians, "the
> salmon he no pass Tumwater falls. It too much big leap. Snake
> Indian he no catch um fish above falls. By and by great *toma-
> nowos* bridge at Cascades he fall in, dam up water, make river
> higher all way up to Tumwater; then salmon he get over. Then
> Snake Indian all time catch um plenty."

This is mighty big talk, because it would mean that the whole run of
fish to the Columbia above the Cascades is a comparatively new run—
that the great runs of the Snake and the Salmon rivers, the run that
reaches Rock Island, the runs that used to find their way above the
Grand Coulee and into British Columbia, have all grown from the few
pioneer fish that first ventured over the newly formed cascades. Even
apart from the fish, this conception of the Bridge of the Gods is gran-
diose, because such a bridge must have been a wonder as great almost
as the Grand Canyon or Death Valley. And Balch is very insistent that
there actually was such a bridge in almost recent times. He quotes the
words of another Indian, a Klikitat, to a pioneer at White Salmon:

> "My father talk one time; long time ago liddle boy, him in
> canoe, his mother paddle, paddle up Columbia, then come to
> *tomanowos* bridge. Squaw paddle canoe under: all dark under
> bridge. He look up, all like one big roof, shut out sky, no see um

sun. Indian afraid, paddle quick, get past quick, no good. Liddle boy no forget how bridge look!"

Balch continues:

Local proof also is not wanting. In the fall, when the freshets are over and the waters of the Columbia are clear, one going out in a small boat just above the Cascades and looking down into the transparent depths can see submerged forest trees beneath him, still standing upright as they stood before the bridge fell in and the river was raised above them. It is a strange, weird sight, this forest beneath the river; the waters watch over the broken tree-tops, fish swim among the leafless branches; it is desolate, spectre-like, beyond all words.

Such evidence, I suppose, will have rotted away by now, and the water backed up behind Bonneville will have buried it still deeper. Perhaps there never was a bridge of the gods; perhaps the Cascades hide nothing more than a slide from a mountainside; perhaps the salmon always found their way back into Idaho and Montana and British Columbia. I haven't inquired very deeply, because I like Balch's picture and would as soon keep it in error as lose it in truth.

Ann and I crossed the Hood River bridge a few miles above Bonneville and followed the Washington bank back to Portland again. From there we turned up the Willamette Valley—Balch says that should be Wallamet, which is certainly closer to the common pronunciation—because there were things we had to see there and because it is the loveliest valley in the west and we still half wish we lived there. From the Willamette we turned up the Mackenzie, stopping at the Waterville bridge to watch the great panicky Chinooks milling and circling in the shallow water below the weir that holds them from their spawning grounds. The Mackenzie is little more than a stream here, because the Eugene power canal has taken off much of its water; but above Leaburg it is a good-sized river and as wild and white over a bottom of big, round boulders as any river I know. It is also a fine fly-fisherman's river, full of big red-sided rainbows that come nobly to floating deer-hair patterns in the strongest water. We fished a little, because it would have been almost sacrilege not to, but I was more concerned to know the river than the fishing, and we did not catch any really good fish.

From the head of the Mackenzie we followed the Deschutes, another fly-fisherman's river, back down to the Columbia again. From the mouth of the Deschutes we turned briefly back to The Dalles, where the river flows through a deep and narrow lava channel that is as impressive as its broadest reaches. Above The Dalles, all the way to the big bend between Plymouth and Pasco the Columbia is lonely, a wide swift river with gravel bars and rocky islands, flowing among sandy hills made rugged by outcrop of black rock ramparts. Sometimes there are willows near the water, sometimes poplars enclosing a rare farm. Occasionally a heron rises on slow wings, or there are gulls flying, strangely far from salt water. But for the most part the country is sand and sagebrush and rocks, and the flow of so much water through it seems at once tragic and fine.

We turned away at the big bend to follow the Snake and the Salmon back into Idaho, but in a few days we came back to the Columbia again, passed the irrigated lands near the mouth of the Yakima and came into another waste of sagebrush and tumbleweed, rock and sand and gravel. It is a windy desolate country, huge and lonely, with the grotesque and incredible wonders of the Grand Coulee already beginning to grow up out of the ground; but it fitted a mood of breathless wonder already built in us by all we had seen, and we loved it. We found the Columbia's own way through the narrow gap in the Saddle Mountains and knew we were coming near the end, for Rock Island Dam, a little below Wenatchee, is the farthest ascent of the Chinooks since Coulee Dam was finished.

Still below Rock Island we turned away from the river and so came into the Grand Coulee, the dry bed of what was once the greatest river on earth. We stopped at the dry falls and tried, as every dutiful tourist must, to imagine a wall of water four hundred feet high and five miles wide pouring over them. I looked down at the lakes at the foot of the falls and felt that prehistoric monsters might still live in them; I felt for a single quick moment that I knew that fish had run up from the sea to the foot of the falls and perhaps spawned and died in the more sheltered places of the river bed. But the Grand Coulee is death and desolation now, a geologist's delight and a fisherman's hell. Somewhere along the road we picked up an old man who lived and farmed under the shadow of Steamboat Rock. As we went along he showed us the pass he had come down through thirty-three years earlier, then a good spring that came up out of the rock and then a breastwork thrown up by the Indians to serve their last stand in that part of the country. When we came to his farm and stopped, he showed us one more thing, a great yellow cross in the road that marks the place where a car crashed into his haywagon, killing its own two passengers and one of his horses. We were sorry to leave the old man and go back to remembering that the waters of half a continent had once poured over Steamboat Rock in a fall wider than the Dry Falls and twice as high.

We came to Coulee Dam at last and found it almost finished, with the water already pouring over its face. Perhaps I was exhausted by bigness, or perhaps I had expected too much. Coulee Dam is big, but it is not beautiful. It did not seem to me then as impressive as it should have. I tried to feel it impressive, but could not; I saw the fierceness and length of the race below it and understood that no salmon could be drawn from that into a ladder or an elevator, then I felt ready to leave and find the live and free Columbia again.

We found it between Bridgeport and Wenatchee, running with green snow water among orchards and rocky range hills, breaking white in rapids, accepting tributaries that came in beautifully over gravel bars. And at Rock Island it was the real Columbia again, with Chinooks and bluebacks and steelheads using it. Rock Island is the oldest and by far the most beautiful of the three Columbia River dams, a long, low curve, wide and graceful, set among high, steep hills, dry, grassy, hardened by rock outcrop. The two days we spent there were sunny and windy, and the Columbia was in fine spring freshet; the whole main curve of the dam was hidden under a tremendous roll of green water, utterly smooth, brilliant in the sun with an infinite depth of color and light, crashing down into a heavy roar of arching waves and leaping white spray.

The fish turned into ladders on both sides of the dam and were trapped there. We were at the right trap, on the west bank of the river and M. J. Hanavan, the biologist, was with us. Mr. Uber, who is in charge of the fish work at the damsite, came down a little later. He raised the brail, a horizontal grating that made the floor of the trap, until the fish were forced up and we could see them.

The work at Rock Island is the solution of the problem made by Coulee Dam. A hundred and twenty miles downstream from Coulee, it is the nearest place at which the fish can be held and saved from wasting themselves in the wild water below the dam. So the ladders that used to pass them over Rock Island are turned into traps and the fish are taken from there in tank trucks to Leavenworth Hatchery or the spawning streams that enter the Columbia between Rock Island and Coulee. No great proportion of the Chinook run reaches Rock Island—some nine or ten thousand compared with a count of three or four hundred thousand at Bonneville in a normal year; but nine thousand big fish are a lot to handle, particularly when you add to them some twenty thousand bluebacks out of a run of a hundred thousand and five or six thousand steelheads. We had followed one fish to a spawning tributary of the lower Columbia, and we had followed others back into Idaho to their spawning places near the Salmon River; now we were to follow others from the Columbia to the farthest spawning tributaries that were still open to them.

Soon after Uber had lifted the brail, a big tank truck came down to pick up its load. The truck backed up to the elevator, shot out a load of stale water and took on a thousand gallons of fresh water. Uber raised the brail a little higher in the trap and turned a strong flow of water through the elevator. This passed into the trap, and the fish turned toward it immediately and began to seek a way through the bars and into the elevator. After a little while Uber opened the gate, and they began to move in, a little nervously, with the same hesitations and turnings they use in crossing the counting plates at Bonneville, but always passing through in the end because their maturity compels them against the current and there is no release until the proper spawning place is found.

About fifty Chinooks swam in, some of them big fish of thirty pounds or more. There were several steelhead with them and a few jacks, the precociously mature males that follow the Chinook run. Then the gate was closed, the elevator was raised and the fish, with another thousand gallons of water, were shot down from it into the truck. The water already in the tank cushioned their fall, splashing and spilling out over the roadway. The driver closed the hatch, started the auxiliary engine that draws air over the ice compartment and pumps it through the water in the tank, then climbed into his cab and drove off.

Leavenworth was not yet operating, and it was sixty miles to Nason Creek, on the Stevens Pass highway, where the fish were to be dumped to find natural spawning. I was glad of that because I do not care much for hatcheries and I wanted my fish to spawn naturally. The truck stopped once on the way while Hanavan took a water sample and tested it; then we came up into the green timber and the swift streams of the Cascades again. Fish that had climbed five hundred miles of the Columbia were back within a hundred miles of salt water. I wondered how many of those in the truck would have homed to this Wenatchee Valley anyway, Rock Island trap or no. I thought: Not many, because the Wenatchee run had gone far down long before Coulee Dam was built. Yet it may grow again from this freighting of fish by road, and the other runs to the Methow, Entiat and Okanogan rivers may grow, perhaps breeding fish that will home to them as unfailingly as the runs of a hundred years ago. When that time comes, the ladders at Rock Island will be opened again perhaps, and the trucks and Leavenworth will have little work to do unless the spawners crowd the streams and there is a surplus to be cared for.

The highway came close to Nason Creek and the truck stopped in a wide space of clear gravel, then backed out on a ramp built over a good pool in the creek. We looked in the tank again (carefully because a fish will sometimes try to jump out) and saw them moving restlessly against the black steel walls. The driver went down and clamped a metal chute under the round rear door of the tank, then tripped the clamp on the door. For a fraction of a second only water came out; then there were fish in it, struggling against it, plunging down into Nason Creek; then there was only a trickle of water from the truck and two or three last fish flopping out and down. We watched and could see many of them in the pool, lying well in the stream, already sheltering behind boulders or close to the bottom. There were six miles of Nason Creek open to them between fences. They had some three months to search their way about it before their spawning time would come.

We climbed the Wenatchee Valley again the next day and stopped for a little while beside the pool in Nason Creek before going on through Stevens Pass to the coast again. I knew the book was all mine now and I could write it as it should be written, with the feel of the Columbia in it.

JUNE

June is the midsummer month, yet in the temperate latitude of southern England and the British Columbia coast it is not full summer; growth is still fresh and young, and the rivers still have the flow of stored-up winter snow or rain. All the summer months are trout fisher's months, I suppose, wherever trout swim and feed. Yet June is generally a quiet month on the Campbell, and in most of the lakes near sea level the surface water is almost too warm for good fly-fishing. Some of the mountain streams make good fishing, but it is too early for the really cold ones.

In June, were I near enough to it, I would always go into the Kilipi River, which flows into Nimpkish Lake. Once I had a trap line up the valley, and in the winters I used to catch fine trout for food as they lay behind the late-spawning coho salmon. But in June I fished there for fun and caught, not many fish, but always fish that surprised me.

Generally, I had to go there over a short weekend, leaving a logging camp after work on Saturday, walking through to Nimpkish Lake, then rowing six or eight miles up or down the lake to the mouth of the river. That left time to make a quick camp, cook supper and fish through the river's straight swift run from my camp to the lake. Sometimes I caught nothing on that first evening, once I caught two fine cutthroats, each over three pounds, which ran out into the lake so far that I waded almost shoulder deep to hold them and turn them. Once I hooked, on the fly and fairly in the mouth, a five-pound sockeye salmon; this was surprising enough, because properly organized sockeyes are not supposed to take fly or bait of any kind at all readily. It was the more surprising because sockeyes don't run to the Kilipi; but I was reaching well out into the lake at the time, and perhaps a passing school had turned momentarily into the fresh flow of current. I saw no others roll or jump.

On the Sunday I usually fished the canyon and the water below it, but sometimes I walked the five or six miles through to the meadows, to see them in their summer green; the Kilipi meadows are always full of deer as no other place I know, and the deer are bold and calm. It is almost as though, knowing little of the rifle, they place a human being's power of harming them on a par with that of the cougar: they watch cautiously, even suspiciously; they bound away if you come upon them too suddenly or too closely; but generally they stand with heads arrogantly raised, eyes impersonally curious, unless one is within a hundred feet or so—half a dozen easy springs for a hunting cougar. I like the meadows if only for the deer, but there are many birds there too. The snipe nest there, and ruffed grouse drum steadily through the day among the crab apples and cedars. Song sparrows are always there, summer and winter, warblers are quick in the swamp grass, and at different times I have seen goldfinches and vireos, bluebirds, meadow larks, kinglets, red-winged blackbirds, flickers with the lovely flash of orange under their wings, downy woodpeckers and the swooping flight and scarlet crests of pileated woodpeckers.

Bears love the meadows in fall, when the salmon are running, but they come there in summer as well, to roll in cool mud wallows and rub themselves against the trunks of big crab apples. The trout, like the bears, are interested mainly in the salmon runs, but a few of them seem to stay there through the year. A small fork of the river runs through the meadows, deep and slow and very clear. Once I came quietly to the deepest pool of all, ten or twelve feet from smooth surface to pale gravel, and saw three good trout lying quite still on the bottom. It seemed almost foolish to fish for them with anything less interesting than a worm, but I tied on a big dry sedge and cast it well above the nearest fish. Three times I floated it over him, and the third time I thought I saw him move. Perhaps it was less than a movement, simply a stiffening of the body, a tightening of muscles. I cast again, and as the fly touched the water, he started up. He came slowly, his body tilted only a little, with a feathery lightness of flying, up and up and up through brilliant water that seemed lighter and clearer than air. He met the fly perfectly, dropped back under it for a moment, then quietly took it. I fished for the rest of the afternoon but could not move the others.

It is a little like that in the canyon. I have never seen many fish there in June, but the few that are there can be seen; one sees them from above and knows the climb down is worth while. Nearly always they are deep down in the pools, apparently little concerned with feeding, and nearly always they are big cutthroats, beautifully colored. But they do feed there, and they seem to love best of all the bright, blue-green cedar borer beetles. All trout seem to like these beetles, and I made up my own clumsy imitation long ago—a body of emerald green and blue seal's fur, ribbed with bronze peacock herl and gold thread, wings of green peacock and a light blue hackle tied above them. I fish it drowned, with little movement, and in the Kilipi it was often an hour's work to get the fly down to where the trout would take an interest in it. But the take was always worth while, the solemn opening and closing of a great mouth, the twist of a wide body against the strike and a strong run, deep down. Once only I hooked a summer steelhead somewhere far below me in a pool that I had not examined from above. I was standing on a little pinnacle of rock from which I could not move, and it was nearly half an hour before I could bring him back to it. Then, as I reached down to slip a finger in his gills, I fell in. For a few moments I floundered about, trying to climb back on the rock without losing my rod, then I gave up with a good grace and swam to the tail of the pool, praying that the line would not tangle my legs. It did not, and when I climbed out again the fish was still hooked.

But for all its surprises and delights, the Kilipi never gave me really good June fishing, though some northwest rivers have. Almost any stream with a real stock of nonmigratory trout should be at its best in June, when there are plentiful hatches of fly and the water is cool and lively enough to keep the fish active. June is transition from spring to summer, a month when everything has its full vigor, before anything is stale or mature. In June May flies may be thick on the water, stone-fly nymphs may still be crawling up the rocks to split their cases and fly away, midges will be dancing in clouds near the water's edge and falling spent on the water to move fish that the angler finds it difficult to tempt with his larger flies; and on June evenings may come the early sedge hatches.

None of these interest the summer steelhead; yet June is perhaps the best steelhead month of all the year. The fish are not so numerous then as later, in September and early October when the fall run is in. But those that have come up from salt water are perfect, bright and clean, still several months from the full maturity and the slowing bulk of developed ovaries and milt sacs. When a June fish takes, he is into his run before you can move to raise the rod, and that run is fierce and long and dangerous. Almost always a June fish is a jumping fish, a bold, wild, jumping fish, and he is little concerned to keep within the limits of the pool in which he has taken the fly.

Good summer steelhead runs are less common than good winter runs. Oregon rivers and northern California rivers draw fine runs. Some rivers in Washington state have good runs, and the North Fork of the Stillaguamish has been set aside by a wise authority for fly-fishing only. In British Columbia there are many rivers with summer-run fish, but most of them are not easily accessible to anglers. For some reason, the rivers on the east coast of Vancouver Island, accessible from the Island Highway, draw few summer fish. The Campbell has no true summer run; the Oyster, the Courtenay, the Qualicum rivers and all the smaller streams between them, in spite of good winter runs, do not draw summer fish. I believe the Cowichan had a fair run at one time, but Indian fishing killed it. North of Seymour Narrows, rivers such as the Nimpkish have runs, and several of the mainland rivers have really fine runs. There is one in particular that I mean to try out now that the war is over; it comes to a river in Ramsay Arm, near the mouth of Bute Inlet.

Nearly all the rivers on the west coast of Vancouver Island have summer runs, but only one of them is easily reached—the Stamp River at Alberni. The Stamp is General Money's river and always will be so far as I am concerned. The General lived at Qualicum until he died in 1941, and there he built the big hotel and the golf course. He was the wisest and best fisherman I have ever known in British Columbia, and he was also probably the keenest. A few months before he died, Ann and I stopped at his house on our way up the Island. It was a cold, wet December evening, and we found him just changed after a day of searching for winter fish in one of the Qualicum rivers. All the clothes he had worn during the day were hung to dry in the warmest place in the house. He had been really wet, right to the skin, and his day had given him a move from only a single fish, but the General was happy and satisfied with it and was already making plans for the next day.

When you fished with General Money, you fished as his guest; and never was host more gracious or better informed on the possibilities of his domain. It was a June day when I first went down to the Stamp with him, a sunny day after rain the night before. We drove to the cottage he had built on the high bank above his favorite pool, put up our rods and walked to the edge of the clifflike bank. General Money's Pool is at a good, wide bend of the river; above it there is a straight reach of fast water as far as the mouth of the Ash and below it a broken rapid that gathers itself through two or three hundred yards to a narrow pool under the far bank. From where we were standing we had a clear view of the pool and its bottom, except when a light breeze ruffled the surface, and after looking for a while we knew that there were fish in it—three together, well down the pool and near the middle, and a fourth a little below them and well over to the far side. The General was pleased. "Water's in fine shape," he said. "I'm glad I got you out today."

We walked down the steep trail to the pool, and he settled himself in his favorite place under the big trees near the head.

"Fish this top part through," he told me, "in case there's something there. You'll cover those three fish from the kidney stones—you'll see them, two light-colored, kidney-shaped stones on this side. When they're under your feet, you ought to be reaching the fish. Then you might reach the other one with a long cast from the flat rock just below the kidney stones. It won't be much good below that."

I fished carefully down, came to the kidney stones, cast well across and felt a good heavy pull as the fly came round in midstream. The fish ran without hesitation, hard for the tail of the pool. I put on a heavy strain, and he jumped out twice, still going away, tumbling over himself and splashing the shining water high at each fall. The jumps slowed him a little, and he turned and came back up the pool very fast; opposite me, only thirty or forty feet out, he jumped again beautifully, very high out of the water. For a moment after that he was quiet. The General was beside me now.

"You must get him," he said. "It would be too bad to lose the first fish of the day."

"I'd like to keep him away from the others," I said. "We don't want to disturb the pool too much."

"Don't worry about that, man. Make sure of him."

But the fish ran straight across, and I worked upstream a little so that I had a chance to hold him well above the best part of the pool. After five more good minutes the General gaffed him for me.

"Go and catch another one," he said.

"No, sir. You fish now."

"Go on and fish. I like to watch you."

More than anything, I wanted to watch him, but it seemed too late to say that now. I washed my fly and looked over my gut, then started in again well above the stones. When they were under my feet again, I realized that I was a little breathless and anxious. It suddenly occurred to me that the General was watching me, closely and critically. I had done well enough with the first fish, but I began to wonder if I might not bungle something now, and I remembered how I hate to put a man in some good favorite place where I know there are fish and see him spoil it. The fly swung round without a touch, and I cast again. Still nothing, and nothing to a third cast. I felt disappointed, but I moved on down and left them then. It seemed better to do that than chance putting them off altogether. At the flat rock I drew more line off the reel and reached well over toward the far side. It was a good cast, but short of the fish, I felt sure, and I wondered if I could handle two or three more yards of line. I took them out, picked up, measured out an ordinary cast, then picked up and cast again with all the drive I could put into the rod. The last loop of line left my hand and I felt the pull of its leaving come cleanly against the reel. The fly curled over, carrying the gut out to its full length, and began fishing. I saw a brown-backed shape come up to meet it, waited a moment, then tightened on him. He began to jump at once, again and again and again, all across the tail of the pool. The General was coming along the bank behind me.

"Lightly hooked," I said. "He won't stay on long."

"I know, I know," he said. "Try and get him though. Bring him into this side, if you can, and I'll go below you and try to put the gaff in him."

The fish had come up the pool a little, but he started down and began jumping again. At the tail of the pool he was right on the surface, working almost gently against me, and I thought for a moment I could swing him across to where the General was waiting. Then the fly came away.

"Rotten luck," the General said. "If anyone had told me you could get over to that fish with only thigh boots and an eleven-foot rod, I'd never have believed him."

That was the most tactful and graceful remark any man has ever made to me after the loss of a good fish. I went back from the pool with a feeling of merit that was completely without justification but extremely pleasant.

We rested the pool for fifteen or twenty minutes, then the General himself started down it. He was a tall slim man, very straight, with a long, brown face, deeply lined, and blue eyes bright and quick to smile against the brownness. He moved out gracefully and easily until he was in water over his hips; then he began to put out line with his doublehanded thirteen-foot rod. He was spey casting, rolling the line out in a long loop that lifted the fly from the water in front of him and carried it over and out in a straight smooth cast that covered the whole water. He worked his fly across, deep and slow, moved down a step or two and cast again, letting the big shining curve of the rod carry the burden of the work. He had fished this pool a thousand times, made each cast he was making now a thousand times before, but his mind was with his fly, working it down to the fish, bringing it easily into the swifter water near his own bank, holding it with the long rod so that it would not cross too quickly, ready to meet the fierce, quick pull of a taking fish with a tightening of the line at the right moment. I watched him cast again, and judged that he was almost at the kidney stones. The fly came in midstream, a shade too quickly, I thought, and the General lowered his rod point. Then the fish took. I saw the rod lift and bend and saw clearly the delayed boil of the fish's deep turn. The big rod dipped to him, met his runs and his jumps, humored him away from the rocks and bad water at the tail of the pool, brought him up and held him at last on his side and ready for the gaff. I set the gaff and brought him ashore, and the General looked at him, his eyes and face alight with the pleasure of it. "I thought we could take another," he said.

It was on one of the last days I fished with him, not much over a year before he died, that he caught a fish in his pool by a new method. It was an August day, and the river was very low—too low, the General said, for someone had closed the gate at the dam and made a drop of a foot or more during the night. I was almost glad because I had planned to fish the greased line anyway; the low water and the hot bright day were perfect for it. The General said he just wanted to sit in the shade and watch; his doctor had warned him a few days earlier that he must show his heart a little consideration.

So I started down with the greased line and a tiny silver-bodied fly that I had tied the night before. I fished carefully, by the book, casting a slack line well across, lifting the belly of the line each time before the current could draw on it, holding the fly right up under the surface in a slow, easy drift all the way across. The fish came again as I reached the kidney stones and came as a good fish sometimes does to the greased line, with a long slashing rise that threw water a foot into the air. For once I did the rest of it right—pointed my rod straight downstream, held it well into my own bank and let the delayed pull on the belly of the line set the hook. When the General gaffed him, he said with something like awe in his voice, "Look at that fly. Right in the back corner of the mouth, exactly the way it's supposed to be."

That was the best of all the days we had together. We ate our lunch in the shade and drank bottles of cool stout. Then I went upstream with the General's big rod and left him to fish his pool with the greased line. Something told me to fish the heavy white water, and I was hardly getting the fly well out before I hooked a fish. He started downstream, and I glanced quickly along the river to pick a place to gaff him, then looked down to the pool where the General was fishing. I saw his rod come up and knew that he was into one as well. Suddenly I was afraid. I thought of the sharp stab of excitement that comes with the surface rise to the greased line, of the long strain of the fight with a small fly and light gut, of those last anxious moments as the fish comes within reach of the gaff. I began to run downstream, caring nothing about my own fish, which tumbled on ahead of me. I wondered if I could break in him—it's not always so easy when you want to. Then I saw he was close to shore, and I reached for my gaff almost without thinking. He started out as I came up to him, but I made a lucky stroke and caught him just above the tail. In a moment I had him on the bank, tapped him on the head, dropped the rod and started on again.

As I came down to the big pool, I saw the General was getting his gaff ready. I shouted, "I'll do that, sir," but he looked back and smiled and shook his head. Then I saw him lean forward and gaff his fish with an easy, gentle stroke. He waded ashore and I met him.

"That's wonderful sport," he said. "We should have tried it long ago." He knelt beside his fish and freed the fly from the corner of the jaw. "I'm going to send away for a light rod as soon as we get home. You must help me pick one out of the catalogue."

We took the fish back in the shade and sat down. "That's my day's fishing," the General said. "I'm getting old. But we've found something new for the river after all these years."

Lewington's Carrier

For a year after I left school I studied history with Dr. T. H. Davies, rector of the parish of Headbourne Worthy, near Winchester. Attached to the rectory were several scattered fields of glebe; they were strategically placed fields and of good variety, ranging from marsh and meadowland to the high ground near the school and the narrow wood along the Pilgrim's Way. In good partridge country, where the landowners also preserved pheasants and ducks, this meant fairly important sporting possibilities of which Denis, the rector's son, and I availed ourselves to the full. We even managed to extend them a little by friendly agreements with one or two of the near-by farmers. And occasionally we took casual evening strolls across the stubble fields that marched with our glebe, then stirred out early the next morning with our guns to see if the chance shift of wildlife population had lasted through the night. Acre for acre, there were probably not many properties in the south of England that showed a finer yield of game that year. And we achieved considerable variety too: snipe, teal, mallard, pheasants, partridges, rabbits, pigeons, hares, besides crows, hawks, weasels and other vermin which, we easily persuaded ourselves, more than made up for the few pheasants and partridges that might, with some logic, have been considered poached.

Within a mile of the rectory flowed the Itchen, one of the finest trout streams in England. Unfortunately there was very little we could do about that. In the winter we managed to get very occasional permission to try for grayling, but in the trout season we were without privilege and could only admire the gliding water and the fine fish that lay between the trailing weed beds. There were some really big fish in the reach, and I watched them a lot at their wise, quiet feeding. The river was of noble proportions there below the rectory, and the best fish were splendidly difficult to approach and seemed to have about them a quiet air of confidence in their own good judgment which implied that they could treat artificial flies with complete contempt in the midst of the most tempting hatch of naturals; but I felt satisfied that I could have found a way to move them. Once or twice, picking days of bad weather, we hid a rod in our long plus fours and went down to a place where head-high sedges hid us. We would put the rod together with eager, trembling hands, watching for rises as we worked. Generally, when the rod was up, there was no good fish in sight, and we made only a few haphazard, frightened casts, then took the rod down and went home. Once I hooked a good fish, tried to hurry him out and lost him in a weed bed. That was excitement of a really high quality. On another evening, after a day of storm, I was down among the high rushes alone. It was a very quiet evening, and for some reason I determined not to be nervous. The rushes hid me from sight, but they served equally to hide the approach of a keeper or a legitimate fisherman, and that, generally, was a worrying thought that stayed right with us. On this evening I felt I could disregard it—no one would come. A good fish was rising well across the stream, on the far side of a weed bed that made a little island above the surface. It was a difficult chance, and I suspected the fish was feeding on nymphs rather than on surface flies, but I gave him the floating fly first. Four or five times I laid it perfectly above him, watched it drift over him and recovered without hooking the weed bed. The next cast hooked the weeds some way below him, but the light gut broke easily, and he went on feeding. I changed to a dark Greenwell nymph, cast once more and saw him bulge. He ran at once, straight up along the weed bed, past the head of it and into the clear. I got him to the bank almost easily and decided that I had tried my luck far enough. That was the only fish we ever had to show for ourselves in daylight fishing.

We tried several times in the dark of hot July nights. I have always thought night fishing an overrated form, both for entertainment and results, and we found it that way on the Itchen, except on one night. We had gone some little way upstream from the rectory to a place where a fine lawn came down to the river from a big house on the far side. There were lights on in the house, and we could hear people talking and laughing. In the river several fish were rising steadily, and after a little while we found most of the rises. I decided to fish a dry coachman, so that we would have some chance of seeing the white wings against the dark water. Three fish were rising quite regularly close under a wall at the foot of the lawn opposite us, and I began to try to cover them. Time after time the fly went down and was disregarded. Denis said at last, "I think you must be short of them." So I pulled off a yard more line and felt the fly hit the brick wall. It fell back, came over a fish and disappeared in a good ring. I tightened, felt I had him, then forgot fish and rod and everything in sudden terror. I heard Denis gasp in the dark beside me. From somewhere within fifty or a hundred yards of us had come the sharp quick sound of a running reel.

When I felt my rod again the fish was gone. Denis and I lay down and waited, a little way back from the bank.

"Somebody's fishing," I whispered.

"Yes," Denis said. "Pulling line off his reel."

"Sounded too long for that. I think he had a fish on."

We waited and listened. I could still see two fish rising steadily over by the wall. The sound did not come again, and we grew bolder. I cast for the second fish, rose him, hooked him and lost him. The sound of the other fisherman's reel came again, from a little farther away.

"What do you think he's doing?" Denis asked.

"Catching fish," I said, but I wasn't convinced. There was something wrong about the sound, it was a tearing off of line that started and stopped abruptly and seemed to fit no natural circumstance of fishing.

"Have you got that light?" I asked. "I want to look at the fly."

The barb was broken from the hook, as I had thought it might be. Crouching well down in the grass and shielding the light, we tied on a new fly. The sound came again, from about where it had been the first time. We strained our eyes toward it and listened hard. It came again, exactly as before, lasting the same four or five seconds, starting and stopping abruptly. It seemed mysterious and frightening because one could not picture the man's actions from hearing it. "I'm going to get that other fish anyway," I said. I did, first cast. The other fisherman must have hooked a fish at the same moment, because his reel started to run again; time after time it whirred out, and all the while he seemed to be coming closer to us. I hurried my fish all I could. The moon was coming up, and in a few minutes the meadows would be almost as light as in daytime. The screeching of the reel went on, and I began to wonder if he would hear my own much lighter check. The fish was on his side now. We scooped him out somehow and ran back from the bank. Still the other reel gave tongue to the intermittent runs of its fish. Then Denis began to laugh.

"Shut up," I said. "And let's get out of here."

He still laughed.

"Do you know what that is?" he asked.

"No," I said irritably. "I'm damned if I do."

"It's a screech owl," Denis said. "Listen."

We didn't always have to poach. Besides the glebe and the few farmers' fields we could walk through with good right, there was Lewington's meadow, just below the church. And there was the churchyard itself for that matter, which was bordered by the same little stream that flowed along Lewington's meadow. Mr. Lewington was the village baker, a baker second to none in the world for fresh currant bread and half a dozen other good things. He was also a small but very intensive livestock farmer, drawn into it by a deep love of animals rather than by any simple economic reason. His rich little meadow supported, and his low, many-roomed barn sheltered, besides the bakery horse, a herd of goats, many turkeys, big white ducks, guinea hens, chickens and several cats.

Mr. Lewington was well disposed toward us for a number of reasons, and he gave us free range of his meadow and full rights on the little stream that we called Lewington's Carrier. In return for this we undertook to control the surplus of rats that plagued his buildings in spite of all his cats could do. Denis and I did a lot of ratting and were well equipped for it with traps and snares and ferrets and terriers. But Lewington's rats were difficult because the barn and some of the other buildings offered them so many hiding places. We kept traps set there all the time, and the necessity of baiting and resetting brought us often to the meadow.

The carrier was a good clear little stream, varying in width from a yard or so to twelve feet or more. It flowed into the Itchen two or three fields below Lewington's, so there were nearly always good trout in it, and besides the trout many small pike, most of them fish of a pound or less, but some as large as two or three pounds. We found the trout generally impossible to catch; they seldom fed really well and they were very nervous in the small water, so we spent a lot of time on the pike. We started out with some vague idea that by clearing out all the pike we might attract more trout to the stream and give ourselves a better chance to catch them. So we went after the pike with nets at first but were not very successful; then we tried shooting them and did little better that way. We filled ink bottles with black powder, corked them tightly and made them into effective little bombs with a length of fuse and a small detonator. They exploded satisfactorily under water, but the pike wouldn't wait to be stunned or killed, and the bombs had no effect at long range. Finally we gave up complicated methods and went out with trout rods and small treble hooks and snagged them. It wasn't by any means an easy sport, but we grew really skillful after a while and learned to spot the fish quickly, stalk them cunningly, drop the hooks lightly just beyond them, allowing for the drift of the current, then set them in side or back with a single swift draw. Even a one-pound pike, hooked in that way, put up a really good little fight, and several times we came back from the meadow or the churchyard with three or four of them. But they never seemed much fewer, and the trout remained scarce and wary as ever.

Those trout were something of a challenge to me and to my county patriotism. Here was I, a good Dorset trout fisher, completely beaten by a few good Hampshire trout. Denis would remind me of this once in a while, and the thing was no less bitter to me because I knew that the Hampshire trout streams were so greatly superior to ours in Dorset. I liked to think that if we had their trout streams, we could surely do wonderful things. So I walked often along the carrier and hoped to find a feeding fish. Sometimes I found one, and then I used all the skill I had, creeping up on him, setting my best flies out for him in my best manner. Nearly always something went wrong—the fly dragged or hooked a tuft of grass or simply scared the fish and sent him off upstream under a great gliding wave that disturbed everything else in the carrier. When, as happened rarely, I did hook a fish, it was always a small one. The big fish that fed by the mouth of the culvert that brought the stream under the road took my fly once, and I struck too soon. The fish that hung just above the fence at the end of the meadow rose once, far short. The other good ones for the most part disregarded me or swept away and left me at my first preparatory move.

Then, one hot June day, everything was changed. Yet I remember far better than the change in the fish what happened afterward in Mr. Lewington's barn. The day had been very hot, and, with a wisdom I don't always keep about me when there's a chance of going fishing, I told Denis that there might be a good rise of fish in the very late afternoon. We went through Mr. Lewington's barnyard sometime after five-thirty, and he was not yet back with the bakery wagon. The rise was already on when we got down to the carrier; at least the big fish by the fence at the lower end of the meadow was rising. I had a small, dark-hackled olive on, and we had spotted the rising fish from thirty or forty feet out in the meadow. We stayed where we were, and I began to let out line, keeping the fly in the air till I thought I had enough to cover the fish. It was a long chance, because the recovery of the first cast would almost certainly hook the fly firmly in the edge of the bank, and a quiver of a grass tussock was usually all that was necessary to put that particular fish off his feed. But the first cast was right; the fish came up to a natural, took that and broke the surface again to our fly before the little rings of his first rise had spread. He did his best, that fish, running down under the wire of the fence until we thought of jumping into the stream to follow him, but he came back and was netted. Denis took the rod then, and we found another good one rising in the bend. He let the dark-olive float past him twice, but Denis offered it to him once more, setting it on the water a bare two inches above his nose, and that time he had it.

Between there and the road we spoiled two chances at good fish, but we were feeling so good that it hardly mattered. Below the mouth of the culvert there is a miniature pool, and a fish was rising near the tail of this.

"You take him," Denis said.

"No, you," I told him. "I want the other one, the one that rises under the culvert."

"How do you know he's there?"

My fish rose as Denis spoke, a neat tiny rise about a foot below the mouth of the culvert. Denis knelt, ready to cast for the lower fish, and I said, "Hold him from going up if you can. Stand up and walk backward as soon as you hook him."

Denis nodded. We were both excited, and I was afraid it might spoil his cast, but he made it beautifully; the fish came to him, he tightened, started him down, and the hook came away. We both watched the culvert anxiously. One full minute passed, then our fish rose again in the same place, just a foot short of the concrete face of the culvert.

"Do you want to try for him?" I asked.

Denis shook his head, and for a moment I was almost sorry. It didn't look so easy now. I knew it wasn't easy because I had tried it fifty times before and had only put the fly over him properly once or twice. But he was a fraction farther down from the culvert this time than ever before.

"I'm going to throw the fly at the concrete and let it bounce off to him," I said.

I tried it and it worked. The fly dropped perfectly. The fish pushed his nose under it, backed down with it for six inches, a foot, two feet. Then he turned away and went back to his place. A moment later we saw his tiny rise again.

I let out a great blast of tightly held breath.

"Gosh," Denis said, "I thought he was surely going to take it."

I brought my cast back and broke the fly off.

"What are you going to do?" Denis asked.

"Change," I said. "Orange quill I think. That old boy's particular."

I looked in my box and wondered. The orange quills were there, tiny and neat on No. 17 hooks. Beside them were some beautiful red quills and half a dozen Yorkshire tups I had bought from Chalkley's the day before. For a moment longer I hesitated; then I knew the orange quill was right, if I could put it over him.

I tried the same cast. The fly was short of the concrete and flipped up under the culvert, showing the fish far too much gut. Quite without hope, I watched it ride the smooth current down. Then there was a great sucking rise that echoed up under the culvert, and the fly was gone. I struck, and he took line for his home, somewhere far under the road. But it must have been straight and clear of snags under there because he came back safely, and five minutes later we had him.

"What an evening," Denis said. "We couldn't have done much better on the Test at Longparish."

So we came very happily into Mr. Lewington's barnyard and began to look for him to tell him of our sport and ask after his rats. We found him in the barn, milking a goat, a turkey perched on one shoulder, a big red hen on the other. More goats wandered in and out, the ducks were there, up from the carrier, and a score of chickens and turkeys. One of the cats was drinking out of the pail as the old gentleman milked.

"Scat," said Mr. Lewington as we came to the door, and he brushed the cat away. A moment later he was contrite.

"'Tis all my fault. I allus gives 'em milk out of the fust bucket and tonight I didn't do it. Dunno what's come over me."

He got up and poured some milk out of the pail into a pan.

"There," he said. "Do 'ee drink it up now." The cats clustered round the pan and began to lap.

"How're the rats, Mr. Lewington?" I asked. "We thought of changing the traps round, because they haven't caught anything the last couple of nights."

Mr. Lewington set the pail down with a thump. "Do 'ee come along and I'll show 'ee." He stood up and bustled out of the barn. We followed.

"Every night I see 'un. Durnedest gert big old buck you ever did see. In t' stable he is, every night. He's got t' mare so nervous she won't 'ardly eat 'er hoats."

He opened the stable door and there was the rat, every bit as big as two big rats, sitting up a foot or so behind the mare's hoofs. Mr. Lewington whooped and charged forward, the mare started violently, the rat disappeared.

"He's gone," Denis said sensibly. "You won't see him again tonight."

But Mr. Lewington was busy at the mare's manger, crouching his short body and striking a match to look for something.

"I see 'un go in there," he was saying. "That's where 'e always do go. There's three on us here tonight, and we'll 'ave un this time."

Denis and I moved up and saw that he was trying to look through the narrow triangular tunnel made by a slanting board nailed behind the manger. "That's where 'ee always do go, and that's where 'e's gone tonight. Do 'ee look through other end while I 'old up a light this end for 'ee to zee."

I went round and looked through. The match flared, and I saw outlined against it a huge curved back, ugly and almost hairless.

"He's there," I said. "Shall I get a stick and poke him out?"

"No," Mr. Lewington said. "Do 'ee keep un there, both on 'ee. Don't let un get out." And he bustled out of the barn.

"What's he gone for?" I asked Denis.

"I don't know. Something lethal I imagine."

Mr. Lewington came back. In one hand he had a candle in a lantern and in the other a .410 shotgun.

"You can't shoot him in there," I said.

"Can't I?" said Mr. Lewington.

He set the lantern up on a bale of straw opposite one end of the rat's hiding place.

"You'll frighten the mare," Denis said.

"You'll burn the stable down," I said.

"She'll be all right," Mr. Lewington said. "Out t' way now while I finish un."

"Take the mare out," I said.

Mr. Lewington was at the far end of the tunnel, sighting along his gun. "Move t' lantern up a mite," he said. "I can't see un."

I moved the lantern up and stepped back quickly. There was a roar and a flash. The mare plunged, reared and wheeled out of the stable. The lantern shattered to pieces. I saw a glow of red on the bale of straw and crushed it out with my coat sleeve.

"I got un," Mr. Lewington said. "Couldn't not have. Light that 'ere candle again so's we can see un."

I found the candle, lighted it and held it near the mouth of the tunnel.

"See him?" I asked.

There was a long pause from Mr. Lewington's end.

"No," he said at last. "'Ee ain't there."

Denis came back with the mare. "Did you find him?"

"Oh, he's dead, all right," I said confidently. "Just crawled away somewhere."

"Couldn't not be," Mr. Lewington said. "Could 'ee?"

"No," Denis said. "We'll find him tomorrow."

We found him two days later in a trap we had set in the stable, without a mark on him. We took him away and put shotgun pellets in him, then brought him back for Mr. Lewington.

Pacific Salmon

The word salmon is practically synonymous with game fish. The manifold virtues of the Atlantic salmon established this, but his Pacific cousins do a lot for anglers too. What is more, they are in many ways the most spectacular natural resource available to mankind and a major item of the world's food supply. One need not be an angler to be very much interested in them; but anglers have many special reasons for interest, and most men who have fished on the Pacific coast have a healthy curiosity, not only about the salmon runs themselves, but about the industry that depends on them.

Pacific salmon are confusing chiefly because so very much confusing stuff has been written about them. There is confusion, to start with, about their relationship to Atlantic salmon. They are related, but that is about all. They differ widely from the Atlantic salmon in both habits and physical characteristics, and for this sufficient reason they are classed by biologists as a separate genus: *Oncorhynchus* instead of *Salmo*.

The next confusion comes from the several species of Pacific salmon. There are five completely separate species, and each species is physically different from the others, different in life history, different in feeding and other habits. All five species are commercially important: at least two are directly important to anglers, and the other three are indirectly important.

As though five species were not enough, there is further confusion in that each species has several common names: the Chinook salmon of the Columbia, for instance, becomes the king salmon in Puget Sound, the spring salmon, and also the tyee, of British Columbia, and king salmon again in Alaska. These are local names, of course, but they are the only names that ordinary people know and use, and the locality where each has its meaning is no little county or bailiwick, but an area measured in tens of thousands of square miles and populated by hundreds of thousands. The Chinook has a right to the title "king" or "tyee," because he is by far the largest of Pacific salmon, commonly weighing between twenty and fifty pounds at maturity and occasionally as much as a hundred pounds. Just why my fellow British Columbians and I call him "spring salmon" I am not sure, but probably because many rivers have two quite distinct runs of Chinooks, one in the spring, which is earlier than all the other salmon runs, and the other in late summer or fall. But the Columbia River is the great and famous home of this salmon, and for the purposes of this book it is as well to keep to the Columbia name Chinook.

Because of his size, the Chinook is probably the best known of all the Pacific salmon. But the coho, or silver, salmon deserves equally well of anglers because he is a great fighter, a jumping fool who takes the fly readily in salt or fresh water. Cohos are much smaller than Chinooks, averaging about eight pounds and rarely weighing more than twenty, but they bear at least an equal part with the Chinooks in supporting the commercial troll fishery.

The sockeye is as definitely a fish of the Fraser River as the Chinook is of the Columbia. On the Columbia they call the sockeye the "blueback," which is a pity, because that is the name given to immature cohos by British Columbia fishermen. Commercially the sockeye is also known as the "red salmon," from the bright-red color of his flesh. This redness holds up well in canning and makes the sockeye, pound for pound, commercially the most valuable of the five species.

The humpback is a little fish, averaging about four pounds. The commercial name, more widely used all the time, is "pink salmon," but most fishermen still use the affectionate "humpie," which seems to fit better and mean more than pink. The humpback takes fly or spoon in salt water but is important chiefly to net fishermen.

The dog salmon also has been given an approved commercial name, "chum salmon," but I haven't heard it used very much by fishermen. Dogs are fine fish, but until recently the industry paid little attention to them. I like to think that when I first watched the big dog salmon runs fifteen or sixteen years ago, they were a true picture of the abundant wealth of all the salmon runs before the coming of the white fishermen; but intensive fishing since then has done much to cut them down to size.

These, then, are the five salmon that make millions of dollars a year for the industry in Alaska, British Columbia, Washington and Oregon. Around the Kamchatka Peninsula, in the Okhotsk Sea and the Bering Sea, the Russians and Japanese take another hundred million or so of the same fish for their canneries and salteries. And so the world eats salmon.

But we are not yet out of all the confusions. There is a favorite misconception, greatly encouraged by the newspapers, that all Pacific salmon go down to the sea soon after hatching from the egg, live and grow there for exactly four years, then return to spawn. The truth is somewhat less simple. If we were to take the life histories of all five species, lump them together and strike an average, an approximate four-year cycle might be the answer. But there are wide variations from this average, not only between species but within species. The little humpback is the only one of the five with an invariable life history: he goes down to salt water just as soon as he can swim freely and returns to spawn exactly two years after his parents made the same journey. The coho is almost as constant: he spends a full year in the river, then goes to sea and returns to spawn just three years after his parents. But a few cohos return in the fourth year, and a good number of males mature precociously and return after a single year in salt water.

The dog salmon is a fairly good example of a four-year fish. Like the humpbacks, they seem to go to sea as soon as they are free-swimming fry, and they return at the end of the three, four or five years—the great majority at the end of four years. The sockeye and the Chinook have the least predictable life histories. Most sockeyes go to sea after one year of feeding in a fresh-water lake, but some go down almost at once, and a few spend two full years in fresh water. Most of them return after three or four years in salt water, at four or five years of age, that is; but some individuals mature at three, six, seven and eight years. There is a great variation between the runs of different rivers: the Fraser River run is chiefly made up of four-year-olds; while nearly half the fish running to Rivers Inlet and the Skeena River are five- or six-year-olds, and more than 80 per cent of the Nass River run are five-years-old or older.

The majority (about four-fifths) of Chinooks go to sea as soon as they are free-swimming, and nearly all return after four or five years in salt water. This means, of course, that fish will be fairly often returning at four, five, six and seven years of age, though there will be more four- and five-year-olds than anything else. Again with Chinooks, there is some variation between the runs of different rivers: in the Yukon River, for instance, which has a big run of Chinooks, most of the fish spend at least one year in fresh water and six in salt water before maturing; a fair proportion spend two years in fresh water and do not return to spawn until they are eight years old. There is a fairly well-supported theory that this delay is due to the slower growth rate in waters farther north.

The seaward movement of Pacific salmon is essentially a feeding movement. The young fish go down from the rivers when they have reached a certain stage of development, and they find there the abundance they need to grow them to full maturity. Generally speaking, this feeding migration is a northward movement, made so partly by the set of the current along the Pacific coast and partly by other factors. The extent of the movement varies considerably, for some fish travel little, if at all, beyond the influence of their own rivers, while others may go as far as seven or eight hundred miles northward before they turn back in the spawning migration. The seaward limit of the migration is somewhere near the hundred-fathom line, which is usually about thirty or forty miles offshore; beyond the hundred-fathom line the bottom drops off quite steeply toward the extreme depths of the ocean proper, and the abundance of feed is not so great as it is in the shallower water of the continental shelf.

Since the feeding migration is generally a northward movement, the spawning migration must be generally a southward movement. As the sexual organs of the fish mature, certain stimulations are released in them, and one response is a tendency to swim against the current. The eddies of the Japan Current make a fairly constant northward current along the coast of British Columbia, and by swimming against this with a steadily growing determination, the maturing fish draw gradually southward until they find their own rivers again and ascend them.

The feeding habits of the various Pacific salmon, like most of their other habits, vary considerably. All species feed very heavily on crustaceans, chiefly euphausiid shrimps, but the sockeye is the only species that keeps closely to this feed throughout its life history. Humpbacks, toward the end of their second and last year in salt water, feed a good deal on herring and launce fish. Dog salmon, though they certainly feed on both shrimps and herrings, are probably less selective than any of the other species. Cohos feed on crustaceans almost exclusively until their second summer in salt water, when they turn to herrings and launce fish with a voracity that grows them from silvery three-pounders into mature fish of ten pounds in a short six months. Young Chinooks, like young cohos, feed largely on crustaceans, but they turn to smelts and squid and launce fish as they grow larger, then to herrings and pilchards. Both cohos and Chinooks may turn back to feeding on shrimps whenever they come upon them in their ranging.

The abundance of the Pacific salmon runs produces a fishery whose yield no local market can absorb in fresh form. This was true before the white man reached the coast at all, and the Indians of the Columbia River and other parts of the coast ran what was undoubtedly a commercial fishery in the fullest sense of the term. They fished primarily for their own use, and they certainly ate fresh fish as they fished. But they smoked fish and dried fish for winter use, and they pounded dried fish into pemmican, a powdery meal which they packed into primitive sacks lined with fish skins and used in trade with other Indians.

Their fishing methods were fairly primitive but quite good enough to take big catches from the superabundance of fish that ran to every river and creek and stream along the coast. The Indians of Puget Sound used an ingenious reef net made of willow bark, which they set and worked over the kelp-covered reefs on flood tide so effectively that they could kill as many as three thousand salmon on a single run of tide. In other places, generally in rivers and the spawning tributaries, they used nets much like the modern haul or drag seines, floating or fixed traps, weirs, dip nets, spears, gaffs and even the bow and arrow. Occasionally they trolled with bone hooks and strips of herring for bait.

Almost all these methods have their counterparts in the modern industry, larger and more efficient, but essentially the same. The Indian fishery was limited by the fishing population, by the materials available and by the consuming population within reach. The white fishery was limited at first in the same way, but it overcame the limitations one by one until the sole limitation became the number of fish available.

The modern industry produces fresh, salt and even smoked fish, but the bulk of the product is canned fish; efficient canneries have wholly solved the problem of limited local markets, and now the whole world is a market. Up and down the coast there are between two and three hundred salmon canneries normally operating, half of them in Alaska, thirty or forty in British Columbia, perhaps twenty in the Columbia

River and the others wherever the fish run well. Together they pack some ten million cases of salmon a year. Since it takes on the average about twelve sockeyes to make up a case, or ten cohos, or four Chinooks, or sixteen humpbacks, or nine dog salmon, it seems fairly safe to say that the canning industry uses at least a hundred million salmon a year. But there are big variations in all these figures from year to year, because the runs are not steady: the run of humpbacks to Puget Sound, for instance, yielded nearly six million fish in 1935 and less than a quarter of a million in 1936. This was a regular and expected variation, and it is repeated in greater or lesser degree in all humpback runs—one year is good and the next year is bad. Annual variations in the runs of the other species are less marked, but there are variations, and, unless man interferes by closing off spawning areas or by fishing too hard, they perpetuate themselves. A big year always yields, in due course of the cycle, a big year, and a small year always yields a small year.

Gill nets, traps, purse seines and trolling are the principal methods of fishing. Except in the really big rivers, such as the Fraser and the Columbia, few fish are taken in fresh water; the boats go out to sea and meet the fish as they are coming in on their spawning migration. Gill-net boats are probably the most numerous; these are small boats, about thirty feet long and powered by eight- or ten-horsepower gas engines. They are usually run by one or two men and carry some three hundred fathom of a net which is made of fine twine in a mesh just wide enough to allow the fish to slide his gills and pectoral fins through; as the thick part of his body comes against the mesh he is held, and when he tries to draw out, his fins or gills tangle in the mesh.

Most gill nets are drift nets; that is, the fisherman runs out the full length of his net between a small floating buoy and his boat, then kills his engine and lets the boat, buoy and net drift through a stretch of channel where the fish should be running. The net is kept at stretch vertically by a cork line at the surface and a lead line below, so that it makes a great curtain that fish are bound to strike. In clean water gill-netters can fish only at night, when the mesh is more or less invisible to the fish, but many of the coast rivers carry glacial silt well down into the inlets and channels where the fish pass, and in those waters the boats often fish night and day.

Traps are still used in Oregon and Alaska, though Washington prohibited their use in 1935, and the only traps in British Columbia are two or three which operate at the southern end of Vancouver Island. Most traps are made of heavy netting stretched on piles driven into the bottom. In the usual design there is a lead, a straight line of piling which carries a solid wall of web and extends for a thousand feet or more across the normal course of the migrating fish. As the fish turn along this lead they come through a narrow recurved entrance into a semicircular enclosure known as the "big heart." Trying to find a way out of this, they come into the small heart, which leads them through a funnel-shaped entrance into the pot; from there they come through a still narrower entrance of the same type into the spiller, a small enclosure, from which they are easily brailed when it is time for the trap to be emptied. Strategically placed traps are most efficient means of catching fish—too efficient, many people think and public opinion is strongly against their use both in Washington and British Columbia. Yet no type of gear is more easily controlled and regulated than are traps, for the simple reason that they are fixed. A single fishery officer can keep close watch and order the trap closed or opened as the escapement of spawning fish beyond the trap demands. Traps also do much to reduce the hardships and hazards of fishing, and they permit fishermen to live a home life in permanent settlements. Two questions about traps have not been satisfactorily answered: Do they destroy and waste more immature fish than other types of gear? Do they employ fewer men than other types of gear? Without really good answers to these questions, it is impossible to say whether the pros or the cons are right.

Purse seiners are big boats, forty to seventy feet long with fifty or a hundred Diesel horsepower. They have a crew of eight or ten men who fish, not for wages, but for shares of the catch. The boats are broad in the beam, with wide round sterns to carry the big nets, and they roll mightily in the trough of a heavy sea. The nets are usually about three hundred fathoms long and ten fathoms deep, of heavy twine in a four-inch mesh. They have the usual cork line and lead line to spread them in the water, except that the lead line has a number of iron rings attached to it. The purse line, heavy rope, passes through these rings, and by taking it in during a set, the net is pursed—that is, the lead line is drawn up on the rings until the depth of the net comes into a bag that prevents the fish from diving down and escaping.

Making a purse seine set, like most types of fishing, can be pretty hard work. When the fish are running thinly and the crew is making several sets a day to catch enough fish to pay for their grub, it is a depressing business. But when there is a real run of sockeyes or humps going through and every set means a chance of big money, there is a fine, keen excitement in the work. When the dog salmon are running late in the year and the winter southeasters have started, the work is harder than ever, cold, wet work and often dangerous. But the dog salmon run is the one that makes up for bad seasons, and the boats go out and make sets that often circle four thousand fish or more. Sometimes several boats are needed to carry the fish of a single haul, and sometimes ambitious skippers load their boats until the net table is level with the water; then, if a little slop comes up, boat and load may go down together. Men take big chances when the stakes are big.

Humpbacks and sockeyes are the purse-seiner's real gold though, and a purse seiner's real time is a summer dawn when the inside waters are still except for the creases and whirls of the tide. A good skipper knows the fish and the waters he fishes, and his crew gives him its whole faith. The boat cruises along, hunting fish. Fish show, perhaps jumping, perhaps finning, perhaps only by bubbles that wobble to the surface from three or four fathoms down. The set is made with swift and eager efficiency. The big skiff slides into the water from its place on top of the net, the skiff man is at the oars almost as it touches. He rows, steadily and strongly, holding one end of the net while the big boat circles the school of fish, paying the long net out, cork line, web, lead line and purse line, smoothly over the roller on the stern. The long circle is closed in a few short minutes, the winch brings the purse line in until there is webbing all around the fish and under them. The crew brings in the net over the live roller on the turntable, slowly closing the great circle of cork line. The fish show rarely at first, then more frequently, until the circle is close against the boat and only a few feet in diameter. Then the brail, a huge dip net hung on blocks from the boom, goes down and brings up load after load of bright silver fish until the net is empty. The boat and its crew may be richer by fifty dollars—or five thousand.

The trollers are, of all commercial fishermen, most nearly anglers; their problems are angler's problems, with feeding fish, but multiplied and magnified. Trollers hook bottom and lose gear; trollers change spoons as anglers change flies; trollers argue and theorize and think and wonder as anglers do; they play their hunches and gauge their luck as all fishermen do. A good troller, like a good angler or a good purse-seine captain, has some indefinite advantage compounded of knowledge and experience and thoroughness that his fellows have not.

Trollers are little men and very independent. They own their own boats and their own gear, and they go their own way to find their own fish. Their boats are of every shape and size and kind, from rowboats up to fifty-foot, Diesel-powered, deep-sea craft that would make a yachtsman jealous. The little boats, and some of the big ones, fish inside waters. In the Gulf of Georgia big catches of young cohos are made during the early part of the summer, a wasteful slaughter of fish that would double or triple their weight within a few months; but for the most part the inside trollers everywhere have to depend on the spasmodic movements of cohos and Chinooks. Sometimes a run of feeding cohos makes good fishing, and sometimes a movement of herring draws schools of young and hungry Chinooks; but the main runs of spawning fish are no longer feeding freely when they reach the inside waters but are fed to full development, intent on the business ahead. The bright spoons of the inside trollers draw only the careless or quick-tempered or unlucky ones. But for all that, inside trolling is a fine, free, easy way of life for many men, and inside trollers are often good and wise fishermen.

Probably the greatest trolling grounds in the world are the banks off the west coast of Vancouver Island, where a great proportion of the Columbia River Chinooks go to feed. The Columbia fish run farther north than that, as far as the north coast of the Queen Charlotte Islands, and the fishermen follow them all the way, the Americans fishing offshore, beyond the three-mile limit, Canadians fishing with them and also in their own territorial waters. The Americans fish chiefly for Chinooks, because they are a long way from their home ports and the cohos do not keep well on ice. But the Canadians fish heavily for cohos also, as the Americans do in their own territorial waters. American trollers land yearly in Washington, Oregon and California some fifteen or twenty million pounds of salmon, and the cohos make up perhaps as much as one-third of this total. The British Columbia trollers land about a million Chinooks—fish, not pounds—and anywhere from one to three million or more cohos each year.

A troller carries two slender cedar poles some forty to sixty feet long, which stand upright against his mast. When he starts to fish, he lowers his poles until they project horizontally from each side of the boat, to spread his lines. Usually a big troller fishes six or eight stainless-steel lines, two on each main pole, two out over the stern and two more from bow poles which project ahead of and out from the boat. Each line is held almost straight down in the water by a thirty- or forty-pound ball of lead and carries several spoons, perhaps two or three for Chinooks, occasionally as many as seven or eight for cohos, which trail out from the main line on shorter lines of their own. This is modern and highly efficient gear, made possible only recently by the wide use of power reels, called "gurdies," which are driven by shaft and clutch from the main engine, to bring in the lines when a fish is hooked.

The outside trollers fish from dawn till dark, in all weathers, often riding the great Pacific swells for a week or more at a time before turning back with their catch. Good trollers make big money in years when the run is right and the price is right; but the money they make is usually a straight return on skill and investment—to stay out where the fish are a boat must be big enough to carry fish and ice, and seaworthy to stand whatever weather comes. To handle such a boat and fish her properly, a troller needs not only fishing knowledge but seamanship and mechanical skill and a fair share of courage.

I have said that the Pacific salmon runs are probably the most spectacular natural resource on the face of the earth. Their greatness is less than it once was, but even today this annual movement of millions upon millions of great gleaming fish through the length and breadth of the continental shelf toward their spawning in the high tributaries is a tremendous thing. The salmon runs, more surely and easily than almost any other resource, can be made to last and serve indefinitely, can even be grown back to, or beyond, their full glory. The base of the resource is the sea, which gives life to myriads of diatoms. So long as there are euphausiid shrimps to feed on the diatoms, so long as there are herrings to feed on the euphausiids, so long as there are salmon to feed on the herrings and so turn the diatoms at last to man's use, the ocean base of the resource is solid. And there will be salmon and more salmon to complete this cycle so long as they are allowed to enter the rivers to their spawning in sufficient numbers, so long as the way to the spawning beds is kept clear and easy and open and so long as the rivers are kept clean and fresh and pure. It is as simple as that.

PLAIN FISHING

FRANK R. STOCKTON

"**W**ell, sir," said old Peter, as he came out on the porch with his pipe, "so you come here to go fishin'?"

Peter Gruse was the owner of the farmhouse where I had arrived that day, just before suppertime. He was a short, strong-built old man, with a pair of pretty daughters, and little gold rings in his ears. Two things distinguished him from the farmers in the country round about: one was the rings in his ears, and the other was the large and comfortable house in which he kept his pretty daughters. The other farmers in that region had fine large barns for their cattle and horses, but very poor houses for their daughters. Old Peter's earrings were indirectly connected with his house. He had not always lived among those mountains. He had been on the sea, where his ears were decorated, and he had traveled a good deal on land, where he had ornamented his mind with many ideas which were not in general use in the part of his State in which he was born. This house stood a little back from the highroad, and if a traveler wished to be entertained, Peter was generally willing to take him in, provided he had left his wife and family at home. The old man himself had no objection to wives and children, but his two pretty daughters had.

These two young women had waited on their father and myself at suppertime, one continually bringing hot griddle cakes, and the other giving me every opportunity to test the relative merits of the seven different kinds of preserves, which, in little glass plates, covered the unoccupied spaces on the tablecloth. The latter, when she found that there was no further possible way of serving us, presumed to sit down at the corner of the table and begin her supper. But in spite of this apparent humility, which was only a custom of the country, there was that in the general air of the pretty daughters which left no doubt in the mind of the intelligent observer that they stood at the wheel in that house. There was a son of fourteen, who sat at table with us, but he did not appear to count as a member of the family.

"Yes," I answered, "I understood that there was good fishing here-abouts, and, at any rate, I should like to spend a few days among these hills and mountains."

"Well," said Peter, "there's trout in some of our streams, though not as many as there used to be, and there's hills a plenty, and mountains too, if you choose to walk fur enough. They're a good deal furder off than they look. What did you bring with you to fish with?"

"Nothing at all," I answered. "I was told in the town that you were a great fisherman, and that you could let me have all the tackle I would need."

"Upon my word," said old Peter, resting his pipe-hand on his knee and looking steadfastly at me, "you're the queerest fisherman I've seed yet. Nigh every year, some two or three of 'em stop here in the fishin' season, and there was never a man who didn't bring his jinted pole, and his reels, and his lines, and his hooks, and his dry-good flies, and his whisky flask with a long strap to it. Now, if you want all these things, I haven't got 'em."

"Whatever you use yourself will suit me," I answered.

"All right, then," said he. "I'll do the best I can for you in the mornin'. But it's plain enough to me that you're not a game fisherman, or you wouldn't come here without your tools."

To this remark I made answer to the effect, that though I was very fond of fishing, my pleasure in it did not depend upon the possession of all the appliances of professional sport.

"Perhaps you think," said the old man, "from the way I spoke, that I don't believe them fellers with the jinted poles can ketch fish, but that ain't so. That old story about the little boy with the pin hook who ketched all the fish, while the gentleman with the modern improvements, who stood alongside of him, kep' throwin' out his beautiful flies and never got nothin', is a pure lie. The fancy chaps, who must have ev'rythin' jist so, gen'rally gits fish. But for all that, I don't like their way of fishin', and I take no stock in it myself. I've been fishin', on and off, ever since I was a little boy, and I've caught nigh every kind there is, from the big jewfish and cavalyoes down South, to the trout and minnies round about here. But when I ketch a fish, the first thing I do is to try to git him on the hook, and the next thing is to git him out of the water jist as soon as I kin. I don't put in no time worryin' him.

There's only two animals in the world that likes to worry smaller creeturs a good while afore they kill 'em; one is the cat, and the other is what they call the game fisherman. This kind of a feller never goes after no fish that don't mind being ketched. He goes fur them kinds that loves their home in the water and hates most to leave it, and he makes it jist as hard fur 'em as he kin. What the game fisher likes is the smallest kind of a hook, the thinnest line, and a fish that it takes a good while to weaken. The longer the weak'nin' business kin be spun out, the more the sport. The idee is to let the fish think there's a chance fur him to git away. That's jist like the cat with her mouse. She lets the little creetur hop off, but the minnit he gits fur enough down, she jabs on him with her claws, and then, if there's any game left in him, she lets him try agen. Of course, the game fisher could have a strong line and a stout pole and git his fish in a good sight quicker, if he wanted to, but that wouldn't be sport. He couldn't give him the butt and spin him out, and reel him in, and let him jump and run till his pluck is clean worn out. Now, I likes to git my fish ashore with all the pluck in 'em. It makes 'em taste better. And as fur fun, I'll be bound I've had jist as much of that, and more, too, than most of these fellers who are so dreadful anxious to have everythin' jist right, and think they can't go fishin' till they've spent enough money to buy a suit of Sunday clothes. As a gen'ral rule they're a solemn lot, and work pretty hard at their fun. When I work I want to be paid fur it, and when I go in fur fun I want to take it easy and comfortable. Now I wouldn't say so much agen these fellers," said old Peter, as he arose and put his empty pipe on a little shelf under the porch roof, "if it wasn't for one thing, and that is, that they think that their kind of fishin' is the only kind worth considerin'. The way they look down upon plain Christian fishin' is enough to rile a hitchin' post. I don't want to say nothin' agen no man's way of attendin' to his own affairs, whether it's kitchen gardenin', or whether it's fishin', if he says nothin' agen my way; but when he looks down on me, and grins me, I want to haul myself up, and grin him, if I kin. And in this case, I kin. I s'pose the house cat and the cat fisher (by which I don't mean the man who fishes for catfish) was both made as they is, and they can't help it; but that don't give 'em no right to put on airs before other bein's, who gits their meat with a square kill. Good night. And sence I've talked so much about it, I've a mind to go fishin' with you tomorrow myself."

The next morning found old Peter of the same mind, and after breakfast he proceeded to fit me out for a day of what he called "plain Christian trout fishin'." He gave me a reed rod, about nine feet long, light, strong, and nicely balanced. The tackle he produced was not of the fancy order, but his lines were of fine strong linen, and his hooks were of good shape, clean and sharp, and snooded to the lines with a neatness that indicated the hand of a man who had been where he learned to wear little gold rings in his ears.

"Here are some of these feather insects," he said, "which you kin take along if you like." And he handed me a paper containing a few artificial flies. "They're pretty nat'ral," he said, "and the hooks is good. A man who come here fishin' gave 'em to me, but I shan't want 'em today. At this time of year grasshoppers is the best bait in the kind of place where we're goin' to fish. The stream, after it comes down from the mountain, runs through half a mile of medder land before it strikes into the woods agen. A grasshopper is a little creetur that's got as much conceit as if his jinted legs was fishpoles, and he thinks he kin jump over this narrer run of water whenever he pleases; but he don't always do it, and them of him that don't git snapped up by the trout that lie along the banks in the medder is floated along into the woods, where there's always fish enough to come to the second table."

Having got me ready, Peter took his own particular pole, which he assured me he had used for eleven years, and hooking on his left arm a good-sized basket, which his elder pretty daughter had packed with cold meat, bread, butter, and preserves, we started forth for a three-mile walk to the fishing ground. The day was a favorable one for our purpose, the sky being sometimes overclouded, which was good for fishing, and also for walking on a highroad; and sometimes bright, which was good for effects of mountain scenery. Not far from the spot where old Peter proposed to begin our sport, a small frame house stood by the roadside, and here the old man halted and entered the open door without knocking or giving so much as a premonitory stamp. I followed, imitating my companion in leaving my pole outside, which appeared to be the only ceremony that the etiquette of those parts required of visitors. In the room we entered, a small man in his shirt sleeves sat mending a basket handle. He nodded to Peter, and Peter nodded to him.

"We've come up a-fishin'," said the old man. "Kin your boys give us some grasshoppers?"

"I don't know that they've got any ready ketched," said he, "for I reckon I used what they had this mornin'. But they kin git you some. Here, Dan, you and Sile go and ketch Mister Gruse and this young man some grasshoppers. Take that mustard box, and see that you git it full."

Peter and I now took seats, and the conversation began about a black cow which Peter had to sell, and which the other was willing to buy if the old man would trade for sheep, which animals, however, the basket mender did not appear just at that time to have in his possession. As I was not very much interested in this subject, I walked to the back door and watched two small boys in scanty shirts and trousers and ragged straw hats, who were darting about in the grass catching grasshoppers, of which insects, judging by the frequent pounces of the boys, there seemed a plentiful supply.

"Got it full?" said their father when the boys came in.

"Crammed," said Dan.

Old Peter took the little can, pressed the top firmly on, put it in his coattail pocket, and rose to go. "You'd better think about that cow, Barney," said he. He said nothing to the boys about the box of bait; but I could not let them catch grasshoppers for us for nothing, and I took a dime from my pocket, and gave it to Dan. Dan grinned, and Sile looked sheepishly happy, and at the sight of the piece of silver an expression of interest came over the face of the father. "Wait a minute," said he, and he went into a little room that seemed to be a kitchen. Returning, he brought with him a small string of trout. "Do you want to buy some fish?" he said. "These is nice fresh ones. I ketched 'em this mornin'."

To offer to sell fish to a man who is just about to go out to catch them for himself might, in most cases, be considered an insult, but it was quite evident that nothing of the kind was intended by Barney. He probably thought that if I bought grasshoppers, I might buy fish. "You kin have 'em for a quarter," he said.

It was derogatory to my pride to buy fish at such a moment, but the man looked very poor, and there was a shade of anxiety on his face which touched me. Old Peter stood by without saying a word. "It might be well," I said, turning to him, "to buy these fish, for we may not catch enough for supper."

"Such things do happen," said the old man.

"Well," said I, "if we have these we will feel safe in any case." And I took the fish and gave the man a quarter. It was not, perhaps, a professional act, but the trout were well worth the money, and I felt that I was doing a deed of charity.

Old Peter and I now took our rods, and crossed the road into an enclosed lot, and thence into a wide stretch of grassland, bounded by hills in front of us and to the right, while a thick forest lay to the left. We had walked but a short distance, when Peter said: "I'll go down into the woods, and try my luck there, and you'd better go along upstream, about a quarter of a mile, to where it's rocky. P'raps you ain't used to fishin' in the woods, and you might git your line cotched. You'll find the trout'll bite in the rough water."

"Where is the stream?" I asked.

"This is it," he said, pointing to a little brook, which was scarcely too wide for me to step across, "and there's fish right here, but they're hard to ketch, fur they git plenty of good livin', and are mighty sassy about their eatin'. But you kin ketch 'em up there."

Old Peter now went down toward the woods, while I walked up the little stream. I had seen trout brooks before, but never one so diminutive as this. However, when I came nearer to the point where the stream issued from between two of the foothills of the mountains, which lifted their forest-covered heights in the distance, I found it wider and shallower, breaking over its rocky bottom in sparkling little cascades.

Fishing in such a jolly little stream, surrounded by this mountain scenery, and with the privileges of the beautiful situation all to myself, would have been a joy to me if I had had never a bite. But no such ill luck befell me. Peter had given me the can of grasshoppers after putting half of them into his own bait box, and these I used with much success. It was grasshopper season, and the trout were evidently on the lookout for them. I fished in the ripples under the little waterfalls; and every now and then I drew out a lively trout. Most of these were of moderate size, and some of them might have been called small. The large ones probably fancied the forest shades, where old Peter went. But all I caught were fit for the table, and I was very well satisfied with the result of my sport.

About an hour after noon I began to feel hungry, and thought it time to look up the old man, who had the lunch basket. I walked down the bank of the brook, and some time before I reached the woods I came to a place where it expanded to a width of about ten feet. The water here was very clear, and the motion quiet, so that I could easily see to the bottom, which did not appear to be more than a foot below the surface. Gazing into this transparent water, as I walked, I saw a large trout glide across the stream, and disappear under the grassy bank which overhung the opposite side. I instantly stopped. This was a much larger fish than any I had caught, and I determined to try for him.

I stepped back from the bank, so as to be out of sight, and put a fine grasshopper on my hook; then I lay, face downward, on the grass, and worked myself slowly forward until I could see the middle of the stream; then quietly raising my pole, I gave my grasshopper a good swing, as if he had made a wager to jump over the stream at its widest part. But as he certainly would have failed in such an ambitious endeavor, especially if he had been caught by a puff of wind, I let him come down upon the surface of the water, a little beyond the middle of the brook. Grasshoppers do not sink when they fall into the water, and so I kept this fellow upon the surface, and gently moved him along, as if, with all the conceit taken out of him by the result of his ill-considered leap, he was ignominiously endeavoring to swim to shore. As I did this, I saw the trout come out from under the bank, move slowly toward the grasshopper, and stop directly under him. Trembling with anxiety and eager expectation, I endeavored to make the movements of the insect still more natural, and, as far as I was able, I threw into him a sudden perception of his danger, and a frenzied desire to get away. But, either the trout had had all the grasshoppers he wanted, or he was able, from long experience, to perceive the difference between a natural exhibition of emotion and a histrionic imitation of it, for he slowly turned, and, with a few slight movements of his tail, glided back under the bank. In vain did the grasshopper continue his frantic efforts to reach the shore; in vain did he occasionally become exhausted, and sink a short distance below the surface; in vain did he do everything that he knew, to show that he appreciated what a juicy and delicious morsel he was, and how he feared that the trout might yet be tempted to seize him; the fish did not come out again.

Then I withdrew my line, and moved back from the stream. I now determined to try Mr. Trout with a fly, and I took out the paper old Peter Gruse had given me. I did not know exactly what kind of winged insects were in order at this time of the year, but I was sure that yellow butterflies were not particular about just what month it was, so long as the sun shone warmly. I therefore chose that one of Peter's flies which was made of the yellowest feathers, and, removing the snood and hook from my line, I hastily attached this fly, which was provided with a hook quite suitable for my desired prize. Crouching on the grass, I again approached the brook. Gaily flitting above the glassy surface of the water, in all the fancied security of tender youth and innocence, came my yellow fly. Backward and forward over the water he gracefully flew, sometimes rising a little into the air, as if to view the varied scenery of the woods and mountains, and then settling for a moment close to the surface, better to inspect his glittering image as it came up from below, and showing in his every movement his intense enjoyment of summertime and life.

Out from his dark retreat now came the trout; and settling quietly at the bottom of the brook, he appeared to regard the venturesome insect with a certain interest. But he must have detected the iron barb of vice beneath the mask of blitheful innocence, for, after a short deliberation, the trout turned and disappeared under the bank. As he slowly moved away, he seemed to be bigger than ever. I must catch that fish! Surely he would bite at something. It was quite evident that his mind was not wholly unsusceptible to emotions emanating from an awakening appetite, and I believed that if he saw exactly what he wanted, he would

not neglect an opportunity of availing himself of it. But what did he
want? I must certainly find out. Drawing myself back again, I took off
the yellow fly, and put on another. This was a white one, with black
blotches, like a big miller moth which had fallen into an ink pot. It
was certainly a conspicuous creature, and as I crept forward and sent
it swooping over the stream, I could not see how any trout, with a
single insectivorous tooth in his head, could fail to rise to such an
occasion. But this trout did not rise. He would not even come out from
under his bank to look at the swiftly flitting creature. He probably
could see it well enough from where he was.

But I was not to be discouraged. I put on another fly; a green one
with a red tail. It did not look like any insect that I had ever seen, but
I thought that the trout might know more about such things than I.
He did come out to look at it, but probably considering it a product of
that modern aestheticism which sacrifices natural beauty to mediaeval
crudeness of color and form, he returned without evincing any disposition to countenance this style of art.

It was evident that it would be useless to put on any other flies, for
the two I had left were a good deal bedraggled, and not nearly so
attractive as those I had used. Just before leaving the house that morning Peter's son had given me a wooden matchbox filled with worms for
bait, which, although I did not expect to need, I put in my pocket. As
a last resort I determined to try the trout with a worm. I selected the
plumpest and most comely of the lot; I put a new hook on my line; I
looped him about it in graceful coils, and cautiously approached the
water, as before. Now a worm never attempts to leap wildly across a
flowing brook, nor does he flit in thoughtless innocence through the
sunny air, and over the bright transparent stream. If he happens to fall
into the water, he sinks to the bottom; and if he be of a kind not
subject to drowning, he generally endeavors to secrete himself under a
stone, or to burrow in the soft mud. With this knowledge of his nature
I gently dropped my worm upon the surface of the stream, and then
allowed him to sink slowly. Out sailed the trout from under the bank,
but stopped before reaching the sinking worm. There was a certain
something in his action which seemed to indicate a disgust at the sight
of such plebeian food, and a fear seized me that he might now swim
off, and pay no further attention to my varied baits. Suddenly there
was a ripple in the water, and I felt a pull on the line. Instantly I
struck; and then there was a tug. My blood boiled through every vein
and artery, and I sprang to my feet. I did not give him the butt: I did
not let him run with yards of line down the brook; nor reel him in, and
let him make another mad course upstream: I did not turn him over as
he jumped into the air; nor endeavor, in any way, to show him that I

understood those tricks, which his depraved nature prompted him to play upon the angler. With an absolute dependence upon the strength of old Peter's tackle, I lifted the fish. Out he came from the water, which held him with a gentle suction as if unwilling to let him go, and then he whirled through the air like a meteor flecked with rosy fire, and landed on the fresh green grass a dozen feet behind me. Down on my knees I dropped before him as he tossed and rolled, his beautiful spots and colors glistening in the sun. He was truly a splendid trout, fully a foot long, round and heavy. Carefully seizing him, I easily removed the hook from the bony roof of his capacious mouth thickly set with sparkling teeth, and then I tenderly killed him, with all his pluck, as old Peter would have said, still in him.

I covered the rest of the fish in my basket with wet plantain leaves, and laid my trout king on this cool green bed. Then I hurried off to the old man, whom I saw coming out of the woods. When I opened my basket and showed him what I had caught, Peter looked surprised, and, taking up the trout, examined it.

"Why, this is a big fellow," he said. "At first I thought it was Barney Sloat's boss trout, but it isn't long enough for him. Barney showed me his trout, that gen'rally keeps in a deep pool, where a tree has fallen over the stream down there. Barney tells me he often sees him, and he's been tryin' fur two years to ketch him, but he never has, and I say he never will, fur them big trout's got too much sense to fool round any kind of victuals that's got a string to it. They let a little fish eat all he wants, and then they eat him. How did you ketch this one?"

I gave an account of the manner of the capture, to which Peter listened with interest and approval.

"If you'd a stood off and made a cast at that feller, you'd either have caught him at the first flip, which isn't likely, as he didn't seem to want no feather flies, or else you'd a skeered him away. That's all well enough in the tumblin' water, where you gen'rally go fur trout, but the man that's got the true feelin' fur fish will try to suit his idees to theyrn, and if he keeps on doin' that, he's like to learn a thing or two that may do him good. That's a fine fish, and you ketched him well. I've got a lot of 'em, but nothin' of that heft."

After luncheon we fished for an hour or two, with no result worth recording, and then we started for home.

When we reached the farm the old man went into the barn, and I took the fish into the house. I found the two pretty daughters in the large room, where the eating and some of the cooking was done. I opened my basket, and with great pride showed them the big trout I had caught. They evidently thought it was a large fish, but they looked at each other, and smiled in a way that I did not understand. I had expected from them, at least, as much admiration for my prize and my skill as their father had shown.

"You don't seem to think much of this fine trout that I took such trouble to catch," I remarked.

"You mean," said the elder girl, with a laugh, "that you bought of Barney Sloat."

I looked at her in astonishment.

"Barney was along here today," she said, "and he told about your buying your fish of him."

"Bought of him!" I exclaimed indignantly. "A little string of fish at the bottom of the basket I bought of him, but all the others, and this big one, I caught myself."

"Oh, of course," said the pretty daughter, "bought the little ones and caught all the big ones."

"Barney Sloat ought to have kept his mouth shut," said the younger pretty daughter, looking at me with an expression of pity. "He'd got his money, and he hadn't no business to go telling on people. Nobody likes that sort of thing. But this big fish is a real nice one, and you shall have it for your supper."

"Thank you," I said, with dignity, and left the room.

I did not intend to have any further words with these young women on this subject, but I cannot deny that I was annoyed and mortified. This was the result of a charitable action. I think I was never more proud of anything than of catching that trout; and it was a very considerable downfall suddenly to find myself regarded as a mere city man fishing with a silver hook. But, after all, what did it matter? But the more I said this to myself, the more was I impressed with the fact that it mattered a great deal.

The boy who did not seem to be accounted a member of the family came into the house, and as he passed me he smiled good-humoredly, and said: "Buyed 'em!"

I felt like throwing a chair at him, but refrained out of respect to my host. Before supper the old man came out on to the porch where I was sitting. "It seems," said he, "that my gals has got it inter their heads that you bought that big fish of Barney Sloat, and as I can't say I seed you ketch it, they're not willin' to give in, 'specially as I didn't git no such big one. 'Tain't wise to buy fish when you're goin' fishin' yourself. It's pretty certain to tell agen you."

"You ought to have given me that advice before," I said, somewhat shortly. "You saw me buy the fish."

"You don't s'pose," said old Peter, "that I'm goin' to say anythin' to keep money out of my neighbor's pockets. We don't do that way in these parts. But I've told the gals they're not to speak another word about it, so you needn't give your mind no worry on that score. And now let's go in to supper. If you're as hungry as I am, there won't be many of them fish left fur breakfast."

For two days longer I remained in this neighborhood, wandering alone over the hills, and up the mountainsides, and by the brooks, which tumbled and gurgled through the lonely forest. Each evening I brought home a goodly supply of trout, but never a great one like the noble fellow for which I angled in the meadow stream.

On the morning of my departure I stood on the porch with old Peter waiting for the arrival of the mail driver, who was to take me to the nearest railroad town.

"I don't want to say nothin'," remarked the old man, "that would keep them fellers with the jinted poles from stoppin' at my house when they comes to these parts a-fishin'. I ain't got no objections to their poles; 'tain't that. And I don't mind nuther their standin' off, and throwin' their flies as fur as they've a mind to; that's not it. And it ain't even the way they have of worryin' their fish. I wouldn't do it myself, but if they like it, that's their business. But what does rile me is the cheeky way in which they stand up and say that there isn't no decent way of fishin' but their way. And that to a man that's ketched more fish, of more different kinds, with more game in 'em, and had more fun at it, with a lot less money and less tom-foolin' than any fishin' feller that ever come here and talked to me like an old cat tryin' to teach a dog to ketch rabbits. No, sir; agen I say that I don't take no money fur entertainin' the only man that ever come out here to go a-fishin' in a plain, Christian way. But if you feel tetchy about not payin' nothin', you kin send me one of them poles in three pieces, a good strong one, that'll lift Barney Sloat's trout, if ever I hook him."

I sent him the rod; and next summer I am going up to see him use it.

A TALE OF THE TROUT STREAM

WILLIAM DAVENPORT
HULBERT

It was winter, and the trout stream ran low in its banks, hidden from the sky by a thick shell of ice and snow. But the trout stream was used to that, and it slipped along in the semidarkness, undismayed, talking to itself in low, murmuring tones, and dreaming of the time when spring should come back and all the rivers should be full.

Mingled with its waters, and borne onward and downward by its current, were multitudes of the tiniest bubbles and particles of air—most of them too small to be seen by the human eye, yet large enough to be the very breath of life to thousands and thousands of living creatures. They went wherever the water could go, and some of them worked down into the gravel of the riverbed, and there, between the pebbles, they found a vast number of little balls of yellow-brown jelly, each about as large as a small pea. And the air bubbles touched the trout eggs gently, and in some wonderful way their oxygen passed in through the pores of the shells, and the little lives within were quickened and stirred.

Through each of those thin, leathery, semitransparent shells you could have seen, if you had examined it closely, a pair of bright, beady eyes and a little thread of a backbone. The backbones were all too long to lie straight, and had to curl up inside the eggs like so many horseshoes, and along the outside of each one a set of the tiniest and daintiest muscles was getting ready for a long pull, and a strong pull, and a pull all together. And one day, late in the winter, the muscles in one particular egg pulled with all their might, the backbone straightened,

337

the shell was ripped open, and the tail of a new Brook Trout wriggled itself out into the water.

But his head and shoulders were still inside, and for a while it looked as if he would never get them out. A long, narrow fin ran aft from the middle of his back, around the end of his tail, and forward again on the under side of his body; and with this for an oar he struggled and writhed and squirmed, and went bumping blindly about among the pebbles like a kitten with its head in the cream pitcher. And at last he backed free of the shell in which he had lain for several months, and lay down on a stone to rest and meditate.

The Troutlet had to lie on his side, for attached to his breast was a large, round, transparent sac, which contained a goodly portion of the yolk of the egg. If you had examined it with a microscope you would have seen a most strange and beautiful sight. His heart was pumping blood into it through little arteries which kept branching and dividing, and in the very smallest of these branches a wonderful process was going on. Somehow, by life's marvelous and mysterious alchemy, the blood was laying hold of the material of the yolk, turning it into more blood, and carrying it away to be used in building up bone and muscle.

With a full haversack to draw on in such a convenient manner, the baby Trout was not obliged, for the present, to think about hustling around in search of a living. This was very fortunate, for the stream was full of beasts of prey, who would be only too glad to gobble him up; and, besides, his frail little body was so delicate that he could not bear the light. So he simply dived down deeper into the gravel and stayed there, and for some weeks he led a very quiet life among the pebbles.

His yolk sac was gradually shrinking, and after a month or so it drew itself up into a little cleft in his breast and almost disappeared. It could no longer supply food enough for his growing body. And other changes had come. The embryonic fin which had made his tail so like a paddle was gone, the true dorsal and caudal and anal fins had taken their proper shape, and he looked a little less like a tadpole, and a little more like a fish. He was stronger, and he no longer dreaded the light; and so at last he came up out of the gravel bed to study swimming, and to take his rightful place in the world of moving, murmuring waters.

He had hardly emerged from his hiding place in the gravel when a queer, big-headed little fish darted at him from under a big stone, with his jaws open and an awful cavity yawning behind them. The Troutlet dodged between a couple of pebbles and escaped, but another youngster behind him was caught and swallowed alive. This was his first meeting with the stargazer, who kills more babies than ever Herod did. Then there were minnows, and herrings, and chubs, and lizards, and frogs, and weasels, and watersnakes, and other butchers of all sorts and sizes, too numerous to mention. Perhaps the worst of all were the older trout, who never seemed to have any scruples at all about eating their young relations. I don't believe that more than one or two in a thousand of the small fry ever lived to maturity. Our young friend spent most of his time in the shallow water near the banks, hidden as much as possible under chips and dead leaves, and behind stones.

His first taste of food was a great experience, and gave him some entirely new ideas of life. He was lying with his head upstream, as was his usual habit, when a particularly.fat, plump little larva came drifting down with the current. He looked very tempting, and our friend sallied out from under a little black stick and caught him on the fly, just as he had seen the stargazer catch his own brother. The funny little creature wriggled deliciously on his tongue, and he held him between his jaws for a moment in a kind of ecstasy; but he couldn't quite make up his mind to swallow him, and presently he spat him out again. It was the first time he had ever done such a thing, and he felt rather overwhelmed; but an hour or two later he tried it again, and this time the living morsel did not stop in his mouth, but went straight on down.

Henceforth he could take care of himself. He was no longer an embryo; he was a real fish, a genuine *Salvelinus fontinalis,* as carnivorous as the biggest and fiercest of his relations. The cleft in his breast might close up now, and the last remnant of the yolk sac vanish forever.

It must be admitted, however, that he did not look much like a mature trout. He was less than three-quarters of an inch long, and his enormous head, bulging eyes, and capacious mouth were out of all proportion to his small and feeble body. But time and food were all that were needed to set these matters right; and he had learned how to get the food, while the time came of itself. I should be afraid to guess how many tiny water creatures, insects and larvae and crustacea, found their way down his ravenous little maw; but it is pretty safe to say that he ate more than his own weight in a single day. Consequently he grew rapidly in size and strength and symmetry; and from being a quiet, languid baby, always hiding in dark corners and attending strictly to his own affairs, he became one of the liveliest and most inquisitive little fishes in all the stream.

It would take too long to tell of all his youthful adventures during the next year, and of his many narrow escapes, and the tight places that he got into and out of. Once a kingfisher dived for him, missed him by a hair's breadth, and flew back, scolding and chattering, to his perch on an old stump that leaned far out over the water. And once he had a horrible vision of an immense loon close behind him, with long neck stretched out, and huge bill just ready to make the fatal grab. He dodged and got away, but it frightened him about as badly as anything can frighten a creature with no more nerves than a fish. Many other such adventures he had, but somehow or other he always pulled through, and the next spring he was eating the new crop of young fry with as little concern as the stargazers had shown in trying to eat him. Our friend appeared to be one of those who are foreordained to eat and not be eaten, though it was more than likely that in the end he, too, would meet a violent death. It seems to be a true saying that no brook trout ever dies of old age.

When he was about a year and a half old he noticed that all the larger trout were gathering at the places where the water was shallow, the bottom pebbly, and the current rather rapid, and that they acted as if they had important business on hand. He wanted to do as the others did, and thus it happened that he went back again to the gravelly shallows where the air bubbles had first found him.

The male trout were the first to arrive, and they promptly set to work to prepare nests for their mates, who were expected a little later. It was a simple process—the nest-making. All they did was to shove the gravel aside with their noses and fins and tails, and then fan the sediment away until they had made nice, clean little hollows in the bed of the stream; but there was a good deal of excitement and jealousy over it. The biggest and strongest always wanted the best places. Our Trout was too young to bear a very prominent part in these proceedings, but he and a few companions of his own age and size skirmished around the edges of the nesting ground. And a little later, when the nests began to be put to practical use, the yearlings were very much in evidence. Strictly fresh eggs are as good eating down under the water as they are on land, and partly for this reason, and partly because direct sunshine is supposed to be very injurious to them, the mothers always covered them with gravel as quickly as possible. But very often some of them were caught up by the current and swept away in spite of all precautions, and then our young friend would creep up as near as he dared, and whenever one of the little yellow-brown balls came his way he would gobble it down without any remorse whatever.

A year later our Trout went again to the gravelly shallows, and this time, being six inches long and about thirty months old, he decided to make a nest of his own. He did so, and had just induced a beautiful young fish of the other sex to come and examine it with a view to matrimony, when the biggest old male in the stream appeared on the scene and promptly turned him out of house and home. It was very exasperating, not to say humiliating.

The next time he had better luck. As another summer passed away and the cooler weather came on, he arrayed himself in his wedding finery, decking himself out in his gayest colors, and making a very brave display. In later years he was larger and heavier, but I don't think he was ever much handsomer than in that fourth autumn of his life. His back was a dark, dusky, olive green, with mottlings that were still darker and duskier. His sides were somewhat lighter, almost golden in some places, and scattered irregularly over them were the bright carmine spots which sometimes gave him the name of the Speckled Trout. Beneath, he was usually of a light cream color, but, now that he had put on his best suit, his vest was bright orange, and some of his fins were variegated with red and white, while others were a fiery yellow. He was clothed in thousands on thousands of tiny scales, so small and fine that the eye could hardly separate them; and from the bony shoulder-girdle just behind his gills a raised line, slightly waving, ran back to his tail, like the sheer-line of a ship. There might be other fishes more slender than he, and possibly more graceful; but in him there was something besides beauty—something that told of power, and speed, and doggedness. His broad mouth opened clear back under his eyes, and was armed with rows of strong, sharp teeth which pointed backward, so that when they once fastened themselves in a smaller fish they never let go again. His eyes were large and were set well apart, and the bulge of his forehead between them hinted at more brains than are allotted to some of the people of the stream.

And now he started once more for the shallows, and traveled as he had never traveled before in all his life. Streams are made to swim against—every brook trout knows that—and the faster they run the greater is the joy of breasting them. One moment he was working up the long rapid like a bird in the teeth of the wind, and the next he was gathering all his strength for the great leap to the top of the waterfall; now he rested for a little while in a quiet pool, and now he went swinging round the curves, diving under logs and fallen trees, darting up the still places where the water lay a-dreaming, and wriggling over bars where it was not half deep enough to cover him; until at last he reached the place where so many, many generations of brook trout had begun their existence.

He scooped out a fine large nest, a little apart from those of his rivals; but for some reason the first possible mates who came to look at his location declined to stay. Finally, however, there came one who seemed to be quite satisfied, and of whom our friend had every reason to be proud.

She was not a native of the stream, but of one of the hatcheries of the Michigan Fish Commission, and while he was lying in the gravel-bed, she was one of a company of many thousands who inhabited a number of black wooden troughs that stood in a large, pleasant room, full of the sound of running water. Among all those thousands, she was one of the smartest and most precocious. This was particularly fortunate for her, for there was a very hard and trying experience before her—one in which she would have need of all her strength and vitality, and in which her chances of life would be very small indeed. It came with planting time, when she and a host of her companions were whisked through a rubber siphon, deposited in a large galvanized iron can, and borne away to the trout stream. Their troubles began before they reached their destination, for they were pretty badly cramped for room, and after a while the supply of oxygen in the water became exhausted. Every last one of them would have suffocated if the man who had charge of them hadn't noticed what was going on and pumped some fresh air into the water with a bellows. And when they reached the stream matters were a thousand times worse, for the same fishes and frogs and other enemies that had so persecuted our friend and his brothers and sisters were on hand to welcome these new arrivals. But by dint of strength, speed, agility, and good judgment in selecting hiding places, this particular young trout made her way unharmed through all the dangers of babyhood and early youth, and now she was one of the most beautiful little three-year-old pirates that ever swooped down upon a helpless victim. As she and our friend swam side by side, her nose and the end of her tail were exactly even with his. Her colors were the same that he had worn before he had put on his wedding garment, and if you had seen them together in the early summer, I don't think you could ever have told them apart. They were a well-matched pair.

But they were not to be allowed to set up housekeeping without fighting for the privilege. Hardly had she finished inspecting the nest and made up her mind that it would answer, when a third trout appeared and tried to do as the big bully had done the year before. This time, however, our young friend's blood was up, and though the enemy was considerably larger than he, he was ready to strike for his altars and his fires. It was a comical little duel, down there under the water. One would almost have thought they were at play, rather than fighting for the possession of a wife and a home, for at first they did nothing but make quick rushes and ram each other in the ribs, each one poking his snout into the other's fat sides as if he were trying to tickle him. It seemed only a trial of strength and speed and dexterity; and if our Trout was not quite as powerful as the other, yet he proved himself more than his match in quickness and agility. And then suddenly his mouth opened, and the sharp teeth of his lower jaw tore a row of bright scales from his adversary's side, and left a long, deep gash behind. That settled it.

The nesting season cannot last forever, and by and by, when the days were very short and the nights were very long, and the frost began to take hold, the last trout went in search of better feeding grounds.

One of the Trout's most exciting adventures, and the one which probably taught him more than any other, came in the following summer. The stream had grown rather too warm for comfort, and he had formed the habit of spending a great deal of his time in deep, quiet pools, where icy springs bubbled out of the bank and imparted a delightful coolness to the water. It was delicious to idle away a long, hot July afternoon in the wash below one of these fountains, having a lazy, pleasant time, and enjoying the caressing touch of the cold water as it slid along his body from nose to tail. And one sunshiny day a fly lit on the surface almost directly over his head—a bright, gaily-colored fly of a species which was entirely new to him, but which looked as if it might be very finely flavored. He made a dash and seized it, but he had no sooner got it between his lips than he spat it out again, before the angler had time to strike. Instead of being soft and juicy and luscious, it was stiff and hard and dry, with a long, crooked stinger. It disappeared as suddenly as it had come, and the Trout sank back to the bottom of the pool.

But presently three more flies came down together and lit in a row, one behind another. They were different from the first, and the Trout decided to try his luck once more. He chose the foremost of the three, and found it quite as ill-tasting as its predecessor, but this time the angler's eye and hand were a trifle quicker, and before he could get rid of it the hook was fast in his lip. For the next few minutes he tore around the pool and up and down the stream as if he were crazy, frightening the smaller fishes almost out of their wits.

The first thing he did was to shoot along the surface for several feet, throwing his head from side to side as he went, and doing his best to shake that horrible fly out of his mouth. That didn't help matters in the least, and next he jumped clear out of the water and tried to strike the line with his tail. That was no better, so he rushed off up the stream as hard as he could go, then doubled and dashed away in the other direction, and so went streaking it back and forth as if all the imps of darkness were after him, instead of one pleasant-faced man who was really very good-natured and kind-hearted.

The worst of it was that wherever he went and whatever he did there was always a steady strain on the line—not strong enough to break it or to tear the hook away, but enough to keep him from getting a single inch of slack. If there had been any chance to jerk he would probably have got away in short order. He grew tired after a while, and dived to the bottom of the pool, hoping to lie still for a few minutes, where he could rest and think of some new plan of escape. But that constant tugging on his lip was more than he could stand. It almost seemed as if it would pull the jaw out of his head, and presently he let himself be drawn up again to the surface. Once he was so close to the shore that the angler made a thrust at him with the landing net, and just grazed his side. It frightened him worse than ever, and he raced away again so fast that the reel sang, and the line swished through the water like a knife.

The other two flies were trailing behind, and the short line that held them was constantly catching on his fins and twisting itself around his tail in a way that annoyed him greatly. And yet, as it finally turned out, it was one of those flies that saved his life. He was coming back from that last unsuccessful rush for liberty, fighting for every inch, and only yielding to a strength a thousand times greater than his own, when the trailer suddenly caught on a sunken log and held fast. Instantly the strain on his mouth relaxed, and he began jerking this way and that, backward and forward, right and left, tearing the hole in his lip a little larger at every yank, until the hook came away and he was free. The wound was a painful one, and he carried the scar as long as he lived, but the lesson he learned was worth all it cost.

The year went by, and the Trout increased in size and strength and wisdom, as a trout should. One after another his rivals disappeared, and at last there was only one left who was larger and stronger than he, and the way the fierce, solemn old brute finally departed this life deserves a paragraph all to itself.

It happened—or rather it began—one morning in early spring—just after the ice had gone out. Our Trout was there, and was feeling a trifle sleepy and lazy after the long, dull winter, though he did not fail to keep an eye open for anything good to eat. I hardly think he would have jumped at a fly, for it was not the proper season for insects, and he was rather methodical in his diet; but almost anything else was welcome. The water was high that day, from the melting snows, and many a delicious grub and earth worm had been washed from the bank by the freshet, only to find its way down the throat of some hungry trout. And presently, what should come drifting along but a poor little field mouse, struggling desperately in a vain effort to swim back to the shore. Once before our friend had swallowed a mouse whole, just as you would take an oyster from the half-shell, and he knew that they were very nice indeed. He made a rush for the unlucky little animal, and in another minute he would have had him, but just then the big trout ranged up alongside with an air which seemed to say, "That's my meat. You get out of this!"

Our friend obeyed, and the bully gave a leap and seized the mouse, and then—his time had come.

He fought bravely, but he was fairly hooked, and in a few minutes he was out on the bank, gasping for breath, flopping wildly about, and fouling his beautiful sides with sand and dirt. And that was the end of him.

And so our friend became the King of the Trout Stream.

You are not to suppose, however, that he paid very much attention to his subjects, or that he was particularly fond of giving orders. On the contrary, he had become very solitary and hermit-like in his habits. In his youth he had been fond of society, but of late years his tastes seemed to have changed, and he kept to himself, and lurked in the shady, sunless places till his skin grew darker, and he more and more resembled the shadows in which he lived. His great delight was to watch from the depths of some cave-like hollow under an overhanging bank until a herring, or a minnow, or some other baby-eater came in sight, and then to rush out and swallow him head first.

He took ample revenge on all those pesky little fishes for all that they had done and tried to do to him and his brethren in the early days. The truth is that every brook trout is an Ishmaelite. The hand of every creature is against him, from that of the dragon-fly larva to that of the man with the latest invention in the way of patent fishing tackle. It is no wonder if he turns the tables on his enemies whenever he has a chance, or even if he sometimes goes so far, in his general ruthlessness, as to eat his own offspring.

Yet, in spite of our friend's moroseness and solitary habits, there were certain times and seasons when he did come more or less in contact with his inferiors. In late spring and early summer he liked to sport for a while in the swift rapids—perhaps to stretch his muscles after the dull, quiet life of the winter time, or possibly to free himself from certain little insects which sometimes fastened themselves to his body, and which, for lack of hands, it was rather difficult to get rid of. Here he often met some of his subjects, and later, when the hot weather came on, they all went to the spring holes which formed their summer resorts. And at such times he never hesitated to take advantage of his superior size and strength. He always picked out the coolest and most comfortable places in the pools, and helped himself to the choicest morsels of food; and the others took what was left, without question. And when the summer was gone, and the water grew cold and invigorating, and once more he put on his wedding garment and hurried away to the gravelly shallows, how different was his conduct from what it had been when he was a yearling! Then he was only a hanger-on; now he selected his nest and his mate to suit himself, and nobody ever dared to interfere.

Other changes had come beside those in his relations to his fellow trout. The curving lines of his body were not quite as graceful as they once had been, and at times he wore a rather lean and dilapidated appearance, especially during the six months from November to May. His tail was not as handsomely forked as when he was young, but was nearly square across the end, and was beginning to be a little frayed at the corners. His lower jaw had grown out beyond the upper, and at its extremity it was turned up in a wicked-looking hook which amounted almost to a disfigurement, but which was often very convenient in hustling smaller trout out of the way. Even his complexion had changed, as we have already seen. As to size, he succeeded, after many years of living and ruling, in attaining a weight of nearly three pounds, which made him considerably larger and heavier than his old enemy had been. Altogether, he was less prepossessing than in former days, and decidedly more formidable.

But the two great interests of his every-day life were the same that they had always been—namely, to get enough to eat, and to keep out of the way of his enemies. For enemies he still had, and would continue to have as long as he lived. The fly fishermen came every spring and summer, and only the wisdom born of experience kept him from falling into their hands. Several times he met with an otter, and had to run for his life. Once a bear, fishing for suckers, came near catching a brook trout. He certainly could not complain of any lack of excitement.

And when the end came it was a violent one, and so inglorious that I am almost ashamed to tell it. He, the King of the Trout Stream—he, who had so often run Fate's gauntlet and escaped with his body unharmed and his wits sharper than ever—he, who knew the wiles of the fly fishermen better than any other trout in the river, fell a victim to a little Indian boy with a piece of edging for a rod, coarse string for a line, and salt pork for bait.

I'm sure it wouldn't have happened if he had stayed at home, but one spring he took it into his head to go on an exploring expedition out into Lake Superior.

I understand that his cousins in the streams of eastern Canada sometimes visit salt water in somewhat the same manner, and that they thereupon lose the bright trimmings of their coats and become a plain silver-gray. Superior did not affect our friend in that way, but something worse happened to him—he lost his common sense. Perhaps his interest in his new surroundings was so great that he forgot the lessons of wisdom and experience which it had cost him so much to learn.

In the course of his wanderings he came to where a school of yellow perch was loafing in the shadow of a wharf, and just as he pushed his way in among them, that little white piece of fat pork sank slowly down through the green water. It was something new to the Trout, and the perch seemed to think it was good to eat, and so, although the string was in plain sight, and ought to have been a sufficient warning, he exercised his royal prerogative, shouldered those yellow-barred plebeians aside, and took the tid-bit for himself. It is too humiliating; let us draw a veil over that closing scene.

The King of the Trout Stream had gone the way of his fathers, and another reigned in his stead.

A FATAL SUCCESS

HENRY VAN DYKE

Beekman De Peyster was probably the most passionate and triumphant fisherman in the Petrine Club. He angled with the same dash and confidence that he threw into his operations in the stock market. He was sure to be the first man to get his flies on the water at the opening of the season. And when we came together for our fall meeting, to compare notes of our wanderings on various streams and make up the fish stories for the year, Beekman was almost always "high hook." We expected, as a matter of course, to hear that he had taken the most and the largest fish.

It was so with everything that he undertook. He was a masterful man. If there was an unusually large trout in a river, Beekman knew about it before any one else, and got there first, and came home with the fish. It did not make him unduly proud, because there was nothing uncommon about it. It was his habit to succeed, and all the rest of us were hardened to it.

When he married Cornelia Cochrane, we were consoled for our partial loss by the apparent fitness and brilliancy of the match. If Beekman was a masterful man, Cornelia was certainly what you might call a mistressful woman. She had been the head of her house since she was eighteen years old. She carried her good looks like the family plate; and when she came into the breakfast room and said good morning, it was with an air as if she presented every one with a check for a thousand dollars. Her tastes were accepted as judgments, and her preferences had the force of laws. Wherever she wanted to go in the summertime, there the finger of household destiny pointed. At Newport, at Bar Harbour, at Lenox, at Southampton, she made a record. When she was joined in holy wedlock to Beekman De Peyster, her father and mother heaved a sigh of satisfaction, and settled down for a quiet vacation in Cherry Valley.

It was in the second summer after the wedding that Beekman admitted to a few of his ancient Petrine cronies, in moments of confidence (unjustifiable, but natural), that his wife had one fault.

"It is not exactly a fault," he said, "not a positive fault, you know. It is just a kind of a defect, due to her education, of course. In everything else she's magnificent. But she doesn't care for fishing. She says it's stupid—can't see why any one should like the woods—calls camping out the lunatic's diversion. It's rather awkward for a man with my habits to have his wife take such a view. But it can be changed by training. I intend to educate her and convert her. I shall make an angler of her yet."

And so he did.

The new education was begun in the Adirondacks, and the first lesson was given at Paul Smith's. It was a complete failure.

Beekman persuaded her to come out with him for a day on Meacham River, and promised to convince her of the charm of angling. She wore a new gown, fawn-color and violet, with a picture hat, very taking. But the Meacham River trout was shy that day; not even Beekman could induce him to rise to the fly. What the trout lacked in confidence the mosquitoes more than made up. Mrs. De Peyster came home much sunburned, and expressed a highly unfavorable opinion of fishing as an amusement and of Meacham River as a resort.

"The nice people don't come to the Adirondacks to fish," said she; "they come to talk about the fishing twenty years ago. Besides, what do you want to catch that trout for? If you do, the other men will say you bought it, and the hotel will have to put in another for the rest of the season."

The following year Beekman tried Moosehead Lake. Here he found an atmosphere more favorable to his plan of education. There were a good many people who really fished, and short expeditions in the woods were quite fashionable. Cornelia had a camping-costume of the most approved style made by Dewlap on Fifth Avenue—pearl gray with linings of rose silk—and consented to go with her husband on a trip up Moose River. They pitched their tent the first evening at the mouth of Misery Stream, and a storm came on. The rain sifted through the canvas in a fine spray, and Mrs. De Peyster sat up all night in a waterproof cloak, holding an umbrella. The next day they were back at the hotel in time for lunch.

"It was horrid," she told her most intimate friend, "perfectly horrid. The idea of sleeping in a shower-bath, and eating your breakfast from a tin plate, just for sake of catching a few silly fish! Why not send your guides out to get them for you?"

But, in spite of this profession of obstinate heresy, Beekman observed with secret joy that there were signs, before the end of the season, that Cornelia was drifting a little, a very little but still perceptibly, in the direction of a change of heart. She began to take an interest, as the big trout came along in September, in the reports of the catches made by the different anglers. She would saunter out with the other people to the corner of the porch to see the fish weighed and spread out on the grass. Several times she went with Beekman in the canoe to Hardscrabble Point, and showed distinct evidences of pleasure when he caught large trout. The last day of the season, when he returned from a successful expedition to Roach River and Lily Bay, she inquired with some particularity about the results of his sport; and in the evening, as the company sat before the great open fire in the hall of the hotel, she was heard to use this information with considerable skill in putting down Mrs. Minot Peabody of Boston, who was recounting the details of her husband's catch at Spencer Pond. Cornelia was not a person to be contented with the back seat, even in fish stories.

When Beekman observed these indications he was much encouraged, and resolved to push his educational experiment briskly forward to his customary goal of success.

"Some things can be done, as well as others," he said in his masterful way, as three of us were walking home together after the autumnal dinner of the Petrine Club, which he always attended as a graduate member. "A real fisherman never gives up. I told you I'd make an angler out of my wife; and so I will. It has been rather difficult. She is 'dour' in rising. But she's beginning to take notice of the fly now. Give me another season, and I'll have her landed."

Good old Beekman! Little did he think—But I must not interrupt the story with moral reflections.

The preparations that he made for his final effort at conversion were thorough and prudent. He had a private interview with Dewlap in regard to the construction of a practical fishing costume for a lady, which resulted in something more reasonable and workmanlike than had ever been turned out by that famous artist. He ordered from Hook & Catchett a lady's angling outfit of the most enticing description—a split-bamboo rod, light as a girl's wish, and strong as a matron's will; an oxidized silver reel, with a monogram on one side, and a sapphire set in the handle for good luck; a book of flies, of all sizes and colors, with the correct names inscribed in gilt letters on each page. He surrounded his favorite sport with an aureole of elegance and beauty.

And then he took Cornelia in September to the Upper Dam at Rangeley.

She went reluctant. She arrived disgusted. She stayed incredulous. She returned—Wait a bit, and you shall hear how she returned.

The Upper Dam at Rangeley is the place, of all others in the world, where the lunacy of angling may be seen in its incurable stage. There is a cozy little inn, called a camp, at the foot of a big lake. In front of the inn is a huge dam of gray stone, over which the river plunges into a great oval pool, where the trout assemble in the early fall to perpetuate their race. From the tenth of September to the thirtieth, there is not an hour of the day or night when there are no boats floating on that pool, and no anglers trailing the fly across its waters. Before the late fishermen are ready to come in at midnight, the early fishermen may be seen creeping down to the shore with lanterns in order to begin before cock crow. The number of fish taken is not large—perhaps five or six for the whole company on an average day—but the size is sometimes enormous—nothing under three pounds is counted—and they pervade thought and conversation at the Upper Dam to the exclusion of every other subject. There is no driving, no dancing, no golf, no tennis. There is nothing to do but fish or die.

At first, Cornelia thought she would choose the latter alternative. But a remark of that skillful and morose old angler, McTurk, which she overheard on the verandah after supper, changed her mind.

"Women have no sporting instinct," said he. "They only fish because they see men doing it. They are imitative animals."

That same night she told Beekman, in the subdued tone which the architectural construction of the house imposes upon all confidential communications in the bedrooms, but with resolution in every accent, that she proposed to go fishing with him on the morrow.

"But not on that pool, right in front of the house, you understand. There must be some other place, out on the lake, where we can fish for three or four days, until I get the trick of this wobbly rod. Then I'll show that old bear, McTurk, what kind of an animal woman is."

Beekman was simply delighted. Five days of diligent practice at the mouth of Mill Brook brought his pupil to the point where he pronounced her safe.

"Of course," he said patronizingly, "you haven't learned all about it yet. That will take years. But you can get your fly out thirty feet, and you can keep the tip of your rod up. If you do that, the trout will hook himself, in rapid water, eight times out of ten. For playing him, if you follow my directions, you'll be all right. We will try the pool tonight, and hope for a medium-sized fish."

Cornelia said nothing, but smiled and nodded. She had her own thoughts.

At about nine o'clock Saturday night, they anchored their boat on the edge of the shoal where the big eddy swings around, put out the lantern and began to fish. Beekman sat in the bow of the boat, with his rod over the left side; Cornelia in the stern, with her rod over the right side. The night was cloudy and very black. Each of them had put on the largest possible fly, one a "Bee Pond" and the other a "Dragon"; but even these were invisible. They measured out the right length of line, and let the flies drift back until they hung over the shoal, in the curly water where the two currents meet.

There were three other boats to the left of them. McTurk was their only neighbor in the darkness on the right. Once they heard him swearing softly to himself, and knew that he had hooked and lost a fish.

Away down at the tail of the pool, dimly visible through the gloom, the furtive fisherman, Parsons, had anchored his boat. No noise ever came from that craft. If he wished to change his position, he did not pull up the anchor and let it down again with a bump. He simply lengthened or shortened his anchor rope. There was no click of the reel when he played a fish. He drew in and paid out the line through the rings by hand, without a sound. What he thought when a fish got away, no one knew, for he never said it. He concealed his angling as if it had been a conspiracy. Twice that night they heard a faint splash in the water near his boat, and twice they saw him put his arm over the side in the darkness and bring it back again very quietly.

"That's the second fish for Parsons," whispered Beekman, "what a secretive old Fortunatus he is! He knows more about fishing than any man on the pool, and talks less."

Cornelia did not answer. Her thoughts were all on the tip of her own rod. About eleven o'clock a fine, drizzling rain set in. The fishing was very slack. All the other boats gave it up in despair; but Cornelia said she wanted to stay out a little longer, they might as well finish up the week.

At precisely fifty minutes past eleven, Beekman reeled up his line, and remarked with firmness that the holy Sabbath day was almost at hand and they ought to go in.

"Not till I've landed this trout," said Cornelia.

"What? A trout! Have you got one?"

"Certainly; I've had him on for at least fifteen minutes. I'm playing him Mr. Parsons' way. You might as well light the lantern and get the net ready; he's coming in towards the boat now."

Beekman broke three matches before he made the lantern burn; and when he held it up over the gunwale, there was the trout sure enough, gleaming ghostly pale in the dark water, close to the boat, and quite tired out. He slipped the net over the fish and drew it in—a monster.

"I'll carry that trout, if you please," said Cornelia, as they stepped out of the boat; and she walked into the camp, on the last stroke of midnight, with the fish in her hand, and quietly asked for the steel-yard.

Eight pounds and fourteen ounces—that was the weight. Everybody was amazed. It was the "best fish" of the year. Cornelia showed no sign of exultation, until just as John was carrying the trout to the icehouse. Then she flashed out—

"Quite a fair imitation, Mr. McTurk—isn't it?"

Now McTurk's best record for the last fifteen years was seven pounds and twelve ounces.

So far as McTurk is concerned, this is the end of the story. But not for the De Peysters. I wish it were. Beekman went to sleep that night with a contented spirit. He felt that his experiment in education had been a success. He had made his wife an angler.

He had indeed, and to an extent which he little suspected. That Upper Dam trout was to her like the first taste of blood to the tiger. It seemed to change, at once, not so much her character as the direction of her vital energy. She yielded to the lunacy of angling, not by slow degrees (as first a transient delusion, then a fixed idea, then a chronic infirmity, finally a mild insanity) but by a sudden plunge into the most violent mania. So far from being ready to die at Upper Dam, her desire now was to live there—and to live solely for the sake of fishing—as long as the season was open.

There were two hundred and forty hours left to midnight on the thirtieth of September. At least two hundred of these she spent on the pool; and when Beekman was too exhausted to manage the boat and the net and the lantern for her, she engaged a trustworthy guide to take Beekman's place while he slept. At the end of the last day her score was twenty-three, with an average of five pounds and a quarter. His score was nine, with an average of four pounds. He had succeeded far beyond his wildest hopes.

The next year his success became even more astonishing. They went to the Titan Club in Canada. The ugliest and most inaccessible sheet of water in that territory is Lake Pharaoh. But it is famous for the extraordinary fishing at a certain spot near the outlet, where there is just room enough for one canoe. They camped on Lake Pharaoh for six weeks, by Mrs. De Peyster's command; and her canoe was always the first to reach the fishing ground in the morning, and the last to leave it in the evening.

Some one asked him, when he returned to the city, whether he had good luck.

"Quite fair," he tossed off in a careless way; "we took over three hundred pounds."

"To your own rod?" asked the inquirer, in admiration.

"No—o—o," said Beekman, "there were two of us."

There were two of them, also, the following year, when they joined the Natasheebo Salmon Club and fished that celebrated river in Labrador. The custom of drawing lots every night for the water that each member was to angle over the next day, seemed to be especially designed to fit the situation. Mrs. De Peyster could fish her own pool and her husband's too. The result of that year's fishing was something phenomenal. She had a score that made a paragraph in the newspapers and called out editorial comment. One editor was so inadequate to the situation as to entitle the article in which he described her triumph "The Equivalence of Woman." It was well meant, but she was not at all pleased with it.

She was now not merely an angler, but a "record" angler of the most virulent type. Wherever they went, she wanted, and she got, the pick of the water. She seemed to be equally at home on all kinds of streams, large and small. She would pursue the little mountain-brook trout in the early spring, and the Labrador salmon in July, and the huge speckled trout of the northern lakes in September, with the same avidity and resolution. All that she cared for was to get the best and the most of the fishing at each place where she angled. This she always did.

And Beekman—well, for him there were no more long separations from the partner of his life while he went off to fish some favorite stream. There were no more homecomings after a good day's sport to find her clad in cool and dainty raiment on the verandah, ready to welcome him with friendly badinage. There was not even any casting of the fly around Hardscrabble Point while she sat in the canoe reading a novel, looking up with mild and pleasant interest when he caught a larger fish than usual, as an older and wiser person looks at a child playing some innocent game. Those days of a divided interest between man and wife were gone. She was now fully converted, and more. Beekman and Cornelia were one; and she was the one.

The last time I saw the De Peysters he was following her along the Beaverkill, carrying a landing net and a basket, but no rod. She paused for a moment to exchange greetings, and then strode on down the stream. He lingered for a few minutes longer to light a pipe.

"Well, old man," I said, "you certainly have succeeded in making an angler of Mrs. De Peyster."

"Yes, indeed," he answered—"haven't I?" Then he continued, after a few thoughtful puffs of smoke, "Do you know, I'm not quite so sure as I used to be that fishing is the best of all sports. I sometimes think of giving it up and going in for croquet."

OLD RED

CAROLINE GORDON

PART ONE

When the door had closed behind his daughter, Mister Maury went to the window and stood a few moments looking out. The roses that had grown in a riot all along that side of the fence had died or been cleared away, but the sun lay across the garden in the same level lances of light that he remembered. He turned back into the room. The shadows had gathered until it was nearly all in gloom. The top of his minnow bucket just emerging from his duffel bag glinted in the last rays of the sun. He stood looking down at his traps all gathered neatly in a heap at the foot of the bed. He would leave them like that. Even if they came in here sweeping and cleaning up—it was only in hotels that a man was master of his own room—even if they came in here cleaning up he would tell them to leave all his things exactly as they were. It was reassuring to see them all there together, ready to be taken up in the hand, to be carried down and put into a car, to be driven off to some railroad station at a moment's notice.

As he moved towards the door he spoke aloud, a habit that was growing on him:

"Anyhow I won't stay but a week. . . . I ain't going to stay but a week, no matter what they say. . . ."

Downstairs in the dining room they were already gathered at the supper table: his white-haired, shrunken mother-in-law; his tall sister-in-law who had the proud carriage of the head, the aquiline nose, but not the spirit of his dead wife; his lean, blond, new son-in-law; his black-eyed daughter who, but that she was thin, looked so much like him, all of them gathered there waiting for him, Alexander Maury. It

361

occurred to him that this was the first time he had sat down in the
bosom of the family for some years. They were always writing saying
that he must make a visit this summer or certainly next summer—
". . . all had a happy Christmas together, but missed you. . . ."
They had even made the pretext that he ought to come up to inspect
his new son-in-law. As if he hadn't always known exactly the kind of
young man Sarah would marry! What was the boy's name? Stephen,
yes, Stephen. He must be sure and remember that.

He sat down and shaking out his napkin spread it over his capacious
paunch and tucked it well up under his chin in the way his wife had
never allowed him to do. He let his eyes rove over the table and
released a long sigh.

"Hot batter bread," he said, "and ham. Merry Point ham. I sure am
glad to taste them one more time before I die."

The old lady was sending the little Negro girl scurrying back to the
kitchen for a hot plate of batter bread. He pushed aside the cold plate
and waited. She had bridled when he spoke of the batter bread and a
faint flush had dawned on her withered cheeks. Vain she had always
been as a peacock, of her housekeeping, her children, anything that
belonged to her. She went on now, even at her advanced age, making
her batter bread, smoking her hams according to that old recipe she
was so proud of, but who came here now to this old house to eat or to
praise?

He helped himself to a generous slice of batter bread, buttered it,
took the first mouthful and chewed it slowly. He shook his head.

"There ain't anything like it," he said. "There ain't anything else
like it in the world."

His dark eye roving over the table fell on his son-in-law. "You like
batter bread?" he enquired.

Stephen nodded, smiling. Mister Maury, still masticating slowly,
regarded his face, measured the space between the eyes—his favorite
test for man, horse or dog. Yes, there was room enough for sense
between the eyes. How young the boy looked! And infected already
with the fatal germ, the *cacoëthes scribendi.* Well, their children—if he
and Sarah ever had any children—would probably escape. It was like
certain diseases of the eye, skipped every other generation. His own
father had had it badly all his life. He could see him now sitting at the
head of the table spouting his own poetry—or Shakespeare's—while
the children watched the preserve dish to see if it was going around.
He, Aleck Maury, had been lucky to be born in the generation he had.
He had escaped that at least. A few translations from Heine in his
courting days, a few fragments from the Greek; but no, he had kept
clear of that on the whole. . . .

His sister-in-law's eyes were fixed on him. She was smiling faintly. "You don't look much like dying, Aleck. Florida must agree with you."

The old lady spoke from the head of the table. "I can't see what you do with yourself all winter long. Doesn't time hang heavy on your hands?"

Time, he thought, *time!* They were always mouthing the word, and what did they know about it? Nothing in God's world! He saw time suddenly, a dull, leaden-colored fabric depending from the old lady's hands, from the hands of all of them, a blanket that they pulled about between them, now here, now there, trying to cover up their nakedness. Or they would cast it on the ground and creep in among the folds, finding one day a little more tightly rolled than another, but all of it everywhere the same dull gray substance. But time was a banner that whipped before him always in the wind! He stood on tiptoe to catch at the bright folds, to strain them to his bosom. They were bright and glittering. But they whipped by so fast and were whipping always ever faster. The tears came into his eyes. Where, for instance, had this year gone? He could swear he had not wasted a minute of it, for no man living, he thought, knew better how to make each day a pleasure to him. Not a minute wasted and yet here it was already May. If he lived to the Biblical three-score-and-ten, which was all he ever allowed himself in his calculations, he had before him only nine more Mays. Only nine more Mays out of all eternity and they wanted him to waste one of them sitting on the front porch at Merry Point!

The butter plate which had seemed to swim before him in a glittering mist was coming solidly to rest upon the white tablecloth. He winked his eyes rapidly and, laying down his knife and fork, squared himself about in his chair to address his mother-in-law:

"Well, ma'am, you know I'm a man that always likes to be learning something. Now this year I learned how to smell out fish." He glanced around the table, holding his head high and allowing his well-cut nostrils to flutter slightly with his indrawn breaths. "Yes, sir," he said, "I'm probably the only white man in this country knows how to smell out feesh."

There was a discreet smile on the faces of the others. Sarah was laughing outright. "Did you have to learn how or did it just come to you?"

"I learned it from an old nigger woman," her father said. He shook his head reminiscently. "It's wonderful how much you can learn from niggers. But you have to know how to handle them. I was half the winter wooing that old Fanny. . . ."

He waited until their laughter had died down. "We used to start off

every morning from the same little cove and we'd drift in there together at night. I noticed how she always brought in a good string so I
says to her: 'Fanny, you just lemme go 'long with you.' But she
wouldn't have nothing to do with me. I saw she was going to be a hard
nut to crack, but I kept right on. Finally I began giving her
presents. . . ."

Laura was regarding him fixedly, a queer glint in her eyes. Seeing
outrageous pictures in her mind's eye, doubtless. Poor Laura. Fifty
years old if she was a day. More than half her lifetime gone and all of
it spent drying up here in the old lady's shadow. She was speaking
with a gasping little titter:

"What sort of presents did you give her, Aleck?"

He made his tones hearty in answer. "I give her a fine string of fish
one day and I give her fifty cents. And finally I made her a present of a
Barlow knife. That was when she broke down. She took me with her
that morning. . . ."

"Could she really *smell* fish?" the old lady asked curiously.

"You ought to a seen her," Mister Maury said. "She'd sail over that
lake like a hound on the scent. She'd row right along and then all of a
sudden she'd stop rowing." He bent over and peered into the depths of
imaginary water. " 'Thar they are, White Folks, thar they are. Cain't
you smell 'em?' "

Stephen was leaning forward, eyeing his father-in-law intently.
"Could you?" he asked.

"I got so I could smell feesh," Mister Maury told him. "I could
smell out the feesh but I couldn't tell which kind they were. Now
Fanny could row over a bed and tell just by the smell whether it was
bass or bream. But she'd been at it all her life." He paused, sighing.
"You can't just pick these things up. . . . Who was it said 'Genius is
an infinite capacity for taking pains?' "

Sarah was rising briskly. Her eyes sought her husband's across the
table. She was laughing. "Sir Izaak Walton," she said. "We'd better go
in the other room. Mandy wants to clear the table."

The two older ladies remained in the dining room. Mister Maury
walked across the hall to the sitting room, accompanied by Steve and
Sarah. He lowered himself cautiously into the most solid-looking of
the rocking chairs that were drawn up around the fire. Steve stood on
the hearthrug, his back to the fire.

Mister Maury glanced up at him curiously. "What you thinking
about, feller?" he asked.

Steve looked down. He smiled but his gaze was still contemplative.
"I was thinking about the sonnet," he said, "in the form in which it
first came to England."

Mister Maury shook his head. "Wyatt and Surrey," he said. "Hey, nonny, nonny. . . . You'll have hardening of the liver long before you're my age." He looked past Steve's shoulder at the picture that hung over the mantelshelf: Cupid and Psyche holding between them a fluttering veil and running along a rocky path towards the beholder. It had been hanging there ever since he could remember; would hang there, he thought, till the house fell down or burned down, as it was more likely to do with the old lady wandering around at night carrying lighted lamps the way she did. "Old Merry Point," he said. "It don't change much, does it?"

He settled himself more solidly in his chair. His mind veered from the old house to his own wanderings in brighter places. He regarded his daughter and son-in-law affably.

"Yes, sir," he said, "this winter in Florida was valuable to me just for the acquaintances I made. Take my friend, Jim Yost. Just to live in the same hotel with that man is an education." He paused, smiling reminiscently into the fire. "I'll never forget the first time I saw him. He came up to me there in the lobby of the hotel. 'Professor Maury,' he says, 'you been hearin' about me for twenty years and I been hearin' about you for twenty years. And now we've done met.' "

Sarah had sat down in the little rocking chair by the fire. She leaned towards him now, laughing. "They ought to have put down a cloth of gold for the meeting," she said.

Mister Maury regarded her critically. It occurred to him that she was, after all, not so much like himself as the sister whom, as a child, he had particularly disliked. A smart girl, Sarah, but too quick always on the uptake. For his own part he preferred a softer natured woman.

He shook his head. "Nature does that in Florida," he said. "I knew right off the reel it was him. There were half a dozen men standing around. I made 'em witness. 'Jim Yost,' I says, 'Jim Yost of Maysville or I'll eat my hat.' "

"Why is he so famous?" Sarah asked.

Mister Maury took out his knife and cut off a plug of tobacco. When he had offered a plug to his son-in-law and it had been refused, he put the tobacco back in his pocket. "He's a man of imagination," he said slowly. "There ain't many in this world."

He took a small tin box out of his pocket and set it on the little table that held the lamp. Removing the top, he tilted the box so that they could see its contents: an artificial lure, a bug with a dark body and a red, bulbous head, a hook protruding from what might be considered its vitals.

"Look at her," he said. "Ain't she a killer?"

Sarah leaned forward to look and Steve, still standing on the hearthrug, bent above them. The three heads ringed the light. Mister Maury disregarded Sarah and addressed himself to Steve. "She takes nine strips of pork rind," he said, "nine strips cut just thick enough." He marked off the width of the strips with his two fingers on the table, then, picking up the lure and cupping it in his palm, he moved it back and forth quickly so that the painted eyes caught the light.

"Look at her," he said, "look at the wicked way she sets forward."

Sarah was poking at the lure with the tip of her finger. "Wanton," she said, "simply wanton. What does he call her?"

"This is his Devil Bug," Mister Maury said. "He's the only man in this country makes it. I myself had the idea thirty years ago and let it slip by me the way I do with so many of my ideas." He sighed, then, elevating his tremendous bulk slightly above the table level and continuing to hold Steve with his gaze, he produced from his coat pocket the oilskin book that held his flies. He spread it open on the table and began to turn the pages. His eyes sought his son-in-law's as his hand paused before a gray, rather draggled-looking lure.

"Old Speck," he said. "I've had that fly for twenty years. I reckon she's taken five hundred pounds of fish in her day. . . ."

The fire burned lower. A fiery coal rolled from the grate and fell on to the hearthrug. Sarah scooped it up with a shovel and threw it among the ashes. In the circle of the lamplight the two men still bent over the table looking at the flies. Steve was absorbed in them, but he spoke seldom. It was her father's voice that, rising and falling, filled the room. He talked a great deal but he had a beautiful speaking voice. He was telling Steve now about Little West Fork, the first stream ever he put a fly in. "My first love," he kept calling it. It sounded rather pretty, she thought, in his mellow voice. "My first love. . . ."

PART TWO

When Mister Maury came downstairs the next morning the dining room was empty except for his daughter, Sarah, who sat dawdling over a cup of coffee and a cigarette. Mister Maury sat down opposite her. To the little Negro girl who presented herself at his elbow he outlined his wants briefly: "A cup of coffee and some hot batter bread, just like we had last night." He turned to his daughter. "Where's Steve?"

"He's working," she said. "He was up at eight and he's been working ever since."

Mister Maury accepted the cup of coffee from the little girl, poured half of it into his saucer, set it aside to cool. "Ain't it wonderful," he said, "the way a man can sit down and work day after day? When I think of all the work I've done in my time . . . Can he work *every* morning?"

"He sits down at his desk every morning," she said, "but of course he gets more done some mornings than others."

Mister Maury picked up his saucer, found the coffee cool enough for his taste. He sipped it slowly, looking out of the window. His mind was already busy with his day's program. No water—no running water—nearer than West Fork, three miles away. He couldn't drive a car and Steve was going to be busy writing all morning. There was nothing for it but a pond. The Willow Sink. It was not much, but it was better than nothing. He pushed his chair back and rose.

"Well," he said, "I'd better be starting."

When he came downstairs with his rod a few minutes later the hall was still full of the sound of measured typing. Sarah sat in the dining room in the same position in which he had left her, smoking. Mister Maury paused in the doorway while he slung his canvas bag over his shoulders. "How you ever going to get anything done if you don't take advantage of the morning hours?" he asked. He glanced at the door opposite as if it had been the entrance to a sick chamber. "What's he writing about?" he enquired in a whisper.

"It's an essay on John Skelton."

Mister Maury looked out at the new green leaves framed in the doorway. "John Skelton," he said, "God Almighty!"

He went through the hall and stepped down off the porch onto the ground that was still moist with spring rains. As he crossed the lower yard he looked up into the branches of the maples. Yes, the leaves were full grown already even on the late trees. The year, how swiftly, how steadily it advanced! He had come to the far corner of the yard. Grown up it was in pokeberry shoots and honeysuckle, but there was a place to get through. The top strand of wire had been pulled down and fastened to the others with a ragged piece of rope. He rested his weight on his good leg and swung himself over onto the game one. It gave him a good, sharp twinge when he came down on it. It was getting worse all the time, that leg, but on the other hand he was learning better all the time how to handle it. His mind flew back to a dark, startled moment, that day when the cramp first came on him. He had been sitting still in the boat all day long and that evening when he stood up to get out his leg had failed him utterly. He had pitched forward among the reeds, had lain there a second, face downward, before it came to him what had happened. With the realization came a sharp picture out of his faraway youth. Uncle James, lowering himself ponderously out of the saddle after a hard day's hunting, had fallen forward in exactly the same way, into a knot of yowling little Negroes. He had got up and cursed them all out of the lot. It had scared the old boy to death, coming down like that. The black dog he had had on his shoulder all that fall. But he himself had never lost one day's fishing on account of his leg. He had known from the start how to handle it. It meant simply that he was slowed down that much. It hadn't really made much difference in fishing. He didn't do as much wading but he got around just about as well on the whole. Hunting, of course, had had to go. You couldn't walk all day shooting birds, dragging a game leg. He had just given it up right off the reel, though it was a shame when a man was as good a shot as he was. That day he was out with Tom Kensington, last November, the only day he got out during the bird season. Nine shots he'd had and he'd bagged nine birds. Yes, it was a shame. But a man couldn't do everything. He had to limit himself. . . .

He was up over the little rise now. The field slanted straight down before him to where the pond lay, silver in the morning sun. A Negro cabin was perched halfway up the opposite slope. A woman was hanging out washing on a line stretched between two trees. From the open door little Negroes spilled down the path towards the pond. Mister Maury surveyed the scene, spoke aloud:

"Ain't it funny now? Niggers always live in the good places."

He stopped under a wild cherry tree to light his pipe. It had been hot crossing the field, but the sunlight here was agreeably tempered by the branches. And that pond down there was fringed with willows. His eyes sought the bright disc of the water then rose to where the smoke from the cabin chimney lay in a soft plume along the crest of the hill.

When he stooped to pick up his rod again it was with a feeling of sudden keen elation. An image had risen in his memory, an image that was familiar but came to him infrequently of late and that only in moments of elation: the wide field in front of his uncle's house in Albemarle, on one side the dark line of undergrowth that marked the Rivanna River, on the other the blue of Peters' Mountain. They would be waiting there in that broad plain when they had the first sight of the fox. On that little rise by the river, loping steadily, not yet alarmed. The sun would glint on his bright coat, on his quick turning head as he dove into the dark of the woods. There would be hullabaloo after that and shouting and riding. Sometimes there was the tailing of the fox— that time Old Whiskey was brought home on a mattress! All of that to come afterwards, but none of it ever like that first sight of the fox there on the broad plain between the river and the mountain.

There was one fox, they grew to know him in time, to call him affectionately by name. Old Red it was who showed himself always like that there on the crest of the hill. "There he goes, the damn, impudent scoundrel. . . ." Uncle James would shout and slap his thigh and yell himself hoarse at Whiskey and Mag and the pups, but they would already have settled to their work. They knew his course, every turn of it, by heart. Through the woods and then down again to the river. Their hope was always to cut him off before he could circle back to the mountain. If he got in there among those old field pines it was all up. But he always made it. Lost 'em every time and dodged through to his hole in Pinnacle Rock. A smart fox, Old Red. . . .

He descended the slope and paused in the shade of a clump of willows. The little Negroes who squatted, dabbling in the water, watched him out of round eyes as he unslung his canvas bag and laid it on a stump. He looked down at them gravely.

"D'you ever see a white man that could conjure?" he asked.

The oldest boy laid the brick he was fashioning out of mud down on a plank. He ran the tip of his tongue over his lower lip to moisten it before he spoke. "Naw, suh."

"I'm the man," Mister Maury told him. "You chillun better quit that playin' and dig me some worms."

He drew his rod out of the case, jointed it up and laid it down on a stump. Taking out his book of flies he turned the pages, considering. "Silver Spinner," he said aloud. "They ought to take that . . . in May. Naw, I'll just give Old Speck a chance. It's a long time now since we had her out."

The little Negroes had risen and were stepping quietly off along the path towards the cabin, the two little boys hand in hand, the little girl following, the baby astride her hip. They were pausing now before a dilapidated building that might long ago have been a hen house. Mister Maury shouted at them: "Look under them old boards. That's the place for worms." The biggest boy was turning around. His treble "Yassuh" quavered over the water. Then their voices died away. There was no sound except the light turning of the willow boughs in the wind.

Mister Maury walked along the bank, rod in hand, humming: "Bangum's gone to the wild boar's den. . . . *Bangum's* gone to the wild boar's den. . . ." He stopped where a white, peeled log protruded six or seven feet into the water. The pond made a little turn here. He stepped out squarely upon the log, still humming. The line rose smoothly, soared against the blue and curved sweetly back upon the still water. His quick ear caught the little whish that the fly made when it clove the surface, his eye followed the tiny ripples made by its flight. He cast again, leaning a little backwards as he did sometimes when the mood was on him. Again and again his line soared out over the water. His eye rested now and then on his wrist. He noted with detachment the expert play of the muscles, admired each time the accuracy of his aim. It occurred to him that it was four days now since he had wet a line. Four days. One whole day packing up, parts of two days on the train and yesterday wasted sitting there on that front porch with the family. But the abstinence had done him good. He had never cast better than he was casting this morning.

There was a rustling along the bank, a glimpse of blue through the trees. Mister Maury leaned forward and peered around the clump of willows. A hundred yards away Steve, hatless, in an old blue shirt and khaki pants, stood jointing up a rod.

Mister Maury backed off his log and advanced along the path. He called out cheerfully: "Well, feller, do any good?"

Steve looked up. His face had lightened for a moment but the abstracted expression stole over it again when he spoke. "Oh, I fiddled with it all morning," he said, "but I didn't do much good."

Mister Maury nodded sympathetically. *"Minerva invita erat,"* he said. "You can do nothing unless Minerva perches on the roof tree. Why, I been castin' here all morning and not a strike. But there's a boat tied up over on the other side. What say we get in it and just drift around?" He paused, looked at the rod Steve had finished jointing up. "I brought another rod along," he said. "You want to use it?"

Steve shook his head. "I'm used to this one," he said.

An expression of relief came over Mister Maury's face. "That's right," he said, "a man always does better with his own rod."

The boat was only a quarter full of water. They heaved her over and dumped it out, then dragged her down to the bank. The little Negroes had come up, bringing a can of worms. Mister Maury threw them each a nickel and set the can in the bottom of the boat. "I always like to have a few worms handy," he told Steve, "ever since I was a boy." He lowered himself ponderously into the bow and Steve pushed off and dropped down behind him.

The little Negroes still stood on the bank staring. When the boat was a little distance out on the water the boldest of them spoke:

"You reckon 'at ole jawnboat going to hold you up, Cap'm?"

Mister Maury turned his head to call over his shoulder. "Go 'way, boy. Ain't I done tole you I's a conjure?"

The boat dipped ominously. Steve changed his position a little and she settled to the water. Sitting well forward, Mister Maury made graceful casts, now to this side, now to that. Steve, in the stern, made occasional casts but he laid his rod down every now and then to paddle though there was really no use in it. The boat drifted well enough with the wind. At the end of half an hour seven sizable bass lay on the bottom of the boat. Mister Maury had caught five of them. He reflected that perhaps he really ought to change places with Steve. The man in the bow certainly had the best chance at the fish. "But no," he thought, "it don't make any difference. He don't hardly know where he is now."

He stole a glance over his shoulder at the young man's serious, abstracted face. It was like that of a person submerged. Steve seemed to float up to the surface every now and then, his expression would lighten, he would make some observation that showed he knew where he was, then he would sink again. If you asked him a question he answered punctiliously, two minutes later. Poor boy, dead to the world and would probably be that way the rest of his life. A pang of pity shot through Mister Maury and on the heels of it a gust of that black fear that occasionally shook him. It was he, not Steve, that was the queer one. The world was full of people like this boy, all of them going around with their heads so full of this and that they hardly knew what they were doing. They were all like that. There was hardly any-body—there was *nobody* really in the whole world like him. . . .

Steve, coming out of his abstraction, spoke politely. He had heard that Mister Maury was a fine shot. Did he like to fish better than hunt?

Mister Maury reflected. "Well," he said, "they's something about a covey of birds rising up in front of you . . . they's something . . . and a good dog. Now they ain't anything in this world that I like better than a good bird dog." He stopped and sighed. "A man has got to come to himself early in life if he's going to amount to anything. Now I was smart, even as a boy. I could look around me and see all the men of my family, Uncle Jeems, Uncle Quent, my father, every one of 'em weighed two hundred by the time he was fifty. You get as heavy on your feet as all that and you can't do any good shooting. But a man can fish as long as he lives. . . . Why, one place I stayed last summer there was an old man ninety years old had himself carried down to the river every morning. Yes, sir, a man can fish as long as he can get down to the water's edge. . . ."

There was a little plop to the right. He turned just in time to see the fish flash out of the water. He watched Steve take it off the hook and drop it on top of the pile in the bottom of the boat. Six bass that made and two bream. The old lady would be pleased. "Aleck always catches me fish," she'd say.

The boat glided over the still water. There was no wind at all now.

The willows that fringed the bank might have been cut out of paper. The plume of smoke hung perfectly horizontal over the roof of the Negro cabin. Mister Maury watched it stream out in little eddies and disappear into the bright blue.

He spoke softly: "Ain't it wonderful . . . ain't it wonderful now that a man of my gifts can content himself a whole morning on this here little old pond?"

PART THREE

Mister Maury woke with a start. He realized that he had been sleeping on his left side again. A bad idea. It always gave him palpitations of the heart. It must be that that had waked him up. He had gone to sleep almost immediately after his head hit the pillow. He rolled over, cautiously, as he always did since that bed in Leesburg had given down with him and, lying flat on his back, stared at the opposite wall.

The moon rose late. It must be at its height now. That patch of light was so brilliant he could almost discern the pattern of the wallpaper. It hung there, wavering, bitten by the shadows into a semblance of a human figure, a man striding with bent head and swinging arms. All the shadows in the room seemed to be moving towards him. The protruding corner of the washstand was an arrow aimed at his heart, the clumsy old-fashioned dresser was a giant towering above him.

They had put him to sleep in this same room the night after his wife died. In the summer it had been, too, in June; and there must have been a full moon for the same giant shadows had struggled there with the same towering monsters. It would be like that here on this wall every full moon, for the pieces of furniture would never change their position, had never been changed, probably, since the house was built.

He turned back on his side. The wall before him was dark but he knew every flower in the pattern of the wallpaper, interlacing pink roses with thrusting up between every third cluster the enormous, spreading fronds of ferns. The wallpaper in the room across the hall was like it too. The old lady slept there, and in the room next to his own, Laura, his sister-in-law, and in the east bedroom downstairs, the young couple. He and Mary had slept there when they were first married, when they were the young couple in the house.

He tried to remember Mary as she must have looked that day he first saw her, the day he arrived from Virginia to open his school in the old office that used to stand there in the corner of the yard. He could see Mister Allard plainly, sitting there under the sugar tree with his chair tilted back, could discern the old lady—young she had been then!—hospitably poised in the doorway, hand extended, could hear her voice: "Well, here are two of your pupils to start with. . . ." He remembered Laura, a shy child of nine hiding her face in her mother's skirts, but Mary that day was only a shadow in the dark hall. He could not even remember how her voice had sounded. "Professor Maury," she would have said and her mother would have corrected her with "Cousin Aleck. . . ."

That day she got off her horse at the stile blocks she had turned as she walked across the lawn to look back at him. Her white sun-bonnet had fallen on her shoulders. Her eyes, meeting his, had been dark and startled. He had gone on and had hitched both the horses before he leaped over the stile to join her. But he had known in that moment that she was the woman he was going to have. He could not remember all the rest of it, only that moment stood out. He had won her, she had become his wife, but the woman he had won was not the woman he had sought. It was as if he had had her only in that moment there on the lawn. As if she had paused there only for that one moment and was ever after retreating before him down a devious, a dark way that he would never have chosen.

The death of the first baby had been the start of it, of course. It had been a relief when she took so definitely to religion. Before that there had been those sudden, unaccountable forays out of some dark lurking place that she had. Guerrilla warfare and trying to the nerves, but that had been only at first. For many years they had been two enemies contending in the open. . . . Towards the last she had taken mightily to prayer. He would wake often to find her kneeling by the side of the bed in the dark. It had gone on for years. She had never given up hope. . . .

Ah, a stout-hearted one, Mary! She had never given up hope of changing him, of making him over into the man she thought he ought to be. Time and again she almost had him. And there were long periods, of course, during which he had been worn down by the conflict, one spring when he himself said, when she had told all the neighbors, that he was too old now to go fishing any more. . . . But he had made a comeback. She had had to resort to stratagem. His lips curved in a smile, remembering the trick.

It had come over him suddenly, a general lassitude, an odd faintness in the mornings, the time when his spirits ordinarily were at their highest. He had sat there by the window, almost wishing to have some ache or pain, something definite to account for his condition. But he did not feel sick in his body. It was rather a dulling of all his senses. There were no longer the reactions to the visible world that made his days a series of adventures. He had looked out of the window at the woods glistening with spring rain; he had not even taken down his gun to shoot a squirrel.

Remembering Uncle Quent's last days he had been alarmed, had decided finally that he must tell her so that they might begin preparations for the future—he had shuddered at the thought of eventual confinement, perhaps in some institution. She had looked up from her sewing, unable to repress a smile.

"You think it's your mind, Aleck. . . . It's coffee. . . . I've been giving you a coffee substitute every morning. . . ."

They had laughed together over her cleverness. He had not gone back to coffee but the lassitude had worn off. She had gone back to the attack with redoubled vigor. In the afternoons she would stand on the porch calling after him as he slipped down to the creek. "Now, don't stay long enough to get that cramp. You remember how you suffered last time. . . ." He would have forgotten all about the cramp until that moment but it would hang over him then through the whole afternoon's sport and it would descend upon him inevitably when he left the river and started for the house.

Yes, he thought with pride. She was wearing him down—he did not believe there was a man living who could withstand her a lifetime— she was wearing him down and would have had him in another few months, another year certainly. But she had been struck down just as victory was in her grasp. The paralysis had come on her in the night. It was as if a curtain had descended, dividing their life sharply into two parts. In the bewildered year and a half that followed he had found himself forlornly trying to reconstruct the Mary he had known. The pressure she had so constantly exerted upon him had become for him a part of her personality. This new, calm Mary was not the woman he had lived with all these years. She had lain there—heroically they all said—waiting for death. And lying there, waiting, all her faculties engaged now in defensive warfare, she had raised, as it were, her lifelong siege; she had lost interest in his comings and goings, had once even encouraged him to go for an afternoon's sport! He felt a rush of warm pity. Poor Mary! She must have realized towards the last that she had wasted herself in conflict. She had spent her arms and her strength against an inglorious foe when all the time the real, the invincible adversary waited. . . .

He turned over on his back again. The moonlight was waning, the contending shadows paler now and retreating towards the door. From across the hall came the sound of long, sibilant breaths, ending each one on a little upward groan. The old lady. . . . She would maintain till her dying day that she did not snore. He fancied now that he could hear from the next room Laura's light, regular breathing and downstairs were the young couple asleep in each other's arms. . . .

All of them quiet and relaxed now, but they had been lively enough at dinner time. It had started with the talk about Aunt Sally Crenfew's funeral tomorrow. Living now as he had for some years, away from women of his family, he had forgotten the need to be cautious. He had spoken up before he thought:

"But that's the day Steve and I were going to Barker's Mill. . . ."

Sarah had cried out at the idea. "Barker's Mill!" she had said, "right on the Crenfew land . . . well, if not on the very farm, in the very next field. It would be a scandal if he, Professor Maury, known by everybody to be in the neighborhood, could not spare one afternoon, one insignificant summer afternoon, from his fishing long enough to attend the funeral of his cousin, the cousin of all of them, the oldest lady in the whole family connection. . . ."

Looking around the table he had caught the same look in every eye; he had felt a gust of that same fright that had shaken him there on the pond. That look! Sooner or later you met it in every human eye. The thing was to be up and ready, ready to run for your life at a moment's notice. Yes, it had always been like that. It always would be. His fear of them was shot through suddenly with contempt. It was as if Mary were there laughing with him. *She* knew that there was not one of them who could have survived as he had survived, could have paid the price for freedom that he had paid. . . .

Sarah had come to a stop. He had to say something. He shook his head.

"You think we just go fishing to have a good time. The boy and I hold high converse on that pond. I'm starved for intellectual companionship I tell you. . . . In Florida I never see anybody but niggers. . . ."

They had all laughed out at that. "As if you didn't *prefer* the society of niggers!" Sarah said scornfully.

The old lady had been moved to anecdote:

"I remember when Aleck first came out here from Virginia, Cousin Sophy said: 'Professor Maury is so well educated. Now Cousin Cave Maynor is dead who is there in the neighborhood for him to associate with?' 'Well,' I said, 'I don't know about that. He seems perfectly satisfied with Ben Hooser. They're off to the creek together every evening soon as school is out.' "

Ben Hooser. . . . He could see now the wrinkled face, overlaid with that ashy pallor of the aged Negro, smiling eyes, the pendulous lower lip that, drooping away, showed always some of the rotten teeth. A fine nigger, Ben, and on to a lot of tricks, the only man really that he'd ever cared to take fishing with him.

But the first real friend of his bosom had been old Uncle Teague, the factotum at Hawkwood. Once a week or more likely every ten days he fed the hounds on the carcass of a calf that had had time to get pretty high. They would drive the spring wagon out into the lot; he, a boy of ten, beside Uncle Teague on the driver's seat. The hounds would come in a great rush and rear their slobbering jowls against the wagon wheels. Uncle Teague would wield his whip, chuckling while he threw the first hunk of meat to Old Mag, his favorite.

"Dey goin' run on dis," he'd say. "Dey goin' run like a shadow. . . ."

He shifted his position again, cautiously. People, he thought . . . people . . . so bone ignorant, all of them. Not one person in a thousand realized that a fox-hound remains at heart a wild beast and must kill and gorge and then, when he is ravenous, kill and gorge again. . . . Or that the channel cat is a night feeder. . . . Or . . . His daughter had told him once that he ought to set all his knowledge down in a book. "Why?" he had asked. "So everybody else can know as much as I do?"

If he allowed his mind to get active, really active, he would never get any sleep. He was fighting an inclination now to get up and find a cigarette. He relaxed again upon his pillows, deliberately summoned pictures before his mind's eye. Landscapes—and streams. He observed their outlines, watched one flow into another. The Black River into West Fork, that in turn into Spring Creek and Spring Creek into the Withlicocchee. Then they were all flowing together, merging into one broad plain. He watched it take form slowly: the wide field in front of Hawkwood, the Rivanna River on one side, on the other Peters' Mountain. They would be waiting there till the fox showed himself on that little rise by the river. The young men would hold back till Uncle James had wheeled Old Filly, then they would all be off pell-mell across the plain. He himself would be mounted on Jonesboro. Almost blind, but she would take anything you put her at. That first thicket on the edge of the woods. They would break there, one half of them going around, the other half streaking it through the woods. He was always of those going around to try to cut the fox off on the other side. No, he was down off his horse. He was coursing with the fox through the trees. He could hear the sharp, pointed feet padding on the dead leaves, see the quick head turned now and then over the shoulder. The trees kept flashing by, one black trunk after another. And now it was a ragged mountain field and the sage grass running before them in waves to where a narrow stream curved in between the ridges. The fox's feet were light in the water. He moved forward steadily, head down. The hounds' baying grew louder. Old Mag knew the trick. She had stopped to give tongue by that big rock and now they had all leaped the gulch and were scrambling up through the pines. But the fox's feet were already hard on the mountain path. He ran slowly, past the big boulder, past the blasted pine to where the shadow of the Pinnacle Rock was black across the path. He ran on and the shadow swayed and rose to meet him. Its cool touch was on his hot tongue, his heaving flanks. He had slipped in under it. He was sinking down, panting, in black dark, on moist earth while the hounds' baying filled the valley and reverberated from the mountainside.

Mister Maury got up and lit a cigarette. He smoked it quietly, lying back upon his pillows. When he had finished smoking he rolled over on his side and closed his eyes. It was still a good while till morning, but perhaps he could get some sleep. His mind played quietly over the scene that would be enacted in the morning. He would be sitting on the porch after breakfast, smoking, when Sarah came out. She would ask him how he felt, how he had slept.

He would heave a groan, not looking at her for fear of catching that smile on her face—the girl had little sense of decency. He would heave a groan, not too loud or overdone. "My kidney trouble," he would say, shaking his head. "It's come back on me, daughter, in the night."

She would express sympathy and go on to talk of something else. She never took any stock in his kidney trouble. He would ask her finally if she reckoned Steve had time to drive him to the train that morning. He'd been thinking about how much good the chalybeate water of Estill Springs had done him last year. He might heave another groan here to drown her protests. "No. . . . I better be getting on to the Springs. . . . I need the water. . . ."

She would talk on a lot after that. He would not need to listen. He would be sitting there thinking about Elk River, where it runs through the village of Estill Springs. He could see that place by the bridge now: a wide, deep pool with plenty of lay-bys under the willows.

The train would get in around one o'clock. That nigger, Ed, would hustle his bags up to the boarding house for him. He would tell Mrs. Rogers he must have the same room. He would have his bags packed so he could get at everything quick. He would be into his black shirt and fishing pants before you could say Jack Robinson. . . . Thirty minutes after he got off the train he would have a fly in that water.

THROUGH THE
BAD BEND

JOHN FOX, JR.

A wildly beautiful cleft through the Cumberland Range opens into the head of Powell's Valley, in Virginia, and forms the Gap. From this point a party of us were going bass-fishing on a fork of the Cumberland River over in the Kentucky mountains. It was Sunday, and several Kentucky mountaineers had crossed over that day to take their first ride on the cars, and to see "the city"—as the Gap has been prophetically called ever since it had a crossroads store, one little hotel, two farmhouses, and a blacksmith's shop. From them we learned that we could ride down Powell's Valley and get to the fork of the Cumberland by simply climbing over the mountain. As the mountaineers were going back home the same day, Breck and I boarded the train with them, intending to fish down the fork of the river to the point where the rest of the party would strike the same stream, two days later.

At the second station down the road a crowd of Virginia mountaineers got on board. Most of them had been drinking, and the festivities soon began. One drunken young giant pulled his revolver, swung it back over his shoulder—the muzzle almost grazing a woman's face behind him—and swung it up again to send a bullet crashing through the top of the car. The hammer was at the turning-point when a companion caught his wrist. At the same time, the fellow's sister sprang across the aisle, and, wrenching the weapon from his grasp, hid it in her dress. Simultaneously his partner at the other end of the car was drawing a .45 Colt's half as long as his arm. A quick panic ran through the car, and in a moment there was no one in it with us but the mountaineers, the conductor, one brakeman, and one other man, who sat still in his seat, with one hand under his coat. The prospect was neither pleasant nor peaceful, and we rose to our feet and waited. The disarmed giant was raging through the aisle searching and calling, with mighty oaths, for his pistol. The other had backed into a corner of the car, waving his revolver, turning his head from side to side to avoid a surprise in the rear, white with rage, and just drunk enough to shoot. The little conductor was unmoved and smiling, and, by some quiet mesmerism, he kept the two in subjection until the station was reached.

The train moved out and left us among the drunken maniacs, no house in sight, the darkness settling on us, and the unclimbed mountain looming up into it. The belligerents paid no attention to us, however, but disappeared quickly, with an occasional pistol shot and a yell from the bushes, each time sounding farther away. The Kentucky mountaineers were going to climb the mountain. A storm was coming, but there was nothing else to do. So we shouldered our traps and followed them.

There were eight of us—an old man and his two daughters, the husband of one of these, the sweetheart of the other, and a third man, who showed suspicion of us from the beginning. This man with a flaring torch led the way; the old man followed him, and there were two mountaineers deep between the girls and us, who went last.

It was not long before a ragged line of fire cut through the blackness overhead, and the thunder began to crash and the rain to fall. The torch was beaten out, and for a moment there was a halt. Breck and I could hear a muffled argument going on in the air above us, and, climbing toward the voices, we felt the lintel of a mountain cabin and heard a long drawl of welcome.

The cabin was one dark room without even a loft, the home of a newly married pair. They themselves had evidently just gotten home, for the hostess was on her knees at the big fireplace, blowing a few coals into a blaze. The rest of us sat on the two beds in the room waiting for the firelight, and somebody began talking about the trouble on the train.

"Did you see that feller settin' thar with his hand under his coat while Jim was tryin' to shoot the brakeman?" said one. "Well, Jim killed his brother a year ago, an' the feller was jus' waitin' fer a chance to git Jim right then. I knowed that."

"Who was the big fellow who started the row, by flourishing his pistol around?" I asked.

A man on the next bed leaned forward and laughed slightly. "Well, stranger, I reckon that was me."

This sounds like the opening chapter of a piece of fiction, but we had really stumbled upon this man's cabin in the dark, and he was our host. A little spinal chill made me shiver. He had not seen us yet, and I began to wonder whether he would recognize us when the light blazed up, and whether he would know that we were ready to take part against him in the car, and what would happen, if he did. When the blaze did kindle, he was reaching for his hip, but he drew out a bottle of apple-jack and handed it over the foot of the bed.

"Somebody ought to 'a' knocked my head off," he said.

"That's so," said the younger girl, with sharp boldness. "I never seed sech doin's."

The old mountaineer, her father, gave her a quick rebuke, but the man laughed. He was sobering up, and, apparently, he had never seen us before. The young wife prepared supper, and we ate and went to bed—the ten of us in that one room. The two girls took off their shoes and stockings with frank innocence, and warmed their bare feet at the fire. The host and hostess gave up their bed to the old mountaineer and his son-in-law, and slept, like the rest of us, on the floor.

We were wakened long before day. Indeed it was pitch dark when, after a mountain custom, we stumbled to a little brook close to the cabin and washed our faces. A wood-thrush was singing somewhere in the darkness, and its cool notes had the liquid freshness of the morning. We did not wait for breakfast, so anxious were the Kentuckians to get home, or so fearful were they of abusing their host's hospitality, though the latter urged us strenuously to stay. Not a cent would he take from anybody, and I know now that he was a moonshiner, a feudsman, an outlaw, and that he was running from the sheriff at that very time.

With a parting pull at the apple-jack, we began, on an empty stomach, that weary climb. Not far up the mountain Breck stopped, panting, while the mountaineers were swinging on up the path without an effort, even the girls; but Breck swore that he had heart disease, and must rest. When I took part of his pack, the pretty one looked back over her shoulder and smiled at him without scorn. Both were shy, and had not spoken a dozen words with either of us. Halfway up we overtook a man and a boy, one carrying a tremendous demijohn and the other a small hand-barrel. They had been over on the Virginia side selling moonshine, and I saw the light of gladness in Breck's eye, for his own flask was wellnigh empty from returning our late host's courtesy. But both man and boy disappeared with a magical suddenness that became significant later. Already we were suspected as being revenue spies, though neither of us dreamed what the matter was.

We reached the top after daybreak, and the beauty of the sunrise over still seas of white mist and wave after wave of blue Virginia hills was unspeakable, as was the beauty of the descent on the Kentucky side, down through primeval woods of majestic oak and poplar, under a trembling world of dew-drenched leaves, and along a tumbling series of waterfalls that flashed through tall ferns, blossoming laurel, and shining leaves of rhododendron.

The sun was an hour high when we reached the foot of the mountain. There the old man and the young girl stopped at a little cabin where lived the son-in-law. We, too, were pressed to stop, but we went on with the suspicious one to his house, where we got breakfast. There the people took pay, for their house was weather-boarded, and they were more civilized; or perhaps for the reason that the man thought us spies. I did not like his manner, and I got the first unmistakable hint of his suspicions after breakfast. I was down behind the barn, and he and another mountaineer came down on the other side.

"Didn't one o' them fellers come down this way?" I heard him ask.

I started to make my presence known, but he spoke too quickly, and I concluded it was best to keep still.

"No tellin' whut them damn fellers is up to. I don't like their occupation."

That is, we were the first fishermen to cast a minnow with a reel into those waters, and it was beyond the mountaineer's comprehension to understand how two men could afford to come so far and spend time and a little money just for the fun of fishing. They supposed we were fishing for profit, and later they asked us how we kept our fish fresh, and how we got them over the mountain, and where we sold them. With this idea, naturally it was a puzzle to them how we could afford to give a boy a quarter for a dozen minnows, and then, perhaps, catch not a single fish with them.

When I got back to the house, Breck was rigging his rod, with a crowd of spectators around him. Such a rod and such a fisherman had never been seen in that country before. Breck was dressed in a white tennis shirt, blue gymnasium breeches, blue stockings, and white tennis shoes. With a cap on his shock of black hair and a .38 revolver in his belt, he was a thing for those women to look at and to admire, and for the men to scorn—secretly, of course, for there was a look in his black eyes that forced guarded respect in any crowd. The wonder of those mountaineers when he put his rod together, fastened the reel, and tossed his hook fifty feet in the air was worth the morning's climb to see. At the same time they made fun of our rods, and laughed at the idea of getting out a big "green pyerch"—as the mountaineers call bass—with "them switches." Their method is to tie a strong line to a long hickory sapling, and, when they strike a bass, to put the stout pole over one shoulder and walk ashore with it. Before the sun was over the mountain, we were wading down the stream, while two boys carried our minnows and clothes along the bank. The news of our coming went before us, and every now and then a man would roll out of the bushes with a gun and look at us with much suspicion and some wonder. For two luckless hours we cast down that too narrow and too shallow stream before we learned that there was a dam two miles farther down, and at once we took the land for it. It was after dinner when we reached it, and there the boys left us. We could not induce them to go farther. An old miller sat outside his mill across the river, looking at us with some curiosity, but no surprise, for the coming of a stranger in those mountains is always known miles ahead of him.

We told him our names and that we were from Virginia, but were natives of the Bluegrass, and we asked if he could give us dinner. His house was half a mile farther down the river, he said, but the women folks were at home, and he reckoned they would give us something to eat. When we started, I shifted my revolver from my pocket to a Kodak camera case that I had brought along to hold fishing tackle.

"I suppose I can put this thing in here?" I said to Breck, not wanting to risk arrest for carrying concealed weapons and the confiscation of the pistol, which was valuable. Breck hesitated, and the old miller studied us keenly.

"Well," he said, "if you two air from Kanetucky, hit strikes me you ought to know the laws of yo' own State. You can carry it in thar as baggage," he added, quietly, and I knew that my question had added another fagot to the flame of suspicion kindling against us.

In half an hour we were in the cool shade of a spreading apple tree in the miller's yard, with our bare feet in thick, cool grass, while the miller's wife and his buxom, red-cheeked daughter got us dinner. And a good dinner it was; and we laughed and cracked jokes at each other till the sombre, suspicious old lady relaxed and laughed, too, and the girl lost some of her timidity and looked upon Breck with wide-eyed admiration, while Breck ogled back outrageously.

After dinner a scowling mountaineer led a mule through the yard and gave us a surly nod. Two horsemen rode up to the gate and waited to escort us down the river. One of them carried our baggage, for no matter what he suspects, the mountaineer will do anything in the world for a stranger until the moment of actual conflict comes. In our green innocence, we thought it rather a good joke that we should be taken for revenue men, so that, Breck's flask being empty, he began by telling one of the men that we had been wading the river all the morning, that the water was cold, and that, anyway, a little swallow now and then often saved a fellow from a cold and fever. He had not been able to get any from anybody—and couldn't the man *do* something? The mountaineer was touched, and he took the half-dollar that Breck gave him, and turned it over, with a whispered consultation, to one of two more horsemen that we met later on the road. Still farther on we found a beautiful hole of water, edged with a smooth bank of sand—a famous place, the men told us, for green "pyerch." Mountaineers rolled out of the bushes to watch us while we were rigging up, some with guns and some without. We left our pistols on the shore, and several examined them curiously, especially mine, which was hammerless. Later, I showed them how it worked, and explained that one advantage of it was that, in close quarters, the other man could not seize your pistol, get his finger or thumb under your hammer, and prevent you from shooting at all. This often happens in a fight, of course, and the point appealed to them strongly, but I could see that they were wondering why I should be carrying a gun that was good for close quarters, since close quarters are rarely necessary except in case of making arrests. Pretty soon the two men who had gone for Breck's "moonshine" returned, and a gleam rose in Breck's eye and went quickly down. Instead of a bottle, the boy handed back the half-dollar.

"I couldn't git any," he said. He lied, of course, as we both knew, and the disappointment in Breck's face was so sincere that his companion, with a gesture that was half sympathy, half defiance, whisked a bottle from his hip.

"Well, by—I'll give him a drink!"

It was fiery, white as water, and so fresh that we could taste the smoke in it, but it was good, and we were grateful. All the afternoon, from two to a dozen people watched us fish, but we had poor luck, which is never a surprise, fishing for bass. Perhaps the fish had gone to nesting, or the trouble may have been the light of the moon, during which they feed all night, and are not so hungry through the day; or it may have been any of the myriad reasons that make the mystery and fascination of catching bass. At another time, and from the same stream, I have seen two rods take out one hundred bass, ranging from one to five pounds in weight, in a single day. An hour by sun, we struck for the house of the old man with whom we had crossed the mountain, and, that night, we learned that we had passed through a locality alive with moonshiners, and banded together with such system and determination that the revenue agents rarely dared to make a raid on them. We were supposed to be two spies who were expected to come in there that spring. We had passed within thirty yards of a dozen stills, and our host hinted where we might find them. We thanked him, and told him we preferred to keep as far away from them as possible. He was much puzzled. He also said that we had been in the headquarters of a famous desperado, who was the leader of the Howard faction in the famous Howard-Turner feud. He was a non-combatant himself, but he had "feelin's," as he phrased it, for the other side. He was much surprised when we told him we were going back there next day. We had told the people we were coming back, and next morning we were foolish enough to go.

As soon as we struck the river, we saw a man with a Winchester sitting on a log across the stream, as though his sole business in life was to keep an eye on us. All that day we were never out of sight of a mountaineer and a gun; we never had been, I presume, since our first breakfast on that stream. Still, everybody was kind and hospitable and honest—how honest this incident will show. An old woman cooked dinner especially for us, and I gave her two quarters. She took them, put them away, and while she sat smoking her pipe, I saw something was troubling her. She got up presently, went into a room, came back, and without a word dropped one of the quarters into my hand. Half a dollar was too much. They gave us moonshine, too, and Breck remarked casually that we were expecting to meet our friends at Uncle Job Turner's, somewhere down the river. They would have red whiskey from the Bluegrass and we would be all right. Then he asked how far down Uncle Job lived. The remark and the question occasioned very badly concealed excitement, and I wondered what had happened, but I did not ask. I was getting wary, and I had become quite sure that the fishing must be better down, very far down, that stream. When we started again, the mountaineers evidently held a quick council of war. One can hear a long distance over water at the quiet of dusk, and they were having a lively discussion about us and our business over there. Somebody was defending us, and I recognized the voice as belonging to a red-whiskered fellow, who said he had lived awhile in the Bluegrass, and had seen young fellows starting to the Kentucky River to fish for fun. "Oh, them damn fellers ain't up to nothin'," we could hear him say, with the disgust of the cosmopolitan. "I tell ye, they lives in town an' they likes to git out this way!"

I have always believed that this man saved us trouble right then, for next night the mountaineers came down in a body to the house where we had last stopped. But we had gone on rather hastily, and when we reached Uncle Job Turner's, the trip behind us became more interesting than ever in retrospect. All along we asked where Uncle Job lived, and once we shouted the question across the river, where some women and boys were at work, weeding corn. As usual, the answer was another question, and always the same—what were our names? Breck yelled, in answer, that we were from Virginia, and that they would be no wiser if we should tell—an answer that will always be unwise in the mountains of Kentucky as long as moonshine is made and feuds survive. We asked again, and another yell told us that the next house was Uncle Job's. The next house was rather pretentious. It had two or three rooms, apparently, and a loft, and was weatherboarded; but it was as silent as a tomb. We shouted "Hello!" from outside the fence, which is etiquette in the mountains. Not a sound. We shouted again— once, twice, many times. It was most strange. Then we waited, and shouted again, and at last a big gray-haired old fellow slouched out and asked rather surlily what we wanted.

"Dinner."

He seemed pleased that that was all, and his manner changed immediately. His wife appeared; then, as if by magic, two or three children, one a slim, wild, dark-eyed girl of fifteen, dressed in crimson homespun. As we sat on the porch I saw her passing through the dark rooms, but always, while we were there, if I entered one door she slipped out of the other. Breck was more fortunate. He came up behind her the next day at sundown while she was dancing barefooted in the dust of the road, driving her cows home. Later I saw him in the cow pen, helping her milk. He said she was very nice, but very shy.

We got dinner, and the old man sent after a bottle of moonshine, and in an hour he was thawed out wonderfully.

We told him where we had been, and as he slowly began to believe us, he alternately grew sobered and laughed aloud.

"Went through thar fishin', did ye? Wore yo' pistols? Axed whar thar was branches whar you could ketch minners? Oh, Lawd! Didn't ye know that the stills air al'ays up the branches? Tol' 'em you was goin' *to meet a party at my house, and stay here awhile fishin'?* Oh, Lawdy! Ef that ain't a good un!"

We didn't see it, but we did later, when we knew that we had come through the "Bad Bend," which was the headquarters of the Howard leader and his chief men; that Uncle Job was the most prominent man of the other faction, and lived farthest up the river of all the Turners; that he hadn't been up in the Bend for ten years, and that we had given his deadly enemies the impression that we were friends of his. As Uncle Job grew mellow, and warmed up in his confidences, something else curious came out. Every now and then he would look at me and say:

"I seed you lookin' at my pants." And then he would throw back his head and laugh. After he had said this for the third time, I did look at his "pants," and I saw that he was soaking wet to the thighs—why, I soon learned. A nephew of his had killed a man at the county seat only a week before. Uncle Job had gone on his bond. When we shouted across the river, he was in the cornfield, and when we did not tell our names, he got suspicious, and, mistaking our rod-holders for guns, had supposed that his nephew had run away, and that we were officers come to arrest him. He had run down the river on the other side, had waded the stream, and was up in the loft with his Winchester on us while we were shouting at his gate. He told us this very frankly. Nor would even he believe that we were fishing. He, too, thought that we were officers looking through the Bad Bend for some criminal, and the least innocent mission that struck him as plausible was that, perhaps, we might be looking over the ground to locate a railroad, or prospecting for coal veins. When Uncle Job went down the road with us the next morning, he took his wife along, so that no Howard would try to ambush him through fear of hitting a woman. And late that afternoon, when we were fishing with Uncle Job's son in some thick bushes behind the house, some women passed along in the path above us, and, seeing us, but not seeing him, scurried out of sight as though frightened. Little Job grinned.

"Them women thinks the Howards have hired you fellers to layway dad."

The next morning I lost Breck, and about noon I got a note from him, written with a trembling lead pencil, to the effect that he believed he would fish up a certain creek that afternoon. As the creek was not more than three feet wide and a few inches deep, I knew what had happened, and I climbed one of Job's mules and went to search for him. Breck had stumbled upon a moonshine still, and, getting hilarious, had climbed a barrel and was making to a crowd of mountaineers a fiery political speech. Breck had captured that creek, "wild-cat" still and all, and to this day I never meet a mountaineer from that region who does not ask, with a wide grin, about Breck.

When we reached the county seat, the next day, we met the revenue deputy. He said the town was talking about two spies who were up the Fork. We told him that we must be the spies. The old miller was the brains of the Bend, he said, both in outwitting the revenue men and in planning the campaign of the Howard leader against the Turners, and he told us of several fights he had had in the Bad Bend. He said that we were lucky to come through alive; that what saved us was sticking to the river, hiring our minnows caught, leaving our pistols on the bank to be picked up by anybody, the defence of the red-whiskered man from the Bluegrass, and Breck's popularity at the still. I thought he was exaggerating—that the mountaineers, even if convinced that we were spies, would have given us a chance to get out of the country —but when he took me over to a room across the street and showed me where his predecessor, a man whom I had known quite well, was shot through a window at night and killed, I was not quite so sure.

But still another straw of suspicion was awaiting us. When we reached the railroad again—by another route, you may be sure— Breck, being a lawyer, got permission for us to ride on a freight train, and thus save a night and a day. The pass for us was technically charged to the mail service. The captain and crew of the train were overwhelmingly and mysteriously polite to us—an inexplicable contrast to the surliness with which passengers are usually treated on a freight train. When we got off at the Gap, and several people greeted us by name, the captain laughed.

"Do you know what these boys thought you two were?" he asked, referring to his crew. "They thought you were freight 'spotters.'"

The crew laughed. I looked at Breck, and I didn't wonder. He was a ragged, unshaven tramp, and I was another.

Months later, I got a message from the Bad Bend. Breck and I mustn't come through there any more. We have never gone through there any more, though anybody on business that the mountaineers understand, *can* go more safely than he can cross Broadway at Twenty-third Street, at noon. As a matter of fact, however, there are two other forks to the Cumberland in which the fishing is very good indeed, and just now I would rather risk Broadway.

FISH ARE SUCH LIARS!

ROLAND PERTWEE

There had been a fuss in the pool beneath the alders, and the small rainbow trout, with a skitter of his tail, flashed upstream, a hurt and angry fish. For three consecutive mornings he had taken the rise in that pool, and it injured his pride to be jostled from his drift just when the May fly was coming up in numbers. If his opponent had been a half-pounder like himself, he would have stayed and fought, but when an old hen fish, weighing fully three pounds, with a mouth like a rat hole and a carnivorous, cannibalistic eye rises from the reed beds and occupies the place, flight is the only effective argument.

But Rainbow was very much provoked. He had chosen his place with care. Now the May fly was up, the little French chalk stream was full of rising fish, and he knew by experience that strangers are unpopular in that season. To do one's self justice during a hatch, one must find a place where the fly drifts nicely overhead with the run of the stream, and natural drifts are scarce even in a chalk stream. He was not content to leap at the fly like a hysterical youngster who measured his weight in ounces and his wits in milligrams. He had reached that time of life which demanded that he should feed off the surface by suction rather than exertion. No living thing is more particular about his table manners than a trout, and Rainbow was no exception.

"It's a sickening thing," he said to himself, "and a hard shame." He added: "Get out of my way," to a couple of fat young chub with negroid mouths who were bubbling the surface in the silly, senseless fashion of their kind.

"Chub indeed!"

But even the chub had a home and he had none—and the life of a homeless river dweller is precarious.

"I will not and shall not be forced back to midstream," he said.

For, save at eventide or in very special circumstances, trout of personality do not frequent open water where they must compete for every insect with the wind, the lightning-swift sweep of swallows and martins, and even the laborious pursuit of predatory dragon-flies with their bronze wings and bodies like rods of colored glass. Even as he spoke he saw a three-ouncer leap at a dapping May fly which was scooped out of his jaws by a passing swallow. Rainbow heard the tiny click as the May fly's body cracked against the bird's beak. A single wing of yellowy gossamer floated downward and settled upon the water. Under the shelving banks to right and left, where the fly, discarding its nymph and still too damp for its virgin flight, drifted downstream, a dozen heavy trout were feeding thoughtfully and selectively.

"If only some angler would catch one of them, I might slip in and occupy the place before it gets known there's a vacancy."

But this uncharitable hope was not fulfilled, and with another whisk of his tail he propelled himself into the unknown waters upstream. A couple of strands of rusty barbed wire, relic of the war, spanned the shallows from bank to bank. Passing beneath them he came to a narrow reach shaded by willows, to the first of which was nailed a board bearing the words Pêche Réservée. He had passed out of the communal into private water—water running languidly over manes of emerald weed between clumps of alder, willow herb, tall crimson sorrel and masses of yellow iris. Ahead, like an apple-green rampart, rose the wooded heights of a forest; on either side were flat meadows of yellowing hay. Overhead, the vast expanse of blue June sky was tufted with rambling clouds. "My scales!" said Rainbow. "Here's water!"

But it was vain to expect any of the best places in such a reach would be vacant, and to avoid a recurrence of his unhappy encounter earlier in the morning, Rainbow continued his journey until he came to a spot where the river took one of those unaccountable right-angle bends which result in a pool, shallow on the one side, but slanting into deeps on the other. Above it was a water break, a swirl, smoothing, as it reached the pool, into a sleek, swift run, with an eddy which bore all the lighter floating things of the river over the calm surface of the little backwater, sheltered from above by a high shelving bank and a tangle of bramble and herb. Here in this backwater the twig, the broken reed, the leaf, the cork, the fly floated in suspended activity for a few instants until drawn back by invisible magnetism to the main current.

Rainbow paused in admiration. At the tail of the pool two sound fish were rising with regularity, but in the backwater beyond the eddy the surface was still and unbroken. Watching open-eyed, Rainbow saw not one but a dozen May flies, fat, juicy, and damp from the nymph, drift in, pause, and carried away untouched. It was beyond the bounds of possibility that such a place could be vacant, but there was the evidence of his eyes to prove it; and nothing if not a tryer, Rainbow darted across the stream and parked himself six inches below the water to await events.

It so happened that at the time of his arrival the hatch of fly was temporarily suspended, which gave Rainbow leisure to make a survey of his new abode. Beyond the eddy was a submerged snag—the branch of an apple tree borne there by heavy rains, water-logged, anchored, and intricate—an excellent place to break an angler's line. The river bank on his right was riddled under water with old rat holes, than which there is no better sanctuary. Below him and to the left was a dense bed of weeds brushed flat by the flow of the stream.

"If it comes to the worst," said Rainbow, "a smart fish could do a get-away here with very little ingenuity, even from a cannibalistic old hen like—hullo!"

The exclamation was excited by the apparition of a gauzy shadow on the water, which is what a May fly seen from below looks like. Resisting a vulgar inclination to leap at it with the violence of a youngster, Rainbow backed into the correct position which would allow the stream to present the morsel, so to speak, upon a tray. Which it did—and scarcely a dimple on the surface to tell what had happened.

"Very nicely taken, if you will accept the praise of a complete stranger," said a low, soft voice, one inch behind his line of sight.

Without turning to see by whom he had been addressed, Rainbow flicked a yard upstream and came back with the current four feet away. In the spot he had occupied an instant before lay a great old trout of the most benign aspect, who could not have weighed less than four pounds.

"I beg your pardon," said Rainbow, "but I had no idea that any one —that is, I just dropped in *en passant,* and finding an empty house, I made so bold—"

"There is no occasion to apologize," said Old Trout seductively. "I did not come up from the bottom as early today as is my usual habit at this season. Yesterday's hatch was singularly bountiful and it is possible I did myself too liberally."

"Yes, but a gentleman of your weight and seniority can hardly fail to be offended at finding—"

"Not at all," Old Trout broke in. "I perceive you are a well-conducted fish who does not advertise his appetite in a loud and splashing fashion."

Overcome by the charm of Old Trout's manner and address, Rainbow reduced the distance separating them to a matter of inches.

"Then you do not want me to go?" he asked.

"On the contrary, dear young sir, stay by all means and take the rise. You are, I perceive, of the rainbow or, as they say here in France, of the Arc-en-ciel family. As a youngster I had the impression that I should turn out a rainbow, but events proved it was no more than the bloom, the natural sheen of youth."

"To speak the truth, sir," said Rainbow, "unless you had told me to the contrary, I would surely have thought you one of us."

Old Trout shook his tail. "You are wrong," he said. "I am from Dulverton, an English trout farm on the Exe, of which you will have heard. You are doubtless surprised to find an English fish in French waters."

"I am indeed," Rainbow replied, sucking in a passing May fly with such excellent good manners that it was hard to believe he was feeding. "Then you, sir," he added, "must know all about the habits of men."

"I may justly admit that I do," Old Trout agreed. "Apart from being hand-reared, I have in my twelve years of life studied the species in moods of activity, passivity, duplicity, and violence."

Rainbow remarked that such must doubtless have proved of invaluable service. It did not, however, explain the mystery of his presence on a French river.

"For, sir," he added, "Dulverton, as once I heard when enjoying 'A Chat about Rivers,' delivered by a much-traveled sea trout, is situated in the west of England, and without crossing the Channel I am unable to explain how you arrived here. Had you belonged to the salmon family, with which, sir, it is evident you have no connection, the explanation would be simple, but in the circumstances it baffles my understanding."

Old Trout waved one of his fins airily. "Yet cross the Channel I certainly did," said he, "and at a period in history which I venture to state will not readily be forgotten. It was during the war, my dear young friend, and I was brought in a can, in company with a hundred yearlings, to this river, or rather the upper reaches of this river, by a young officer who wished to further an entente between English and French fish even as the war was doing with the mankind of these two nations."

Old Trout sighed a couple of bubbles and arched his body this way and that.

"There was a gentleman and a sportsman," he said. "A man who was acquainted with our people as I dare to say very few are acquainted. Had it ever been my lot to fall victim to a lover of the rod, I could have done so without regret to his. If you will take a look at my tail, you will observe that the letter *W* is perforated on the upper side. He presented me with this distinguishing mark before committing me, with his blessing, to the water."

"I have seldom seen a tail more becomingly decorated," said Rainbow. "But what happened to your benefactor?"

Old Trout's expression became infinitely sad. "If I could answer that," said he, "I were indeed a happy trout. For many weeks after he put me into the river I used to watch him in what little spare time he was able to obtain, casting a dry fly with the exquisite precision and likeness to nature in all the likely pools and runs and eddies near his battery position. Oh, minnows! It was a pleasure to watch that man, even as it was his pleasure to watch us. His bravery too! I call to mind a dozen times when he fished unmoved and unstartled while bullets from machine guns were pecking at the water like herons and thudding into the mud banks upon which he stood."

"An angler!" remarked Rainbow. "It would be no lie to say I like him the less on that account."

Old Trout became unexpectedly stern.

"Why so?" he retorted severely. "Have I not said he was also a gentleman and a sportsman? My officer was neither a pot-hunter nor a beast of prey. He was a purist—a man who took delight in pitting his knowledge of nature against the subtlest and most suspicious intellectual forces of the wild. Are you so young as not yet to have learned the exquisite enjoyment of escaping disaster and avoiding error by the exercise of personal ingenuity? Pray, do not reply, for I would hate to think so hard a thing of any trout. We as a race exist by virtue of our brilliant intellectuality and hypersensitive selectivity. In waters where there are no pike and only an occasional otter, but for the machinations of men, where should we turn to school our wits? Danger is our mainstay, for I tell you, Rainbow, that trout are composed of two senses—appetite, which makes of us fools, and suspicion, which teaches us to be wise."

Greatly chastened not alone by what Old Trout had said but by the forensic quality of his speech, Rainbow rose short and put a promising May fly onto the wing.

"I am glad to observe," said Old Trout, "that you are not without conscience."

"To tell the truth, sir," Rainbow replied apologetically, "my nerve this morning has been rudely shaken, but for which I should not have shown such want of good sportmanship."

And with becoming brevity he told the tale of his eviction from the pool downstream. Old Trout listened gravely, only once moving, and that to absorb a small blue dun, an insect which he keenly relished.

"A regrettable affair," he admitted, "but as I have often observed, women, who are the gentlest creatures under water in adversity, are a thought lacking in moderation in times of abundance. They are apt to snatch."

"But for a turn of speed, she would certainly have snatched me," said Rainbow.

"Very shocking," said Old Trout. "Cannibals are disgusting. They destroy the social amenities of the river. We fish have but little family life and should therefore aim to cultivate a freemasonry of good-fellowship among ourselves. For my part, I am happy to line up with other well-conducted trout and content myself with what happens along with my own particular drift. Pardon me!" he added, breasting Rainbow to one side. "I invited you to take the rise of May fly, but I must ask you to leave the duns alone." Then, fearing this remark might be construed to reflect adversely upon his hospitality, he proceeded: "I have a reason which I will explain later. For the moment we are discussing the circumstances that led to my presence in this river."

"To be sure—your officer. He never succeeded in deluding you with his skill?"

"That would have been impossible," said Old Trout, "for I had taken up a position under the far bank where he could only have reached me with a fly by wading in a part of the river which was in view of a German sniper."

"Wily!" Rainbow chuckled. "Cunning work, sir."

"Perhaps," Old Trout admitted, "although I have since reproached myself with cowardice. However, I was at the time a very small fish and a certain amount of nervousness is forgivable in the young."

At this gracious acknowledgment the rose-colored hue in Rainbow's rainbow increased noticeably—in short, he blushed.

"From where I lay," Old Trout went on, "I was able to observe the maneuvers of my officer and greatly profit thereby."

"But excuse me, sir," said Rainbow, "I have heard it said that an angler of the first class is invisible from the river."

"He is invisible to the fish he is trying to catch," Old Trout admitted, "but it must be obvious that he is not invisible to the fish who lie beside or below him. I would also remind you that during the war every tree, every scrap of vegetation, and every vestige of natural cover had been torn up, trampled down, razed. The river banks were as smooth as the top of your head. Even the buttercup, that very humorous flower that tangles up the back cast of so many industrious anglers, was absent. Those who fished on the Western Front had little help from nature."

Young Rainbow sighed, for, only a few days before, his tongue had been badly scratched by an artificial alder which had every appearance of reality.

"It would seem," he said, "that this war had its merits."

"My young friend," said Old Trout, "you never made a greater mistake. A desire on the part of our soldiery to vary a monotonous diet of bully beef and biscuit often drove them to resort to villainous methods of assault against our kind."

"Nets?" gasped Rainbow in horror.

"Worse than nets—bombs," Old Trout replied. "A small oval black thing called a Mills bomb, which the shameless fellows flung into deep pools."

"But surely the chances of being hit by such a—"

"You reveal a pathetic ignorance," said Old Trout. "There is no question of being hit. The wretched machine exploded under water and burst our people's insides or stunned us so that we floated dead to the surface. I well remember my officer coming upon such a group of marauders one evening—yes, and laying about him with his fists in defiance of King's Regulations and the Manual of Military Law. Two of them he seized by the collar and the pants and flung into the river. Spinning minnows, that was a sight worth seeing! 'You low swine,' I heard him say; 'you trash, you muck! Isn't there enough carnage without this sort of thing?' Afterward he sat on the bank with the two dripping men and talked to them for their souls' sake.

" 'Look ahead, boys. Ask yourselves what are we fighting for? Decent homes to live in at peace with one another, fields to till and forests and rivers to give us a day's sport and fun. It's our rotten job to massacre each other, but, by gosh, don't let's massacre the harmless rest of nature as well. At least, let's give 'em a running chance. Boys, in the years ahead, when all the mess is cleared up, I look forward to coming back to this old spot, when there is alder growing by the banks, and willow herb and tall reeds and the drone of insects instead of the rumble of those guns. I don't want to come back to a dead river that I helped to kill, but to a river ringed with rising fish—some of whom were old comrades of the war.' He went on to tell of us hundred Dulverton trout that he had marked with the letter *W*. 'Give 'em their chance,' he said, 'and in the years to come those beggars will reward us a hundred times over. They'll give us a finer thrill and put up a cleaner fight than old Jerry ever contrived.' Those were emotional times, and though you may be reluctant to believe me, one of those two very wet men dripped water from his eyes as well as his clothing.

"'Many's the 'appy afternoon I've 'ad with a roach pole on Brentford Canal,' he sniffed, 'though I've never yet tried m' hand against a trout.' 'You shall do it now,' said my officer, and during the half-hour that was left of daylight that dripping soldier had his first lesson in the most delicate art in the world. I can see them now—the clumsy, wet fellow and my officer timing him, timing him—'one and two, and one and two, and—' The action of my officer's wrist with its persuasive flick was the prettiest thing I have ever seen."

"Did he carry out his intention and come back after the war?" Rainbow asked.

"I shall never know," Old Trout replied. "I do not even know if he survived it. There was a great battle—a German drive. For hours they shelled the river front, and many falling short exploded in our midst with terrible results. My own bank was torn to shreds and our people suffered. How they suffered! About noon the infantry came over—hordes in field gray. There were pontoons, rope bridges and hand-to-hand fights on both banks and even in the stream itself."

"And your officer?"

"I saw him once, before the water was stamped dense into liquid mud and dyed by the blood of men. He was in the thick of it, unarmed, and a German officer called on him to surrender. For answer he struck him in the face with a light cane. Ah, that wrist action! Then a shell burst, smothering the water with clods of fallen earth and other things."

"Then you never knew?"

"I never knew, although that night I searched among the dead. Next day I went downstream, for the water in that place was polluted with death. The bottom of the pool in which I had my place was choked with strange and mangled tenants that were not good to look upon. We trout are a clean people that will not readily abide in dirty houses. I am a Dulverton trout, where the water is filtered by the hills and runs cool over stones."

"And you have stayed here ever since?"

Old Trout shrugged a fin. "I have moved with the times. Choosing a place according to the needs of my weight."

"And you have never been caught, sir, by any other angler?"

"Am I not here?" Old Trout answered with dignity.

"Oh, quite, sir. I had only thought, perhaps, as a younger fish enthusiasm might have resulted to your disadvantage, but that, nevertheless, you had been returned."

"Returned! Returned!" echoed Old Trout. "Returned to the frying-pan! Where on earth did you pick up that expression? We are in France, my young friend; we are not on the Test, the Itchen, or the

Kennet. In this country it is not the practice of anglers to return anything, however miserable in size."

"But nowadays," Rainbow protested, "there are Englishmen and Americans on the river who show us more consideration."

"They may show you consideration," said Old Trout, "but I am of an importance that neither asks for nor expects it. Oblige me by being a little more discreet with your plurals. In the impossible event of my being deceived and caught, I should be introduced to a glass case with an appropriate background of rocks and reeds."

"But, sir, with respect, how can you be so confident of your unassailability?" Rainbow demanded, edging into position to accept an attractive May fly with yellow wings that was drifting downstream toward him.

"How?" Old Trout responded. "Because—" Then suddenly: "Leave it, you fool!"

Rainbow had just broken the surface when the warning came. The yellow-winged May fly was wrenched off the water with a wet squeak. A tangle of limp cast lapped itself round the upper branches of a willow far upstream and a raw voice exclaimed something venomous in French. By common consent the two fish went down.

"Well, really," expostulated Old Trout, "I hoped you were above that kind of thing! Nearly to fall victim to a downstream angler. It's a little too much! And think of the effect it will have on my prestige. Why, that incompetent fool will go about boasting that he rose me. Me!"

For some minutes Rainbow was too crestfallen even to apologize. At last: "I am afraid," he said, "I was paying more heed to what you were saying than to my own conduct. I never expected to be fished from above. The fly was an uncommonly good imitation and it is a rare thing for a Frenchman to use Four-X gut."

"Rubbish," said Old Trout testily. "These are mere half-pound arguments. Four-X gut, when associated with a fourteen-stone shadow, should deceive nothing over two ounces. I saved your life, but it is all very provoking. If that is a sample of your general demeanor, it is improbable that you will ever reach a pound."

"At this season we are apt to be careless," Rainbow wailed. "And nowadays it is so hard, sir, to distinguish the artificial fly from the real."

"No one expects you to do so," was the answer, "but common prudence demands that you should pay some attention to the manner in which it is presented. A May fly does not hit the water with a splash, neither is it able to sustain itself in midstream against the current. Have you ever seen a natural insect leave a broadening wake of cutwater behind its tail? Never mind the fly, my dear boy, but watch the manner of its presentation. Failure to do that has cost many of our people their lives."

"You speak," said Rainbow, a shade sulkily, "as though it were a disgrace for a trout ever to suffer defeat at the hands of an angler."

"Which indeed it is, save in exceptional circumstances," Old Trout answered. "I do not say that a perfect upstream cast from a well-concealed angler, when the fly alights dry and cocked and dances at even speed with the current, may not deceive us to our fall. And I would be the last to say that a grasshopper skillfully dapped on the surface through the branches of an overhanging tree will not inevitably bring about our destruction. But I do most emphatically say that in such a spot as this, where the slightest defect in presentation is multiplied a hundred-fold by the varying water speeds, a careless rise is unpardonable. There is only one spot—and that a matter of twelve yards downstream—from which a fly can be drifted over me with any semblance to nature. Even so, there is not one angler in a thousand who can make that cast with success, by reason of a willow which cramps the back cast and the manner in which these alders on our left sprawl across the pool."

Rainbow did not turn about to verify these statements because it is bad form for a trout to face downstream. He contented himself by replying, with a touch of acerbity: "I should have thought, sir, with the feelings you expressed regarding sportsmanship, you would have found such a sanctuary too dull for your entertainment."

"Every remark you make serves to aggravate the impression of your ignorance," Old Trout replied. "Would you expect a trout of my intelligence to put myself in some place where I am exposed to the vulgar assaults of every amateur upon the bank? Of the green boy who lashes the water into foam, of the purblind peasant who slings his fly at me with a clod of earth or a tail of weed attached to the hook? In this place I invite attention from none but the best people—the expert, the purist."

"I understood you to say that there were none such in these parts," grumbled Rainbow.

"There are none who have succeeded in deceiving me," was the answer. "As a fact, for the last few days I have been vastly entranced by an angler who, by any standard, is deserving of praise. His presentation is flawless and the only fault I can detect in him is a tendency to overlook piscine psychology. He will be with us in a few minutes, since he knows it is my habit to lunch at noon."

"Pardon the interruption," said Rainbow, "but there is a gallant hatch of fly going down. I can hear your two neighbors at the tail of the pool rising steadily."

Old Trout assumed an indulgent air. "We will go up if you wish," said he, "but you will be well advised to observe my counsel before taking the rise, because if my angler keeps his appointment you will most assuredly be *meunièred* before nightfall."

At this unpleasant prophecy Rainbow shivered. "Let us keep to weed," he suggested.

But Old Trout only laughed, so that bubbles from the river bed rose and burst upon the surface.

"Courage," said he; "it will be an opportunity for you to learn the finer points of the game. If you are nervous, lie nearer to the bank. The natural fly does not drift there so abundantly, but you will be secure from the artificial. Presently I will treat you to an exhibition of playing with death you will not fail to appreciate." He broke off and pointed with his eyes. "Over you and to the left."

Rainbow made a neat double rise and drifted back into line. "Very mellow," he said—"very mellow and choice. Never tasted better. May I ask, sir, what you meant by piscine psychology?"

"I imply that my angler does not appreciate the subtle possibilities of our intellect. Now, my officer concerned himself as vitally with what we were thinking as with what we were feeding upon. This fellow, secure in the knowledge that his presentation is well-nigh perfect, is content to offer me the same variety of flies day after day, irrespective of the fact that I have learned them all by heart. I have, however, adopted the practice of rising every now and then to encourage him."

"Rising? At an artificial fly? I never heard such temerity in all my life," gasped Rainbow.

Old Trout moved his body luxuriously. "I should have said, appearing to rise," he amended. "You may have noticed that I have exhibited a predilection for small duns in preference to the larger *Ephemeridae*. My procedure is as follows: I wait until a natural dun and his artificial May fly are drifting downstream with the smallest possible distance separating them. Then I rise and take the dun. Assuming I have risen to him, he strikes, misses, and is at once greatly flattered and greatly provoked. By this device I sometimes occupy his attention for over an hour and thus render a substantial service to others of my kind who would certainly have fallen victim to his skill."

"The river is greatly in your debt, sir," said Young Rainbow, with deliberate satire.

He knew by experience that fish as well as anglers are notorious liars, but the exploit his host recounted was a trifle too strong. Taking a sidelong glance, he was surprised to see that Old Trout did not appear to have appreciated the subtle ridicule of his remark. The long, lithe body had become almost rigid and the great round eyes were focused upon the surface with an expression of fixed concentration.

Looking up, Rainbow saw a small white-winged May fly with red legs and a body the color of straw swing out from the main stream and describe a slow circle over the calm surface above Old Trout's head. Scarcely an inch away a tiny blue dun, its wings folded as closely as the pages of a book, floated attendant. An upward rush, a sucking kerr-rop, and when the broken water had calmed, the dun had disappeared and the May fly was dancing away downstream.

"Well," said Old Trout, "how's that, my youthful skeptic? Pretty work, eh?"

"I saw nothing in it," was the impertinent reply. "There is not a trout on the river who could not have done likewise."

"Even when one of those two flies was artificial?" Old Trout queried tolerantly.

"But neither of them was artificial," Rainbow retorted. "Had it been so, the angler would have struck. They always do."

"Of course he struck," Old Trout replied.

"But he didn't," Rainbow protested. "I saw the May fly go down with the current."

"My poor fish!" Old Trout replied. "Do you presume to suggest that I am unable to distinguish an artificial from a natural fly? Are you so blind that you failed to see the prismatic colors in the water from the paraffin in which the fly had been dipped? Here you are! Here it is again!"

Once more the white-winged insect drifted across the backwater, but this time there was no attendant dun.

"If that's a fake I'll eat my tail," said Rainbow.

"If you question my judgment," Old Trout answered, "you are at liberty to rise. I dare say, in spite of a shortage of brain, that you would eat comparatively well."

But Rainbow, in common with his kind, was not disposed to take chances.

"We may expect two or three more casts from this fly and then he will change it for a bigger. It is the same program every day without a variation. How differently my officer would have acted. By now he would have discovered my little joke and turned the tables against me. Aye me, but some men will never learn! Your mental outfit, dear Rainbow, is singularly like a man's," he added. "It lacks elasticity."

Rainbow made no retort and was glad of his forbearance, for every word Old Trout had spoken was borne out by subsequent events. Four times the white-winged May fly described an arc over the backwater, but in the absence of duns Old Trout did not rise again. Then came a pause, during which, through a lull in the hatch, even the natural insect was absent from the river.

"He is changing his fly," said Old Trout, "but he will not float it until the hatch starts again. He is casting beautifully this morning and I hope circumstances will permit me to give him another rise."

"But suppose," said Rainbow breathlessly, "you played this game once too often and were foul hooked as a result?"

Old Trout expanded his gills broadly. "Why, then," he replied, "I should break him. Once round a limb of that submerged apple bough and the thing would be done. I should never allow myself to be caught and no angler could gather up the slack and haul me into midstream in time to prevent me reaching the bough. Stand by."

The shadow of a large, dark May fly floated cockily over the backwater and had almost returned to the main stream when a small iron-blue dun settled like a puff of thistledown in its wake.

The two insects were a foot nearer the fast water than the spot where Old Trout was accustomed to take the rise. But for the presence of a spectator, it is doubtful whether he would have done so, but Young Rainbow's want of appreciation had excited his vanity, and with a rolling swoop he swallowed the dun and bore it downward.

And then an amazing thing happened. Instead of drifting back to his place as was expected, Old Trout's head was jerked sideways by an invisible force. A thin translucent thread upcut the water's surface and tightened irresistibly. A second later Old Trout was fighting, fighting, fighting to reach the submerged apple bough with the full weight of the running water and the full strength of the finest Japanese gut strained against him.

Watching, wide-eyed and aghast, from one of the underwater rat holes into which he had hastily withdrawn, Rainbow saw the figure of a man rise out of a bed of irises downstream and scramble upon the bank. In his right hand, with the wrist well back, he held a light split-cane rod whose upper joint was curved to a half-circle. The man's left hand was detaching a collapsible landing net from the ring of his belt. Every attitude and movement was expressive of perfectly organized activity. His mouth was shut as tightly as a steel trap, but a light of happy excitement danced in his eyes.

"No, you don't, my fellar," Rainbow heard him say. "No, you don't. I knew all about that apple bough before ever I put a fly over your pool. And the weed bed on the right," he added, as Old Trout made a sudden swerve half down and half across stream.

Tucking the net under his arm the man whipped up the slack with a lightning-like action. The maneuver cost Old Trout dear, for when, despairing of reaching the weed and burrowing into it, he tried to regain his old position, he found himself six feet farther away from the apple bough than when the battle began.

Instinctively Old Trout knew it was useless to dash downstream, for a man who could take up slack with the speed his adversary had shown would profit by the expedient to come more quickly to terms with him. Besides, lower down there was broken water to knock the breath out of his lungs. Even where he lay straining and slugging this way and that, the water was pouring so fast into his open mouth as nearly to drown him. His only chance of effecting a smash was by a series of jumps, followed by quick dives. Once before, although he had not confessed it to Rainbow, Old Trout had saved his life by resorting to this expedient. It takes the strain off the line and returns it so quickly that even the finest gut is apt to sunder.

Meanwhile the man was slowly approaching, winding up as he came. Old Trout, boring in the depths, could hear the click of the check reel with increasing distinctness. Looking up, he saw that the cast was almost vertical above his head, which meant that the moment to make the attempt was at hand. The tension was appalling, for ever since the fight began his adversary had given him the butt unremittingly. Aware of his own weight and power, Old Trout was amazed that any tackle could stand the strain.

"Now's my time," he thought, and jumped.

It was no ordinary jump, but an aerial rush three feet out of the water, with a twist at its apex and a cutting lash of the tail designed to break the cast. But his adversary was no ordinary angler, and at the first hint of what was happening he dropped the point of the rod flush with the surface.

Once and once more Old Trout flung himself into the air, but after each attempt he found himself with diminishing strength and with less line to play with.

"It looks to me," said Rainbow mournfully, "as if my unhappy host will lose this battle and finish up in that glass case to which he was referring a few minutes ago." And greatly affected, he burrowed his nose in the mud and wondered, in the event of this dismal prophecy coming true, whether he would be able to take possession of the pool without molestation.

In consequence of these reflections he failed to witness the last phase of the battle, when, as will sometimes happen with big fish, all the fight went out of Old Trout, and rolling wearily over and over, he abandoned himself to the clinging embraces of the net. He never saw the big man proudly carry Old Trout back into the hayfield, where, before proceeding to remove the fly, he sat down beside a shallow dike and lit a cigarette and smiled largely. Then, with an affectionate and professional touch, he picked up Old Trout by the back of the neck, his forefinger and thumb sunk firmly in the gills.

"You're a fine fellar," he said, extracting the fly; "a good sportsman and a funny fish. You fooled me properly for three days, but I think you'll own I outwitted you in the end."

Rummaging in his creel for a small rod of hard wood that he carried for the purpose of administering the quietus, he became aware of something that arrested the action. Leaning forward, he stared with open eyes at a tiny *W* perforated in the upper part of Old Trout's tail.

"Shades of the war! Dulverton!" he exclaimed. Then with a sudden warmth: "Old chap, old chap, is it really you? This is red-letter stuff. If you're not too far gone to take another lease of life, have it with me."

And with the tenderness of a woman, he slipped Old Trout into the dike and in a tremble of excitement hurried off to the *auberge* where the fishermen lodged, to tell a tale no one even pretended to believe.

For the best part of an hour Old Trout lay in the shallow waters of the dike before slowly cruising back to his own place beneath the overhanging bank. The alarming experience through which he had passed had made him a shade forgetful, and he was not prepared for the sight of Young Rainbow rising steadily at the hatch of fly.

"Pardon me, but a little more to your right," he said, with heavy courtesy.

"Diving otters!" cried Young Rainbow, leaping a foot clear of the water. "You, sir! You!"

"And why not?" Old Trout replied. "Your memory must be short if you have already forgotten that this is my place."

"Yes, but—" Rainbow began and stopped.

"You are referring to that little circus of a few minutes ago," said Old Trout. "Is it possible you failed to appreciate the significance of the affair? I knew at once it was my dear officer when he dropped the artificial dun behind the natural May fly. In the circumstances I could hardly do less than accept his invitation. Nothing is more delightful than a reunion of comrades of the war." He paused and added: "We had a charming talk, he and I, and I do not know which of us was the more affected. It is a tragedy that such friendship and such intellect as we share cannot exist in common element."

And so great was his emotion that Old Trout dived and buried his head in the weeds. Whereby Rainbow did uncommonly well during the midday hatch.

WEATHER PROPHET

EDMUND WARE SMITH

Once I came up in February because I had to see how the lake country looked under snow. Steve Ireland met me at Mopang, and we started for Privilege in the pung, with a northeaster building steadily behind us. Steve yelled into his turned-up collar: "Travel eight hundred miles to spend one day in a blizzard. Jesus!"

"Maybe it'll clear."

"Doc Musgrave says it'll hold northeast for two days. He don't often miss."

Whenever Steve mentioned Dr. Delirious Musgrave, there was a note in his voice of troubled fascination. I had always wanted to meet the doctor. His personality seemed to weigh on Steve's mind. I wanted to hear Steve talk about him now, but a quickened bitterness of the storm made talk an effort.

We were crossing the wake of an old burn where the blown snow towered around us, and the wind struck sharp. When at length we came into the shelter of the spruces, the wind seemed far away. You could hear it roaring in the branches, and the snow swept down like spilled veils, but the storm was at arm's length, momentarily.

Steve lifted his chin above his collar, and said:

"He claims the day he does he'll die."

"Does what?" I asked, my wits half numbed.

"Figures wrong on the weather."

"Oh, Doc Musgrave?"

"Yuh," said Steve, resettling his chin.

We put a blanket on old Chub in the Privilege stable, fed him his oats, and floundered up the hill above the lake to Steve's cabin. It was nice inside. You could smell peeled spruce, oakum chinking and wood smoke. The wind sent the fine snow hissing against the windows, reminding us of our comfort within.

"This time of year," Steve said, as he primed the pump, "there ain't much doin', only ice fishin'."

"I don't mind. I got to dreaming about winter on the lake, and had to come and see."

"You're seein' it, all right. You better stay over a few days."

"I can't do it. I'll have to go in the morning."

I opened the bottom draft of the stove, and the fire woke up and made the chimney roar. "Maybe if the storm holds, I'll be snowbound."

"He claimed it would," Steve said. A gust rattled the stovepipe in its guy wires, and Steve added: "Listen to that."

We ate fried salt pork, pickerel and tea. Steve inquired for all my friends he had guided. I asked about Uncle Jeff Coongate, Neilly Winslow, the Iron Duke and Jim Scantling. Steve said they were all smart, and let it go at that, but when I mentioned Peter Deadwater, the Indian, he perked up.

"Say! Peter's wife's goin' to have a kid."

"Honest?"

"Fact, so help me. Talk about a happy Injun."

"I thought Peter and Sadie couldn't have any kids."

"Well," Steve said, "they thought there wa'nt no hope, an' so'd everyone. They been wantin' one twelve years."

"When's the baby due?"

"Peter figures apple-blossom time. He's been poundin' ash, an' got a cradle built, an' a basket, an' a doe-skin suit with pants to it, soft as silk. It's a caution, the way that Injun works. Changed his whole character. He ain't touched a drop of lemon extrac' nor essence of pep'mint, not for five-six months. Just works, an' tends Sadie, an' lays plans for that kid."

"That's wonderful, Steve."

"It's the Lord's mercy. Let's wash the dishes."

We cleaned up, and got out the ice-fishing equipment. We were ready to start for the lake, when Steve spotted a gap in the chinking. A fine spray of snow had blasted through, building a hard white mound on the floor. Steve got a mallet and caulking iron and closed the gap with a twist of oakum. "Some storm, to find a hole that small," he said.

"Steve, didn't you say you drove Doc Musgrave's buggy for him, when you were little?"

"Yuh. We was good friends in them days."

"Aren't you now?"

"It's mighty queer, but he don't care for me now, me nor anyone at all."

A moment later we were out in the blizzard, toting our fishing gear down to the lake. I was more than ever determined to meet the doctor some day; but now his prophecy of weather was of direct concern. We chiseled our holes in the lee of Genius Island, but shelter was scant. The snow gave visible shape to the turbulence in the sky, and my forehead ached with cold.

The tip-ups were active, but we couldn't hook a trout. "They're slapping it with their tails," Steve said. "You can watch 'em do it, if you lay still over a hole."

I tried it, shading my eyes with my hands. Down there in the deep clear water, you could see the togue swimming along slowly in single file. They would bump the bait with their noses, and, as they swam by, bat it with their tails.

"Can you see 'em?" Steve asked.

He was kneeling on the opposite side of the hole, facing me. I glanced toward him, but my answer froze. Just behind Steve, and to one side of him, stood Peter Deadwater, the Indian. He was wearing snowshoes—the long, narrow Cree model for open travel. Suspended from a thong in his left hand were two lake trout of about six pounds. Steve saw my astonished expression, and turned.

"You ghost," he said to the Indian.

"No." Peter made an up-and-down motion with his free hand.

"Heard us chiseling," Steve explained to me; and the Indian grunted.

I stood up and brushed off the snow. "Hear good news, Peter," I said. "Congratulations."

Peter grunted again.

"How things with Sadie?" Steve asked.

Peter shrugged. While we took up our sets, he stood perfectly still in the exact spot where we had first seen him. Steve kept glancing at him curiously, and, when we were ready to go, said:

"Peter. You come my cabin. Get warm. Tea. Pickerel chowder."

Peter declined with a headshake and held out one of the lake trout, saying: "Namaycush."

"Come help eat," Steve said, taking the trout.

"I go home. Sadie hot. Crazy talk."

Steve looked quickly at me. "He means Sadie's sick." Then he turned to Peter. "How long Sadie hot? How long talk crazy?"

"Morning."

"This morning?"

Peter Deadwater nodded, his eyes vacant.

"She got pain some place?"

Peter touched his forehead, then put his hand down over his stomach, groaned, and stared at Steve.

"You go home. Take trout to Sadie. I get doctor. See?"

Peter moved away a few steps, turned on his long webs, and came back. "Doctor cross lake to Injun Village in storm?"

"Yes."

"Tell him open water Leadmine Point. Spring-hole. Tell him very danger spring-hole."

"I know," Steve said. "I tell him."

Peter started off, the snow blowing shoulder high around him. Ten steps and he had vanished. It was six miles, due southwest across the lake to the Indian Village. In the falling dark, even with the northeast gale full on his back, it would be a bitter journey.

Steve and I hid our tackle on Genius Island and went straight in to Privilege. I had to stop behind a shed at the public landing to get out of the wind for a minute. I thought my forehead was frozen, but it wasn't. Steve drew off a mitten and blew on his knuckles. "You're goin' to get a hell of a start," he said. "Doc Musgrave talks like he wasn't there at all."

"What? How do you mean?"

The shed trembled in a gust. In the dark you could still see the snow-shapes racing. Steve said: "Well, he don't say 'I done this,' nor 'I done that.' You'll think he's talkin' about someone else that ain't anywheres around. Once, when I was a kid, he told me why. Thought I'd forget, p'raps, but I didn't. He told me it was his other self he is talkin' about—the man he might of been, he said. But all the time it's really him, because he ain't no one else. But you got to talk to him like he was."

"Are you going to drive him across the lake tonight?"

Steve put on his mitten. "You can't work a horse on the lake. Four bad reefs in the ice between Genius Island and Caribou Rock. He'll go on snowshoes."

In the back room of Sam Lurch's barbershop in Privilege, we found Dr. Musgrave. He was a man in his early fifties. He sat on the wood box, a bottle between his knees, apparently entranced by the gleaming nickel stove-rail. The air in the room was hot and foul, but Musgrave wore a heavy sheepskin coat. The lamplight showed the birthmark which spread from his right temple over his entire right cheek to his jaw. His upward glance was too swift for me to see his eyes. With no sign of recognition for Steve, whom he had known since boyhood, he resumed his staring at the nickel rail. Steve had told me what to expect, but no warning could have prepared me for talking face to face with a man who not only dreamed he wasn't there, but demanded that others honor his unreality.

"Well," Steve said to him, "he said it would hold northeast for two days."

"Yes," said Musgrave. "He is an authority on the weather, as well as on rum, axe wounds and obstetrics."

Outside, the wind rose shrieking. You could hear the hard snow batter the walls like shot. As if at this corroboration of his prophecy, Musgrave grinned and leaned closer to the stove.

When the gust had spent itself, Steve said: "Would he cross the lake tonight to tend a sick woman in the Injun Village?"

After a long silence, Musgrave said: "He would think hard during such a trip—think himself into a stupor."

To see the man actually sitting there, yet talking of himself as if he were absent, gave me the shivers.

"He would have his coat collar up," he went on, "and his face wrapped to the eyes. He would keep the wind dead fair on his back, and—"

Steve moved toward the doctor nervously. "He would want to keep the wind heavy on his right shoulder. That would bear him inside of the open spring-hole off Leadmine Point."

Dr. Musgrave took a small drink from the bottle, replaced it between his knees, and, as if Steve had not spoken, resumed:

"—his thoughts would keep him company, and he would hum. His humming, and the cadence of his steps, would make him forget the night."

"But," said Steve, his voice rising, "he would want to keep his mind on that spring-hole. If the wind backs into the north, it would veer the doctor off course. He would walk right into *open water* in the dark."

"He stated that the wind would hold northeast," said Musgrave, complacently. "And it will."

"Even so, he'll pass within two hundred yards of the spring-hole!" Steve took a radium-dialed compass from his pocket and held it out to Musgrave in his open palm. "The snow is blowing so he won't even see his feet," he went on, his voice growing unsteady. "Wouldn't he take this?"

"Does a prophet need a compass?"

The man on the wood box seemed to ignore our presence as well as his own, and, while we humored his strange conceit, the purpose of our visit had been obscured. When I could bear the suspense no longer, I began speaking to him, unnaturally, in the third person:

"Is he equipped to take a six-months baby from the wife of Peter Deadwater? While the men discuss the weather, the Indian's woman lies out of her head with fever."

"He has performed Caesareans in this country under strange conditions," Musgrave answered, "and with strange instruments. Once he cauterized an amputation with a heated abutment spike. And he did a transfusion with the quill of a goose."

"But the Indian woman has been delirious since morning," I said. "The man with Steve Ireland thinks it may be emergency."

"Ah, yes, no doubt," replied Musgrave, blandly, "but the doctor hates cold—cold and terror, they are the same." He picked up the rum bottle and held it to the light. As near as I could judge, he had drunk half the contents. He removed the cork, took another swallow, and said: "Northeast for two days."

"Maybe the Indian's woman will die," I said, "and they are all here, talking."

"Maybe," said Musgrave, rising.

In the act of buttoning his coat collar to the throat, he turned toward us, and I saw him full face in the light. I knew why Steve Ireland both feared and pitied him. Above the doctor's straight, merciless mouth, were the eyes of a child; and I saw in these features the evidence of a man divided. You looked into his wide child's eyes, and pitied. You remembered his mouth, and shrank from him.

Steve went to him, begging: "Would the doctor please take a friend for company tonight? The friend that used to drive the buggy for him?"

"No."

Musgrave jerked his snowshoes from a peg, and kneeled to tie their lampwick lashings. Whether Steve was driven by a superstition about putting on snowshoes indoors, or by his dread that the wind would shift, I do not know. But when Musgrave stood up, Steve clutched him by the shoulders, and shook him, saying:

"If he walks into that spring-hole, *both* of him will go under the ice together—the one he is, and that other one, too!"

For an instant, as Steve backed away, the child part dominated Musgrave's face. He seemed touched that anyone should go to such lengths to warn him away from danger; and, in the only natural sentence I heard him speak, he said: "That's all right, Stevie—I'll be there in two hours."

He put on the pack which I assumed contained his instrument bag, and we followed him out into the blizzard. At the lake shore, he said: "He will go on from here alone." He hesitated for just a moment, then turned away, and walked off in the dark.

For two or three minutes after he had vanished, we stood looking out over the howling blackness of the lake. Then we turned wearily up the hill to Steve's cabin.

The warmth, the smell of broiling trout, and the leaky kettle's hiss could not remove the spell of Dr. Musgrave. Steve kept glancing at the black windows. It was as if he thought he might actually see the wind's direction.

"Steve," I said, "how wide is that spring-hole?"

"Better than a quarter-mile, when I last saw it."

After we had eaten, I lay in my bunk; but, despite my snow-burned face and eyes, there was no drowsiness. And there was none for Steve. He looked at his watch, and said: "It's thirty-eight minutes, now."

"Where would he be, about?"

"Mouth of Hardwood Cove."

Presently, as if Musgrave were with us in the cabin, we began to talk his way. To Steve Ireland, whom I had known fourteen years, I said: "The men lay in comfort wondering if the wind would change."

Steve got up, opened the door, and looked out into the whirlpools of the sky. He had to use his strength to close it, and the cold wind drove in a spray of snow and tore the ammunition-company calendar from its hook. "One of the men knows the wind is changing," he said.

"Where would he be now?"

Steve answered so quickly that I knew he was with Musgrave almost step for step: "Forty-three minutes—off Bear Trap Landing."

"They thought of how, in summer, they had paddled often across the six miles to Peter Deadwater's shack."

Steve got out his compass and set it on the table. He looked again at his watch. "The men couldn't rest good."

"No," I said. "They were thinking of the other man, counting on the wind to hold him on course, and the wind veering him toward the open water, and the Indian waiting, and his wife hot and crazy talking."

"For Chris' sake!" Steve cried. "I'm goin' outside and see for certain."

When Steve came in again, his face looked numb. His hair, powdered white with snow, made him seem prematurely old. He went to the stove and sat on the deacon seat, his back to the warmth. He kept looking at his watch, while the snow melted, glistening in his hair.

"Well?" I asked.

"The wind's due north—changed, with never a lull to warn him."

Steve got a lumberman's blueprint map of the lake, and spread it on the bench beside him. With a pencil he drew a straight line due southwest from Privilege six miles to the Indian Village on the far shore.

Along that line he marked various points, and the times he estimated it would take Musgrave to pass them, at a speed of three miles per hour. Hardwood Cove, 38 mins. Bear Trap Landing, 43 mins.

At Caribou Rock, an hour and five mins., Steve drew a gradual curve on the map. The curve bore left—southward, as the wind veered into the north. A mile south of Caribou Rock, he drew in the spring-hole off Leadmine Point. Then he looked at his watch again, and said: "Munson Reef—an hour and twelve minutes."

"My God, Steve! How many, many times we fished that spring-hole in hot weather when the trout were deep."

Steve made a dot on the penciled line which curved and then straightened toward the open water. He sat tense, his watch under his eyes, his pencil poised.

"Sometimes," Steve said, "when we was makin' calls away out somewheres away from the villages, he was mighty nice. He was kind. He would tell me to stop the buggy by a field of daisies, or hockweed. Them things made him happy. If he saw a doe deer on the lake shore, that would make him happy, too, or a loon callin'. It was the same with insects, any livin' thing, or anything that was pretty to look at. He could explain them things. I thought the world was flat, till he told me why it ain't. He said I was the only one he could talk to, or that could talk to him. I was eleven years old, then. . . ." Steve's pencil point touched the map, as he checked the time. "Little Mopang Bar—hour an' eighteen minutes."

"Steve! How close is he to it—now?"

"Seven minutes."

Steve brushed his hand over his damp hair, and wiped the wet palm on his thigh. "It was when I got older that he changed toward me. But I guess he thought 'twas me that changed. He wouldn't talk to me no more, nor he didn't want me 'round. He said people was no good after they stopped bein' children. But *he* was good, them times with me, when I was a boy. There wa'nt a thing he wouldn't do for people that was ailin'. But outside of for that, he wouldn't go near no one."

Steve got up from the bench, took off a stove lid and stirred the fire. A furious wind-blast drew back down the stovepipe, and the fine ash rose in the room.

"Big Mopang Bar," Steve said, "hour an' twenty-three minutes."

"That leaves him three minutes!"

"Two. . . . I wonder how Peter's woman's makin' out?"

"But he knows the lake, Steve. Maybe, when he got out there alone, with the storm, and the darkness—maybe he remembered what you said, and kept the wind heavy on his right shoulder. That would save him. He would pass Leadmine Point inside the spring-hole."

Steve looked intently at his watch. I saw his lips move, as he checked over the last minutes. Then he stopped counting. He was so quiet it was as if he had stopped breathing. After a long time he folded the map, put the watch back in his pocket, and stood up.

"Well," he said, "I liked him, just the same. It's like I was with him out there tonight, right beside him the whole way, till he drowned. Only nothin' I could do to help him, like watchin' a blind man walk off a cliff, an' your voice gone."

"Steve, I can't believe it!"

"That's 'cause you don't want to, an' I don't, neither."

Steve crossed to the table and turned down the lamp. He stood there with the dim light on his face, until I had stretched out under my blankets. "All set?" he said.

"Sure—maybe he made it all right."

"Maybe." Steve blew out the lamp and we lay in the dark, listening to the long-drawn fury of the storm.

Morning broke clear with a light north wind. Steve had the bacon frying. The cabin was warm, and bright sunlight streamed through the windows. I looked out, and saw the lake stretching white and lovely below us. That view, so peaceful now, so immaculate, made the night seem unreal.

"Steve, how do you feel this morning?"

"Frisky," he said. "That was bad last night."

Yet in Steve's voice there was uncertainty. I felt it, perhaps in his very cheerfulness. When we had eaten, and were on our way down to the stable, Steve said: "Would it trouble you if I got Jim Scantling to drive you to Mopang this mornin'? I want to cross the lake."

"No, Steve, of course not. I'd stay and go with you, if I could."

"Well, I just got an awful hankerin' to make it across," Steve explained.

Jim and Steve hooked up, and old Chub's breath blew white in the cold. We climbed to the seat, and I reached down to shake hands with Steve. "Let me know about things, will you?" I asked.

"Sure. I'll write you a letter. So-long."

I looked around once to see Steve striking off across the white-glaring lake toward the Indian Village.

Dere frend,

I seen from his drifted tracks right where it begun to change on him near Caribou Rock. I followed the curve of them until I dassent go no closer the open water, where his tracks run off I seen one of his mittens layin on the ice where he tried to claw back on but that is all so I swung back and went to the Peter Deadwater shack and the priest was there. Peter's woman was dead and the baby was dead.

Well my good frend I must close now as there is a diver comin from Eastport to dive for him and I am to lay a boom on the ice for him to work off of, but they will never find him as the currents will draw him under, as ever your frend Steve Ireland.

P.S. I told Peter how we tried to get the doctor to him and he said all right.

THE TROUT

JESSE HILL FORD

At the time Coy was eight he had been fishing with his grandfather five years—since he could first remember, when they fished for bream near Royal in the lily pad ponds belonging to old man Paris Austin. Later, after the dam at Muscle Shoals was built, they began journeying to a camp near Guntersville to fish in the backwaters of the Tennessee River. It was twenty miles from Royal, Alabama, where they lived, to the Tennessee River backwaters, and because Grandfather Rickman didn't drive, they would have to get someone to take them there in the car, with their yellow can poles tied to the outside of it and the minnow buckets rattling inside. Usually Catherine, Coy's aunt, drove them to the fish camp on Goodluck Road, where they rented a boat and paddled out to the drowned trees where the white perch bedded, and there they would sit, with Catherine gone into Guntersville to visit friends for the day while Coy and Grandfather Rickman fished.

It was July, and the boat leaked, so that Coy took turns with the old man bailing out the boat with a pork and beans can, while they drifted and paddled among the trees the river had killed when the dam pushed it out of its banks. They had left the bank early that morning, and when Grandfather Rickman remarked that they had not got a fish and it was nine thirty, the paper label had come off the bean can and was sloshing in the water at Coy's feet. The water reminded him of summer leaves, and the snake doctors which lit on his cork or teetered now and then on the end of the yellow cane pole he held reminded him of airplanes. In the other end of the boat, Grandfather Rickman sat bent forward, looking intently at his own cork, floating beside a shattered gray stump. He seemed a very old and skinny man, hidden except for his face and hands by a long-sleeved shirt and cotton trousers and a felt hat which shaded his light-blue eyes.

Looking back at his own cork, Coy saw a remarkable thing, for it had gone down and under the surface in a swoop. He raised the tip of his pole at once and felt the tug of the fish for an instant before his line came up limp out of the water. The minnow's head was all that remained on the hook.

"I think I had a trout," he said.

"No," said his grandfather, who always spoke in a hushed voice for fear he would alarm the fish, "it was only a gar." And as though to prove the truth of what he said, Grandfather Rickman's pole bent suddenly and he raised the ugly fish to the surface before the hook came with the old man's minnow bitten in two. The gar thrashed the surface once before it faded back, slowly, like a sinking log.

"It felt like a big trout," Coy said.

"The garfish keep the other fish from biting," said his grandfather. "They're mean." He dipped his paddle in the water to move the boat on. "They'll get all our minnows," the old man said. "The scamps."

Coy took up the bean can and began to bail. The water which leaked in was pleasant and cool to his bare feet, and he wished he knew how to swim, for the sun was merciless and hot. He wore only a pair of shorts, and everywhere else he was brown. He was always brown by the middle of June, lean and brown and growing, and Tennessee seemed far away, for his parents lived in Nashville and he went to school there and associated the city with wintertime. But he thought of Alabama as long summers and elm trees shading his grandmother's house and the smell of cow feed when his grandfather milked every morning and nightfall; of dew on the early-morning grass and of days when the rains flooded the streets of Royal, and the very air which blew and sifted through the rain made the cushions of a chair damp to sit on. And there were the long days, such as this, when they fished until the water turned brassy gold with the sun's decline and the honking of the car horn called them back to the bank.

Paddling back without fish on the stringer was a deep-hurting sense of defeat to Coy, a sensation of dying which his grandfather seemed not to feel, for to the old man, fishing did not have to mean catching fish. To the old man, fishing was a still and quiet patience, a hushed attitude of body, broken only by a laugh of pleasure when Coy pulled a fish out, or a cry of "Hey!" when the old man himself brought a white-sided perch up and into the boat. To Coy, paddling back with a full stringer of fish meant going back with a deep sense of victory in his breast.

"No," said Grandfather Rickman, when they had reached the new spot and were fishing again, near an old bleached tree which had fallen from the bank out into the river, "you'll know a trout if you ever feel one. It's like hooking the bottom, and all of a sudden the bottom begins to move, and then it goes wild, and that fish comes straight up out of the water. It makes a trout mad to hook him."

Coy remembered seeing one trout, a trout Mr. Vilous Lee had caught in one of Mr. Paris Austin's ponds. Mr. Vilous was a butcher, a vindictive fisherman who set out poles at several places along the bank trying to catch catfish, and he had seen the big trout the week before and had rigged an enormous pole with a minnow on the line nearly as long as his hand. Then he had crept far up the bank under the shade of a catalpa tree and waited. He had waited there all day from early morning until midafternoon, when Grandfather Rickman finally shouted, "Watch out, Vilous!" And with that the butcher had run down the long grassy stretch to the bank of the pond. The trout was already hung when he reached the big pole, and the butcher yanked the fish straight out of the water and, laughing in a wild, ugly way, he walked up the bank with the trout still dangling on the line. Coy's father, who was there that day, had said the fish was a large-mouth bass and that, mistakenly, the North Alabama fishermen called these fish trout. But the fish was still a trout to Coy, and to Grandfather Rickman, and to Mr. Vilous Lee. Far up the bank, the trout had struggled free of the hook and fallen to the grass, and the butcher had flung himself on the fish, reaching his rough fingers through its gills and raising it high in the air, making the creature writhe and bleed to be held so cruelly.

They had ridden back into town and weighed the trout on the scales at the grocery where the butcher worked—six pounds. It was the biggest fish Coy had ever seen caught, and he had dreamed afterward that someday he would catch a trout, but, having caught one, he would not feel such a cruel delight. The butcher's cruelty seemed somehow to be tied up with his taking a large spoonful of baking soda occasionally and gagging it down with water. Grandfather Rickman had said Vilous was ruining his stomach by the habit, and sure enough, only a few months before, the butcher had died. When Coy had come back to Royal from Nashville, at the summer's beginning, he had gone to the grocery store and seen a new butcher behind the counter. The new butcher had worked in Birmingham, he said. His name was Clisby, and he didn't fish.

"What happened to Mr. Vilous Lee?" Coy asked, dipping up a can of water from the bottom of the boat and pouring it quietly out into the river.

"Why, you know what happened," Grandfather Rickman said softly. "He died. They buried him."

"But why did Mr. Lee die?"

"They say it was his stomach. He had an operation in Birmingham. Then he came home and got all right, I thought. We went out to the ponds some last fall, before the weather got too cold."

"And then what?"

"Well, he had a spell this spring, and we only went fishing one time."

"Was he still taking soda, Grandpapa?"

"I think he had gone back to his bad habits. Yes," Grandfather Rickman said, after a pause, "I'm sure of it."

Coy thought of Mr. Vilous Lee dying, of a dark-red something in his stomach which the doctors had not been able to help, and he remembered the butcher's thick, freckled hands, and the strange sweet smell of his breath, and the wild, angry look of his eyes. Coy knew instinctively that the butcher *drank,* and that the smell was whisky, and he felt his grandfather's dispassionate disapproval of the habit.

"I didn't like him," Coy said. "He hurt my feelings."

Grandfather Rickman smiled. "You took his catfish off the line. He didn't like for anyone to touch his poles after he had set them out. He didn't think a fish was his unless he had taken it off the hook. You shouldn't dislike him for that." The old man spoke as though the butcher were still alive. "He gave us many a ride to the ponds," he said, after a moment.

"But I still didn't like him," Coy said.

"Well, Vilous never understood children," Grandfather Rickman said. "He didn't know what to say to them. He couldn't talk to a kid. But he was a good friend to me, Coy." Grandfather Rickman's voice had fallen now, for he had felt the butcher's death again, and his face was grave and sad.

Coy bailed the water out, scraping the can until the boat bottom was just barely damp. Then, while he watched, the water began seeping in again. It came in so slowly that he had no patience for it, and he shifted his pole to fish on the other side of the boat, away from the snags beside the old tree, out away from everything, away from the bank, where nothing would bite, where he knew the fish would not be. But he was bored.

Then the fish struck. Coy felt him before he realized the cork was gone under, and he lifted the pole in his trembling arms, fighting against the strength of the fish with his own strength, going so hard upward with the light pole that it bent sharply.

"Easy!" cried Grandfather Rickman. "Play him easy!"

But the pole broke just then, and Coy pulled in the broken half and held it, his body frozen still by the sight of the trout coming out of the water and landing with a splash. The fish skittered sideways around the end of the boat toward the bank and went down deep again, moving back suddenly toward the river.

"Let him get tired," Grandfather Rickman cautioned. But Coy was already drawing in the broken pole. He reached the line and began frantically pulling the fish in toward the boat.

"No!" cried Grandfather Rickman. "You'll lose him! You'll lose him!"

And just as the old man yelled the second time, the fish came out of the water again, and this time, as he landed, the hook came loose and the line went sick and limp. The trout lay near the surface an instant, nearly exhausted, not realizing it was free. But then, with a flash of its green body, it was gone. Coy drew the hook out of the water and held it in his trembling fingers. It was bent straight. Then he looked at Grandfather Rickman.

"Why couldn't you listen to me?" Grandfather Rickman said. "That was a trout."

Coy could feel himself collapsing inside to an indrawn knot of sorrow in his stomach. Holding the broken cane pole across his lap, he began to weep. "A trout," he cried. "A trout!" There would never be such a victory so close again, and he felt the loss and the anguish slowly killing him.

"There," said Grandfather Rickman. "It's all right." The old man came cautiously forward to pick up the empty bean can. He sat down and began bailing out the boat. "You did the only thing you knew how to do. But if it happens again, don't try to pull him out of the water. Wear him down first."

Coy wiped his eyes on his arm, smelling the salt sweat and the sun in his skin. He nodded, struggling to recover. But he knew the trout would never strike again. It was gone back into the deep cool mystery of the green water, to remain there now, buried forever.

DUD DEAN AND THE ENCHANTED

H.W.H.

ARTHUR R.
MacDOUGALL, JR.

The Lady was a most alert and intelligent person. I met her at a bookstore in modern Babylon, where she presided over books, clerks, and cash registers. And she asked, "Where can I find a professional guide in Maine who knows how to prepare a palatable meal, make a bough bed, paddle a canoe, and where to find the white orchid, *Cypripedium acaule albiflorum?*" Before I could attempt to answer the question, the lady added, "He must *know* the wilderness, and above all, he must be a gentleman."

I looked at the lady, who was neat and trim but forty years old plus ten. And it seemed to me that she need not worry about men who were not gentlemen. And then, while I sought for words that would not betray my private amusement, I thought of Dud Dean, who would have replied to a question with such stipulations in a courtly manner.

"Lady," I said, "there are doubtless scores of such men who are registered guides in Maine, but I only know one of them. He is much older than you and I, and his mind and personality are more mature. He knows the birds and flowers by their names, although he often calls them names that are not found in the books. And he is a gentleman with the best of manners."

"And what are the wages one must pay such a paragon?"

"Wait a moment. I only told you that I knew such a guide. I didn't say that he was available. Dud Dean picks and chooses his clientelle. One must persuade Dud that he is worth the while. Your money would be a secondary consideration."

"You intrigue me," the lady said. "And how do I approach this

Dud? And is he none other than the lauded Dud Dean of your stories? And would he really know where *Cypripedium acaule albiflorum* grows?"

"Dud would call them lady's-slippers or white moccasins. And I am sure that he would know a score of places where they bloom in June."

The lady tapped her white teeth with the rubber end of a pencil. "Now that I have gone so far," she said, "I should tell you the rest. I expect to attach myself to a man in June. The gentleman grew up in Maine. The white moccasin flowers are only an aside. One can buy almost anything in this city, but if it had a glory, that is soiled or dead. We, this man and I, have a hunger in us, not so much to see the rare white orchid as to keep a tryst where such a triumph of the ancient earth survives. It isn't easily said, and I wonder if you understand."

I assumed that I did understand. And I said, "If you will come to Bingham, I will take you to Dud Dean's house, and then you and he can talk about the project to your heart's content. If you are fortunate enough to enlist Dud Dean, he can make your dream come true."

When I had told Dud about the lady and her projected vacation and her projected husband, he smiled quizzically. Then he said, "Nope. I'm too old to lead honeymooners eround. Besides, I long ago had to give up guidin' parties with womenfolks. Nancy's jealous."

Nancy Dean had been washing dishes, and of course Dud had made the speech for her to hear. She came from the kitchen to the sitting-room. Nancy is one of those rare persons who grow more and more attractive as they ripen in wisdom, and with charity for all. Now she came to us smiling.

"To the contrary," she said, "I have always wanted Dud to guide ladies. They have a most delightful effect upon him. He calls to mind all his old gallantries. He gets his hair cut and his mustache trimmed. Furthermore, it has been a long time since the opportunity came to guide honeymooners. Why, I would love to go myself, if I were a guide! And I think, Dudley, that it was kind of Mr. Macdougall to think of you, and to recommend you to these people."

"Pshaw, Nancy, how many times have I heard you say that a man sh'ud keep his eyes on Greeks that come bearin' gifts? Mak's like all parsons. Thar's sunthin' up his sleeves. Besides, w'ud yer trust him to size up a strange woman? Like ducks yer w'ud. What erbout her man? Has he got fallen arches? Can he take blackflies an' bog water? Can he sleep with the stub end of a fir bough in the small of his back? Er is he old enough to know better, but don't?"

"They grew up in little Maine towns," I said. "He came from a little village in Washington County. She grew up in Aroostook. And they are dreaming about white moccasins, and all that."

"Crotch. Is that supposed to prove sunthing, Mak?"

"Dudley," said Nancy.

"Hump. Wel-el, no harm if I talk with them. When they come to Bingham, bring 'em eround. My garden is planted. Chores purty well caught up. Bring 'em up here. Nancy will size 'em up, and if she decides that I am good enough fer sech folks I have no doubt that I'm their man."

Five weeks after that day, the lady, Mrs. Pendmaster Davis, wrote a letter to me, and that is the rest of the story.

Dear Mr. Macdougall,

I am happy! Your friend was the most delightful and entrancing man! To that, we both agree. Pend and I have reviewed our honeymoon and the endless little delights that Dud contrived for us. We have them like a rosary to tell over and over—and I am not irreverent.

First thing. Dud asked us, "Which is most important—the lady's-slippers er *trout?*"

I said, "Trout," because I knew how dearly Pend loves to fish for trout. And he has caught them in England, Scotland, and in the Pyrenees, as well as almost everywhere in North America.

But Pend said, "The lady's-slippers. There is no question about that."

Honestly, I think that your old friend was pleased. But he almost insisted on giving us physical examinations. How careful and wise he is! When at last we convinced him that we really wanted to go afoot into a remote corner of the wilderness, and that I was prepared to undergo the torments of the blackfly, and what else, he said:

"C'ud you even stand bein' lost? Reason I ask is that I've got a sartin place in mind which I hain't seen fer fifty years. Since then, thar's been a big fire in thar, an' since the fire it's been logged over. So I might have to poke eround afore we got thar. But I am mortally sure that we can find your white moccasins, an' find them no end. And thar's bound to be some trout to catch. But to git thar, we'd have to go to Big Enchanted Pond, cross it, and then climb up into Bulldog Mountain."

"Enchanted!" Did anyone ever have a honeymoon in a more fittingly named place? Of course we were enthusiastic. Pend said, "I have been lost with men in whom I had less confidence. And, by gosh, I managed to enjoy it. As for our lady, she has already risked more than that. Lead on, MacDuff."

Then the men bought our supplies. And your Mr. Dean loaned Pend one of his huge packbaskets. They carried fifty pounds each. All because Pend was determined that a honeymoon would be spoiled unless there was plenty to eat.

I do not believe that Dud Dean was even puzzled about where he was or where to go ahead. I know that Pend did not worry for a moment. He said to me, "This man is the genuine old guide. We need not fret." And yet, Dud had not gone that way for fifty years. Think of it, a lifetime!

We walked from the road that goes to Spencer Lake. What a breathless beauty there is in all that country! The Upper Enchanted! Verily. Dud told us about the terrible forest fire of 1895—the very year Pend was born. Dud showed us huge pine trunks that still lie where they fell after that fire. Pend cut into one with his axe. It was still sound under the outer grey shell. And Dud called to our attention the marine rock at the height of land—as one goes down to Enchanted Pond. That man is a matchless entertainer, because his own interests are so varied.

Dud told us about the legend that Enchanted Pond is bottomless beneath its deepest water. He pointed out the place at the lower end where some old lumberman had built a dam between those magnificent granite mountains.

And Pend caught three gloriously colored trout in that blue water, while Dud rowed us to the Bulldog Mountain shore. By the way, Pend did not keep those trout. I have had so much to learn about men and fishermen in these few weeks—things I might have learned years ago, if Pend had come into the store for a copy of your book, *Dud Dean and His Country,* years ago instead of a few months ago. Dud Dean! And His Country! We'll never forget that man or his country—not ever.

The mountain was steep. Did you know that once there was a profile of a bulldog on the east end, until it slid off and away during a springtime deluge? What a savage name, Bulldog! Must there be a bulldog in the Enchanted Country? No. The Enchanted is rid of that. I am glad it is gone. But there is a great raw scar where the profile was.

Now we come to our weather. That old joke about the Maine man who said to the tourist who had complained about the weather, "What kind of weather do yer want? We've got all kinds," is no whimsy. There never was a lovelier day than when we started up the mountain. The sky was as blue as the ribbon that Alice wore into Wonderland. Then, as if by magic, the cumulus clouds grew forebodingly dark. It was as if the demons were angry because we had invaded their mountain. And how it rained!

Dud explained, with that solemn face he puts on, that it does not rain cats and dogs in the Enchanted—not even bulldogs. Instead, according to Dud, it rains rain, although sometimes it rains lady's-slippers—white fer when she gets up in the morning, gold fer when she eats her dinner (at noon, of course) and pink fer when she goes to dance across the sunset. And then he added that he had known it to rain *trout* in the Enchanted, but that kind, he said, hardly ever take a fly, unless a fellow has the Pink Lady.

"I have a Pink Lady," said Pend. And I guess that I was, after such an interpolation!

Dud pretended not to comprehend the implication. He said, "Then I guess, maybe, yer c'ud git some trout if yer sh'ud try real hard. But yer know, thar was once a tribe of Indians that lived up an' down the Kennebec. And among them was a girl so purty that they called her 'Flower-of-the-rising-sun.' Of course, all the young fellers loved her. One of them was a big, tall chap who went by the name of Moxie, an' he courted her morning, noon, an' almost all night. So they were wed. Then the young man made a terrible mistake. Took his young wife with him when he went into the Enchanted to fish fer trout. Fer a little time they was happy an' contented—until early one morning, when Moxie woke up. He looked fer his wife. She had left his side. He hurried outside the wigwam, and thar he saw her walkin' over the lake, where the risin' sun made a path.

"Moxie called to her, but she did not hear him. He ran to the lake, and went after her in his birch canoe. No use. She jist went away, up the mountain, an' thar she vanished out of mortal sight. Poor Moxie! Not even a yeller leaf was turned upside down. Not even a twig had been rolled on its side. An' he never found her. So after a while he left the Enchanted; wandered off, down country, an' where Moxie Mountain is he died of a broken heart. Yer can see him any clear day, with his great shoulders an' chest heaved up ag'inst the sky.

"But what the Enchanted did with Flower-of-the-rising-sun, no man knows. Yer see, it ain't safe in here, but the trout don't know it. As fer fishermen, what do they know but trout?"

Of course, your old friend was talking to help us forget the drenching rain. Once he turned to look at us, and asked, "W'udn't you rather go back to the camps on the big lake? They're nice an' comfortable. We c'ud sleep dry, an' then come up here tomorrow."

Pend looked to me. And I said, "No."

"Ye're sure?"

I was. But I was weary and very, very wet. At noontime we stopped at a little spring. And there Dud and Pend cooked our dinner. The rain continued. And once more Dud asked me, "Don't yer want to go back to the camps?"

I am so glad that I refused to turn back. So glad!

When we went on, Dud said, "Mind now, that I'm goin' it purty blind. Maybe I can't find that pond tonight. It's a small mark in this big country. And maybe it ain't thar anymore, like Flower-of-the-rising-sun. Queer things happen up here, an' ordinary things happen queerly. Even the trout, in this pond I'm lookin' fer, is strange. Some folks declare that thar ain't a trout in it to go over half a pound. An' some persons have fished in here to go back home vowin' that thar's no trout at all. And a few folks whisper erbout tremendous trout that haunt the place."

Pend asked, "But what do you say?"

"I say that it strikes me as odd that when I come in here fifty years ago, the weather was jist like it is this very afternoon. We was young fellers, Mat Markham an' me. Thar was mighty heavy timber up here on the mountain. Take that an' the rainstorm, an' the light was dim. Arter a while, we both figgered that we was good an' lost. So we started settin' a line—yer know, pickin' out a tree straight ahead of us, goin' to that, an' then pickin' another. Mat was kinda superstitious. He still is. I 'member that he said, 'If I ever git out of this godforsaken place, I'll never set foot on it ag'in.' And b'crotch, he was as good as his word, becuz he's never been in here since that time. I've always wanted to come in here, but until now this an' that has lured me elsewhere.

"When Mat an' me had gone over the divide, an' started down, the rain kinda pindled—good deal as it's doin' now. Mat kept on moaning, but I didn't pay much attention of course. All of a sudden, I seen a big round raft of fog, like an old circus tent, but kinda moving, writhing, an' rolling. I scootched down, so's I c'ud see under the fog, an' then I seen the pond, level, an' lookin' like an old kitchen floor that has been scoured with sand an' mopped an' mopped fer a hundred years by generations of peeticular women.

" 'Look,' I says to Mat, who was still grumblin' erbout the rain an' foolish fools like us. 'Look,' I says. An' then I p'inted like this—"

Mr. Macdougall, your Dud is a magician. When Pend and I looked where Dud had pointed, just as he had pointed for his friend fifty years ago, we saw a pond, or part of a pond. And there was a cloud of fog lying over it, like a circus tent!

"Great guns, man," exclaimed Pend. "You have an instinct for the abrupt. Is that the pond you were looking to find?"

"Don't know yit. Maybe. Anyhow, it's a pond. Or will it fold up in that cloud an' vanish away?"

Pend said, "We will soon find out!"

So he ran down to the shore of the pond, where he splashed his right hand in the water. "It's real," he said, while laughing back at us.

"C'ud be," said Dud.

But what a ghost of a pond it was, under that weird raft of mountain fog. It was grey and lonely. And for a moment, no more, I wished that I were back on Madison Avenue. And then I remembered how unearthy the skyscrapers look in fog and storm. One sees a few lower stories, but the rest are swallowed up, as if the building were immaterial or upside down in a vague, formless sea.

"Fust," said Dud, "good sense makes camp. Let's see . . . Ayah, over this way thar's a spring, er thar was fifty years ago."

We followed Dud.

"Here," he said. And I saw the sweetest little spring that came as by kindly magic from under a mound of soft moss. "And thar," said Dud. And I saw a single plant of *Cypripedium acaule* with ten blossoms on the one plant.

Dud smiled at me. "Ye'll have to excuse us, becuz they're only pink ones. An' I don't mind if yer laugh at me, when I tell yer that they was here fifty years ago."

Pend had brought that tent with the wonderfully light but waterproof material—floor and all. And he and Dud were only a few moments setting it up.

"There is plenty of room for the three of us," I said.

Dud Dean laughed at me. "If yer don't mind," he said, "I will put up my own shelter-half where Mat an' me built us a leanto so long ago. Now, when we're all shipshape, why not cook up sunthin' until it's real hot. I'll go explore to see if them cedars still grow near the south shore, where Mat an' me made our raft. Say, do yer know this is the most fun I've had since the day Mat fell inter a springhole on the shore of Middle Carry Pond. We was hedgehoggin' erlong the shore, lookin' fer a boat that had come up missing, as Mont Spinney said when his wife run off with the butter money. The shore, yer see, looked all firm an' trustworthy, but when Mat stepped in that place he jist went out of sight inter a deep springhole. An' the poor feller was so cold when he wallowed out that he kept saying, 'Colder'n hell, colder'n hell,' till Mak give him a lecture fer what he called apostasy.

" 'What d'yer mean by that?' says Mat.

" 'I mean that hell is *not* cold,' says Mak."

Pend and I began to unpack. And in a few moments we heard Dud's axe. He had found the cedars. Pend explained to me that cedar was a light wood, and that it made a buoyant raft.

When Dud came back, he was poling a large raft. And he had a bundle of dry kindling wood tied and fastened on his shoulders. The fire was quickly kindled, and I am sure that mortals never ate more delicious food than our hot biscuits and beef stew. And then we went to bed. And then we slept like small children—children in the Enchanted Country!

Dud awakened us. And I smelled bacon and coffee. "I figgered," he said, "that it w'ud be all right to wake yer up, becuz the weather has improved. Besides, the trout are puddlin' out front."

Did you ever try to dress in a sleeping-bag? There are difficulties. Dud called again. "I wish that ye'd hurry. Thar's an old she otter and her kits out in the pond. It's int'restin' to watch 'em cut up."

I just wrapped a blanket around me and went out. What a handsomely graceful creature an otter is. There were four of them, diving, rising, and chasing each other in the water. How could one ever forget that strong, swift gracefulness!

At the further end of the pond (it was shaped like a football) the trout continued to rise. "Puddling" Dud called it, "becuz they're only takin' nymphs near the surface."

Otters, trout, nymphs, and the earliest daylight in the Enchanted!

Of course, breakfast was delicious. "Coffee," said Dud, "must be part good spring water—none of your chemically diluted, polluted stuff that is as vile as bogwater! But, as Mat says, 'To make good coffee, fust take some coffee, put it in a *coffee-pot* full of b'ilin' water, an' then let it be so long as it takes to whistle, *Comin' Through the Rye.*' "

Pend and I decided to christen the pond "Ghost Lake." And then we embarked on Dud's raft. Of course I should have died if they had made me stay ashore, although I offered to do so, nevertheless. But the men insisted that I should go.

Pend fished with flies. And I was so proud to observe that Dud Dean approved of Pend's skill. It was all so beautifully done. The dry flies appeared to be so small and fragile—number twelves and fourteens, I think. Pend cast into the circles made by the feeding trout. And those vividly colored fish rose with astonishing savageness. And when hooked, they fought with all the grace of the otters.

When one went free, Pend would say, "Bully for you, mister." Then Dud Dean would chuckle. I counted all the fish that Dud actually netted to remove the flies. There were forty of them—"none under half a pound, an' some of 'em almost big e-nough to scare a hot-house trout to death."

They saved one, an unimaginably beautiful thing. "Plenty fer three of us," said Dud. "An' now, let's go find the lady's-slippers, if yer really meant what yer said."

The sun had risen. The pond was a strange pale green and warm with a golden light when we left the camp. It was amusing to me to witness Dud's apologetic way when the first lady's-slippers that he found were a great bed of *Cypripedium calceolus pubescens,* the big yellow moccasin. "Y'know," he said, "I had fergotten all erbout them yeller slippers. Yer don't see 'em very often."

As a matter of fact, I had never seen them growing in the wild way. The large bed was mixed with ferns. The blossoms were like pure gold in that damp, dark setting of forest shadows. And there were so many of them! So amazingly abundant in that lavish place that I could not believe my eyes.

But all that was only to prepare us for the white slippers around the little lost bog, where like figments of utter beauty the enchanted white moccasins grew. When your raw-boned old friend pushed a screen of ferns aside to show us the first patch, I loved him . . . that greatly simple man.

"Here they are," he said. "And to me, it seems as though I had only left them here a few hours ago. But it was fifty years ago. Ask Mat Markham." Then I detected an anxiety in his voice. "I 'spose that ye'll want to pick some?"

"Just one," I said.

I thought for a moment that he was going to hug me. "Glory be!" he said. "I reckon that the Indian girl c'ud spare yer more than that."

Pend and I took color shots, as we had of the yellow moccasins. We have shown the slides to our friends. The question we always expect never fails to be asked: "Where are they?" And I do not need to pretend vagueness to protect the stand, because I only know that they are somewhere on the other side of a mountain—somewhere in the Enchanted.

"B'fore we go back to camp," said Dud Dean, "I'd be pleased to have the lady try my little flyrod down here off the old beaver dam at the foot of this little bog. The trout in thar are little fellers, but the Lord has dressed 'em up real purty."

That was my first lesson in fly fishing. And the fly was a Red Ibis. I loved fly fishing in spite of the blackflies that beset us. Dud Dean was patient and cheerful when I tangled the line in cedars that grew too near the water. What fun it was to catch those handsome little trout.

And that was how our week began! We fell in love with your friend. He is a great soul and a charming gentleman. He is a mystic, but his big hands were made to hold an axe. He is a big, rawboned weather-beaten man, but he can remember where he saw white lady's-slippers growing fifty years ago.

Our days in that Enchanted Country were too swift, as I suppose days are sure to be when one is altogether happy and content. The last night was clear and lighted by a full moon. And is there a place on earth where the moonlight falls so magically as near a mountain top! Dud came to us where we sat looking out on the little lake. And he said, "If the idea sh'ud appeal to you folks, I w'ud like to show yer sunthin' strange and beautiful."

A pleasant sense of excitement filled me. Pend whispered to me, "I have an intuition that we shall never forget this, whatever he has in mind."

We followed Dud along the west shore of the pond—no flashlights, because Dud said, "They'd be handy, but I w'udn't dare."

He led us to the strangest thing—an old dead pine (very ancient) that seemed to be fast in the soft soil of the shore, but lying its full length out in the pond.

"It's always been here," he said. "The water is real shallow, an' the bottom is hard shale and sand. So if anyone fell off, 'tw'udn't do 'em any harm. Matter of fact, we c'ud wade to the end of the log, if that was necessary. But the pine is as stidy as a board walk."

And then he walked out. I did not think that I could do it in that half-light, but with Pend's help I did. Dud was waiting for us at the end. And he whispered, "Look at the bottom."

The bottom was silver white.

"Sand," said Dud. "In the daytime yer can see it bubbling. Thar's a tremendous spring here, but it's always gentle—no gushing. Now, jist keep still an' watch."

As I watched, the water seemed to become clearer, or the moonlight brighter.

"Now," whispered Dud.

A school of little trout swam over the white sand, turned, and came back.

"Not yit," whispered Dud. "It hain't here yit."

Pend whispered in my ear, "I suspect that I know what he wants us to see. Watch."

Suddenly, as if they had been summoned from far away, the small trout were gone. And, without a visible approach, I saw a huge fish posed motionless over the sand. And I felt that queer excitement that is older than our Race. And I saw the larger stripe of white-white on the creature's pectoral fins. I saw its eyes!

"Wait," whispered Dud.

And there, beside the first trout, lay another giant. They lay side by side, and I saw that they were perfectly matched.

"Wait," whispered Dud.

And there were three more, and then I saw another. There were six immense trout—as if they had materialized from the clean water and the white sand. My eyes began to doubt, or I to doubt my eyes. I moved nearer to Pend, to touch him for assurance. And the trout were gone!

Dud chuckled. "It w'ud always be that way," he said.

We walked back to the camp without speaking. Dud placed wood on the red coals. It caught fire, and the yellow light was welcome.

"Were they real?" I asked, feeling silly to do so, but unable to keep back the question.

"Of course they were real," said Pend.

But Dud Dean chuckled. "Speakin' fer myself, I'll have to say that I don't know. All I know is that's what I saw off that log when it was full moonlight fifty years ago. I was there to git a pail of water, but I went back after Mat Markham. And I know what Mat said. He says, "Be you tryin' to fool me? Nobudy ever catched a trout that big. Nobudy ever heard of a big trout bein' catched in this pond. It's a crotchly lie, that's what it is!" And all the time, Mat stood thar lookin' at them trout jist the same as we did tonight.

"So much as I know, Mat was right when he said that no one ever claimed to git any really big trout in here. We didn't. And nor have we this time. In most waters, trout grow slow. I don't see any reason to think that trout grow fast in this little pond. It appears to be fair-to-middlin' trout water an' that's all.

"But if I was to let myself go, I w'ud take my oath that them *big* trout we saw tonight was the same trout that I saw fifty years ago. Yes sir, by crotch, I'll never forget them trout. C'udn't. But yer may watch an' wait until kingdom-come an' ye'll never see them trout in the daylight. They don't even seem to be nearabouts in the daytime. So it figgers out this way: only time ye'll ever see 'em is late in a moonlight night. So I don't know. Sometimes I have wondered if it was a trick the moonlight played, but yer saw the smaller trout before the big ones come in tonight. W'ud yer say that it was a trick of the moonlight on the bottom, Pend?"

Pend replied, "No, it wasn't an illusion."

"Wel-el, maybe it's the Enchanted—eh? Maybe it's like pink, and white, and yellow lady's-slippers. All I know is that I've seen them trout twice. I guess I'm not apt to see them ever ag'in. But maybe you folks will. Yer know, I w'ud have been bad disapp'inted if storm er clouds had hidden the full moon tonight. Wel-el, hope yer sleep sound. So goodnight."

When he had gone to his own camp, Pend and I sat together near the dying fire. And I said, "What do you really think, dear?"

"Think? Why I think that Dud Dean was like an old priest out there tonight. And deep in my heart, I think that the grand old fellow was passing something on to us, something he has loved, and that he wanted to share with us. God bless him."

GOD'S HOOKS

HOWARD WALDROP

They were in the End of the World Tavern at the bottom of Great Auk Street.

The place was crowded, noisy. As patrons came in, they paused to kick their boots on the floor and shake the cinders from their rough clothes.

The air smelled of wood smoke, singed hair, heated and melted glass.

"Ho!" yelled a man at one of the noisiest tables to his companions, who were dressed more finely than the workmen around them. "Here's old Izaak now, come up from Staffordshire."

A man in his seventies, dressed in brown with a wide white collar, bagged pants, and cavalier boots, stood in the doorway. He took off his high-brimmed hat and shook it against his pantsleg.

"Good evening, Charles, Percy, Mr. Marburton," he said, his gray eyes showing merry above his full white mustache and Vandyke beard.

"Father Izaak," said Charles Cotton, rising and embracing the older man. Cotton was wearing a new-style wig, whose curls and ringlets flowed onto his shoulders.

"Mr. Peale, if you please, sherry all round," yelled Cotton to the innkeeper. The older man seated himself.

"Sherry's dear," said the innkeep, "though our enemy, the King of France, is sending two ships' consignments this fortnight. The Great Fire has worked wonders."

"What matters the price when there's good fellowship?" asked Cotton.

"Price is All," said Marburton, a melancholy round man.

"Well, Father Izaak," said Charles, turning to his friend, "how looks the house on Chancery Lane?"

"Praise to God, Charles, the Fire burnt but the top floor. Enough remains to rebuild, if decent timbers can be found. Why, the lumbermen are selling green wood most expensive, and finding ready buyers."

"Their woodchoppers are working day and night in the north, since good King Charles gave them leave to cut his woods down," said Percy, and drained his glass.

"They'll not stop till all England's flat and level as Dutchman's land," said Marburton.

"If they're not careful, they'll play hob with the rivers," said Cotton.

"And the streams," said Izaak.

"And the ponds," said Percy.

"Oh, the fish!" said Marburton.

All four sighed.

"Ah, but come!" said Izaak. "No joylessness here! I'm the only one to suffer from the Fire at this table. We'll have no long faces till April! Why, there's tench and dace to be had, and pickerel! What matters the salmon's in his Neptunian rookery? Who cares that trout burrow in the mud, and bite not from coat of soot and cinders? We've the roach and the gudgeon!"

"I suffered from the Fire," said Percy.

"What? Your house lies to east," said Izaak.

"My book was at bindery at the Office of Stationers. A neighbor brought me a scorched and singed bundle of title pages. They fell sixteen miles west o'town, like snow, I suppose."

Izaak winked at Cotton. "Well, Percy, that can be set aright soon as the Stationers reopen. What you need is something right good to eat." He waved to the barkeep, who nodded and went outside to the kitchen. "I was in early and prevailed on Mr. Peale to fix a supper to cheer the dourest disposition. What with shortages, it might not pass for kings, but we are not so high. Ah, here it comes!"

Mr. Peale returned with a huge, round platter. High and thick, it smelled of fresh-baked dough, meat, and savories. It looked like a cooked pond. In a line around the outside, halves of whole pilchards stuck out, looking up at them with wide eyes, as if they had been struggling to escape being cooked.

"Oh, Izaak!" said Percy, tears of joy springing to his eyes. "A stargazey pie!"

Peale beamed with pleasure. "It may not be the best," he said, "but it's the End o' the World!" He put a finger alongside his nose and laughed. He took great pleasure in puns.

The four men at the table fell to, elbows and pewter forks flying.

They sat back from the table, full. They said nothing for a few minutes, and stared out the great bow window of the tavern. The shop across the way blocked the view. They could not see the ruins of London which stretched—charred, black, and still smoking—from the Tower to the Temple. Only the waterfront in that great length had been spared.

On the fourth day of that Great Fire, the King had given orders to blast with gunpowder all houses in the way of the flames. It had been done, creating the breaks that, with a dying wind, had brought it under control and saved the city.

"What the city has gone through this past year!" said Percy. "It's lucky, Izaak, that you live down country, and have not suffered till now."

"They say the Fire didn't touch the worst of the Plague districts," said Marburton. "I would imagine that such large crowds milling and looking for shelter will cause another one this winter. Best we should all leave the city before we drop dead in our steps."

"Since the comet of December, year before last, there's been nothing but talk of doom on everyone's lips," said Cotton.

"Apocalypse talk," said Percy.

"Like as not it's right," said Marburton.

They heard the clanging bell of a crier at the next cross street.

The tavern was filling in the late-afternoon light. Carpenters, tradesmen covered with soot, a few soldiers all soiled came in.

"Why, the whole city seems full of chimneysweeps," said Percy.

The crier's clanging bell sounded, and he stopped before the window of the tavern.

"New edict from His Majesty Charles II to be posted concerning rebuilding of the city. New edict from Council of Aldermen on rents and leases, to be posted. An Act concerning movements of trade and shipping to new quays to become law. Assize Courts sessions to begin September 27, please God. Foreign nations to send all manner of aid to the City. Murder on New Ogden Street, felon apprehended in the act. Portent of Doom, monster fish seen in Bedford."

As one, the four men leaped from the table, causing a great stir, and ran outside to the crier.

*　　*　　*

"See to the bill, Charles," said Izaak, handing him some coins. "We'll meet at nine o' the clock at the Ironmongers' Company yard. I must go see to my tackle."

"If the man the crier sent us to spoke right, there'll be no other fish like it in England," said Percy.

"Or the world," said Marburton, whose spirits had lightened considerably.

"I imagine the length of the fish has doubled with each county the tale passed through," said Izaak.

"It'll take stout tackle," said Percy. "Me for my strongest salmon rod."

"I for my twelve-hair lines," said Marburton.

"And me," said Izaak, "to new and better angles."

The Ironmongers' Hall had escaped the Fire with only the loss of its roof. There were a few workmen about, and the Company secretary greeted Izaak cordially.

"Brother Walton," he said, "what brings you to town?" They gave each other the secret handshake and made The Sign.

"To look to my property on Chancery Lane, and the Row," he said. "But now, is there a fire in the forge downstairs?"

Below the Company Hall was a large workroom, where the more adventurous of the ironmongers experimented with new processes and materials.

"Certain there is," said the secretary. "We've been making new nails for the roof timbers."

"I'll need the forge for an hour or so. Send me down the small black case from my lockerbox, will you?"

"Oh, Brother Walton," asked the secretary. "Off again to some pellucid stream?"

"I doubt," said Walton. "But to fish, nonetheless."

Walton was in his shirt, sleeves rolled up, standing in the glow of the forge. A boy brought down the case from the upper floor, and now Izaak opened it, and took out three long gray-black bars.

"Pump away, boy," he said to the young man near the bellows, "and there's a copper in it for you."

Walton lovingly placed the metal bars, roughened by pounding years before, into the coals. Soon they began to glow redly as the teenaged boy worked furiously on the bellows-sack. He and Walton were covered with sweat.

"Lovely color, now," said the boy.

"To whom are you prenticed?" asked Walton.

"To the Company, sir."

"Ah," said Walton. "Ever seen angles forged?"

"No, sir, mostly hinges and buckles, nails like. Sir Abram Jones sometimes puddles his metal here. I have to work most furious when he's here. I sometimes don't like to see him coming."

Walton winked conspiratorially. "You're right, the metal reaches a likable ruddy hue. Do you know what this metal is?"

"Cold iron, wasn't it? Ore beaten out?"

"No iron like you've seen, or me much either. I've saved it for nineteen years. It came from the sky, and was given to me by a great scientific man at whose feet it nearly fell."

"No!" said the boy. "I heard tell of stones falling from the sky."

"I assure you, he assured me it did. And now," said Izaak, gripping the smallest metal bar with great tongs and taking it to the anvil, "we shall tease out the fishhook that is hidden away inside."

Sparks and clanging filled the basement.

They were eight miles out of northern London before the air began to smell more of September than of Hell. Two wagons jounced along the road toward Bedford, one containing the four men, the other laden with tackle, baggage, and canvas.

"This is rough enough," said Cotton. "We could have sent for my coach!"

"And lost four hours," said Marburton. "These fellows were idle enough, and Izaak wanted an especially heavy cart for some reason. Izaak, you've been most mysterious. We saw neither your tackles nor your baits."

"Suffice to say, they are none too strong nor none too delicate for the work at hand."

Away from the town, there was a touch of coming autumn in the air.

"We might find nothing there," said Marburton, whose spirits had sunk again. "Or some damnably small salmon."

"Why then," said Izaak, "we'll have Bedfordshire to our own, and all of September, and perhaps an inn where the smell of lavender is in the sheets and there are twenty printed ballads on the wall!"

"Hmmph!" said Marburton.

At noon of the next day, they stopped to water the horses and eat.

"I venture to try the trout in this stream," said Percy.

"Come, come," said Cotton. "Our goal is Bedford, and we seek Leviathan himself! Would you tempt sport by angling here?"

"But a brace of trouts would be fine now."

"Have some more cold mutton," said Marburton. He passed out bread and cheese and meat all around. The drivers tugged their fore-locks to him and put away their rougher fare.

"How far to Bedford?" asked Cotton of the driver called Hum-phrey.

"Ten miles, sir, more or less. We should have come farther but, what with the Plague, the roads haven't been worked in above a year."

"I'm bruised through and through," said Marburton.

Izaak was at the stream, relieving himself against a tree.

"Damn me!" said Percy. "Did anyone leave word where I was bound?"

Marburton laughed. "Izaak sent word to all our families. Always considerate."

"Well, he's become secretive enough. All those people following him a-angling since his book went back to the presses the third time. Ah, books!" Percy grew silent.

"What, still lamenting your loss?" asked Izaak, returning. "What you need is singing, the air, sunshine. Are we not Brothers of the Angle, out a-fishing? Come, back into the carts! Charles, start us off on 'Tom o' the Town.'"

Cotton began to sing, in a clear sweet voice, the first stanza. One by one the others joined, their voices echoing under the bridge. The carts pulled back on the roads. The driver of the baggage cart sang with them. They went down the rutted Bedford road, September all about them, the long summer after the Plague over, their losses, heartaches all gone, all deep thoughts put away. The horses clopped time to their singing.

Bedford was a town surrounded by villages, where they were stared at when they went through. The town was divided neatly in two by the double-gated bridge over the River Ouse.

After the carts crossed the bridge, they alighted at the doorway of a place called the Topsy-Turvy Inn, whose sign above the door was a world globe turned arse-over-teakettle.

The people who stood by the inn were all looking up the road, where a small crowd had gathered around a man who was preaching from a stump.

"I think," said Cotton, as they pulled their baggage from the cart, "that we're in Dissenter country."

"Of that I'm sure," said Walton. "But once we Anglicans were on the outs and they'd say the same of us."

One of the drivers was listening to the man preach. So was Marburton.

The preacher was dressed in somber clothes. He stood on a stump at two cross streets. He was stout and had brown-red hair that glistened in the sun. His mustache was an unruly wild thing on his lip, but his beard was a neat red spike on his chin. He stood with his head uncovered, a great worn clasp Bible under his arm.

"London burned clean through," he was saying. "Forty-three parish churches razed. Plagues! Fires! Signs in the skies of the sure and certain return of Christ. The Earth swept clean by God's loving mercy. I ask you sinners to repent for the sake of your souls."

A man walking by on the other side of the street slowed, listened, stopped.

"Oh, this is Tuesday!" he yelled to the preacher. "Save your rantings for the Sabbath, you old jailbird!"

A few people in the crowd laughed, but others shushed him.

"In my heart," said the man on the stump, "it is always the Sabbath as long as there are sinners among you."

"Ah, a fig to your damned sneaking disloyal Non-Conformist drivel!" said the heckler, holding his thumb up between his fingers.

"Wasn't I once as you are now?" asked the preacher. "Didn't I curse and swear, play at tipcat, ring bells, cause commotion wherever I went? Didn't God's forgiving Grace . . . ?"

A constable hurried up.

"Here, John," he said to the stout preacher. "There's to be no sermons, you know that!" He waved his staff of office. "And I charge you all under the Act of 13 Elizabeth 53 to go about your several businesses."

"Let him go on, Harry," yelled a woman. "He's got words for sinners."

"I can't argue that. I can only tell you the law. The sheriff's about on dire business, and he'd have John back in jail and the jailer turned out in a trice. Come down off the stump, man."

The stout man waved his arms. "We must disperse, friends. The Sabbath meeting will be at . . ."

The constable clapped his hands over his ears and turned his back until the preacher finished giving directions to some obscure clearing in a woods. The red-haired man stepped down.

Walton had been listening and staring at him, as had the others. Izaak saw that the man had a bag of his tools of the trade with him. He was obviously a coppersmith or brazier, his small anvils, tongs, and taphammers identifying him as such. But he was no ironmonger, so Walton was not duty-bound to be courteous to him.

"Damnable Dissenters indeed," said Cotton. "Come, Father Izaak, let's to this hospitable inn."

A crier appeared at the end of the street. "Town meeting. Town meeting. All free men of the Town of Bedford and its villages to be in attendance. Levies for the taking of the Great Fish. Four of the clock in the town hall."

"Well," said Marburton, "that's where we shall be."

They returned to the inn at dusk.

"They're certainly going at this thing full-tilt," said Percy. "Nets, pikes, muskets."

"If those children had not been new to the shire, they wouldn't have tried to angle there."

"And wouldn't have been eaten and mangled," said Marburton.

"A good thing the judge is both angler and reader," said Cotton. "Else Father Walton wouldn't have been given all the morrow to prove our mettle against this great scaly beast."

"If it have scales," said Marburton.

"I fear our tackle is not up to it," said Percy.

"Didn't Father Walton always say that an angler stores up his tackle against the day he needs it? I'll wager we get good sport out of this before it's over."

"And the description of the place! In such a narrow defile, the sunlight touches it but a few hours a day. For what possible reason would children fish there?"

"You're losing your faith, Marburton. I've seen you up to your whiskers in the River Lea, snaggling for salmon under a cutbank."

"But I, praise God, know what I'm about."

"I suppose," said Izaak, seating himself, "that the children thought so too."

They noticed the stout Dissenter preacher had come in and was talking jovially with his cronies. He lowered his voice and looked toward their table.

Most of the talk around Walton was of the receding Plague, the consequences of the Great Fire on the region's timber industry, and other matters of report.

"I expected more talk of the fish," said Percy.

"To them," said Cotton, "it's all the same. Just another odious county task, like digging a new canal or hunting down a heretic. They'll be in holiday mood day after tomorrow."

"They strike me as a cheerless lot," said Percy.

"Cheerless, but efficient. I'd hate to be the fish."

"You think we won't have it to gaff long before the workmen arrive?"

"I have my doubts," said Marburton.

"But you always do."

Next morning, the woods became thick and rank on the road they took out of town. The carts bounced in the ruts. The early sun was lost in the mists and the trees. The road rose and fell again into narrow valleys.

"Someone is following us," said Percy, getting out his spyglass.

"Probably a pedlar out this way," said Cotton, straining his eyes at the pack on the man's back.

"I've seen no cottages," said Marburton. He was taking kinks out of his fishing line.

Percy looked around him. "What a Godless-looking place."

The trees were more stunted, thicker. Quick shapes, which may have been grouse, moved among their twisted boles. An occasional cry, unknown to the four anglers, came from the depths of the woods. A dull boom, as of a great door closing, sounded from far away. The horses halted, whinnying, their nostrils flared.

"In truth," said Walton from where he rested against a cushion, "I feel myself some leagues beyond Christendom."

The gloom deepened. Green was gone now, nothing but grays and browns met the eye. The road was a rocky rut. The carts rose, wheels teetering on stones, and agonizingly fell. Humphrey and the other driver swore great blazing oaths.

"Be so abusive as you will," said Cotton to them, "but take not the Lord's name in vain, for we are Christian men."

"As you say." Humphrey tugged his forelock.

The trees reached overhead, the sky was obscured. An owl swept over, startling them. Something large bolted away, feet drumming on the high bank over the road.

Percy and Cotton grew quiet. Walton talked, of lakes, streams, of summer. Seeing the others grow moody, he sang a quiet song. A driver would sometimes curse.

A droning, flapping sound grew louder, passed to their right, veered away. The horses shied then, trying to turn around in the road, almost upsetting the carts. They refused to go on.

"We'll have to tether them here," said Humphrey. "Besides, Your Lordship, I think I see water at the end of the road."

It was true. In what dim light there was, they saw a darker sheen down below.

"We must take the second cart down there, Charles," said Walton, "even if we must push it ourselves."

"We'll never make it," said Percy.

"Whatever for?" asked Cotton. "We can take our tackle and viands down there."

"Not my tackle," said Walton.

Marburton just sighed.

They pushed and pulled the second cart down the hill; from the front they kept it from running away on the incline, from the back to get it over stones the size of barrels. It was stuck.

"I can't go on," said Marburton.

"Surely you can," said Walton.

"Your cheerfulness is depressing," said Percy.

"Be that as it may. Think trout, Marburton. Think salmon!"

Marburton strained against the recalcitrant wheel. The cart moved forward a few inches.

"See, see!" said Walton. "A foot's good as a mile!"

They grunted and groaned.

They stood panting at the edge of the mere. The black sides of the valley lifted to right and left like walls. The water itself was weed-choked, scummy, and smelled of the sewer ditch. Trees came down to its very edges. Broken and rotted stumps dotted the shore. Mist rose from the water in fetid curls.

Sunlight had not yet come to the bottom of the defile. To left and right, behind, all lay in twisted woody darkness. The valley rose like a hand around them.

Except ahead. There was a break, with no trees at the center of the cleft. Through it they saw, shining and blue-purple against the cerulean of the sky, the far-off Chiltern Hills.

"Those," said a voice behind them, and they jumped and turned and saw the man with the pack. It was the stout red-haired preacher of the day before. "Those are the Delectable Mountains," he said.

"And this is the Slough of Despond."

He built a small lean-to some hundred feet from them.

The other three anglers unloaded their gear and began to set it up.

"What, Father Walton? Not setting up your poles?" asked Charles Cotton.

"No, no," said Izaak, studying the weed-clotted swamp with a sure eye. "I'll let you young ones try your luck first."

Percy looked at the waters. "The fish is most likely a carp or other rough type," he said. "No respectable fish could live in this mire. I hardly see room for anything that could swallow a child."

"It is Leviathan," said the preacher from his shelter. "It is the Beast of Babylon, which shall rise in the days before Antichrist. These woods are beneath his sway."

"What do you want?" asked Cotton.

"To dissuade you, and the others who will come, from doing this. It is God's will these things come to pass."

"Oh, Hell and damn!" said Percy.

"Exactly," said the preacher.

Percy shuddered involuntarily. Daylight began to creep down to the mere's edge. With the light, the stench from the water became worse.

"You're not doing very much to stop us," said Cotton. He was fitting together an eighteen-foot rod of yew, fir, and hazelwood.

"When you raise Leviathan," said the preacher, "then will I begin to preach." He took a small cracked pot from his large bag, and began to set up his anvil.

Percy's rod had a butt as thick as a man's arm. It tapered throughout its length to a slender reed. The line was made of plaited, dyed horsehair, twelve strands at the pole end, tapering to nine. The line was forty feet long. Onto the end of this, he fastened a sinker and a hook as long as a crooked little finger.

"Where's my baits? Oh, here they are." He reached into a bag filled with wet moss, pulled out a gob of worms, and threaded seven or eight, their ends wriggling, onto the hook.

The preacher had started a small fire. He was filling an earthen pot with solder. He paid very little attention to the anglers.

Percy and Marburton, who was fishing with a shorter but thicker rod, were ready before Cotton.

"I'll take this fishy spot here," said Percy, "and you can have that grown-over place there." He pointed beyond the preacher.

"We won't catch anything," said Marburton suddenly and pulled the bait from his hook and threw it into the water. Then he walked back to the cart and sat down, and shook.

"Come, come," said Izaak. "I've never seen you so discouraged, even after fishless days on the Thames."

"Never mind me," said Marburton. Then he looked down at the ground. "I shouldn't have come all this way. I have business in the city. There are no fish here."

Cajoling could not get him up again. Izaak's face became troubled. Marburton stayed put.

"Well, I'll take the fishy spot then," said Cotton, tying onto his line an artificial fly of green with hackles the size of porcupine quills.

He moved past the preacher.

"I'm certain to wager you'll get no strikes on that gaudy bird's wing," said Percy.

"There is no better fishing than angling fine and far off," answered Cotton. "Heavens, what a stink!"

"This is the place," said the preacher without looking up, "where all the sins of mankind have been flowing for sixteen hundred years. Not twenty thousand cartloads of earth could fill it up."

"Prattle," said Cotton.

"Prattle it may be," said the preacher. He puddled solder in a sandy ring. Then he dipped the pot in it. "It stinks from mankind's sins, nonetheless."

"It stinks from mankind's bowels," said Cotton.

He made two backcasts with his long rod, letting more line out the wire guide at the tip each time. He placed the huge fly gently on the water sixty feet away.

"There are no fish about," said Percy, down the mire's edge. "Not even gudgeon."

"Nor snakes," said Cotton. "What does this monster eat?"

"Miscreant children," said the preacher. "Sin feeds on the young."

Percy made a clumsy cast into some slime-choked weeds.

His rod was pulled from his hands and flew across the water. A large dark shape blotted the pond's edge and was gone.

The rod floated to the surface and lay still. Percy stared down at his hands in disbelief. The pole came slowly in toward shore, pushed by the stinking breeze.

Cotton pulled his fly off the water, shook his line, and walked back toward the cart.

"That's all for me, too," he said. They turned to Izaak. He rubbed his hands together gleefully, making a show he did not feel.

The preacher was grinning.

"Call the carters down," said Walton. "Move the cart to the very edge of the mere."

While they were moving the wagon with its rear facing the water, Walton went over to the preacher.

"My name is Izaak Walton," he said, holding out his hand. The preacher took it formally.

"John Bunyan, mechanic-preacher," said the other.

"I hold no man's religious beliefs against him, if he be an honest man, or an angler. My friends are not of like mind, though they be both fishermen and honest."

"Would that Parliament were full of such as yourself," said Bunyan. "I took your hand, but I am dead set against what you do."

"If not us," said Walton, "then the sheriff with his powder and pikes."

"I shall prevail against them, too. This is God's warning to mankind. You're a London man. You've seen the Fire, the Plague?"

"London is no place for honest men. I'm of Stafford."

"Even you see London as a place of sin," said Bunyan. "You have children?"

"I have two, by second wife," said Walton. "Seven others died in infancy."

"I have four," Bunyan said. "One born blind." His eyes took on a faraway look. "I want them to fear God, in hope of eternal salvation."

"As do we all," said Walton.

"And this monster is warning to mankind of the coming rains of blood and fire and the fall of stars."

"Either we shall take it, or the townsmen will come tomorrow."

"I know them all," said Bunyan. "Mr. Nurse-nickel, Mr. By-your-Leave, Mr. Cravenly-Crafty. Do ye not feel your spirits lag, your backbone fail? They'll not last long as you have."

Walton had noticed his own lassitude, even with the stink of the slough goading him. Cotton, Percy and Marburton, finished with the cart, were sitting disconsolately on the ground. The swamp had brightened some; the blazing blue mountain ahead seemed inches away. But the woods were dark, the defile precipitous, the noises loud as before.

"It gets worse after dark," said the preacher. "I beg you, take not the fish."

"If you stop the sheriff, he'll have you in prison."

"It's prison from which I come," said Bunyan. "To jail I shall go back, for I know I'm right."

"Do your conscience," said Walton, "for that way lies salvation."

"Amen!" said Bunyan, and went back to his pots.

Percy, Marburton, and Charles Cotton watched as Walton set up his tackle. Even with flagging spirits, they were intrigued. He'd had the carters peg down the trace poles of the wagon. Then he sectioned together a rod like none they had seen before. It was barely nine feet long, starting big as a smith's biceps, ending in a fine end. It was made of many split laths glued seamlessly together. On each foot of its length past the handle were iron guides bound with wire. There was a hole in the handle of the rod, and now Walton reached in the wagon and took out a shining metal wheel.

"What's that, a squirrel cage?" asked Percy.

They saw him pull line out from it. It clicked with each turn. There was a handle on the wheel, and a peg at the bottom. He put the peg through the hole in the handle and fastened it down with an iron screw.

He threaded the line, which was thick as a pen quill, through the guides, opened the black case, and took out the largest of the hooks he'd fashioned.

On the line he tied a strong wire chain, and affixed a sinker to one end and the hook on the other.

He put the rod in the wagon seat and climbed down to the back and opened his bait box and reached in.

"Come, my pretty," he said, reaching. He took something out, white, segmented, moving. It filled his hand.

It was a maggot that weighed half a pound.

"I had them kept down a cistern behind a shambles," said Walton. He lifted the bait to show them. "Charles, take my line after I bait the angle; make a handcast into the edge of those stumps yonder. As I was saying, take your gentles, put them in a cool well, feed them on liver or pork for the summer. They'll eat and grow and not change into flies, for the changing of one so large kills it. Keep them well fed; put them into wet moss before using them. I feared the commotion and flames had collapsed the well. Though the butcher shop was gone, the baits were still fat and lively."

As he said the last word, he plunged the hook through the white flesh of the maggot.

It twisted and oozed onto his hand. He opened a small bottle. "And dowse it with camphire oil just before the cast." They smelled the pungent liquid as he poured it. The bait went into a frenzy.

"Now, Charles," he said, pulling off fifty feet of line from the reel. Cotton whirled the weighted hook around and around his head. "Be so kind as to tie this rope to my belt and the cart, Percy," said Walton.

Percy did so. Cotton made the hand-cast, the pale globule hitting the water and sinking.

"Do as I have told you," said Walton, "and you shall not fail to catch the biggest fish."

Something large between the eyes swallowed the hook and five feet of line.

"And set the hook sharply, and you shall have great sport." Walton, seventy years old, thin of build, stood in the seat, jerked far back over his head, curving the rod in a loop.

The waters of the slough exploded, they saw the shallow bottom and a long dark shape, and the fight was on.

The preacher stood up from his pots, opened his clasp Bible, and began to preach in a loud strong voice.

"Render to Caesar," he said: Walton flinched and put his back into turning the fish, which was heading toward the stumps. The reel's clicks were a buzz. Bunyan raised his voice: "Those things which are Caesar's, and to God those things which are God's."

"Oh, shut up!" said Cotton. "The man's got trouble enough!"

The wagon creaked and began to lift off the ground. The rope and belt cut into Walton's flesh. His arms were nearly pulled from their sockets. Sweat sprang to his forehead like curds through a cheesecloth. He gritted his teeth and pulled.

The pegs lifted from the ground.

Bunyan preached on.

The sunlight faded, though it was late afternoon. The noise from the woods grew louder. The blue hills in the distance became flat, gray. The whole valley leaned over them, threatening to fall over and kill them. Eyes shined in the deeper woods.

Walton had regained some line in the last few hours. Bunyan preached on, pausing long enough to light a horn lantern from his fire.

After encouraging Walton at first, Percy, Marburton and Cotton had become quiet. The sounds were those of Bunyan's droning voice, screams from the woods, small pops from the fire, and the ratcheting of the reel.

The fish was fighting him on the bottom. He'd had no sight of it yet since the strike. Now the water was becoming a flat black sheet in the failing light. It was no salmon or trout or carp. It must be a pike or eel or some other toothed fish. Or a serpent. Or cuttlefish, with squiddy arms to tear the skin from a man.

Walton shivered. His arms were numb, his shoulders a tight aching band. His legs where he braced against the footrest quivered with fatigue. Still he held, even when the fish ran to the far end of the swamp. If he could keep it away from the snags, he could wear it down. The fish turned, the line slackened, Walton pumped the rod up and down. He regained the lost line. The water hissed as the cording cut through it. The fish headed for the bottom.

Tiredly, Walton heaved, turned the fish. The wagon creaked.

"Blessed are they that walk in the path of righteousness," said Bunyan.

The ghosts came in over the slough straight at them. Monkey-demons began to chatter in the woods. Eyes peered from the bole of every tree. Bunyan's candle was the only light. Something walked heavily on a limb at the woods' edge, bending it. Marburton screamed and ran up the road.

Percy was on his feet. Ghosts and banshees flew at him, veering away at the last instant.

"You have doubts," said Bunyan to him. "You are assailed. You think yourself unworthy."

Percy trotted up the stony road, ragged shapes fluttering in the air behind him, trying to tug his hair. Skeletons began to dance across the slough, acting out pantomimes of life, death, and love. The Seven Deadly Sins manifested themselves.

Hell yawned opened to receive them all.

Then the sun went down.

"Before you join the others, Charles," said Walton, pumping the rod, "cut away my coat and collar."

"You'll freeze," said Cotton, but climbed into the wagon and cut the coat up the back and down the sleeves. It and the collar fell away.

"Good luck, Father Walton," he said. Something plucked at his eyes. "We go to town for help."

"Be honest and trustworthy all the rest of your days," said Izaak Walton. Cotton looked stunned. Something large ran down from the woods, through the wagon, and up into the trees. Cotton ran up the hill. The thing loped after him.

Walton managed to gain six inches on the fish.

Grinning things sat on the taut line. The air was filled with meteors: burning, red, thick as snow. Huge worms pushed themselves out of the ground, caught and ate demons, then turned inside out. The demons flew away.

Everything in the darkness had claws and horns.

"And lo! the seventh seal was broken, and there was quietness on the earth for the space of half an hour," read Bunyan.

He had lit his third candle.

Walton could see the water again. A little light came from somewhere behind him. The noises of the woods diminished. A desultory ghost or skeleton flitted grayly by. There was a calm in the air.

The fish was tiring. Walton did not know how long he had fought on, or with what power. He was a human ache, and he wanted to sleep. He was nodding.

"The townsmen come," said Bunyan. Walton stole a fleeting glance behind him. Hundreds of people came quietly and cautiously through the woods, some extinguishing torches as he watched.

Walton cranked in another ten feet of line. The fish ran, but only a short way, slowly, and Walton reeled him back. It was still a long way out, still another hour before he could bring it to gaff. Walton heard low talk, recognized Percy's voice. He looked back again. The people had pikes, nets, a small cannon. He turned, reeled the fish, fighting it all the way.

"You do not love God!" said Bunyan suddenly, shutting his Bible.

"Yes I do!" said Walton, pulling as hard as he could. He gained another foot. "I love God as much as you."

"You do not!" said Bunyan. "I see it now."

"I love God!" yelled Walton and heaved the rod.

A fin broke the frothing water.

"In your heart, where God can see from his high throne, you lie!" said Bunyan.

Walton reeled and pulled. More fin showed. He quit cranking.

"God forgive me!" said Walton. "It's fishing I love."

"I thought so," said Bunyan. Reaching in his pack, he took out a pair of tin snips and cut Walton's line.

Izaak fell back in the wagon.

"John Bunyan, you son of a bitch!" said the sheriff. "You're under arrest for hampering the King's business. I'll see you rot."

Walton watched the coils of line on the surface slowly sink into the brown depths of the Slough of Despond.

He began to cry, fatigue and numbness taking over his body.

"I denied God," he said to Cotton. "I committed the worst sin." Cotton covered him with a blanket.

"Oh, Charles, I denied God."

"What's worse," said Cotton, "you lost the fish."

Percy and Marburton helped him up. The carters hitched the wagons, the horses now docile. Bunyan was being ridden back to jail by constables, his tinker's bag clanging against the horse's side.

They put the crying Walton into the cart, covered him more, climbed in. Some farmers helped them get the carts over the rocks.

Walton's last view of the slough was of resolute and grim-faced men staring at the water and readying their huge grapples, their guns, their cruel hooked nets.

They were on the road back to town. Walton looked up into the trees, devoid of ghosts and demons. He caught a glimpse of the blue Chiltern Hills.

"Father Izaak," said Cotton. "Rest now. Think of spring. Think of clear water, of leaping trout."

"My dreams will be haunted by God the rest of my days," he said tiredly. Walton fell asleep.

He dreamed of clear water, leaping trouts.

This story is for Chad Oliver, Punisher of Trouts.

STUBB KILLS A WHALE

HERMAN MELVILLE

If to Starbuck the apparition of the Squid was a thing of portents, to Queequeg it was quite a different object.

"When you see him 'quid," said the savage, honing his harpoon in the bow of his hoisted boat, "then you quick see him 'parm whale."

The next day was exceedingly still and sultry, and with nothing special to engage them, the Pequod's crew could hardly resist the spell of sleep induced by such a vacant sea. For this part of the Indian Ocean through which we then were voyaging is not what whalemen call a lively ground; that is, it affords fewer glimpses of porpoises, dolphins, flying-fish, and other vivacious denizens of more stirring waters, than those off the Rio de la Plata, or the in-shore ground off Peru.

It was my turn to stand at the foremast-head; and with my shoulders leaning against the slackened royal shrouds, to and fro I idly swayed in what seemed an enchanted air. No resolution could withstand it; in that dreamy mood losing all consciousness, at last my soul went out of my body; though my body still continued to sway as a pendulum will, long after the power which first moved it is withdrawn.

Ere forgetfulness altogether came over me, I had noticed that the seamen at the main and mizen mast-heads were already drowsy. So that at last all three of us lifelessly swung from the spars, and for every swing that we made there was a nod from below from the slumbering helmsman. The waves, too, nodded their indolent crests; and across the wide trance of the sea, east nodded to west, and the sun over all.

Suddenly bubbles seemed bursting beneath my closed eyes; like vices my hands grasped the shrouds; some invisible, gracious agency preserved me; with a shock I came back to life. And lo! close under our lee, not forty fathoms off, a gigantic Sperm Whale lay rolling in the water like the capsized hull of a frigate, his broad, glossy back, of an Ethiopian hue, glistening in the sun's rays like a mirror. But lazily undulating in the trough of the sea, and ever and anon tranquilly sprouting his vapory jet, the whale looked like a portly burgher smoking his pipe of a warm afternoon. But that pipe, poor whale, was thy last. As if struck by some enchanter's wand, the sleepy ship and every sleeper in it all at once started into wakefulness; and more than a score of voices from all parts of the vessel, simultaneously with the three notes from aloft, shouted forth the accustomed cry, as the great fish slowly and regularly spouted the sparkling brine into the air.

"Clear away the boats! Luff!" cried Ahab. And obeying his own order, he dashed the helm down before the helmsman could handle the spokes.

The sudden exclamations of the crew must have alarmed the whale; and ere the boats were down, majestically turning, he swam away to the leeward, but with such a steady tranquility, and making so few ripples as he swam, that thinking after all he might not as yet be alarmed, Ahab gave orders that not an oar should be used, and no man must speak but in whispers. So seated like Ontario Indians on the gunwales of the boats, we swiftly but silently paddled along; the calm not admitting of the noiseless sails being set. Presently, as we thus glided in chase, the monster perpendicularly flitted his tail forty feet into the air, and then sank out of sight like a tower swallowed up.

"There go flukes!" was the cry, an announcement immediately followed by Stubb's producing his match and igniting his pipe, for now a respite was granted. After the full interval of his sounding had elapsed, the whale rose again, and being now in advance of the smoker's boat, and much nearer to it than to any of the others, Stubb counted upon the honor of the capture. It was obvious, now, that the whale had at length become aware of his pursuers. All silence of cautiousness was therefore no longer of use. Paddles were dropped, and oars came loudly into play. And still puffing at his pipe, Stubb cheered on his crew to the assault.

Yes, a mighty change had come over the fish. All alive to his jeopardy, he was going "head out"; that part obliquely projecting from the mad yeast which he brewed.

"Start her, start her, my men! Don't hurry yourselves; take plenty of time—but start her; start her like thunder-claps, that's all," cried Stubb, spluttering out the smoke as he spoke. "Start her, now; give 'em the long and strong stroke, Tashtego. Start her, Tash, my boy—start her, all; but keep cool, keep cool—cucumbers is the word—easy, easy —only start her like grim death and grinning devils, and raise the buried dead perpendicular out of their graves, boys—that's all. Start her!"

"Woo-hoo! Wa-hee!" screamed the Gay-Header in reply, raising some old war-whoop to the skies; as every oarsman in the strained boat involuntarily bounced forward with the one tremendous leading stroke which the eager Indian gave.

But his wild screams were answered by others quite as wild. "Kee-hee! Kee-hee!" yelled Daggoo, straining forwards and backwards on his seat, like a pacing tiger in his cage.

"Ka-la! Koo-loo!" howled Queequeg, as if smacking his lips over a mouthful of Grenadier's steak. And thus with oars and yells the keels cut the sea. Meanwhile, Stubb retaining his place in the van, still encouraged his men to the onset, all the while puffing the smoke from his mouth. Like desperadoes they tugged and they strained, till the welcome cry was heard—"Stand up, Tashtego!—give it to him!" The harpoon was hurled. "Stern all!" The oarsmen backed water; the same moment something went hot and hissing along every one of their wrists. It was the magical line. An instant before, Stubb had swiftly caught two additional turns with it round the loggerhead, whence, by reason of its increased rapid circlings, a hempen blue smoke now jetted up and mingled with the steady fumes from his pipe. As the line passed round and round the loggerhead; so also, just before reaching that point, it blisteringly passed through and through both of Stubb's hands, from which the hand-cloths, or squares of quilted canvas some-times worn at these times, had accidentally dropped. It was like hold-ing an enemy's sharp two-edged sword by the blade, and that enemy all the time striving to wrest it out of your clutch.

"Wet the line! wet the line!" cried Stubb to the tub oarsman (him seated by the tub) who, snatching off his hat, dashed the sea-water into it. More turns were taken, so that the line began holding its place. The boat now flew through the boiling water like a shark all fins. Stubb and Tashtego here changed places—stem for stern—a staggering business truly in that rocking commotion.

From the vibrating line extending the entire length of the upper part of the boat, and from its now being more tight than a harpstring, you would have thought the craft had two keels—one cleaving the water, the other the air—as the boat churned on through both opposing ele-ments at once. A continual cascade played at the bows; a ceaseless whirling eddy in her wake; and, at the slightest motion from within, even but of a little finger, the vibrating, cracking craft canted over her spasmodic gunwale into the sea. Thus they rushed; each man with might and main clinging to his seat, to prevent being tossed to the foam; and the tall form of Tashtego at the steering oar crouching almost double, in order to bring down his centre of gravity. Whole Atlantics and Pacifics seemed passed as they shot on their way, till at length the whale somewhat slackened his flight.

"Haul in—haul in!" cried Stubb to the bowsman! and, facing round towards the whale, all hands began pulling the boat up to him, while yet the boat was being towed on. Soon ranging up by his flank, Stubb, firmly planting his knee in the clumsy cleat, darted dart after dart into the flying fish; at the word of command, the boat alternately sterning out of the way of the whale's horrible wallow, and then ranging up for another fling.

The red tide now poured from all sides of the monster like brooks down a hill. His tormented body rolled not in brine but in blood, which bubbled and seethed for furlongs behind in their wake. The slanting sun playing upon this crimson pond in the sea, sent back its reflection into every face, so that they all glowed to each other like red men. And all the while, jet after jet of white smoke was agonizingly shot from the spiracle of the whale, and vehement puff after puff from the mouth of the excited headsman; as at every dart, hauling in upon his crooked lance (by the line attached to it), Stubb straightened it again and again, by a few rapid blows against the gunwale, then again and again sent it into the whale.

"Pull up—pull up!" he now cried to the bowsman, as the waning whale relaxed in his wrath. "Pull up!—close to!" and the boat ranged along the fish's flank. When reaching far over the bow, Stubb slowly churned his long sharp lance into the fish, and kept it there, carefully churning and churning, as if cautiously seeking to feel after some gold watch that the whale might have swallowed, and which he was fearful of breaking ere he could hook it out. But that gold watch he sought was the innermost life of the fish. And now it is struck; for, starting from his trance into that unspeakable thing called his "flurry," the monster horribly wallowed in his blood, over-wrapped himself in impenetrable, mad, boiling spray, so that the imperilled craft, instantly dropping astern, had much ado blindly to struggle out from that phrensied twilight into the clear air of the day.

And now abating in his flurry, the whale once more rolled out into view; surging from side to side; spasmodically dilating and contracting his spout-hole, with sharp, cracking, agonizing respirations. At last, gush after gush of clotted red gore, as if it had been the purple lees of red wine, shot into the frighted air; and falling back again, ran dripping down his motionless flanks into the sea. His heart had burst!

"He's dead, Mr. Stubb," said Daggoo.

"Yes; both pipes smoked out!" and withdrawing his own from his mouth, Stubb scattered the dead ashes over the water; and, for a moment, stood thoughtfully eyeing the vast corpse he had made.

THE SEA DEVIL

ARTHUR GORDON

The man came out of the house and stood quite still, listening. Behind him, the lights glowed in the cheerful room, the books were neat and orderly in their cases, the radio talked importantly to itself. In front of him, the bay stretched dark and silent, one of the countless lagoons that border the coast where Florida thrusts its great green thumb deep into the tropics.

It was late in September. The night was breathless; summer's dead hand still lay heavy on the land. The man moved forward six paces and stood on the sea wall. He dropped his cigarette and noted where the tiny spark hissed and went out. The tide was beginning to ebb.

Somewhere out in the blackness a mullet jumped and fell back with a sullen splash. Heavy with roe, they were jumping less often, now. They would not take a hook, but a practiced eye could see the swirls they made in the glassy water. In the dark of the moon, a skilled man with a cast net might take half a dozen in an hour's work. And a big mullet makes a meal for a family.

The man turned abruptly and went into the garage, where his cast net hung. He was in his late twenties, wide-shouldered and strong. He did not have to fish for a living, or even for food. He was a man who worked with his head, not with his hands. But he liked to go casting alone at night.

He liked the loneliness and the labor of it. He liked the clean taste of salt when he gripped the edge of the net with his teeth as a cast netter must. He liked the arching flight of sixteen pounds of lead and linen against the starlight, and the weltering crash of the net into the unsuspecting water. He liked the harsh tug of the retrieving rope around his wrist, and the way the net came alive when the cast was true, and the thud of captured fish on the floor boards of the skiff.

He liked all that because he found in it a reality that seemed to be missing from his twentieth-century job and from his daily life. He liked being the hunter, skilled and solitary and elemental. There was no conscious cruelty in the way he felt. It was the way things had been in the beginning.

The man lifted the net down carefully and lowered it into a bucket. He put a paddle beside the bucket. Then he went into the house. When he came out, he was wearing swimming trunks and a pair of old tennis shoes. Nothing else.

The skiff, flat-bottomed, was moored off the sea wall. He would not go far, he told himself. Just to the tumbledown dock half a mile away. Mullet had a way of feeding around old pilings after dark. If he moved quietly, he might pick up two or three in one cast close to the dock. And maybe a couple of others on the way down or back.

He shoved off and stood motionless for a moment, letting his eyes grow accustomed to the dark. Somewhere out in the channel a porpoise blew with a sound like steam escaping. The man smiled a little; porpoises were his friends. Once, fishing in the Gulf, he had seen the charter-boat captain reach overside and gaff a baby porpoise through the sinewy part of the tail. He had hoisted it aboard, had dropped it into the bait well, where it thrashed around, puzzled and unhappy. And the mother had swum alongside the boat and under the boat and around the boat, nudging the stout planking with her back, slapping it with her tail, until the man felt sorry for her and made the captain let the baby porpoise go.

He took the net from the bucket, slipped the noose in the retrieving rope over his wrist, pulled the slipknot tight. It was an old net, but still serviceable; he had rewoven the rents made by underwater snags. He coiled the thirty-foot rope carefully, making sure there were no kinks. A tangled rope, he knew, would spoil any cast.

The basic design of the net had not changed in three thousand years. It was a mesh circle with a diameter of fourteen feet. It measured close to fifteen yards around the circumference and could, if thrown perfectly, blanket a hundred and fifty square feet of sea water. In the center of this radial trap was a small iron collar where the retrieving rope met the twenty-three separate drawstrings leading to the outer rim of the net. Along this rim, spaced an inch and a half apart, were the heavy lead sinkers.

The man raised the iron collar until it was a foot above his head. The net hung soft and pliant and deadly. He shook it gently, making sure that the drawstrings were not tangled, that the sinkers were hanging true. Then he eased it down and picked up the paddle.

The night was black as a witch's cat; the stars looked fuzzy and dim. Down to the southward, the lights of a causeway made a yellow necklace across the sky. To the man's left were the tangled roots of a mangrove swamp; to his right, the open waters of the bay. Most of it was fairly shallow, but there were channels eight feet deep. The man could not see the old dock, but he knew where it was. He pulled the paddle quietly through the water, and the phosphorescence glowed and died.

For five minutes he paddled. Then, twenty feet ahead of the skiff, a mullet jumped. A big fish, close to three pounds. For a moment it hung in the still air, gleaming dully. Then it vanished. But the ripples marked the spot, and where there was one there were often others.

The man stood up quickly. He picked up the coiled rope, and with the same hand grasped the net at a point four feet below the iron collar. He raised the skirt to his mouth, gripped it strongly with his teeth. He slid his free hand as far as it would go down the circumference of the net so that he had three points of contact with the mass of cordage and metal. He made sure his feet were planted solidly. Then he waited, feeling the tension that is older than the human race, the fierce exhilaration of the hunter at the moment of ambush, the atavistic desire to capture and kill and ultimately consume.

A mullet swirled, ahead and to the left. The man swung the heavy net back, twisting his body and bending his knees so as to get more upward thrust. He shot it forward, letting go simultaneously with rope hand and with teeth, holding a fraction of a second longer with the other hand so as to give the net the necessary spin, impart the centrifugal force that would make it flare into a circle. The skiff ducked sideways, but he kept his balance. The net fell with a splash.

The man waited for five seconds. Then he began to retrieve it, pulling in a series of sharp jerks so that the drawstrings would gather the net inward, like a giant fist closing on this segment of the teeming sea. He felt the net quiver, and knew it was not empty. He swung it, dripping, over the gunwale, saw the broad silver side of the mullet quivering, saw too the gleam of a smaller fish. He looked closely to make sure no sting ray was hidden in the mesh, then raised the iron collar and shook the net out. The mullet fell with a thud and flapped wildly. The other victim was an angel fish, beautifully marked, but too small to keep. The man picked it up gently and dropped it overboard. He coiled the rope, took up the paddle. He would cast no more until he came to the dock.

The skiff moved on. At last, ten feet apart, a pair of stakes rose up

gauntly out of the night. Barnacle encrusted, they once had marked
the approach from the main channel. The man guided the skiff between them, then put the paddle down softly. He stood up, reached for
the net, tightened the noose around his wrist. From here he could drift
down upon the dock. He could see it now, a ruined skeleton in the
starshine. Beyond it a mullet jumped and fell back with a flat, liquid
sound. The man raised the edge of the net, put it between his teeth. He
would not cast at a single swirl, he decided; he would wait until he saw
two or three close together. The skiff was barely moving. He felt his
muscles tense themselves, awaiting the signal from the brain.

Behind him in the channel he heard the porpoise blow again, nearer
now. He frowned in the darkness. If the porpoise chose to fish this
area, the mullet would scatter and vanish. There was no time to lose.

A school of sardines surfaced suddenly, skittering along like drops
of mercury. Something, perhaps the shadow of the skiff, had frightened them. The old dock loomed very close. A mullet broke water just
too far away; then another, nearer. The man marked the spreading
ripples and decided to wait no longer.

He swung back the net, heavier now that it was wet. He had to turn
his head, but out of the corner of his eye he saw two swirls in the black
water just off the starboard bow. They were about eight feet apart, and
they had the sluggish oily look that marks the presence of something
big just below the surface. His conscious mind had no time to function, but instinct told him that the net was wide enough to cover both
swirls if he could alter the direction of his cast. He could not halt the
swing, but he shifted his feet slightly and made the cast off balance. He
saw the net shoot forward, flare into an oval, and drop just where he
wanted it.

Then the sea exploded in his face. In a frenzy of spray, a great
horned thing shot like a huge bat out of the water. The man saw the
mesh of his net etched against the mottled blackness of its body and he
knew, in the split second in which thought was still possible, that those
twin swirls had been made not by two mullet, but by the wing tips of
the giant ray of the Gulf Coast, *Manta birostris,* also known as clam
cracker, devil ray, sea devil.

The man gave a hoarse cry. He tried to claw the slipknot off his
wrist, but there was no time. The quarter-inch line snapped taut. He
shot over the side of the skiff as if he had roped a runaway locomotive.
He hit the water head first and seemed to bounce once. He plowed a
blinding furrow for perhaps ten yards. Then the line went slack as the
sea devil jumped again. It was not the full-grown manta of the deep
Gulf, but it was close to nine feet from tip to tip and it weighed over a
thousand pounds. Up into the air it went, pearl-colored underbelly

gleaming as it twisted in a frantic effort to dislodge the clinging thing that had fallen upon it. Up into the starlight, a monstrous survival from the dawn of time.

The water was less than four feet deep. Sobbing and choking, the man struggled for a foothold on the slimy bottom. Sucking in great gulps of air, he fought to free himself from the rope. But the slipknot was jammed deep into his wrist; he might as well have tried to loosen a circle of steel.

The ray came down with a thunderous splash and drove forward again. The flexible net followed every movement, impeding it hardly at all. The man weighed a hundred and seventy-five pounds, and he was braced for the shock, and he had the desperate strength that comes from looking into the blank eyes of death. It was useless. His arm straightened out with a jerk that seemed to dislocate his shoulder; his feet shot out from under him; his head went under again. Now at last he knew how the fish must feel when the line tightens and drags him toward the alien element that is his doom. Now he knew.

Desperately he dug the fingers of his free hand into the ooze, felt them dredge a futile channel through broken shells and the ribbonlike sea grasses. He tried to raise his head, but could not get it clear. Torrents of spray choked him as the ray plunged toward deep water.

His eyes were of no use to him in the foam-streaked blackness. He closed them tight, and at once an insane sequence of pictures flashed through his mind. He saw his wife sitting in their living room, reading, waiting calmly for his return. He saw the mullet he had just caught, gasping its life away on the floor boards of the skiff. He saw the cigarette he had flung from the sea wall touch the water and expire with a tiny hiss. He saw all these things and many others simultaneously in his mind as his body fought silently and tenaciously for its existence. His hand touched something hard and closed on it in a death grip, but it was only the sharp-edged helmet of a horseshoe crab, and after an instant he let it go.

He had been under water perhaps fifteen seconds now, and something in his brain told him quite calmly that he could last another forty or fifty and then the red flashes behind his eyes would merge into darkness, and the water would pour into his lungs in one sharp painful shock, and he would be finished.

This thought spurred him to a desperate effort. He reached up and caught his pinioned wrist with his free hand. He doubled up his knees to create more drag. He thrashed his body madly, like a fighting fish, from side to side. This did not disturb the ray, but now one of the great wings tore through the mesh, and the net slipped lower over the fins projecting like horns from below the nightmare head, and the sea devil jumped again.

And once more the man was able to get his feet on the bottom and his head above water, and he saw ahead of him the pair of ancient stakes that marked the approach to the channel. He knew that if he was dragged much beyond those stakes he would be in eight feet of water, and the ray would go down to hug the bottom as rays always do, and then no power on earth could save him. So in the moment of respite that was granted him, he flung himself toward them.

For a moment he thought his captor yielded a bit. Then the ray moved off again, but more slowly now, and for a few yards the man was able to keep his feet on the bottom. Twice he hurled himself back against the rope with all his strength, hoping that something would break. But nothing broke. The mesh of the net was ripped and torn, but the draw lines were strong, and the stout perimeter cord threaded through the sinkers was even stronger.

The man could feel nothing now in his trapped hand, it was numb; but the ray could feel the powerful lunges of the unknown thing that was trying to restrain it. It drove its great wings against the unyielding water and forged ahead, dragging the man and pushing a sullen wave in front of it.

The man had swung as far as he could toward the stakes. He plunged toward one and missed it by inches. His feet slipped and he went down on his knees. Then the ray swerved sharply and the second stake came right at him. He reached out with his free hand and caught it.

He caught it just above the surface, six or eight inches below high-water mark. He felt the razor-sharp barnacles bite into his hand, collapse under the pressure, drive their tiny slime-covered shell splinters deep into his flesh. He felt the pain, and he welcomed it, and he made his fingers into an iron claw that would hold until the tendons were severed or the skin was shredded from the bone. The ray felt the pressure increase with a jerk that stopped it dead in the water. For a moment all was still as the tremendous forces came into equilibrium.

Then the net slipped again, and the perimeter cord came down over the sea devil's eyes, blinding it momentarily. The great ray settled to the bottom and braced its wings against the mud and hurled itself forward and upward.

The stake was only a four-by-four of creosoted pine, and it was old. Ten thousand tides had swirled around it. Worms had bored; parasites had clung. Under the crust of barnacles it still had some heart left, but not enough. The man's grip was five feet above the floor of the bay; the leverage was too great. The stake snapped off at its base.

The ray lunged upward, dragging the man and the useless timber. The man had his lungs full of air, but when the stake snapped he thought of expelling the air and inhaling the water so as to have it finished quickly. He thought of this, but he did not do it. And then, just at the channel's edge, the ray met the porpoise, coming in.

The porpoise had fed well this night and was in no hurry, but it was a methodical creature and it intended to make a sweep around the old dock before the tide dropped too low. It had no quarrel with any ray, but it feared no fish in the sea, and when the great black shadow came rushing blindly and unavoidably, it rolled fast and struck once with its massive horizontal tail.

The blow descended on the ray's flat body with a sound like a pistol shot. It would have broken a buffalo's back, and even the sea devil was half stunned. It veered wildly and turned back toward shallow water. It passed within ten feet of the man, face down in the water. It slowed and almost stopped, wing tips moving faintly, gathering strength for another rush.

The man had heard the tremendous slap of the great mammal's tail and the snorting gasp as it plunged away. He felt the line go slack again, and he raised his dripping face, and he reached for the bottom with his feet. He found it, but now the water was up to his neck. He plucked at the noose once more with his lacerated hand, but there was no strength in his fingers. He felt the tension come back into the line as the ray began to move again, and for half a second he was tempted to throw himself backward and fight as he had been doing, pitting his strength against the vastly superior strength of the brute.

But the acceptance of imminent death had done something to his brain. It had driven out the fear, and with the fear had gone the panic. He could think now, and he knew with absolute certainty that if he was to make any use of this last chance that had been given him, it would have to be based on the one faculty that had carried man to his pre-eminence above all beasts, the faculty of reason. Only by using his brain could he possibly survive, and he called on his brain for a solution, and his brain responded. It offered him one.

He did not know whether his body still had the strength to carry out the brain's commands, but he began to swim forward, toward the ray that was still moving hesitantly away from the channel. He swam forward, feeling the rope go slack as he gained on the creature.

Ahead of him he saw the one remaining stake, and he made himself swim faster until he was parallel with the ray and the rope trailed behind both of them in a deep U. He swam with a surge of desperate energy that came from nowhere so that he was slightly in the lead as they came to the stake. He passed on one side of it; the ray was on the other.

Then the man took one last deep breath, and he went down under the black water until he was sitting on the bottom of the bay. He put one foot over the line so that it passed under his bent knee. He drove both his heels into the mud, and he clutched the slimy grass with his bleeding hand, and he waited for the tension to come again.

The ray passed on the other side of the stake, moving faster now. The rope grew taut again, and it began to drag the man back toward the stake. He held his prisoned wrist close to the bottom, under his knee, and he prayed that the stake would not break. He felt the rope vibrate as the barnacles bit into it. He did not know whether the rope would crush the barnacles, or whether the barnacles would cut the rope. All he knew was that in five seconds or less he would be dragged into the stake and cut to ribbons if he tried to hold on; or drowned if he didn't.

He felt himself sliding slowly, and then faster, and suddenly the ray made a great leap forward, and the rope burned around the base of the stake, and the man's foot hit it hard. He kicked himself backward with his remaining strength, and the rope parted, and he was free.

He came slowly to the surface. Thirty feet away the sea devil made one tremendous leap and disappeared into the darkness. The man raised his wrist and looked at the frayed length of rope dangling from it. Twenty inches, perhaps. He lifted his other hand and felt the hot blood start instantly, but he didn't care. He put his hand on the stake above the barnacles and held on to the good rough honest wood. He heard a strange noise, and realized that it was himself, sobbing.

High above, there was a droning sound, and looking up he saw the nightly plane from New Orleans inbound for Tampa. Calm and serene, it sailed, symbol of man's proud mastery over nature. Its lights winked red and green for a moment; then it was gone.

Slowly, painfully, the man began to move through the placid water. He came to the skiff at last and climbed into it. The mullet, still alive, slapped convulsively with its tail. The man reached down with his torn hand, picked up the mullet, let it go.

He began to work on the slipknot doggedly with his teeth. His mind was almost a blank, but not quite. He knew one thing. He knew he would do no more casting alone at night. Not in the dark of the moon. No, not he.

SPARE THE ROD

PHILIP WYLIE

The eyes of Dexter Heath were the most remarkable feature in a rather dashing ensemble—gray eyes, round, penetrating and vigilant. Next was his hair, which was dark and curly, but curly without pattern, and incredibly unkempt; his hair was like a distant view of some irregular object foundering in a stormy sea. The rest of him was normal for a boy of eleven—snub nose, a voice that was invariably an exclamation, although sometimes hushed, and, under his sun-tanned skin, young muscles of which he was proud to the point of racy braggadocio.

On a late summer afternoon, Crunch Adams, coming down the Gulf Stream Dock to minister to his fishing cruiser, was struck by the posture and attitude of Dexter. Balanced on a rail at the end of the dock, with his chin in his hand, the young man was staring ferociously at the universe, not seeing it, but not liking it, either. Crunch pondered the spectacle of fury in equilibrium for a moment, and then, with a grin, interrupted it.

"What's eating you, Dexter?"

The young man budged a little, put down a tentative foot, and looked at the captain. All traces of wrath had been erased by those slight movements. He seemed calm—even bored. "Nothing," he replied. "Nothing."

Crunch persisted. "Don't kid me. If there had been a nail between your teeth, you'd have ground it to filings."

"I was just thinkin'," Dexter responded lazily. And, indeed, he began thinking. Hard. His broken reverie was not a subject he could discuss. There had been sadness in it, and frenzy at the injustice of the world. His mind had been clamorous with ideas which were antisocial, hostile, and, even, illegal. Dexter did not wish to have any of his secret thoughts heckled out of him. It was therefore necessary to dissemble. Earlier in the afternoon he had indulged in a different sort of day-dream. He recalled it and drew on it for material: "I was just thinkin' what if a brontosorassus came steamin' up the bay."

"A what?"

"Brontosorassus. Swimmin' like a submarine! Neck out. Fangs drip-pin' ooze! You couldn't hang him on any fifty-four-thread. But maybe you could hold him on three-hundred-thread. With a fifty-ought reel. You'd have to fight him night and day—for maybe a couple of weeks!"

"Oh," said Crunch. "A dinosaur." He was still grinning, but he fell in with Dexter's mood. He felt that he now understood the savagery which had been on the young man's face. "I guess you could never hang one. And you certainly couldn't boat an eighty-footer in a forty-foot cruiser."

"You could beach him," Dexter said, pleased at this attention from a great man and yielding his inner sorrow to imagination. "Maybe, if they were still plentiful, you'd have to keep a swassy-cans on the dock."

"Swassy-cans?"

"That's French," said the boy with some small condescension. "My father taught it to me. My father knows most languages, I guess. It's the French word for a seventy-five. A gun. You could have one right here—if you put some cement posts under the dock. Then—Wham! Whang! Zowie! Boy! You'd have to mount her like a antiaircraft gun, too, in case any of those big old peterodackles flew by. Wham! Whacko! Blow a wing off one and steam out and polish her off with a lance! Wham! Boom!"

Crunch chuckled. "Guess you're right. Too bad we didn't live in those days. There'd have been some real fishing, hunh?"

"Fishin'," said Dexter, "and huntin'!"

"Like to wet a line now? I mean—I've got a hand line on the *Posei-don*. And some bait. I'd be glad to rig it for you."

Dexter was grateful, but negative. "No, thanks. I don't care much for this old hand-line stuff. But if I ever had a harpoon in any big old brontosorassus . . ."

Crunch nodded and stepped aboard his boat. He had no precise recollection of his own age of dinosaur hunting, but he felt an indefi-nite kindredship for it. "Maybe," he said as he picked up a square of sandpaper and tore it into suitable sizes, "you'd like to go out with Des and me some day?"

Dexter's head moved forward from his shoulders and his brow puckered. "You mean you'd really take me out?"

Crunch set up a rasp and sizzle on the varnish. "Sure. Sometime. If I get a couple of nice customers who don't mind."

The young man gasped. Then he controlled himself. Life had taught him not to count too many unhatched chickens. "How soon—how soon—do you think you might possibly run across a couple of people like that?"

"Oh . . . soon," Crunch answered. "Any day."

Dexter had put in frequent appearances at the Gulf Stream Dock before Crunch had made that astonishing offer. But, thereafter, he was the most regular of all the juvenile buffs—boys who wistfully watched the boats go out and who, when the boats came in, identified various fish for less knowing adults, with a marked air of superiority. Dexter scrutinized every party that chartered the *Poseidon.* Sometimes he knew at a glance that the customers were not the sort who would care for an eleven-year-old supercargo. Sometimes he had great hopes. But no invitation was forthcoming.

The truth was that Crunch had forgotten the conversation. Small boys were ubiquitous, indistinguishable, and, on a busy fishing dock, often in the way. The *Poseidon's* skipper had noticed Dexter closely enough to like him—to be amused by him—and to make a suggestion which had dropped back into his unconscious mind. Dexter, however, was that rather common but always astounding combination of the dreamer and the man of action. His father, who knew all languages, had told him that one of the cardinal virtues was "initiative." He had explained the word. Dexter eventually enlarged upon its meaning.

In consequence, on one blue and golden morning when the *Poseidon's* outriggers were trailing balaos down the enameled sea, Crunch went below and was startled by the sight of two medium-sized shoes protruding from beneath a pile of pillows, blankets, canvas and gear on the starboard bunk. He grabbed one of the shoes and pulled forth Dexter.

The young man was alarmed, but in control of himself. "I had to do it!" he said. "You invited me! Besides—Mr. and Mrs. Winton fishing out there are two of the nicest people in Miami. My father said so. I heard them charter you last night—so I sneaked here early . . ."

Crunch remembered his offer, then. His first feeling for his stowaway was one of intense sympathy. Mr. and Mrs. Winton would be amused and pleased by the event. There was no doubt of that. But, on the other hand, it had been presumptive of the boy to steal a trip. Crunch had been rather harshly brought up; he felt that contemporary children were less disciplined and respectful than they should be. His

father would have given him a good licking for behavior like young
Mr. Heath's. Crunch weighed the situation. The corners of his mouth
twitched. He hid that reflex with his hand. Sternly, he eyed the boy. "I
suppose you realize that what you've done is a crime on the high
seas?"

"I just thought—since you'd asked me already—"

"If I had a brig," Crunch went on, "as captain, I could throw you in
it. All stowaways are condemned to hard labor. And bread and water—"

"I got my own lunch—right here!" Dexter produced from his
blouse a large and messy-looking sandwich which was inadequately
wrapped in newspaper. "And I'll be only too glad to work . . ."

Crunch nodded and cast his eye about. The *Poseidon* was spic and
span. "You'll go aloft," he said finally, "where my mate can keep his
eye on you. Here's a rag and a can of polish. You can shine all the
brass till it's too bright to look at. And you can also keep your eye on
the baits. If you see anything—don't scream. Just tell Des."

"Gee!" said Dexter. "Golly!" he added. "I was afraid you'd keep me
down here!"

Crunch motioned the boy up the companionway and into the cockpit, where the two Wintons regarded his appearance with moderate
surprise.

"This," said the captain, "is Dexter Heath. A stowaway. I'm putting him to work polishing brass."

Mr. Winton, who was a big man with white hair and a white mustache, burst into hearty laughter. His wife only smiled, and she regarded the boy's struggle of jubilance and discomfiture with a certain
tenderness. "I'm sure he didn't mean any harm, Crunch. How old are
you, son?"

"Eleven," Dexter replied.

"Do you like fishing?"

"My father," Dexter said uncompromisingly, "is the greatest fisherman in the world! Sometimes, he takes me. I will be nearly as good
when I get that old."

"Your father's a great fisherman," Mr. Winton mused. "Heath. I
don't think I've heard about him."

"You would," the boy said, "if—" He broke off. "You can stand a
hundred feet from my father and he can cast a plug into your pocket! I
guess he knows mostly where every fish lives in every canal in the
Glades. He hooked a water moccasin on a plug, once, and reeled it up
and killed it with a stick!"

Mr. Winton whistled and shook his head in awe. Crunch turned
away his face. "Go and polish that brass," he said.

Desperate received the newcomer placidly. Crunch had yelled up his name and the conditions of tolerance to be applied to him. The *Poseidon* sailed along. Dexter put elbow grease in his work and the results began to show. His eye attention, however, was largely for the baits. He labored for perhaps half an hour before he ventured any conversation. Des had been wondering just how long he would keep that humble silence.

"This is the Gulf Stream, isn't it?" the boy inquired.

Des nodded. "Right here, in this dark-blue water, it is. Over yonder, where the water is paler blue, it isn't. You can see the edge."

"Yeah," Dexter murmured. "Like two kinds of tile in a first-class bathroom."

Des pursed his lips, squinted judiciously at the boy, and nodded again. "If you look at that turning buoy out there, you'll see it has a wake behind it. Just as if it was being hauled through the water. But it's anchored. It's the Stream that makes the wake."

"Sure," the boy assented. "I can see it plain." And then, with every atom of his energy, every possible vibration of his vocal chords, he bellowed, "Marlin!"

Crunch dropped a bait and stared. Des whirled from the top controls. Mr. Winton sat up straight. His wife said, "Goodness! Where?"

Dexter was pointing with his polishing rag—pointing palely. His knees were knocking together a little. "Right out there!"

Some fifty feet behind Mr. Winton's bait there was, indeed, a fish. Its length lay yellow under the water. A fin stuck darkly from its back into the air. It was obviously following the bait—following it with a speed not greatly in excess of the *Poseidon*'s and with a peculiar wobbling motion, as if it swam in zigzags.

Crunch stepped toward the canopy and peered at his prisoner with annoyance. "I told you not to yell, Dexter. That's no marlin. It's a lousy hammerhead shark. Speed her up, Des, and we'll get away."

Dexter was not dashed. Instead, he seemed rather more interested. "A hammerhead shark!" he repeated. "A real, live one! Boy, look at her cut around that old bait!"

Des notched up the throttles. The shark began to lose the race.

"A real shark," Dexter went on excitedly. "A man-eater! And I saw it first!"

Then Mr. Winton spoke. Perhaps his words contained the whole truth. But perhaps he understood and shared the feelings of the boy. "What do you say we slow down and let him get the bait? The fishing's slow today, anyhow, and I need a workout. Helen's always telling me to take more exercise."

"Boy!" murmured Dexter, in a low tone, but one that held audible hope.

"If you want to do it . . ." said Crunch, who was not much on fighting hammerheads. Mako sharks, or whites, or threshers, were different. He waved Des to slow down.

Out beyond the *Poseidon*'s wake, the shark was plunging back and forth in an effort to pick up the scent of the bait. When Des slowed the boat, the shark got it, and came boiling through the sea. His ugly, scimitar-shaped foreface broke water as he engulfed the small fish. The line drifted down from the clothespin at the outrigger tip. Mr. Winton reeled until it was taut and he struck hard several times. The shark gradually became aware that there was a thorn in its jaws and a hampering line hitched to the thorn. First he swam off in a logy manner. Then he essayed a short run. After that, he went fast and far.

"I saw him swallow it!" Dexter kept saying.

Mr. Winton screwed up the drag on the side of his reel. The extra tension bent the rod in a bow. The reel kept humming.

"Like a big amberjack," Mrs. Winton said. "Only—not so fast."

"He's got about three hundred and fifty yards," her husband finally muttered. "That's a good deal."

Crunch grinned. "You asked for it."

Presently the run stopped. Hammerheads, as a rule, make one exciting and fairly fast run. After that they merely resist—lunging lazily, throwing their weight around, bracing dead against the angler's pull. They are not sporty fish. They do not jump. They lack flash and fire and heart. But any fish that weighs three or four hundred pounds provides a tussle on twenty-four-thread line.

Mr. Winton worked hard. It was a warm day. Perspiration ran from him. He called for a glass of water. He called for his sun helmet. He dried his slippery hands on his trousers. He rocked back in the fighting chair and winked up at Dexter, who was standing on the edge of the canopy with, as Mr. Winton later said, "his eyes popping and his tongue hanging out."

"I can see him!" the boy presently yelled. "He's turning over on his side!"

And so he was. A moment later, the shark quit. He came in without a struggle—so much dead weight pulled through the water like a boat on a painter. Crunch went to the stern. He picked up a long knife. Dexter was panting—as if he had manipulated the tackle through the whole fight. He saw Crunch grab the leader and shorten it. He saw him reach down to the water. Dexter held his breath. The skipper actually grabbed one of the hideous eye stalks in his bare hand. Then the muscles in his arms and the muscles along his back bulged, and hardened like rocks. He pulled the great fish—a fish which in that instant seemed bigger to Dexter than any "brontosorassus"—at least a third of its length out of water. He hooked one eye stalk over the gunwale and held the other while he plunged the knife deep into the white bellyside. "I hate sharks," he said coldly.

Dexter gasped. The shark trembled as the knife point found its heart. Blood poured from it. But, still calmly, Crunch put down the knife, picked up a pair of pliers, and went after the hook. The curved jaws snapped convulsively inches from the captain's hand. Nevertheless, he got the hook out with a quick, hard wrench, and he let the hammerhead slide back into the water. It sank, trailing crimson, stone dead.

Mr. Winton fanned himself with his helmet. "How'd you like it, son?"

Dexter swallowed. "Gee!" he murmured. "Imagine! Barehanded! I guess that's about the bravest thing I ever heard of."

Crunch laughed. "Nothing to it—if you know how to handle 'em."

"And," Mrs. Winton added, "if you're as strong as a derrick."

It had been a day for Dexter. A champion day. The fishing had not been much—two bonitos and a mackerel. But they had supplemented his sandwich lunch with a piece of chocolate cake, two pears, three hard-boiled eggs, some pickles and potato chips. They had forgotten, after the fight with the shark, that he was a prisoner. He'd been allowed to troll a feather on a casting rod for more than two hours. He hadn't had a strike, but that did not matter. He'd "fished the Stream." Not many kids could say that. He'd seen a big one take out line by the hundreds of yards. You could tell people that, without adding that the "big one" was just a shark.

As the *Poseidon* came in, the world seemed especially elegant to Dexter. The sun was going down in a yellow sky and the whole bay—the islands, the palms, the buildings, the lawns—was gleaming in amber opulence. It made reality theatrical, and only the sight of the Gulf Stream Dock brought the boy out of the mood. Then he became quiet. His thanks were effusive, but not as effusive as his day-long behavior had been. He apologized for stowing away. He went ashore rather solemnly. He had to get home for supper, he said.

"I like that kid," Mr. Winton chuckled.

His wife agreed. "He's marvelous. Who are his people?"

Crunch shrugged. "Darned if I know. I like him, too. He's here a lot. The fellows let him fish—and sometimes he makes a nickle running an errand. I think I heard somebody say that his mother is dead."

It was on the next morning that Des missed the rod. The casting rod with which Dexter had fished. But he didn't think of Dexter right away. "I put it in its regular place on the rack," he told Crunch. "I remember doing it. Who'd swipe that? If somebody wanted dough, why didn't they take an expensive outfit? I made that rod myself two years ago—and there were rods worth five times as much hanging there!"

Crunch did not think of Dexter, either. Not then.

They did when the skipper of the *Firefly* happened to say, "That kid you took out was down here looking for you fellows last night. At least, I think it was him. When I called to him, he beat it."

"Was he carrying a rod and reel?" Des asked.

"Couldn't say. He was maybe carrying something. Skulking along out of the range of the floodlights. You missing one?"

Neither Des nor Crunch replied to that. They went back to their boat. "I'd have bet a week's charter that kid wouldn't touch anything," Crunch said.

"I guess he didn't. At least, I hope he didn't. As far as that goes, the whole outfit wasn't worth more than twenty-five bucks. I can easily—"

"I don't like kids that steal," the captain interrupted angrily. "Still —what can we do? Ask him? Go to his house and ask his father? When you think how he'd feel if somebody else took the rod?"

There the matter dropped. Or, rather, it drifted. Dexter did not show up for three or four days, which was suspicious, but when he did put in an appearance he was as bland and poised as ever. They saw him often, after that. Sometimes he fished for snappers and grunts. Once he did a job of brass polishing on the *Firefly*. Two or three times he hosed down the *Merdora*. But neither Crunch nor Des were happy about the youngster. If he had taken the rod, something should be done about it. If he had not, they would have given a good deal to be certain of the fact. They discussed the situation occasionally, but to no purpose.

It was Desperate's idea to invite him to go fishing again.

"What'll that prove?" Crunch asked.

"I dunno. We'd get to know him better. Kids are funny. We might find that the rod came back all by itself—which would save us buying a new reel and line and me doing a lot of work. Or we might be able to ask him if he took it—and find out he didn't. Which would make me feel a lot better."

"Yeah," Crunch replied. "Me, too. And I'd also feel free to do a little snooping around the dock. There are four or five guys here dumb enough to think we might not recognize that rod if it was rewound and repainted."

"I haven't seen it yet, anyhow," Des said. "If I do! . . ."

"If you do," Crunch grinned, "let me start the trouble."

They asked the Graymonds first. The Graymonds were summer visitors from Tennessee. They'd never fished in salt water. They said they'd be delighted to have an "extra" mate.

Then they asked Dexter.

He was sitting on a soap box at the time, cutting out long, thick strips of bonito belly for Red. He looked at them with an expression which neither could quite analyze. They decided it changed—from a sort of alarm to eagerness.

"I thought you were mad at me," Dexter said.

"What for?" Crunch asked that question quickly.

"Stowing away."

"Oh. No. You worked that out. We'll be going tomorrow at nine, if you'd like to come along. Bottom fishing—down the reef a ways. Anchored all day. You may have a chance to fish. Somebody swiped one of our casting rods, but you could use a hand line."

"I'll go."

He did not seem especially pleased. Crunch said as much.

Dexter gazed at him in a hurt manner. "Can't a fellow be overwhelmed?" he asked tremulously.

"He didn't do it," Des said later that evening.

And Crunch nodded. "Guess not. And that's a relief!"

Mrs. Graymond found the "extra" mate shy and rather uncommunicative.

She was a dark-haired, dark-eyed girl and she had a way with boys. A most successful way, as a rule. She simply treated them as if they were twice their age. But Dexter did not seem to have an opinion about the outcome of the World's Series, he was not expecting to play football in the fall, he had no dog, and he was willing to admit that he liked fishing—but not with any emphasis or detail.

Indeed, after a quarter of an hour of lopsided conversation, Dexter embarrassedly asked Crunch if he could go "up topside" and shine a little brass. Crunch sent him up. And Desperate respected the boy's vast quietude.

It was a very tragic quietude. The one thing Dexter had wanted in his whole life more than the friendship of two such dramatic, important persons as Crunch and his mate, was that rod. He had taken it. Stolen it so craftily that even though he had been spotted on the night of the theft, he was positive nobody could testify he had been carrying away the precious tackle. Indeed, when the skipper of the *Firefly* had called to him, the rod, line and reel had been hidden underneath the dock in a spot from which Dexter had later retrieved it by means of a temporarily borrowed dinghy.

Now—they had taken him fishing. As he polished brass—and

glanced up occasionally with sadness at the broad back of the best mate on the Gulf Stream—Dexter reflected that he had sort of hoped they might vaguely suspect him and would in consequence merely become negative toward him. They couldn't prove anything. And he would never tell. He would go on lying, even if they tortured him worse than the Indians. But the fact that they had invited him to go out—and even to fish—was an almost unendurable kindness. It showed they trusted him.

If he had known their true anxiety over the suspicion of his deed, Dexter would probably have tried to slip overboard unnoticed. On the other hand, when his conscience smote him with the epithet of "thief," he did not flinch. He merely stuck out his chin and squinted back any dampness in his eyes. Maybe he was a thief, but there are things worse than robbery.

It was in the company of such fierce feelings that he watched them cut the *Poseidon*'s speed, make ready the anchor, pick an exact spot over a favorite patch of rocks after much searching through a glass-bottomed bucket, and come to an easy rest. In the distance were the V-shaped outriggers of boats trolling the Stream, the spindly legs of Fowey Rock Light, a few sails, and the smoke-plumed hulls of a pair of tankers beating south inside the current. Under the *Poseidon*'s keel were the irregular blurs of a coral bottom—lumps and caverns, minia-ture mountains and dark valleys of a size to hide groupers, jewfish, sharks.

The baits went overboard and Dexter was summoned from the com-parative obscurity of his place aloft. He was given a hand line by Crunch, who said, "Now, son, hang a whopper!" Desperate grinned at him. He wondered how he could stand it all day long.

They fished with dead shrimp and chunks of balao. Mrs. Graymond used a rod like the one Dexter had stolen. Its twin. Her husband chose a larger rig with a bigger hook, a heavier hunk of bait, and a reel that buzzed instead of clicked. The three lines soaked up salt water.

"Just about like perch fishing, isn't it?" Mrs. Graymond said.

Dexter smiled back at her smile. "Perch?"

"We catch them in Tennessee. And catfish. And bass, sometimes. Quite big ones. Two pounds—even three."

Her husband nodded. "I was thinking the same thing. I'd expected, somehow, that salt-water fishing would be different."

Then—it was different. His rod jerked. His reel whirred. His arms shot up and down. "Whoa!" he shouted. "Must be loose from that anchor! I've got bottom, captain!"

"You've got a fish," Crunch said.

Mr. Graymond opened his mouth as if to make a denial. Then—the grouper really ran. If he'd had bottom, the *Poseidon* would have to have been going at its top speed; even Mr. Graymond could reason that far, although his reasoning processes were seriously compromised by the situation. Crunch set him in the fighting chair and helped to thrust the bucking ferrule of the rod into the gimbal.

It was a pretty fight, though clumsy, and marred by a mild profanity of amazement. Even Dexter almost forgot his burden of trouble. Until Crunch reached over with a gaff and scooped in the fish.

Just an old grouper, Dexter said to himself at that point. His reason was the violent behavior of the Graymonds. *You'd think,* Dexter went on thinking, *it was a blue marlin. Or some kind of swordfish, or something.*

"But it's a monster!" Mrs. Graymond gasped. "A perfect giant! How much does he weigh!"

"Oh," Crunch murmured, "around, say, twenty pounds."

"Why, darling, it's a whale!" She kissed her husband.

Perhaps Mr. Graymond caught sight of Dexter's eyes. "Well, dear . . . it may not be so big for here. You've got to remember, we're pond and stream anglers." He stared, however, into the fishbox, where the grouper displayed its tweedy pattern of browns and its brilliant fins, spread taut. "Still," he said, "it's a doggoned big fish! Doggoned big." He glanced at Dexter defiantly.

But Dexter had lost his cynical expression. Something had hit his line. He was pulling it up, hand over hand, with an expert continuum of effort which gave the fish no slack, no chance to escape. He flipped his fish deftly into the box, without benefit of gaff. The enthralled Tennesseans bumped heads lightly in their eagerness to look. Dexter had caught a pork fish—a vivid yellow chap, eight or nine inches long, with a flat face and black, vertical stripes.

"It's the most gorgeous thing I ever saw!" exclaimed Mrs. Graymond.

"And good to eat," said Dexter.

She turned toward him with surprise. "But—it's *much* too beautiful for that! It ought to be in an aquarium!"

Dexter went to the box for bait.

And the fishing continued. Every fish, it appeared, was too beautiful for Mrs. Graymond to think of eating. Even Dexter, who was a practical individual, began to see the quarry through the lady's eyes. And they were kind of pretty—mighty bright-colored—when you thought of it. Right down to grunts.

The accident happened in the only way it could have happened. And in a place where even the most nervous boatman would hardly expect anything serious to occur. Dexter, liking the Graymonds almost against his will, and passionately eager to do anything to aid Crunch and Des, had undertaken to remove fish from the hooks and to put on baits for the customers. He was perfectly competent for the chore. He had weeks of dock fishing behind him.

Relieved of the duty, Crunch had gone below to prepare a special chowder from the grouper. Desperate had already occupied himself with the rearrangement of gear on the foredeck. Thus the two novices and the youngster were left alone. Mrs. Graymond hooked a fish. Dexter went to her side to give advice. It was a pretty good-sized fish —a snapper, he hoped—and his attention was entirely focussed, on the lady.

Mr. Graymond also hooked a fish. Not wishing to disturb his thrilling wife, and imagining himself by then a fairly proficient fisherman, he fought the creature in silence. It ran and it shook and it bent his rod but he dragged it to the surface. Then, seeing that Dexter was still busy, he undertook to copy the boy's trick of flicking his quarry aboard. He wound the line up to the swivel, blocked the reel spool with his thumb, braced his feet, and gave a tremendous heave. His fish was yanked out of the water. It rose into the air, writhing. It landed in the cockpit. It spat out the hook. And Mr. Graymond yelled.

Crunch and Des, separately, interpreted the yell as evidence of another triumph. It was not. It was a yell of sheer horror.

For the thing in the boat was horrible. A thing like a fat snake, five feet long, a sickly rich green, with a sharp, reptilian mouth, terrible teeth, and brilliant, evil eyes. Even as Mr. Graymond yelled, it slithered into a knot and struck like a rattlesnake, at the support of a chair. It bounced from that and struck again, biting fiercely on a glove. Dexter wheeled and saw it and turned ash-pale. Mrs. Graymond also saw, and she tried to scream and could not. She tried to move, but her legs would not budge.

"Keep away from it!" Dexter said hoarsely. "It'll bite! It's deadly poison!"

That it would bite was obvious. It was, even then, striking a pail. That the green moray is poisonous is a technical problem, since the toxicology of slimes and fish poisons is an unfinished science. Certainly morays make bad wounds that are slow to heal. Certainly men have suffered fearful infections from their bites, or from bacteria that entered the bites. Certainly all the boatmen in Florida waters would be hard put to choose between a big moray and a rattlesnake, if one had to be let loose in a cockpit.

Dexter's husky advice was heeded by the terrified man. He jumped backwards mechanically and found himself, somehow, standing on one of the couches. But his wife was still transfixed. The moray saw her—and started for her.

Dexter had been standing behind her. He came around in front. In coming, he grabbed the only thing handy—a gaff. The moray turned toward him. As it struck, Dexter clipped it with the gaff. Savagely, the green, repugnant monster plunged again and the boy hit it again, knocking it back. His gaff was too short for such work, and he knew it. He knew that if he missed, the moray would not. But he struck a third time. Mrs. Graymond came to galvanic life. She realized the boy had made a place which would permit her to jump to the side of her husband. She jumped. And, at last, she screamed.

Seeing that the lady was clear, Dexter lost no time in leaping up on one of the fishing chairs.

Then Crunch came, fast. He had recognized the scream as one not of exultation. He snatched up the long-handled gaff—which Dexter hadn't been able to reach—and he broke the moray's back with it.

It took two hours and a half, together with one of the tastiest dishes in all the experience of the Graymonds, to start the fishing again. They called Dexter a hero and the bravest kid they had ever seen and Mr. Graymond patted his back and Mrs. Graymond kissed him. There were long discussions of the venomousness of the big eels, and there was a brief but tense altercation between husband and wife over the uncourageous behavior of the former. Dexter noted a look in Crunch's eye which eased away a full half of his sadness. Then the lines were wet again, no more morays were caught, and Mr. Graymond made no further attempts to fling fish aboard unaided.

It turned out to be a good day, with a fine catch of panfish, and two more groupers. A day marked by An Adventure to Tell People Back Home. The Graymonds began to refer to the battle in that fashion. Dexter slipped back into his melancholy. The sun moved down. The anchor went up. And, in the purpling evening, the *Poseidon* hummed paint-slick down the Government Cut toward home.

Dexter was sitting alone on the canopy top when Mr. Graymond came up beside him. He didn't say anything. He just shook Dexter's hand, and his own head, and went away. But he had left something in Dexter's palm. The boy looked at it. And—for him—the sun shone brightly, the sea was perfumed, there were flowers on every tree. It was a five-dollar bill.

His first impulse was to shout for Crunch. Five dollars was a fortune. It would pay for the rod. But Dexter was a youth accustomed to consideration. Maybe four dollars would foot the bill. Or even three. His ideas about money, in sums larger than ten or fifteen cents, were not merely vague. They scarcely existed. If three were enough . . .

what he could do with the other two would be! . . . But he sturdily thrust back temptation. He leaned over the cockpit.

"Captain Adams," he said in a low tone, "would you come here a minute? It's important."

Crunch recognized the tone. He had been hoping to hear it all day. "Take over," he said quickly to his mate. "I'll see the kid."

He climbed up on the canopy. He sat down beside the boy. He was smiling. "O.K., Dexter. What's important?"

Dexter handed him the five dollars. "That's for the rod I stole."

Crunch took the money. "Oh," he said somewhat numbly. "Where'd you?—"

"Mr. Graymond gave it to me. A reward, I guess, for saving that Mrs. Graymond's life, or maybe her leg."

"I see. Yeah. Look, Dex. About swiping the rod. Why?"

Dexter was crying a little, then. Things had broken too well for a man to bear. But he started to talk. Every sentence made the going tougher. Crunch didn't interrupt. He just sat there, watching the causeway slide past, watching the boat swing as Des prepared to back her in.

"I had to," the youngster began. "You gotta believe I had to! If you didn't, I'd about die!" He swallowed. "Look. You know about 'business reverses'? Pop's been having what he calls that. It really means we don't have any money. Until they started, we had enough. We had a wonderful time! We'd get up together, and I'd help get breakfast, and eat lunch at school, and, evenings, we'd cook at home and sometimes we'd go out for dinner to a real restaurant! Then . . . when Saturdays came . . ."

Dexter had to pull himself together. "When—Saturdays came—he'd take me out in the Glades—fishing in the canal! We'd drive in our car, and I'd fish a jack pole and he'd cast plugs. I—I—I told you he could put one in your pocket a hundred feet away. It's true! Then—when we had to sell the car—we couldn't go so far and we had to fish in places that weren't so good—but we hardly never missed a Saturday! He's—he knows all the birds—and how to catch snakes—and we saw deer and 'coons and possums! And then . . ."

The boy's voice went lower—close to inaudibility. His words ran fast. "School was coming. I had to have shoes and knickers and books and things—and Pop sold his rod and his reel and his tackle box and he had about a million plugs and he sold them and said he didn't care to fish with an old jack pole so we didn't go out together any more. He didn't tell me he sold those things to get my school stuff ready—but I found out from the man that bought them. Pop had a chance to sell—

and he knew we'd have to buy all my stuff in a few weeks. I found that out. So I knew."

He didn't get any further than that. He couldn't. But there was no need of it.

The *Poseidon* was edging toward the dock. Crunch jumped to the top controls while Des made fast the bow lines. Crunch didn't particularly want Dexter to see him at that instant, anyway. His jaw was set like steel. When the *Poseidon* was snug, Crunch looked at the hunched back of the boy. Then his eye traveled ashore, and he saw a man standing there. A medium-sized man, an unimportant-looking man, with a good face, full of worry. The man's eyes were hurt, and in his hand was the rod Des had made—the one his son had stolen.

Des helped the passengers ashore. Immediately afterward, the man —Mr. Heath—accosted the mate. He spoke rapidly, nervously. "My boy must have stolen this. He left it in my room a few days ago with a note saying he had found it. As soon as I had time—I traced it— through the tackle shops. Somebody recognized your work . . ."

Des just stood.

But the boy heard his father's voice. He leaped up with a tearing, ecstatic cry. "It's all right, Pop! It's yours! I just paid five bucks for it!"

The man, gray, embarrassed, gazed at his son. He spoke the first words that came into his head—spoke them bitterly. "Five bucks— when it's worth twenty-five! See here, son! . . ."

Dexter slid down into the cockpit. He was not breathing, or even seeing. He was sick. Sicker, perhaps, than he would ever be again in his life. He leaped ashore, and eluded Desperate's panicky effort to catch him. He ran away down the dock—to be alone.

Crunch dropped down, also, and came ashore. The Graymonds were waiting for their catch to be put on the fish rack. They realized something was wrong. They stood by, puzzled and unhappy.

Crunch took the gray-faced man by the arm. It was quivering. "Look," he began urgently. "I can't explain now. But you've got to believe me, Mr. Heath! This is a mighty important moment in your kid's life! He's a fine kid, Mr. Heath! I only hope mine grows up half that swell! But I want you to let me handle this my way. I want you to keep that rod—"

"I couldn't, Captain! I—I'm kind of broken up about it. I came home that night to tell my son I had found a job—a good one—and there was the stolen rod and the lying note! I've tried to teach him— about stealing—lying—and it half killed me! I decided not to say a thing about the job, till my boy confessed the theft. He—" Mr. Heath stammered. "He did it—for me. That is—for motives which were decent. If you . . ."

Crunch squeezed the father's arm hard. He also swallowed. "Look, Mr. Heath. I know all that! You keep the rod. Do you hear me? You've gotta! You've got to trust my judgment!" His blistering blue gaze held on the gray eyes of the other man.

"All right," said Mr. Heath, sighing. "All right. I'll trust you. I'm sort of mixed up—anyway . . ."

Crunch raced away—butting into people on the dock. He found Dexter hiding, on the ground, under the truck that took away fish carcasses. Dexter was racked by crying. Crunch seized his foot, pulled him out, and stood him up.

"Go away!" Dexter said in near strangulation. "I don't want any favors! I thought that five bucks was plenty."

Crunch shook him. "Listen!" His own voice was wild and tight. "Listen, Dex! I want you to get square with me! You gave that rod to your dad. He's gotta keep it. You got to pay for all of it. That's what I'm here to tell you."

"How can I? Twenty-five!—"

"I told you to shut up! Now, shut up! I'm doing the talking! You owe me twenty bucks. All right. There's just about twenty days before school begins. From now on—every day—you're working for me all day. A dollar a day. And lunches," Crunch added hastily. "A dollar a day and lunches. If you don't earn all of it—if you're a couple of days short—then you can go out a few Saturdays! You shine brass, and watch baits . . ."

Dexter shook his head miserably. "I—I ain't no good! You know that! I steal, and I think hammerheads are marlins. . . ."

"No good?" The man's voice was incredulous. "No good! Son, you got bait eyes like a hawk's! You can see a fin before even the fish knows he's coming up! You're the rarin'est, tearin'est moray fighter I ever saw milling in a cockpit! No good! Why—you're worth any three eighteen-year-old mates on the Gulf Stream Dock! Now! You working for me—or not?"

Dexter had listened. He wiped a wet sleeve wetter. "Gee!—" He hesitated, and dared it—"Gee, *Crunch,* you're a swell guy!"

Crunch slapped his shoulder and caught up his arm.

They went back along the dock together in a swift, easy lope, taking care not to butt into anybody.

ONCE ON A SUNDAY

PHILIP WYLIE

Somewhere up the river a noon whistle blew; quiet came over the boatyard. The band saw stopped screaming first; mallets and hammers fell silent; old man Kane's handsaw was last. Crunch Adams, acting yard superintendent that day, picked up the box of lunch his wife, Sari, had prepared for him and walked over to the lean, gnarled shipwright. Crunch inspected the intricately worked chunk of madeira —looked his thoughts—and the old fellow nodded with satisfaction.

Crunch sat in the shade of a cabbage palm, out of the heat. Kane moved beside him and opened a pasteboard shoebox. The two men began to eat. Multiple riffles moved along the turgid river at their feet.

"Mullet," Crunch said.

"Mullet," the old man agreed.

The backdrop of Miami glittered in the sunlight and murmured with an abnormal springtime industry occasioned by the presence of thousands of soldiers and sailors. By and by Crunch's eyes traveled purposefully to the blue-grey sides of the hauled crash boat on which they were working. "Navy'd like to have her back in the water tomorrow night."

"No doubt," said the skillful old man. "But it's Sunday."

The *Poseidon*'s skipper nodded. "Yeah." He let time pass. They watched a brace of pelicans float up the river on stiff wings. "Enemy works on Sunday, though. Usually attacks then, if possible."

Mr. Kane spat. "Swine."

"Short-handed," Crunch went on. "We are. Everybody is. If we could get that piece fitted tomorrow morning, they could paint it later—"

"I'm a strict Presbyterian," the old man replied firmly. "At eleven tomorrow, I'll be in church, that's where I'll be."

"I know how it is." Crunch's expression was innocent. "I fished a Presbyterian minister once—on a Sunday."

"You don't *say!*"

Desperate, the *Poseidon*'s mate, was swabbing down. The sun was a red disc—a stagy decoration; it emitted no glare but it dyed the line of boats at the Gulf Stream Dock a faint orange. Soon it would be gone. Crunch and Sari were up on the pier, laughing with the last customer. A tall stranger made his way past them, stared at the boats' names, and walked lithely to the stern of the *Poseidon.*

"Are you Crunch Adams?" he asked. His "r's" burred with a trace of Scotland and the voice that pronounced them had a slow sonority.

"I'm Des, the mate. Crunch is yonder."

The eyes of the stranger were cavernous. His nose was large and beaklike; above the six-foot level of his craggy head was a shock of iron-grey hair. Des wondered what sort of man he was and had a partial answer when the man saw young Bill Adams. Bill was three, then—proudly toting a suitcase for his father. The evening breeze stirred his blond curls. He tugged and grunted—a scale model of Hercules, in a blue sunsuit. A twinkle came in the man's recessed eyes and his broad mouth broke into a smile. "Likely lad!"

"Crunch's. The skipper's."

"I've been told he's the best. It shows—in the offspring."

Des began to like the guy. "Hey, Crunch!" he called.

"My problem," said the man, as he and the two charter-boatmen put their heads together, "is as difficult as it is simple. I'm a minister o' the gospel—a Presbyterian—though I wouldn't like it to be held against me."

Crunch and Des chuckled.

"When I went to school in Edinburgh—which was a considerable long while ago—I used to slip out as often as the opportunity afforded and cast a fly for trout and sometimes for salmon. I haven't wet a line since." He rubbed his chin. "My daughter spends her winters here with her husband, who's a man of means. I've joined them for a few days' vacation and my son-in-law insists I put in a few on the sea. He's footing the bill—and a man ought to keep in good with his son-in-law, don't you think?" He beamed.

"Very sound," Crunch said.

"But there's more to it than that," the man went on. "Do you mind if I light a pipe? It's safe on these gasoline boats?"

Crunch struck the match.

The prospective customer sat down with a sigh of composure. He sniffed the air. "Salty. I like it. Smells as good as the recollection of a frith. Unfortunately, for the past twenty-five years, I've hardly smelled it at all. I've been preaching the gospel inland. Not that it isn't as desperately needed there as on the coasts. I am simply explaining the rest of my predicament—an altogether happy one, as it chances. This vacation I'm on comes between my old church and a new one I'm to take directly after Christmas. What's that yonder?" He pointed with the stem of his pipe.

Crunch looked in time to see the triangular top of a dark fin ease into the blue water. "Porpoise."

"You don't say! They come here in this Bay?"

"Some of 'em live in here."

"Well!" He watched the big mammal rise and blow. "Fine creature! But to get to the point. Where I'm taking the new pastorate, fishing is partly a business and largely a recreation, besides. It's in New Jersey, at a place called Antasquan—a big town or small city, whichever you will. Some of my new congregation are commercial fishermen, and some of the wealthier ones are boat-owners, like yourselves. They go out for big tunny, I understand. Then, there's something called 'blues' they're partial to—"

"We know a little about it," Crunch said appreciatively. "We've fished a few summers from the Manasquan nearby."

The minister smiled. "Which, no doubt, is one of the reasons my son-in-law stipulated you two! What can a man expect in a corporation lawyer, though, except guile? At any rate, I've got a congregation of fishermen—and golf players, to boot. Being a Scot, I can handle the golf, on week days, though it somewhat drains my congregations on the Sabbath, I hear. As fishing does, to an even greater degree, in the summer. But I like to know something of the pursuits of the men I preach to. So I'm doubly glad to be able to take advantage of this vacation to find out what I can of salt-water fishing. Have I made myself clear?"

"You sure have, Mr.—?"

"McGill. The Reverend Doctor Arthur McGill. And if, in the heat of excitement in the three days I've got to fish, it should become necessary to use a shorter term, you'll find I respond to 'Mac.' "

He shook hands with them to seal the bargain.

When he was gone, Des grinned at the descending twilight. "The trouble is, there aren't enough ministers like that. If there were, I'd go to church oftener, myself."

"Just what I was thinking," his skipper agreed.

The Reverend Doctor Arthur McGill appeared on the Gulf Stream Dock at seven o'clock the following morning—a green-visored hat flopping above his grey mane and a huge hamper carried lightly over his bony arm. He took the gap between dock and stern in an easy stride and deposited the basket.

It was a cool, breezy day—it would be choppy outside—but, if he knew it, he did not seem concerned. "Bracing weather," he said. "I hadn't expected it of the tropics. I rose before the servants and picked my own grapefruit from a tree in the yard. There was something burning out toward the Everglades and it recalled my autumn fire anywhere in the world. But the grapefruit was a distinctly pagan note; it made me understand a little why it is that north country men always have a sense of guilt in the south. It ought to be snowing and blowing —and here you are picking fruit!"

Des was already hanging the bow lines on the dolphins. The *Poseidon* pushed into the ship channel and started east. At the jetty-mouth, the outgoing tide, bulled by the easterly wind, threw up an unpredictable maelstrom of lumpy current; the *Poseidon* tossed, smashed hard and found her sea gait for the day. Three warm December weeks had changed, overnight, into the Floridian equivalent of a winter day—a day with a twelve-mile breeze and a temperature in the shade of sixty —a "cold" day, in the opinion of the natives.

Crunch cut baits. The minister wrapped an elbow around one of the canopy supports and watched, his eyes bright under his tangled brows. Once or twice, the skipper glanced at him covertly; he wasn't going to be seasick. He took in each detail, as the strip was sliced wafer-thin, tapered, pointed, beveled, and pierced for the hook. "It's an art, I can see that."

"The idea is to make it flutter in the water—like a fish with a busy tail." Crunch dropped over a bait on a leader and tested it to make sure it would not spin and wind up—or unwind—the line. He handed the rod to Reverend McGill and, under the same intense scrutiny, he arranged two balao on the outrigger lines. Then, because his passenger looked quizzical, he explained the operation of outriggers.

"You see," said the minister, "I'm a dub and a tyro and I have plenty of need to learn all this. A congregation of fishing enthusiasts will listen with a polite and patronizing interest if their dominie discusses the fine points of netting fishes in the Sea of Galilee two thousand years ago. But if you can bring the matter up to date—put it in terms of outriggers, so to speak—and use it in an illustration, you may even wake up the habitual sleepers."

Crunch laughed. "I get the idea, parson. Now. About 'blues.' Being a part-time Jersey fisherman myself, I understand the Jersey attitude. It's cold today—and we may run along like this for hours without a strike—so I'll explain what they do off the 'Squan Inlet—and why. Their fishing is done this way—and other ways."

"I'd appreciate it." The minister snuggled into the fighting chair and pulled his muffler tighter.

Crunch was deep in a lucid description of the art of chumming for tuna—remembering to cite the fact that Jersey old-timers still call them "horse mackerel"—when there was a splash behind the center bait. Reverend McGill went taut as his reel warbled.

"Bonita!" Crunch said. "Just hang on till he gets that run out of his system."

Reverend McGill hung on—and hung on properly—with his rod high enough so that no sudden bend could snap it over the stern and low enough so that he had room to lift it and take in slack in the event the fish turned suddenly. It did. The rod went higher and the minister began to reel. He brought the bonita to within a few yards of the boat and it sounded a good seventy-five feet. His rod tip shivered with the rapid tail action. He pumped the fish up, under Crunch's instruction. It sounded again—ran again—and came to gaff.

Crunch brought it aboard and the exhilarated minister looked. "Magnificent creature! Herringbone back—and the underside as white and sleek as alabaster! Funny thing! It's almost as big as any fish I ever caught in my life—and yet it pulled so hard I expected a fish my own size!"

"Bonitas are strong," Crunch said. He resumed his discussion of chumming. His back was turned to the water when Reverend McGill had his second strike. The minister handled the fish with considerable skill. "'Cuda," Crunch said, after a moment.

It proved to be a barracuda. Crunch flipped it over the gunwale, showed the ferocious teeth by clamping the fish's head under the lid of the box in the stern, and removed the hook with pliers in a gingerly fashion. The *Poseidon* ran steadily for some two hours after that. Then there was a bluish flash under one of the outrigger baits and its line drifted gently down to the water only to spring tight like the wire of a snare. Crunch eyed the line as it cut the surface—pointing, in a curve, to a fish that was barely under water. "Dolphin," he explained. "Get ready for him to jump. And when he does jump—watch him."

When the fish jumped, it was quite a sight. This particular dolphin at the particular instant was green and silver. Sometimes they are luminous cobalt and silver or gold—with pale blue spots. Sometimes they are almost pure gold or silver. Their rainbow patterns cannot be predicted—they change in seconds—and they range through all the natural colors save red and those with red in them, as well as through the spectra of precious metals.

"I know," the minister said quietly and between breaths, when Crunch gaffed the dolphin, "why people write poetry about them." He watched Crunch bait up again and went back to his vigil. "It's amazing," he continued, "what eyes you have. Now, in all three strikes, all I saw was a flicker and a lot of spray. But—each time—you saw the fish and named it correctly."

Crunch laughed. "I didn't see the fish, itself, any time. Except, as you say, an impression of a fish. I could tell what they were by the way your rod tip behaved—by the angle at which the fish fought—by a lot of little things."

"They must be fine points, for fair! I don't suppose you reveal them to the novitiate—the lucky novitiate, I might add?"

"Why not?" Crunch grinned benignly. "Take—the bonita. He was first. He hits hard and fast, usually at a sharp angle to the course of the bait. When he feels the hook he puts on every ounce of power he's got. He goes away, maybe for thirty yards or so, and then, still feeling the hook, he goes down. He'll bore straight down or go down in a spiral, like an auger. Now there's a fish out here that's related to the tuna, called an albacore. He does the same thing. But when the albacore swims, it's like a glide, all power and no wiggle. With a bonita there's the wiggle. A flutter. You see it in the rod tip. You feel it in your arms."

"You do that," the minister agreed.

"'Cuda's can sound—or run—or jump. In fact, they usually give a jump or two like a pike or a muskie. On the same tackle, they're even stronger, I believe. But they do one thing that's characteristic—they jerk. If you get one near the boat you can see him do it under water. He'll yank his head back and forth trying to get rid of the hook or to break the line, just the way a bulldog yanks."

"And the dolphin?"

"He always skims along at a terrific rate right below the surface. You can tell that because your line, instead of boring down into the sea, will be stretching out over it for a long way. Then the dolphin will circle, first one way and then the other, in big arcs. That is, he will unless he's foul-hooked. Hooked from the outside, in the back, say. Or hooked through the eye. In that case, he's very apt to sound—and if you haven't seen him when he hit, you'll be hard put to guess what you're fighting. Of course, you occasionally do see dolphin before they hit, because they sometimes make several bounds into the air to get the bait, as if they were impatient with the resistance of the water."

"I see." The minister mused, "Funny, that. If you're fishing for salmon—you take salmon. You know what you've got when you have your rise. Trout, too, unless you happen to encounter a chub or dace. Here, though, the possibilities are vast."

"There are hundreds."

The minister thought that over. "And what would a sailfish be like? That is, if we were to have the fantastic good fortune—?"

So Crunch told him about the ways of sailfish. And in the end, he was, as usual, completely at a loss: "What I've said goes for the average sailfish. But you're continually running into the exception. The fellow who just gulps the bait and runs. The one who strikes like a bonita—with only a flash under the bait. And then, when you know it was a sail because you saw its high fin and its bill—and you hook it—it'll possibly turn out to be a white marlin."

"I presume, in the three days I have, there's no chance of that?"

"I dunno," Crunch answered. "There's always some chance. They're tailing today, though. I've seen a couple. They don't strike, as a rule, when they're running south from a cold snap."

The minister nodded. Crunch knew by his attitude during the discussion of sailfish that the Reverend Doctor McGill had a very definite dream about his three days of deep-sea angling and the dream was centered around that particular breed of fish. In his mind's eye, the minister wanted not only what knowledge of marine angling he could glean from the period, but a particular object, a mounted sail, to hang, probably, in his study, where the visiting members of his new congregation could observe it and admire. Reverend McGill did not say so. He was too humble a man. But Crunch knew.

While the skipper was contemplating that matter, the novice in the *Poseidon*'s stern had another strike. The reel sang. The fish ran. Then it went deep. The rod tip fluttered. "A bonita!" the preacher cried with certainty.

"Well—it's not quite like a bonita. A little, just a shade, less powerful. Not quite so vicious. It might be a small bonita, at that. But I think it's a kingfish."

It was a kingfish. The minister chuckled. "You're not giving away all your trade secrets in one day!"

"Well, that one wasn't easy. I couldn't be sure myself. If we call three quarters of them correctly we're doing fine."

"I won't be so rash and conceited on the next," the minister promised. But there wasn't any "next." They ate the excellent lunch in the big hamper. They trolled the length of the island that is Miami Beach.

Then they turned south and went as far as the old lighthouse. But there were no more strikes upon which the minister could test his fresh knowledge.

That evening the *Poseidon* came in as late as the winter sun would allow. "I've had a wonderful day," the minister said. "I've thought of at least six new sermons. I've settled in my head a minute point of ethics brought to me by one of my former flock which stuck me for a long time. I've caught four prime fish—whoppers, all—and two of 'em, you say, are superb eating. There's a good fifteen pounds of meat for the larders of myself and the friends of my son-in-law. And I'll never be able to thank you enough. The best part of it all is," his eyes crinkled, "we'll be at it again in the morning—and the day after, also. That's what they mean when they call this place a paradise on earth!"

Crunch stopped the recital and carefully poured a cup of coffee from his thermos. He raised his eyebrows enquiringly at old man Kane. The shipwright nodded and held out a cup from which he had been drinking milk. "Thanks, Crunch. So—what happened? Did he get a sail?"

"No," Crunch said. He peered reminiscently at the murky river and tossed a coral pebble to break the immaculate surface. "No. Doctor McGill never caught a sail, so far as I am aware."

"I'm disappointed."

"Maybe he wasn't! Des and I got fond of that gent. Whatever a good man is, he's it. And by that I mean he was both a man, and good. We fished Friday, from seven till dark, and got skunked. It was raw and windy with low clouds. Not a strike. But the old boy saw a whale, a fine-back, that came up close to the *Poseidon* and cruised along, blowing—and he insisted it made the day worth while.

"Then—Saturday came. His last day. He was going home Monday and he was planning to take in a couple of Miami preachers Sunday and Sunday night. So we started at six, in the dark, and we dragged a bait till night. He caught one grouper over the reef, and a rock hind, and he had one sailfish rise. I swear the old boy's hair stood on end. The sail came like an upside-down yacht with her keel out, and it followed the bait for a mile, but it never hit. Old Mac McGill stood up the whole time, muttering. First I thought he was praying and then I had a kind of shock because I thought he was swearing, but he wasn't doing either—he was just coaching the fish—like a quarterback on the bench when his team's in a spot. The fish never did hit, just eyed that bait, wallowed behind it, and finally swam away. And then it got dark and we came in and the dominie's vacation was over. He said he'd be back some day when his pocketbook could stand it and he said he'd had more fun than ever before in his life. His eyes shot sparks and he meant every word of it. He was disappointed, I am certain, but not as much disappointed as pleased. Des and I, of course, tried to make up for the thin fishing by telling him as many stories as we could—and by giving him as much dope as we knew how."

"A good sport," Kane nodded.

"The real thing. Well, he shook our hands and thanked us and went away. Mr. Williams, the dock manager, had us down Sunday for a party—we didn't know the people—and we sat around Saturday evening feeling pretty low about the preacher. Sunday, we got down about seven and our party hadn't shown up. So we just sat around some more. Lots of people get a special kick out of deep-sea fishing for the main and simple reason that you don't have to get out at the crack of dawn. I mean, they'll hit at noon just as often as they'll hit at daybreak, which isn't like freshwater stuff. Anyway—"

During the night the wind had hauled. The norther had blown itself out and the Trade Wind, dawdling back from the southeast, had taken its place, pushing the cold air aside, dissipating the lowering clouds, and substituting the regimented wool-balls of Caribbean cumulus. The thermometer, between midnight and sunrise, had gone up fifteen degrees and a balminess characteristic of Florida had supplanted the sharp chill. Even the first level bars of sunshine were warm and it was certain that by noon the temperature in the shade would be eighty. On such days, after a cold-weather famine, the sailfish are likely to be ravenous. Crunch knew it, and Des, and they wondered in their separate silences what Reverend McGill would think about it. Because he knew, too. They'd told him how, as a rule, the sailfish would come up fighting on these days when the weather broke.

By nine o'clock, they were getting restless. Their party hadn't appeared. All the other boats were out, with the exception of one, engine parts of which were strewn over its stern cockpit for repair. Des was commenting on the laggardliness of some people when Crunch said, "Look. There's Reverend McGill."

The minister stepped from a car. He was wearing a neat serge suit and a high, starched collar. He walked down the dock with a sheepish expression and said, "That was my son-in-law. Off to play golf—like too many in my own congregations! I went along with him this far—I can walk the balance of the way to the kirk." Then he realized that the boats had gone. "How does it happen you're still hanging to the pilings?"

"We were chartered," Des said bitterly, "by some slug-a-bed named Ellsworth Coates."

The minister turned pale. He swallowed. "That," he finally murmured, "is the name of my son-in-law—the heathen tempter!"

Crunch merely glanced up at the tall man on the dock. Then he squinted across the Bay. He neither smiled nor frowned—just squinted. "I guess he must have seen the weather prediction—and realized what it would probably be like out there today."

Reverend McGill sat down shakily. "It's like him! The lawyer's guile! Dropping me here to walk to church! And with you two boys waiting, steam up and bait in the box! What does he take me for—a weakling? Is some crafty second-rate, amoral attorney to be the first to make me break the Sabbath? Not that, in the proper cause, I mightn't! I'm none of your hardshell preachers! I've been known far and wide as a liberal man, these long years! But a precedent is a precedent and I've kept the Lord's day, in my own fashion, as an example. Fie to Ellsworth—the wretch!"

"This might turn out to be a good cause," Des said. "After all, it's a day in a hundred, and you wanted your future parish to feel you were one of them."

"It could be a day in a million!" the minister said scornfully.

Time passed—a good deal of time. Crunch began to repair a light rod which had lost a guide in an encounter with a wahoo. Up where the Gulf Stream Dock joined the Florida shore a school of big jack got under a walloping school of small mullet. The result was aquatic chaos: fish showered into the air as if they were being tossed up in barrelfuls by Davy Jones himself. The minister watched, goggle-eyed, and said something that Crunch thought was, "It's more than flesh can withstand!" But Crunch wasn't certain.

And then the *Clarissa B.* came in. She came in because one of her four passengers, a novice, had been taken ill—although the sea was smooth: only a vague ground swell kept it from being as calm as pavement. The *Clarissa,* as she approached, throwing two smart wings of water from her bows, was flying four sailfish flags.

"Four of them!" Reverend McGill whispered disconsolately. "I could have stood two—or possibly three—!"

The boat turned, backed in smartly, and deposited her shaky passenger with little ceremony: the other anglers were manifestly annoyed at the interruption and anxious to get back on the Gulf Stream. She pulled away from her slip again—showing four forked tails above her gunwales.

"Good fishing, eh?" Crunch called to the skipper.

"They'll jump in the boat!" he yelled back. "It's red-hot! We've already had a triple and two doubleheaders and a single!" He turned his wheel and purred into the blue distance.

Reverend McGill sighed and stood up. He shook out his full length of supple anatomy. He brushed back his iron-grey hair. "In any event," he said, grinning, "I'll not rationalize. I had it on the tip of my tongue to say that the Reverend Doctor Stone, whom I had intended to hear this morning, isn't so much of a preacher-man. We'll agree that he's the finest preacher in the south—and that by going fishing, I'm committing a mortal sin of the first magnitude. But—boys—let's get a lunch on board and make all the haste we can to violate the canon that has to do with this precious and altogether magnificent day!" He took off his collar as he came aboard.

By four o'clock in the afternoon, the lone passenger was stunned. In the interim, no less than seven sailfish had come up from the purple depths and done their best to be caught by the cleric. But in each instance that gentleman, through bad luck and inexperience, had failed to bring his fish to boat. In testament of his effort there was a broken rod. There were blisters on his fingers. There was a burn on his left arm where the running line had cut him. There was an empty reel from which the line had been stripped. And there was on the deck, a leader to which was still attached the upper half of a broken hook. But no sailfish flag flew from the *Poseidon*'s outrigger.

The loquacious Reverend McGill was dour, and his accent had become more Scottish. "I will nae say it's injustice," he proclaimed morosely, "an' a' would not ha' missed this day for the worrld—but it's a sterrn way to remind a mon of his evil intent!"

Crunch and Des exchanged glances. "There'll be more of 'em, parson," Des said encouragingly. "Just—take it easy."

And, even while he spoke, the outrigger line on the port side fell again and a big boil of water showed briefly where the bait had been. The line came tight and the minister struck to set the hook. The fish ran off rapidly for about forty yards and sounded. "It's no sailfish this time," he cried. "A bonita, I think. At least, perhaps we'll ha' one small fishie to show for our sins!"

Crunch looked critically at the bend in the rod. "If it's a bonita, it's the father of all bonitas," he said quietly.

"Very unlikely," Reverend McGill replied as he jockeyed to get in a few feet of slack. "Nothing sensational. The last two hours, I've realized I was predestined to have misfortune to the end of the day. But at least my face will be saved. I'll never have to exhibit a sailfish I caught on Sunday and acknowledge my guilt. The deed will be a secret between the two of us—and my son-in-law—who will use it, no doubt, for some blackmailing tomfoolery, one day. Now—he's coming toward us nicely!"

The fish swam toward the *Poseidon* for several yards. Then it turned, still deep under the water, and ran three hundred yards with the speed of an express train. The reel screamed. Crunch yelled. Des brought the *Poseidon* around in a fast arc. They chased the fish at full throttle for five hundred yards more before the minister stopped losing line from a spool that was by then no thicker than his thumb.

"It must be a sailfish, after all," Reverend McGill murmured.

"It's no sailfish," Crunch replied. His mouth was tight and he shot an enquiring glance at Des.

"What then?"

"I dunno. I dunno, Reverend. Maybe a marlin—"

"A marlin! It isn't possible—!"

"I think," Des called, "it's an Allison tuna. Better take it easy, Mac. You've got a long fight on your hands if it is."

"I'll gentle it like a baby," the angler promised. "I'm getting a bit of line, now." He tried tentatively and then with fury. "He's running to us—*to* us—faster than I can reel!"

Crunch waved—and waved again. The *Poseidon* leaped away from the fish but even at full gun she barely made enough speed so that the man on the rod could keep his line taut. Presently Crunch signalled again and the boat stood still. "Mac," as Des had called him in the stress of excitement, began to horse his fish toward the boat, lifting slowly until his bowed rod came high, dropping the tip swiftly, and winding in the slack thus gained. Two feet at a time, he brought the fish toward the place where the two guides leaned in tense concentration and where he labored sweatily. When the reel-spool was well filled with line, the fish turned and raced away again—a hundred yards, two, three. The process was repeated. The fish ran.

On the fifth struggle to the boat Reverend McGill gasped, "It's a new tribulation! I've hung a whale! Every joint in me is protesting—!"

"Stay with it," Crunch breathed fervently.

"Mon—I'm a *Scot.*"

He stayed with it. Stayed with it until it tired and until, an hour and three quarters after he had hooked it, a head and jaws rolled out of water not forty feet from the *Poseidon*. Crunch felt himself grow weak. He just stood there. Des said in a small voice, "You see it?"

"Yeah."

"What is it?"

"I dunno." Crunch repeated the words as if they angered him. "I dunno. It was red—wasn't it?"

"Yeah. It was red."

"But it wasn't a snapper," Crunch continued. "Not a snapper—not a monster mangrove snapper. I never saw it before. Mac—take it mighty easy, now. It's something new you've got there."

"I couldn't put any strength on it if I had to," the minister said grittily. Then he did put on strength. The fish made a last flurry—a rush, a mighty splash—and Crunch got the leader in his gloved hand. Swiftly, skillfully, he rammed home the gaff. The tail hammered on the boat's hull like a piston. Des jumped clear down from the canopy without hanging and made a noose around the leader. He dropped the rope into the sea. The two men pulled, and the fish came aboard tail first.

It was red, scarlet, from mouth to caudal. Its underside was greenish-white. It had big fins and a square tail. It was toothed. Its eyes were green. It gasped like a grouper and flopped heavily. They guessed it weighed about a hundred and eighty.

The minister flexed his raging arms slowly, caught some of his wind, stirred his back a little as if he were afraid any further motion would shatter it, and he looked and looked at the fish. "You mean—this is one you boys can't give a name to?"

Crunch said slowly, "No, Mac. And I don't think anybody—any taxidermist, any ichthyologist—can give it a name, either. I think it's a new one. Somebody comes in with a brand-new one every year or so, around these parts. Tonight you're gonna, Mac."

"Whatever the name is," Des said with the voice of a man who had seen a miracle, "part of it will probably be McGill—forever."

Crunch walked stiffly to the radio telephone. He put in a call for Hal—and for Bob Breastedt—the two foremost piscatorial authorities on the coast. "It's built like an amberjack—something," he said into the transmitter. "Fought like one—more or less. But it has scales like a tarpon, almost, and fins like a bass, and the darned thing's red all over!"

The experts came to the dock to meet the *Poseidon*—and so did the reporters.

It was a new one. Part of its long scientific name eventually became McGillia.

Many weeks later, Crunch had a letter from the minister. It was postmarked "Antasquan, N.J." It said, in part:

". . . and the celebrated catch we made that memorable day has become a not unmixed blessing. It served the purpose of giving my new flock an advance notice that I'm a fisherman of distinction. Indeed, the reputation carried ahead of me by the national publicity was so great that I'm alarmed whenever I remember that next summer I'll have to go out and show my lack of proficiency on the blues and the school tuna—not to mention the great horse mackerel. However, I'll take my chances on that.

"The point is, the fact that I caught the fish on the Sabbath was one which the press associations did not glaze over. On the contrary, they prominently noted it, and my congregation here was quick to make the discovery. Some of them chided me. And all of those who fish, and those who play golf, are smugly planning to be absent from their pews as soon as the spring weather breaks. After all, their dominie fishes on Sunday! This, however, has set me thinking—this—and the lesson in wiliness I learned from my son-in-law.

"Even now, war work is engaging the daytime hours of some of my people on Sunday—so I have stressed the evening service. It is already a feature in this city and the kirk is full every Sunday night though it was formerly sparsely attended at that hour. Come spring, my friends, and I expect to have most of the golfers and anglers in the evening habit and it'll be another bit of triumph I can credit to you and your fine ship! In short, I'm punished by the richly deserved lampoons of a fine group of people—and rewarded with an evening attendance that beats the old morning service average!

"The fish itself arrived in due course—splendidly mounted and a thing of wonder. In that, I lost out, also—because I still have no symbol of my dubious skill to hang on my study wall. One of my parishioners is on the board of the American Museum of Natural History—and there the creature hangs. Still—I think the day was well spent—for myself and my fellow men—don't you?"

Crunch rose and stretched. He looked at his watch. One o'clock. Presently, the sound of the band saw rent the air. The boatyard resumed work for the U.S. Navy. Crunch had been reading the letter—having taken it from his hip pocket at the proper moment. He handed it, now, to the old shipwright, who stared blankly.

"You mean—you brought this thing here this morning?"

"Sure," Crunch said.

"You knew I was going to tell you I wouldn't work tomorrow?"

Crunch nodded. "Yep. But we need you—if we're going to get that job back in the water on time for Uncle Sam."

Kane glanced down at the name of the church on the letterhead. He sucked his teeth. "Well," he said slowly, "if that preacher can go fishing—and have it turn out all right—I guess I can work."

"It was for a cause. So's this."

"I still don't get it! You planned to tell me this story—and brought the letter to prove it was the truth—"

"I'm like the preacher's son-in-law," Crunch said as he walked away. "Guileful."

LABRADOR-UNGAVA

HAROLD F. BLAISDELL

The frontiers of fishing have been pushed back so rapidly in recent years that very few remain. It is futile to hope to find virgin fishing in regions which can be reached by automobile. Even beyond the last roads there are wide belts of territory which are relatively easy to reach by plane or boat, and whose waters see many fishermen. Only by flying hundreds of miles beyond the last overland approach can one find what every fisherman dreams of: unfished waters which teem with fish, exactly as they have for centuries. In spite of our rapidly mounting affluence and the wonders of modern transportation, very few fishermen have been fortunate enough to fish waters which fall into this category.

In this class I am including only those waters which truly lie beyond the beyond. If one has the necessary means, it is fairly simple to fish waters which fall just short of this category. But to reach waters which perhaps no civilized man has ever fished is quite another matter. To do so it is necessary to invade country so remote and hostile that it is shunned by all but the most daring and competent pilots.

Ever since I can remember I have dreamed of fishing such waters, and three years ago my dreams finally came true. At that time Norm Hathaway and his partner Smudge Grant were operating a recently opened fishing camp in western Labrador. They were looking for publicity in the form of magazine articles and invited me to sample their fishing in the hope that it would provide the necessary material. Since Pete and I had teamed up on similar, but less ambitious, projects, I sold them the idea of including Pete in on the deal. He would play his usual role of photographer and member of the party who generally catches the fish worth writing about and photographing.

With only the vaguest notion of what was in store for us, we drove to Bangor, Maine, from where we would fly with Norm and Smudge to the camp in Labrador. This, we learned, was a distance of approximately a thousand miles. A thousand-mile flight in a commercial plane is nothing to get excited about, but Pete and I were to learn that to fly a thousand miles in a tiny plane is another matter altogether.

Early the next morning we took off into a cloudless sky which seemed to guarantee ideal flying conditions. Pete flew with Smudge in a Piper "Apache" equipped with wheels; Norm and I took off from the Penobscot River in a Cessna rigged with pontoons.

We landed at Van Buren to clear customs, then headed for Seven Islands, Quebec, where we would take on gas. It had been smooth sailing up to then, but in crossing the St. Lawrence we ran into bumpy going. Our perfect day had turned into something quite different, and when we sat down at Seven Islands it was in weather that had become downright nasty.

We headed north from Seven Islands and began climbing to clear the Laurentide escarpment. The air was as full of holes as Swiss cheese, and we bounced and banged along in a steady series of tooth-jarring impacts. Rain hammered at the plane and visibility diminished.

We were in touch with Smudge and Pete by radio, and when the weather steadily grew worse Smudge announced that they were turning back toward Seven Islands. We continued on, and soon we were over the Labrador plateau, a region which, from the air, seemed to be made up of almost as much water as land. Norm assured me that a forced landing, which seemed a likely possibility, would be nothing more serious than an inconvenience. He could kill the motor anywhere and bring the plane down safely, he declared. So he elected to continue on.

The iron mining town of Schefferville, Quebec, is connected with the outside world only by a 350-mile railroad which ends at Seven Islands. We picked up the railroad after our climb and followed it as a guideline. By that time the weather had forced us down to an altitude of only a few hundred feet.

Our flight plan called for us to land at Schefferville, but the seaplane base was too socked-in for a safe landing. Norm canceled the plan by radio and declared his intention of heading directly for the fishing camp, sixty-five air miles east of Schefferville. There, he hoped, we'd have enough visibility for a landing.

We had been in the air over ten hours when Norm announced that we were only a few miles from the camp. But ahead of us lay a solid bank of fog and clouds, and he appended this welcome announcement with one which was not as encouraging. He didn't dare proceed, he said; the camp was guarded by low, but very substantial hills, and it would be foolhardy to risk an approach until the hills could be plainly seen.

Talk about frustration! It seemed that we had come a thousand miles, only to spend a cold and wretched night in the little plane only a few miles from our destination. But I resigned myself to this unpleasant development prematurely, and with too little respect for Norm's skill as a pilot.

He banked the plane and studied the situation carefully while we flew in a tight circle.

"We're in a pocket of visibility that seems to be drifting toward the camp," he said. "We'll keep circling, and if the pocket moves over the camp we'll duck in."

Sure enough, after we had flown several circles, the hills Norm feared suddenly came into view.

"We've got it made," Norm declared. "We'll be drinking coffee in the cook shack inside of ten minutes."

To my inexpressible relief, we were. By that time the weather had closed in completely again, and the rain came down in sheets. A delay of only a few minutes in our arrival, and we would have spent the night in the plane exactly as I had anticipated.

It was only late August, but the next day was so cold and wretched that fishing was out of the question. As the wind howled and rain beat on the roof, I rather envied Pete. He and Smudge were undoubtedly drowning their frustration in some snug bar in Seven Islands.

Early the next morning I was startled from a sound sleep by a plane which buzzed the camp at little more than treetop level. I crawled from my sleeping bag and stumbled outside the plywood cabin. Every cloud had been swept from the sky, and the plane gleamed in the rays of the rising sun as it made another pass over the camp. It was Smudge's Piper, and the buzzing was to serve notice that Smudge and Pete would soon be waiting in Schefferville for Norm to pick them up in the seaplane.

Less than two hours later they were eating breakfast in the cook shack and telling their story between bites. After returning to Seven Islands they had decided to make another try with the mistaken idea that the weather had cleared. It had done so only to the extent of decoying them beyond the point of no return. Then conditions became so hopeless that they had no choice but to attempt a forced landing.

They were following the railroad, and during its construction airstrips had been bulldozed here and there along its course. These had long been abandoned and neglected and were in sorry shape. But with luck, Smudge had managed to bring the plane down safely on one of the rough and rutted strips.

There they had spent two cold and miserable nights in the ruins of what had been a tool shack. We had foolishly stowed gear in the two planes with no eye for such an emergency, and this compounded their plight. Fortunately, they had their sleeping bags with them and enough food to make out. But their heavy clothing and rain gear were in the Cessna with Norm and me. Launching the plane that morning had been a difficult and risky business, but their luck had held.

Now that we were regrouped, Norm and Smudge disclosed plans which they had kept secret. They had prospected for fishing over much of Labrador, and during one prospecting trip they had landed near an Eskimo village on the coast. There they were told of a spot so teeming with arctic char that the Eskimos called it the "Home of the Fish." Following directions that were anything but specific, they had found the place—and had discovered the fishing to be every bit as spectacular as described.

Later they flew a tent, supplies and extra gas to a deep fjord a considerable distance from the actual fishing spot. The outlet of the fjord was alive with arctic char, they said, and the chosen campsite would provide access to both places. Pete and I were to be the first guests to sample the fishing.

Our destination lay approximately 250 miles northeast of the permanent fishing camp, and where we would be beyond radio contact with Schefferville. I listened as Norm gave the approximate fix of the fishing spot and left instructions to notify the airbase at Schefferville if we weren't back within five days. The sobering implications of this precaution intruded on my visions of big fish, but only momentarily.

Although the task looked impossible, Norm soon had all our gear stowed in the little plane, with room for Pete and me to cram ourselves into the rear compartment. Very shortly thereafter the four of us were aloft and headed for the coast. It was the beginning of a never-to-be-forgotten experience.

Labrador is an immense plateau which tilts upward in the direction of the coast. The western part includes chains of lakes and rivers which stretch in all directions as far as the eye can see. The region is totally uninhabited and virtually impenetrable. Because of this, the waters, which make up approximately twenty percent of the total area, are largely unfished and await exploration. Since vast areas of virgin wilderness are foreign to common experience, such an expanse of unfished water is hard to imagine in the abstract. Only when one can look down upon it from a plane does it become a conceivable reality, and for a fisherman the sight is almost overwhelming. As I drank in the full implication, I was all but intoxicated by the realization that I was at last where I had always dreamed of being: in a region where fish lived and flourished beyond all human encroachment, with every mile taking us deeper into this exotic context.

The land below us was sparsely spiked with spruce trees. The ground was covered with deep moss in which a network of caribou trails was constantly visible. As we continued northeast the tree growth dwindled, the lakes became fewer and the brown carpet of moss gave way to outcroppings of naked rock. Rushing streams appeared as the land became more elevated and irregular, and patches of perennial snow lay on shaded slopes and in depressions. Finally, as we neared the coast, snowcapped mountains loomed ahead.

The coast of Labrador is a region of ominous grandeur, the sight of which inspires exotic emotions that are beyond description. Mountains of naked rock rise to heights of several thousand feet, lending abysmal perspective to the many fjords which thrust inland from the sea. The effect is so awesome that the Eskimos refer to the section as the "Home of the Spirits," and one is tempted to believe that the name derives from more than superstition alone. It is a land so openly hostile to human presence that guardianship by evil spirits seems a strong possibility.

Close to the coast, we flew over a fjord so deep that the bottom of the earth seemed to have fallen away. Norm guided the little plane down into this chasm, and we had the experience of flying between walls of rock which rose high above us on both sides. Moments later we could make out a tiny patch of green on a small shelf on the shore of the fjord. It was the tent in which we would spend the night. Satisfied that it was still standing, Norm pulled the plane out of the deep canyon and headed it for the river in which we were to fish for arctic char.

In making our approach we first flew out over the sea, crossing a bay in which floated icebergs of dazzling whiteness. Soon we came opposite the mouth of a rushing river, and Norm pointed the nose of the plane directly upstream. A few miles from the sea we reached the place where the river was born, the outlet of a large and beautiful lake which threaded its way inland among towering mountains. Norm eased the plane down on the calm surface of the lake, and as we stepped ashore a startled Canada goose led her flotilla of half-grown goslings toward the safety of the opposite shore.

As we drew on waders and set up rods, Pete and I experienced emotions that are denied all but the most fortunate fishermen. We had left our homes to travel over 1600 miles, many of these across a land utterly devoid of human habitation. We had watched the proof of the almost incredible remoteness of our destination flow beneath us, and we were appropriately attuned to the exotic nature of the package we were about to open. If our hands trembled as we fumbled our rods together, it was not without good reason.

Unlike the many dreams which fail to materialize, ours came true to the last detail. We hiked around the shore of the lake to where the river began, and there drank in a spectacle which had not been apparent from the air. Tons of white water came thundering out of the lake, spewing over a dike of solid granite in a great chute of leaping foam. Below, the escaping water spread to form an enormous pool of conflicting currents before flowing off to the sea.

Pete, Norm and Smudge cast big Dardevles into the pool almost simultaneously. With a devotion to duty beyond all normal call, I first dug into my pack for a camera. Before I could ready it, all three fishermen were fast to wildly fighting fish. Their spinning reels buzzed in unison, so loudly that I could hear them above the roar of the river, and three arctic char tore downriver as though they had no intention of stopping until they reached the sea. I snapped a picture of the trio braced against bucking rods, then hastened to heave out my own lure with feverish anticipation.

I let the spoon sink well down into the swirling current, then felt it smacked almost as soon as I started to retrieve it. My line streaked straight toward the tossing foam, and a glistening body of gunmetal hue hurtled high above violent water in a magnificent leap. In another instant the frantic fish headed straight down the pool in a run that took nearly a hundred yards of line from my spinning reel. I had questioned Norm about the fighting qualities of arctic char, and he had told me that in his opinion they would outfight Atlantic salmon. Moments after hooking my first char I was ready to agree.

The great pool was alive with fish, and for the remainder of the afternoon there were few moments when one or more of us didn't have a fish on. Pete caught the biggest, a char of twelve pounds, but we all had fish break off which undoubtedly were larger. This was practically unavoidable, due to the nature of the pool and the great force of the current which each hooked fish immediately used to advantage. Many reacted to the sting of the hook by making a single, wild leap; all took off downriver at full speed, sometimes running an estimated hundred yards or more of line without stopping. They would then bulldog against the rod while they regained strength and take off in another downstream dash which often threatened to clean the reel. The pool spread back from the fast water in a backwater so enormous that it was impossible to follow a hooked fish; we had to stand pat, put on all the pressure we dared and hope for the best. When it became a case of either stopping a fish or letting him clean the reel, the line sometimes parted under the increased pressure.

My previous impressions of arctic char had been gained only from pictures of highly colored fish. As a result, I had expected fish which outdid the brook trout with respect to coloration and was surprised when the char we caught exhibited only neutral colors. They were a metallic blue-gray along their backs and sides and sparsely peppered with light gray spots. Their bellies were a gleaming white.

This lack of coloration, I learned, was due to the fact that the fish were fresh from the sea. As they moved inland to spawn they, the males in particular, would take on the vivid colors I had seen in pictures.

The char were so eager to hit a spoon that I jumped to the conclusion that they would certainly go for a big streamer. I set up a fly rod with high expectations, but my efforts with it came to naught. I suspected at the time that the trouble was inability to sink the streamer deeply enough. Later experience convinced me that arctic char are just hard to take on flies. In any event, it was very difficult, at least for me, to fish vainly with a fly for any significant period of time while those around me were hooking fish on spoons almost as fast as they could land them.

As is often the case, the heaviest and strongest fish were the least inclined to leap, and their first runs invariably took them so far downstream that we could only estimate their size from the savage power of the runs. We came away with no actual idea of the size of the fish which broke our lines, but some of them must have been truly tremendous. As an example, Pete had one on for a solid hour, and the fish seemed as strong as ever when Pete finally had to break him off.

He hooked the fish late in the afternoon, and during the hour-long battle never regained any of the line taken out in the first sizzling run. The sun sank behind the mountains, and at last Norm announced that our departure couldn't be postponed any longer. Pete would either have to bring in the fish or break him off.

Pete grimly tightened the drag of his reel and began cranking slowly. His line lifted from the water under the strain until it stood clear for many yards downstream. More reeling extracted the last bit of stretch from the great length of nylon. Pete ceased reeling, ounces short of the breaking point, but the big char refused to yield under the pressure. Reluctantly, Pete gave the reel handle a few more turns, and the tortured line finally parted. It was a heartbreaking experience, but not a total loss. For the rest of his days, Pete will cherish the conviction that for a thrill-packed hour he was fast to an arctic char that would have challenged all records.

We climbed above mountains whose tops reflected the rapidly waning daylight, but the deep fjords already were vast pools of shadow and darkness. I had lost all sense of direction and orientation, but Norm and Smudge held a running consultation in which they checked off what, to them, were recognizable landmarks. Just when it seemed that darkness would overtake us, Norm guided the plane down into the somber depths of the fjord in which our tent was pitched.

The hard nip of frost was already in the air as we built a fire and fried steaks. By the time we had finished eating, the wet waders which I had draped over the tail of the plane were frozen stiff. As I recall, it was the first day of September, but Norm told us that the ground was likely to be deep with snow before the month was half over.

Night came on with a rush, and as we yarned around the fire we were treated to a display of northern lights which I can still see vividly in retrospect, but for which I can find no adequate words of description. What seemed to be the beams of giant searchlights swept the skies above us, while vertical curtains of brilliant and ever-changing hues danced and undulated as though wafted about by angry storms. It was a spectacle of magnificent beauty, but also one of implied threat. It conveyed the disturbing feeling that human presence was frowned on, and that our intrusion might at any moment make us the unfortunate victims of cosmic wrath. Then, even more keenly than before, I shared the Eskimos' awe of that magnificent but ominous region.

Early the next morning we crowded into the plane and flew down the fjord, landing just above a rips below which the outlet became a tidal river. Norm and Smudge promised that here we would find even more char than existed in the big pool we had fished the previous day, but they added that they would not run as large.

It was a beautiful place to fish, posing none of the difficulties which had contributed to the loss of so many big fish the previous afternoon. A smooth, sandy bottom made wading easy, and the flow of the river was even and sedate. And talk about fish! Almost every cast brought a prompt strike from arctic char which ranged from those of two pounds in weight to six-pounders, and which fought like supercharged demons.

To my great delight, fish were breaking the surface within easy reach, so once more I rigged up a fly rod with great anticipation. In the meantime, Pete, Norm and Smudge were taking fish on medium-size Dardevles as fast as they could whip one char down and cast for another.

But although I floated a dry fly among dozens of rising fish, none paid it the slightest attention. Finally, unable to stand the torture of going fishless in the midst of plenty, I waded ashore to swap my fly rod for a spinning outfit.

Norm saw me making the change and shouted to ask if I had any wet flies. When I told him I had plenty, he asked if he might borrow a few, as well as my fly rod. I placed a box of wet flies beside the fly rod and told him to help himself.

Norm had the wisdom to guess that the char were taking something just under the surface. He began fishing a sunken wet fly among them, allowing it to come over them with a dead drift. After a prolonged period of casting he finally hooked and landed a char, and at the end of an equal interval he hooked another. In the meantime, I had caught at least a dozen fish on a spoon.

Norm proved that arctic char can be caught on flies. But it took considerable time and effort to take a pair of fish from a river that was fairly teeming with them. Before I could make a second try the fish suddenly stopped rising, and my hope of taking at least one arctic char on a fly went down the drain. But I had experimented enough to conclude that if all arctic char behaved as did those which we had encountered, they are a relatively poor bet for the fly fisherman.

We had caught so many of these fish that we had lost all sense of actual numbers, so that afternoon we decided to fly back to the base camp. Norm and Smudge had wanted us to take and photograph char (we had snapped dozens of pictures); now that that had been accomplished, they were equally eager for us to sample the fishing for big brook trout and ouananiche in their home waters.

On the flight to the coast we had flown over a particularly inviting lake which Norm declared to be fully as large as Moosehead Lake in Maine. Many lesser streams ran into the lake, but it was fed also by what obviously was a very large river. The lake was an unknown quantity to Norm and Smudge, and although such a thing is hard to imagine nowadays, it probably had never been fished by a sport fisherman. Just the thought of heaving out a lure at the mouth of that river was enough to make one's pulse quicken, and Norm had declared that we would try it on the way back if possible.

Pete and I looked forward to prospecting that unfished lake, which most certainly must have held some huge fish. Unfortunately, we didn't get to do so. It was late in the afternoon as we came over the lake, and we were still at least a hundred miles from our home base. Our reserve cushion of gas was minimal, Norm declared, and after carefully weighing the risks involved he decided against the stopover.

The temptation to fish that lake was tantalizing, and Pete and I often speculate about what results would have been had we gone down for a try. Maybe we will never know. On the other hand, maybe Norm has that remote lake in mind as an objective for another trip.

Not only is Labrador one of the few regions where unknown and unnamed lakes and rivers still exist, but the fish which exist in its waters are made up of the species most ardently sought by sport fishermen—and they all grow to trophy size.

Labrador is one of the few areas in the world where really large brook trout are abundant. Many of the lakes and streams which hold big brookies have populations of ouananiche which include fish up to ten pounds in weight. In both the streams and lakes, right along with the brook trout and salmon, are lake trout which reach enormous sizes. Moreover, the lakers will take flies and lures near the surface, for the water never grows so warm that it drives them into the depths.

The fishing season is relatively short, restricted to July, August and no more than the first half of September. Norm told us that during July and the first half of August, large hatches of mayflies resulted in dry fly fishing that had few, if any, equals. In the waters surrounding the base camp, the daily take with dry flies (per fisherman) was almost certain to include several brookies of more than four pounds, plus ouananiche of equal, or greater, size.

Unfortunately, freezing nights and chilly days had put an end to the hatches by the time we arrived. In fact, they seemed to have put an end to the fishing in general; we spent the first day after our return fishing proven spots with disappointing results.

That evening Norm voiced the opinion that perhaps the trout and salmon had moved into smaller streams preparatory to spawning, and that we might locate them by acting accordingly. Norm and Smudge had to fly to Schefferville the next day to arrange details concerning closing camp for the year, but a guide would take Pete and me to a small stream which Norm looked on as a good bet.

The stream was nothing more than a short connection between lakes, half a mile long and small enough for easy wading. Still hoping for surface fishing, we tied on dry flies and began working upstream. We had hardly started when Pete let out a whoop that brought me on the run with camera ready. I arrived in time to photograph him in the act of landing a brook trout of over four pounds, a male fish decked out in spawning colors of spectacular beauty.

Needless to say, we went at the stream in earnest with dry flies, but to our bitter disappointment we couldn't raise another fish. I fished carefully through a long, boulder-studded pool that had to hold trout if any were present anywhere. Failing to get a single strike, I finally decided it was time to give up the hope of bringing fish to a dry fly.

I changed leaders, tied on a big streamer and cast it across the current. It arced across the stream without results, and I twitched it upstream close to the shoreline. As it came abreast of a foam-covered pocket it was suddenly seized amid a mighty swirl and a flash of brilliant red and orange. I was fast to a brookie that was a near twin of the one Pete had taken. When I had landed the fish after a stubborn and powerful battle, a second cast brought a wallop from another lunker. I yelled to Pete to come and take *my* picture.

After photographing me with the second fish, Pete switched to a streamer, waded across the stream above the pool and then took up a position directly across from mine. For the next hour, and without moving, we had a taste of what paradise would be if fishermen could have their say.

Brook trout of all sizes came to our streamers in what was almost a regular pattern. A fish of three pounds or more would be followed by several smaller trout—brookies that would arouse envy if taken in close-to-home waters, but small by the standards which gave a dream-like quality to our happy circumstance. Then, after several lesser trout had struck, there would come another rod-plunging belt from another whopper, and the cycle would be repeated.

When at last the trout in the pool ceased hitting, I asked Pete to estimate the number we had caught. He said that in his opinion we had taken at least a hundred. It had seemed that to me, but I had hesitated to voice an estimate for by that time I was too overwhelmed by the experience to trust my judgment.

I had only trout in mind when I moved downstream to refish water that had yielded nothing to dry flies. Consequently, I was quite unprepared for the enormous ouananiche which came to my streamer on the first cast. The big fish showed most of its length and bulk as it hit, and at the sight I yelled to Pete that I had hooked a salmon of at least ten pounds.

With all due allowance for my excitement, I doubt that I exaggerated by much, if at all. The reel wailed as the dynamic fish tore across the pool—then the line suddenly went slack. I had given the fish no pressure to work against save for the light drag of the reel, but the hook must have engaged only superficially. At any rate, it simply let go.

Numb with disappointment, I cast again and got another hard strike. This turned out to be from a ouananiche of over five pounds which ran and leaped like a fish gone mad before I finally netted it. But by following the huge ouananiche that had come off, this splendid fish seemed hardly more than a pygmy.

We kept only a few of the largest fish for photographing, but if it could have been done without injury to the fish, I would have liked to photograph our total take for the day. I'd like such a photograph if for no other reason than to prove that it hadn't all been a fantastic dream.

All good things come to an end, but with luck they can repeat themselves. Norm and Smudge were forced to give up their fishing camp the following year. Their lease was canceled by the Newfoundland government because of anticipated hydroelectric developments. Smudge entered into a partnership in developing a fishing camp on the George River in northern Quebec. In the meantime I had placed an article about the first trip, and the following year Smudge invited Pete and me to fish the George for Atlantic salmon with another article in mind.

The camp on the George, the George River Lodge, is located about fifty miles upriver from Ungava Bay. It is buried in the wild wasteland that is typical of the Labrador-Ungava region, but this time, thank goodness, our trip was uneventful.

We drove from Pittsford to Montreal, flew via Quebec Air to Schefferville and were flown from there to the George River in a twin-engine seaplane. Compared to our trip to the Labrador coast, this jaunt seemed almost indecently easy.

The George is one of the great rivers of northern Quebec, and one of the finest Atlantic salmon rivers in North America. It is huge and brawling, and anything but easy to fish. Difficulties arise not only because of the wild character of the river itself, but also because of subarctic winds and cold which make casting difficult and prolonged fishing a test of endurance.

We arrived during the last few days of August, but the next day a freezing sleet storm kept everybody in camp. The weather cleared that night, but not before blanketing the land with fully six inches of snow. I caught my first George River salmon, a fourteen-pound fish, against the wintry background commonly pictured on Christmas cards.

Not only does the George River have an annual run of large salmon, but it holds brook trout of trophy size, plus many lake trout. Lakers up to ten pounds rise to flies cast for salmon, and fish of several times that weight are there for any who choose to go after them with king-size hardware.

The salmon run begins around the middle of August and reaches its peak in September. The trout fishing, excellent earlier, falls off about the time the salmon begin showing, but with salmon in the river all attention focuses on this king of freshwater game fish. Splendid brook trout are landed with what amounts to indifference, and inadvertent hang-ups with lakers are looked on as a nuisance. The lakers are strong and heavy, but comparatively sluggish. Their refusal to burn themselves out in fast runs results in a dull and drawn-out battle that is to be deplored when one is eager to tie into a salmon.

The salmon which run the George average larger than those common to most North American salmon rivers. This is due in part to the fact that some weigh as much as thirty pounds, but more to the fact that grilses are virtually absent. These smaller salmon, which return to rivers to spawn after spending a comparatively short time in the sea, make up a large part of the take on many salmon streams. Smudge Grant assured us that we would take few, if any, salmon weighing under ten pounds, and this proved to be true. We caught no salmon that were appreciably under the ten-pound mark, nor did we see any brought in by other fishermen.

We were new at the game, but I suspect that the George River poses problems for experienced salmon fishermen accustomed to smaller and tamer rivers. No holding pools exist on the George, for one thing, and there is no opportunity to fish for previously located fish. Most of the water lies completely beyond reach, too violent to be fished from canoe or boat and unapproachable by wading. The fisherman must endure the frustration of seeing salmon break, roll and leap in midriver while forced to confine his efforts to only the edges of the massive flow. This is not as prohibitive to his chances as it may sound, for at various points the salmon favor the easier shoreline current, and in such places plenty of fish pass within casting range.

Pete and I came well stocked with conventional salmon flies: standard patterns of wet flies in a variety of sizes, plus bushy dry flies which we hoped we could use to good effect. Contrary to our hopes, none of our flies produced the desired results. Apparently, something out of the ordinary was needed to attract the salmon's attention in the tossing currents of that mighty river.

This was proven when one of the fishermen began taking salmon on a fly which I have mentioned in a previous chapter, and which I had seen Norm Hathaway use with telling effect in Labrador. Its construction has already been described, and from the description it can be seen that it violates the artistic standards to which conventional salmon flies usually adhere.

We had seen bands of caribou every day, and along their trails we had seen hair which they apparently shed in thickly matted patches of fleece. Pete had tucked a patch in his fishing vest to take home to his oldest boy who is a budding naturalist, and it provided us with material for duplicating the crude and shaggy fly that had proven its effectiveness. I had a spool of rod-winding thread in my kit, and from the caribou hair I fashioned copies on hooks stripped of dressing that had proven to be ineffective.

The next morning, Pete made a noisy job of stomping into his waders as it was just turning light. Given back twenty years, I would have been quick to join him. But my older bones still ached from the previous day's fishing, and I only groaned and scrounged deeper into the comfort of my sleeping bag.

We were eating breakfast when Pete returned, bouncing with excitement. A huge salmon had walloped one of the caribou hair creations almost immediately, and during the remaining time Pete had been playing the big fish. He had had him almost within tailing distance several times, only to have the salmon make yet another long run. Finally, the fish apparently took a turn around a sunken rock and then snapped the leader.

We weren't long in getting to the river. As usual, a wind of nearly gale force made casting an arm-wearying job, but by timing the gusts, and beefing into each cast, it was possible to drop the hair flies on currents the salmon were using. For perhaps the tenth time I cast as far as I could manage, and then watched the buoyant hair fly leave a wake as it cut across the current on a tight line. It dipped under as waves and small whirlpools engulfed it, but always it bobbed to the surface again and resumed its course. I was thinking how much it resembled a mouse swimming valiantly for its life, when it suddenly disappeared in the center of a violent swirl. The line came taut against the rod, then it ripped upward as a dozen pounds of salmon climbed high above the water.

There followed one of the hardest days of fishing I have ever put in. A guide brought us our lunches at noon, and apart from the short time it took us to gobble sandwiches, and the time devoted to photography, we stood waist-deep in icy water, flailing with leaden arms against a wind that showed us no mercy. Despite insulated underwear and heavy woolen outer garments, we were chilled to the bone from almost the first minute. When we finally quit that evening I felt as though I had been frozen and then beaten with a length of rubber hose.

But we were as happy and fulfilled as we were cold and bone weary. During the day we had landed six salmon weighing from ten to seventeen pounds. We had hooked and lost others and had had strikes which we missed. Furthermore, we had found the answer to our needs in the rough hair flies, for they continued to produce throughout the remainder of our stay.

As a result of writing a couple of articles about the Labrador-Ungava region, I have been asked many questions by interested fishermen. This has been rather embarrassing, for one hardly becomes an authority on a region so vast and little known with the help of only two trips of short duration. Yet I am keenly aware of a fisherman's burning desire to fish where few others have fished, and I have tried to be as helpful as my very limited experience will permit.

In answering queries I have tried to point out both the good and the bad in order to help the fisherman decide if a Labrador-Ungava trip can fulfill a lifelong ambition. It did just that for Pete and me, but I'm sure that there are others for whom such a trip would be unpleasant and disappointing.

In the first place, if my experience is a valid criterion, the weather is likely to be hostile and even downright bitter. Both of our trips carried over into September, and that must be taken into account. But if one hopes to catch Atlantic salmon he has no choice but to go late in the season and should expect to encounter freezing weather.

The weather enters the picture from another angle, for the success of any trip depends absolutely on conditions which will permit flying. One can be grounded for days on end, and there is never any assurance that a trip will not be ruined because of the inability to fly. Pete and I were relatively lucky, but we listened to stories about parties who spent most of their allotted time waiting for the weather to clear.

Relatively few comforts can be offered by fishing camps in the far north. Distance and transportation difficulties preclude all but the most basic necessities. If trips are made to outlying waters, one must be prepared to put up with much less.

I'm sure that most people are quite unaware of the vastness of the uninhabited and impassable regions which exist in Labrador and northern Quebec. I can assure you that if you penetrate these regions deeply you will be beyond any prompt help from the outside in case of an emergency. The need for medical attention could arise when foul weather made flying impossible; plane damage or malfunction would result in a serious predicament. These risks are part of the deal and could offset the most spectacular fishing for those who could not accept them with equanimity.

The country is wild and rugged, and I have reached an age when I find the physical demands of such a trip to be exhausting. I have gladly paid the price of creaking joints and aching muscles for exotic fishing, but this could be a no-go factor for those who feel that no fishing is worth suffering for.

I have been asked many questions about tackle, mainly by those of the opinion that a considerable amount of specialized tackle would have to be bought. Pete and I chose our equipment from what we had at hand and found it to be entirely adequate. I feel sure that the rods and reels any other fisherman uses on his home waters would suffice for him equally well. Spare rods are a wise precaution and plenty of extra spinning line almost a must. Fly reels should be well filled with backing; hardware and flies should run to medium and large sizes. Waders are of vital importance.

The prospective Atlantic salmon fisherman may hesitate to tackle fish which may exceed twenty pounds in weight with a fly rod which has never stood up to anything larger than trout. But any rod which will deliver long casts is adequate if equipped with a reel which holds sufficient backing—a couple of hundred yards if one wants to be on the safe side.

I took two fly rods with me on the trip to the George River. One was an 8-foot Orvis which handles a No. 8 line, the other a 7½-foot Orvis which takes a No. 7 line. I found the 8-footer to be perfectly adequate, and when Pete stepped on the butt of his rod he used the 7½-foot rod and found it to be up to the job.

Actually, the greatest need for backbone in a salmon rod comes when making long casts, rather than while playing fish. Salmon wear themselves out by leaping and making long runs, and the reel, rather than the rod on which it is mounted, is the instrument which plays the chief part in their undoing.

Although the cost of a Labrador-Ungava trip need not include expenses for special tackle, it adds up to what, by my standards, is a sizable amount of money. Most outfitters take over at Schefferville, and furnish air transportation to fishing sites as part of their services. Round-trip plane fare from Montreal to Schefferville is about $150.00. A week at a fishing camp costs between $400.00 and $500.00 during the first part of the season. The charge for a week during the salmon run, or for a trip such as Pete and I took for arctic char, is about double that figure.

What do you get for your time, effort and money? If our two trips are valid measurements, you come away with the memory of a thrilling experience that will stay fresh in your mind for the rest of your days. You will have seen wild, primitive country and wildlife that has little fear of man. And you will have fished waters that teem with big fish, and which, as yet, have suffered no significant depletion at the hands of mankind.

Unfortunately, the fish of cold, subarctic waters grow and reproduce at a much slower rate than those of warmer regions, so the consequence of only moderate fishing pressure is rapid deterioration. For the present, Labrador-Ungava is a land of many unfished waters, but this circumstance cannot endure for long. The exotic, primitive quality of each unfished lake and stream will soon be destroyed by the inexorable expansion of civilization's frontiers.

The rate of this expansion is so rapid that it is sadly obvious that it can be only a few years before the few remaining regions that have been spared encroachment will be swallowed up and stripped of that grandeur and dignity which can exist nowhere but beyond the limits of human invasion.

We who are living today have the dubious distinction of being among the last ever to know the exquisite and deeply moving emotions which derive from setting foot on land that has defied all human influence. The more remote sections of Labrador-Ungava still fall in this category, and the fisherman who fishes in this still wild and untamed land will be among the last to savor one of the most exotic of all human experiences.

THE DOORS OF HIS FACE, THE LAMPS OF HIS MOUTH

ROGER ZELAZNY

'm a baitman. No one is born a baitman, except in a French novel where everyone is. (In fact, I think that's the title, *We are All Bait, Pfft!*) How I got that way is barely worth telling and has nothing to do with neo-exes, but the days of the beast deserve a few words, so here they are.

The Lowlands of Venus lie between the thumb and forefinger of the continent known as Hand. When you break into Cloud Alley it swings its silverblack bowling ball toward you without a warning. You jump then, inside that firetailed tenpin they ride you down in, but the straps keep you from making a fool of yourself. You generally chuckle afterwards, but you always jump first.

Next, you study Hand to lay its illusion and the two middle fingers become dozen-ringed archipelagoes as the outers resolve into greengray peninsulas; the thumb is too short, and curls like the embryo tail of Cape Horn.

You suck pure oxygen, sigh possibly, and begin the long topple to the Lowlands.

There, you are caught like an infield fly at the Lifeline landing area —so named because of its nearness to the great delta in the Eastern Bay—located between the first peninsula and "thumb." For a minute it seems as if you're going to miss Lifeline and wind up as canned seafood, but afterwards—shaking off the metaphors—you descend to scorched concrete and present your middle-sized telephone directory of authorizations to the short, fat man in the gray cap. The papers show that you are not subject to mysterious inner rottings and etcetera. He then smiles you a short, fat, gray smile and motions you toward the bus which hauls you to the Reception Area. At the R.A. you spend three days proving that, indeed, you are not subject to mysterious inner rottings and etcetera.

Boredom, however, is another rot. When your three days are up, you generally hit Lifeline hard, and it returns the compliment as a matter of reflex. The effects of alcohol in variant atmospheres is a subject on which the connoisseurs have written numerous volumes, so I will confine my remarks to noting that a good binge is worthy of at least a week's time and often warrants a lifetime study.

I had been a student of exceptional promise (strictly undergraduate) for going on two years when the *Bright Water* fell through our marble ceiling and poured its people like targets into the city.

Pause. The Worlds Almanac re Lifeline: ". . . Port city on the eastern coast of Hand. Employees of the Agency for Non-terrestrial Research compromise approximately 85% of its 100,000 population (2010 Census). Its other residents are primarily personnel maintained by several industrial corporations engaged in basic research. Independent marine biologists, wealthy fishing enthusiasts, and waterfront entrepreneurs make up the remainder of its inhabitants."

I turned to Mike Dabis, a fellow entrepreneur, and commented on the lousy state of basic research.

"Not if the mumbled truth be known."

He paused behind his glass before continuing the slow swallowing process calculated to obtain my interest and a few oaths, before he continued.

"Carl," he finally observed, poker playing, "they're shaping Tensquare."

I could have hit him. I might have refilled his glass with sulfuric acid and looked on with glee as his lips blackened and cracked. Instead, I grunted a noncommittal.

"Who's fool enough to shell out fifty grand a day? ANR?"

He shook his head.

"Jean Luharich," he said, "the girl with the violet contacts and fifty or sixty perfect teeth. I understand her eyes are really brown."

"Isn't she selling enough face cream these days?"

He shrugged.

"Publicity makes the wheels go 'round. Luharich Enterprises jumped sixteen points when she picked up the Sun Trophy. You ever play golf on Mercury?"

I had, but I overlooked it and continued to press.

"So she's coming here with a blank check and a fishhook?"

"Bright Water, today," he nodded. "Should be down by now. Lots of cameras. She wants an Ikky, bad."

"Hmm," I hmmed. "How bad?"

"Sixty day contract, Tensquare. Indefinite extension clause. Million and a half deposit," he recited.

"You seem to know a lot about it."

"I'm Personal Recruitment. Luharich Enterprises approached me last month. It helps to drink in the right places.

"Or own them." He smirked, after a moment.

I looked away, sipping my bitter brew. After awhile I swallowed several things and asked Mike what he expected to be asked, leaving myself open for his monthly temperance lecture.

"They told me to try getting you," he mentioned. "When's the last time you sailed?"

"Month and a half ago. The *Corning."*

"Small stuff," he snorted. "When have you been under, yourself?"

"It's been awhile."

"It's been over a year, hasn't it? That time you got cut by the screw, under the *Dolphin?"*

I turned to him.

"I was in the river last week, up at Angleford where the currents are strong. I can still get around."

"Sober," he added.

"I'd stay that way," I said, "on a job like this."

A doubting nod.

"Straight union rates. Triple time for extraordinary circumstances," he narrated. "Be at Hangar Sixteen with your gear, Friday morning, five hundred hours. We push off Saturday, daybreak."

"You're sailing?"

"I'm sailing."

"How come?"

"Money."

"Ikky guano."

"The bar isn't doing so well and baby needs new minks."

"I repeat—"

". . . And I want to get away from baby, renew my contact with basics—fresh air, exercise, make cash. . . ."

"All right, sorry I asked."

I poured him a drink, concentrating on H_2SO_4, but it didn't transmute. Finally I got him soused and went out into the night to walk and think things over.

Around a dozen serious attempts to land *Ichthyform Leviosaurus Levianthus,* generally known as "Ikky," had been made over the past five years. When Ikky was first sighted, whaling techniques were employed. These proved either fruitless or disastrous, and a new procedure was inaugurated. Tensquare was constructed by a wealthy sportsman named Michael Jandt, who blew his entire roll on the project.

After a year on the Eastern Ocean, he returned to file bankruptcy. Carlton Davits, a playboy fishing enthusiast, then purchased the huge raft and laid a wake for Ikky's spawning grounds. On the nineteenth day out he had a strike and lost one hundred and fifty bills' worth of untested gear, along with one *Ichthyform Levianthus*. Twelve days later, using tripled lines, he hooked, narcotized, and began to hoist the huge beast. It awakened then, destroyed a control tower, killed six men, and worked general hell over five square blocks of Tensquare. Carlton was left with partial hemiplegia and a bankruptcy suit of his own. He faded into waterfront atmosphere and Tensquare changed hands four more times, with less spectacular but equally expensive results.

Finally, the big raft, built only for one purpose, was purchased at auction by ANR for "marine research." Lloyd's still won't insure it, and the only marine research it has ever seen is an occasional rental at fifty bills a day—to people anxious to tell Leviathan fish stories. I've been baitman on three of the voyages, and I've been close enough to count Ikky's fangs on two occasions. I want one of them to show my grandchildren, for personal reasons.

I faced the direction of the landing area and resolved a resolve.

"You want me for local coloring, gal. It'll look nice on the feature page and all that. But clear this—If anyone gets you an Ikky, it'll be me. I promise."

I stood in the empty Square. The foggy towers of Lifeline shared their mists.

Shoreline a couple eras ago, the western slope above Lifeline stretches as far as forty miles inland in some places. Its angle of rising is not a great one, but it achieves an elevation of several thousand feet before it meets the mountain range which separates us from the Highlands. About four miles inland and five hundred feet higher than Lifeline are set most of the surface airstrips and privately owned hangars. Hangar Sixteen houses Cal's Contract Cab, hop service, shore to ship. I do not like Cal, but he wasn't around when I climbed from the bus and waved to a mechanic.

Two of the hoppers tugged at the concrete, impatient beneath flying haloes. The one on which Steve was working belched deep within its barrel carburetor and shuddered spasmodically.

"Bellyache?" I inquired.

"Yeah, gas pains and heartburn."

He twisted setscrews until it settled into an even keening, and turned to me.

"You're for out?"

I nodded.

"Tensquare. Cosmetics. Monsters. Stuff like that."

He blinked into the beacons and wiped his freckles. The temperature was about twenty, but the big overhead spots served a double purpose.

"Luharich," he muttered. "Then you *are* the one. There's some people want to see you."

"What about?"

"Cameras. Microphones. Stuff like that."

"I'd better stow my gear. Which one am I riding?"

He poked the screwdriver at the other hopper.

"That one. You're on video tape now, by the way. They wanted to get you arriving."

He turned to the hangar, turned back.

"Say 'cheese.' They'll shoot the close-ups later."

I said something other than "cheese." They must have been using telelens and been able to read my lips, because that part of the tape was never shown.

I threw my junk in the back, climbed into a passenger seat, and lit a cigarette. Five minutes later, Cal himself emerged from the office Quonset, looking cold. He came over and pounded on the side of the hopper. He jerked a thumb back at the hangar.

"They want you in there!" he called through cupped hands. "Interview!"

"The show's over!" I yelled back. "Either that, or they can get themselves another baitman!"

His rustbrown eyes became nailheads under blond brows and his glare a spike before he jerked about and stalked off. I wondered how much they had paid him to be able to squat in his hangar and suck juice from his generator.

Enough, I guess, knowing Cal. I never liked the guy, anyway.

Venus at night is a field of sable waters. On the coasts, you can never tell where the sea ends and the sky begins. Dawn is like dumping milk into an inkwell. First, there are erratic curdles of white, then streamers. Shade the bottle for a gray colloid, then watch it whiten a little more. All of a sudden you've got day. Then start heating the mixture.

I had to shed my jacket as we flashed out over the bay. To our rear, the skyline could have been under water for the way it waved and rippled in the heatfall. A hopper can accommodate four people (five, if you want to bend Regs and underestimate weight), or three passengers with the sort of gear a baitman uses. I was the only fare, though, and the pilot was like his machine. He hummed and made no unnecessary noises. Lifeline turned a somersault and evaporated in the rear mirror at about the same time Tensquare broke the fore-horizon. The pilot stopped humming and shook his head.

I leaned forward. Feelings played flopdoodle in my guts. I knew every bloody inch of the big raft, but the feelings you once took for granted change when their source is out of reach. Truthfully, I'd had my doubts I'd ever board the hulk again. But now, now I could almost believe in predestination. There it was!

A tensquare football field of a ship. A-powered. Flat as a pancake, except for the plastic blisters in the middle and the "Rooks" fore and aft, port and starboard.

The Rook towers were named for their corner positions—and any two can work together to hoist, co-powering the graffles between them. The graffles—half gaff, half grapple—can raise enormous weights to near water level; their designer had only one thing in mind, though, which accounts for the gaff half. At water level, the Slider has to implement elevation for six to eight feet before the graffles are in a position to push upward, rather than pulling.

The Slider, essentially, is a mobile room—a big box capable of moving in any of Tensquare's crisscross groovings and "anchoring" on the strike side by means of a powerful electromagnetic bond. Its winches could hoist a battleship the necessary distance, and the whole craft would tilt, rather than the Slider come loose, if you want any idea of the strength of that bond.

The Slider houses a section operated control indicator which is the most sophisticated "reel" ever designed. Drawing broadcast power from the generator beside the center blister, it is connected by short-wave with the sonar room, where the movements of the quarry are recorded and repeated to the angler seated before the section control.

The fisherman might play his "lines" for hours, days even, without seeing any more than metal and an outline on the screen. Only when the beast is graffled and the extensor shelf, located twelve feet below waterline, slides out for support and begins to aid the winches, only then does the fisherman see his catch rising before him like a fallen Seraph. Then, as Davits learned, one looks into the Abyss itself and is required to act. He didn't, and a hundred meters of unimaginable tonnage, undernarcotized and hurting, broke the cables of the winch, snapped a graffle, and took a half-minute walk across Tensquare.

We circled till the mechanical flag took notice and waved us on

down. We touched beside the personnel hatch and I jettisoned my gear
and jumped to the deck.

"Luck," called the pilot as the door was sliding shut. Then he
danced into the air and the flag clicked blank.

I shouldered my stuff and went below.

Signing in with Malvern, the de facto captain, I learned that most of
the others wouldn't arrive for a good eight hours. They had wanted
me alone at Cal's so they could pattern the pub footage along
twentieth-century cinema lines.

Open: landing strip, dark. One mechanic prodding a contrary hopper. Stark-o-vision shot of slow bus pulling in. Heavily dressed
baitman descends, looks about, limps across field. Close-up: he grins.
Move in for words: "Do you think this is the time? The time he *will* be
landed?" Embarrassment, taciturnity, a shrug. Dub something—"I
see. And why do you think Miss Luharich has a better chance than
any of the others? It is because she's better equipped? [Grin.] Because
more is known now about the creature's habits than when you were
out before? Or is it because of her will to win, to be a champion? Is it
any one of these things, or is it all of them?" Reply: "Yeah, all of
them." "—Is that why you signed on with her? Because your instincts
say, 'This one will be it'?" Answer: "She pays union rates. I couldn't
rent that damned thing myself. And I want in." Erase. Dub something
else. Fadeout as he moves toward hopper, etcetera.

"Cheese," I said, or something like that, and took a walk around
Tensquare, by myself.

I mounted each Rook, checking out the controls and the underwater video eyes. Then I raised the main lift.

Malvern had no objections to my testing things this way. In fact, he
encouraged it. We had sailed together before and our positions had
even been reversed upon a time. So I wasn't surprised when I stepped
off the lift into the Hopkins Locker and found him waiting. For the
next ten minutes we inspected the big room in silence, walking
through its copper coil chambers soon to be Arctic.

Finally, he slapped a wall.

"Well, will we fill it?"

I shook my head.

"I'd like to, but I doubt it. I don't give two hoots and a damn who
gets credit for the catch, so long as I have a part in it. But it won't
happen. That gal's an egomaniac. She'll want to operate the Slider,
and she can't."

"You ever meet her?"

"Yeah."

"How long ago?"

"Four, five years."

"She was a kid then. How do you know what she can do now?"

"I know. She'll have learned every switch and reading by this time. She'll be up on all theory. But do you remember one time we were together in the starboard Rook, forward, when Ikky broke water like a porpoise?"

"How could I forget?"

"Well?"

He rubbed his emery chin.

"Maybe she can do it, Carl. She's raced torch ships and she's scubaed in bad waters back home." He glanced in the direction of invisible Hand. "And she's hunted in the Highlands. She might be wild enough to pull that horror into her lap without flinching.

". . . For John Hopkins to foot the bill and shell out seven figures for the corpus," he added. "That's money, even to a Luharich."

I ducked through a hatchway.

"Maybe you're right, but she was a rich witch when I knew her.

"And she wasn't blonde," I added, meanly.

He yawned.

"Let's find breakfast."

We did that.

When I was young I thought that being born a sea creature was the finest choice Nature could make for anyone. I grew up on the Pacific coast and spent my summers on the Gulf or the Mediterranean. I lived months of my life negotiating coral, photographing trench dwellers, and playing tag with dolphins. I fished everywhere there are fish, resenting the fact that they can go places I can't. When I grew older I wanted bigger fish, and there was nothing living that I knew of, excepting a Sequoia, that came any bigger than Ikky. That's part of it. . . .

I jammed a couple of extra rolls into a paper bag and filled a thermos with coffee. Excusing myself, I left the galley and made my way to the Slider berth. It was just the way I remembered it. I threw a few switches and the shortwave hummed.

"That you, Carl?"

"That's right, Mike. Let me have some juice down here, you double-crossing rat."

He thought it over, then I felt the hull vibrate as the generators cut in. I poured my third cup of coffee and found a cigarette.

"So why am I a double-crossing rat this time?" came his voice again.

"You knew about the cameramen at Hangar Sixteen?"

"Yes."

"Then you're a double-crossing rat. The last thing I want is publicity. 'He who fouled up so often before is ready to try it, nobly once more.' I can read it now."

"You're wrong. The spotlight's only big enough for one, and she's prettier than you."

My next comment was cut off as I threw the elevator switch and the elephant ears flapped above me. I rose, settling flush with the deck. Retracting the lateral rail, I cut forward into the groove. Amidships, I stopped at a juncture, dropped the lateral, and retracted the longitudinal rail.

I slid starboard, midway between the Rooks, halted, and threw on the coupler.

I hadn't spilled a drop of coffee.

"Show me pictures."

The screen glowed. I adjusted and got outlines of the bottom.

"Okay."

I threw a Status Blue switch and he matched it. The light went on. The winch unlocked. I aimed out over the waters, extended the arm, and fired a cast.

"Clean one," he commented.

"Status Red. Call strike." I threw a switch.

"Status Red."

The baitman would be on his way with this, to make the barbs tempting.

It's not exactly a fishhook. The cables bear hollow tubes; the tubes convey enough dope for any army of hopheads; Ikky takes the bait, dangled before him by remote control, and the fisherman rams the barbs home.

My hands moved over the console, making the necessary adjustments. I checked the narco-tank reading. Empty. Good, they hadn't been filled yet. I thumbed the Inject button.

"In the gullet," Mike murmured.

I released the cables. I played the beast imagined. I let him run, swinging the winch to stimulate his sweep.

I had an air conditioner on and my shirt off and it was still uncomfortably hot, which is how I knew that morning had gone over into noon. I was dimly aware of the arrivals and departures of the hoppers. Some of the crew sat in the "shade" of the doors I had left open, watching the operation. I didn't see Jean arrive or I would have ended the session and gotten below.

She broke my concentration by slamming the door hard enough to shake the bond.

"Mind telling me who authorized you to bring up the Slider?" she asked.

"No one," I replied. "I'll take it below now."

"Just move aside."

I did, and she took my seat. She was wearing brown slacks and a baggy shirt and she had her hair pulled back in a practical manner. Her cheeks were flushed, but not necessarily from the heat. She attacked the panel with a nearly amusing intensity that I found disquieting.

"Status Blue," she snapped, breaking a violet fingernail on the toggle.

I forced a yawn and buttoned my shirt slowly. She threw a side glance my way, checked the registers, and fired a cast.

I monitored the lead on the screen. She turned to me for a second.

"Status Red," she said levelly.

I nodded my agreement.

She worked the winch sideways to show she knew how. I didn't doubt she knew how and she didn't doubt that I didn't doubt, but then—

"In case you're wondering," she said, "you're not going to be anywhere near this thing. You were hired as a baitman, remember? Not a Slider operator! A baitman! Your duties consist of swimming out and setting the table for our friend the monster. It's dangerous, but you're getting well paid for it. Any questions?"

She squashed the Inject button and I rubbed my throat.

"Nope," I smiled, "but I am qualified to run that thingamajigger— and if you need me I'll be available, at union rates."

"Mister Davits," she said, "I don't want a loser operating this panel."

"Miss Luharich, there has never been a winner at this game."

She started reeling in the cable and broke the bond at the same time, so that the whole Slider shook as the big yo-yo returned. We skidded a couple of feet backward. She raised the laterals and we shot back along the groove. Slowing, she transferred rails and we jolted to a clanging halt, then shot off at a right angle. The crew scrambled away from the hatch as we skidded onto the elevator.

"In the future, Mister Davits, do not enter the Slider without being ordered," she told me.

"Don't worry. I won't even step inside if I am ordered," I answered. "I signed on as a baitman. Remember? If you want me in here, you'll have to *ask* me."

"That'll be the day," she smiled.

I agreed, as the doors closed above us. We dropped the subject and headed in our different directions after the Slider came to a halt in its berth. She did say "good day," though, which I thought showed breeding as well as determination, in reply to my chuckle.

Later that night Mike and I stoked our pipes in Malvern's cabin. The winds were shuffling waves, and a steady spattering of rain and hail overhead turned the deck into a tin roof.

"Nasty," suggested Malvern.

I nodded. After two bourbons the room had become a familiar woodcut, with its mahogany furnishings (which I had transported from Earth long ago on a whim) and the dark walls, the seasoned face of Malvern, and the perpetually puzzled expression of Dabis set between the big pools of shadow that lay behind chairs and splashed in cornets, all cast by the tiny table light and seen through a glass, brownly.

"Glad I'm in here."

"What's it like underneath on a night like this?"

I puffed, thinking of my light cutting through insides of a black diamond, shaken slightly. The meteor-dart of a suddenly illuminated fish, the swaying of grotesque ferns, like nebulae—shadow, then green, then gone—swam in a moment through my mind. I guess it's like a spaceship would feel, if a spaceship could feel, crossing between worlds—and quiet, uncannily, preternaturally quiet; and peaceful as sleep.

"Dark," I said, "and not real choppy below a few fathoms."

"Another eight hours and we shove off," commented Mike.

"Ten, twelve days, we should be there," noted Malvern.

"What do you think Ikky's doing?"

"Sleeping on the bottom with Mrs. Ikky if he has any brains."

"He hasn't. I've seen ANR's skeletal extrapolation from the bones that have washed up—"

"Hasn't everyone?"

". . . Fully fleshed, he'd be over a hundred meters long. That right, Carl?"

I agreed.

". . . Not much of a brain box, though, for his bulk."

"Smart enough to stay out of our locker."

Chuckles, because nothing exists but this room, really. The world outside is an empty, sleet drummed deck. We lean back and make clouds.

"Boss lady does not approve of unauthorized fly fishing."

"Boss lady can walk north till her hat floats."

"What did she say in there?"

"She told me that my place, with fish manure, is on the bottom."
"You don't Slide?"
"I bait."
"We'll see."
"That's all I do. If she wants a Slideman she's going to have to ask nicely."
"You think she'll have to?"
"I think she'll have to."
"And if she does, can you do it?"
"A fair question," I puffed. "I don't know the answer, though."

I'd incorporate my soul and trade forty percent of the stock for the answer. I'd give a couple years off my life for the answer. But there doesn't seem to be a lineup of supernatural takers, because no one knows. Supposing when we get out there, luck being with us, we find ourselves an Ikky? Supposing we succeed in baiting him and get lines on him. What then? If we get him shipside, will she hold on or crack up? What if she's made of sterner stuff than Davits, who used to hunt sharks with poison-darted air pistols? Supposing she lands him and Davits has to stand there like a video extra.

Worse yet, supposing she asks for Davits and he still stands there like a video extra or something else—say, some yellowbellied embodiment named Cringe?

It was when I got him up above the eight-foot horizon of steel and looked out at all that body, sloping on and on till it dropped out of sight like a green mountain range . . . And that head. Small for the body, but still immense. Fat, craggy, with lidless roulettes that had spun black and red since before my forefathers decided to try the New Continent. And swaying.

Fresh narco-tanks had been connected. It needed another shot, fast. But I was paralyzed.

It had made a noise like God playing a Hammond organ. . . .

And looked at me!

I don't know if seeing is even the same process in eyes like those. I doubt it. Maybe I was just a gray blur behind a black rock, with the plexi-reflected sky hurting its pupils. But it fixed on me. Perhaps the snake doesn't really paralyze the rabbit, perhaps it's just that rabbits are cowards by constitution. But it began to struggle and I still couldn't move, fascinated.

Fascinated by all that power, by those eyes, they found me there fifteen minutes later, a little broken about the head and shoulders, the Inject still unpushed.

And I dream about those eyes. I want to face them once more, even if their finding takes forever. I've got to know if there's something inside me that sets me apart from a rabbit, from notched plates of reflexes and instincts that always fall apart in exactly the same way whenever the proper combination is spun.

Looking down, I noticed that my hand was shaking. Glancing up, I noticed that no one else was noticing.

I finished my drink and emptied my pipe. It was late and no songbirds were singing.

I sat whittling, my legs hanging over the aft edge, the chips spinning down into the furrow of our wake. Three days out. No action.

"You!"

"Me?"

"You."

Hair like the end of the rainbow, eyes like nothing in nature, fine teeth.

"Hello."

"There's a safety rule against what you're doing, you know."

"I know. I've been worrying about it all morning."

A delicate curl climbed my knife then drifted out behind us. It settled into the foam and was plowed under. I watched her reflection in my blade, taking a secret pleasure in its distortion.

"Are you baiting me?" she finally asked.

I heard her laugh then, and turned, knowing it had been intentional.

"What, me?"

"I could push you off from here, very easily."

"I'd make it back."

"Would you push me off, then—some dark night, perhaps?"

"They're all dark, Miss Luharich. No, I'd rather make you a gift of my carving."

She seated herself beside me then, and I couldn't help but notice the dimples in her knees. She wore white shorts and a halter and still had an offworld tan to her which was awfully appealing. I almost felt a twinge of guilt at having planned the whole scene, but my right hand still blocked her view of the wooden animal.

"Okay, I'll bite. What have you got for me?"

"Just a second. It's almost finished."

Solemnly, I passed her the wooden jackass I had been carving. I felt a little sorry and slightly jackass-ish myself, but I had to follow through. I always do. The mouth was split into a braying grin. The ears were upright.

She didn't smile and she didn't frown. She just studied it.

"It's very good," she finally said, "like most things you do—and appropriate, perhaps."

"Give it to me." I extended a palm.

She handed it back and I tossed it out over the water. It missed the white water and bobbed for awhile like a pigmy seahorse.

"Why did you do that?"

"It was a poor joke. I'm sorry."

"Maybe you are right, though. Perhaps this time I've bitten off a little too much."

I snorted.

"Then why not do something safer, like another race?"

She shook her end of the rainbow.

"No. It has to be an Ikky."

"Why?"

"Why did you want one so badly that you threw away a fortune?"

"Many reasons," I said. "An unfrocked analyst who held black therapy sessions in his basement once told me, 'Mister Davits, you need to reinforce the image of your masculinity by catching one of every kind of fish in existence.' Fish are a very ancient masculinity symbol, you know. So I set out to do it. I have one more to go. Why do you want to reinforce *your* masculinity?"

"I don't," she said. "I don't want to reinforce anything but Luharich Enterprises. My chief statistician once said, 'Miss Luharich, sell all the cold cream and face powder in the System and you'll be a happy girl. Rich, too.' And he was right. I am the proof. I can look the way I do and do anything, and I sell most of the lipstick and face powder in the System—but I have to be *able* to do anything."

"You do look cool and efficient," I observed.

"I don't feel cool," she said, rising. "Let's go for a swim."

"May I point out that we are making pretty good time?"

"If you want to indicate the obvious, you may. You said you could make it back to the ship, unassisted. Change your mind?"

"No."

"Then get us two scuba outfits and I'll race you under Tensquare.

"I'll win, too," she added.

I stood and looked down at her, because that usually makes me feel superior to women.

"Daughter of Lir, eyes of Picasso," I said, "you've got yourself a race. Meet me at the forward Rook, starboard, in ten minutes."

"Ten minutes," she agreed.

And ten minutes it was. From the center blister to the Rook took maybe two of them, with the load I was carrying. My sandals grew very hot and I was glad to shuck them for flippers when I reached the comparative cool of the corner.

We slid into harnesses and adjusted our gear. She had changed into a trim one-piece green job that made me shade my eyes and look away, then look back again.

I fastened a rope ladder and kicked it over the side. Then I pounded on the wall of the Rook.

"Yeah?"

"You talk to the port Rook, aft?" I called.

"They're all set up," came the answer. "There's ladders and drag-lines all over that end."

"You sure you want to do this?" asked the sunburnt little gink who was her publicity man, Anderson yclept.

He sat beside the Rook in a deckchair, sipping lemonade through a straw.

"It might be dangerous," he observed, sunken-mouthed. (His teeth were beside him, in another glass.)

"That's right," she smiled. "It *will* be dangerous. Not overly, though."

"Then why don't you let me get some pictures? We'd have them back to Lifeline in an hour. They'd be in New York by tonight. Good copy."

"No," she said, and turned away from both of us.

She raised her hands to her eyes.

"Here, keep these for me."

She passed him a box full of her unseeing, and when she turned back to me they were the same brown that I remembered.

"Ready?"

"No," I said, tautly. "Listen carefully, Jean. If you're going to play this game there are a few rules. First," I counted, "we're going to be directly beneath the hull, so we have to start low and keep moving. If we bump the bottom, we could rupture an air tank. . . ."

She began to protest that any moron knew that and I cut her down.

"Second," I went on, "there won't be much light, so we'll stay close together, and we will *both* carry torches."

Her wet eyes flashed.

"I dragged you out of Govino without—"

Then she stopped and turned away. She picked up a lamp.

"Okay. Torches. Sorry."

". . . And watch out for the drive-screws," I finished. "There'll be strong currents for at least fifty meters behind them."

She wiped her eyes again and adjusted the mask.

"All right, let's go."

We went.

She led the way, at my insistence. The surface layer was pleasantly warm. At two fathoms the water was bracing; at five it was nice and cold. At eight we let go the swinging stairway and struck out. Ten-square sped forward and we raced in the opposite direction, tattooing the hull yellow at ten-second intervals.

The hull stayed where it belonged, but we raced on like two dark-side satellites. Periodically, I tickled her frog feet with my light and traced her antennae of bubbles. About a five meter lead was fine; I'd beat her in the home stretch, but I couldn't let her drop behind yet.

Beneath us, black. Immense. Deep. The Mindanao of Venus, where eternity might eventually pass the dead to a rest in cities of unnamed fishes. I twisted my head away and touched the hull with a feeler of light; it told me we were about a quarter of the way along.

I increased my beat to match her stepped-up stroke, and narrowed the distance which she had suddenly opened by a couple meters. She sped up again and I did, too. I spotted her with my beam.

She turned and it caught on her mask. I never knew whether she'd been smiling. Probably. She raised two fingers in a V-for-Victory and then cut ahead at full speed.

I should have known. I should have felt it coming. It was just a race to her, something else to win. Damn the torpedoes!

So I leaned into it, hard. I don't shake in the water. Or, if I do it doesn't matter and I don't notice it. I began to close the gap again.

She looked back, sped on, looked back. Each time she looked it was nearer, until I'd narrowed it down to the original five meters.

Then she hit the jatoes.

That's what I had been fearing. We were about halfway under and she shouldn't have done it. The powerful jets of compressed air could easily rocket her upward into the hull, or tear something loose if she allowed her body to twist. Their main use is in tearing free from marine plants or fighting bad currents. I had wanted them along as a safety measure, because of the big suck-and-pull windmills behind.

She shot ahead like a meteorite, and I could feel a sudden tingle of perspiration leaping to meet and mix with the churning waters.

I swept ahead, not wanting to use my own guns, and she tripled, quadrupled the margin.

The jets died and she was still on course. Okay, I was an old fuddy-duddy. She *could* have messed up and headed toward the top.

I plowed the sea and began to gather back my yardage, a foot at a time. I wouldn't be able to catch her or beat her now, but I'd be on the ropes before she hit deck.

Then the spinning magnets began their insistence and she wavered. It was an awfully powerful drag, even at this distance. The call of the meat grinder.

I'd been scratched up by one once, under the *Dolphin,* a fishing boat of the middle-class. I *had* been drinking, but it was also a rough day, and the thing had been turned on prematurely. Fortunately, it was turned off in time, also, and a tendon-stapler made everything good as new, except in the log, where it only mentioned that I'd been drinking. Nothing about it being off-hours when I had a right to do as I damn well pleased.

She had slowed to half her speed, but she was still moving crosswise, toward the port, aft corner. I began to feel the pull myself and had to slow down. She'd made it past the main one, but she seemed too far back. It's hard to gauge distances under water, but each red beat of time told me I was right. She was out of danger from the main one, but the smaller port screw, located about eighty meters in, was no longer a threat but a certainty.

She had turned and was pulling away from it now. Twenty meters separated us. She was standing still. Fifteen.

Slowly, she began a backward drifting. I hit my jatoes, aiming two meters behind her and about twenty back of the blades.

Straightline! Thankgod! Catching, softbelly, leadpipe on shoulder SWIMLIKEHELL! maskcracked, not broke though AND UP!

We caught a line and I remember brandy.

Into the cradle endlessly rocking I spit, pacing. Insomnia tonight and left shoulder sore again, so let it rain on me—they can cure rheumatism. Stupid as hell. What I said. In blankets and shivering. She: "Carl, I can't say it." Me: "Then call it square for that night in Govino, Miss Luharich. Huh?" She: nothing. Me: "Any more of that brandy?" She: "Give me another, too." Me: sounds of sipping. It had only lasted three months. No alimony. Many $ on both sides. Not sure whether they were happy or not. Wine-dark Aegean. Good fishing. Maybe he should have spent more time on shore. Or perhaps she shouldn't have. Good swimmer, though. Dragged him all the way to Vido to wring out his lungs. Young. Both. Strong. Both. Rich and spoiled as hell. Ditto. Corfu should have brought them closer. Didn't. I think that mental cruelty was a trout. He wanted to go to Canada. She: "Go to hell if you want!" He: "Will you go along?" She: "No." But she did, anyhow. Many hells. Expensive. He lost a monster or two. She inherited a couple. Lot of lightning tonight. Stupid as hell. Civility's the coffin of a conned soul. By whom?—Sounds like a bloody neo-ex. . . . But I hate you, Anderson, with your glass full of teeth and her new eyes. . . . Can't keep this pipe lit, keep sucking tobacco. Spit again!

*　*　*

Seven days out and the scope showed Ikky.

Bells jangled, feet pounded, and some optimist set the thermostat in the Hopkins. Malvern wanted me to sit out, but I slipped into my harness and waited for whatever came. The bruise looked worse than it felt. I had exercised every day and the shoulder hadn't stiffened on me.

A thousand meters ahead and thirty fathoms deep, it tunneled our path. Nothing showed on the surface.

"Will we chase him?" asked an excited crewman.

"Not unless she feels like using money for fuel." I shrugged.

Soon the scope was clear, and it stayed that way. We remained on alert and held our course.

I hadn't said over a dozen words to my boss since the last time we went drowning together, so I decided to raise the score.

"Good afternoon," I approached. "What's new?"

"He's going north-northeast. We'll have to let this one go. A few more days and we can afford some chasing. Not yet."

Sleek head . . .

I nodded. "No telling where this one's headed."

"How's your shoulder?"

"All right. How about you?"

Daughter of Lir . . .

"Fine. By the way, you're down for a nice bonus."

Eyes of perdition!

"Don't mention it," I told her back.

Later that afternoon, and appropriately, a storm shattered. (I prefer "shattered" to "broke." It gives a more accurate idea of the behavior of tropical storms on Venus and saves lots of words.) Remember that inkwell I mentioned earlier? Now take it between thumb and forefinger and hit its side with a hammer. Watch your self! Don't get splashed or cut—

Dry, then drenched. The sky one million bright fractures as the hammer falls. And sounds of breaking.

"Everyone below?" suggested loudspeakers to the already scurrying crew.

Where was I? Who do you think was doing the loudspeaking?

Everything loose went overboard when the water got to walking, but by then no people were loose. The Slider was the first thing below decks. Then the big lifts lowered their shacks.

I had hit it for the nearest Rook with a yell the moment I recognized the pre-brightening of the holocaust. From there I cut in the speakers and spent half a minute coaching the track team.

Minor injuries had occurred, Mike told me over the radio, but nothing serious. I, however, was marooned for the duration. The Rooks do not lead anywhere; they're set too far out over the hull to provide entry downwards, what with the extensor shelves below.

So I undressed myself of the tanks which I had worn for the past several hours, crossed my flippers on the table, and leaned back to watch the hurricane. The top was black as the bottom and we were in between, and somewhat illuminated because of all that flat, shiny space. The waters above didn't rain down—they just sort of got together and dropped.

The Rooks were secure enough—they'd weathered any number of these onslaughts—it's just that their positions gave them a greater arc of rise and descent when Tensquare makes like the rocker of a very nervous grandma. I had used the belts from my rig to strap myself into the bolted-down chair, and I removed several years in purgatory from the soul of whoever left a pack of cigarettes in the table drawer.

I watched the water make teepees and mountains and hands and trees until I started seeing faces and people. So I called Mike.

"What are you doing down there?"

"Wondering what you're doing up there," he replied. "What's it like?"

"You're from the Midwest, aren't you?"

"Yeah."

"Get bad storms out there?"

"Sometimes."

"Try to think of the worst one you were ever in. Got a slide rule handy?"

"Right here."

"Then put a one under it, imagine a zero or two following after, and multiply the thing out."

"I can't imagine the zeros."

"Then retain the multiplicand—that's all you can do."

"So what are you doing up there?"

"I've strapped myself in the chair. I'm watching things roll around the floor right now."

I looked up and out again. I saw one darker shadow in the forest.

"Are you praying or swearing?"

"Damned if I know. But if this were the Slider—if only this were the Slider!"

"He's out there?"

I nodded, forgetting that he couldn't see me.

Big, as I remembered him. He'd only broken surface for a few moments, to look around. *There is no power on Earth that can be com-*

pared with him who was made to fear no one. I dropped my cigarette. It was the same as before. Paralysis and an unborn scream.

"You all right, Carl?"

He had looked at me again. Or seemed to. Perhaps that mindless brute had been waiting half a millenium to ruin the life of a member of the most highly developed species in business. . . .

"You okay?"

. . . Or perhaps it had been ruined already, long before their encounter, and theirs was just a meeting of beasts, the stronger bumping the weaker aside, body to psyche. . . .

"Carl, dammit! Say something!"

He broke again, this time nearer. Did you ever see the trunk of a tornado? It seems like something alive, moving around in all that dark. Nothing has a right to be so big, so strong, and moving. It's a sickening sensation.

"Please answer me."

He was gone and did not come back that day. I finally made a couple of wisecracks at Mike, but I held my next cigarette in my right hand.

The next seventy or eighty thousand waves broke by with a monotonous similarity. The five days that held them were also without distinction. The morning of the thirteenth day out, though, our luck began to rise. The bells broke our coffee-drenched lethargy into small pieces, and we dashed from the galley without hearing what might have been Mike's finest punchline.

"Aft!" cried someone. "Five hundred meters!"

I stripped to my trunks and started buckling. My stuff is always within grabbing distance.

I flipflopped across the deck, girding myself with a deflated squiggler.

"Five hundred meters, twenty fathoms!" boomed the speakers.

The big traps banged upward and the Slider grew to its full height, m'lady at the console. It rattled past me and took root ahead. Its one arm rose and lengthened.

I breasted the Slider as the speakers called, "Four-eighty, twenty!"

"Status Red!"

A belch like an emerging champagne cork and the line arced high over the waters.

"Four-eighty, twenty!" it repeated, all Malvern and static. "Baitman, attend!"

I adjusted my mask and hand-over-handed it down the side. Then warm, then cool, then away.

Green, vast, down. Fast. This is the place where I am equal to a squiggler. If something big decides a baitman looks tastier than what he's carrying, then irony colors his title as well as the water about it.

I caught sight of the drifting cables and followed them down. Green to dark green to black. It had been a long cast, too long. I'd never had to follow one this far down before. I didn't want to switch on my torch.

But I had to.

Bad! I still had a long way to go. I clenched my teeth and stuffed my imagination into a straightjacket.

Finally the line came to an end.

I wrapped one arm about it and unfastened the squiggler. I attached it, working as fast as I could, and plugged in the little insulated connections which are the reason it can't be fired with the line. Ikky could break them, but by then it wouldn't matter.

My mechanical eel hooked up, I pulled its section plugs and watched it grow. I had been dragged deeper during this operation, which took about a minute and a half. I was near—too near—to where I never wanted to be.

Loathe as I had been to turn on my light, I was suddenly afraid to turn it off. Panic gripped me and I seized the cable with both hands. The squiggler began to glow, pinkly. It started to twist. It was twice as big as I am and doubtless twice as attractive to pink squiggler-eaters. I told myself this until I believed it, then I switched off my light and started up.

If I bumped into something enormous and steel-hided my heart had orders to stop beating immediately and release me—to dart fitfully forever along Acheron, and gibbering.

Ungibbering, I made it to green water and fled back to the nest.

As soon as they hauled me aboard I made my mask a necklace, shaded my eyes, and monitored for surface turbulence. My first question, of course, was: "Where is he?"

"Nowhere," said a crewman; "we lost him right after you went over. Can't pick him up on the scope now. Musta dived."

"Too bad."

The squiggler stayed down, enjoying its bath. My job ended for the time being, I headed back to warm my coffee with rum.

From behind me, a whisper: "Could you laugh like that afterwards?"

Perceptive Answer: "Depends on what he's laughing at."

Still chuckling, I made my way into the center blister with two cupfuls.

"Still hell and gone?"

Mike nodded. His big hands were shaking, and mine were steady as a surgeon's when I set down the cups.

He jumped as I shrugged off the tanks and looked for a bench.

"Don't drip on that panel! You want to kill yourself and blow expensive fuses?"

I toweled down, then settled down to watching the unfilled eye on the wall. I yawned happily; my shoulder seemed good as new.

The little box that people talk through wanted to say something, so Mike lifted the switch and told it to go ahead.

"Is Carl there, Mister Dabis?"

"Yes, ma'am."

"Then let me talk to him."

Mike motioned and I moved.

"Talk," I said.

"Are you all right?"

"Yes, thanks. Shouldn't I be?"

"That was a long swim. I—I guess I overshot my cast."

"I'm happy," I said. "More triple-time for me. I really clean up on that hazardous duty clause."

"I'll be more careful next time," she apologized. "I guess I was too eager. Sorry—" Something happened to the sentence, so she ended it there, leaving me with half a bagful of replies I'd been saving.

I lifted the cigarette from behind Mike's ear and got a light from the one in the ashtray.

"Carl, she was being nice," he said, after turning to study the panels.

"I know," I told him. "I wasn't."

"I mean, she's an awfully pretty kid, pleasant. Headstrong and all that. But what's she done to you?"

"Lately?" I asked.

He looked at me, then dropped his eyes to his cup.

"I know it's none of my bus—" he began.

"Cream and sugar?"

Ikky didn't return that day, or that night. We picked up some Dixieland out of Lifeline and let the muskrat ramble while Jean had her supper sent to the Slider. Later she had a bunk assembled inside. I piped in "Deep Water Blues" when it came over the air and waited for her to call up and cuss us out. She didn't, though, so I decided she was sleeping.

Then I got Mike interested in a game of chess that went on until daylight. It limited conversation to several "checks," one "checkmate," and a "damn!" Since he's a poor loser it also effectively sabotaged subsequent talk, which was fine with me. I had a steak and fried potatoes for breakfast and went to bed.

Ten hours later someone shook me awake and I propped myself on one elbow, refusing to open my eyes.

"Whassamadder?"

"I'm sorry to get you up," said one of the younger crewmen, "but Miss Luharich wants you to disconnect the squiggler so we can move on."

I knuckled open one eye, still deciding whether I should be amused.

"Have it hauled to the side. Anyone can disconnect it."

"It's at the side now, sir. But she said it's in your contract and we'd better do things right."

"That's very considerate of her. I'm sure my Local appreciates her remembering."

"Uh, she also said to tell you to change your trunks and comb your hair, and shave, too. Mister Anderson's going to film it."

"Okay. Run along; tell her I'm on my way—and ask if she has some toenail polish I can borrow."

I'll save on details. It took three minutes in all, and I played it properly, even pardoning myself when I slipped and bumped into Anderson's white tropicals with the wet squiggler. He smiled, brushed it off; she smiled, even though Luharich Complectacolor couldn't completely mask the dark circles under her eyes; and I smiled, waving to all our fans out there in videoland. —Remember, Mrs. Universe, you, too, can look like a monster-catcher. Just use Luharich face cream.

I went below and made myself a tuna sandwich, with mayonnaise.

Two days like icebergs—bleak, blank, half-melting, all frigid, mainly out of sight, and definitely a threat to peace of mind—drifted by and were good to put behind. I experienced some old guilt feelings and had a few disturbing dreams. Then I called Lifeline and checked my bank balance.

"Going shopping?" asked Mike, who had put the call through for me.

"Going home," I answered.

"Huh?"

"I'm out of the baiting business after this one, Mike. The Devil with Ikky! The Devil with Venus and Luharich Enterprises! And the Devil with you!"

Up eyebrows.

"What brought that on?"

"I waited over a year for this job. Now that I'm here, I've decided the whole thing stinks."

"You knew what it was when you signed on. No matter what else you're doing, you're selling face cream when you work for face cream sellers."

"Oh, that's not what's biting me. I admit the commercial angle irritates me, but Tensquare has always been a publicity spot, ever since the first time it sailed."

"What, then?"

"Five or six things, all added up. The main one being that I don't care any more. Once it meant more to me than anything else to hook that critter, and now it doesn't. I went broke on what started out as a lark and I wanted blood for what it cost me. Now I realize that maybe I had it coming. I'm beginning to feel sorry for Ikky."

"And you don't want him now?"

"I'll take him if he comes peacefully, but I don't feel like sticking out my neck to make him crawl into the Hopkins."

"I'm inclined to think it's one of the four or five other things you said you added."

"Such as?"

He scrutinized the ceiling.

I growled.

"Okay, but I won't say it, not just to make you happy you guessed right."

He, smirking: "That look she wears isn't just for Ikky."

"No good, no good." I shook my head. "We're both fission chambers by nature. You can't have jets on both ends of the rocket and expect to go anywhere—what's in the middle just gets smashed."

"That's how it *was.* None of my business, of course—"

"Say that again and you'll say it without teeth."

"Any day, big man"—he looked up—"any place . . ."

"So go ahead. Get it said!"

"She doesn't care about that bloody reptile, she came here to drag you back where you belong. You're not the baitman this trip."

"Five years is too long."

"There must be something under that cruddy hide of yours that people like," he muttered, "or I wouldn't be talking like this. Maybe you remind us humans of some really ugly dog we felt sorry for when we were kids. Anyhow, someone wants to take you home and raise you—also, something about beggars not getting menus."

"Buddy," I chuckled, "do you know what I'm going to do when I hit Lifeline?"

"I can guess."

"You're wrong. I'm torching it to Mars, and then I'll cruise back home, first class. Venus bankruptcy provisions do not apply to Martian trust funds, and I've still got a wad tucked away where moth and corruption enter not. I'm going to pick up a big old mansion on the Gulf and if you're ever looking for a job you can stop around and open bottles for me."

"You are a yellowbellied fink," he commented.

"Okay," I admitted, "but it's her I'm thinking of, too."

"I've heard the stories about you both," he said. "So you're a heel and a goofoff and she's a bitch. That's called compatibility these days. I dare you, baitman, try keeping something you catch."

I turned.

"If you ever want that job, look me up."

I closed the door quietly behind me and left him sitting there waiting for it to slam.

The day of the beast dawned like any other. Two days after my gutless flight from empty waters I went down to rebait. Nothing on the scope. I was just making things ready for the routine attempt.

I hollered a "good morning" from outside the Slider and received an answer from inside before I pushed off. I had reappraised Mike's words, sans sound, sans fury, and while I did not approve of their sentiment or significance, I had opted for civility anyhow.

So down, under, and away. I followed a decent cast about two hundred-ninety meters out. The snaking cables burned black to my left and I paced their undulations from the yellowgreen down into the darkness. Soundless lay the wet night, and I bent my way through it like a cock-eyed comet, bright tail before.

I caught the line, slick and smooth, and began baiting. An icy world swept by me then, ankles to head. It was a draft, as if some one had opened a big door beneath me. I wasn't drifting downwards that fast either.

Which meant that something might be moving up, something big enough to displace a lot of water. I still didn't think it was Ikky. A freak current of some sort, but not Ikky. Ha!

I had finished attaching the leads and pulled the first plug when a big, rugged, black island grew beneath me. . . .

I flicked the beam downward. His mouth was opened.

I was rabbit.

Waves of the death-fear passed downward. My stomach imploded. I grew dizzy.

Only one thing, and one thing only. Left to do. I managed it, finally. I pulled the rest of the plugs.

I could count the scaly articulations ridging his eyes by then.
The squiggler grew, pinked into phosphorescence . . . squiggled!
Then my lamp. I had to kill it, leaving just the bait before him.
One glance back as I jammed the jatoes to life.

He was so near that the squiggler reflected on his teeth, in his eyes.
Four meters, and I kissed his lambent jowls with two jets of backwash
as I soared. Then I didn't know whether he was following or halted. I
began to black out as I waited to be eaten.

The jatoes died and I kicked weakly.

Too fast, I felt a cramp coming on. One flick of the beam, cried
rabbit. One second, to know . . .

Or end things up, I answered. No, rabbit, we don't dart before
hunters. Stay dark.

Green waters finally, to yellowgreen, then top.

Doubling, I beat off toward Tensquare. The waves from the explosion behind pushed me on ahead. The world closed in, and a
screamed, "He's alive!" in the distance.

A giant shadow and a shock wave. The line was alive, too. Happy
Fishing Grounds. Maybe I did something wrong. . . .

Somewhere Hand was clenched. What's bait?

A few million years. I remember starting out as a one-celled organism
and painfully becoming an amphibian, then an air-breather. From
somewhere high in the treetops I heard a voice.

"He's coming around."

I evolved back into homosapience, then a step further into a hang-
over.

"Don't try to get up yet."

"Have we got him?" I slurred.

"Still fighting, but he's hooked. We thought he took you for an
appetizer."

"So did I."

"Breathe some of this and shut up."

A funnel over my face. Good. Lift your cups and drink. . . .

"He was awfully deep. Below scope range. We didn't catch him till
he started up. Too late, then."

I began to yawn.

"We'll get you inside now."

I managed to uncase my ankle knife.

"Try it and you'll be minus a thumb."

"You need rest."

"Then bring me a couple more blankets. I'm staying."

I fell back and closed my eyes.

* * *

Someone was shaking me. Gloom and cold. Spotlights bled yellow on the deck. I was in a jury-rigged bunk, bulked against the center blister. Swaddled in wool, I still shivered.

"It's been eleven hours. You're not going to see anything now."

I tasted blood.

"Drink this."

Water. I had a remark but I couldn't mouth it.

"Don't ask how I feel," I croaked. "I know that comes next, but don't ask me. Okay?"

"Okay. Want to go below now?"

"No. Just get me my jacket."

"Right here."

"What's he doing?"

"Nothing. He's deep, he's doped but he's staying down."

"How long since last time he showed?"

"Two hours, about."

"Jean?"

"She won't let anyone in the Slider. Listen, Mike says come on in. He's right behind you in the blister."

I sat up and turned. Mike was watching. He gestured; I gestured back.

I swung my feet over the edge and took a couple of deep breaths. Pains in my stomach. I got to my feet and made in into the blister.

"Howza gut?" queried Mike.

I checked the scope. No Ikky. Too deep.

"You buying?"

"Yeah, coffee."

"Not coffee."

"You're ill. Also, coffee is all that's allowed in here."

"Coffee is a brownish liquid that burns your stomach. You have some in the bottom drawer."

"No cups. You'll have to use a glass."

"Tough."

He poured.

"You do that well. Been practicing for that job?"

"What job?"

"The one I offered you—"

A bolt on the scope!

"Rising, ma'am! Rising!" he yelled into the box.

"Thanks, Mike. I've got it in here," she crackled.

"Jean!"

"Shut up! She's busy!"

"Was that Carl?"

"Yeah," I called. "Talk later," and I cut it.

Why did I do that?

"Why did you do that?"

I didn't know.

"I don't know."

Damned echoes! I got up and walked outside.

Nothing. Nothing.

Something?

Tensquare actually rocked! He must have turned when he saw the hull and started downward again. White water to my left, and boiling. An endless spaghetti of cable roared hotly into the belly of the deep.

I stood awhile, then turned and went back inside.

Two hours sick. Four, and better.

"The dope's getting to him."

"Yeah."

"What about Miss Luharich?"

"What about her?"

"She must be half dead."

"Probably."

"What are you going to do about it?"

"She signed the contract for this. She knew what might happen. It did."

"I think you could land him."

"So do I."

"So does she."

"Then let her ask me."

Ikky was drifting lethargically, at thirty fathoms.

I took another walk and happened to pass behind the Slider. She wasn't looking my way.

"Carl, come in here!"

Eyes of Picasso, that's what, and a conspiracy to make me Slide . . .

"Is that an order?"

"Yes—No! Please."

I dashed inside and monitored. He was rising.

"Push or pull?"

I slammed the "wind" and he came like a kitten.

"Make up your own mind now."

He balked at ten fathoms.

"Play him?"

"No!"

She wound him upwards—five fathoms, four . . .

She hit the extensors at two, and they caught him. Then the graffles.
Cries without and a heat lightning of flashbulbs.
The crew was Ikky.
He began to struggle. She kept the cables tight, raised the graf-
fles . . .
Up.
Another two feet and the graffles began pushing.
Screams and fast footfalls.
Giant beanstalk in the wind, his neck, waving. The green hills of his
shoulders grew.
"He's big, Carl!" she cried.
And he grew, and grew, and grew uneasy . . .
"Now!"
He looked down.
He looked down, as the god of our most ancient ancestors might
have looked down. Fear, shame, and mocking laughter rang in my
head. Her head, too?
"Now!"
She looked up at the nascent earthquake.
"I can't!"
It was going to be so damnably simple this time, now the rabbit had
died. I reached out.
I stopped.
"Push it yourself."
"I can't. You do it. Land him, Carl!"
"No. If I do, you'll wonder for the rest of your life whether you
could have. You'll throw away your soul finding out. I know you will,
because we're alike, and I did it that way. Find out now!"
She stared.
I gripped her shoulders.
"Could be that's me out there," I offered. "I am a green sea serpent,
a hateful, monstrous beast, and out to destroy you. I am answerable to
no one. Push the Inject."
Her hand moved to the button, jerked back.
"Now!"
She pushed it.
I lowered her still form to the floor and finished things up with
Ikky.
It was a good seven hours before I awakened to the steady, sea-
chewing grind of Tensquare's blades.
"You're sick," commented Mike.
"How's Jean?"

"The same."

"Where's the beast?"

"Here."

"Good." I rolled over. ". . . Didn't get away this time."

So that's the way it was. No one is born a baitman, I don't think, but the rings of Saturn sing epithalamium the sea-beast's dower.